Heather Hutchins

LAYOPeetate

No more samples
New crap
School Sucks!

V.P.
H + H = 2
♥
WOOP!! hoop

ERIK

Senior YEAR!

THE English Beat!
SKA!

"H. y. y. y. y."
Heather

♥
Liddy, kelley

RUN D.M.C.

Kelley loves Heather
Heather loves Erik
but I know in that
unnatural body because
she loves me
I love her
I HORNY boyfriend!

Heather
Hutchins

THE English Beat!

History is bunk!

ERIK
+
HEATHER

Magruder's
AMERICAN
GOVERNMENT

1984

Revised by **William A. McClenaghan**

Department of Political Science
Oregon State University

Allyn and Bacon, Inc.

Boston   Rockleigh NJ   Atlanta
Dallas   Sacramento   Warrensburg MO
London   Sydney   Toronto

AMERICAN GOVERNMENT, first
published in 1917, and revised
annually, is an enduring symbol of
the author's faith in American ideals
and American institutions. The life of
Frank Abbott Magruder (1882–1949)
was an outstanding example of
Americanism at its very best. His
career as a teacher, author, and
tireless worker in civic and religious
undertakings remains an inspiring
memory to all who knew him.

Features and Skill Features by:
Catherine Cornbleth, Department of
Education, University of Pittsburgh
and
William A. McClenaghan

Senior Editor: Donald B. Armin
Design: L. Christopher Valente
Design Production: Janet Hobbs/
Virginia Pierce/Dorothy Spence
Technical Art: Burt Rush, Visual Services
Preparation Services Manager:
Martha E. Ballentine
Buyer: Roger Powers
Cover Design: John Martucci
Cover Materials from:
McClenaghan Collection and the J.
Doyle Dewitt Collection (Edmund
Sullivan/Curator)
Photo Research: Susan Richardson/
Mary Stuart Lang/Susan Van Etten

Library of Congress Catalog Card Number:
17-13472

Printed in the United States of America

ISBN   0-205-8132-0

456789   88 87 86 85 84

PREFACE

If a nation expects to be ignorant and free, . . .
it expects what never was and never will be.

Thomas Jefferson

This is a book about government—and, more particularly, about government in the United States. Over the course of its 24 chapters and more than 600 pages, we shall consider the ways in which government in this country is organized, the ways in which it is controlled by the people, the many things that it does, and the various ways in which it does them.

American Government, 1984, is the latest in a long line of editions of this book. The first one appeared in 1917, and this one is the 64th edition. Every edition of this book has had one basic purpose: to describe, analyze, and explain the American system of government.

American Government, 1984, is a thoroughly and carefully revised book. Altogether, the many changes which have been made appear on more than 300 of its pages.

All of the many changes within the book illustrate a very important point:

The American system of government is extraordinarily dynamic. Change—growth, adaptation, innovation—is a basic element of its character. While it is true that its fundamental principles and its basic structure have remained constant over time, many of its other characteristics have changed. And they continue to do so—from year to year and, frequently, from one day to the next, and sometimes remarkably.

To underscore the critical importance of this fact of continuing change, dwell for a moment on the phrase "the American system of government." You will come across it again and again, for it is an apt description of government in the United States. And, as you will soon discover, that system is a very complex one.

It is complex because it is made up of many different parts, performing many different functions. And it is a system because all of its many different parts are interrelated. The whole cannot be understood without a knowledge of its several interacting parts; and those parts cannot be understood without a knowledge of the

whole. Given all of this, the vital effects of ongoing change in the system are obvious.

Every effort has been made to see that this book is as accurate, as up-to-date, as readable, and as interesting and useable as possible. The wealth of factual information it contains has been drawn from the most current and reliable of sources. This is not a book on current events, however. It does contain much data and draws many examples from the contemporary scene. But they are purposefully woven into the context of its primary objective: the description, analysis, and explanation of the American system of government.

Some criticize textbooks because, they say, they are "too large" and "too factual," and they sometimes argue that they should be more "interpretive." *This* textbook includes that material which we believe to be absolutely necessary to a basic knowledge and understanding of the American governmental system. If it is a "large" one, it is because its subject is a very large *and* a very *important* one.

Every book, no matter its subject, reflects in at least some degree, the biases of its author. And this book is no exception. We have made a very conscious effort to minimize their appearance, and to present a fair and balanced view of government in the United States. But, inevitably, those biases are present. Whenever they appear, they should be subjected to critical examination by the reader, of course. One of them is outstandingly obvious: the conviction that the American system of government, although it contains some and sometimes glaring imperfections, is in fact and should be government of the people, by the people, and for the people.

One final comment here—from both the original author, the late Frank Abbott Magruder, and the present one: Over the years we have received much valuable help from the many teachers and students who have used this book in classrooms across the nation. Their comments, suggestions, criticisms, and questions have played a large part in the making of each new edition—and they continue to be more than welcome, of course.

William A. McClenaghan
Department of Political Science
Oregon State University
Corvallis, Oregon

CONTENTS

vii

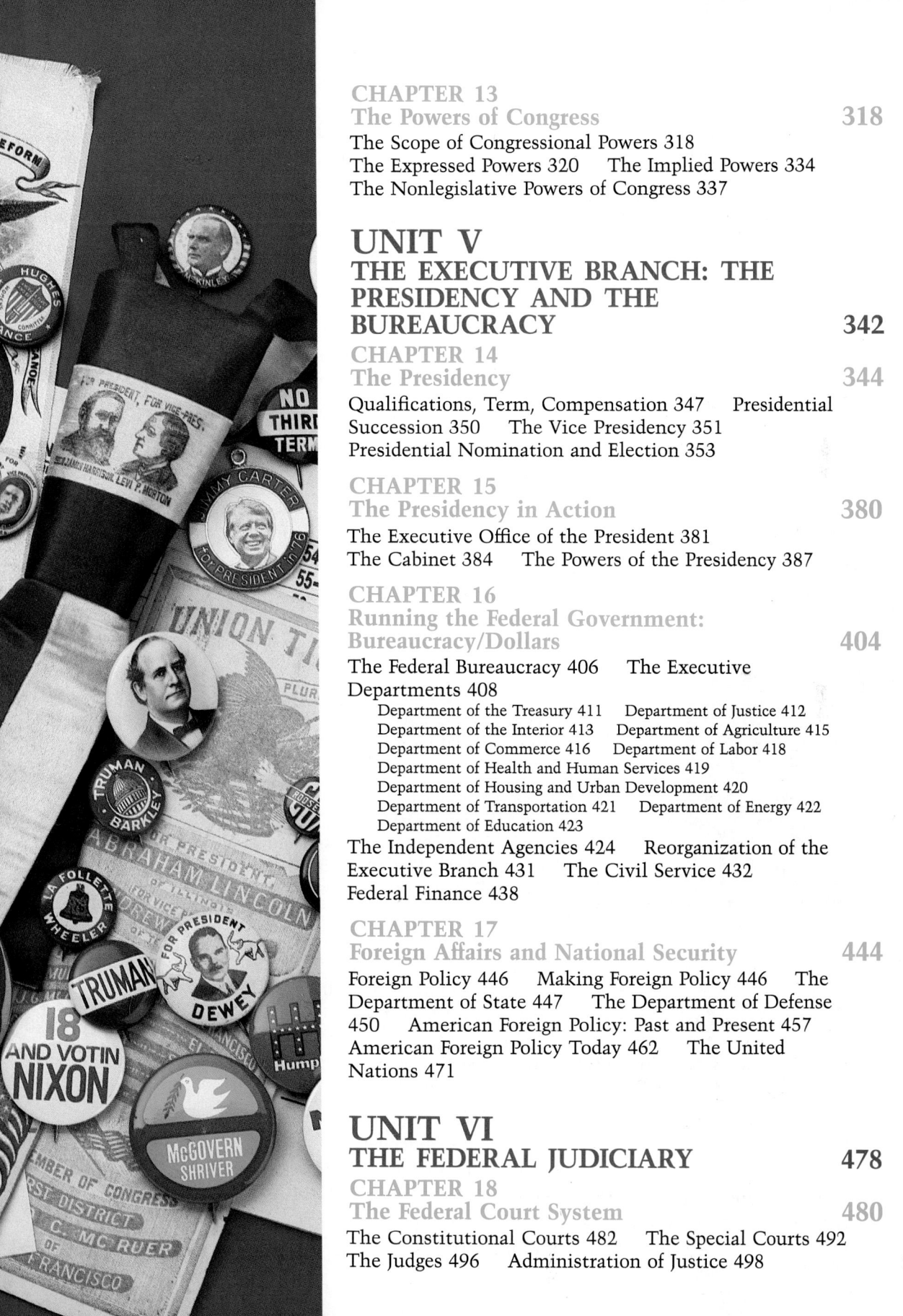

FEATURES

SKILL FEATURES

MAPS, GRAPHS, CHARTS, DIAGRAMS

TABLES

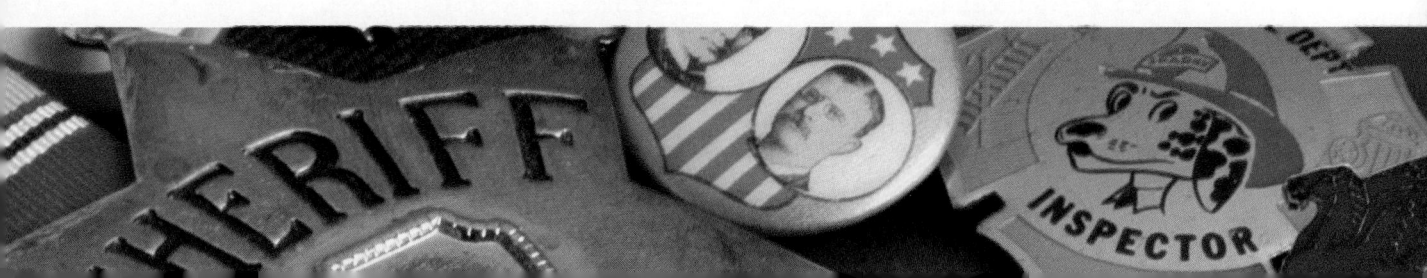

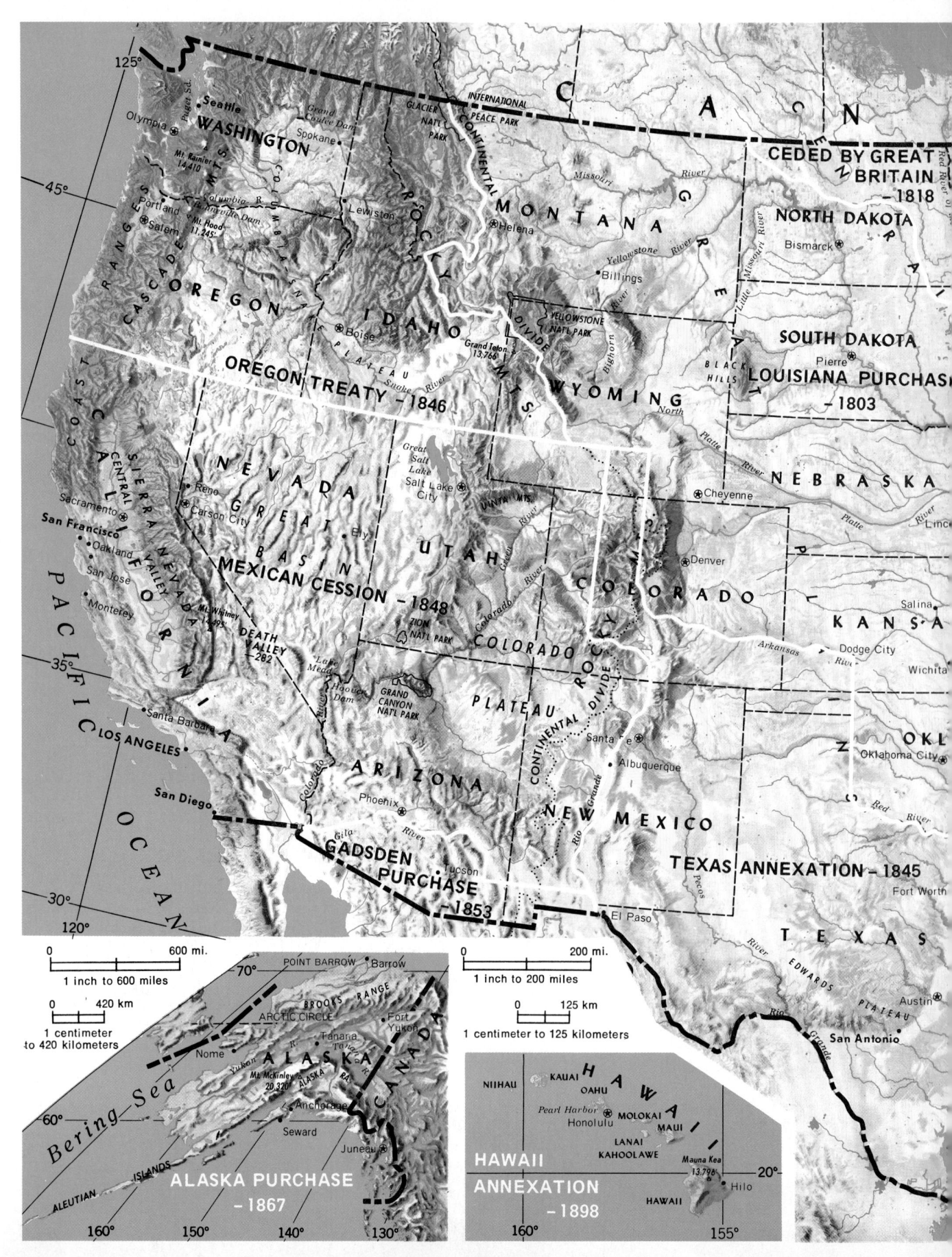

CANADA

CEDED BY GREAT BRITAIN –1818

WASHINGTON
Seattle
Olympia
Puget Sd.
Grand Coulee Dam
Spokane
Mt. Rainier 14,410
Portland
Mt. Hood 11,245
Columbia R.
Bonneville Dam
Salem
GLACIER NAT'L PARK
INTERNATIONAL PEACE PARK
CONTINENTAL
Lewiston

OREGON
COAST RANGES
CASCADE

MONTANA
Helena
Billings
Missouri
River
Yellowstone River
Bighorn

NORTH DAKOTA
Bismarck

IDAHO
Boise
PLATEAU
Snake River
Grand Teton 13,766
YELLOWSTONE NAT'L PARK
DIVIDE
ROCKY
MTS.

OREGON TREATY –1846

SOUTH DAKOTA
Pierre
BLACK HILLS

LOUISIANA PURCHASE –1803

WYOMING
North
Platte
GREAT

NEVADA
Reno
Carson City
SIERRA NEVADA
CENTRAL
CALIFORNIA
Sacramento
San Francisco
Oakland
San Jose
Monterey
VALLEY
Ely
GREAT
BASIN

MEXICAN CESSION –1848

Great Salt Lake
Salt Lake City
UINTA MTS.
Green River

UTAH
ZION NAT'L PARK

Mt. Whitney 14,495
DEATH VALLEY –282
Lake Mead
Hoover Dam
GRAND CANYON NAT'L PARK
Colorado River
COLORADO PLATEAU

COLORADO
Denver
ROCKY
DIVIDE
CONTINENTAL

NEBRASKA
Cheyenne
Platte
River
PLAINS

KANSAS
Salina
Dodge City
Arkansas River
Wichita

ARIZONA
Phoenix
Gila River
Colorado R.
Tucson
San Diego
Santa Barbara
LOS ANGELES

GADSDEN PURCHASE –1853

NEW MEXICO
Santa Fe
Albuquerque
Rio Grande
El Paso

TEXAS ANNEXATION –1845
Fort Worth

OKLA
Oklahoma City
Red River

TEXAS
EDWARDS PLATEAU
Austin
San Antonio
Pecos
Rio Grande

PACIFIC OCEAN

125°
45°
120°
35°
30°

Scale bars (lower left):
0 — 600 mi.
1 inch to 600 miles
0 — 420 km
1 centimeter to 420 kilometers

ALASKA inset:
POINT BARROW
Barrow
70°
BROOKS RANGE
ARCTIC CIRCLE
Nome
Fort Yukon
Yukon R.
Tanana
Tanana R.
ALASKA
Mt. McKinley 20,320
ALASKA RA.
Anchorage
CANADA
Seward
Juneau
60°
Bering Sea
ALEUTIAN ISLANDS
160° 150° 140° 130°

ALASKA PURCHASE –1867

Scale bars (center):
0 — 200 mi.
1 inch to 200 miles
0 — 125 km
1 centimeter to 125 kilometers

HAWAII inset:
NIIHAU
KAUAI
OAHU
HAWAII
Pearl Harbor
Honolulu
MOLOKAI
LANAI
MAUI
KAHOOLAWE
Mauna Kea 13,798
HAWAII
Hilo
20°
160° 155°

HAWAII ANNEXATION –1898

THE UNITED STATES

0   200 mi.   0   250 km

1 inch to 200 miles   2 centimeters to 250 kilometers

Lambert Conformal Conic Projection

UNIT ONE

The Foundations of the American Governmental System

On a Friday in late May in 1787 a group of men met in Philadelphia to design a new government for their new country. The government they produced, after nearly four months of discussion, argument, and compromise, was put into written form in the remarkable document that is the Constitution of the United States.

This book is about that government. It is a government which has continued and prospered, adapting itself to changes that its Framers could not possibly have imagined would take place over the course of nearly two hundred years.

The American system of government is not simple. On the contrary, it is probably the most complicated of the more than 160 such systems that now exist in the world. The basic purpose of this book is to help you understand it.

In Unit One of this book, we set the scene for our study. We consider the foundations of the American system of government. We look at its origins and development, the fundamental principles on which it is built, and the structure of the American federal system—that is, the division of powers between the National Government and the States. In Unit Two we turn to American civil rights—how government protects and promotes individual freedoms; we explore the politics of American democracy in Unit Three. In Units Four, Five, and Six, we deal respectively with the legislative, executive, and judicial branches of the Federal Government and with the shaping of national policy in many areas. Finally, in Unit Seven, we turn to the many facets of State and local government.

The Statue of Liberty, symbol of America as a land of opportunity and freedom.

1

Modern Political and Economic Systems

To help you to
Learn ▪ Know ▪ Understand

The basic nature of the state and government in the modern world.

The major forms of government in the world today.

The basic concepts of American democracy.

The basic features of the major economic systems in the world today.

Government is a contrivance of human wisdom to provide for human wants.
Edmund Burke

The Constitution's opening words read: "We the People of the United States. . . ." No other words in all of that remarkable document are more important or more meaningful. For here, in these seven words, the Constitution proclaims the very essence of the American system of government.

As Americans, we take great and justifiable pride in that system of government. It is self-government under law—government of the people, by the people, and for the people. It is a government in which "We the People" rule, and a government which exists only to do our bidding.

We take pride, too, in the fact that our system of government is and has been for generations, the envy of peoples the world over. Many other nations have tried governmental systems much like ours. But none of them has lasted for so long, nor has any of them been developed on so large a scale.

As we take that pride, however, it seems wise to remember this: We have learned much from—and we owe much to—some of those other peoples and nations. As we shall see, our debts to the ancient Greeks and to the not-so-ancient English are especially large.

The nation's Capitol, scene of the inauguration of the 40th President of the United States.

It seems wise to remember another fact, too: Systems of self-government have been exceedingly rare over the course of human history. Authoritarian systems—whether known as tyrannies, despotisms, or dictatorships—have been much more durable and considerably more numerous.

"We the People" rule the world's largest, and the world's most powerful democracy. Yet, more than four billion other people and more than 160 other nations share our globe.

Viewed against such a backdrop, then, this also seems wise: That we begin our study of the American system of government with a brief look at the many forms of government to be found in the world today. Much of what exists, and many of the things that happen, in even the farthest corners of the globe can have an immediate and an important effect upon our daily lives. They may even affect the very future of our existence as a nation.

Governments in the World Today

Government is among the oldest of all human inventions. More than 2300 years ago, Aristotle wrote that "man is by nature a political animal." When he did so, he was only recording what, even then, had been obvious for thousands of years.

Government was invented at that point at which people first realized that they could not survive without some form of authority, some power, that could regulate both their own and their neighbors' conduct.

The State

Over the long course of human history, the **state** has emerged as the dominant political unit in the world. It may be defined in these terms: A body of people, living in a defined territory, organized politically, and having the power to make and enforce law without the consent of any higher authority.

There are more than 160 states in the world today. They vary greatly in size and military power, natural resources and economic importance, and many other factors. Each of them, however, has all four of the characteristics set out in our definition: population, territory, sovereignty, and government.[1]

Population.   Clearly there must be people. The size of the population is not essential to the existence of a state, however. The smallest of them all, in terms of population, is San Marino.[2] Nestled high in the Apennines and bounded on all sides by Italy, it has only some 21,000 people. The People's Republic of China is the largest. Its population is now well over one billion—so many that if they were all to line up in single file the Chinese people could encircle the globe more than 20 times.

Territory.   Just as there must be people, so must there be land, territory with known and recognized boundaries. Here, too, San Marino ranks as the smallest state in the world. It has an area of only some 63 square kilometers (24 square miles). The largest is the Soviet Union, with 22,403,000 square kilometers (8,650,000 square miles)— about one-sixth the land surface of the earth. The total area of the United States is 9,372,614 square kilometers (3,618,770 square miles).

Sovereignty.   Every state is **sovereign.** That is, every state has supreme and absolute power within its own territory. It may make its own policies, chart its own courses of action, both foreign and domestic. It is neither subordinate nor responsible to any outside authority.

Thus, as a sovereign state, the United States may determine its own form of government. It may frame its own economic system, may shape its own foreign policies, and may decide as it will on all other matters—and so, too, may all other states.[3]

The *location* of sovereignty within a state—who, in fact, holds that power—is of supreme importance. If the people are sovereign, then the government is democratic. If, on the other hand, the power is held by a single person or a small group, a dictatorship exists.

Government.   Every state is politically organized. That is, every state has a **government**. Government is the institution through which the public policies of a state are made and enforced and all of its other affairs are conducted. To put the definition another way, government is the agency through which the state exerts its will and works to accomplish its goals. It consists of the machinery and the personnel by which the state is ruled (governed).

Origins of the State

For centuries historians, political scientists, philosophers, and others have pondered the question of the origin of the state. What factor or set of circumstances first brought it into being?

Over time, many different answers have been offered, but history provides

---

[1]Note that what we have defined here—the *state*— is a *legal* entity. In popular usage, a state is often called a "nation" or a "country." In a strict sense, however, **nation** is an *ethnic* term, referring to races or other large groups of people. **Country** is a *geographic* term, referring to a particular place, region, or area of land.

[2]The Vatican is not cited here primarily because the United States does not recognize it as a sovereign state. Nor is the principality of Monaco cited; its several legal ties to France deny its sovereignty.

[3]In this book, *state* printed with a small "s" denotes a state in the family of nations, such as France, The United States, and the Soviet Union. *State* printed with a capital "S" refers to a State in the American Union, such as California, Illinois, and North Carolina.

no conclusive evidence to support any of them. The four which have been most widely accepted are:

The Force Theory. Many scholars have long believed that the state was born of force. They hold that it developed because one man—or perhaps a small group of men—claimed control over an area and forced all within it to submit to his—or their—rule. When that rule was established, they argue, all of the basic elements of the state—population, territory, sovereignty, and government—were present.

The Evolutionary Theory. Others claim that the state developed naturally and gradually out of the early family. They hold that the primitive family, of which the father was the head and thus the "government," was the first stage in human political development. Over countless years the original family became a network of closely related families—a clan. In time the clan became a tribe. When the tribe first turned to settled agriculture—when it gave up its nomadic ways and first tied itself to the land—the state was born.

The Divine Right Theory. Some theorists have argued that the state arose as the result of the "divine right of kings." They claim that God gave those of royal birth the right to rule other men. As unsound as this idea may seem today, it was widely accepted in the 17th and 18th centuries. And much of the thought upon which present-day demo-cratic government rests was first developed as an argument against the "divine-right" theory.

The Social Contract Theory. In terms of our political system, the most significant of the theories of the origin of the state is that of the "social contract." It was developed in the 17th and 18th centuries by such philosophers as John Locke, James Harrington, and Thomas Hobbes in England and Jean Jacques Rousseau in France.

Hobbes wrote that in his earliest history man lived in unbridled freedom, in a "state of nature." Each man could do as he pleased and in any manner he chose, at least so far as he was physically capable of so doing. That which he could take by force was his, and for as long as he could hold it. But all men were similarly free. Thus, each man was only as safe as his own physical prowess and watchfulness could make him. His life in the state of nature, wrote Hobbes, was "nasty, brutish, and short."

Men overcame their unpleasant condition, says the theory, by agreeing with one another to create a state. By *contract*, men within a given area joined together, each agreed to give up to the state as much power as was needed to promote the safety and well-being of all. In the contract (that is, through a constitution), the members of the state created a government to exercise the powers which they had voluntarily granted to the state.

Reproduced by permission of Johnny Hart and Field Enterprises

In short, the **social contract** theory argues that the state arose out of a voluntary act of free men. It holds that the state exists only to serve the will of the people, that they are the sole source of political power, and that they are free to give or to withhold that power as they choose. The theory seems farfetched to many of us today. But the great concepts it fostered—popular sovereignty, limited government, and individual rights—were, as we shall see, immensely important to the shaping of our own governmental system.[4]

 FOR REVIEW

1. What is a state? What are its four main characteristics?

2. What is the difference between a state and a government?

3. Why is the location of sovereignty within a state so important?

4. Why is the social contract theory so significant in terms of the development of the American political system?

Forms of Government

No two governments are, or ever have been, exactly alike. Clearly this must be so, for governments are the products of human needs and human experiences. And all of them have been shaped by many other factors—geography, climate, history, customs, resources, the capacities of the people, and several others.

Political scientists have developed a number of different bases upon which to classify—and so to describe and to analyze—governments.

Three of those classifications are especially important and useful for our purposes—classifications according to: (1) the geographical distribution of governmental power within the state, (2) the nature of the relationship between the **legislative** (lawmaking) and the **executive** (law-executing) branches of the government, and (3) the number of persons who may take part in the governing process.

(1) Geographic Distribution of Power. In every system of government the power to govern is located in one or more places, geographically. From this standpoint, three basic forms of government exist: *unitary* governments, *federal* governments, and *confederate* governments.

Unitary Government. A **unitary** government is often described as a centralized government. It is one in which all of the powers held by the government belong to a single central agency. Local units of government are created by and for the convenience of the central government, and whatever powers they have come only from that source.

Most governments in the world are unitary in form. Great Britain gives us a classic illustration of the type. All of the power that the British government has is held by one central organ, the Parliament. Local governments do exist but solely to relieve Parliament of burdens it could perform only with much difficulty and inconvenience. Though it isn't likely, Parliament could do away with all agencies of local government in Great Britain at any time.

Be careful *not* to confuse the unitary form of government with a dictatorship. In the unitary form *all of the powers the government possesses* are concentrated in the central government. But that government might not have *all* power. In Great Britain, for example, the powers held by the government are strictly lim-

---

[4]The Declaration of Independence (see text, pages 626–627) laid its justification for revolution on the social contract theory, arguing that the king and his ministers had violated the contract. Thomas Jefferson called the document "pure Locke."

President Reagan addresses the lawmakers of the National Government—the Congress. Also in attendance are the Justices of the Supreme Court (at right, front row).

ited. British government is unitary and is also, at the same time, democratic.

Federal Government. A **federal** government is one in which the powers of government are divided between a central government and several regional (local) governments. This *division of powers* is made on a geographic basis by an authority superior to both the central and the local governments, and it cannot be changed by either level acting alone.

In the United States, for example, the National Government has certain powers and the 50 States have others. This division of powers is set out in the Constitution of the United States. The Constitution stands above both levels of government and cannot be changed unless the people, acting through both the National Government and the States, agree to that change.

Australia, Canada, Mexico, New Zealand, Switzerland, West Germany, Yugoslavia, and some 20 other states also have federal forms of government today. (Note that the government of each of the 50 States in the American Union is unitary, not federal, in form.)

Confederate Government. A **confederation** is an alliance of independent states. A central organ (the confederate government) has the power to handle only those matters of common concern which the member states have assigned to it. Typically, confederate governments have had limited powers and only in such fields as defense and foreign commerce.

There are no confederations in the world today. But, in our own history, the United States under the Articles of Confederation (1781–1789) and the Confederate States (1861–1865) are examples of the form.

(2) Relationship Between Legislative and Executive Branches. Viewing governments from the standpoint of the relationship between their legislative (lawmaking) and their executive (law-executing) agencies yields two basic forms: *presidential* and *parliamentary*.

Britain's House of Commons, which is the lower chamber of its parliament. Virtually all the powers of government are lodged in this House.

Presidential   Government. The **presidential** form features a *separation of powers* between the executive and legislative branches of the government. The two branches are independent of and co-equal with one another. The chief executive (president) is chosen independently of the legislature, holds office for a fixed term, and has broad powers not subject to the direct control of the legislature.

Usually, as in the United States (and each of the 50 States) a written constitution provides for the separation of powers between the branches of government. Thus, the Constitution of the United States provides for the selection of the President, independently of the Congress, for a fixed four-year term. It also assigns to the President and to the Congress their separate fields of power.

Parliamentary   Government. In the **parliamentary** form, the executive is made up of the prime minister (or premier) and that official's cabinet. They themselves are members of the legislative branch (the parliament). The prime minister is the leader of the majority party—or of a coalition of two or more parties—in parliament, and is chosen to office by that body. With its approval, he or she selects the members of the cabinet from among the members of parliament. The executive is thus chosen by the legislature, is a part of it, and is subject to its direct control.

The prime minister and the cabinet—very often called "the government"—remain in office only as long as their policies and administration have the confidence and support of a majority in parliament. If they are defeated on an important matter (if they do not receive a "vote of confidence"), they must resign from office. Then a new "govern-

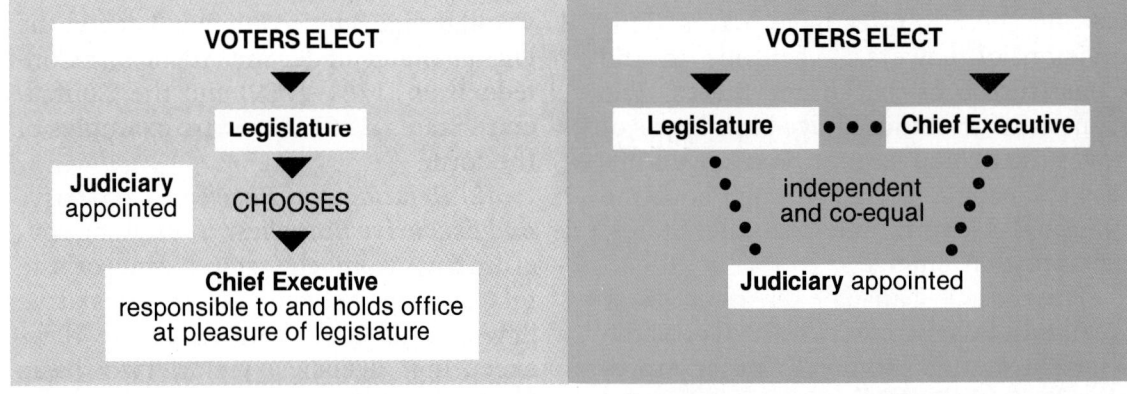

PARLIAMENTARY GOVERNMENT

VOTERS ELECT
▼
Legislature
▼
CHOOSES
▼
Chief Executive
responsible to and holds office
at pleasure of legislature

Judiciary appointed

PRESIDENTIAL GOVERNMENT

VOTERS ELECT
▼   ▼
Legislature • • • Chief Executive
independent
and co-equal
Judiciary appointed

ment" must be formed. Either parliament chooses a new prime minister or, as often happens, a general election is held in which all of the seats in parliament go before the voters. The British, most European, and a majority of all other governments in the world today are parliamentary in form.

(3) The Number Who May Participate. What is perhaps the most meaningful of classifications of government is that based upon the number of persons who may take part in the governing process. Here we have two basic forms to consider: *dictatorships* and *democracies.*

Dictatorship. Where the power to govern is held by one person or held by a small group, a **dictatorship** exists. It is probably the oldest, and certainly the most common, form of government known to history.

All dictatorships are **authoritarian.** That is, they are governmental systems in which those in power hold absolute and unchallengeable authority over the people.

Modern dictatorships have tended to be **totalitarian,** as well. That is, they exercise dictatorial (authoritarian) power over just about every aspect of human affairs; their power embraces all (the *totality of*) matters of human concern.

The best examples of dictatorship in the 20th century are those which existed in Fascist Italy (from 1922 to 1943) and Nazi Germany (from 1933 to 1945), and those which now exist in the Soviet Union (where the present dictatorial regime was established in 1917) and the People's Republic of China (where the dictatorship came to power in 1949).

One-man dictatorships have been and are rather uncommon. They are not unknown, however. The recently-deposed regime in Uganda is a classic example of the point. Idi Amin Dada seized control of the government of that

Adolf Hitler and his Nazi Party ruled Germany from 1933 to 1945. Hitler's dictatorship was crushed by the Allied victory in World War II.

East African state in 1971. Immediately, Amin proclaimed himself the country's "President-for-Life." For eight years he ruled with a harsh and **autocratic** (absolute, unlimited) hand. His government was finally overturned by the armies of Tanzania in 1979.

Dictatorships are much more often dominated by the will of a small, tight-knit group. Yuri Andropov, the leader of the Soviet Union, may be properly described as a dictator. But, in fact, he has no power to act without the support and approval of the powerful *politburo* (executive council) of the Communist Party of the USSR.

The primary characteristic of any dictatorship is that *it is not responsible to the people and cannot be limited by them.* Dictatorships often present the outward appearance of control by the people. Popular elections are generally held. But elections are rigidly controlled and typically, the voter is offered the candidates of only one political party. There is often an elected legislative body but only to rubber-stamp the policies and programs of the dictatorship.

Public support is mobilized through massive propaganda programs and absolute control of the educational system. Opposition is put down, often ruthlessly, by a secret police. Only one political party, highly organized and rigidly disciplined, is allowed. Freedom of speech, thought, and association—so vital in democracy—are not tolerated.

Typically, dictatorial regimes are quite militaristic in character. They usually gain power by force; many of the major posts in the government are held by militarists. What is more, after crushing all effective opposition at home, they may turn to foreign aggression and other adventures to enhance the country's military power and prestige.

Benito Mussolini stated the basic philosophy of the modern-day totalitarian dictatorship when he proclaimed:

> All is in the state and for the state, nothing outside the state, nothing against the state.

Democracy. In the **democratic** form of government, supreme political authority rests with the people. The people hold the sovereign power and government is conducted only by and with their consent.[5]

Abraham Lincoln gave immortality to this definition of democracy in the Gettysburg Address in 1863: "government of the people, by the people, for the people." Nowhere is there a better, more concise statement of the American understanding of the term.

A democracy may be either *direct* or *indirect* in form. A **direct** (or *pure*) **democracy** exists where the will of the people is translated into public policy (law) directly by the people themselves in mass meetings. Clearly, such a system can be made to work only in very small communities where it is possible for the citizens to meet in a given place and where the problems of government are few and simple.

Direct democracy does not exist at the national level anywhere in the world today. But the old New England town meeting and the *Landsgemeinde* in a few of the smaller Swiss cantons are excellent examples of direct democracy in action.[6]

In the United States we are more familiar with the *indirect* form—that is, with *representative democracy*. In a **representative democracy** the popular will is expressed through a small group of persons chosen by the people to act as their representatives. These agents of the people are responsible for the day-to-day conduct of government. And they are held accountable to the people for that conduct, especially at periodic elections.

To put it another way, representative democracy is government by popular consent—government with the consent of the governed.

There are some who insist that the United States is a *republic* rather than a democracy. They hold that, in a **republic,** the sovereign power is held by the electorate and is exercised by representatives chosen by and held responsible to the electorate. For them, democracy may be defined only in terms of direct democracy. To most Americans, however, the terms democracy, republic, representative democracy, and republican form of government generally mean the same thing.

---

[5]The word *democracy* is derived from the Greek words *demos*, meaning "the people," and *kratia* meaning "rule" or "authority." The Greek word *demokratia* means, literally, "rule by the people."

[6]The *Landsgemeinde*, like the original New England town meeting, is an assembly open to all local citizens qualified to vote. In a more limited sense, lawmaking by initiative petition is also an example of direct democracy (see page 533).

WHAT DOES "DEMOCRACY" MEAN?

"A word fitly spoken. . . ."

Proverbs, 25:11.

What, precisely, does the word *democracy* mean? That may seem a strange question to ask here—in the midst of several pages in which we try to answer it. It may seem strange, too, in the light of this: No term is more widely used in American politics and, certainly, no concept is more central to our whole system of government.

But anyone who has ever made a serious attempt to answer that question has quickly discovered this: Democracy is a very difficult word to define—and it is for several reasons.

For one thing, it has no *referent.* That is, it is a word much like "good," "truth," "justice," and so on. You cannot see it, or touch it, or hear it; it does not call to mind some tangible object or some sharply etched picture.

And the word can mean different things to different people. The Soviet Union claims to be democratic. So does the United States. Clearly, they and we are not using the word in the same way.

There is yet another problem here. We often use the term in two quite distinct senses. Thus, we speak of democracy as an *ideology* (a theory, a set of beliefs)—for example, "the democratic way of life." And we also refer to it as a *process* (a practice, a way of doing things)—"making democracy work." Any useful definition of the term must cover both of these aspects of it.

1. Check the definition(s) of democracy in (at least one) standard dictionary. What do you find? Where else might you look for a good explanation of the term?
2. What does democracy mean to you —in your own words?

"The Small Society," by Brickman. Washington Star Syndicate Inc.

Today, most of the states of the Western World are representative democracies—but, certainly, some are more democratic than others.

Basic Concepts of Democracy

There is nothing inevitable about democracy. It does not exist here simply because we regard it as the best of all possible political systems. Nor will it continue to exist for that reason.

Rather, it exists in this country because we believe in its basic concepts. And it will continue to exist only for as long as we continue to subscribe to —and practice—those concepts.

The basic concepts of democracy—as we understand and apply the term in the United States—are:

(1) A recognition of the fundamental worth and dignity of each and every person.

(2) A respect for the equality of all persons.

(3) A faith in majority rule and an insistence upon minority rights.

(4) An acceptance of the necessity of compromise.

(5) An insistence upon the widest possible area of individual freedom.

Of course, these ideas may be, and often are, worded in other ways. No matter what the wording, however, they form the very *minimum* that must be agreed to by anyone who professes to believe in democracy.

Fundamental Worth of the Individual.   Democracy is firmly based upon a belief in the fundamental importance of the individual. Democracy insists that *each person's worth and dignity must be recognized and respected by all other individuals, and by all of society, at all times.*

This concept of the sanctity of the individual is of overriding importance in democratic thought. Anything and everything a democratic society does must and should be done within the limits of this great, *central* concept.

At various times the welfare of one or a few individuals is subordinated to the interests of the many in a democracy, of course. People can be (and are) forced to do several things, both large and small, and whether they want to or not. The examples of this are many, and they range all the way from paying taxes or registering for the draft on down to stopping at a stop sign

When these or similar things are done, a democratic society is serving the interests of the many. But it is *not* serving them simply as the interests of a mass of people who happen to outnumber the few. Rather, it is serving the many who, *as individuals,* together make up that society.

Equality of All Persons.   Hand-in-hand with the belief in the sanctity of the individual, democracy stresses the equality of all individuals. It holds, with Jefferson, that "all men are created equal."

Certainly, democracy does *not* insist upon an equality of *condition* for all persons. Thus, it does not claim that all are born with the same mental or physical abilities. Nor does it argue that all persons have a right to an equal share of worldly goods.

Rather, the democratic concept of equality insists that all are entitled to: (1) *equality of opportunity* and (2) *equality before the law.* That is, the democratic concept of equality holds that no person should be held back for any such artificial or arbitrary reasons as those based upon race, color, religion, or sex. It holds that each person must be free to develop himself or herself as fully as he or she can (or cares to) and that each person should be treated as the equal of all others by the law.

We have come a great distance toward reaching the goal of equality for all in this country. But only the willfully blind will not see this point: We are still a considerable distance from a genuine, universally recognized, and universally respected equality for all of our people.

Majority Rule and Minority Rights. In a democracy public policy is to be made *not* by the dictate of a ruling few but in accord with the will of the people.

But what is the "popular will," and how is it to be determined? How, that is, are public policy questions to be decided and public policies made? There must be some standard, some device, by which these crucial questions can be answered. The only satisfactory device democracy knows is that of *majority rule.*

An ancient Arab proverb tells us that it is better to knock heads together than to count them. In effect, it suggests that we are more likely to find out what is inside those heads by breaking them open than we are by simply counting them. But, again, and most emphatically, democracy *does* believe in counting them.

Democracy is firmly committed to the proposition that a majority of the people will be right more often than they will be wrong. It also believes that the majority will be right more often than one person or small group.

Democracy may be quite usefully described as an experiment—a trial-and-error process, designed to find satisfactory ways to order human relations. Notice that it does *not* say that the majority will always be "right," that it will *always* arrive at the best of all possible decisions on public matters. In fact, the democratic process (the process of majority rule) does not intend to come up with "right" or "best" answers. Rather, it searches for *satisfactory* solutions to public problems.

Of course, democracy insists that the decisions that are made will more often be *more* rather than *less* satisfactory. It does admit the possibility of mistakes, however—the possibility that "wrong" or less satisfactory answers will sometimes be found. And it also recognizes that seldom is any solution to a public problem so satisfactory that it cannot be improved. So, the process of experimentation, of seeking answers to public questions, is a continuous one.

Certainly, a democracy cannot work without the principle of majority rule. Unchecked, however, a majority could destroy its opposition and, in the process, destroy democracy, as well. Thus, democracy insists upon majority rule *restrained by minority rights*. The majority must always recognize the right of any minority to become, if it can, by fair and lawful means, itself the majority.

The majority must always be willing to listen to a minority's argument, to hear its objections, to bear its criticisms, and to welcome its suggestions. Anything less contradicts the very meaning of democracy.

Necessity of Compromise. In a democracy public decision-making is (must be) very largely a matter of give-and-take. It is a matter of **compromise**— the process of blending and adjusting, of reconciling competing views and interests, in order to find the position most acceptable to the largest number.

Compromise is an essential part of the democratic concept for two major reasons. *First*, remember that democracy puts the *individual* first and, at the same time, insists that each individual is the *equal* of all others. How—in a society made up of many individuals (and groups) with many quite different opinions and interests—can public decisions be made except by compromise? *Secondly*, few public questions have only "two sides." Most have many different sides and can be answered in several ways. As a case in point, take the apparently simple question of how a city should pay for the paving of a public street. Should it charge the costs to those who own property along the street? Or should all of the city's residents pay the costs from the city's general treasury? Or should the city and the adjacent property owners share the costs? What of those who will use the street but do not live in the city? Should they have to pay a toll or buy a license for that use?

Again, the point here is that *most* public policy questions can be answered in several different ways. But the fact remains that *some* answer must be found.

It would be impossible for the people in a democratic society to decide most public questions without the element of compromise. Remember, however, that compromise is a *process*, it is never an end in itself. Not all compromises are good, and not all are necessary. There are some things—such as the equality of all persons—that should never be the subject of any kind of compromise if democracy is to survive.

Individual Freedom.   From all that has been said to this point, it should be clear that democracy can thrive only in an atmosphere of individual freedom. But democracy *does not* and *cannot* insist upon complete freedom for the individual. Absolute freedom can exist only in a state of **anarchy**—in the total absence of government. And anarchy can only lead, inevitably and quickly, to rule by the strong and ruthless.

Democracy does insist, however, that each individual must be as free to do as he or she pleases as the freedom of all will allow. Justice Oliver Wendell Holmes once had this to say about the relative nature of each individual's rights: "The right to swing my fist ends where the other man's nose begins."

Drawing the line between the rights of one individual and those of another is a far-from-easy task. But the drawing of that line is a continuingly necessary and vitally important function of democratic government. It is because, as John F. Kennedy once said: "The rights of every man are diminished when the rights of one man are threatened."

Striking the proper balance between freedom for the individual and the rights of society as a whole is similarly difficult—and vital. Abraham Lincoln once stated democracy's problem here in these words:

> Must a government of necessity be too *strong* for the liberties of its own people, or too *weak* to maintain its own existence?

The problem goes to the very heart of democracy. Human beings desire both liberty and authority. Democratic government must work, constantly, to strike the proper balance between the two. The authority of government must be adequate to the needs of society. But that authority must never be allowed to become so great that it restricts the individual beyond necessity.

Democracy looks upon all civil rights as vital, but it places its highest value on those guarantees necessary to the free exchange of ideas: on *freedom of expresssion* and *freedom of thought.* Several years ago, the President's Committee on Civil Rights made the point this way:

> In a free society there is faith in the ability of the people to make sound, rational judgments. But such judgments are possible only when the people have access to all relevant facts and to all prevailing interpretations of the facts. How can such judgments be formed on a sound basis if arguments, viewpoints, or opinions are arbitrarily suppressed? How can the concept of the marketplace of thought in which truth ultimately prevails retain its validity if the thought of certain individuals is denied the right of circulation?

We shall return to the whole subject of individual rights later—especially in Chapters 5 and 6. We shall also return to each of the other basic democratic concepts in many pages of this book.

✓ FOR REVIEW

1. What is the basic characteristic of a unitary government? A confederate government? A federal government? Which of these forms is the most common today?
2. What is the basic characteristic of a presidential government? A par-

liamentary government? Which of these forms is the most common today?

3. What is the basic characteristic of a dictatorial government? A democratic government? Which of these forms is the most common today?

4. What does the text suggest are the basic concepts of democracy?

Capitalism, Socialism, Communism

What are the functions which, whatever its form, a government ought to undertake? What should it have the power to do? What should it not be allowed to do? Certainly these questions may be asked of just about all areas of human activity. But these questions are raised most often, and most significantly, in the realm of economic affairs.

Questions of politics and of economics are, in fact, inseparable. Many of the most important and most difficult questions governments face are economic ones. What, for example, should be the relationship between management and labor in a nation's economy? On what basis should goods and services be distributed and exchanged within the nation? Should such basic industries as transportation, steel, and oil be privately or publicly owned and operated?

What provisions, if any, ought to be made for the welfare of the elderly? And what of the poor, the physically or mentally handicapped, and those who are otherwise disadvantaged?

Clearly, these are critical *economic* questions—and, just as clearly, they are critical *political* questions, as well.

Three major economic systems predominate in the world today: *capitalism*, *socialism*, and *communism*.

Brokers who buy and sell stocks are subject to government regulations designed to prevent fraudulent trading practices.

Capitalism

The American economic system—and that found in several other nations today—is known as **capitalism.** It is based upon private ownership, individual initiative, profit, and competition. Capitalism is often described, as well, as the **free enterprise** or **private enterprise** system.

Basic Nature of the Capitalistic System. In the capitalistic system the means by which goods and services are produced are held, very largely, as private property. That is, the instruments of production, of distribution, and of exchange (as factories, mines, stores, farms, railroads, airlines, banks) are privately owned and managed.

Those who own these means hire labor and *compete* with one another to produce goods and services at a *profit*. Competition is the lifeblood of the system. Profit is what makes the system work. The **profits** of an enterprise are its earnings, that is, the returns realized by

The particular shape of a nation's economic system has very real and very profound effects upon the shape of everyone's daily life. At left: Customers wait for a government-run meat market to open in Soviet-dominated Poland. Right: A meat counter in a privately-owned supermarket in New York.

the owners over and above the costs of doing business. In short, profits are the rewards received for the risks taken and the initiative shown.

Generally speaking, any person or group may start an enterprise—try to produce or sell goods or offer services—and the risks and rewards are theirs. Most of the larger and many of the smaller businesses in the United States today are in fact owned by large numbers of persons—by stockholders who own shares in them. Some 30 million persons in the United States own shares in some 11,000 business firms today.

Typically, part of the profits earned by an enterprise is paid out to shareholders as *dividends* and part is reinvested in the business. Thus, the investor receives a return on his or her investment, the business expands, more jobs are created, individual purchasing power increases, and a still higher standard of living results.

Laissez-Faire Theory. American capitalism as we know it today bears only a distant resemblance to classical capitalistic economics. The beginnings

of capitalism are found in the concepts of *laissez-faire*, a doctrine developed in the late 18th and early 19th centuries.[7]

Under ***laissez-faire*** theory, government should play only a very limited—really a "hands off"—role in society. Its activities should be confined to three areas: (1) the conduct of foreign relations and national defense, (2) the maintenance of police and courts to protect private property and the health, safety, and morals of the people, and (3) the performance of certain necessary functions which cannot be provided by private enterprise at a profit.

The theory was given its classic expression by Adam Smith in *The Wealth of Nations*, first published in London in 1776. Its basic assumption was well summarized in Thomas Jefferson's often quoted remark: "That government is best which governs least." Its supporters insisted that government's place in economic affairs ought to be limited to those functions designed to protect and

---

[7]The term *laissez-faire* comes from a French idiom meaning "to let alone." Translated literally, it means "allow to act."

promote the unhampered, free play of competition and the operation of the law of supply and demand.

The theory of *laissez-faire* economics never operated in fact in this country, even in the earliest days of the Republic. Even so, it is clear that the concepts of *laissez-faire* had, and still have, a profound effect upon the nature of our economic system. Most business enterprises in the United States are owned by private persons, not by government. They are financed with private capital, not with public funds. And, they are managed by private citizens, not by public officials.

A "Mixed Economy." While the American economic system is essentially private in character, government has always played a considerable, and an increasing, role in it. Indeed, our system may be properly described as a **mixed economy.** That is, it is one in which private enterprise is combined with and supported by considerable government regulation and promotion.

A vast amount of economic regulation and promotion takes place at all levels of government in the United States—National, State, and local. To give only a very few examples, economic activities are regulated by government in this country through: antitrust laws, labor-management relations statutes, pure food and drug laws, the regulation of environmental pollution, the policing of investment practices, and city and county zoning ordinances and building codes.

Also, the nation's economic life is promoted in a great number of public ways; for example: by direct subsidies, public roads and highways, such services as the postal system and weather reports, public housing programs, research at State universities, loan programs for different purposes, and planting and marketing advice to farmers.

Our economy is also "mixed" in the sense that some enterprises and functions which might be carried on privately are, in fact, operated by government. Public education, the postal system, the monetary system, some forms of public transportation, and roadbuilding are examples of long standing.

How much should government participate, regulate and promote, police and serve? Many of our most heated political debates center on this question. In the search for answers, we tend to follow the general rule expressed by Abraham Lincoln 120 years ago:

The legitimate object of government is to do for the community of people whatever they need to have done, but cannot do so well for themselves, in their separate and individual capacities.

Most Americans believe that a well-regulated capitalistic system—one of free choice, individual incentive, private enterprise—is the best guarantee of the better life for everyone.

Socialism

Socialism is a philosophy of *economic collectivism*. It advocates the collective—that is, the social, public—ownership of the instruments of production, distribution, and exchange. It holds that the means by which goods and services are produced should be *publicly* owned and managed.

Socialism rejects the ideas of private ownership, competition, and profit which lie at the heart of capitalist thought and practice.

The roots of socialism lie deep in history. Almost from the beginning there have been those who have dreamed and planned for a society built upon socialist doctrine. Most of the earlier socialists foresaw a collective economy arising out of and managed by voluntary private action. With few exceptions, they believed they could reach their goals without government action. For this reason, early socialist doctrine is often called "private socialism."

Socialism in its modern form—that is, *state socialism*—has emerged only over the course of the past 100 years or so. Only since the middle of the 1800s have most socialists argued that the reaching of their goal is too big a task for private action alone.

The most extreme form of socialism today is *communism.* Most socialists outside the Soviet and Chinese orbits are *evolutionary socialists,* or, as they are often called, *social democrats.* They believe that socialism can best be brought about gradually and peaceably, by lawful means, and by working within the established framework of govern-

A day care center in Denmark, a country in which this and other kinds of social services (such as dental and medical care and housing for the aged) are provided by the government.

ment. They believe that, even after they have won control of government, the new order should be introduced only in stages. The first stage, they believe, should be the **nationalization** (socialization, public ownership) of a few key enterprises, such as banking, transportation, and the steel industry.

Evolutionary socialists argue that political democracy, with its emphasis on popular participation in government, is incomplete. For them, true democracy can exist only when the people share in the management of their economic destinies. The British Labor Party and the major socialist parties of Western Europe and the Scandinavian countries are the major examples of evolutionary socialism in action today.[8]

Socialists insist that their philosophy is based on justice because it aims at a more nearly equal distribution of both wealth and opportunity among people. Opponents of socialism condemn it because they believe that it kills individual initiative and denies to the capable and the industrious their just rewards. Many also feel that the greater government regulation needed for socialism can only lead to dictatorship.

The complexities of today's society have led to vast expansion of government functions in the United States and most other countries. Many of the activities undertaken by government in this country in the past 50 years or so have been attacked by opponents who insist that they are "socialistic" and thus ill-advised and a threat to the nation and its future.

---

[8]Although socialism and communism are often identified with each other, the socialists of the noncommunist world (the evolutionary socialists) are generally bitter foes of the communists. They share many of the ideas supported by the Russian, Chinese, and other Marxists. But most evolutionary socialists do not accept the theory of the class struggle, the necessity of violent revolution, and the dictatorship of the proletariat—all fundamental to Marxian communism.

Communism

As we know it today, communism was born in 1848 with the publication of *The Communist Manifesto*. A brief, inflammatory pamphlet, it was written by Karl Marx with the aid of his close colleague, Friedrich Engels. In *The Communist Manifesto* and his later and very extensive writings, Marx laid down the cardinal premises of *scientific socialism*, or communism.[9]

From the death of Marx in 1883, and that of Engels in 1895, communism has been interpreted and expanded by his followers. The most important of the latter-day "high priests of communism" have been Vladimir Ilyich Lenin, Josef Stalin, Nikita Khrushchev and Leonid Brezhnev in the Soviet Union, and Mao Tse-tung in the People's Republic of China. The doctrines they have developed are very clearly both political and economic in nature.[10]

Communist Theory. Communist ideology rests upon four basic, and closely related, propositions: (1) its theory of history, (2) the labor theory of value, (3) its theory of the nature of the state, and (4) its concept of the dictatorship of the proletariat.

(1) The Communist Theory of History. According to Marx, all of human history has been a story of the "class struggle." The communists say that there have always been two opposing classes in society—one an oppressor (dominating) class and the other an oppressed (dominated) class. Thus, in the Middle Ages those two classes were the nobility and their serfs. Today, say the communists, the capitalists (the *bourgeoisie*) keep the workers (the *proletariat*) in bondage. Workers in capitalistic countries are described as "wage slaves," who are paid barely enough to allow them to eke out a starvation living as they toil for their masters.

The communists hold that the class struggle has become so bitter and the divisions between the classes is now so sharp that a revolt of the masses and the downfall of the bourgeoisie are inevitable. They see their function as that of speeding up the "natural" course of history, by violence if need be.

(2) The Labor Theory of Value. The communist ideology also holds that the value of any commodity is determined by the amount of labor needed to produce it. In other words, a suit of clothes is worth so much because it takes so much labor to produce it. Because the laborer produced the suit and thus created its value, the communists claim that the laborer should receive that value in full. They are bitterly opposed to the free enterprise profit system and condemn profits as "surplus value" which should go to the worker.

(3) The Nature of the State. To the communists, the state is the instrument or "tool" of the dominating class—a tool with which the bourgeoisie keeps the proletariat in bondage. Because the bourgeoisie has so firm a hold on the state and its power, said Lenin, it is only through a "violent and bloody revolution" that the situation can be changed.

The communists see a number of other institutions in this same light. Thus, Marx described religion as the "opiate of the people." Religious beliefs, he wrote, are a drug fed to the people, a hoax through which they are led to tolerate their supposed harsh lot in this life in the hope of gaining a "fictional afterlife."

(4) The Dictatorship of the Proletariat. The communists do not

---

[9]The term *scientific socialism* was used to separate Marxian thought from the older and less extreme forms of socialism. In later years, Marx and his followers came to prefer the term *communism*.

[10]Capitalism is also a political and an economic doctrine, but in a much more limited sense. To the capitalist, the proper role of government is that of stimulator, servant, and regulator or referee.

foresee a proletariat able to govern themselves after a revolution. Rather, the proletariat would need "guidance and education"—from the Communist Party, of course. Hence, the dogma calls for a *dictatorship of the proletariat*. That is, a totalitarian regime is to be set up to lead the people to the theoretical goal of communism: a "free classless society." As that goal is reached, it is claimed, the state will "wither away." The cardinal principle of the new society would then be: "From each according to his ability, to each according to his need."

Evaluation of Communism. The Soviet Union presents the outstanding example of communism in action. Strictly speaking, the Russians do not practice pure communism today, but an extreme form of socialism.[11]

Their present system stems from the October Revolution of 1917 when Lenin and his followers came to power.[12] Immediately, Lenin tried to set up a communist system. The attempt made the chaos of Russia's defeat and withdrawal from World War I even worse, and it failed. The inefficient and the lazy received as much as the efficient and the industrious. Workers and peasants rebelled. The new government imposed

Jay Justus, *Minneapolis Star*

Communist predictions of a breakdown in our system of free enterprise have proven to be both false and foolish.

severe reprisals; many thousands were executed. Finally, the Soviet leaders changed their approach, turning to their version of socialism. The Soviets now say they are working *toward* the eventual goal of pure communism.

More than 130 years of Marxist theory and more than 60 years of Soviet communism have exposed many of the fallacies of communist doctrine. We shall note the major fallacies of this doctrine here.

Marx argued that the divisions between the bourgeoisie and the proletariat would become deeper and deeper, to the point where capitalism would collapse under its own weight. The rich, said Marx, would become richer and the poor would become poorer. The struggle between the bourgeoisie and the proletariat would grind the middle class down into the ranks of the proletariat.

In fact, the contrary has happened.

---

[11]According to Marx, the guiding principle in a communist society should be "From each according to his ability, to each according to his need." But compare this with this provision (Article 13) of the Soviet Constitution of 1977: "The State shall control the measure of labor and consumption in accordance with the principle: 'From each according to his ability, to each according to his work.' . . . Socially useful work and its results shall determine a citizen's status in society."

[12]The revolution occurred on October 25, 1917, by the Julian calendar then in use in Russia. By the western (Georgian) calendar, now also used in the Soviet Union, the date was November 7. The communists did not, as is often supposed, revolt against the old czarist regime. Rather, they overthrew a fledgling democratic government headed by Alexander Kerensky. The Kerensky government had been created as a result of a revolution in March of 1917. It was this earlier, noncommunist revolt that deposed the czarist tyranny.

The economic gap between workers and owners has narrowed almost to the point of extinction, especially in the United States. Marx and his followers failed to foresee the tremendous growth of the middle class. The poor have not become poorer; they have, in fact, become much, much richer.

Communist theory has little room for individual initiative and incentive, so vital in our own economic system. One of the basic differences between our system and the communists' is that: Where we try to promote *equality of opportunity*, the communists argue for *equality of condition*.

Experience has forced the communists to recognize the importance of incentive, however. The labor theory of value has been very largely ignored in communist practice. Income in the Soviet Union today is based largely on the amount or the importance of the work one does. Thus, scientists, managers, administrators, teachers, and others in the professions receive larger incomes and many more privileges than do the masses in the working class.

The state has not been the tool of the dominant class in the non-communist world. Rather, the state—acting through government controlled by, and responsive to, the will of the people—has become a major agent in improving the welfare of the people.

Marx predicted that the emergence of communism would promote peace among the nations of the world. In fact, quite the opposite has occurred.

Marx, and then Lenin and later Soviet leaders, were confident that communism would appeal to workers throughout the world, regardless of nationality. Thus, the *Manifesto* closed with this cry: "Workingmen of all countries, unite!" But, in fact, the communist dogma has not lessened nationalistic sentiments. That point has been demonstrated time and again—in Poland and elsewhere in Eastern Europe, and by the swords-point relationships between the Soviet Union and the other major communist power today, the People's Republic of China.

The state in the Soviet Union, the People's Republic of China, and other communist countries shows no sign of "withering away." Indeed, under communism the power of the state has been sharply *increased*. The dictatorships established in these countries have become the most totalitarian the world has ever seen. All forms of opposition are ruthlessly put down. Basic freedoms are not permitted, lest the people examine and question the policies of the state. Fear is a weapon in the hands of the ruling group. The dictatorship easily perpetuates itself.

✓ FOR REVIEW

1. Upon what key factors is capitalism based?
2. According to *laissez-faire* theory, what is the proper role of government in society?
3. Why may the American economic system be described as a "mixed" one?
4. What is the basic tenet of the socialist philosophy?
5. Why is modern socialism often given the label of "state socialism"?
6. Who founded present-day communism? When?
7. What are the four central propositions upon which communist theory is built?
8. What fallacies in communist theory and practice are noted in the text?

SUMMARY

We begin our study of the American system of government with a look at the different political and economic systems in the world today.

The *state* is the dominant unit in the political structure of the world. All of the more than 160 states in the world today have four essential characteristics: (1) population, (2) territory, (3) sovereignty, and (4) government.

While no two governments are the same, each may be classified in several ways on the basis of certain factors. On the basis of (1) geographic distribution of power, governments are *unitary, confederate,* or *federal* in form; (2) legislative-executive relationships, they are either *presidential* or *parliamentary;* and (3) the number who may participate, *democratic* or *dictatorial.*

Especially in the American context, *democracy* rests upon five basic concepts: (1) the fundamental worth and dignity of every person; (2) the equality of all persons; (3) majority rule limited by minority rights; (4) the necessity of compromise; and (5) the widest possible area of individual freedom.

Capitalism is an economic doctrine based upon private ownership of the means by which goods and services are produced and upon individual initiative, competition, and profit.

Socialism is a philosophy of economic collectivism, advocating public ownership of at least the major instruments of production, distribution, and exchange. Evolutionary socialists are to be distinguished from revolutionary socialists; most of the latter are communists.

Communism is an extreme form of socialism. It is built on four central concepts: (1) its theory of history; (2) the labor theory of value; (3) its theory of the nature of the state; and (4) the dictatorship of the proletariat.

CHAPTER REVIEW

Key Terms/Concepts

Anarchy (14)
Authoritarian (9)
Autocratic (9)
Capitalism (15)
Communism (18)
The Communist Manifesto (19)
Competition (15)
Compromise (13)
Confederation (7)
Democracy (10)
Dictatorship (9)
Direct/indirect democracy (10)
Divine right (5)
Equality (12)
Executive (6)
Federal (7)
Free enterprise (15)
Government (4)
Legislative (6)
Majority rule (12)
Minority rights (12)
Mixed economy (17)
Parliamentary government (8)
Presidential government (8)
Private enterprise (15)
Profit (15)
Proletariat (19)
Representative democracy (10)
Republic (10)
Social contract (5)
Socialism (17)
Sovereignty (4)
State/state (3,4)
Totalitarian (9)
Unitary government (6)

Keynote Questions

1. What is *sovereignty*? Why is it the one characteristic of a state that sets it apart from all other political units?
2. What is the difference between a *state* and a *government*?
3. Summarize the *social contract theory*. What importance did it have to the shaping of the American governmental system?
4. Describe and compare these forms of government: unitary, federal, confederate; parliamentary, presidential; dictatorial, democratic.
5. What are the basic concepts upon which American democracy rests?
6. What are the essential features of the three major economic systems to be found in the world today? How do they differ with regard to the ownership of: (a) property? (b) the instruments of production, distribution, and exchange?
7. Why are the terms "free enterprise" and "mixed economy" used to describe the American economic system?
8. Cite three of the fallacies of communist doctrine.

For Thought and Discussion

1. In 1733 Alexander Pope penned these lines, in his "Essay on Man":

   For forms of government let fools contest;
   Whate'er is best administer'd is best.

   What do you think of Pope's view of forms of government?
2. Why have so few of all of the governments the world has ever known been democratic in form? Why have most democracies lasted for only relatively brief periods of time?
3. Democracy has been described as "a never-ending search for truth." How would you phrase this description, in your own words? Why must the search be never-ending?
4. Do you agree with this observation by Lord Bryce: "No government demands so much from the citizens as democracy and none gives back so much." And this one by John F. Kennedy: "Ask not what your country can do for you; ask what you can do for your country."
5. Karl Marx predicted that successful communist revolutions would take place first in the more highly industrialized nations, first in Germany and England and then in the United States. History has proved him quite wrong, however. Communist revolutions have taken place, instead, in some of the world's under-developed and predominantly agricultural countries. Why?

Suggested Activities

1. Prepare a series of posters or other displays to illustrate the basic concepts of democracy cited in the text.
2. Make a list of: (a) examples of the ways in which economic activities are regulated by the National, State, and local governments in your area; (b) examples of the ways in which the three levels of government aid the economy of your locale; and (c) the publicly conducted enterprises in your community.
3. Invite the owner of a local business to discuss with the class the various ways in which government regulates and aids his or her business.
4. Stage a debate or class forum on one of the following topics: (a) *Resolved*, That the United States is a republic, not a democracy; (b) *Resolved*, That government should strive to promote equality of opportunity for all but not equality of condition.

CHAPTER 2

To Form A More Perfect Union

CHAPTER OBJECTIVES

To help you to
Learn ▪ Know ▪ Understand

The historical and theoretical origins of the American governmental system.

The development of that system through the colonial period to the coming of Independence.

The governmental arrangements set up by the first State constitutions and by the Articles of Confederation.

The events and the processes involved in the creation and the adoption of the Constitution of the United States.

We hold these truths to be self-evident, that all men are created equal, that they are endowed by their Creator with certain unalienable Rights, that among these are Life, Liberty, and the pursuit of Happiness.

The Declaration of Independence

Government did not suddenly come to the United States with the Declaration of Independence in 1776. Nor was it created by the Framers of the Constitution in 1787. Instead, its roots reach deep into the past. Indeed, its origins may be traced to the very beginnings of western civilization.

Those who built the American system of government worked with what they knew. They built with a knowledge of ideas and of **institutions** (established customs, laws, practices) gained in their own lives, of course. They worked, too, with a knowledge that had come to them from centuries of experience, tradition, thought, and deed.

In this chapter we focus upon the origins of the American governmental system. We shall review its historical development through the creation of the Constitution in the late 1780s. As we do so, keep this point in mind: The job of building government in the United States did not end some 200 years ago. Nor has it been completed since. Rather, it is a continuing and a never-ending process, as we shall see.

24

When the Declaration of Independence was written (lower left) in 1776, the nation was largely rural, made up mostly of scattered farms and small settlements.

The Colonial Period

The English Heritage

Peoples from many lands came to explore and to settle in different parts of what was to become the United States. The English, French, Dutch, Spanish, Swedes, and others all played a part in colonizing America. But it was the English who came in the largest numbers. And it was the English who soon controlled the 13 colonies that stretched for some 1300 miles (1780 kilometers) along the Atlantic seaboard.[1]

The earliest English settlers were pioneers. They had had to brave the dangers of the sea to come to America. Once here, they had to clear the wilderness, build homes and farms, and deal with the Indians. Quite literally, they had to hack out their own economic futures in the New World. But they brought with them the knowledge of a political system that had been developing in England for centuries. And so they carried much of their political future with them, ready-made.

Most importantly, those early settlers brought with them three ideas that were to loom large in the shaping of government in the United States.

Ordered Government. They saw the need for an orderly regulation of their relationships with one another—that is, for government. And they quickly created local governments, based upon those they had known in England.

Many of the offices and units of government they established can be found at the local level around the country yet today—the offices of sheriff, coroner, assessor, and justice of the peace, the grand jury, counties, townships, and several others.

[1]England first began to claim territory in North America with the voyages of John Cabot in 1496 and 1498. By 1664, when it seized Holland's colonial holdings (New Netherlands), England held all of the Atlantic coast from the Gulf of Saint Lawrence south to Florida. With the end of the French and Indian War, in 1763, it had eliminated all French claims in North America; and in 1763 it also acquired Florida from Spain. Thus, on the eve of the American Revolution, England controlled all of the present-day United States east of the Mississippi.

Limited Government. Those first colonists brought with them, too, the idea that government is *not* all-powerful. That is, that government is *limited* in what it may do and that each person has certain rights that government cannot injure or take away.

The concept of limited government was deeply rooted in England by the time the first English ships reached the New World. It had been planted there in such historic documents as the Magna Carta in 1215, the Petition of Right in 1628, and the Bill of Rights and the Act of Toleration in 1689.

Representative Government. The early English settlers also carried another very important concept to America: representative government. The idea that government should serve the people had also been developing in England for centuries. With it had come a growing insistence that the people should have a voice in deciding what government should and should not do. This notion of "government of, by, and for the people" found fertile soil in America.

We have built upon, and changed and added to, those ideas and institutions that came to us from England, of course. Still, there is much in the American government of today that bears the English stamp. Surely, this should not be surprising. The colonial period of American history lasted for over a century and a half, from 1607 to 1775. And, there has not been an independent United States for a very much longer time.

Government in the Colonies

The 13 colonies were established separately, over a span of 125 years. Over that long period, they developed from outlying trading posts and isolated farm settlements into organized communities. The first of them, Virginia, was founded with the first permanent English settlement in the New World, at Jamestown in 1607. The Pilgrims began the settlement of the second one, Massachusetts, when they landed at Plymouth in 1620. The others came into being during the next several decades. Georgia was the last to be formed, with the settlement of Savannah in 1733.

Each of the colonies was born out of a different set of circumstances, and so each had its own character. Thus, Virginia was set up as a commercial venture. Its first colonists were employees of the Virginia Company, a private trading corporation.[2] Massachusetts, on the other hand, was first settled by the Pilgrims (in 1620) and by the Puritans (in 1628). They came to America in search of greater personal and religious freedom. Georgia was founded largely as a haven for debtors, as a refuge for the victims of England's harsh poor laws.

But the differences between and among the colonies is really of little moment. Of much greater importance is the fact all of them were shaped by their English origins.

Three Types of Colonies. Each of the colonies was established on the basis of a **charter,** a written grant of authority from the King.[3] Over time, these instruments of government produced three kinds of colonies—and so three kinds of colonial government: *royal, proprietary,* and *charter.*

---

[2]In 1606 King James I had given the company the exclusive right to trade and colonize along the Atlantic coast from New England to the Carolinas. Under its original charter the company was divided into two parts. The Virginia Company of London was to operate in Virginia and the Carolinas and The Virginia Company of Plymouth in New England.

The Company was patterned after the highly profitable East India Company, set up in 1600 to trade with India. But there were large differences between India and North America; most importantly, India was densely populated but the North American continent was largely uninhabited. Neither branch of the Virginia Company prospered and England's major interest in the New World soon turned from trade to settlement.

[3]Except for Georgia. Its charter was granted by Parliament in 1732.

The first representative legislature to meet in America met in the chancel of the church at Jamestown, Virginia, in the summer of 1619.

Royal Colonies. The **royal colonies** were those subject to the direct control of the Crown. On the eve of the Revolution in 1775 there were eight of them: New Hampshire, Massachusetts, New York, New Jersey, Virginia, North Carolina, South Carolina, and Georgia.

The Virginia colony was not the quick success its sponsors had promised. So, in 1624, the King revoked the London Company's charter and Virginia became the first royal colony. Later, as the original charters of other colonies were cancelled or withdrawn, they, too, became royal colonies. Georgia was the last to join their list, in 1752.

Gradually, a pattern of government emerged for each of the royal colonies. The King named a governor. He was the colony's chief executive and usually its most influential resident. A council, also named by the King, served as an advisory body to the royal governor. In time, the governor's council became the upper house of the colonial legislature.

It also became the highest court in the colony. The lower house of the legislature was elected by those property owners qualified to vote.[4] It owed much of its influence to the fact that it shared with the governor and his council the "power of the purse"—*i.e.*, the power to tax and the power to spend. The governor, advised by the council, appointed the judges for the courts of the colony.

The laws passed by the legislature had to be approved by the governor and also by the Crown. The royal governors often ruled with a stern hand, following instructions received from London. Much of the resentment that finally flared into revolution was fanned by their actions.

---

[4]In 1619 the London Company allowed the creation of a legislature in Virginia. It held its first meeting in the church at Jamestown on July 30, 1619, and was the first representative body to meet in the New World. It was made up of burgesses elected from each settlement in the colony. The term "burgesss" was used because the local settlements were expected to grow into boroughs (towns), as in England.

The Proprietary Colonies.   At the time of the Revolution there were three proprietary colonies: Maryland, Pennsylvania, and Delaware. The name came from the term **proprietor**—a person to whom the King had made a grant of land in the New World. By charter, that land could be settled and governed much as the proprietor (owner) chose.

In 1634 the King had granted Maryland to Lord Baltimore and in 1681 Pennsylvania to William Penn. In 1682 Penn also acquired Delaware, which had first been settled by the Dutch in 1631 and by the Swedes in 1638.[5]

The governments of these three colonies were much like those in the royal colonies. The governor, however, was appointed by the proprietor. In effect, the proprietor (the landlord) stood between his colony and the king. In Maryland and Delaware the legislature was **bicameral** (made up of two houses). The members of the upper house, who were also the members of the governor's council, were chosen by the proprietor. The members of the lower house were elected by the freemen (property owners) of the colony. In Pennsylvania the legislature was a **unicameral** (one-house) body. The governor's council had no legislative authority; it merely advised the governor. As in the royal colonies, appeals from the decisions of the courts could be carried to the King and his Privy Council in London.

The Charter Colonies.   Connecticut and Rhode Island were charter colonies. They were based upon charters granted (in 1662 and 1663, respectively) to the colonists themselves, as a group. Thus, they were largely self-governing. Power over colonial affairs was held by the colonists rather than by a trading company, a proprietor, or the Crown.[6]

The governors of Connecticut and Rhode Island were elected each year by the freemen of the colony. Although the King's approval was required, it was not often asked. The members of both houses of the legislature were not subject to the governor's veto nor was the Crown's approval needed. Colonial judges were appointed by the legislature, but appeals could be taken from their courts to the King in Council.

The Connecticut and the Rhode Island charters were so liberal for their time that, with independence, they were kept as State constitutions—until 1818 and 1843, respectively. In fact, many historians say that had Britain allowed the other colonies so much freedom and self-government, the Revolution might never have occurred.

☑ FOR REVIEW

1. What major political concepts did the early English settlers bring?
2. Identify and describe the three types of colonial government in pre-Revolutionary America.

The Colonies and England[7]

The 13 colonies, which had been separately established, were separately controlled under the King—from London, largely through the Privy Council and the Board of Trade.

Parliament took little part in the management of the colonies. While it did become more and more interested in matters of trade, it left matters of colo-

---

[5]New York (New Netherlands before its capture from the Dutch in 1664), New Jersey, North Carolina, South Carolina, and Georgia also began as proprietary colonies. Each of them later became a royal colony.

[6]The Massachusetts Bay Colony was established as the first charter colony in 1629. But its charter was later revoked and Massachusetts became a royal colony in 1691. Religious dissidents from Massachusetts founded both Connecticut (in 1633) and Rhode Island (in 1636).

[7]England became Great Britain, by the Act of Union with Scotland, in 1707.

nial administration almost entirely to the Crown.[8]

Over the century and a half that followed the first settlement at Jamestown, the colonies developed within that framework of royal control. In *theory*, they were governed in all important matters from London. But London was 3000 miles (4800 kilometers) away. So, in *practice*, the colonists became used to a large measure of self-government.

In time, each colonial legislature assumed broad lawmaking powers. Many found the power to the purse to be very effective, as we've noted—and they often bent a governor to their will by not voting the money for his salary until he came to terms with them.

By the mid-1700s, the relationship between Britain and the colonies had become—in fact, if not in form—*federal*. The central government in London was responsible for colonial defense and for foreign affairs. It also provided a uniform system of money and credit, and a common market for colonial trade. Beyond that, the colonies were allowed a fairly wide measure of self-rule. Little was taken from them in direct taxes to pay for the services of the central government. And the few regulations set by Parliament, mostly about trade, were largely ignored.

This all changed, and dramatically, in the early 1760s, however. George III came to the throne in 1760, and shortly Britain began to deal more firmly with its American possessions. Restrictive

trading acts were expanded and enforced; and new taxes were imposed, mostly to support British troops in North America.

Many colonists took strong exception to these moves. They objected to taxes they had had no part in levying—it was "taxation without representation." They saw little if any need for the troops —the power of the French had been broken in the French and Indian War (1754–1763). They were British subjects and loyal to the Crown. But they flatly refused to agree that Parliament had the right to control what they believed to be their own local affairs.

The King's ministers were poorly informed and stubborn. They pushed ahead with their policies, despite the resentments they stirred in America. Within a few years the colonists were to be forced to a fateful choice—to submit or to revolt.

The Colonies Unite

There were several attempts to bring about colonial union long before the fateful 1770s.

Early Attempts. In 1643 the Massachusetts Bay, Plymouth, New Haven, and Connecticut settlements formed the New England Confederation, a "league of friendship" for defense against the Indians. As the Indian danger passed and frictions grew between the settlements, the confederation lost importance and finally died in 1684. In 1697 William Penn offered an elaborate plan for intercolonial cooperation, largely in trade, defense, and criminal matters. It was given little attention, however, and was soon forgotten.

The Albany Plan, 1754. In 1754 the Board of Trade called a meeting of seven of the northern colonies[9] at Alba-

---

[8]Parliament is the central and dominant organ in present-day British government, as we noted in Chapter 1. Much of earlier English political history can be told in terms of the centuries-long struggle for supremacy between King and Parliament, however. That conflict was largely settled by England's Glorious Revolution of 1688, but it did continue on through the American colonial period and into the 19th century. But, here, an important point in American political history: despite its growing power in British government, Parliament paid little attention to the colonies until late in the colonial period.

---

[9]Connecticut, Maryland, Massachusetts, New Hampshire, New York, Pennsylvania, and Rhode Island.

ny, to take up the problems of colonial trade and the danger of French and Indian attacks. Here, Benjamin Franklin offered what came to be known as the Albany Plan of Union.

Franklin wanted an annual congress (assembly or conference) of delegates from each of the 13 colonies. That body would have power to raise military and naval forces, make war and peace with the Indians, regulate trade with them, levy taxes, and collect customs duties.

Franklin's plan was ahead of its time. It was agreed to by the Albany meeting, but it was turned down by the colonies and by the Crown. His plan was to be remembered later, however, when independence came.

The Stamp Act Congress, 1765. The harsh tax and trade policies of the 1760s fanned resentment in the colonies. A number of new laws had been passed by Parliament, among them the Stamp Act of 1765. That law required the use of tax stamps on all legal documents, on certain business agreements, and on all newspapers circulating in the colonies.

The new taxes were widely denounced—in part because the rates were severe, but largely because they amounted to "taxation without representation." In October of 1765 nine of the colonies[10] sent delegates to the Stamp Act Congress in New York. They prepared a strong protest against the new British policies, a Declaration of Rights and Grievances, and sent it off to the King. Their actions marked the first time a significant number of the colonies had joined to oppose the home government.

Parliament repealed the Stamp Act, but frictions mounted. New laws were passed and new policies made to tie the colonies more closely to London. Resentment and anger were expressed in wholesale evasion of the laws. There was mob violence at several ports and many colonists **boycotted**—refused to buy or sell—English goods. On March 3, 1770, British troops in Boston fired on a jeering throng, killing five in what came to be known as the Boston Massacre.

Organized resistance grew and was carried on through Committees of Correspondence, which had grown out of a group formed by Samuel Adams in Boston in 1772. Within a year these committees were to be found throughout the colonies, providing a network for cooperation and the exchange of information among the patriots.

Protests multiplied, and in many places. The famous Boston Tea Party came on December 16, 1773. A group of men, dressed as Indians and protesting a new monopoly on tea, boarded three ships in Boston harbor and dumped their offending cargoes into the sea.

The First Continental Congress, 1774. In the spring of 1774 Parliament passed yet another set of laws, this time to punish the colonists for the troubles in Boston and elsewhere. These new laws—denounced in America as "the Intolerable Acts"—caused the Massachusetts and the Virginia assemblies to call a general meeting of all of the colonies.

Fifty-five delegates, from every colony except Georgia, met in Philadelphia on September 5, 1774. Many of the most able men of the day were there: Samuel and John Adams from Massachusetts; Roger Sherman from Connecticut; Stephen Hopkins from Rhode Island; John Dickinson and Joseph Galloway from Pennsylvania; John Jay and Philip Livingston from New York; George Washington, Richard Henry Lee, and Patrick Henry from Virginia; and John Rutledge from South Carolina.

[10]All except Georgia, New Hampshire, North Carolina, and Virginia.

A society of patriots, known as the Sons of Liberty, raises the Liberty Pole in 1776 as the news of independence reached their community.

For nearly two months the members of this First Continental Congress debated the worsening situation. A Declaration of Rights, protesting Britain's colonial policies, was addressed to George III. The delegates urged each of the colonies to refuse all trade with England until the hated taxes and trade regulations were repealed.

The meeting adjourned on October 26, with a call for a second congress to assemble the following May.

But the British government would not compromise, let alone reverse its policies. It reacted to the Declaration of Rights as it had to other expressions of colonial discontent—with even stricter and more repressive measures.

☑ FOR REVIEW────────────

1. By the mid-1700s, the governmental relationship between Britain and the colonies had become what —in fact, if not in form? Why?

2. How did that relationship change in the 1760s?

Independence

The Second Continental Congress

The Second Continental Congress met in Philadelphia on May 10, 1775. By then, the Revolution had begun. The "shot heard 'round the world" had been fired. The battles of Lexington and Concord had been fought three weeks earlier, on April 19th.

Each of the 13 colonies—soon to be States—was now represented. Most of those who had attended the First Continental Congress were again present. Important newcomers were Benjamin Franklin of Pennsylvania and John Hancock of Massachusetts.

Hancock was chosen president of the Congress.[11] Almost at once, a "continental army" was organized, and George Washington was appointed its commander in chief. Thomas Jefferson then

───────────────

[11]Peyton Randolph, who had also served as president of the First Continental Congress, was originally chosen to the office. He resigned on May 24, however, because the Virginia House of Delegates, of which he was the Speaker, had been called into session. Hancock was then elected to succeed him.

took Washington's place in the Virginia delegation.

The Second Continental Congress became, by force of circumstance, our first national government. It served as the first government of the United States for five fateful years—from the signing of the Declaration of Independence in July of 1776 until the Articles of Confederation went into effect on March 1, 1781. During that time, it prosecuted a war, raised armies and a navy, borrowed money, bought supplies, created a monetary system, made treaties with foreign powers, and performed as any government would have had to under the circumstances.

The unicameral Congress exercised both legislative and executive powers. In legislative matters each colony (later State) had one vote. Executive functions were handled through committees.

The Declaration of Independence

On June 7, 1776, Richard Henry Lee of Virginia proposed to the Second Continental Congress:

> *Resolved,* That these United Colonies are, and of right ought to be, free and independent States, that they are absolved from all allegiance to the British Crown, and that all political connection between them and the State of Great Britain is, and ought to be, totally dissolved.

A committee of five of the ablest men in the Congress—Benjamin Franklin, John Adams, Roger Sherman, Robert Livingston, and Thomas Jefferson—was named to prepare a proclamation of independence. Their momentous product, the Declaration of Independence,[12] was almost wholly the work of the young and brilliant Jefferson.

---

[12]The full text of the Declaration appears on pages 626–627.

On July 2 the final break came. The delegates unanimously agreed to Lee's resolution. Two days later, July 4, 1776, the Declaration of Independence was adopted and announced to the world.

Much of the Declaration speaks of "the repeated injuries and usurpations" that led the colonists to revolt. It proclaims the independence of the United States, of course. At its heart, in its second paragraph, it declares:

> We hold these truths to be self-evident, that all men are created equal, that they are endowed by their Creator with certain unalienable Rights, that among these are Life, Liberty and the pursuit of Happiness. That to secure these rights, Governments are instituted among Men, deriving their just powers from the consent of the governed; That whenever any Form of Government becomes destructive of these ends, it is the Right of the People to alter or to abolish it, and to institute new Government, laying its foundations on such principles and organizing its power in such form, as to them shall seem most likely to effect their Safety and Happiness.

With these brave words the United States of America was born. The 13 colonies became free and independent States.

The First State Governments

In January of 1776 New Hampshire adopted a constitution to replace its royal charter. Some three months later South Carolina had done so, too. Then, on May 10th, nearly two months before the Declaration of Independence, Congress urged each of the colonies to adopt

> such governments as shall, in the opinion of the representatives of the people, best conduce to the happiness and safety of their constituents.

Mounted messengers carried the news of independence throughout the 13 colonies.

Most of the States adopted written constitutions in 1776 and 1777. With minor changes, Connecticut and Rhode Island transformed their charters into new fundamental laws. Assemblies or conventions were commonly used to draft or adopt these new documents. Massachusetts set a lasting precedent in the constitution-making process. There, a convention submitted its product to the voters for ratification. The Massachusetts constitution of 1780 is the oldest of the present-day State constitutions. In fact, it is the oldest written constitution in force anywhere in the world today.[13]

The first State constitutions differed, and sometimes widely, in detail. Yet, they shared many common features.

Popular Sovereignty Each of the new constitutions was based upon the principle of *popular sovereignty*. Each of them insisted that government could exist and function *only* with the consent of the governed.

Limited Government The twin concept of *limited government* was also a major feature of each of the documents. Those powers that were granted to government were granted very sparingly and were hedged with many restrictions.

Civil Liberties Seven of the new documents[14] contained a bill of rights, setting out the "unalienable rights" held by the people. In every State it was made clear that the sovereign people held certain rights that government must at all times respect.

Separation of Powers and Checks and Balances The powers that were given to the new State governments were purposefully divided among three distinct branches—executive, legislative, and judicial. Each branch was given powers with which to check—restrain—each of the other branches.

The new State constitutions were rather brief documents. Most of the authority given to State government rested with the legislature. The **suffrage**—the right to vote—was limited to those adult males who could meet property ownership and other high qualifications.

FOR REVIEW

1. What was the Second Continental Congress? How and why did it become our first national government?

2. Who wrote the Declaration of Independence? Why are the opening lines of its second paragraph so important?

3. What, in brief, was the nature of the first State governments?

---

[13]From independence until that constitution became effective in 1780, Massachusetts relied on its colonial charter in force prior to 1691 as its fundamental law. We shall return to the subject of State constitutions later, in Chapter 19. But, for now, this important point: The earliest of those documents were, within a very few years, to have a marked effect upon the drafting of the Constitution of the United States.

[14]Delaware, Maryland, Massachusetts, New Hampshire, North Carolina, Pennsylvania, and Virginia.

The Confederation and the Critical Period

Our First National Constitution.

The First and Second Continental Congresses rested on no legal base. They were called in haste, to meet an emergency, and they were intended to be temporary. Something more regular and lasting was clearly needed.

Richard Henry Lee's resolution which had led to the Declaration of Independence also called upon the Second Continental Congress to propose "a plan of confederation." Off and on—for 17 months—that body considered the problem of uniting the former colonies. Finally, on November 15, 1777, the Articles of Confederation were approved.

The Articles did not go into effect immediately, however. The **ratifications** (formal approval) of all 13 States were needed. Eleven States agreed to the document within a year. Delaware added its approval in mid-1779. But Maryland did not ratify until February 27, 1781. The Second Continental Congress then set March 1, 1781, as the date upon which the Articles were to become effective.

The Articles established "a firm league of friendship" among the States. Each State kept "its sovereignty, freedom, and independence, and every power, jurisdiction, and right . . . not . . . expressly delegated to the United States, in Congress assembled." The States came together "for their common defense, the security of their liberties, and their mutual and general welfare."

Governmental Structure. The government set up by the Articles was simple indeed. A Congress was the sole organ created. It was a single-chambered body, made up of delegates chosen yearly by the States in whatever way their legislatures might direct. Each State had one vote in the Congress.

There was neither an executive nor a judicial branch. These functions were to be handled by committees of the Congress. Each year the Congress chose one of its members as its president—that is, as its presiding officer, but not as the president of the United States. Civil officers—for example, postmasters—were appointed by the Congress.

Powers of Congress. Several important powers were given to the Congress. It could make war and peace; send and receive ambassadors; enter into treaties; borrow money; set up a monetary system; build a navy; raise an army, by asking the States for troops; fix uniform standards of weights and measures; and settle disputes among the States.

State Obligations. By agreeing to the Articles, the States had pledged themselves to several things. They agreed to obey the Articles and acts of the Congress; provide the funds and troops requested by Congress; treat citizens of other States fairly and equally with their own; give full faith and credit to the public acts, records, and judicial

WEAKNESSES IN THE ARTICLES OF CONFEDERATION

- One vote for each State, regardless of size.
- Congress had no power to lay and collect taxes or duties.
- Congress had no power to regulate foreign and interstate commerce.
- No executive to enforce acts of Congress.
- No national court system.
- Amendment only with consent of all of the States.
- A 9/13 majority required to pass laws.
- Articles only a "firm league of friendship."

PERSONALITY PROFILE

MERCY OTIS WARREN (1728–1814)

Women were largely excluded from active politics until well into this century. Still, many did play an important part in shaping the nation.

Mercy Otis Warren of Massachusetts was one of the most effective propagandists for American independence. Both her brother, James Otis, and her husband, James Warren, were major political figures; and she knew many of the other leading personalities of the day, as well.

Her letters to Abagail Adams often criticized the limited opportunities available to women. Nonetheless, she was able to make a number of contributions to the public life of her time.

She wrote several plays (published anonymously) which poked fun at the British and predicted the Revolution. Some of her writings were printed in newspapers and helped to arouse the spirit of Independence. Later, she op-

posed the Constitution and, in 1788, published her *Observations of the New Constitution.* In 1805 she completed a three-volume history of the American Revolution, which is still valued for its profiles of many of the leading personalities of the period.

1. What more can you learn of Mercy Otis Warren?
2. What do you think led some women to break with tradition and become actively involved in politics?

proceedings of every other State; surrender fugitives from justice to each other; submit their disputes to Congress for settlement; and allow open travel and trade between and among the States.

In short, the Congress possessed only those powers "expressly delegated" to it by the Articles. The States retained those powers not given to the Congress. They were primarily responsible for protecting life and property and for promoting the general welfare (the "safety and happiness") of the people.

Weaknesses. The powers of the Congress appear, at first glance, to have been considerable. Several important ones were not given to it, however. The

lack of them, together with other weaknesses, soon proved the Articles could not meet the needs of the time.

The Congress was not given the power to tax. It could raise money only by borrowing and by asking the States for funds. Borrowing was at best a poor source: The Second Continental Congress had borrowed heavily to support the Revolution, and many of those debts had not been repaid. And while the Articles were in force, not one State came close to meeting the financial requests made by the Congress.

Nor did Congress have the power to regulate trade between and among the States. And the lack of a central mechanism to regulate commerce was one of the major factors that led to the adoption of the Constitution, as we shall see.

The Congress had no power to make the States obey the Articles or the laws it made. It could exercise the powers it did have only with the consent of nine of the 13 State delegations. And, finally, the Articles themselves could be changed—**amended**—only with the consent of all 13 of the State legislatures.[14]

The Critical Period, the 1780s.

The long Revolutionary War finally ended on October 18, 1781. America's victory was confirmed by the Treaty of Paris in 1783. Peace brought the new nation's economic and political problems into sharp focus. The weaknesses of the Articles soon surfaced.

With a central government unable to act, the States bickered among themselves and grew increasingly jealous and suspicious of one another. They refused to support the new central government, financially and in almost every other way. Several of them made agreements with foreign governments, even though that was forbidden by the Articles. Most even organized their own military forces.

George Washington complained: "We are one nation today and 13 tomorrow. Who will treat with us on such terms?"

The States taxed each other's goods and even banned some trade. They printed their own money, often with little backing. Economic chaos spread. Prices soared. Sound credit vanished. Debts, public and private, went unpaid.

In Shays' Rebellion, angry farmers seized several courts in Massachusetts to prevent the loss of their property to creditors and tax collectors.

Violence broke out in a number of places. Shays' Rebellion in western Massachusetts in 1786 was only the most spectacular of several incidents.

The Articles had not created a government able to deal with the nation's troubles. Inevitably, there were demands for a stronger, more effective national government. Those who were most threatened by economic and political instability—large property owners, merchants, traders, and other creditors—soon took the lead in efforts to that end. The movement to change began to take concrete form in 1785.

The Meetings at Mount Vernon and Annapolis

Maryland and Virginia, plagued by trade disputes, took the first step. Ignoring the Congress, the two States agreed to a conference on those problems. Their representatives met at Alexandria, in Virginia, in March of 1785. At George Washington's invitation, they moved their sessions to his home at Mount Vernon. Their negotiations proved so successful that, on January 21, 1786, the Virginia Assembly called for "a joint meeting of [all of] the States to recommend a federal plan for regulating commerce."

---

[14]No amendments were added to the Articles. To get all 13 of the jealous, increasingly unfriendly States to agree on anything seemed to many hopeless. In 1785 the Congress, in a final attempt to solve its money problems, proposed an amendment to permit it to levy import duties. Only New York, reaping income from its own tax on imports, refused to ratify the proposal.

That "joint meeting" opened at Annapolis, in Maryland, on September 11, 1786. Only five of the 13 States attended, however.[15] Disappointed, but still hopeful, the Annapolis Convention called for yet another meeting of the States

> . . . at Philadelphia on the second Monday in May next, to take into consideration the situation of the United States, to devise such further provisions as shall appear to them necessary to render the constitution of the Federal Government adequate to the exigencies of the Union. . . .

By mid-February of 1787, seven of the States had named delegates to the Philadelphia meeting.[16] Then, on February 21st, the Congress, which had been hesitating, also called upon the States to send delegates to Philadelphia

> . . . for the sole and express purpose of revising the Articles of Confederation and reporting to Congress and the several legislatures such alterations and provisions therein as shall when agreed to in Congress and confirmed by the States render the [Articles] adequate to the exigencies of Government and the preservation of the Union.

That Philadelphia meeting became, of course, the Constitutional Convention.

✓ FOR REVIEW

1. What were the Articles of Confederation? When and by whom were they prepared?
2. Describe the government set up by the Articles. What powers were given to Congress?
3. What were the major weaknesses of the Articles?
4. Why is the period the Articles were in force called "the Critical Period" in American history?

The Constitutional Convention

The Philadelphia meeting began on Friday, May 25, 1787.[17] In all, 12 of the States were represented. Rhode Island did not take part in the Convention.[18]

The Framers

In all, 74 delegates were chosen by the several State legislatures. For a number of reasons, only 55 of them actually attended the Convention, however.

Of that 55, surely this much can be said: Never, before or since, has so remarkable a group been brought together in this country. Thomas Jefferson, who was not among them, later called the delegates "an assembly of demi-gods."

They included these outstanding personalities: George Washington, James Madison, Edmund Randolph, and George Mason from Virginia; Benjamin Franklin, Gouverneur Morris, Robert Morris, and James Wilson from Pennsylvania; Alexander Hamilton from New York; William Paterson from New Jersey; Elbridge Gerry and Rufus King from Massachusetts; Luther Martin from Maryland; Oliver Ellsworth and Roger Sherman from Connecticut; John Dick-

---

[15]New York, New Jersey, Pennsylvania, Delaware, and Virginia. Although four other States (New Hampshire, Massachusetts, Rhode Island, and North Carolina) had appointed delegates, none of them attended the Annapolis meeting.

[16]Delaware, Georgia, New Hampshire, New Jersey, North Carolina, Pennsylvania, Virginia.

[17]Not enough of the States were represented on the date originally set, Monday, May 14. Those delegates who were present met and adjourned each day until May 25, when a quorum (majority) of the States were on hand.

[18]The Rhode Island legislature was controlled by the "soft-money" forces there-- mostly debtors and small farmers who were helped by inflation and so were against a stronger central government. The New Hampshire delegation, delayed mostly by lack of funds, did not reach Philadelphia until late July.

inson from Delaware; and John Rutledge and Charles Pinckney from South Carolina.

These were men of wide knowledge and public experience, and of wealth and prestige. Many of them had fought in the Revolution; 39 had been members of the Continental Congress or the Congress of the Confederation, or both. Eight had served in constitutional conventions in their own States; and seven had been State governors. Eight had signed the Declaration of Independence. Thirty-one of the delegates had attended college, in a day when there were only a few colleges in the land; their number included two college presidents and three professors. Two were to become President of the United States, and one a Vice President. Seventeen were later to serve in the Senate and 11 in the House of Representatives.

Is it any wonder that the product of such a gathering was described by the English statesman, William E. Gladstone, a century later, as "the most wonderful work ever struck off at a given time by the brain and purpose of man"?

Remarkably, the average age of the Framers was only 42, and nearly half of

STEPS TO A MORE PERFECT UNION

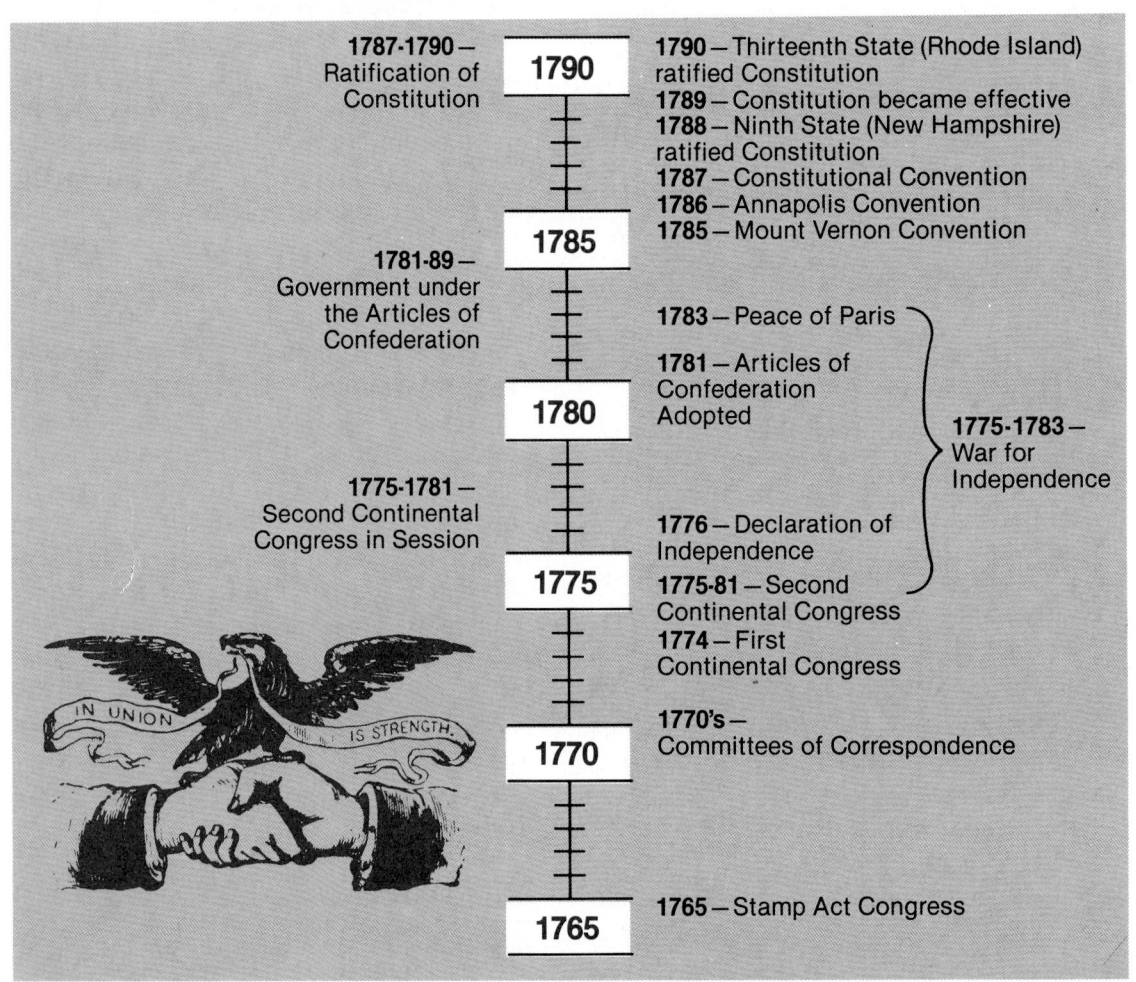

1787-1790 — Ratification of Constitution

1790 — Thirteenth State (Rhode Island) ratified Constitution
1789 — Constitution became effective
1788 — Ninth State (New Hampshire) ratified Constitution
1787 — Constitutional Convention
1786 — Annapolis Convention
1785 — Mount Vernon Convention

1781-89 — Government under the Articles of Confederation

1783 — Peace of Paris
1781 — Articles of Confederation Adopted

1775-1783 — War for Independence

1775-1781 — Second Continental Congress in Session

1776 — Declaration of Independence
1775-81 — Second Continental Congress
1774 — First Continental Congress
1770's — Committees of Correspondence
1765 — Stamp Act Congress

SOME USEFUL TIPS FOR EFFECTIVE STUDY

By now you have read (or at least been exposed to) several textbooks—and you are now nearly 40 pages through this one. How much do you learn—really know and understand and, in fact, remember—when you read a textbook?

Here are five hints, useful guides, to the more effective study of this book. (You may find them of some help with other books in other courses, too.)

1. Always read a text assignment before that material is to be covered in class.

2. First, skim the assigned reading, for an overview of its content. In this preliminary go-through, pay particular attention to such things as the Chapter Objectives, the major headings throughout the chapter, and the Summary and Chapter Review sections at its end.

3. Then, read the assigned material with care. Take orderly notes as you read the assignment, noting the key passages and important points, (Unless this book is your own personal property, do not mark/underline key passages, make notes in the margins, etc.)

4. Answer the review questions as you encounter them. (And, right now, find out what the Glossary, on pages 617–625, is—and how to use it.)

5. Next, reread the assigned material—to pick up the important points you missed the first time. Relearning is a vital part of the learning process.

Your teacher can offer some more, and some very good, help to improve your study habits—and so your learning. He/she will almost certainly emphasize such things as:

1. Class attendance—most teachers cover a good deal of material in class that is not included in the text.

2. A regular study schedule—cramming sometimes helps just before a test, but it almost never results in real learning.

3. Seek help if you need it—that's what teachers are for.

them were only in their 30s. Indeed, most of the real leaders were in that age group—Madison was 36, Gouverneur Morris 35, Randolph 34, and Hamilton 32. At 81, Franklin was the oldest. He was failing, however, and not able to attend many of the meetings. George Washington, at 55, was one of the few older members who played a key part in the making of the Constitution.

By and large, the Framers of the Constitution were of a new generation in American politics. Several of the better known leaders of the Revolutionary pe-riod were not in Philadelphia. Patrick Henry said he "smelt a rat" and refused to attend. Samuel Adams, John Hancock, and Richard Henry Lee were not selected as delegates by their States. Thomas Paine was in Paris. So, too, was Thomas Jefferson, as American minister to France. And John Adams was our envoy to England and Holland at the time.

Organization and Procedure

The Framers met in Independence Hall, probably in the same room in which the Declaration of Independence had been signed 11 years earlier.

They organized immediately, on May 25.[19] George Washington was unanimously elected president of the convention. Then, and at the second session on Monday, May 28, several rules of procedure were adopted. A majority of the States (seven) would be a quorum to conduct business. Each State delegation was to have one vote on all questions. And a majority of the votes cast would carry any proposal.

The delegates also decided to keep their sessions secret. The convention had drawn much public attention—and speculation, too. So, to protect themselves from outside pressures, they adopted a rule of secrecy. And, on the whole, it was well kept.

A secretary (William Jackson) and other minor, nonmember officers were appointed. Jackson kept the convention's *Journal*. But that official record was quite sketchy. It was mostly a listing of members present, motions put, and votes taken—and not always an accurate one, at that.

Fortunately, several of the delegates kept their own accounts of the proceedings—most notably, James Madison. Most of what is known of the work of the convention comes from Madison's careful and voluminous *Notes*. His brilliance and depth of knowledge led his colleagues to hold him in great respect. Quickly, he became the convention's floor leader. Madison contributed more to the Constitution than did any of the others—and, still, he was able to keep a close record of its work. Certainly he deserves the title "Father of the Constitution."

_____

[19]Twenty-eight delegates from seven States were present on that first day. The full number of 55 was not reached until August 6 when John Francis Mercer of Maryland arrived and was seated. Some 40 members attended most of the daily sessions of the convention.

The Framers met on 89 of the 116 days from May 25 through their final meeting on September 17. They did most of their work on the floor of the convention. Some matters were handled by committees, but all questions were ultimately settled by the full body.

The Decision to Write a New Constitution

Recall, the Philadelphia Convention was called to *recommend revisions* in the Articles of Confederation. But almost at once the delegates agreed that they were, in fact, meeting to create a *new* government for the United States. On May 30 they adopted this proposal, which was put by Edmund Randolph of Virginia:

> *Resolved, . . .* that a *national* Government ought to be established consisting of a *supreme* Legislative, Executive and Judiciary.

With this momentous decision, the Framers redefined the purpose of the convention. From that point on, they set about the writing of a new constitution, to *replace* the Articles of Confederation. Their debates were spirited, even bitter. At times the convention seemed near collapse. Once they had passed Governor Randolph's resolution, however, the goal of the majority of the convention never changed.

The Virginia Plan

No State had more to do with the calling of the convention than Virginia. It was not surprising, then, that its delegates should offer the first plan for a new constitution. On May 29 the Virginia Plan, largely the work of Madison, was presented by Randolph.

The Virginia Plan called for a new government with three separate branches—legislative, executive, and judicial. The legislature (Congress) would be *bicameral*—that is, it would have two houses. Representation in each house was to be based either upon each State's population or the amount of money it gave for the support of the central government. The members of the lower house (the House of Representatives) were to be popularly elected in each State. Those of the upper house (the Senate) were to be chosen by the lower house, from lists of persons nominated by the State legislatures.

Congress was to be given all of the powers it held under the Articles. In addition, it was to have the power to legislate "in all cases in which the separate States are incompetent" to act, to veto any State law in conflict with national law, and to use force to make a State obey national law.

A "National Executive" and a "National Judiciary" were to be chosen by Congress. Together, these two branches would form a "council of revision." They could veto acts of Congress; but a veto could be overridden by the two houses. The executive would have "a general authority to execute the national laws." The judiciary would "consist of one or more supreme tribunals, and of inferior tribunals."

The Plan also provided that all State officers should take an oath to support the Union, that each State be guaranteed a republican form of government, and that Congress have the power to admit new States to the Union.

It called, then, for a *thorough* revision of the Articles. Its goal was the creation of a *national* government with greatly expanded powers and, importantly, the power to enforce its decisions.

The Virginia Plan set the agenda for much of the convention's work. But some delegates—especially those from the smaller States of Delaware, Maryland, and New Jersey, and from New

Philadelphia's State House—Independence Hall—where the Constitution was written in 1787 and where the Declaration of Independence had been signed 11 years before.

York[20]—found it too radical. Soon they developed their counter-proposals. On June 15 William Paterson of New Jersey presented the position of the small States.

The New Jersey Plan

Paterson and his colleagues offered several amendments to the Articles, but not nearly so thorough a revision as proposed by the Virginia Plan. The New Jersey Plan would have kept the unicameral Congress of the Confederation, with each of the States equally represented. To those powers Congress already had would be added closely limited powers to tax and to regulate interstate trade.

The New Jersey Plan also called for a "federal Executive" of more than one person. This plural executive would be chosen by the Congress and could be removed by it on the request of a majority of the States' governors. The "federal Judiciary" would be composed of a single "supreme Tribunal," appointed by the executive.

---

[20]The Virginia Plan's major support came from the three largest States: Virginia, Pennsylvania, and Massachusetts. New York was then only the fifth largest. Alexander Hamilton, the convention's most outspoken champion of a stronger central government, was regularly out-voted by his fellow-delegates from New York.

Among their several differences, the major point of disagreement between the two Plans was centered on this question: How should the States be represented in Congress? On the basis of their populations (or financial contributions), as in the Virginia Plan? Or on the basis of State equality, as in the Articles and the New Jersey Plan?

For weeks the question was argued. The lines were sharply drawn. Several delegates, on both sides of the issue, threatened to withdraw. But, finally and fortunately, a compromise was reached. It proved to be one of the truly great compromises of the convention.

A "Bundle of Compromises"

The Constitution, as it was drafted at Philadelphia, has often been called a "bundle of compromises." The description is apt—*if*, that is, it is properly understood.

By no means all, or even most, of what went into the document came from compromises. The Framers were, in fact agreed on many of the basic issues they faced. Thus, nearly all of them were convinced that a *new* central government had to be created—and, too, that that government had to have the powers necessary to deal with the nation's economic and social problems. They were dedicated, too, to the concepts of popular sovereignty and of limited government. None of them questioned for a moment the wisdom of representative government. The principles of separation of powers and checks and balances were accepted almost as a matter of course.

There were differences of opinion among them, certainly, and often very important ones. How could matters have been otherwise? The delegates came from 12 different States which were, in 1787, widely separated in both geographic and economic terms. And, of course, they often reflected the interests of their respective States.

Many disputes did occur, and the compromises by which they were resolved often were reached only after hours and days or even weeks of heated debate. But the point here is that the differences were *not* over the *most fundamental* of questions. Instead, they involved such vital, but lesser, points as these: the details of the structure of Congress, the method by which the President was to be chosen, and the particular limits that should be placed on the several new powers to be given to the new central government.

The Connecticut Compromise

The disagreement over representation in Congress was critical. The large States expected to dominate the new government. The small States feared that they would not be able to protect their interests. Tempers flared, on both sides. Benjamin Franklin was moved to suggest that

> . . . prayers imploring the assistance of Heaven . . . be offered in this Assembly every morning before we proceed to business.

The conflict was finally settled by a compromise first suggested by the Connecticut delegation. It was agreed that Congress should be composed of two houses, a Senate and a House of Representatives. In the smaller Senate the States would be represented equally. In the House representation would be based upon each State's population.

Thus, by combining basic features of the rival Virginia and New Jersey Plans, the conventions's most serious dispute was resolved. The Connecticut Compromise was so pivotal to the writing of the Constitution, and has had such a lasting impact upon the shape of the Government of the United States, that it has been called the Great Compromise.

The Three-Fifths Compromise

Once it had been agreed that the seats in the House would be based on each State's population, this question arose: Should slaves be counted in the populations of the southern States?

Again debate was fierce. Most of the delegates from the slave-holding States argued that they should be counted, of course—and most of the northerners took the opposing view.

Finally, the Framers agreed that all "free persons" should be counted, and so, too, should "three-fifths of all other persons." For the "three-fifths," won by the southerners, the northerners exacted a price. That formula was to be used, too, in fixing the amount of money to be raised in each State by any direct tax levied by Congress. In short, the southerners could count their slaves, but they would also have to pay for them.

Of course, this odd compromise disappeared from the Constitution with the 13th Amendment (which abolished slavery) in 1865. For nearly 120 years, there have been no "all other persons" in this country.

The Commerce and Slave Trade Compromise

The convention generally agreed that Congress had to have the power to regulate foreign and interstate trade. But to many southerners that power carried a dangerous possibility. They worried that Congress, likely to be controlled by northern commercial interests, would act against the interests of the agricultural South.

They were particularly fearful on two counts. First, that Congress would try to support the new government out of export duties—and southern cotton was the major American export of the time. Secondly, that Congress would interfere with the slave trade.

So, before they would agree to the commerce power, the southerners insisted upon certain protections. Accordingly, Congress was forbidden the power to tax the export of goods from any State. And it was also forbidden the power to act on the slave trade for a period of at least 20 years.

Other Compromises

These three compromises were the major ones in the making of the Constitution. But, again, there were many others. The convention spent much of its time, said Franklin, "sawing boards to make them fit."

Those sections of the Constitution which deal with the selection of the President, the treaty-making process, the structure of the national court system, and the amendment process all took their final form as a product of give-and-take among the Framers. And so did many of its other provisions, as we shall see in later chapters.

☑ FOR REVIEW

1. When and where was the Constitution written?
2. Who is known as the "Father of the Constitution"? Why? Who were the other more outstanding delegates to the Constitutional Convention?
3. In what sense were the Framers "a new generation in American politics"?
4. What momentous decision did the Framers make at the beginning of the Convention?
5. What were the Virginia and the New Jersey Plans? The principal point of difference between them?
6. In what sense was the Constitution a "bundle of compromises"? What were the three major compromises reached by the Framers?

Sources of the Constitution

The Framers were well-educated and widely-read. They were familiar with the governments of ancient Greece and Rome and of contemporary England and Europe. And they knew the political writings of their time—including such works as William Blackstone's *Commentaries on the Laws of England*, the Baron de Montesquieu's *The Spirit of the Laws*, Jean Jacques Rousseau's *Social Contract*, John Locke's *Two Treatises of Civil Government*, and much else.

More immediately, the Framers drew upon their own experiences. Remember, they were closely familiar with the Second Continental Congress, the Articles of Confederation, and their own State governments. Much that went into the Constitution came directly—sometimes word for word—from the Articles. And a number of provisions were drawn from the several State constitutions, as well.

The Convention Completes Its Work

For several weeks, through the hot Philadelphia summer, the members took up resolution after resolution. Finally, on September 8, a committee was named "to revise the stile of and arrange the articles which had been agreed to" by the convention. That group, headed by Gouverneur Morris, put the Constitution in its final, clear, concise form.

Then, on September 17, the convention approved its work and 39 names were placed on the finished document.[21]

Wise old Benjamin Franklin put into words what many of the Framers must have thought on that final day:

---

[21]Three of the 42 delegates present on that last day refused to sign the proposed Constitution: Edmund Randolph of Virginia, who later did support ratification and then served as Attorney General and then Secretary of State in the Washington administration; Elbridge Gerry of Massachusetts, who later became Vice President under Madison; and George Mason of Virginia, who continued to oppose the Constitution until his death in 1792. George Read of Delaware signed both for himself and for the absent John Dickinson.

Sir, I agree with this Constitution with all its faults, if they are such; because I think a general Government necessary for us . . . I doubt . . . whether any Convention we can obtain, may be able to make a better Constitution. For when you assemble a number of men to have the advantage of their joint wisdom, you inevitably assemble with those men, all their prejudices, their passions, their errors of opinion, their local interests, and their selfish views. From such an assembly can a perfect production be expected? It therefore astonishes me, Sir, to find this system approaching so near to perfection as it does. . . .

On Franklin's motion, the Constitution was signed, and Madison tells us that

. . . Doct^r Franklin, looking toward the President's chair, at the back of which a rising sun happened to be painted, observed to a few members near him, that Painters had found it difficult to distinguish in their art a rising from a setting sun. I have, said he, often and often in the course of the Session . . . looked at that behind the President without being able to tell whether it was rising or setting. But now at length I have the happiness to know that it is a rising and not a setting sun.

Ratification

The new Constitution was intended to replace the Articles of Confederation. And, remember, the Articles provided that changes could be made in them *only* if *all* of the State legislatures agreed. The Framers had seen how crippling that unanimity requirement could be. So, the new Constitution provided (in Article VII) that

The ratification of the conventions of nine States shall be sufficient for the establishment of this Constitution between the States so ratifying the same.

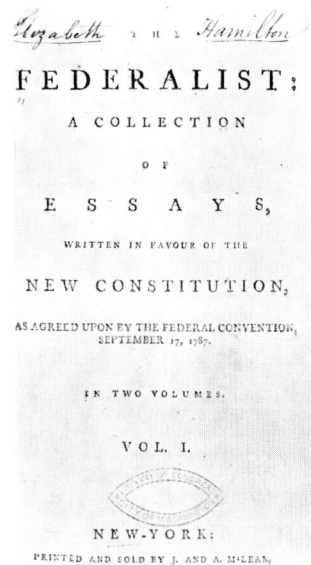

James Madison

Alexander Hamilton

Each of the 85 essays in the remarkable *Federalist* papers was signed with the pen name "Publius." Hamilton probably wrote 51 of them, Madison 26, and John Jay 8.

The Congress of the Confederation agreed to this irregular procedure. After a short debate, it sent the new document on to the States on September 28, 1787.

Federalists and Anti-Federalists. The proposed Constitution was printed, circulated, and debated throughout the country. Two groups quickly emerged in each of the States: the *Federalists*, who favored ratification, and the *Anti-Federalists*, who opposed it.

The Federalists were led by many of those who had attended the Philadelphia Convention. Among them, the most active and the most effective were James Madison and Alexander Hamilton. Their opposition was headed by such well-known Revolutionary War figures as Patrick Henry, Richard Henry Lee, John Hancock, and Samuel Adams.

The Federalists stressed the weaknesses of the Articles. They argued that the many difficulties facing the Republic could be overcome only by a new government based upon the proposed Constitution.

The Anti-Federalists attacked nearly every part of the new document. Many objected to the ratification process, to the absence of any mention of God, to the denial to the States of a power to print money, and to much else.

Two of its major features drew the heaviest fire, however: (1) the much-increased powers of the government and (2) its lack of a bill of rights. (It did not provide for such basic liberties as freedom of speech, press, and religion, nor for the rights of fair trial.) Patrick Henry said of the proposed Constitution:

> I look upon that paper as the most fatal plan that could possibly be conceived to enslave a free people.

Success. The contest was close in several States, but the Federalists finally won in all of them. The Constitution was ratified by the convention called in each State on the date and by the vote that is shown in the table on the next page.

On June 21, 1788, New Hampshire brought the number of ratifying States to nine. Under Article VII, this should have brought the Constitution into effect. But, in fact, it did not. Neither Virginia nor New York had yet ratified, and without either of them the new government could not hope to succeed.

Virginia. Virginia's ratification followed New Hampshire's by just four days. The debates in its convention were intense and brilliant. They were followed closely throughout the State. The Federalists were led by Madison, the young John Marshall, and Governor Edmund Randolph (even though he had refused to sign the Constitution at Philadelphia). Patrick Henry led the opposition and was joined by such outstanding Virginians as James Monroe, Richard Henry Lee, and George Mason (another of the non-signers).

Although George Washington was not a delegate, his strong support for ratification proved vital. With Madison, he was able to move a reluctant Jefferson to agree. Had Jefferson fought as did other Anti-Federalists, Virginia might never have ratified the Constitution.

New York. A narrow vote in the New York convention brought the number of States to 11 on July 26, 1788.

New York ratified only after a long battle. The well-organized Anti-Federalists were led by Governor George Clinton and by two of the State's three delegates to the Philadelphia Convention.[22]

The contest in New York gave rise to a remarkable campaign document: *The Federalist.* This was a collection of 85 essays written in favor of the Constitu-

---

[22]Robert Yates and John Lansing; both had quit Philadelphia in July, arguing that the convention had gone beyond its authority. Alexander Hamilton had been the State's other delegate, of course. Like many other Anti-Federalist leaders, Governor Clinton later supported the Constitution. He was Vice President during Thomas Jefferson's second term and also in James Madison's first term in the Presidency.

RATIFICATION OF THE CONSTITUTION

State	Date	Vote
Delaware	Dec. 7, 1787	30–0
Pennsylvania	Dec. 12, 1787	46–23
New Jersey	Dec. 19, 1787	38–0
Georgia	Jan. 2, 1788	26–0
Connecticut	Jan. 9, 1788	128–40
Massachusetts	Feb. 6, 1788	187–168
Maryland	Apr. 28, 1788	63–11
South Carolina	May 23, 1788	149–73
New Hampshire	June 21, 1788	57–46
Virginia	June 25, 1788	89–79
New York	July 26, 1788	30–27
North Carolina	Nov. 21, 1789*	184–77
Rhode Island	May 29, 1790	34–32

*Second vote; ratification was originally defeated on August 4, 1788, by a vote of 184–84.

tion by Alexander Hamilton, James Madison, and John Jay. They were written in haste, and purposely slanted in favor of ratification. Even so, they remain an excellent commentary on the Constitution and are among the very best of all political writings in the English language.

Inauguration of the New Government

On September 13, 1788, with 11 of the 13 States "under the federal roof," the Congress of the Confederation paved the way for its successor. It chose New York as the temporary capital.[23] And it set the first Wednesday in January as the date on which the States would choose presidential electors. The first Wednesday in February was set as the date on which those electors would vote. Finally, the first Wednesday in March was set as the date for the inauguration of the new government.

---

[23]The District of Columbia did not become the nation's capital until late in the year 1800. Congress moved its sessions to Philadelphia in December of 1790.

George Washington had chaired the Philadelphia convention, and his strong support was a vital part of the campaign for its ratification.

The new Congress did convene on March 4, 1789. It met in Federal Hall, on Wall Street in New York City. Because it lacked a quorum, however, it could not count the electoral votes until April 6. Finally, on that day, it found that George Washington had been elected President by a unanimous vote and John Adams, Vice President with a substantial majority.

Then, on April 30, after an historic trip from Mount Vernon to New York, Washington took the oath of office as the first President of the United States.

✓ FOR REVIEW

1. From what sources did the Framers draw in writing the Constitution?
2. How was the Constitution ratified? What was "irregular" about that process?
3. The Anti-Federalists centered their opposition to the Constitution on what two points?
4. What is *The Federalist?* By whom was it written?

S U M M A R Y

Government in the United States is the product of centuries of development.

The English, who settled the 13 colonies, had much to do with the shaping of the American governmental system. Most importantly, they set the pattern of early government in America and brought with them the ideas of limited government and representative government.

Starting with Jamestown in Virginia in 1607, all 13 colonies were established by 1732. There were three types of colonies: royal, proprietary, and charter. The eight royal colonies were ruled by a royal governor appointed by and directly responsible to the king. The three proprietary colonies were governed under a proprietor who was, in turn, responsible to the king. The two charter colonies, the most democratic, were largely self-governing.

England tightened its control over the colonies in the 1760s. Colonial resistance to the policies of George III led, finally, to revolution in the mid-1770s. Several attempts had been made to head off the break, most notably and finally by the First Continental Congress in 1774.

By the time the Second Continental Congress assembled, on May 10, 1775, the American Revolution had in fact begun. By force of circumstance, that body became our first national government. It carried on the Revolution; proclaimed the Declaration of Independence on July 4, 1776; and wrote our first national constitution, the Articles of Confederation, which became effective on March 1, 1781.

The government created by the Articles proved too weak for the times. The political and economic chaos of the day led to the replacement of the Articles by the present Constitution of the United States.

The Constitution was drafted by a convention which met at Philadelphia from May 25 to September 17 in 1787. It became effective with the formation of the new government in March and April of 1789.

C H A P T E R   R E V I E W

Key Terms/Concepts

Albany Plan of Union (29)
Anti-Federalists (45)
Articles of Confederation (34)
Bicameral (28)
Charter colonies (28)
Commerce and Slave Trade Compromise (43)
Connecticut Compromise (42)
Constitution (40)
Critical Period (36)
Declaration of Independence (32)
Federalists (45)
First Continental Congress (30)
Limited government (26)
New Jersey Plan (41)
Popular sovereignty (33)
Proprietary colonies (28)
Ratification (34,44)
Representative government (26)
Royal colonies (27)
Second Continental Congress (31)
Stamp Act Congress (30)
The Federalist (46)
Three-Fifths Compromise (43)
Unicameral (28)
Virginia Plan (40)

Keynote Questions

1. What three central ideas about government did the early English settlers bring with them, ready-made, to the New World? Why can two of them be said to have contained the "seeds of revolution"?
2. The sentiments and the events that finally led to the Revolution, were very largely centered in those colonies with which of the three types of colonial government established in British North America? Why?
3. Why can it be said that by the mid-1700s the relationship between Britain and the colonies had become federal in fact, if not in form? How did that relationship change in the early 1760s?
4. What body became the first national government of the United States? When, and for how long did it function in that capacity?
5. List the basic political ideas set forth in the second paragraph of the Declaration of Independence.
6. What document became the first

constitution of the United States? When, and for how long was it in force? Describe the basic shape of the governmental system it created.

7. What were the common features of most of the first State constitutions?

8. Why are the 1780s known as the Critical Period of American history?

9. Why can it be said that, on the whole, the Constitution was framed by "a new generation in American politics"?

10. What did Benjamin Franklin mean when he said that the Philadelphia Convention spent much of its time "sawing boards to make them fit"? Cite three major illustrations of his point.

11. On what principal grounds did the Federalists support ratification of the Constitution? On what principal grounds did the Anti-Federalists oppose it?

For Thought and Discussion

1. What can you make of this historical irony? The first representative assembly to meet in the New World met at Jamestown on July 30, 1619. Less than a month later, the first shipload of African slaves to reach any point later to be a part of the United States docked at Jamestown.

2. What did Thomas Jefferson mean when he described the Declaration of Independence as "pure Locke"?

3. It has been said that the Declaration of Independence was both radical and revolutionary but that the Constitution was neither. Why do you agree or disagree with that statement?

4. The Preamble to the Constitution states: "We the People of the United States . . . do ordain and establish this Constitution for the United States of America." Yet, in fact, the Constitution was put together by 55 men at Philadelphia and ratified by conventions in the 13 States. How can one explain the apparent contradiction here?

5. In what particular ways did the Constitution provide for "a more perfect Union" than did the Articles of Confederation?

Suggested Activities

1. Write a short biographical sketch of one or more of these historic figures: George Washington, Benjamin Franklin, James Madison, Thomas Jefferson, Samuel Adams, Patrick Henry, John Hancock, Thomas Paine, Richard Henry Lee, Gouverneur Morris, Alexander Hamilton.

2. On page 44 we noted that several provisions in the Constitution were taken directly from the Articles of Confederation. Prepare an outline of the Articles, and point out those provisions that were put into the Constitution. (The text of the Articles can be found in the *United States Code*, vol. 1, pp. XXXIX–XLIII and in many standard reference works in American history.)

3. Prepare a wall chart or bulletin board display showing the major weaknesses of the Articles of Confederation and how those matters were treated in the Constitution.

4. Stage a debate or class forum on one of these questions: (a) *Resolved*, That the Framers of the Constitution should have provided for a unicameral Congress in which each of the States would be equally represented; (b) *Resolved*, That the 13 States should not have accepted the Constitution proposed by the Philadelphia Convention; (c) *Resolved*, That the Philadelphia Convention should have submitted the proposed Constitution to the people in each State, to accept or reject by popular vote.

3

The Living Constitution

CHAPTER OBJECTIVES

To help you to
Learn ▪ Know ▪ Understand

The basic principles of the American constitutional system.

The essential meaning of those principles in both their historical and current settings.

The processes of constitutional change and development by formal amendment.

The processes of constitutional change and development by informal amendment.

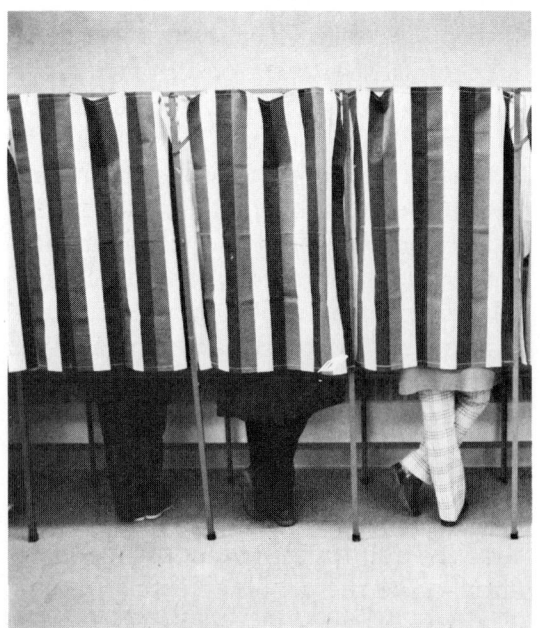

The people made the Constitution and the people can unmake it. It is the creature of their own will, and lives only by their will.

Chief Justice John Marshall
Cohens v. Virginia (1821)

The Constitution of the United States is this nation's fundamental law. It is, by its own terms, "the supreme law of the land"—the highest form of law in the United States.[1]

The Constitution sets out the basic principles upon which the government of the United States was built and upon which it is maintained. It lays out the basic framework and procedures by which—and the limits within which—that government must operate.

The Constitution is a fairly brief document. Its little more than 7000 words can be read, easily, in a half hour. Read it, now—and, as you do, note this: It deals very largely with matters of basic principle. Unlike most other constitutions—those of the 50 States and of most other nations, it is not overweighted with the details of governmental structures and processes.

In this chapter we look, first, at the basic principles of the American constitutional system. Then we turn to the subject of constitutional growth—to the various ways in which the Constitution has changed and been changed over the course of now nearly 200 years.

---

[1]In Article VI, Section 2. You will find the text of the Constitution, together with a two-page outline of its contents, on pages 628-640.

We the People of the United States

insure domestic Tranquility, provide for the common defence, promote the gener... and our Posterity, do ordain and establish this Constitution for the United States...

Article. I.

Section. 1. All legislative Powers herein granted shall be vested in a Congress... of Representatives.

Section. 2. The House of Representatives shall be composed of Members chosen e... in each State shall have the Qualifications requisite for Electors of the most numerous Branch...

The Constitution's opening words, "We the People," clearly affirm the principle of popular sovereignty—the idea that government receives its powers from the people.

The Basic Principles

The Constitution is built upon six basic principles: *popular sovereignty, limited government, separation of powers, checks and balances, judicial review,* and *federalism.*

Popular Sovereignty

In the United States all political power belongs to the people. The people are sovereign. They are the *only* source for any and all governmental power. Government can govern only with the consent of the governed.

This principle of popular sovereignty is woven through all of the Constitution. In its very opening words, in the Preamble, it declares: "We the People of the United States . . . do ordain and establish this Constitution for the United States of America."

Acting through the Constitution, the sovereign people created the Government of the United States and have given to it certain powers. And, through the Constitution and its own fundamental law, each State government has received its powers from the people.

Limited Government

The principle of limited government holds that government is *not* all-powerful, that it may do only *certain* things —*only* those things that the people have seen fit to give it the power to do.

In effect, the principle of limited government is the other side of the coin of popular sovereignty. It is the principle of popular sovereignty stated the other way around: The people are the only source for any and all of government's authority; and government has only that authority the people have given to it.

The highly important concept of limited government may be put another way: Government must obey the law. Put this way, the principle is often called **constitutionalism**—that is, that government must be conducted according to constitutional principles. The concept of limited government is also often described as **the rule of law**—that is, that government and its officers, in all that they do, are always subject to, never above, the law.

In very large part, the Constitution is a statement of limited government. Much of it is written as explicit prohibitions of power to government.[2]

Separation of Powers

Remember our short discussion of the parliamentary and the presidential forms of government, on page 8. In a parliamentary system the basic powers of a government—its legislative, executive, and judicial powers—are all gathered in the hands of a single agency. British government is a good example. In a presidential system, however, these basic powers are divided (separated) among three distinct and independent branches of the government—as in the United States.

The Constitution distributes the powers of the National Government among the Congress (the legislative branch), the President (the executive branch), and the courts (the judicial branch). This **separation of powers** is clearly set forth in three places in the Constitution:

Article I, Section 1 declares: "All legislative powers herein granted shall be vested in a Congress of the United States . . ." Thus, Congress is the *law-making* branch of the National Government.

Article II, Section 1 declares: "The executive power shall be vested in a President of the United States . . ." Thus, the President is given the *law-executing, law-enforcing, law-administering* powers of the National Government.

Article III, Section 1 declares: "The judicial power of the United States shall be vested in one Supreme Court, and in such inferior courts as the Congress may from time to time ordain and establish." Thus, the federal courts, and most importantly the Supreme Court, *interpret and apply* the laws of the United States in cases brought before them.

In defense of this three-part arrangement, James Madison wrote in *The Federalist* No. 47:

> The accumulation of all powers, legislative, executive, and judiciary, in the same hands, whether one, a few, or many, . . . may justly be pronounced the very definition of tyranny.

Checks and Balances

The National Government is organized around three separate branches. As we've just noted, the Constitution gives to each its own distinct field of governmental authority—legislative, executive, and judicial.

These three branches are not entirely separated, however. They are not completely independent of one another. Rather, they are tied together by a complex system of **checks and balances.** Each branch is subject to a number of constitutional checks (restraints) by either or both of the others. Or, in other words, each branch has certain powers with which it can check the operations of the other two.

The major features of the check-and-balance arrangement are set out in the chart on page 53. As you can see, the Congress has the power to make law, but the President may **veto** (reject) any act of Congress. In its turn, Congress can override a veto by a two-thirds vote in each house. Congress can refuse to provide funds requested by the President, or the Senate may refuse to approve a treaty or an appointment made by the President. The President has the power to name all federal judges. Each of

---

[2]See, especially, Article I, Sections 9 and 10; the 1st through the 10th Amendments; and the 13th, 14th, 15th, 19th, 24th, and 26th Amendments.

THE MAJOR FEATURES OF THE AMERICAN SYSTEM OF CHECKS AND BALANCES

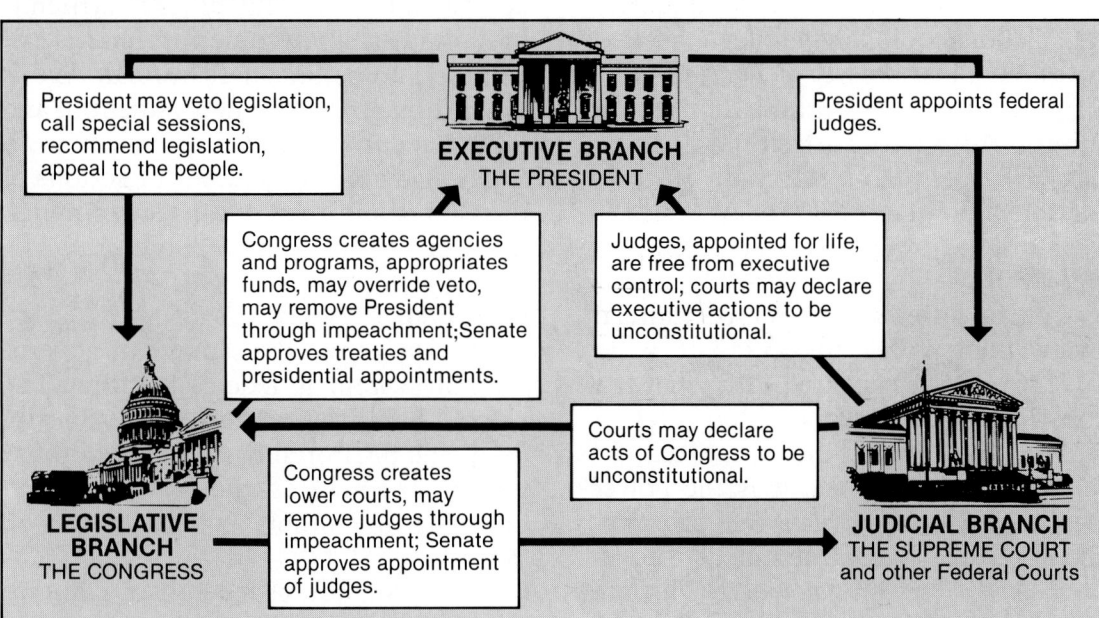

President may veto legislation, call special sessions, recommend legislation, appeal to the people.

EXECUTIVE BRANCH
THE PRESIDENT

President appoints federal judges.

Congress creates agencies and programs, appropriates funds, may override veto, may remove President through impeachment; Senate approves treaties and presidential appointments.

Judges, appointed for life, are free from executive control; courts may declare executive actions to be unconstitutional.

Courts may declare acts of Congress to be unconstitutional.

LEGISLATIVE BRANCH
THE CONGRESS

Congress creates lower courts, may remove judges through impeachment; Senate approves appointment of judges.

JUDICIAL BRANCH
THE SUPREME COURT
and other Federal Courts

those appointments, however, must be approved by the Senate. The courts have the power to decide the constitutionality of acts of Congress and of presidential actions—and to strike down those found to be unconstitutional.

Head-on clashes between the departments do not often happen. The check and balance system operates all the time, however—and in almost routine fashion. And the very fact that it does exist—the fact that each of the branches has its several checks—has an impact on much that happens in Washington. The point can be seen time and again:

Thus, when the President picks someone to serve in come important office in the executive branch—as, say, Secretary of State or as Director of the FBI or of the CIA—the President is quite aware of the fact that the Senate must confirm that appointment. And so, quite purposefully, he picks someone who *will* be approved by the Senate. Or, in a very similar sense, when Congress makes law it does so with a careful eye on both the President's veto power and the power of the courts to review its actions.

Spectacular clashes—direct applications of the check and balance system—do occur, of course. Thus, the President does veto some acts of Congress. And, on rare occasion, Congress does override one of those vetoes. Or, even more rarely, the Senate does sometimes reject one of the President's appointees.

But, again, these and other direct confrontations are not at all common. Both Congress and the President, and even the courts, try to avoid them. The check and balance system makes compromise necessary—and, recall, compromise is an absolutely vital part of democratic government.

The system works. It has prevented "an unjust combination of the majority." Still, and at the same time, it has not very often stalled a close working relationship between the executive and the legislative branches.

But, notice, this has been especially true when the President and a majority in both houses of Congress have been of the same political party. When the other party controls one or both houses on Capitol Hill, partisan frictions tend to play a larger-than-usual part in that relationship—as they do today.

Judicial Review

Courts have the power of **judicial review,** the power to decide if what government does squares with what the Constitution provides.

More exactly, judicial review may be defined in these terms: It is the power of a court to determine the constitutionality of a governmental action. In part, then, it is the power to declare **unconstitutional**—to declare illegal, null and void, of no force and effect—a governmental action found to violate some provision in the Constitution.

The power of judicial review is held by all federal courts and by most State courts, as well.[3]

The Constitution does not provide for judicial review in so many words. But it is clear that the Framers meant that the federal courts—and that most especially the Supreme Court—should have that power.

In practice, the Supreme Court established the power of judicial review in *Marbury* v. *Madison,* in 1803. We shall take a close look at that landmark case in Chapter 18. Since it was decided, the High Court and other federal and State courts have used the power in thousands of cases. In most of them, the challenged governmental action has been upheld.

---

[3]Generally, the power is held by all **courts of record.** These are courts which keep a record of their proceedings and have the power to punish for contempt of court. Usually, only the lowest State courts (*e.g.,* justice of the peace and municipal courts) are not courts of record.

But that is not always the result, of course. To date, the Supreme Court has decided more than 130 cases in which it has found an act or some part of an act of Congress to be unconstitutional. And it has struck down several presidential and other executive branch actions, as well. It has also voided hundreds of actions of the States and their local governments, including more than 900 State laws.

Federalism

As we know, the American governmental system is federal in form. The powers held by government are distributed on a territorial basis. Some of those powers are held by the National Government and others belong to the 50 States.

The principle of federalism came to the Constitution out of both experience and necessity. At Philadelphia, the Framers faced any number of difficult problems—not the least of them: How to build a new, stronger, more effective national government and, at the same time, preserve the existing States and the concept of local self-government.

The colonists had rebelled against the harsh rule of a powerful and distant central government. They had fought for the right to manage their local affairs, without the meddling and dictation of the King and his ministers in far-off London. Surely, they would not now agree to the creation of another such government.

The Framers found their solution in federalism. In short, they constructed the federal arrangement, with its division of powers, as a compromise. It was an alternative to the system of nearly-independent States, loosely tied to one another in the weak Confederation, and a much-feared too-powerful central government.

We shall look at the federal system, at length, in the next chapter.

1. What, in general terms, is the Constitution of the United States?
2. Upon what six basic principles is it built?
3. How do each of these basic principles illustrate the fact that the Constitution is "a statement of limited government"?

Our Changing Constitution

The Constitution of the United States has now been in force for more than 190 years—longer, by far, than the written constitution of any other nation in the world.[4]

In 1789 the young Republic was a small agricultural nation of fewer than four million people, scattered for some 2100 kilometers (1300 miles) along the eastern edge of the continent. The original 13 States, joined together only by horses and sailing ships, struggled to stay alive in a generally hostile world.

Today, the United States has more than 235 million people. The now 50 States stretch across the continent and beyond, and we have many farflung dependencies and commitments. This country is the most powerful on earth. Our modern, highly industrialized and technological society has produced the highest standard of living any nation has ever known.

How has the Constitution, written in 1787, endured and kept up with that astounding change and growth? The answer lies in this highly important fact:

John Hancock argued for the addition of a bill of rights to the Constitution in 1788. Three years later, in 1791, that proposal became reality.

The Constitution of today *is*, and at the same time, *is not* the document of 1787. Many of its words are the same, and much of their meaning remains the same, as well. But some of its words have been changed; some have been taken out, and some have been added. And, too, the meanings of many of its provisions have been modified, as well.

This process of constitutional change, of modification and growth, has come about in two basic ways: (1) by *formal amendment* and (2) by *informal amendment.*

Formal Amendment

The Framers knew that even the wisest of constitution-makers cannot build for all time. And, so, the Constitution provides for its own amendment.

Article V sets out two methods for the _proposal_ and two methods for the _ratification_ of constitutional amendments. So, there are four different methods of formal amendment (see the diagram on the next page).

---

[4]The British constitution dates from well before the Norman Conquest of 1066; but it is not a single, written document. Rather, it is an "unwritten constitution," a collection of principles, customs, traditions and significant parliamentary acts which guide British government and practice.

THE FORMAL AMENDMENT PROCESS

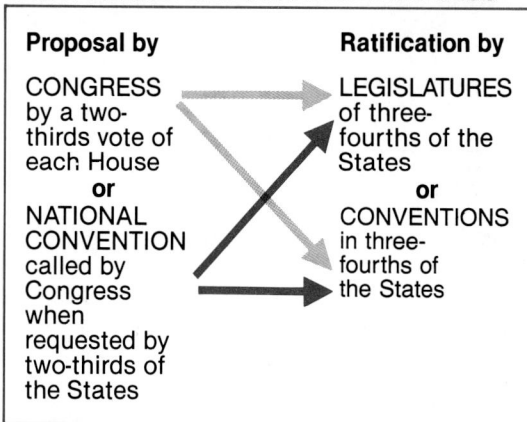

Proposal by	Ratification by
CONGRESS by a two-thirds vote of each House **or** NATIONAL CONVENTION called by Congress when requested by two-thirds of the States	LEGISLATURES of three-fourths of the States **or** CONVENTIONS in three-fourths of the States

First: An amendment may be proposed by a two-thirds vote in each house of Congress and be ratified by three-fourths of the State legislatures. Today, then, 38 State legislatures must approve an amendment in order to make it a part of the Constitution. Twenty-five of the Constitution's now 26 amendments were adopted in this manner.

Second: An amendment may be proposed by Congress and then ratified by conventions, called for that purpose, in three-fourths of the States. Only the 21st Amendment, added in 1933, was adopted in this way.[5]

Third: An amendment may be proposed by a national convention, called by Congress at the request of two-thirds of the State legislatures (today, 34), and ratified by three-fourths of the State legislatures.[6] To date, Congress has not called such a convention.

Fourth: An amendment may be proposed by a national convention and ratified by conventions in three-fourths of the States. Remember that the Constitution itself was adopted in much this same way.

The Constitution places only one restriction on the subjects with which a proposed amendment may deal. Article V declares that "no State, without its consent, shall be deprived of its equal suffrage in the Senate."

Note that the formal amendment process emphasizes the federal character of the governmental system. Proposal takes place at the national level and ratification is a State-by-State matter. And note, too, that our political theory holds that adoption of an amendment represents the expression of the people's sovereign will.

When both houses of Congress pass a resolution proposing an amendment, it is not sent to the President to be signed or vetoed—though the Constitution would seem to call for it.[7] When Congress proposes an amendment it is not making law (not legislating).

The practice of sending proposed amendments to the State legislatures rather than to ratifying conventions is sometimes criticized—especially because it permits a constitutional change without a clear-cut expression by the people. The critics lay their arguments on these points: The State legislators, who do the ratifying are elected to office of a mix of many reasons—party membership, name familiarity, incumbency, their stands on such matters as taxes, schools, welfare programs, and a host of other things. But they are almost never chosen because of their stand on a pro-

---

[5]The 21st Amendment repealed the 18th (which had established national prohibition). Conventions were used to ratify the amendment largely because Congress felt that their popularly elected delegates would be more likely to reflect public opinion on the question of repeal than would State legislators.

[6]The calling of a convention has been a near thing twice in recent years. Between 1963 and 1969, 33 State legislatures—one short of the necessary two-thirds—sought an amendment to erase the Supreme Court's "one-man, one-vote" decisions (see pages 281, 522). And, between 1975 and 1984, 32 States asked for a convention to propose an amendment that would require that the federal budget be balanced each year, except in time of war or other national emergency.

[7]See Article I, Section 7, Clause 3. This practice (not submitting proposed amendments to the President) is an example of the many "informal amendments" to the Constitution—a matter we shall turn to in a moment.

THE 26TH AMENDMENT
AND THE 18-YEAR-OLD VOTE

In 1971, the 26th amendment extended the right to vote to nearly 11 million American 18-, 19-, and 20-year olds. Its proposal won nearly unanimous support in Congress, and the States ratified it in only three months and seven days. At the time, many claimed that the youth vote would soon have a major impact on the nation's politics. But, clearly, that has not been the case.

The Census Bureau reports that only half of all eligible voters between ages of 18 and 24 said they had voted in the 1972 presidential election. In 1976 and 1980 only about 40 percent did so.

There were more than 160 million Americans of voting age in 1980. Only about 86.5 million actually voted, however. The rate of turnout by age group in 1980 was:

Age Group	Percent Voting
18–20	36
21–24	43
25–34	55
35–44	64
45–54	67
55–64	71
65–74	69
over 75	58

1. Why do you think the 26th Amendment was ratified so quickly—in fact, in record-breaking time?
2. Why is the rate of turnout among 18-24-year-olds lower than that of any other age group in the population?
3. Do you think that 18-24-year-olds should vote in larger numbers?

posed amendment to the Federal Constitution. In fact, many of them may have been elected even before the proposal was submitted to the States. On the other hand, the delegates to a ratifying convention would be chosen by the people on the basis of one particular factor: a yes-or-no stand on the proposed amendment.

The Supreme Court has held that a State may not require that an amendment proposed by Congress be approved by a vote of the people of the State before it can be ratified by the State legislature. It made that ruling in a case from Ohio, *Hawke v. Smith,* in 1920. But a State legislature can call for an *advisory* vote by the people before it

acts—as the Court most recently indicated in a case from Nevada, *Kimble v. Swackhamer, 1978.*

If a State rejects a proposed amendment, it is not forever bound by its vote. That is, it may later reconsider and ratify the proposal.

But both the historical precedent and most constitutional scholars agree that the reverse is not true. Once a State has approved an amendment, that action is final and unchangeable.[8]

[8]The Supreme Court has never ruled on this point directly. However, its decisions in related cases indicate that it would hold that a **recision** (a State's attempt to rescind, cancel a ratification) presents a "political question"—that is, one to be decided by Congress rather than the courts.

AMENDMENTS TO THE CONSTITUTION

Amendments	Subject	Year Adopted	Time Required For Ratification
1st–10th	The Bill of Rights	1791	2 years, 2 months 20 days
11th	Immunity of States from certain suits	1795	11 months, 3 days
12th	Changes in Electoral College procedure	1804	6 months, 3 days
13th	Prohibition of slavery	1865	10 months, 3 days
14th	Citizenship, due process, and equal protection	1868	2 years, 26 days
15th	No denial of vote because of race, color, or previous condition of servitude	1870	11 months, 8 days
16th	Power of Congress to tax incomes	1913	3 years, 6 months 22 days
17th	Direct election of U.S. Senators	1913	10 months, 26 days
18th	National (liquor) prohibition	1919	1 year, 29 days
19th	Woman suffrage	1920	1 year, 2 months, 14 days
20th	Change of dates for congressional and presidential terms	1933	10 months, 21 days
21st	Repeal of the 18th Amendment	1933	9 months, 15 days
22nd	Limit on presidential tenure	1951	3 years, 11 months, 3 days
23rd	District of Columbia electoral vote	1961	9 months, 13 days
24th	Prohibition of tax payment as a qualification to vote in federal elections	1964	1 year, 4 months, 9 days
25th	Procedures for determining presidential disability, presidential succession, and for filling a vice presidential vacancy	1967	1 year, 7 months, 4 days
26th	Sets the minimum age for voting in all elections at 18	1971	3 months, 7 days

More than 9000 joint resolutions calling for amendments to the Constitution have been proposed in Congress since 1789. Only 33 of them have been sent on to the States. Of those, only 26 have been finally ratified.[9]

We shall take a brief look at each of those 26 Amendments in a moment. But, first, this very significant point about those formal additions to the Constitution: As important as they are, they have *not* in fact been especially responsible for the extraordinary vitality of the Constitution. That is to say, they have not been a major part of the process by which that document has kept pace with nearly 200 years of far-reaching change in this country.

[9]Two of the seven unratified amendments were offered in 1789, along with the 10 that became the Bill of Rights. One dealt with the distribution of seats in the House of Representatives, the other with congressional pay. A third, proposed in 1810, would have voided the citizenship of anyone accepting a foreign title or other honor. Another, in 1861, would have prohibited any amendment relating to slavery. A fifth, in 1924 would have given Congress the power to regulate child labor. A sixth one, proclaiming the equal rights of women (ERA) was proposed in 1972; but it fell three States short of ratification and died in 1982. A seventh, to give the District of Columbia seats in Congress was proposed in 1978 and is currently before the State legislatures; see page 640.

The 26 Amendments

The *first ten amendments* were all proposed by Congress in 1789 and ratified by the States in 1791. Each of them arose from the controversy surrounding the ratification of the Constitution itself. Many, including Thomas Jefferson, had agreed to support the Constitution only if a listing of the basic rights of the people were added to the document immediately.

These first ten amendments, the **Bill of Rights,** set out the great constitutional guarantees of freedom of expression and belief, freedom and security of the person, and fair and equal treatment before the law. We shall look at them in Chapters 5 and 6. The 10th Amendment spells out the concept of reserved powers in the federal system—a matter we shall look at in the next chapter.

The *11th Amendment* was added in 1795. It declares that a State may not be sued in the federal courts by a citizen of another State or of a foreign state. The *12th Amendment* (1804) made slight changes in the presidential election process.

The *13th, 14th, and 15th Amendments* are often called the Civil War Amendments. The 13th (1865) put an end to slavery and prohibits most other forms of "involuntary servitude." The 14th (1868) defined American citizenship and granted it to former slaves. It also contains the Due Process and Equal Protection Clauses, which protect basic civil rights from infringement by the States. And the 15th Amendment (1870) forbids any restrictions on the right to vote based upon "race, color, or previous condition of servitude."

The *16th Amendment* authorizes a federal income tax. The *17th* provides for the popular election of United States Senators. Both were added in the same year, 1913. The *18th Amendment* (1919) established nationwide prohibition.

The *19th Amendment* (1920) provided for woman suffrage. The *20th* set a new date for the beginning of each regular session of Congress and for the inauguration of the President. The *21st Amendment* repealed the 18th. Both the *20th* and the *21st* Amendments were adopted in 1933.

The *22nd Amendment* was ratified in 1951. It limits a President to two full terms or not more than 10 years in office. The *23rd* (1961) provides for three presidential electors from the District of Columbia. The *24th* (1964) bars the payment of any tax as a qualification for voting in any federal election.

The *25th Amendment* (1967) deals with three matters: presidential succession, a vacancy in the Vice Presidency, and the determination of presidential disability.

The most recent amendment, the *26th*, was ratified in 1971. It sets age 18 as the minimum age for voting in all elections in the United States.

After years of struggle, women in all of the States won the right to vote with the ratification of the 19th Amendment in 1920.

✓ **FOR REVIEW**

1. By what two methods may amendments to the Constitution be proposed?
2. By what two methods may they be ratified?
3. How many amendments have been proposed? Ratified?

Informal Amendment

In the main, the Constitution deals with matters of principle and of basic organization and structure. Most of its sections are brief and undetailed—even skeletal in nature.

Because this is so, the real key to constitutional change and development in the United States lies in the process of **informal amendment.** That is, it lies in those many changes that have been made in the Constitution but which have not involved any changes in its written words.

No one can really understand the Constitution itself—let alone the processes of constitutional change—without understanding this point. Put it this way: There is much—in fact, a great amount—in the Constitution that cannot be seen with the naked eye. There is much that has been put there not by formal amendment but rather by the day-to-day, year-to-year experiences of government under the Constitution.

This highly important process of informal amendment has taken place—and continues to occur—in five separate ways: through (1) *the passage of basic legislation by Congress;* (2) *actions taken by the President;* (3) *decisions of the Supreme Court;* (4) *the activities of political parties;* and (5) *custom.*

Basic Legislation. Congress has been a major agent of informal amendment, and in two different ways. First, it has passed many laws to spell out sever-al of the Constitution's brief provisions. That is, it has added flesh to the bones of those sections the Framers left purposely skeletal, left for Congress to detail as circumstances required.

Take the structure of the federal court system as an example. In Article III, Section 1 the Constitution provides for "one Supreme Court, and . . . such inferior courts as the Congress may from time to time ordain and establish." Beginning with the Judiciary Act of 1789, then, all of the federal courts, except for the Supreme Court, have been set up by acts of Congress. Or, quite similarly, Article II creates only the offices of President and Vice President. All of the many departments, agencies, and offices in the huge executive branch have been created by acts of Congress.

Secondly, Congress has added to the Constitution by the way in which it has used many of its powers. For example, the Constitution gives to Congress the expressed power to regulate foreign and interstate commerce.[10] But what is "foreign commerce"? And what is "interstate commerce"? What, exactly, does Congress have the power to regulate? The Constitution does not say. In passing thousands of statutes under the Commerce Clause, Congress has done much to define its meaning. And, in doing so, it has informally amended—added a great deal to—the Constitution.

Executive Action. The manner in which different Presidents have used their powers has also produced several informal amendments.

For example, the Constitution states that only Congress may declare war.[11] But it also makes the President the Commander in Chief of the armed forces.[12] And, acting under that authori-

---

[10]Article I, Section 8, Clause 3.
[11]Article I, Section 8, Clause 11.
[12]Article II, Section 2, Clause 1.

ty, several Presidents have made war *without* a congressional declaration of war. They have used the armed forces, abroad, in combat, without such a declaration, on no fewer than 150 separate occasions in our history.

Among many other examples that may be cited here is the use of *executive agreements* in the conduct of foreign affairs. An executive agreement is a pact made by the President directly with the head of a foreign state. The principal difference between these agreements and treaties is that they need not be approved by the Senate. But they are as legally binding as treaties; and recent Presidents have often used them instead of the more cumbersome treaty-making process outlined in the Constitution.[13]

Court Decisions. The courts—most tellingly the Supreme Court—interpret and apply the Constitution in many cases they hear. We have already mentioned several of these instances of constitutional interpretation—that is, informal amendment—by the Court; for example, *Marbary* v. *Madison*, 1803. And we shall encounter many more, too—for the Supreme Court is, as Woodrow Wilson once put it, "a constitutional convention in continuous session."

Party Practices. The nation's political parties have also been a major source of informal amendment.

The Constitution does not speak of political parties. In fact, most of the Framers were opposed to their growth. Yet, they have had a major part in the shaping of government and its processes in this country almost from the very beginning. Cases in point are almost without number.

Neither the Constitution nor any law provides for the nomination of candidates for the Presidency. But, from the 1830s on, the major parties have held national conventions to do just that. And, long since, the parties have converted the electoral college from what the Framers intended it to be into a "rubber stamp" for the popular vote in presidential elections. Both houses of Congress are organized, and conduct much of their business, on the basis of party. The President makes appointments to office with an eye to party politics. And on and on. In short, in many ways, government in the United States is government through party.

Custom. Unwritten customs may be as strong as written laws, and many of them have developed in the American governmental system.

Again, there are many examples. By custom, not because the Constitution says so, the heads of the 13 executive departments make up the Cabinet, an advisory body to the President.

On each of the eight occasions when President died in office, the Vice President succeeded to that office—most recently in 1963. Yet, the written words of the Constitution did not provide for this practice until the adoption of the 25th Amendment in 1967. Until then, the Constitution in fact said that the powers and duties of the Presidency—but *not* the office itself—should be transferred to the Vice President.[14] And, again, on and on.

Both the strength and the importance of unwritten customs can be seen in the reaction to the rare circumstances in which one of them was not observed. For nearly 150 years the "no-third-term tradition" was a closely followed rule in presidential politics. It was begun in 1796, when George Washington refused to seek another term as President. In 1940, and again in 1944, however,

[13]Article II, Section 2, Clause 2.

[14]Read, carefully, Article II, Section 1, Clause 6 and then Section 1 of the 25th Amendment.

Franklin Roosevelt broke the custom. He sought and won a third, and then a fourth, term in the White House. As a direct result, the 22nd Amendment was added to the Constitution, in 1951—and so what has been an unwritten custom (an informal amendment) became a written part of the Constitution itself.

1. What are the Constitution's "informal amendments"?
2. In what several ways—through what agents—have these constitutional changes come about?

S U M M A R Y

The Constitution is this nation's fundamental law. It sets forth the six basic principles upon which the American system of government rests:

(1) Popular Sovereignty: The people are sovereign; they are the *only* source for the authority of government.

(2) Limited Government: Government is not all-powerful; it may do *only* those things the people have given it the power to do.

(3) Separation of Powers: The basic powers of government (legislative, executive, and judicial) are divided (separated) among three independent, co-equal branches of government.

(4) Checks and Balances: The three separate branches of government are tied together through a complex system of *checks* (restraints) each may use against the others.

(5) Judicial Review: The courts (most importantly, the Supreme Court) have the power to decide the constitutionality of any action of government.

(6) Federalism: The powers of government are distributed on a territorial basis, between the National Government and the several States.

The formal amendment process is set out in Article V. It provides for four different methods of amendment. Only two have ever been used, however. To date, 26 amendments have been added to the Constitution.

The Constitution has also been changed, has kept up with the developments of nearly 200 years, by "informal amendments." These additions to the Constitution, although they have not changed its written words, are very important. They have been brought about by: (1) basic legislation enacted by Congress; (2) precedent-setting actions by various Presidents; (3) important decisions of the Supreme Court; (4) practices of political parties; and (5) custom.

C H A P T E R   R E V I E W

Key Terms/Concepts

Amendment (55)
Bill of Rights (59)
Checks and Balances (52)
Constitution (50)
Constitutionalism (51)
Executive (52)
Federalism (54)
Formal amendment (55)
Informal amendment (60)
Judicial (52)
Judicial review (53)
Legislative (52)
Limited government (51)
Popular sovereignty (51)
Proposal/ratification (55)
Rule of law (51)
Separation of powers (52)
Supreme law of the land (50)

Keynote Questions

1. Identify and briefly describe each of the six basic principles set out in the Constitution.
2. Why can all of the Constitution be quite properly described as "a statement of limited government"?
3. By what methods can amendments to the Constitution be proposed? By which of them has that in fact been done? How many times thus far?
4. By what methods can proposed amendments be ratified? How many have thus far been ratified? By which method have all but one of them been approved?
5. By what other process has constitutional change occurred in this country?
6. On balance, which of these two processes—formal amendment or the process referred to in question 5—has been more responsible for the changes which have occurred in the American constitutional system?
7. How—through what various means—has that other process been conducted? Cite at least one example of each of them

For Thought and Discussion

1. Select a provision of the Constitution which illustrates one of the basic principles of the constitutional system—*e.g.*, the President's veto power (Article I, Section 7, Clauses 2 and 3), illustrating the principle of checks and balances. Why was the provision included in the Constitution? If the Constitution were to be rewritten today, why would you favor or oppose keeping that provision?
2. On what grounds can it be argued that the first 10 amendments may be viewed, quite properly, as a part of the original Constitution itself?
3. In *The Federalist* No. 51 James Madison wrote:

But what is government itself, but the greatest of all reflections on human nature? If men were angels, no government would be necessary.

Put this in your own words. Which provisions of the Constitution seem to you to be based upon this Madisonian view?

4. Why do you think the author chose as the title for this chapter "The Living Constitution"?
5. In your view, is the Constitution too easily amended—either formally or informally?

Suggested Activities

1. Prepare a chart or poster to show: (a) the principles of separation of powers and checks and balances; (b) the formal amendment process; and/or (c) the informal amendment process.
2. Write a report identifying the reasons and events which led to the adoption of one of the 26 amendments to the Constitution.
3. Compare the provisions of Article V with the amendment processes set out in your State's constitution. Compare, too, the content of the amendments which have been added to these documents. What conclusions can you draw from these comparisons?
4. Stage a debate or class forum on one of the following: (a) *Resolved*, That the Constitution be amended to permit the people to propose constitutional amendments by popular petition and to adopt or reject such amendments by popular vote; (b) *Resolved*, That the President be denied the power to veto acts of Congress; (c) *Resolved*, That the Supreme Court be deprived of its power of judicial review.

4 The Nation and the States: Federalism

CHAPTER OBJECTIVES

To help you to
Learn ▪ Know ▪ Understand

The origins and meaning of federalism.

The division of powers in the American federal system.

The delegated (expressed, implied, inherent) powers of the National Government and the reserved powers of the States.

The Supremacy Clause and the role of the Supreme Court in the federal system.

Federal-State and interstate relations.

The Statehood process.

The Constitution, in all its provisions, looks to an indestructible Union, composed of indestructible States.

Chief Justice Salmon P. Chase
Texas v. White (1868)

Recall that the authors of the Constitution built their proposals for a new system of government for the United States upon the concept of *federalism*. That is, they invented an arrangement in which the powers of government were to be divided geographically—some of the powers were to be held by the new National Government and others by the already existing States.

The Framers had to deal with a number of both difficult and highly important problems at the Philadelphia Convention. Among the most prominent, and complex, of them, was this: How could they design a *strong, national* government, with the power to meet the nation's needs and, at the same time, preserve the existing States?

Few, if any, of the Framers favored a strong centralized (unitary) government in the British pattern. They knew how stoutly the people had fought for the right of local self-government. Still, they knew that the government under the Articles (a confederation) was too weak to deal with the nation's difficulties.

Remember, too, that the authors of the Constitution were dedicated to the concept of limited government. They were convinced that: (1) *any* governmental power is a threat to individual

Under a federal system, each level of government operates through its own agencies, officials, and laws. Here, President Reagan addresses a joint session of Iowa's legislature in 1981, seeking support for his domestic program.

liberty, (2) the use of power must therefore be limited, and (3) to divide governmental power is to restrict it and thus prevent its abuse.

Federalism Defined

A federal system of government is one in which a written constitution divides the powers of government on a territorial basis. The division is made between a central (national) government and several regional (local) governments. Each level has its own field of powers. Neither level, acting alone, can change the basic division of powers the constitution makes between them. Each level operates through its own agencies and acts directly upon the people through its own officials and laws.

In effect, federalism produces a *dual* system of government. It provides for two basic levels of government. Each

has its own sphere of authority; each operates over the same people and the same territory at one and the same time.

Federalism's major strength is that it allows *local* actions in matters of local concern while allowing *national* action in matters of wider concern. Local traditions, needs, and desires may be different in different states. Federalism allows for this. For example: Most forms of gambling are allowed in Nevada but are against the law in most other States. New Jersey buses private as well as public school students free of charge but most States do not. Only in North Carolina does the governor not have the power to veto acts of the legislature. And on and on . . .

Federalism allows and encourages local choice in many matters. It also provides for the strength that comes from union.

National defense and foreign affairs offer ready illustrations of the point, of course. So, too, do domestic affairs. Take, as an example, a natural disaster. When a flood or drought or winter storm or other catastrophe hits some State, the resources of the National Government and all of the other States can be mobilized to aid the stricken area.

The terms *federalism* and *democracy* are not synonymous. Remember: federalism involves a territorial division of the powers of government. Democracy involves the role of the people in the governing process. Still, it is all but impossible to imagine a democratic government operating over any large area in which there is not also present a large degree of local self-government.

☑ F O R   R E V I E W

1. Define federalism.
2. Why did the Framers create a federal system for the United States?
3. How does federalism reinforce the concept of limited government?
4. What is the chief advantage of a federal system?

The Division of Powers

The Constitution sets out the basic design of the American federal system. At base, it provides for a **division of powers** between the National Government on the one hand and the States on the other. That division was intended (implied) in the original Constitution and then spelled out in the 10th Amendment:

> The Powers not delegated to the United States by the Constitution nor prohibited by it to the States, are reserved to the States respectively, or to the people.

The National Government, One of Delegated Powers

The National Government is a government of **delegated powers**. That is, it has only those powers delegated (granted) to it in the Constitution. There are three distinct types of delegated powers: the *expressed*, the *implied*, and the *inherent* powers.

The Expressed Powers. The **expressed powers** are those delegated to the National Government in so many words—spelled out, expressly—in the Constitution.

Most of them are to be found in Article I, Section 8. There, in 18 separate clauses, 27 different powers are expressly given to Congress. They include, among others, the power to lay and collect taxes, to coin money, to regulate foreign and interstate commerce, to raise and maintain armed forces, to declare war, to fix standards of weights and measures, to grant patents and copyrights, and to do many other things.

But, note, several powers are set out elsewhere in the Constitution. Thus, Article II, Section 2 gives several of these powers to the President. They include: the power to act as commander-in-chief of the armed forces, to grant reprieves and pardons, to make treaties, and to name major federal officeholders. Article III grants "the judicial power of the United States" to the Supreme Court and to the other courts in the federal judiciary. And several of the expressed powers are also found in various of the amendments to the Constitution —*e.g.,* the 16th Amendment gives Congress the power to levy an income tax.

The Implied Powers. The **implied powers** are those which are not expressly stated in the Constitution but are *reasonably implied* by those which are.

The constitutional basis for the implied powers is to be found in one of the expressed powers. Article I, Section 8,

THE DIVISION OF POWERS BETWEEN THE NATIONAL GOVERNMENT AND THE STATES

☐ **A** Delegated Powers of the National Government

▨ **B** Reserved Powers of the States

▨ **C** Concurrent Powers

▨ **D** Powers Denied the National Government

▨ **E** Powers Denied the States

☐ **F** Powers Denied both the National Government and the States

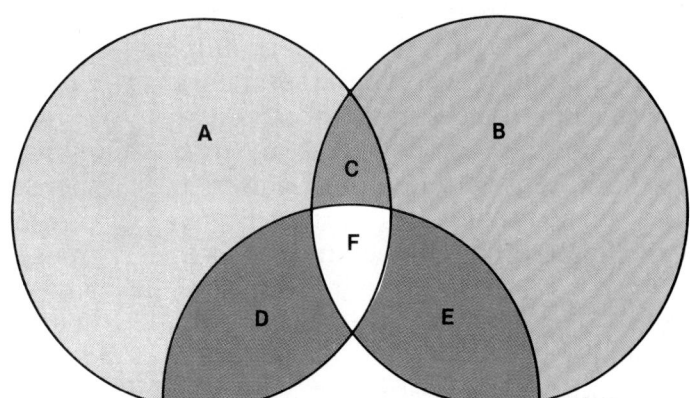

Clause 18 gives to Congress the "necessary and proper" power. The Necessary and Proper Clause reads:

> Congress shall have power . . . to make all laws which shall be necessary and proper for carrying into execution the foregoing powers, and all other powers vested by this Constitution in the Government of the United States, or in any department or officer thereof.

Through congressional and court interpretation, the words "necessary and proper" have come to mean, in effect, "convenient and expedient." Indeed, the Necessary and Proper Clause is sometimes called the Elastic Clause.

To give but a few of the thousands of examples of the exercise of implied powers, note these: Congress has provided for the regulation of labor-management relations, the building of hydro-electric power dams, and the building of a 67,200-kilometer (42,000-mile) interstate highway system. It has made federal crimes of such acts as moving stolen goods, gambling information, or kidnapped persons across State lines. And it has prohibited racial discrimination in access to such places as restaurants, theaters, hotels, and motels.

Congress has taken these actions—and many, many more—because the power to do so is reasonably implied by just *one* of the expressed powers—the power to regulate foreign and interstate commerce.[1]

The Inherent Powers. The **inherent powers** are those which belong to the National Government because it is the national government of a sovereign state in the world community. Although the Constitution does not expressly provide for them, they are powers which national governments have historically possessed. It stands to reason that the Framers intended that these powers would be held by the National Government they created.

The inherent powers are few in number. The chief ones include: the power to regulate immigration, to deport aliens, to acquire territory, to give diplomatic recognition to other states, and to protect the nation against rebellion or internal subversion.

It can be argued that most of the inherent powers are *implied* by one

---

[1] Article I, Section 8, Clause 3. We shall return to the doctrine of implied powers in greater detail in Chapter 13, "The Powers of Congress."

or more of the expressed powers. Thus, the power to regulate immigration is implied by the expressed power to regulate foreign trade. And the power to acquire territory can be drawn from the treaty-making power and the several war powers. But the doctrine of inherent powers holds that it is not necessary to go to those lengths to find these powers in the Constitution. In short, these powers exist because the United States exists.

Powers Denied to the National Government

While the Constitution delegates certain powers to the National Government, it also denies certain powers to it. And it does so in three distinct ways.

First, some powers are denied to the National Government *in so many words*—expressly—in the Constitution.[2] Among them are the power to levy duties on exports; to deny freedom of religion, speech, press, or assembly; to conduct illegal searches or seizures; and to deny to one accused of crime a speedy and public trial, or a trial by jury.

Secondly, several powers are denied to the National Government because of the *silence* of the Constitution. Recall, the National Government is a government of delegated powers; it has only those powers the Constitution gives to it.

Among the many powers not granted to the National Government are these: to create a public school system for the nation, to enact a uniform marriage and divorce law, or to set up units of local government. The Constitution says nothing about these matters. It does not give the National Government the power to do any of these things—expressly, or implicitly, or inherently. And that very silence denies such power to the National Government.

Thirdly, some powers are denied to the National Government because of the nature of the federal system. That is, the National Government cannot be allowed to do those things which would threaten the existence of that system.

For example, in the exercise of its power to tax, Congress cannot tax any of the States (or their local units) in the carrying out of their governmental functions. If it could, it would have the power to destroy (tax out of existence) one or more, or all, of the States.[3]

The States, Governments of Reserved Powers

The Constitution *reserves* power to each of the States. The **reserved powers** are the powers held by the States in the federal system. They are those powers which are not given to the National Government and which are not at the same time denied to the States.

Thus, Alabama (or any other State) may forbid persons under 18 to marry without parental consent or those under 19 to buy liquor. It may require that doctors, lawyers, hairdressers, or plumbers be licensed in order to practice in the State. It may set up public school systems and units of local government, set the conditions under which divorces may be granted, and permit certain forms of gambling and outlaw others.

The sphere of powers held by each of the States is, in a word, huge. They can do all of those things we've suggested and much, much more. They can because nothing in the Constitution forbids them to do so. The National Government can do none of those things because the Constitution does not give it the power to do so. The power to do those things is *reserved* to the States.

[2]Most of the expressed denials of power are found in Article I, Section 9 and in the 1st through the 8th Amendments.

[3]But note that when a State (or one of its local units) performs a so-called "nongovernmental" function—*e.g.,* operating liquor stores, a bus system, a farmer's market, and so forth—it is liable to federal taxes; see page 608.

Powers Denied to the States

Just as the Constitution denies certain powers to the National Government, it does not allow the States to do a number of things.

Some powers are denied to the States *in so many words* by the Constitution.[4] For example, no State may enter into any treaty, alliance, or confederation. Nor may it print or coin money, or deprive any person of life, liberty, or property without due process of law.

There are some powers the States do not have because of the existence of the federal system. Thus, no State (or local government) may tax any of the agencies or functions of the National Government. Remember, too, that each of the States has its own constitution which denies many powers to the State.[5]

Local Governments in the Federal System

Government in the United States is very often looked at in terms of three layers: national, State, and local. However inviting this may be, it is at best misleading. Remember, there are just *two* basic levels in the federal system: the National Government and the 50 States.

There are governments at the local level, of course—everywhere in the country. In fact, there are over 80,000 units of local government in the United States today. We shall take a close look at them later in this book; but, for now, this very important point: All of those thousands of local governments are parts (sub-units) of the various States.

Each of these local units is located *within* one of the 50 States. None of them has an existence apart from its parent State. That is, each of them is a creature of its State. Each of the States, in its constitution and in its laws, has created these units. To whatever extent any of them can provide services, regulate activities, collect taxes, or do anything else, they can only because the State has established them and given them the power to do so. In short, as local governments exercise the powers they possess, they are actually exercising State powers—powers given to them by their parent State.

Another way of putting all of this is to remind you that: Each of the 50 States has a *unitary* form of government.

The Exclusive Powers

The **exclusive powers** are those which, in the federal system, may be used *only* by the National Government. They include most, but not all, of the delegated powers.

Some of the powers delegated to the National Government are also expressly denied to the States, for example—the powers to coin money, make treaties, and lay import duties. Thus, these powers belong solely to—are *exclusive powers* of—the National Government.

Some of the powers given to the National Government but not *expressly* denied to the States are also among the exclusive powers because of the nature of the particular powers involved. For example, the States are not expressly denied the power to regulate interstate commerce. If they were to do so, however, there would be chaos.[6]

---

[4]Most of the expressed prohibitions of power to the States (and, so, to their local governments) are found in Article I, Section 10 and in the 13th, 14th, 15th, 19th, 24th, and 26th Amendments.

[5]Study your own State's constitution on this point - and note, then, the significance of the words "or to the people" in the 10th Amendment. We shall look at the States' constitution in some detail in Chapter 19.

[6]The States may not regulate interstate commerce as such. But in using their different powers, they do *affect* it. For example, in regulating highway speeds the States regulate vehicles operating wholly within the State (*i.e.*, in intrastate commerce) but also those operating from State to State. Generally, the States may affect interstate commerce, but they may not impose an unreasonable burden upon it.

The Concurrent Powers

The **concurrent powers** are those which belong to and are exercised by *both* the National Government and the States. They include, for example, the power to lay and collect taxes, to define crimes and set punishments for them, and to condemn (take) private property for public use.

The concurrent powers are not held and exercised *jointly* by the two basic levels of government—but, rather, *separately* and *simultaneously*. To put their definitions another way: They are those powers which the Constitution does not grant to the National Government exclusively and which does not, at the same time, deny to the States.

☑ FOR REVIEW

1. What is meant by the phrase "division of powers"?

2. Why is the National Government properly described as a government of delegated powers?

3. What are the expressed powers? The implied powers? The inherent powers?

4. Why are the States properly described as governments of reserved powers?

5. On what three bases are powers denied to the National Government? To the States?

6. Where do local governments fit into the federal system?

7. What are the exclusive powers? The concurrent powers?

The Supreme Law of the Land

The division of powers in the American federal system is a very complicated matter, as we have seen. And, as we noted earlier, it produces a dual system of government. That is, it is a system in which two basic levels of government operate over the same territory and the same people at the same time.

In such an arrangement there are certain to be conflicts between the two levels, conflicts between national law on the one hand and State law on the other. Expecting this, the Framers wrote the Supremacy Clause into the Constitution. Article VI, Section 2 declares:

> This Constitution, and the laws of the United States which shall be made in pursuance thereof, and all treaties made or which shall be made under the authority of the United States, shall be the supreme law of the land; . . .

And, Article VI goes on to add:

> . . . and the judges in every State shall be bound thereby, anything in the constitution or laws of any State to the contrary notwithstanding.

The Constitution and the acts and treaties of the United States are "the supreme law of the land." The Constitution stands above all other forms of law in the United States; acts of Congress and treaties stand immediately beneath it.[7]

In other words, the Supremacy Clause forms a "ladder of laws" in the United States. The Constitution stands on the topmost rung. Then come the acts of Congress and treaties. Each State's constitution, supreme over all other forms of that State's law, stands beneath *all* forms of federal law. State

---

[7]Acts of Congress and treaties stand on equal planes with one another. Neither may conflict with any provision in the Constitution. In the rare case of conflict between the provisions of an act and those of a treaty, the more recently adopted takes precedence—as the latest expression of the sovereign people's will. The Supreme Court has regularly held to that position from the first case it decided on the point, *The Head Money Cases,* 1884.

statutes are on the rung beneath the State's constitution. At the base of the ladder are the different forms of local law—city and county charters and ordinances, and so forth.

The Supremacy Clause has been called "the linchpin of the Constitution"—for it joins the National Government and the States into a single government organization, a federal state.

The Supreme Court, the Umpire in the Federal System

The Supreme Court is the "umpire" in the federal system—for one of its chief duties is to apply the Supremacy Clause to the conflicts which that system inevitably produces.

The Court was first called upon to play this role—to settle a clash between a national and a State law—in 1819. The case, *McCulloch* v. *Maryland*, involved the controversial Second Bank of the United States. The Bank had been chartered (established) by an act of Congress in 1816. In 1818 the Maryland legislature, hoping to cripple the Bank, placed a tax on all notes issued by its Baltimore branch. James McCulloch, branch cashier, refused to pay the tax, and he was convicted in the Maryland courts for that refusal.

The Supreme Court unanimously reversed the Maryland courts, however. Speaking for the Court, Chief Justice John Marshall based the decision squarely on the Supremacy Clause:

> If any one proposition could command the universal assent of mankind we might expect it to be this—that the government of the Union, though limited in its powers, is supreme within its sphere of action. . . . [T]he States have no power to retard, impede, burden, or in any manner control, the operation of the constitutional laws enacted by Congress.[8]

Under the leadership of Chief Justice John Marshall, the Supreme Court became a potent force in our system of government.

It is impossible to overstate the significance of the Court's function—past and present—as the umpire of the federal system. Had the Court not taken this role it is quite likely that the federal system—and probably the United States itself—could not have survived its early years. Justice Oliver Wendell Holmes made the point in these words:

> I do not think that the United States would come to an end if we [the Court] lost our power to declare an act of Congress void. I do think the Union would be imperiled if we could not make that declaration as to the laws of the several States.[9]

---

[8]The case is also critically important in the development of the constitutional system because, in deciding it, the Court for the first time upheld the doctrine of implied powers. It also held the National Government to be immune from any form of State taxation; see page 602. We shall return to this landmark case at some length in Chapter 13, "The Powers of Congress."

[9]*Collected Legal Papers* New York: Harcourt, 1920, pages 295–96.

✓ F O R   R E V I E W

1. Why does federalism necessarily produce a dual system of government?

2. What is the Supremacy Clause? The "supreme law of the land"?

3. If a State law conflicts with a national law, which must yield? Is this always true? Why?

4. Why is the Court's decision in *McCulloch* v. *Maryland* of such great importance?

The National Government's Obligations to the States

The Constitution places several obligations upon the National Government for the benfit of the States. Most of them are to be found in Article IV.

Guarantee of a Republican Form of Government

The National Government is required "to guarantee to every State in this Union a republican form of government."[10] The Constitution does not define "republican form of government," and the Supreme Court has regularly refused to do so. It is generally understood to mean a "representative government," however.

The Supreme Court has held that the question of whether or not a State has a republican form of government is a **political question**. That is, it is one to be decided by the political branches of the government—the President and Congress—*not* by the courts (as a judicial question).

The leading case here is *Luther* v. *Borden*, 1849. It grew out of Dorr's Rebellion—a revolt led by Thomas W. Dorr against the State of Rhode Island in 1841–1842. Dorr and his followers had written and proclaimed a new constitution for the State.[11] When they tried to put the new document into operation, however, the governor in office under the original constitution declared martial (military) law. He also called on the Federal Government for help. President John Tyler then took steps to put down the revolt, and it quickly collapsed.

The question of which of the two competing governments was the legitimate one in the State at the time was a major issue in *Luther* v. *Borden*. But, again, the Supreme Court refused to decide the matter.

The only extensive use ever made of the republican-form guarantee came in the period after the Civil War. Congress declared that several Southern States did not have governments of a republican form. It refused to admit Senators and Representatives from those States until they had ratified the 13th, 14th, and 15th Amendments and broadened their laws to recognize the voting and other rights of blacks.

Protection Against Invasion and Domestic Violence

The National Government must also "protect each of them against invasion; and on application of the legislature, or of the executive (when the legislature cannot be convened), against domestic violence."[12]

Foreign Invasion. Today it is very clear that an invasion of any one of the 50 States would be met as an attack upon the United States itself. Hence, this constitutional guarantee is now of little, if any, real significance.

---

[10]Article IV, Section 4.

[11]Recall that Rhode Island had not written a new constitution at the time of independence in 1775; see page 28. Rhode Island's present constitution, which became effective in 1843, came as a direct result of Dorr's rebellion.

[12]Article IV, Section 4.

But, recall, that was not the case in the late 1780s. Then, it was not at all certain that all 13 States would stand together if one of them were attacked by a foreign power. So, before the 13 States agreed to give up their war-making powers, each of them demanded an iron-clad pledge that an attack upon any of them would be met as an attack upon all.

Domestic Violence. The federal system assumes that each of the 50 States will keep the peace within its own borders. However, the Constitution does accept the fact that a State may not be able to control some situations. So, its guarantee of protection against domestic violence in each of them.

Historically, the use of federal force to restore order within a State has been a rare event. The most recent instances occurred nearly 20 years ago. When racial unrest exploded into violence in Detroit during the "long, hot summer" of 1967, President Johnson ordered units of the Regular Army into the city. He acted at the request of Michigan's Governor George Romney, and only after Detroit's police and firefighters, supported by State Police and National Guard units, found they could not control riots, arson, and other pillage in the city's ghetto areas. And in 1968, again at the request of the governors involved, federal troops were sent into Chicago and Baltimore—to help State and local forces put down the violence that had erupted in those two cities following the assassination of Dr. Martin Luther King, Jr.

Normally, a President has sent troops into a State only in answer to a request from its governor (or legislature). But when national laws are being broken, or national functions interfered with, or national property endangered, a President does not need to wait for such a plea.[13]

The ravages of nature—storms, floods, forest fires, and the like—can be far more destructive than human violence. Here, too, acting to protect the States against "domestic violence," the Federal Government stands ready to aid the stricken areas.

Respect for Territorial Integrity

The National Government is constitutionally bound to respect the territorial integrity of each of the States. That is, it must recognize the legal existence and the physical boundaries of each of them.

The whole scheme of the Constitution—its very existence—imposes this obligation. Several of its provisions do so, as well. For example, Congress must include, in both of its houses, members chosen in each one of the States.[14] And Congress, acting alone, cannot create a new State from territory belonging to any one of the existing States. To do so, it first must have the consent of the legislature of the State involved.[15] And, recall, Article V of the Constitution declares that no State can be deprived of its equal representation in the United States Senate without its own consent.

---

[13]President Cleveland ordered federal troops to put an end to rioting in the Chicago railyard during the Pullman Strike in 1894. At the time, he acted despite the objections of Governor William Altgeld of Illinois. The Supreme Court upheld his actions in *In re Debs*, 1896. The Court found that rioters had threatened federal property and impeded the flow of the mails and interstate commerce. Thus, more than "domestic violence" (violence confined within the State) was involved. Most recently, President Eisenhower did so at Little Rock, Arkansas, in 1957, and President Kennedy at the University of Mississippi in 1962 and at the University of Alabama in 1963. In each of those instances the President acted to halt the unlawful obstruction of school integration orders that had been issued by federal courts.

[14]In the House, Article I, Section 2, Clause 1; in the Senate, Article I, Section 3, Clause 1 and 17th Ammendment.

[15]Article, IV, Section 3, Clause 1.

1. What is "a republican form of government" generally understood to mean? Why has the Supreme Court never defined it?
2. Why does the Constitution obligate the National Government to protect each of the States against foreign invasion? Against domestic violence? When is the protection against domestic violence to be provided?
3. How (in what sense) does the Constitution require the National Government to respect the territorial integrity of each State?

Cooperative Federalism

At its very core, federalism involves a division of governmental powers on a territorial basis. That division is the primary and distinctive characteristic of any government which is federal in form —including our own, of course. And, as we have seen over the last several pages, the division of powers in the American federal system is a very complicated matter, indeed.

Federalism produces a dual system of government in the United States. Two basic levels of government operate over the same territory and the same people —and both of them at the same time. Given this complex arrangement, it should come as no surprise that competition, tensions, and conflicts are a regular, ongoing part of American federalism. In short, our governmental system may be likened to a tug-of-war—a continuing power struggle between the National Government and the States.

Keep the central importance of the concept of *divided* powers in mind. But add this vital point to it: The American federal arrangement also involves a broad area of *shared* powers. That is, in addition to the two separate spheres of power held and exercised by the two basic levels of government, there are large, and growing, areas of cooperation between them.

Federal Grants-in-Aid

Perhaps the best known examples of this intergovernmental cooperation are the many federal **grant-in-aid programs** —grants of federal money (or, sometimes, other resources) to the States and/or their cities, counties, and other local units. These grants provide those levels of government with the dollar-help they often need in order to carry out many of their own functions.

The history of these programs can be traced back some 200 years—in fact, to the period before the Constitution. In the Northwest Ordinance of 1787 the Congress under the Articles provided for the government of the territory beyond the Ohio River. And, looking forward to new States on that frontier, it set aside sections of land for the support of public education in those States-to-be. On through the 19th century, federal lands were given to the States for a number of purposes—schools and colleges, roads and canals, flood control work, and several others. (Most of our major State universities were founded as "land-grant colleges"—schools built out of the sale of public lands given to the States by the Morrill Act of 1862.)

Congress began to make grants of federal money quite early, too. In 1808 it gave the States $200,000 to support their militia. Cash grants did not come to play a large role until the Depression years of the 1930s, however. Much of the New Deal program of that era was built around many of them.

Over the years since then, Congress has set up hundreds of grant programs.

In fact, there are now more than 500 of them in operation. There are dozens of separate programs in each of many different areas—in education, mass transit, highway construction, health care, on-the-job training, law enforcement, and many, many others.

Grants-in-aid are based on the taxing power. Article I, Section 8, Clause 3 in the Constitution gives Congress that power in order "to pay the debts, and provide for the common defense and general welfare of the United States."

Over time, most grants have been both *categorical* and *conditional*. That is, Congress has made them for certain closely defined purposes, and it has set certain conditions that the States must meet in order to receive them. Most often, the major "strings" attached to a grant have required a State to (1) use the federal funds only for the purpose specified, (2) make its own contribution (often of an equal amount; sometimes much less), (3) set up a suitable agency and procedures to manage the grant, and (4) obey the federal guidelines set for the program for which the aid is given.

In effect, the grants-in-aid process blurs the division of powers line in the federal system. It permits the Federal Government to operate in many areas in which it would otherwise have no constitutional authority—for example, public education, urban renewal projects, and local mental health programs.

Critics have long made that point. Many of them also object to the narrowly defined (categorical) nature of most of them. They insist that those factors give Washington too much say in policy matters that should be set at the State and local levels.

Block Grants. To meet this latter objection, some categorical grants have been combined into larger programs. That is, Congress has converted them into ***block grants***. These are grants to State and local governments with more broadly defined purposes, and with fewer strings attached.

By 1982 federal grants-in-aid totalled nearly $95 billion. But the Reagan Administration has pushed hard for two major changes here: (1) a sharp cutback in overall spending, and (2) the conversion of most programs from a categorical to the block-grant format. As a result, total grant spending will likely be less than $85 billion in 1984.

Revenue Sharing. The federal revenue sharing program is a newer and entirely separate feature of cooperative federalism. It is an arrangement through which Congress has given to the States, and especially to their principal local units, an annual share of the huge federal tax-take.

The program was first put in place by the State and Local Fiscal Assistance Act of 1972. The law has been revised and extended three times now—most recently in 1983.

For nearly a decade, the States and their local governments received about $6 billion each year. A third of that money went to the States and the other two-thirds was shared by some 39,000 cities, counties, and townships across the country.

The States receive no revenue sharing money today. They were phased out of the program between 1980 and 1983. The current (1983) law provides for the distribution of nearly $5 billion a year.

The revenue sharing and the grants-in-aid programs are strikingly different. Most importantly: (1) no State or local matching funds are involved in the revenue sharing program. And (2) the revenue sharing monies are provided with virtually no strings attached. Congress has placed only one major restriction on the use of revenue sharing funds. They are not to be spent for any function in which discrimination on any of these

A CASE IN POINT

SLICING THE FEDERAL AID PIE

The Tax Foundation is a private research organization specializing in tax matters. Each year it compares each State's federal tax burden (*i.e.,* the total amount of all federal taxes paid in that State) with the total amount of all federal grants-in-aid received by that State and its local governments.

This map, drawn from the Foundation's most recent study, shows how much money the Federal Government collected in each State for every $1.00 of federal grant money that State received in 1982.

Some States "win" and others "lose" in this taxes-paid/aid received comparison. (The amount each State gets back varies from year-to-year, of course—but only somewhat. And, as you can see, that amount varies from State to State each year—and sometimes widely.) For 1982, Texas was the big "loser." Its taxpayers contributed $1.59 to the federal treasury for every dollar it got back. And Mississippi and Vermont were the big "winners"—paying out only 57¢ for each dollar of federal aid.

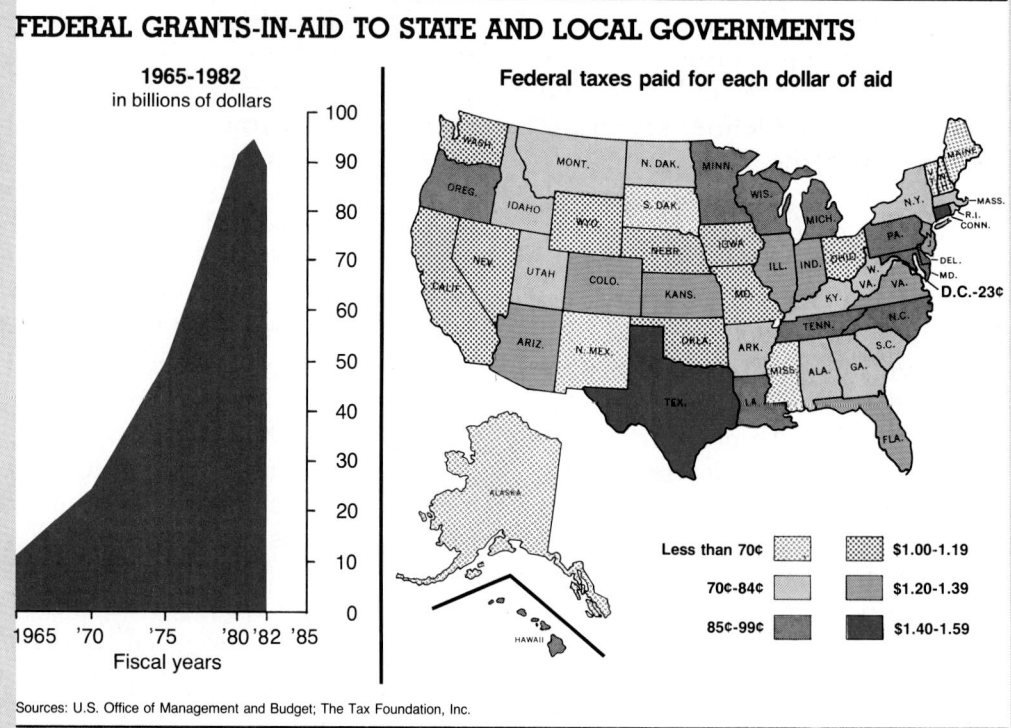

FEDERAL GRANTS-IN-AID TO STATE AND LOCAL GOVERNMENTS

1965-1982
in billions of dollars

Federal taxes paid for each dollar of aid

D.C.-23¢

Less than 70¢ $1.00-1.19
70¢-84¢ $1.20-1.39
85¢-99¢ $1.40-1.59

Fiscal years

Sources: U.S. Office of Management and Budget; The Tax Foundation, Inc.

1. How did your State fare in the taxes-paid to aid-received ratio in 1982?

2. What factors help to explain your State's ranking that year?

bases is practiced: race, color, sex, age, national origin, religious belief, or physical disabilities.

Revenue sharing serves three broad purposes: *First,* It tries to relieve the growing money problems of the States and their local governments. *Second,* it seeks to move power—in the form of control over spending decisions—from the national to the State and local level. *Third,* it works to lessen the burden carried by those least able to pay for the support of State and local activities. It does this by reducing the need to depend on generally more regressive State and local taxes, notably the property tax.

Revenue sharing has been a fairly successful and popular device. Quite understandably, it has strong support from most governors, mayors, and other State and local officials. But it does have its critics. Some argue that it is a "Trojan horse." That is, they say that while it *appears* to return power to the State and local levels, in fact it *increases* their dependence on Washington.

Some critics also argue that, as the Federal Government is putting up the money involved, it should have a much larger say in how it is spent. They want Congress to target specific State and local problem areas—much as it does in the grant-in-aid programs—and so insure more effective use of the funds.

The present (1983) revenue sharing law expires in 1986. Both its supporters and its critics expect a stiff fight over yet another extension of it then.

Other Forms of Federal Aid

The National Government gives aid to the States in a number of other ways. Thus, it shares with them revenues from certain activities. For example, it shares income from the sale of timber from national forest lands, mineral leases on public lands, migratory bird hunting licenses, and leases of power

sites on federal lands. It also makes some direct payments to local governments where there are large federal landholdings. The payments are made *in lieu of* (in place of) the property taxes the local governments cannot collect.

There are many other ways in which the National Government gives help to the States. For example, the FBI aids State and local police in criminal law enforcement. The Census Bureau makes its studies available to State and local schools to help them plan for the future. The Army and Air Force equip and train each State's National Guard units.

State Aid to the National Government

Federal-State cooperation is distinctly a two-way street. The States and their local units also aid the National Government in many ways. For example, national elections are conducted in each State by State and local election officials, financed with State and local funds, and very largely regulated by State laws.

The legal process by which aliens become citizens of the United States (naturalization) takes place in large part in the State courts, rather than in the federal courts. Fugitives from federal justice are often picked up by State and local police. And on and on . . .

✓ **FOR REVIEW**

1. What is meant by "cooperative federalism"?
2. What are federal grants-in-aid? On what grounds do some oppose them? Support them?
3. What is revenue sharing? Its three broad purposes? Its pros and cons?
4. In what ways do the States aid the National Government?

A pier of the Port of New York Authority along the East River, one of several which handle a huge volume of freight and cargo each year.

Interstate Relations

Conflict among the States was a major reason for the adoption of the Constitution in 1789. The fact that the new document strengthened the hand of the National Government—especially in the field of commerce—lessened many of those interstate frictions. So, too, did several of the Constitution's provisions which deal directly with the States' relationships with one another.

Interstate Compacts

As we know, no State may enter into any treaty, alliance, or confederation. The States may, however, with the consent of Congress, enter into **compacts** (agreements) among themselves and with foreign states.[16]

---

[16]Article I, Section 10, Clause 3. The Supreme Court has held that congressional consent is not needed for compacts which do not "tend to increase the political power of the States," *Virginia* v. *Tennessee*, 1893. But it is often difficult to decide whether an agreement is "political" or "nonpolitical." So, most interstate agreements are submitted to Congress as a matter of course.

The States made few compacts until this century—altogether only 26 of them to 1920. Since then, however, and especially since the mid-1930s, they have concluded a still-growing number. New York and New Jersey led the way in 1921—with a compact creating the New York Port Authority to manage and develop the harbor facilities of that great metropolis.

Some 200 compacts are now in force, and many involve several States. All 50 States have joined in two of them, in fact: the Compact for the Supervision of Parolees and Probationers and the Compact on Juveniles. Other agreements, many with multi-State membership, cover a widening range of subjects—including, for example, the development and conservation of such resources as water, oil, wildlife, and fish, forest fire protection, stream and harbor pollution, tax collections, motor vehicle safety, the licensing of drivers, teacher certification, and the cooperative use of public colleges and universities.

Full Faith and Credit

The Constitution commands that

Full faith and credit shall be given in each State to the public acts, records, and judicial proceedings of every other State.[17]

The words "public acts" refer to the laws of a State. "Records" refers to such documents as birth certificates, marriage licenses, deeds to property, car registrations, and the like. The words "judicial proceedings" relate to the outcome of court actions: judgments for debt, criminal convictions, divorce decrees, and so forth.

Suppose that a man dies in Baltimore and leaves a will disposing of some property in Chicago. Illinois must give **full faith and credit** to (respect the validity

---

[17]Article IV, Section 1.

of) the *probating* (proving) of that will as a judicial proceeding of the State of Maryland. One may prove age, marital status, title to property, or similar facts by securing the necessary documents from the State where the record was made.

Exceptions. The Full Faith and Credit Clause is regularly observed and usually operates in a routine way between and among the States. Two exceptions to the rule must be noted, however. *First*, it applies only to *civil* matters; that is, one State will not (cannot) enforce another State's criminal law. *Second*, full faith and credit need not be given to certain divorces granted by one State to residents of another State.

On the second exception, the key question is always this: Was the person who got the divorce in fact a resident of the State which granted it? If so, the divorce will be accorded full faith and credit in other States. If not, then the State granting the divorce did not have the authority to do so and another State may refuse to recognize it.

The matter of interstate (or "quickie") divorces has been a troublesome one for years. And it has been so especially since the Supreme Court's decision in a 1945 case, *Williams* v. *North Carolina*. In that case a man and a woman had traveled to Nevada—where each of them wanted to obtain a divorce so they could marry one another. They lived in Las Vegas for six weeks (the minimum period of State residence required by Nevada's divorce law). They received their divorces, were married, and then immediately returned to North Carolina.

But that State's authorities refused to recognize their Nevada divorces. They were brought to trial and each of them was convicted of the crime of bigamous cohabitation.

On appeal, the Supreme Court upheld North Carolina's denial of full faith and credit to the Nevada divorces. It ruled that the couple had not in fact established *bona fide* (good faith, valid) residence in Nevada. Rather, it held that, through all of this period, they had remained legal residents of North Carolina. In short, the Court found that Nevada did not have the authority to grant their divorces.

A divorce granted by a State court to a *bona fide* resident of that State must be given full faith and credit in all other States. But to become a legal resident of a State a person must intend to reside there permanently, or at least indefinitely. Clearly, the Williamses had not intended to do so.

The *Williams* case, and later ones, cast dark clouds of doubt over the validity of thousands of other interstate divorces. The later marriages of persons involved in them, and/or the frequently tangled estate problems produced by their deaths, suggest the confused and serious nature of the matter.

Extradition

According to the Constitution

A person charged in any State with treason, felony, or other crime, who shall flee from justice, and be found in another State, shall, on demand of the executive authority of the State from which he fled, be delivered up, to be removed to the State having jurisdiction of the crime.[18]

The practice of **extradition** (interstate rendition) is designed to prevent an accused or convicted person from escaping justice by leaving a State. The return

---

[18]Article IV, Section 2, Clause 2. Extradition has been carried on between sovereign states for centuries. The word *extradition* is the term popularly used in the United States for what is technically known in the law as *interstate rendition*.

of a fugitive is most often a routine thing. But a governor does sometimes refuse to surrender someone—and when one does, there the matter ends.

Ever since *Kentucky* v. *Dennison*, in 1861, the Supreme Court has held that a governor cannot be forced to act in an extradition case. So, the Constitution's word "shall" here must be read "may."

Instances of a governor's refusal are not common, but they do happen. In a fairly typical case, in 1978, Governor William Milliken of Michigan refused to return a woman to Alabama. She had been convicted of bank robbery there in 1942. Her part in the crime had been a largely unknowing one; however, she was sentenced to 30 years in prison. She escaped in 1952, made her way to Detroit, and had lived there ever since. Governor Milliken refused to extradite her because, in his view, her 1942 punishment had been too severe. He felt, too, that she had long since paid for her crime in her conscience.

Privileges and Immunities

The Constitution provides:

> The citizens of each State shall be entitled to all privileges and immunities of citizens of the several States.[19]

In short, this means that a resident of one State will not be discriminated against *unreasonably* by another State.

The courts have never given a full list of the privileges and immunities of "interstate citizenship." But these are some of them: The right to pass through or reside in any other State for the purpose of trade, agriculture, professional pursuits, or otherwise. The right to use the courts, make contracts, buy, own, rent, and sell property, and marry.

Of course, the provision does not mean that a resident of one State need not obey the laws of another State while in that State. Nor does it mean that a State may not make *reasonable* discrimination against residents of other States. Thus, any State can require that one live in that State for a certain time before he or she can vote or hold any public office. It may also require a period of residence within the State before it grants a person a license to practice law or medicine or dentistry there; and so on.

The wild fish and game in a State are the common property of the people of that State. So, nonresidents can be asked to pay higher fees for fishing or hunting licenses than those paid by residents (who pays taxes to provide fish hatcheries, enforce game laws, and so on). By the same token, a State university often charges higher tuition to students from other States than it does to those who live in the State.

The Admission of New States

Only Congress has the power to admit new States to the Union. The Constitution places only one restriction on that power. A new State may not be created by taking territory from one or more of the existing States without the consent of the legislature(s) of the State(s) involved.[20]

Congress has admitted 37 States since the original 13 formed the Union.

---

[19]Article IV, Section 2, Clause 1, the provision is reinforced in the 14th Amendment.

[20]Article IV, Section 3, Claus 1. It is sometimes argued that this provision was violated with West Virginia's admission in 1863. That State was formed out of the 40 western counties which had broken away from Virginia over the issue of secession from the Union. The consent required by the Constitution was given by a minority of the members of the Virginia legislature—those who represented the 40 western counties. Congress accepted their action, holding that they were the only group legally capable of acting as the Virginia legislature at the time.

ORIGIN AND ADMISSION OF THE 50 STATES

Order Of Admission	Source Of State Lands	Organized As Territory		Admitted As State	
Delaware	Swedish Charter, 1638; English Charter, 1683	. . .		7 Dec.	1787*
Pennsylvania	English Grant, 1680	. . .		12 Dec.	1787*
New Jersey	Dutch Settlement, 1623; English Charter, 1664	. . .		18 Dec.	1787*
Georgia	English Charter, 1732	. . .		2 Jan.	1788*
Connecticut	English Charter, 1662	. . .		9 Jan.	1788*
Massachusetts	English Charter, 1629	. . .		6 Feb.	1788*
Maryland	English Charter, 1632	. . .		28 Apr.	1788*
South Carolina	English Charter, 1663	. . .		23 May	1788*
New Hampshire	English Charter, 1622 and 1629	. . .		21 June	1788*
Virginia	English Charter, 1609	. . .		25 June	1788*
New York	Dutch Settlement, 1623; English Control, 1664	. . .		26 July	1788*
North Carolina	English Charter, 1663	. . .		21 Nov.	1789*
Rhode Island	English Charter, 1663	. . .		29 May	1790*
Vermont	Lands of New York and New Hampshire	**		4 Mar.	1791
Kentucky	Lands of Virginia	**		1 June	1792
Tennessee	Lands of North Carolina	**		1 June	1796
Ohio	Lands of Virginia; Northwest Territory, 1787	13 July	1787	1 Mar.	1803
Louisiana	Louisiana Purchase, 1803	24 Mar.	1804	30 Apr.	1812
Indiana	Lands of Virginia; Northwest Territory, 1787	7 May	1800	11 Dec.	1816
Mississippi	Lands of Georgia and South Carolina	17 Apr.	1798	10 Dec.	1817
Illinois	Lands of Virginia; Northwest Territory, 1787	3 Feb.	1809	3 Dec.	1818
Alabama	Lands of Georgia and South Carolina	3 Mar.	1817	14 Dec.	1819
Maine	Lands of Massachusetts	**		15 Mar.	1820
Missouri	Louisiana Purchase, 1803	4 June	1812	10 Aug.	1821
Arkansas	Louisiana Purchase, 1803	2 Mar.	1819	15 June	1836
Michigan	Lands from Virginia; Northwest Territory, 1787	11 Jan.	1805	26 Jan.	1837
Florida	Ceded by Spain, 1819	30 Mar.	1822	3 Mar.	1845
Texas	Republic of Texas, 1845	**		29 Dec.	1845
Iowa	Louisiana Purchase, 1803	12 June	1838	28 Dec.	1846
Wisconsin	Lands of Michigan; Northwest Territory, 1787	20 Apr.	1836	29 May	1848
California	Ceded by Mexico, 1848	**		9 Sept.	1850
Minnesota	Northwest Territory, 1787; and Louisiana Purchase, 1803	3 Mar.	1849	11 May	1858
Oregon	Louisiana Purchase, 1803; Treaty with Spain, 1819 and Treaty with Great Britain, 1846	14 Aug.	1848	14 Feb.	1859
Kansas	Louisiana Purchase, 1803; and lands from Texas	30 May	1854	29 Jan.	1861
West Virginia	Part of Virginia to 1863	**		20 June	1863
Nevada	Ceded by Mexico, 1848	2 Mar.	1861	31 Oct.	1864
Nebraska	Louisiana Purchase, 1803	30 May	1854	1 Mar.	1867
Colorado	Louisiana Purchase, 1803	28 Feb.	1861	1 Aug.	1876
South Dakota	Louisiana Purchase, 1803	2 Mar.	1861	2 Nov.	1889
North Dakota	Louisiana Purchase, 1803	2 Mar.	1861	2 Nov.	1889
Montana	Louisiana Purchase, 1803	26 May	1864	8 Nov.	1889
Washington	Louisiana Purchase, 1803; Treaty with Great Britain, 1846	2 Mar.	1853	11 Nov.	1889
Idaho	Louisiana Purchase, 1803; and Oregon Territory	3 Mar.	1863	3 July	1890
Wyoming	Louisiana Purchase, 1803	25 July	1868	10 July	1890
Utah	Ceded by Mexico, 1848	9 Sept.	1850	4 Jan.	1896
Oklahoma	Louisiana Purchase, 1803	2 May	1890	16 Nov.	1907
New Mexico	Ceded by Mexico, 1848	9 Sept.	1850	6 Jan.	1912
Arizona	Ceded by Mexico, 1848; Gadsden Purchase, 1853	24 Feb.	1863	14 Feb.	1912
Alaska	Territory, Purchase from Russia, 1867	24 Aug.	1912	3 Jan.	1959
Hawaii	Territory, Annexed 1898	14 June	1900	21 Aug.	1959

*Date of ratification of U.S. Constitution   **No territorial status before admission to the Union.

Five States—Vermont, Kentucky, Tennessee, Maine, and West Virginia—were created from parts of already existing States. Texas was an independent republic before admission. California was admitted after being ceded to the United States by Mexico. Each of the other 30 States entered the Union only after spending some time as an organized territory.

Admission Procedure

The process of admission is usually simple. The area desiring Statehood first *petitions* (applies to) Congress for admission. If and when it is approved, Congress passes an **enabling act** which directs the framing of a proposed State constitution. After that has been prepared by a convention and approved by a popular vote, it is submitted to Congress. If Congress still agrees to Statehood, it then passes an **act of admission.**

The two newest States, Alaska and Hawaii, abbreviated the usual process. Each adopted a proposed constitution without waiting for an enabling act: Alaska in 1956 and Hawaii in 1950.

Conditions for Admission

Before finally admitting a new State, Congress has often set certain conditions. In 1896 Utah was admitted on condition that its constitution outlaw polygamy. In the act admitting Alaska to the Union in 1959, the State was forever prohibited from claiming title to any lands legally held by an Indian, Eskimo, or Aleut.

Each State enters the Union on an equal footing with each of the other States. Thus, although Congress can set conditions like those just described, it *cannot* impose conditions of a political nature. For example, when Oklahoma was admitted in 1907, Congress said

TERRITORIAL EXPANSION OF THE UNITED STATES AND ACQUISTIONS OF OTHER PRINCIPAL AREAS

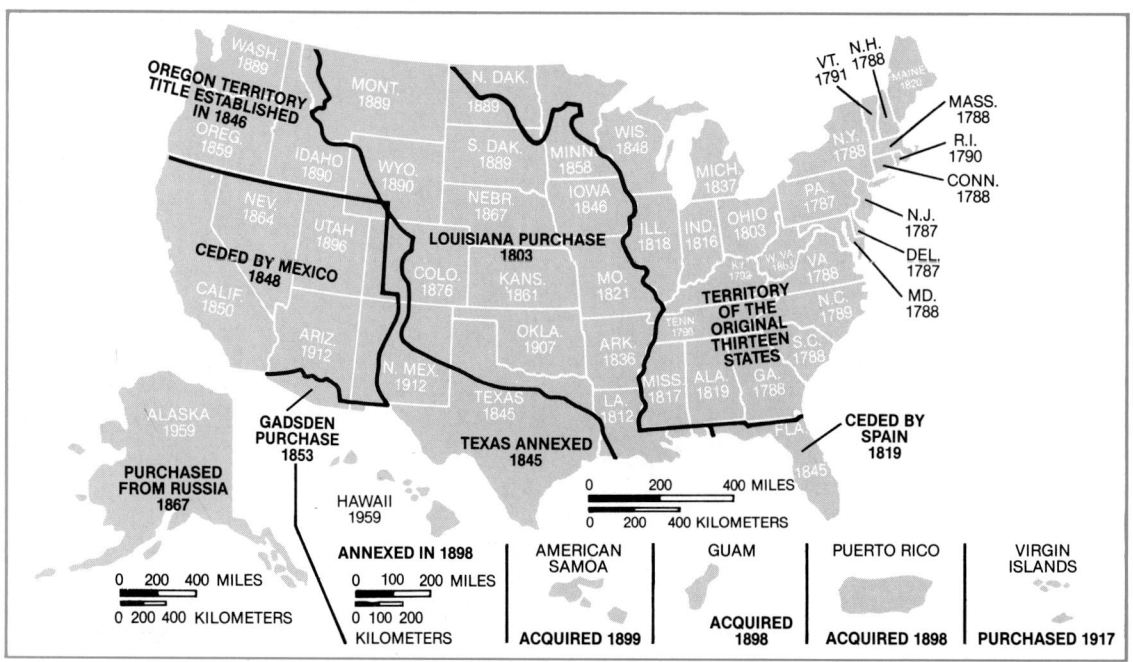

Source: U.S. Bureau of the Census

the State could not remove its capitol from Guthrie to any other place before 1913. In 1910, however, the legislature moved the capital to Oklahoma City. When this step was challenged, the Supreme Court (*Coyle* v. *Smith,* 1911) held that Congress may set conditions for admission as it pleases. *But,* held the Court, the conditions cannot be *enforced* when they compromise the independence of a State to manage its own internal affairs.

One more example here: President Taft vetoed a resolution to admit Arizona in 1911—because its proposed constitution provided that judges could be recalled (removed from office) by popular vote. This meant, said Taft, that a judge would have to keep but one eye on the law and the other on public opinion.

The recall section was then taken out of the document. In 1912 Congress passed, and the President signed, another act of admission. Almost immediately, the new State amended its new constitution, to provide for the recall of judges—and that provision remains a valid part of Arizona's constitution today.

Oklahoma's State Capitol, situated in Oklahoma City since 1910, is fronted by an oil derrick.

☑ FOR REVIEW

1. What are interstate compacts? What agreements are States constitutionally not allowed to make?
2. What, in brief, does the Full Faith and Credit Clause provide? The Extradition Clause? The Privileges and Immunities Clauses?
3. Who has the exclusive power to admit new States to the Union?

S U M M A R Y

A *federal system* is one in which the powers of government are divided on a territorial basis between a central and several regional governments. The Framers created the American federal system to meet the need for a stronger central government and, as well, preserve the existing States.

Our federal system's chief advantage lies in the fact that it allows local matters to be handled in accord with local traditions and needs while matters of wider concern may be handled at the national level.

The Constitution establishes a *division of powers* between the National Government and the States. The National Government has only those powers delegated to it by the Constitution. Its *delegated powers* are of three kinds: (1) the *expressed powers*—those delegated in so many words by the Constitution; (2) the *implied powers*—those reasonably implied by the expressed powers; and (3) the *inherent powers*—those that belong to (inhere in) the National Government because it is the national government of a sovereign state. The Constitution also denies certain powers to the National Government. It does so in three ways: (1) expressly; (2) by its silence; and (3) as a result of its creation of a federal system.

The States possess the *reserved powers* —those not delegated to the National Government and not denied to the States by the Constitution. The States also are denied certain powers—expressly by the Constitution, by the existence of the federal system, and by their own constitutions. Local governments are creatures of, have no legal existence apart from, their States.

The *exclusive powers* are those that belong only to the National Government. The *concurrent powers* are those that may be used by both the National Government and the States.

The Constitution, acts of Congress in accord with it, and treaties made under its authority, are the "supreme law of the land." No form of State law may validly conflict with that supreme law. The Supreme Court fills a crucial role as the umpire in the federal system.

The Constitution places certain obligations on the National Government with regard to the States. It must guarantee to each State a republican form of government, protect each of them against foreign invasion and domestic violence, and respect the territorial integrity of each of them.

The States and the National Government cooperate with one another in many ways, from grant-in-aid programs and revenue sharing to election administration and law enforcement.

The Constitution imposes order on interstate relations through the Full Faith and Credit Clause, the Extradition Clause, and the Privileges and Immunities Clauses. The States may, with the consent of Congress, enter into compacts among themselves.

New States may be admitted to the Union only by Congress, as 37 have thus far.

CHAPTER REVIEW

Key Terms/Concepts

Block grants (75)
Concurrent powers (70)
Cooperative federalism (74)
Delegated powers (66)
Division of powers (66)
Domestic violence (73)
Exclusive powers (69)
Expressed powers ·(66)
Extradition Clause (79)
Federalism (64)

Full Faith and Credit Clause (78)
Grants-in-aid (74)
Implied powers (66)
Inherent powers (67)
Interstate compacts (78)
Interstate rendition (79)
McCulloch v. *Maryland* (71)
Necessary and Proper Clause (66)
Privileges and Immunities Clause (80)

Republican form of government (72)
Reserved powers (68)

Revenue sharing (75)
Supremacy Clause (70)
10th Amendment (68)

Keynote Questions

1. Define *federalism*. Identify and contrast the basic constitutional principle of *separation of powers* and *division of powers*.
2. In what three distinct ways does the Constitution delegate powers to the National Government? What is the Necessary and Proper Clause?
3. What powers does the Constitution assign to the States in the federal system? What does the 10th Amendment provide?

4. On what three separate bases does the Constitution deny powers to the National Government? To the States? What are the concurrent powers?

5. For what does the Supremacy Clause provide?

6. Who or what is the "umpire" in the federal system? Why must that role be performed?

7. What obligations does the Constitution impose upon the National Government with regard to the States?

8. What are federal grants-in-aid? Categorical grants? Block grants? What is revenue sharing?

9. What are interstate compacts? What types of agreements are the States constitutionally forbidden to make?

10. For what does each of these constitutional provisions provide: the Full Faith and Credit Clause? the Extradition Clause? the Privileges and Immunities Clauses?

11. Who has the sole power to admit new States to the Union?

For Thought and Discussion

1. What do you think conditions might be like in what is now the United States if no federal system had been created and the 13 States had tried to continue under the Articles of Confederation?

2. Why do the war powers and the foreign relations powers belong only to the National Government? The power to regulate interstate commerce? The power to coin money?

3. The Constitution (Article I, Section 10, Clause 3) forbids the States to "engage in war." But there is a qualification to this prohibition. Why?

4. In 1954 the Supreme Court held (in *Brown* v. *Topeka Board of Education*) that segregation by race in the public schools was unconstitutional, as a violation of the 14th Amendment's Equal Protection Clause. Why has it been said that the aftermath of that decision offered the most serious challenge to American federalism since 1865?

5. What factors have been most responsible for the growth of the powers of the National Government in recent decades?

6. Read again Justice Holmes' comment (page 71) on the role of the Supreme Court as the "umpire" of the federal system. How might the Union "be imperiled" if the Supreme Court could not declare a State law unconstitutional?

7. Why might a governor be reluctant to call for federal aid during a time when domestic violence broke out in a city in his/her State?

Suggested Activities

1. Using current newspapers and periodicals, find examples of each of the types of power and denials of power shown in the diagram on page 67.

2. Select one of the historical events or court cases referred to in this chapter —*e.g.,* Dorr's Rebellion, *McCulloch* v. *Maryland,* or *Williams* v. *North Carolina.* Study the matter and present your findings to the class.

3. Invite your chief of police or another local law enforcement official to speak to the class on the ways in which different federal agencies cooperate with local police officers.

4. Stage a debate or class forum on one of the following: (a) *Resolved,* That the United States Supreme Court be deprived of its power to declare any form of State law unconstitutional; (b) *Resolved,* That grant-in-aid programs undermine the federal system and reduce the power and importance of the States.

5. Prepare a class report on the admission of your State to the Union.

UNIT TWO

The Unalienable Rights

In Unit One of this book, we examined the basic ideas, the concepts, on which democratic government in the United States is founded. These include a belief in the *fundamental worth and dignity* and in the *equality* of *all* persons. They include faith in the principle of *majority rule* and, at the same time, *respect for minority rights*. They also include recognition of the *necessity of compromise* in making policy decisions. Finally, they include an insistence on the *widest possible area of freedom for the individual.*

To preach freedom, to discuss it, write about it, or make campaign speeches about it, is easy. To practice it, to make sure that it is not being violated or trampled on or taken away, is much more difficult. Critics of American democracy are fond of telling us that we do not always practice what we preach. And, to a point, they are right.

But they are right *only* to a point. We may not always succeed, but we are constantly striving to translate the theory of democracy into the reality of its practice. We, the People of the United States, have come closer to the realization of democracy in practice than have the people of any other nation.

Unit Two of this book illustrates this point. In its two chapters we examine and discuss the rights guaranteed to all Americans by the Constitution. We also see how these guarantees have been applied and extended in practice—especially by court decisions and by laws passed by the Congress.

The Constitution stresses the unparalleled importance of freedom for the individual in this country. Unit Two shows how that emphasis has been—and is still being—translated into fact.

Over the entrance to the Supreme Court Building is the motto: "Equal Justice Under Law."

5

Civil Rights: Fundamental Freedoms

CHAPTER OBJECTIVES

To help you to
Learn ▪ Know ▪ Understand

The fundamental importance of the many constitutional guarantees of civil rights.

The relative nature of those guarantees and their relationship to the concept of limited government.

The relationship between the provisions of the Bill of Rights and the 14th Amendment's Due Process Clause.

The essential meaning of the 1st and 14th Amendments' guarantees of
—religious freedom
—freedom of speech
—freedom of the press
—freedom of assembly and
*   petition*

The God who gave us life gave us liberty at the same time.
Thomas Jefferson

The United States was born out of a struggle for freedom. Those who founded this country loved liberty, and they prized it above all earthly possessions. For them, freedom for their country and freedom for the individual were the greatest of blessings that Providence could bestow. In proclaiming independence, they declared:

> We hold these truths to be self-evident: that all men are created equal; that they are endowed by their Creator with certain unalienable Rights; that among these are Life, Liberty, and the pursuit of Happiness.

In the very next line of the Declaration of Independence, they added:

> That to secure these rights, Governments are instituted among Men. . . .

Later, the Framers of the Constitution repeated this justification for the existence of government. The Preamble to the Constitution declares:

> We the People of the United States, in Order to . . . secure the Blessings of Liberty to ourselves and our Posterity, do ordain and establish this Constitution for the United States of America.

Hundreds of thousands gathered in New York in 1982 in a massive show of support for a freeze on nuclear weapons. *Bottom/left:* A statue of Paul Revere, a symbol of vigilance and devotion to the cause of liberty and independence.

Civil Rights and the Principle of Limited Government

From its very beginnings, government in the United States has been firmly based upon the concept of *limited government*. It rests upon the principle that government has *only* those powers the sovereign people have given to it.

This fact—that government can do only those things the people have given it the authority to do—is best illustrated in the field of civil rights. The Constitution is studded with guarantees of personal freedom—that is, with prohibitions and restrictions upon the power of government to act.

All governments have, and use, authority over individuals. The all-important difference between a democratic government and a dictatorial one lies in the *extent* of that authority. In a dictatorship it is just about unlimited.

In the Soviet Union, for example, opposition to the government is put down as a matter of course, and often harshly. Even such forms of expression as art, music, and literature must glorify the state. In the United States, on the other hand, governmental authority is sharply limited. Peaceable opposition to government is not only allowed, it is encouraged. Justice Robert H. Jackson once put the American position well:

> If there is any fixed star in our constitutional constellation, it is that no official, high or petty, can prescribe what shall be orthodox in politics, nationalism, religion, or any other matter of opinion or force citizens to confess by word or act their faith therein.[1]

---

[1]In *West Virginia Board of Education* v. *Barnette*, 1943; see page 104.

Our System of Civil Rights

In this chapter, and the one to follow, we shall take a close look at each of the many civil rights held by the American people. Before we can do that, however, there are several things you must understand about the over-all nature of those guarantees. Some of these matters are quite complicated; but they are also very crucial to a real understanding of civil rights in the United States.

Historical Background

As we noted in Chapter 2, our system of civil rights guarantees is one of the major pieces of our English heritage. Over centuries, the English people had fought a continuing struggle for individual liberties. The early colonists brought a dedication to that cause with them to the New World.

That commitment to freedom quickly took root and flourished. The Revolutionary War was fought to preserve and to expand the rights of the individual against government. The very first State constitutions contained long lists of the rights held by the people.

The National Constitution, as it was written at Philadelphia, contained a number of important civil rights guarantees—notably in Article I, Sections 9 and 10 and in Article III. Unlike many of the first State documents, however, it did not have a bill of rights, a general listing of the rights of the people.

The outcry that omission raised was so marked that several of the States ratified the original Constitution only with the understanding that such a listing be immediately added. The very first session of Congress in 1789 met that demand with a series of proposed amendments. Ten of them, the Bill of Rights, were ratified by the States and became a part of the Constitution on December 15, 1791. Later amendments, especially the 13th and the 14th, have added to the Constitution's guarantees of personal freedom.

The Courts and Civil Rights

In the United States the courts—and, especially, the Supreme Court of the United States—stand as the major guardian of individual liberties. *All* officers and agencies of government—executive and legislative, national and State and local—are also responsible for protecting the people's rights, of course. But it is the courts that must *interpret* and *apply* the constitutional guarantees whenever a person charges that government has violated his or her liberty.

The fact that the courts do stand guard over our civil rights does *not* mean that we, the people—or any one of us—can sit back in assured safety, however. Nor does the fact that the National Constitution and each of the State constitutions set out long lists of basic rights mean that those rights have been so firmly established that they are ours forever. To preserve and protect those guarantees, each generation must learn and understand them anew—and be willing to fight for them, when necessary. The late Learned Hand, one of our great jurists, put the point this way:

> I often wonder whether we do not rest our hopes too much upon constitutions, upon laws and upon courts. These are false hopes; believe me, these are false hopes. Liberty lies in the hearts of men and women; when it dies there, no constitution, no law, no court can ever do much to help it. While it lies there it needs no constitution, no law, no court to save it.[2]

---

[2]Irving Dillard (ed.), *The Spirit of Liberty: Papers and Addresses of Learned Hand.* (New York: Knopf, 2nd edition, 1953), pages 189–190.

HIGHLIGHTS OF THE BILL OF RIGHTS

Congress OF THE United States
begun and held at the City of New York on
Wednesday the Fourth of March one thousand seven hundred and eighty nine

- Freedom of religion
- Freedom of assembly and petition
- Freedom of speech
- Right to trial by jury
- No cruel and unusual punishments
- Freedom of press
- Right to due process of law
- Protection against illegal searches
- Just compensation for property
- Right to counsel

Civil Rights Relative, Not Absolute

Even though many basic rights are guaranteed to *everyone* in the United States, *no one* has the right to do as he or she pleases. Rather, individuals have the right to do as they please *as long as* they do not interfere with the rights of others to do so. That is, each person's rights are *relative* to the rights of all others.

Thus, each person in the United States has the right of free speech. But no person enjoys *absolute* freedom of speech. One who uses obscene language can be punished by a court for commit-

ting a crime. So, too, can someone who uses words in a way that causes another person to commit a crime—for example, to riot, to destroy private property, or to desert from the armed forces. Or, a person who damages another by what he or she says can be sued for slander.

Our point here can be put another way. Most often, we think of the many different civil rights guarantees in terms that suggest that each and all of them are to be observed all of the time. In fact, there are many situations in which different rights *conflict* with one another.

Take this quick illustration of rights in conflict—free press v. fair trial:

Dr. Samuel Sheppard of Cleveland, Ohio, had been convicted of murdering his wife. His lengthy trial was widely covered in the national news media. Many reporters wrote and broadcast many lurid details (some fact, much fiction) about his love life and other behavior. On appeal, he claimed that that coverage had denied him a fair trial. The Supreme Court agreed and overturned his conviction, *Sheppard* v. *Maxwell*, 1966; see page 142.

Justice Oliver Wendell Holmes once put the relationship between each person's rights in these oft-quoted words:

> The most stringent protection of free speech would not protect a man in falsely shouting fire in a theatre and causing a panic.[3]

Persons to Whom Rights Are Guaranteed

Most rights are extended to *all persons* in the United States. The Supreme Court has often held that the Constitution's word "persons" covers **aliens** (foreign-born residents; non-citizens) as well as citizens.

Not *all* rights are given to aliens, however. Thus, the right to travel freely throughout the country is one of the rights guaranteed to all citizens by the Constitution's two Privileges and Immunities Clauses.[4] But aliens may be, and especially in wartime are, restricted in this regard.

Early in World War II all persons of Japanese descent living on the Pacific Coast were evacuated (moved, forcibly) inland. Some 120,000 persons—two-thirds of them native-born American citizens—were sent to "war relocation camps" set up and run by the Government. The relocation program caused severe economic and personal hardships for many. In 1944 the Supreme Court reluctantly upheld the forced evacuation as a reasonable war-time emergency measure.[5] The action has been strongly criticized ever since. Many Japanese-Americans fought heroically in World War II, and not a single case of *Nisei* (American-born Japanese) disloyalty has ever been found.

Federalism and Civil Rights

Federalism produces this very complex pattern of civil rights guarantees:

(1) Some of the rights guaranteed by the Constitution are guaranteed against the National Government *only*.

(2) Some of those rights are guaranteed against the States (and their local governments) *only*.

(3) Some—a great many of them—are guaranteed against *both* the National Government *and* the States (and their local governments).

(4) Some of the rights guaranteed against a State (and its local governments) arise from the National Constitution while others arise from that State's *own* constitution.

The Scope of the Bill of Rights. Note this very critical fact: The provisions of the Bill of Rights apply against

---

[3]In *Schenck* v. *United States*, 1919; see page 114.

[4]Article IV, Section 2, Clause 1 and the 14th Amendment; see page 80. The guarantee does not extend to citizens under some form of legal restraint—in jail, on bail, committed to a mental institution, etc.

[5]*Korematsu* v. *United States*, 1944; however, on the very same day the Court held (in *Ex parte Endo*) that once the loyalty of any citizen internee had been established, no restriction could be placed on that person's freedom to travel that was not legally imposed on all other citizens.

Today, more than 40 years after the fact, the government appears ready to admit that relocation program was both unnecessary and unjust. In 1980 Congress created a Commission on Wartime Relocation and Internment of Civilians. The Commission, in its final report in 1983, urged that Congress make a "national apology" for the "grave injustice" done to those who were interned.

A woman of Japanese descent waits to be moved to a relocation camp, where she will live for the duration of World War II.

the National Government *only*—not the States.

Remember, these first 10 amendments were added to the Constitution in 1791, to meet one of the major objections to its ratification. They were originally intended as restrictions on the new National Government—not as limits on the already-existing States. And that remains the fact of the matter today.

The Modifying Effect of the 14th Amendment. Again, the provisions of the Bill of Rights apply against the National Government, not the States. This does *not* mean that the States can deny basic civil rights to the people, however.

In part, the States can't do so because each of their own constitutions contains a bill of rights. Also, and at least as importantly, they can't do so because of the 14th Amendment's Due Process Clause. It says:

No State shall . . . deprive any person of life, liberty, or property, without the due process of law.

We shall take a close look at this very important civil rights guarantee in the next chapter. For now, however, we must understand its root meaning.

The Supreme Court has often held that this provision means, at base: No State may deny to any person any right which is "basic or essential to the American concept of ordered liberty."

But just what rights are "basic or essential," and so are a part of the meaning of the 14th Amendment's Due Process Clause? The Court has answered that question in a now long series of cases, as we shall see. In that process, it has ruled that most of the protections set out in the Bill of Rights (and there applicable against the National Government) are also within the meaning of the 14th Amendment (and so applicable against the Sates, as well).

This very complicated matter can be put this way: The Supreme Court has "nationalized the Bill of Rights"—by holding that most of its protections apply against the States, as a part of the meaning of the 14th Amendment's Due Process Clause.

The Court began this historic process in *Gitlow* v. *New York*, in 1925. In that landmark case, Benjamin Gitlow, a communist, had been convicted of criminal anarchy in the State courts. He had made speeches and published a pamphlet calling for the violent overthrow of government. On appeal, the Supreme Court upheld both his conviction and the State law under which he had been tried. In deciding the case, however, the Court made this crucial point: Freedom of speech and freedom of the press—which the 1st Amendment says cannot be denied by the National Government—are also "among the fundamental personal rights and liberties protected by the Due Process Caluse of the 14th Amendment from impairment by the States."

Soon after *Gitlow*, the Court held each of the 1st Amendment's guarantees to be covered by the 14th Amendment. It struck down State laws involving speech (*Fiske* v. *Kansas*, 1927; *Stromberg* v. *California*, 1931), the press, (*Near* v. *Minnesota*, 1931), assembly and petition (*De Jonge* v. *Oregon*, 1937), and religion (*Cantwell* v. *Connecticut*, 1940). In each of those cases it declared a State law unconstitutional as a violation of the 14th Amendment's Due Process Clause.

The Court enlarged the scope of the 14th Amendment's Due Process Clause in several cases decided in the 1960s. It now covers nearly all of the rest of the provisions in the Bill of Rights. Thus, in *Mapp* v. *Ohio*, 1961, it held that the Clause prohibits unreasonable searches and seizures by State and local authorities, and also forbids them the use of any evidence gained by such illegal actions. The 4th Amendment puts the same prohibitions on federal officers.

Since then, the Court has given the same 14th Amendment coverage to:

—the 8th Amendment's ban on cruel and unusual punishment, in *Robinson* v. *California*, 1962.

—the 6th Amendment's guarantee of the right to counsel, in *Gideon* v. *Wainwright*, 1963.

—the 5th Amendment's ban on self-incrimination, in *Malloy* v. *Hogan*, 1964.

—the 6th Amendment's right of persons accused of crime to confront the witnesses against them, in *Pointer* v. *Texas*, 1965.

—the 6th Amendment's right of persons accused of crime to compel witnesses in their behalf, in *Washington* v. *Texas*, 1967.

—the 6th Amendment's guarantee of trial by jury (at least in cases of serious crime), in *Duncan* v. *Louisiana*, 1968; and

—the 5th Amendment's prohibition of double jeopardy, in *Benton* v. *Maryland*, 1969.

We shall return to each of these guarantees shortly—the 1st Amendment rights in this chapter and the others in the next one. For now, however, note the chief point here: The Supreme Court has "nationalized" each of these basic guarantees. By holding that they exist against the States in the 14th Amendment, it has made their basic content and meaning uniform throughout the nation. And, in the process, much of the effect that federalism has on our civil rights system has been sharply reduced.

No Complete Listing of Rights Possible

The Constitution contains many civil rights guarantees. Those protections can be found in Article I, Sections 9 and 10; in Article III, Sections 2 and 3; in the 1st through the 8th Amendments; and in the 13th and 14th Amendments. But nowhere in the Constitution—and, indeed, nowhere else—can one find a complete catalog of all of the rights held by the American people

The too-little noted 9th Amendment declares that there are other rights, beyond those set out in so many words in the Constitution:

The enumeration in the Constitution of certain rights shall not be construed to deny or disparage others retained by the people.

Over the years, the Supreme Court has found that there are, in fact, a number of other rights "retained by the people." For example: The right of a person charged with a crime not to be tried on the basis of evidence gained by an unlawful search or seizure; see page 131.

✓ **F O R   R E V I E W**

1. According to the Declaration of Independence, governments exist for what reason?

2. How do civil rights guarantees illustrate the principle of limited government?

3. Why do the courts stand as the principal guardians of individual liberties in this country?

4. Why does no person have an absolute right to do as he or she pleases?

5. In what sense has the Supreme Court "nationalized" most of the civil rights protections set out in the Bill of Rights?

6. Why is it impossible to list all of the civil rights guaranteed by the Constitution to the American people?

Freedom of Expression

The right to freedom of expression is absolutely indispensable to the idea of democracy. Without it, there simply cannot be a free society.

That basic freedom is enshrined in the 1st Amendment—where freedom of religion, speech, press, assembly, and petition are all protected against the National Government. It declares:

> Congress shall make no law respecting an establishment of religion, or prohibiting the free exercise thereof; or abridging the freedom of speech, or of the press, or the right of the people peaceably to assemble, and to petition the Government for a redress of grievances.

As we've already noted, the 14th Amendment's Due Process Clause extends each of these rights against the States and their local governments.

Freedom of Religion

The 1st and 14th Amendments set out two guarantees of religious freedom. They prohibit (1) an "establishment of religion" (the Establishment Clause) and (2) any arbitrary interference by government in "the free exercise" of religion (the Free Exercise Clause).[6]

Separation of Church and State. The Establishment Clause sets up, in Thomas Jefferson's words, "a wall of separation between church and state." That wall is not infinitely high, however; nor is it one that can't be penetrated. Church and government, while constitutionally separated in the United States, are neither enemies nor even strangers to one another. In fact, their relationship is a friendly one.

Government has done much to encourage churches and religion in this country. Thus, nearly all church-owned property and contributions to churches and religious sects are free from federal, State, and local taxation. Chaplains serve with each branch of the armed forces. Most public officials take an oath of office in the name of God. Sessions of Congress and of most State legislatures and city councils are opened with prayer. The nation's anthem and its coins and currency make reference to God.

The content of the Establishment Clause cannot be described in exact terms. And the exact nature of the "wall of separation" remains a matter of continuing and often heated controversy.

Only comparatively few cases involving the Clause have thus far been decided by the Supreme Court. In fact, the

---

[6]Also, Article VI, Section 3 provides that ". . . no religious test shall ever be required as a qualification to any office or public trust under the United States." In *Torcaso* v. *Watkins*, 1961, the Supreme Court held that the 14th Amendment puts the same restriction upon the States. In that case the Court struck down a section of the Maryland constitution that required all public officeholders in that State to declare a belief in the existence of God.

The 1st Amendment forbids any interference in the "free exercise" of religion. *Above/left:* Protestants at worship. *Above/right:* A service in a Jewish synagogue. *Below:* Catholic worshippers attend mass at a Ukrainian Orthodox Church.

Court did not rule on its meaning until as recently as 1947. A few earlier cases did bear on the question, but none of them involved a direct consideration of the meaning of the "wall of separation."

In *Pierce* v. *Society of Sisters*, 1925, for example, the Court held an Oregon compulsory school attendance law unconstitutional. That law required parents to send their children to *public*

schools. It had been designed to do away with the private—and most of all the **parochial** (*i.e.*, church-related)—schools in the State. In destroying it, the Court did not reach the Establishment Clause question. Instead, it found the law to be an interference with the liberty of parents to direct the upbringing of their children—and, so, in conflict with the Due Process Clause of the 14th Amendment.

Cochran v. *Louisiana*, 1930, was another of those earlier cases. There the Court upheld a State law allowing the use of public funds to supply "schoolbooks to the school children of the State." Under it, textbooks were furnished to pupils in both public and private schools, including those in parochial schools. The law had not been attacked on Establishment Clause grounds, however. Rather, Cochran and others had charged that it violated the 14th Amendment's guarantee against the deprivation of property without due process—because it allowed the spending of public money for what they said was a private purpose. In turning down that argument, the Court found that "the school children and the State alone are the beneficiaries" of the law, not the schools they attend.

The first direct ruling on the Establishment Clause came in *Everson* v. *Board of Education*—a 1947 case often called the *New Jersey School Bus Case*. There the Court upheld a State law that provided for the public (tax-supported) busing of students who attended parochial schools. It was attacked as a support of religion—because, its critics said, it relieved parochial schools of the need to pay for busing and so freed up their money for other (and religious) purposes. The Court did not agree, however. It found the law to be a safety measure, intended to benefit school children, no matter what schools they

might attend. In deciding the case, the Court said that the Establishment Clause

> means at least this: Neither the State nor the Federal Government can set up a church. Neither can pass laws which aid one religion, aid all religions, or prefer one religion over another. . . . No tax in any amount, large or small, can be levied to support any religious activities or institutions, whatever they may be called, or whatever form they adopt to teach or practice religion. Neither the State nor the Federal Government can, openly or secretly, participate in the affairs of any religious organization or groups and *vice versa*.

Since that decision, most of the Court's Establishment Clause cases have involved in one way or another, with religion and education.

Released Time. Two of those cases have dealt with "released time" programs in public schools. Such programs, now found in most of the States, allow those students who wish to do so to be "released" from school time in order to attend classes in religious instruction.

In *McCollum* v. *Board of Education*, 1948, the Court struck down the program then used in Champaign, Illinois—because public school classrooms and other public facilities were being used for religious purposes.

In *Zorach* v. *Clauson*, 1952, however, New York City's program, much like the one in Illinois, was upheld—because New York's program requires that the religious classes be held *away* from the schools, in *private* places.

Prayers and the Bible. Two other decisions have involved the recitation of prayers and the reading of the Bible in public schools.

In *Engel* v. *Vitale*, 1962, the Court outlawed the use, even on a voluntary basis, of a nondenominational prayer written by the New York State Board of Regents. The "Regents' prayer" of New York read:

> Almighty God, we acknowledge our dependence upon Thee, and we beg Thy blessings upon us, our parents, our teachers, and our country.

The Supreme Court held that

> the constitutional prohibition against laws respecting an establishment of religion must at least mean that in this country it is no part of the business of government to compose official prayers for any group of the American people to recite as part of a religious program carried on by government.

To those who held that the Regents' prayer posed no real threat of "an establishment of religion," the Court quoted the author of the 1st Amendment, James Madison:

From *Straight Herblock* (Simon & Schuster, 1964)

"Every schoolchild should be made to pray against government interference with private lives."

It is proper to take alarm at the first experiment on our liberties. . . . Who does not see that the same authority which can establish Christianity, in exclusion of all other Religions, may establish with the same ease any particular sect of Christianity, in exclusion of all other Sects?

In 1963 two cases, one from Pennsylvania and the other from Maryland, were combined for decision by the Court. In *Abington School District* v. *Schempp*, the practice of reading from the Bible—as required by State law—and of reciting the Lord's Prayer at the beginning of each school day was challenged. In *Murray* v. *Baltimore School Board*, a board rule that required each day to open with "reading, without comment, a chapter in the Holy Bible and/or the use of the Lord's Prayer" was also challenged.

The Court ruled that in each case there was a violation of

> the command of the 1st Amendment that the government maintain strict neutrality, neither aiding nor opposing religion.

Most recently, the Court struck down a Kentucky law requiring that copies of the Ten Commandments be posted in all public school classrooms, *Stone* v. *Graham*, 1980.

To sum up these rulings, the Supreme Court has held that the public schools—which are agencies of government—cannot sponsor religious exercises. Specifically, it has ruled that the Establishment Clause forbids the organized reciting of prayers, the devotional reading of the Bible, and the posting of the Ten Commandments in the public schools. But it has *not* held that individuals cannot pray, when and as they choose, in the schools—or in any other place. Nor has it held that the Bible cannot be studied, in a literary or historic frame, in the schools.

These rulings have stirred strong feelings, and in many places. Many proposals have been made to amend the Constitution to allow "voluntary prayer" in the public schools. (And, despite them, both organized prayers and Bible readings are to be found in many public classrooms today.

Chaplains in Congress and the State Legislatures. Daily sessions of both houses of Congress and most of the State legislatures are begun with prayer. In Congress, and in many State legislatures, the opening prayer is offered by a chaplain paid with public funds.

The Supreme Court has ruled that that practice—unlike prayers in the public schools—is constitutionally permissible, *Marsh* v. *Chambers*, 1983. The Court rested its distinction between school prayers and legislative prayers on the point that prayers have been offered in the nation's legislative bodies throughout our history—"from colonial times through the founding of the Republic and ever since."

Evolution. In *Epperson* v. *Arkansas*, 1968, the Court struck down a State law forbidding the teaching of the scientific theory of evolution in the public schools of that State. The Court held that the Establishment Clause

> forbids alike the preference of a religious doctrine or the prohibition of theory which is deemed antagonistic to a particular dogma. . . . The State has no legitimate interest in protecting any or all religions from views distasteful to them.

Tax Exemptions. Every State exempts houses of worship, and other church-owned property used for religious purposes, from both State and local taxation. The Supreme Court has upheld this practice. It ruled that it does not violate the wall of separation in *Walz* v. *Tax Commission of the City of New York* in 1970.

Walz had challenged the exemption of churches from local property taxes. He argued that these exemptions made his and others' property tax bills higher than they would otherwise be. Therefore, he claimed, they amounted to a public support of religion.

The Court turned down his plea. It found that those exemptions are only evidence of a State's "benevolent neutrality" toward religion, not support of it. Said the Court, the exemptions "create only a minimal and remote"—and therefore permissible—"involvement between church and state."

But those church-related schools which discriminate on the basis of race can be denied a tax-exempt status under federal law, *Bob Jones University* v. *United States* and *Goldsboro Christian Schools* v. *United States*, 1983. (Organizations with that status do not pay unemployment and social security taxes; and contributions may be claimed as federal income tax deductions.)

The schools involved in two 1983 cases argued that their racial policies reflect their sincerely held religious beliefs. The Supreme Court granted that point. It held that, nevertheless, the nation's interest in eradicating racial discrimination in education "substantially outweighs whatever burden denial of tax benefits places on [those schools in the] exercise of their religious beliefs."

State Aid to Parochial Schools. Most recent Establishment Clause cases have centered on this highly controversial question: What forms of State aid to parochial schools are constitutional?

Several States give help to private schools, including those which are church-related—for transportation, textbooks, laboratory equipment, standardized testing, and much else. Pressures to expand that aid have grown as school operating costs have soared.

Those who favor such aid note that large numbers of students attend parochial schools who would otherwise have to be educated at public expense. They point to the fact that the Supreme Court has held that parents have a legal right to send their children to those schools (*Pierce* v. *Society of Sisters*). To give that right real meaning, they say, some aid must be given—to relieve some of the double buden carried by parents who must pay taxes to support the public schools their children do not attend.

Many also insist that the church-run schools pose no real church-state problems—because, they say, those schools devote most of their time to **secular** (nonreligious) subjects rather than to **sectarian** (religious) ones.

Those who oppose that aid argue that the public schools play an important democratizing role in bringing pupils of various religious backgrounds together. Many of them object to separating children in schools on the basis of religion—and especially because religious differences are often related to ethnic, social, and economic distinctions among people.

Many of them argue, too, that those parents who choose to send children to parochial schools should accept the financial consequences of that choice, not expect others to do so. And many also insist that church beliefs are bound to have an effect upon the teaching of nonreligious subjects in church-run schools.

The Supreme Court has been picking its way through cases arising out of State aid programs for more than ten years now.[8]

In the first of them, *Board of Education* v. *Allen*, 1968, it upheld a New York law providing secular textbooks for

Parochial schools can recieve State aid, but only for nonsectarian (nonreligious) purposes.

students in parochial schools. The Court applied what has come to be known as "the child-benefit theory"—that the aid is directed to the student, not to the school.

In deciding *Allen*, the Court emphasized that a State may aid *only* secular education in church-related schools. But drawing the line between that aid which supports only the nonreligious activities of a parochial school and that which promotes its religious purposes has proved to be a quite troublesome task.

Excessive Entanglement. Since 1971, the Court has been developing and applying a three-pronged test for this purpose—the **excessive entanglement standard.** To be constitutional, a State's school aid law must meet these requirements: (1) the purpose of the aid must be clearly secular, not religious; (2) its primary effect must neither advance nor inhibit religion; and (3) it must avoid an "excessive entanglement of government with religion."

[8]For about as long, Congress has been considering proposals to allow tuition tax credits—income tax exemptions for parents who pay private school tuitions.

In other words, as the Court put it in the first case in which it used the test: The Establishment Clause is designed to prevent three main evils: "sponsorship, financial support, and active involvement of the sovereign in religious activity," *Lemon* v. *Kurtzman*, 1971.

In *Lemon*, the Court struck down a Pennsylvania law. It provided for reimbursements (money payments) to private schools to cover their costs for teachers' salaries, textbooks, and other teaching materials in nonreligious courses. At the same time, the Court also voided a Rhode Island law giving salary supplements to the teachers of secular courses in private elementary schools, *Earley*, v. *DiCenso*, 1971.

In both cases the Court held that the State programs were of direct benefit to the parochial schools—and so to the churches sponsoring them. It held that they required such close State supervision that they produced an excessive entanglement of government with religion.

The Court has been using its excessive entanglement standard for more than a decade now—upholding some programs and rejecting others. Thus, it has ruled that grants of public money cannot be made to parochial schools for maintenance and repairs nor for tuition reimbursements to parents whose children attend those schools—in a New York case, *Committee for Public Education* v. *Nyquist*, 1973.

It has allowed the use of public funds to lend textbooks to students in parochial schools in a Pennsylvania case, *Meek* v. *Pittinger*, 1975. In that same case, however, it rejected the loan of such things as films, projectors, and recorders, and grants for counselling and speech therapy. And it banned public payments for field trips by parochial school students—in a case from Ohio, *Wolman* v. *Walter*, 1977.

Two New York cases may help to lay out the shape of the Court's standard here. In *Levitt* v. *Committee for Public Education*, 1973, it struck down a program in which the State repaid church-related schools for their costs in certain testing and reporting functions. That ruling focused on the point that many of the tests had been prepared by teachers in those schools—and so could be considered a part of their program of religious instruction.

But in *Committee for Public Education* v. *Regan*, 1980, the Court allowed the State to pay church-related schools to administer, grade, and report the results of standardized tests prepared by the State Department of Education.

The Court has taken a more generous view in cases involving public aid to church-related colleges and universities. Thus, in *Tilton* v. *Richardson*, 1971, it upheld federal grants to such institutions for the construction of academic buildings to be used for nonreligious purposes. It could find no excessive entanglement in these "one-shot" grants.[9]

Certainly, the Court's future holds many other "parochaid" cases.

The Free Exercise of Religion. The second part of the constitutional guarantee of religious freedom is set out in the Free Exercise Clause. That Clause guarantees to each person the right to *believe* whatever that person chooses to believe in matters of religion. No law— and no other action by government— may violate that *absolute* constitutional right. It is protected by both the 1st and the 14th Amendments.

---

[9]It has also sustained two similar State programs— one in South Carolina (*Hunt* v. *McNair*, 1973) and the other in Maryland (*Roemer* v. *Maryland Board of Public Works*, 1976). But in *Tilton* the Court did hold one section of the Higher Education Facilities Act of 1963 unconstitutional. That section limited to 20 years a college's obligation not to use a federally-financed building for religious instruction or worship. The Court ruled that such buildings may *never* be used for those purposes.

No person has an absolute right to *act* as he or she chooses, however. The Free Exercise Clause does *not* give one the other to do any of those things which violate the criminal laws, offend the public morals, or otherwise threaten the health, welfare, or safety of the community.

The Supreme Court laid down the basic shape of the Free Exercise Clause in the very first case it heard on the point—*Reynolds* v. *United States*, 1879. Reynolds, a Mormon living in Utah, had two wives. That circumstance (polygamy) was allowed by the teachings of his church; but it was prohibited by a federal law banning the practice in any of the territories of the United States.

Reynolds was tried and convicted under the law. On appeal, he argued that the law violated his constitutional right to the free exercise of his religious beliefs. The Supreme Court did not agree. It held that the 1st Amendment does not forbid Congress the power to punish those actions which are "violations of social duties or subversive of good order." To hold otherwise, said the Court

> would be to make the professed doctrines of religious belief superior to the law of the land, and in effect permit every citizen to become a law unto himself. Government would exist only in name under such circumstances.

The Court has held to that position ever since. Over the years, it has approved many regulations of human conduct in the face of free-exercise challenges.

For example, it has upheld laws requiring the vaccination of school children (*Jacobson* v. *Massachusetts*, 1905); forbidding the use of poisonous snakes in religious rites (*Bunn* v. *North Carolina*, 1949); and requiring business to be closed on Sundays—"blue laws" (*McGowan* v. *Maryland*, 1961).

Religious groups may be required to have a permit to hold a parade on the public streets (*Cox* v. *New Hampshire*, 1940); and laws regarding child labor must be obeyed if children are used to sell religious literature (*Prince* v. *Massachusetts*, 1944). Those who have religious objections to military service can nonetheless be drafted (*Welsh* v. *United States*, 1970).[10] And the Hare Krishna can be required to limit their religious tracts and other fund-raising at a State fair to a booth or to some other fixed location, even though such activities are a part of their ritual (*Heffron* v. *International Society of Krishna Consciousness*, 1981).

But, over time, the Court has also found many actions by governmments to be contrary to the free-exercise guarantee. It did so for the first time in one of the landmark Due Process cases we cited on page 94, *Cantwell* v. *Connecticut*, 1940. There, it struck down a law requiring a license (an official permit) before any person could solicit money for a religious cause.

There are many other cases in that line: Thus, Amish children cannot be forced to attend school beyond the 8th grade—because that sect's centuries-old "self-sufficient agrarian lifestyle essential to their religious faith is threatened . . . by modern education" (*Wisconsin* v. *Yoder*, 1972). (But the Amish, who believe in taking care of their own, must pay social security taxes, just as all other employers do (*United States* v. *Lee*, 1982.)

A State cannot forbid ministers to hold elected public offices (*McDaniel*

---

[10]The Court has made this ruling many times. *Welsh* is the leading case from the Vietnam War period. There, the Court held that the only persons who could not be drafted because of their beliefs (conscientious objectors) were those "whose consciences, spurred by deeply held moral, ethical, or religious beliefs, would give them no rest if they allowed themselves to become part of an instrument of war." On compulsory military service (the draft), see pages 129, 457.

Sometimes called the "plain people," Amish folk chat after church worship. The Supreme Court has held that Amish children are exempt from State compulsory school attendance laws beyond the 8th grade.

v. *Paty*, 1978). Nor can it deny unemployment compensation benefits to a worker who quit a job because it involved some conflict with his or her religious beliefs (*Sherbert* v. *Verner*, 1963; *Thomas* v. *Indiana*, 1981).[11]

Several important religious freedom cases have been carried to the Supreme Court by the Jehovah's Witnesses—a fundamentalist group which very actively promotes its beliefs. Perhaps the stormiest of the many controversies that sect has stirred arose out of the Witnesses' refusal to obey compulsory flag salute requirements. That contro-

versy, and the two notable Court decisions it produced, tells us much about the Free Exercise Clause. It also shows how difficult many 1st Amendment questions can be for the courts.

The Witnesses refuse to salute the flag because they see such conduct as a violation of the Bible's commandment against idolatry.[12] In *Minersville School District* v. *Gobitis*, 1940, the Court upheld a Pennsylvania school board regulation requiring students to salute the flag at the beginning of each school day. Gobitis instructed his children not to do so, and they were expelled. He went to court, basing his case on the constitutional guarantee. He finally lost in the Supreme Court, however. It declared

---

[11]Typically, State unemployment compensation laws bar such benefits to those who leave jobs voluntarily and "without good cause in connection with the work." In *Sherbert*, a Seventh Day Adventist lost her job in a South Carolina textile mill when she refused to work on Saturdays (her sabbath day). In *Thomas*, a Jehovah's Witness who worked for a machinery company quit after he was transferred from one section of the company (being closed down) to another (where gun turrets for tanks were made); he left because, he said, his religious beliefs would not allow him to work on war materials.

---

[12]Specifically, these verses from Chapter 20 in the Book of Exodus:

"2. Thou shalt have no other gods before me.

"4. Thou shalt not make unto thee any graven images. . . .

"5. Thou shalt not bow down thyself to them, nor serve them . . . ."

that the board's rule was not an infringement of religious liberty; rather, it held that it was a lawful attempt to promote patriotism and national unity.

Just three years later, in a remarkable turnabout, the Court reversed that decision. In *West Virginia Board of Education* v. *Barnette*, 1943, it held, a compulsory flag salute law unconstitutional. Justice Robert H. Jackson's words we quoted on page 89 are from the Court's powerful opinion in that case. And so are these:

> To believe that patriotism will not flourish if patriotic ceremonies are voluntary and spontaneous instead of a compulsory routine is to make an unflattering estimate of the appeal of our institutions to free minds.

☑ F O R　R E V I E W

1. What civil rights guarantees are set out in the 1st Amendment? Against whom do they apply?
2. What is the Establishment Clause? Does it provide for a complete separation of church and state?
3. Does the Constitution prohibit released time programs in public schools? Organized prayer or Bible readings? Tax exemptions for churches? All forms of "parochaid"?
4. What is the Free Exercise Clause? What is the basic shape of the right it guarantees?

Freedom of Speech and Press

The 1st and 14th Amendment's protections of free speech and a free press serve *two* fundamentally important purposes. They are intended:

(1) To guarantee to *each person* a right of free expression—in the spoken and the written word, and by all other means of communication, as well; and

(2) To ensure to *all persons* a full, wide-ranging discussion of public affairs.

That is, they give us the right to have our say and the right to hear what others have to say.

Most often, we think of these great freedoms in terms of that first purpose. The second one is just as important, however. Our system of government depends upon the ability of the people to make sound, reasoned judgments on matters of public concern. Clearly, such judgments can be made only where the people can know all of the facts in a given matter *and* can hear and weigh any and all interpretations of those facts —all opinions about that matter.

Justice Oliver Wendell Holmes once underscored the importance of that second purpose this way:

> Persecution for the expression of opinions seems to me perfectly logical. If you have no doubt of your premises and want a certain result with all your heart, you naturally express your wishes in law and sweep away all opposition. . . . But when men have realized that time has upset many fighting faiths, they may come to believe even more than they believe the very foundations of their own conduct that the ultimate good desired is better reached by free trade in ideas— that the best test of truth is the power of the thought to get itself accepted in the competition of the market. . . . That at any rate is the theory of our Constitution.[13]

Before we can turn to the more exact meanings of the 1st and 14th Amendments here, you must understand two other points:

---

[13]Dissenting in *Abrams* v. *United States*, 1919.

First, the guarantees of free speech and press are intended, most of all, to protect the expression of *unpopular* views. The opinions of the majority need, after all, little or no constitutional protection. Again, in Justice Holmes' words:

> . . . if there is any principle of the Constitution that more imperatively calls for attachment than any other it is the principle of free thought—not free thought for those who agree with us but freedom for the thought that we hate.[14]

Secondly, some forms of expression are *not* protected by the Constitution. No person has an unbridled right of free speech or free press. Many reasonable restrictions may be (and are) placed upon those rights.

We shall see many illustrations of this point on the next several pages. For now, this one: No person has a right to *libel* or *slander* another.[15]

Obscenity.   Obscenity is not protected by the 1st and 14th Amendments. Even so, no civil rights issue has given the Supreme Court more difficulty in recent years.

The Court has wrestled several times with these questions: What language, what printed matter, what films and other materials are, in fact, obscene? And what restrictions can be properly placed on such materials?[16] The leading case on the point today is *Miller* v. *California*, 1973. There the Court laid down a three-part test to determine what material is obscene and what is not.

A book or film or other piece of material is legally obscene if: (1) "the average person applying contemporary [local] community standards," finds that the work, taken as a whole, "appeals to the prurient interest"—*i.e.*, tends to excite lust, produce lewd emotions; (2) "the work depicts or describes, in a patently offensive way," a form of sexual conduct specifically dealt with in an anti-obscenity law; and (3) "the work, taken as a whole, lacks serious literary, artistic, political, or scientific value."

That the problem is a very knotty one can be seen from these cases: In *Stanley* v. *Georgia*, 1969, the Court ruled that a State cannot make it a crime for a person to possess obscene materials for his or her own use in his or her own home.[17] Yet, in two 1971 cases it upheld laws that punish those who send obscene materials in interstate commerce or through the mails or import them from abroad (*United States* v. *Thirty-Seven Photographs; United States* v. *Reidel*). In short, the Court has upheld the right of a person to read a dirty book or see a dirty movie in his or her own home. But, at the same time, it has upheld the laws that deny to that person

---

[14]Dissenting in *United States* v. *Schwimmer*, 1929.

[15]**Libel** (the printed word) and **slander** (the spoken word) involve the use of words *maliciously* (with vicious purpose) to injure a person's character or reputation or expose that person to public contempt, ridicule, or hatred. Truth is generally an absolute defense against a libel or slander claim. The law is less protective of public officials, however. In *New York Times* v. *Sullivan*, 1964, the Supreme Court held that public officials cannot recover damages for a published criticism, even if exaggerated or false, unless "the statement was made with reckless disregard . . . of whether it was false or not." Several later decisions have extended that ruling to cover "public figures" and even private individuals who become involved in newsworthy events.

[16]Congress passed the first of a series of laws to keep obscene matter from the mails in 1872. The current law was upheld by the Court in *Roth* v. *United States*, 1957. It excludes "every obscene, lewd, lascivious, or filthy" piece of material. The Court found the law a proper exercise of the postal power (Article I, Section 8, Clause 7) and so not prohibited by the 1st Amendment. *Roth* marked the Court's first attempt to find an adequate definition of obscenity.

[17]Films were involved in the case. Said the Court: "If the 1st Amendment means anything, it means that the State has no business telling a man, sitting alone in his own home, what books he may read or what films he may watch." But, in *United States* v. *Orito*, 1973, it held that the "zone of privacy" protected by *Stanley* does not go beyond one's own home.

When a group of American Nazis requested permission to parade through a largely Jewish suburb of Chicago, the courts held that, as anti-Semitic as their views may be, the Nazi Party had a right to parade peacefully.

the principal means of obtaining them.[18]

Prior Restraint. The Constitution allows government to punish *some* utterances, *after* they are made. But, with almost no exceptions, it cannot place any "prior restraint" on spoken or on written words. That is, except in the most extreme situations, it cannot curb ideas *before* they are expressed.

Near v. *Minnesota*, 1931, is a leading case on the point. There the Supreme Court struck down a State law that

---

[18]Another chief source of such things is, of course, so-called "adult book stores." Although most of the items they sell cannot be mailed, shipped across State lines, or legally imported, these "porno shops" are usually well-supplied. The 1st Amendment does not forbid a city to regulate the location of "adult entertainment establishments" through its zoning ordinances, *Young* v. *American Mini Theatres*, 1976—and many cities now do so. A city cannot use its zoning laws to ban all live entertainment in commercial establishments, however, *Schad* v. *Borough of Mount Ephraim*, 1981 (in that case, nude dancing in an adult book store). Also, the 1st Amendment is not violated by a State law that prohibits nude dancing in all bars or nightclubs that serve liquor, *New York State Liquor Authority* v. *Bellanca*, 1981, or a city ordinance regulating "head shops," which sell items for use with illegal drugs, *Village of Hoffman Estates* v. *The Flipside*, 1982.

CASE STUDY

WHAT SHOULD (CAN) STUDENTS READ?

In 1982 the Supreme Court held that the 1st Amendment limits a school board's authority to remove books from the shelves of high school libraries. That holding came in a New York case, *Board of Education, Island Trees Union Free School District* v. *Pico.*

In 1976 the local school board ordered the removal of several books from the library at Island Trees High School. Among those books: *The Naked Ape*, by Desmond Morris; *Slaughterhouse-Five*, by Kurt Vonnegut, Jr.; *Soul on Ice*, by Eldridge Cleaver; *The Fixer*, by Bernard Malamud; and *Go Ask Alice*, of anonymous authorship.

When the board's action was publicized, it issued a press release in which the several banned books were described as "anti-American, anti-Christian, anti-Semitic, and just plain filthy." And it declared: "It is our duty, our moral obligation, to protect the children in our schools from this moral danger as surely as from physical and medical dangers."

Steven Pico and several other students took the matter to the federal courts in early 1977. (Pico was then a 17-year-old senior and president of the student council at Island Trees High School.) They sued the board, arguing that its action had violated their 1st Amendment rights.

In 1979 a federal District Court ruled **summarily** (*i.e.*, without holding a formal trial) in the school board's favor. It found that, while the removal of the books might reflect a "misguided educational philosophy," the board had acted within its authority to remove "educationally unsuitable" materials from school libraries.

The students appealed, and the Court of Appeals for the Second Circuit reversed that ruling in 1980. It ordered a trial in the lower federal court.

The school board then took that order to the Supreme Court, but lost. The High Court held that the matter must come to trial. It ruled that the District Court must determine why the board acted as it did. If it acted to remove vulgar or otherwise unsuitable material, its action was constitutionally permissible; but if the board acted to remove unpopular ideas from the library, it violated the 1st Amendment. Said the Court: "Our Constitution does not permit the official suppression of ideas." (And when he learned of the Court's decision, said Steven Pico: "Most young people have bought what they have heard [in school] about the Constitution and the 1st Amendment, and they believe that school is the place to be exposed to a diversity of ideas.")

1. How can you discover what has happened in this controversy since the Supreme Court's ruling? In short, what is the status of the case today?

2. Can you discover what other books were also removed from the school's library? Are (any of) these books in your school's library? Have you read any of them?

3. On whose side do you come down in this case—with the board or with the students? Why?

prohibited the publication of any "malicious, scandalous, and defamatory" periodical. Acting under that law, a local court had issued an order forbidding the continued publication of *The Saturday Press,* a weekly published in Minneapolis. The paper had printed several articles that charged public corruption and which attacked "grafters" and "Jewish gangsters" in that city. The Court held that the guarantee of a free press does not allow a "prior restraint" on publication, except in such extreme cases as wartime or when a publication is obscene or incites readers to violence.

The Court has purposely refused to say that all forms of prior censorship are unconstitutional. But it has said that "a prior restraint on expression comes to this Court with a 'heavy presumption' against its constitutionality," *Nebraska Press Association* v. *Stuart,* 1976.[19] It has used that general rule several times —for example, in the famous Pentagon Papers Case, *New York Times* v. *United States,* 1971. The *Times* and several other newspapers had obtained copies of a set of classified documents. The documents, widely known as "The Pentagon Papers," were officially titled *History of U.S. Decision-Making Process on Viet Nam Policy.* They had been stolen from the Defense Department and then leaked to the press. The Government sought a court order to bar their publication. But the Court rejected that plea. It held that the Government had not shown that printing the documents would endanger the nation's security— and so had not overcome the "heavy presumption" against prior censorship.

On some few occasions the Court has allowed prior restraints, however. Thus, it has upheld regulations that pro-

hibit passing out political literature on military bases without the approval of military authorities, *Greer* v. *Spock,* 1976. The most recent such case is *Snepp* v. *United States,* 1980. There the Court backed a prior censorship regulation of the Central Intelligence Agency. The CIA requires all of its agents to sign a contract in which they agree not to publish anything about the Agency or its activities without its approval. A former agent, Frank Snepp, wrote a book, *Decent Interval,* about the CIA's activities in South Vietnam. He did not submit his book to the Agency for screening before its publication. The Government then sued him for breach of contract—and, over his 1st Amendment objections, the Court upheld the Government's right to do so.

Confidentiality. Do news reporters have a constitutional right to withhold certain information from government? Or, may they be forced to testify before a grand jury, in court, or before a legislative committee—and there be required to name their sources and reveal other confidential information?

These questions are of immediate importance to those who gather and report the news. They also have a direct impact upon the free flow of information—and, therefore, on the public's right to know.

Many reporters and most news organizations insist that they must have the right to refuse to testify, the right to "protect their sources." They argue that without it they cannot assure **confidentiality** to their sources—that is, cannot guarantee them that they will remain anonymous. Unless they can do that, they say, many of their sources will not give them information they must have in order to keep the public informed.

Both State and federal courts have generally rejected the news media argument. In recent years several reporters

---

[19]A case in which a county judge had ordered the media not to report certain details of a sensational murder trial. The Court held the "gag order" to be unconstitutional.

have refused to obey court orders directing them to give information. As a consequence, a number of reporters have gone to jail. Their willingness to pay the penalty for contempt of court testifies to the importance of the issues involved.

In the leading case. *Branzburg* v. *Hayes*, 1972, the Supreme Court held that the 1st Amendment does not grant any special privileges to reporters. They, "like other citizens, [must] respond to relevant questions put to them in the course of a valid grand jury investigation or criminal trial." If any special exemptions are to be given to the news media, said the Court, they must come from Congress and the State legislatures.

To date, Congress has not acted on the Court's suggestion. However, some 20 States have passed so-called "shield laws." These laws do give reporters some protection against having to disclose their sources or reveal other confidential information.

Motion Pictures. The question of whether motion pictures are protected by the constitutional guarantees of freedom of expression reached the Supreme Court early in the history of the movie industry. In *Mutual Film Corporation* v. *Ohio*, 1915, the Court upheld a State law that prohibited the showing of any film that was not of "moral, educational, or amusing and harmless character." It viewed the showing of motion pictures as "a business pure and simple, originated and conducted for profit like other spectacles, not to be regarded . . . as part of the press of the country or as organs of public opinion." Nearly all of the States and thousands of local communities then set up strong movie censorship programs.

The Court overturned that 1915 decision in 1952, however. In *Burstyn* v. *Wilson*, involving movie censorship in New York, it held that "liberty of expression by means of motion pictures is

Because they make use of publicly-owned airwaves, Congress has regulated television and radio broadcasting much more extensively than newspapers and other printed media.

guaranteed by the 1st and 14th Amendments."

Movie censorship as such is not unconstitutional, however. A State or a community can ban an obscene picture. But, to be constitutional, a censorship law must provide for a prompt judicial hearing. At that hearing the government must prove to the court that the film in question is in fact obscene, *Teitel Film Corporation* v. *Cusack*, 1968.

Radio and Television. Radio and television do not enjoy as much freedom as the Constitution guarantees to other means of expression.

Congress has provided for the extensive regulation of radio and television broadcasting in the oft-amended Federal Communications Act of 1934. This law is administered by the Federal Communications Commission; see page 427.

The Supreme Court has several times upheld federal regulation of broadcasting as a proper exercise of the com-

Members of the United Auto Workers union show their support for workers of another union on strike at a meat-packing plant.

merce power (Article I, Section 8, Clause 3). Unlike newspapers and other print media, both radio and television use public property—the publicly-owned airwaves—for their broadcasts. In short, they have no legal right to do so without the public's permission—*i.e.*, without a proper license, *National Broadcasting Co.* v. *United States*, 1942.

The Court has put the nub of the matter this way:

There is no "unabridgeable 1st Amendment right to broadcast comparable to the right of every individual to speak, write, or publish." However, "this is not to say that the 1st Amendment is irrelevant to broadcasting. But . . . it is the right of the viewers and

the listeners, not the right of the broadcasters, which is paramount."[20]

Symbolic Speech. Ideas, views, opinions are usually communicated in one of two eays. They are either presented *orally*—as in a conversation or a speech, or in some *published* form—as in a newspaper, a book, a leaflet, a recording, or a film.

But, notice, conduct—the way in which a person behaves or does a particular thing—can also be a means of expression. This way of saying something has come to be called **symbolic speech.**

Take **picketing** in a labor dispute as a fairly common example. It involves the patrolling of a business site by workers who are on strike. By their conduct, they attempt to inform the public of the controversy and to persuade customers and others not to deal with the firm involved. Picketing is, then, a form of expression. So long as it is peaceful, it is protected by the 1st and 14th Amendments.[21]

What conduct amounts to symbolic speech and is therefore protected by the Constitution? Clearly, the answer cannot be *all* conduct. If it were, murder, arson, robbery, or any other crime could be excused on grounds that the person who committed the crime meant to say something by doing so.

But drawing the line between protected speech and punishable conduct is

---

[20]*Red Lion Broadcasting Co.* v. *FCC,* 1969, in which the Court upheld the **fairness doctrine**—an FCC rule which says that radio and television broadcasters must present all sides of important public issues. The FCC also enforces the **equal time doctrine**, set out in the Communications Act of 1934. It provides that if a radio or television station or network makes air time available to one candidate for a public office it must offer time to all other candidates for that office, and on the same terms.

[21]The leading case on the point is *Thornhill* v. *Arizona,* 1940. There, the Court struck down a State law that made it a crime for one to loiter about or picket a place of business in order to influence others not to trade or work here. But picketing which is "set in a background of violence" may be prevented.

really not that easy. Things that happen in real life present problems in much more complex, less clear-cut terms.

Generally, the Supreme Court has been sympathetic to the symbolic speech argument. But it has not given blanket 1st Amendment protection to that means of expression. As a quick sampling, take a look at these cases:

United States v. *O'Brien*, 1968, involved four young men who had burned their draft cards as a protest against the war in Vietnam. They were then convicted of violating a federal law that makes it a crime to destroy or mutilate the cards. O'Brien defended his conduct by arguing that the 1st Amendment protects "all modes of communication of ideas by conduct." The Court upheld his conviction. Speaking for the majority, Chief Justice Earl Warren declared: "We cannot accept the view that an apparently limitless variety of conduct can be labelled 'speech' whenever the person engaging in the conduct intends thereby to express an idea."[22]

A police officer does not have a constitutional right to have long hair—even if he believes it to be a "a means of expressing his attitude and lifestyle," *Kelley* v. *Johnson*, 1976.

Giving money to a candidate for public office is a "symbolic expression of support" for that candidate. Nevertheless, the limits Congress has placed on the amount that individuals may contribute to the campaigns of candidates for federal office do not violate the 1st Amendment, *Buckley* v. *Valeo*, 1976. And the limits it has put on the

amounts that individuals may give to political action committees are also constitutional, *California Medical Association* v. *Federal Election Commission*, 1981.

Tinker v. *Des Moines School District*, 1969, on the other hand, is one of several cases in which the Court has come down on the side of symbolic speech. A small group of students in the Des Moines public schools had worn black armbands to class. By that quiet behavior they meant to publicize their opposition to the war in Vietnam. For it, they were suspended. The Court ruled that school officials had overstepped their authority here and violated the Constitution. Said the Court: "It can hardly be argued that either students or teachers shed their constitutional rights to freedom of speech or expression at the schoolhouse gate."

The Court reversed the Massachusetts conviction of a man who was sentenced to six months in jail for treating the American flag "contemptuously." He had worn a flag patch on the seat of his pants, as a protest against Nixon administration policies, *Smith* v. *Goguen*, 1974.

In another protest, a college student in Seattle hung an American flag outside his window, upside down, with a peace symbol attached. His conviction under a State law forbidding "improper use" of the flag was overturned, *Spence* v. *Washington*, 1974.

Advertising. Until quite recently, it was generally thought that "commercial speech"—advertising—was not protected by the 1st and 14th Amendments. In *Bigelow* v. *Virginia*, 1975, however, the Court held unconstitutional a State law that prohibited the newspaper advertising of abortion services. And in 1976 it struck down another Virginia law, forbidding the advertising of prescription drug prices, *Virginia State*

[22]The Court upheld the law under which O'Brien was punished. It found the cards to be a necessary part of the machinery of selective service. It ruled that acts of dissent by conduct can be punished if: (1) the object of the protest (here the war and the draft) is within the constitutional powers of the Government, (2) the incidental restriction on expression is no greater than necessary, and (3) the Government's real interest in the matter is not to squelch dissent.

Board of Pharmacy v. *Virginia Citizens Consumer Council.*

It made similar rulings in two 1977 cases. In *Carey* v. *Population Services International* it voided a New York law forbidding the advertisement of contraceptives; and in *Bates* v. *Arizona Bar* it invalidated rules that forbade attorneys to advertise their services and fees.

The Court has also ruled that corporations ("artificial persons" in law) are entitled to freedom of speech. It first did so in a symbolic speech case—where it overturned a State law that prohibited corporations from spending money to influence votes in an issue election, *First National Bank of Boston* v. *Bellotti*, 1978. More recently, it has held that a public utility cannot be prevented from inserting statements on controversial public issues in the monthly bills it sends to its customers, *Consolidated Edison* v. *Public Service Commission of New York*, 1980. However, no group has a constitutional right to put political pamphlets (or anything else) in home mailboxes unless that material bears the correct amount of postage, *U.S. Postal Service* v. *Council of Greenburgh Civic Associations*, 1981.

Another recent case involved advertising, but with a different twist. In *Wooley* v. *Maynard*, 1977, the Court held that a State cannot force its citizens to act as "mobile billboards"—not, at least, when the words used conflict with their religious or moral beliefs. The Maynards, Jehovah's Witnesses, objected to the New Hampshire State motto on their automobile license plates. To them, the words ("Live Free or Die") clashed with their belief in "everlasting life"—and so they covered those words with tape. For this, Maynard was arrested three times, and on the third occasion he was jailed for 15 days. On appeal, the Supreme Court sided with the Maynards and ordered the State of New Hampshire to take no further action against them.

☑ FOR REVIEW

1. For what two important purposes does the Constitution guarantee freedom of expression?
2. The guarantees of free speech and press are especially intended to protect the expression of what views?
3. May government impose a "prior restraint" on speech, writing, or other forms of expression?
4. Is obscenity entitled to the constitutional protections of free expression? Are motion pictures? Radio and TV broadcasting?
5. What is symbolic speech? Commercial speech?

"You have the right to remain silent . . . You have the right to counsel . . . You have the right to read the classified ads . . . "

Stayskal © 1977 *Chicago Tribune*

National Security.   What of those who seek to destroy this country and its form of government? Are they, too, protected by the constitutional guarantees of freedom of expression?

Remember, the guarantees of free speech and press are especially intended to protect *unpopular* opinions. The expression of opinions with which most of

The Supreme Court has ruled that a city may ban commercial billboards, but its ban cannot be so broad as to forbid billboards with political advertisements, public service messages, and other noncommercial material (*Metromedia, Inc.* v. *City of San Diego*, 1981).

us agree really need little or no constitutional protection.

At the same time, however, recognize this point: Government has an undoubted right to protect itself and the nation against **internal subversion**—against domestic threats to the nation's security. But how far can it go in doing so? How can government protect itself and at the same time preserve individual freedoms and democratic procedures?

Clearly, government may punish espionage, sabotage, and treason. These are forms of action, conduct. **Espionage** is the practice of spying for a foreign power. **Sabotage** involves an act of destruction intended to hinder a nation's war or defense effort. **Treason** is specifically defined in the Constitution (Article III, Section 3). It can consist only in levying war against or adhering to the enemies of the nation; see page 148.

Sedition presents a much more delicate problem, however—for it involves the use of spoken or written words. **Sedition** is the incitement (the prompting, urging, fomenting) of resistance to lawful authority; it does not necessarily involve acts of violence or betrayal.

Congress first acted to curb opposition to government in the Alien and Sedition Acts of 1798.[23] Those laws gave the President power to deport undesirable aliens and made "any false, scandalous, and malicious" criticism of the government a crime. They were intended to stifle the opponents of President John Adams and the Federalist Party.

The Alien and Sedition Acts were undoubtedly unconstitutional but they were never tested in the courts. Some 25 persons were fined or jailed for violating them. They were a major issue in the elections of 1800, and a major reason for the defeat of the Federalists that year. In 1801 President Jefferson pardoned all who had been sentenced under the acts and Congress soon repealed them.

---

[23]This is the collective title given to a number of different laws passed by Congress at the time. They arose out of what President John Adams called this nation's "half war" with France. The French navy was seizing American merchant ships in the Atlantic to keep American goods from reaching England, with which France was then at war. The most important of these laws, the Sedition Act of 1798, made it a crime to write, utter, or publish "any false, scandalous, and malicious" statements "with intent to defame" the government or any of its officers or "to incite against them the hatred of the good people of the United States." Violations were punishable by a maximum fine of $2000 and two years in prison. The first person convicted under the acts was Matthew Lyon, a member of Congress from Vermont. He had accused President Adams of "a continual grasp for power . . . an unbounded thirst for ridiculous pomp, foolish adulation and selfish avarice."

Congress passed another sedition law during World War I, as part of the Espionage Act of 1917. That law made it a crime to encourage disloyalty, interfere with the draft, obstruct recruiting, incite insubordination in the armed forces, or hinder the sale of government bonds. It also made it a crime to "willfully utter, print, write or publish any disloyal, profane, scurrilous, or abusive language about the form of government of the United States."

The law was challenged, and upheld, several times. (More than 2000 persons were tried and convicted under its terms.) In the most important of those challenges, *Schenck* v. *United States*, 1919, the Supreme Court laid down the famous *clear and present danger rule.*

Schenck, the general secretary of the Socialist Party, and another party member, had been convicted of trying to obstruct the war effort, in violation of the 1917 law. They had sent some 15,000 strongly worded leaflets to men who had been called to military service, urging them to resist the draft.

The Supreme Court upheld both the law and the convictions. Speaking for the Court, Justice Holmes said:

> We admit that in many places and in ordinary times the defendants in saying all that was said in the circular would have been within their constitutional rights. But the character of every act depends upon the circumstances in which it is done. . . .

And, he then said:

> Words can be weapons. . . . The question in every case is whether the words used are used in such circumstances and are of such nature as to create a clear and present danger that they will bring about the substantive evils [*i.e.,* actions] that Congress has a right to prevent.

In short, the **clear and present danger rule** holds that: words can be outlawed, and those who utter them can be punished when their use creates an immediate danger that criminal acts will follow.

But—and this is the vital nub of the matter—*what* words used in *what* circumstances constitute a clear and present danger? That question can be answered only on the basis of the facts in each case to which the rule is applied.

Congress had made the Espionage Act of 1917 effective only in time of war. In 1940, however, it passed a new sedition law—the Smith Act, and made it applicable in peacetime.[24] It later passed two other such statutes: the Internal Security (McCarran) Act of 1950 and the Communist Control Act of 1954.

The Smith Act makes it unlawful for any person to teach or advocate the violent overthrow of government in the United States, or to organize or knowingly be a member of any group with such an aim. It also forbids **conspiring** (joining, plotting) with others to commit any of those acts.

The Supreme Court first upheld the constitutionality of the Smith Act in *Dennis* v. *United States* in 1951. Eleven of the top leaders of the Communist Party had been convicted of teaching and advocating violent overthrow. On appeal, they argued that the law violated the 1st Amendment's speech and press guarantees. They also claimed that no act of theirs constituted a clear and present danger to this country.

The Court disagreed:

> An attempt to overthrow the government by force, even though doomed from the outset because of inadequate numbers or power of the revolutionists, is a suffi-

---

[24]The Smith Act was passed as the United States moved ever closer to direct involvement in World War II.

cient evil for Congress to prevent. . . . We reject any principle of governmental helplessness in the face of preparation for revolution, which principle, carried to its logical conclusion, must lead to anarchy.

The Court has since modified that holding, however. In several later cases it has sharply limited the use of the Smith Act. Thus, in *Yates* v. *United States*, 1957, it upset the teaching and advocating convictions of a number of lesser party leaders. Their convictions were reversed with this holding: Merely to urge someone to *believe* something, in contrast to urging someone to *do* something, cannot be made illegal. That is, the Smith Act can be applied only to those who teach or advocate *action* to bring about forcible overthrow.

The Court has upheld the "knowing membership" clause of the Smith Act, *Scales* v. *United States*, 1961. But it has also ruled that it is only those who are active members of the Communist Party and those with a "specific intent" to overthrow the government, that the Smith Act intends to punish, *Noto* v. *United States*, 1961. It is not its intent to punish those who are passive, or simply paper-affiliated members of the Communist Party.

The end result of the major Smith Act cases has been this: While the Court has upheld the constitutionality of the law, it has so construed its provisions as to make successful prosecutions under it very difficult.

The McCarran Act has proven to be an even less effective sedition law. Its major provisions require that all "communist-action" and "communist-front" organizations register with the Attorney General. They must report every year, naming their officers and listing all of their members. The act also created the Subversive Activities Control Board, to decide which groups are in fact subject to the law.

The Board first ordered the Communist Party to register in 1953, and the

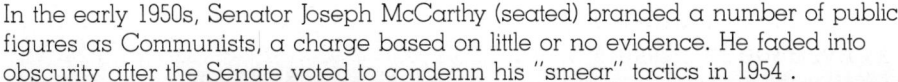

In the early 1950s, Senator Joseph McCarthy (seated) branded a number of public figures as Communists, a charge based on little or no evidence. He faded into obscurity after the Senate voted to condemn his "smear" tactics in 1954 .

Supreme Court held that it could be forced to do so in *Communist Party* v. *SACB*, 1961. It never actually had to do so, however—largely for this reason: Any person who came forward to register the party, as required by the McCarran Act, could then be charged as a "knowing member" under the Smith Act. In 1965 the Court held that no person could be forced into this position. To do so would contradict the 5th Amendment's guarantee against self-incrimination, *Albertson* v. *SACB*, 1965.[25]

The Court further limited the effectiveness of the McCarran Act by holding other parts of it to be unconstitutional. Thus, it struck down a provision denying members of communist organizations the right to obtain or use passports. In *Aptheker* v. *Rusk*, 1964, it found that that section of the law was so broadly and loosely worded that it contradicted the 5th Amendment's Due Process Clause.

The net effect of court response to the McCarran Act has been to leave it a hollow shell. That result was far from unexpected. The several court decisions have parallelled President Truman's veto that Congress overrode in passing the law in the first place.

The Communist Control Act declares the Communist Party in this country to be "a conspiracy to overthrow the Government of the United States." Its goal was to outlaw the Party and keep its candidates off the ballot in any election in this country. As a practical matter, the 1954 law failed in that purpose. In 1980, as in every election since 1968, a Communist Party candidate for President appeared on the ballot in a number of States.

Two factors have made the matter of internal subversion less prominent today than it was only a few years ago. One is the over-all ineffectiveness of the sedition laws. The other, that U.S.—Soviet relations, while still strained, are not as tense as they were in the Cold War period of the 1950s and 1960s.

☑ FOR REVIEW

1. What is sedition? Is it constitutionally protected? How does it differ from espionage, sabotage, or treason?

2. What were the Alien and Sedition Acts? Were they constitutional?

3. What is the "clear and present danger rule"?

4. What is the Smith Act? The McCarran Act? The Communist Control Act? What is the general shape of each of those laws today?

Freedom of Assembly and Petition

The 1st Amendment also guarantees

the right of the people peaceably to assemble, and to petition government for a redress of grievances.

These rights are protected by the 14th Amendment's Due Process Clause, as well. As we noted on page 94, the Supreme Court first made that holding in *DeJonge* v. *Oregon*, 1937—and it has repeated it many times since.[26]

The Constitution here protects the right of the people to assemble—to gath-

---

[25]One practical effect of this decision was to leave the SACB with no real functions to perform. It finally passed out of existence when Congress stopped funding it in 1973.

[26]DeJonge had been convicted of violating the State's law prohibiting acts of "criminal syndicalism" —which the law defined as "the doctrine which advocates crime, physical violence, sabotage, or any unlawful acts" to bring about "industrial or political change or revolution." DeJonge had helped to conduct and had spoken at a public meeting sponsored by the Communist Party. For that behavior alone, he was sentenced to seven years in prison. The Court held that the 14th Amendment includes the rights of assembly and petition, declared the State law unconstitutional, and reversed DeJonge's conviction.

er with one another—to express their views on public matters. It protects their right to organize—as in political parties and pressure groups—to influence public policy. And it protects their right to bring their views to the attention of public officials—by such means as written petitions, letters, or advertisements, lobbying, or parades, marches, or other demonstrations.

But, notice, it is the right of *peaceable* assembly and petition that are guaranteed. The Constitution does not give people the right to incite others to violence, to riot, to block a public street, to close a school, or otherwise to endanger life, property, or public order.

Government may make and enforce *reasonable* rules covering the time, place, and manner of assemblies. It must have that power, in order to keep the public peace. Thus, the Supreme Court has upheld a city ordinance that prohibits making noise or causing any other diversion near a school if that action disturbs normal school activities, *Grayend* v. *City of Rockford,* 1972.

But rules for keeping the public peace must be more than reasonable. They must also be exactly drawn and fairly administered. In *Coates* v. *Cincinnati,* 1971, the Court struck down a city ordinance that made it a crime for three or more persons to assemble on a public sidewalk and there conduct themselves in a manner annoying to passersby. It found that law to be too vague and loosely worded. It also struck down an ordinance that banned all picketing around school buildings, except that picketing involved in a labor dispute. *Police Department of Chicago* v. *Mosley,* 1972. Here the Court found that the ordinance went beyond time-and-place regulation and dealt with the *content* of an assembly.

The responsibility of public officials to control traffic or to keep a demonstra-

tion from growing into a riot can be—and sometimes is—used as an excuse to prevent speech. The line between crowd control and thought control can be very thin—and not always easy to recognize.

Over the past several years, most of the Court's freedom of assembly cases have involved organized demonstrations—mass meetings, parades, marches, sit-ins, picketing, and the like. Demonstrations are, of course, assemblies—ways of communicating ideas and opinions.

Most demonstrations take place in *public* places—on streets and sidewalks, in parks or public buildings, and so on. They do because it is the *public* the demonstrators want to reach. They want to bring their message to those who may not be aware of it, and to reach those who may not agree with them.

Demonstrations almost always involve some degree of conflict. Mostly, they are held to protest something, and so a clash of ideas is present. Many times there is also a conflict with the normal use of streets or other public facilities. It is hardly surprising, then,

The right of free speech is protected by the 1st Amendment, but inciting to riot or disturbing the public peace is not.

that the heat generated by a demonstration can sometimes rise to a very serious level.

Given all of this, the Supreme Court has often upheld State and local laws that require advance notice and permits for demonstrations in public places. In an early leading case, *Cox,* v. *New Hampshire,* 1941, it unanimously approved such a law:

> The authority of a municipality to impose regulations in order to assure the safety and convenience of the people in the use of public highways has never been regarded as inconsistent with civil liberties but rather as one of the means of safeguarding the good order on which they ultimately depend. . . . The question in a particular case is whether the control is exercised so as to deny . . . the right of assembly and the opportunity for the communication of thought and the discussion of public questions.

"Right to demonstrate" cases raise many basic and thorny questions. How and to what extent can demonstrators and their demonstrations be regulated? Does the Constitution require that police officers allow an unpopular group to continue to demonstrate when its activities have excited others to violence? When, in the name of public peace and safety, can police properly order demonstrators to disband?

Among these cases, *Gregory* v. *Chicago,* 1969, remains typical. Dick Gregory and several others had been arrested by Chicago police and charged with disorderly conduct. They had marched, under police protection, singing and chanting and carrying placards, from city hall to the mayor's home, some five miles away. Marching in the streets around the mayor's house, they demanded the firing of the city's school superintendent and an end to *de facto* segregation in the city's schools.

A crowd of several hundred onlookers and residents of the all-white neighborhood quickly gathered. Soon, insults and threats, rocks, eggs, and other missles were thrown at the marchers. The police tried to keep order; but, after about an hour, they decided that serious violence was about to break out. At that point, they ordered the demonstrators to leave the area. When Gregory and the others failed to do so, they were arrested.

Their convictions were unanimously overturned by the High Court. It noted that the marchers had done no more than use their constitutional rights of assembly and petition. The disorders were caused by the neighborhood residents and others, not by the demonstrators. No matter how reasonable the police order, or how laudable the police motives, so long as the demonstrators acted peacefully, as they did, the Court ruled that they could not be punished.[27]

What of demonstrations on private property—for example, at large shopping

"Step Carefully"

LePelly in *The Christian Science Monitor* © TCSPS

DEMOCRATIC PROCESS

MASS MARCHING FOR CAUSES

---

[27]At least not under an ordinance making disorderly conduct a crime—for Gregory and the others had not acted in a disorderly way. But the Court made it clear that its decision might have been different if Chicago had acted under some specifically-drawn time-place-manner ordinance—for example, one forbidding a demonstration in a residential neighborhood after a certain hour in the evening.

Picketers at a supermarket urge customers not to buy lettuce produced on farms that do not employ union workers.

centers? So far, the Court has heard only a few cases raising this question. However, at least this much can be said at this point: The rights of assembly and petition do not give people a right to trespass on private property. They do not have a constitutional right to convert private property to their own uses, even if they try to do so in order to express political views.

Privately owned shopping centers are not public streets, sidewalks, parks, and other "places of public assembly." Because they are not, no one has a constitutional right to do such things as hand out political leaflets or ask people to sign petitions in those places. But, of course, private owners can allow peaceful political activities on their property if they choose to do so.

The comments we have just made are based on the leading case here, *Lloyd Corporation* v. *Tanner*, 1972. However, since that case the Court has held this:

A State supreme court may interpret the provisions of that State's own constitution in such a way as to require the owners of shopping centers to allow the reasonable exercise of the right of peti-

tion on their private property. In that event, there is no violation of the property owners' rights under any provision in the Federal Constitution, *PruneYard Shopping Center* v. *Robbins*, 1980. (In that case, several California high school students had set up a card table in the shopping center, passed out pamphlets, and asked passersby to sign petitions to be sent to the President and Congress.)

☑ **FOR REVIEW**

1. At base, what does the constitutional guarantee of freedom of assembly and petition intend to protect?

2. May government ever regulate the rights of assembly and petition? If so, for what basic purpose?

3. Why do most demonstrations take place in public places? Why do they almost always involve some degree of conflict?

4. Does the Constitution guarantee a right to demonstrate on private property?

S U M M A R Y

The Constitution's many guarantees of civil rights are a major demonstration of the constitutional principle of limited government. Each of them is a prohibition or a restriction on the things that government may do.

Those guarantees are relative, however, not absolute; and, at times, different rights come into conflict with one another. With only minor exceptions, those rights belong to all persons—aliens as well as citizens.

Federalism produces a very complicated pattern of civil rights guarantees in this country. Much of that complication has been lessened over time, however—largely by the Supreme Court's interpretation and application of the 14th Amendment's Due Process Clause. The provisions of the Bill of Rights apply against the National Government *only*. In a now long series of cases, however, the Court has ruled that most of the protections set out in the Bill of Rights (applicable against the National Government) are also within the meaning of the 14th Amendment (and so applicable against the States and their local governments, as well).

No all-inclusive listing of civil rights guarantees is possible; the seldom-noted 9th Amendment assures this. The 1st Amendment protects freedom of expression. In broadest germs, it guarantees freedom of religion (in both the Establishment Clause and the Free Exercise Clause), freedom of speech and press, and freedom of assembly and petition. All of these 1st Amendment protections of the right of expression are extended against the States by the 14th Amendment's Due Process Clause. All of the other constitutional guarantees of civil rights have to do with fair and equal treatment under the law, and we consider those rights in the next chapter.

C H A P T E R   R E V I E W

Key Terms/Concepts

Bill of Rights (90)
Child-benefit theory (100)
Civil rights (90)
Clear and present danger rule (114)
Demonstrations (117)
Due Process Clauses (93)
Espionage (113)
Establishment Clause (95)
Excessive entanglement standard (100)

1st Amendment (95)
14th Amendment (93)
Free Exercise Clause (101)
Freedom of assembly and petition (116)
Freedom of expression (95)
Freedom of religion (95)
Freedom of speech (104)
Freedom of the press (104)

Internal subversion (113)
Libel (105)
Limited government (89)
Nationalization of civil rights (93)
9th Amendment (94)
Obscenity (105)
Parochial schools (97)
Picketing (110)
Prior restraint (106)

Relative nature of civil rights (91)
Sabotage (113)
Secular/Sectarian (100)
Sedition (113)
Separation of church and state (95)
Shield laws (109)
Slander (105)
Symbolic speech (110)
Treason (113)

Keynote Questions

1. Why does each of the many civil rights guaranteed in the Constitution amount to a statement of the principle of limited government?
2. Do all of the many rights guaranteed by the Constitution belong to all persons in the United States?
3. What is the Bill of Rights? Why was it added to the Constitution? When?
4. What is the relationship between the many provisions of the Bill of Rights and the 14th Amendment's Due Process Clause?
5. Why is there nowhere (nor can there be) a complete listing of all of the rights held by the American people?
6. Why are the guarantees set out if the 1st Amendment often called the "fundamental freedoms"?
7. Does the Establishment Clause provide for a complete separation of church and state in this country?
8. What is the basic shape of the guarantee in the Free Exercise Clause?
9. The guarantees of freedom of speech, press, assembly, and petition serve what two fundamentally important democratic purposes?
10. Those guarantees are especially intended to protect the expression of what views? Do they protect all forms of expression?
11. May government ever regulate the exercise of the rights of assembly and petition? If so, for what basic purpose?

For Thought and Discussion

1. Think about each of these comments:

They that can give up liberty in order to obtain a little temporary safety deserve neither liberty nor safety.

Benjamin Franklin.

Those who deny liberty to others deserve it not for themselves.

Abraham Lincoln.

2. Among the many cases cited in this chapter, select three in which you disagree with the Supreme Court's decision. Explain the reason(s) for your disagreement in each case.
3. On page 105, we noted the fact that it is against the law to send obscene materials through the mails, to ship them in interstate commerce, or to import them. How, then, can you explain the fact that "porno shops" are well-supplied with those materials in many places?
4. Do you agree that the law of libel and slander should be more tolerant of criticisms of public officials than of private persons? Why, or why not?
5. What does this observation mean: It is only through the loyalty of free citizens that the freedom of loyal citizens can be preserved?

Suggested Activities

1. Talk with the mayor, city manager, chief of police, and/or other public officials to discover (and then report upon) those measures, if any, that they take to regulate the holding of assemblies (of various kinds) in the streets, parks, auditoriums, and other public places in your community.
2. Talk with all (or at least several) members of the local clergy (ministers, priests, rabbis, and so on) to discover (and then report upon) their attitudes toward tax exemptions for churches and church-related properties in your community.
3. Talk with one or more local newspaper editors and/or radio or television station managers to discover (and then report upon) the precautions they take to avoid suits for libel.
4. Stage a debate or forum on this question: *Resolved,* That those who seek to destroy this country and its free institutions are not entitled to the protections set out in the Constitution.

CHAPTER

6

Civil Rights: Equal Justice Under Law

CHAPTER OBJECTIVES

To help you to
Learn ▪ Know ▪ Understand

The concept of due process of law and its pivotal place in the American system of civil rights.

The many constitutionally guaranteed rights to freedom and security of the person.

The many constitutionally guaranteed rights of persons accused of crime.

The many constitutionally guaranteed rights to equality under the law.

I have a dream that one day this nation will rise up and live out the true meaning of its creed: We hold these truths to be self-evident, that all men are created equal.

Martin Luther King, Jr.

In Chapter 5 we took a close look at the 1st Amendment freedoms—those constitutional guarantees of freedom of expression that lie at the heart of democratic belief and practice. Now we turn to those constitutional guarantees that are intended to ensure fair and equal treatment to all persons under the law.

Though it has had many successes, the American democratic system has not succeeded in extending the guarantees of fair and equal treatment to *all* persons in the United States—and most of all not to blacks or other ethnic minorities. At least it has not *yet* succeeded in doing so. None of our public problems is a more compelling one today.

Due Process of Law

The Constitution contains two Due Process Clauses. The 5th Amendment declares that the Federal Government cannot deprive any person of "life, liberty, or property without due process of law." And the 14th Amendment places the same restriction upon each of the States (and, very importantly, upon all of their local governments, as well).

The aim of the civil rights movement of the 1960s was to show the need for legislation making segregation and discrimination by race unlawful in public places, employment, housing, and voting. Here, marchers walk (in 1965) to Montgomery, Alabama, to show their support for voting rights for blacks.

It has often been said that these two provisions, and their meanings, are harder to understand than any other part of the Constitution. This may be true. But the fact remains that a thorough grasp of them is absolutely essential to an understanding of the American scheme of civil rights.

It is impossible to define the two due process guarantees in exact and complete terms. Over the years, the Supreme Court has quite consistently and purposely refused to give them an exact definition.[1] At base, however, they mean this: Government, in whatever it does, must act *fairly* and in accord with established *rules;* it may not act unfairly, arbitrarily, capriciously, unreasonably.

---

[1] Instead, it has relied on finding the meaning of due process on a case-by-case basis. The Court first described this approach more than a century ago, in *Davidson* v. *New Orleans*, 1878, as the "gradual process of judicial inclusion and exclusion, as the cases presented for decision shall require." It has followed this case-by-case approach ever since.

Procedural and Substantive Due Process

As the two Due Process Clauses have been interpreted and applied by the Supreme Court, the meaning of due process has developed along two lines—one *procedural*, the other *substantive.*

Procedural Due Process. The concept of due process began and developed in English and then American law as a procedural concept. That is, government, in all that it does, must act fairly, use fair procedures.

Substantive Due Process. But fair procedures are of little value if they are used to administer unfair laws. The Supreme Court recognized this fact toward the end of the last century. It began to hold that due process requires that both the ways in which government acts *and* the laws under which it acts must be fair.

In short, these two basic meanings of due process can be put this way: Procedural due process has to do with the *how* (the methods) of governmental action. Substantive due process involves the *what* (the policies) of governmental action.

Many of cases can be used to illustrate these two elements of due process. For now, take *Rochin* v. *California*, 1952, as an illustration of procedural due process.

Rochin was a suspected narcotics pusher. Acting on a tip, three Los Angeles County deputy sheriffs went to his rooming house. They found the outside door to the building open, entered, and then forced their way into Rochin's room. They found him sitting on a bed and spotted two capsules lying on a night stand beside it. When one of the deputies asked "Whose stuff is this?" Rochin grabbed the capsules, popped them into this mouth, and, although all three officers jumped him, was able to swallow them.

Rochin was taken to a hospital, where his stomach was pumped. The capsules were recovered and found to contain morphine. Rochin was then prosecuted for violating the State's narcotics laws. The capsules were to be the chief evidence against him and he was convicted and sentenced to 60 days in jail.

The Supreme Court overturned his conviction. It held that the deputies had violated the 14th Amendment's guarantee of procedural due process. Said the unanimous Court:

> This is conduct that shocks the conscience. Illegally breaking into the privacy of the petitioner, the struggle to open his mouth and remove what was there, the forcible extraction of his stomach's contents—this course of proceeding by agents of government to obtain evidence is bound to offend even hardened sensibilities. They are methods too close to the rack and the screw . . .

As an example of substantive due process, take a case we talked about earlier, *Pierce* v. *Society of Sisters*, 1925. It involved an *initiative* measure.[2] In 1922 the voters of the State of Oregon had adopted a new school attendance law. It required that all persons between the ages of eight and 16 who had not completed the eighth grade had to attend *public* schools. The law's purpose was to destroy the private (and especially the parochial schools) in the State.

A Roman Catholic order challenged the constitutionality of the law. It sued the governor, to prevent him from enforcing it. On appeal, the Supreme Court held that the law violated the 14th Amendment's Due Process Clause.

The Court did not find that the State had enforced the law unfairly. Rather, the Court said that the law itself, in its contents, "unreasonably interferes with the liberty of parents to direct the upbringing and education of children under their control." It also held that the law denied to private school teachers and administrators the liberty to "be engaged in an undertaking . . . long regarded as useful and meritorious."

The 14th Amendment and the Bill of Rights

On pages 93–94 we made the point that the Supreme Court has held that the 14th Amendment's Due Process Clause includes within its meaning many (most) of the provisions of the Bill of Rights. In a long series of decisions, dating from 1925, the Court has *incorporated* those basic rights into the 14th Amendment and thus "nationalized" them. By holding that those rights are protected against the States through the 14th Amendment, as well as against the

---

[2]The **initiative** is a process by which a group may propose a law by gathering signatures on petitions; see page 511.

National Government in the Bill of Rights, the Court has made their meaning uniform throughout the country.

Does all this seem complicated? It is. But an understanding of it is crucial to an understanding of the meaning and importance of the 14th Amendment's Due Process Clause—and so to most of our civil rights law. The landmark cases in which the Supreme Court held that various of the Bill of Rights guarantees are within the meaning of the 14th Amendment are set out in the table on this page.[3]

Due Process and the Police Power
In the federal system, the reserved powers of the States include the very

broad and very important police power —the power of each State to act to protect and promote the public health, public safety, public morals, and general welfare.[4] It is, at base, the power of each State (and its local governments) to safeguard the well-being of its people.

The extent of the police power— what a State can and cannot do in exercising it—is decided by the courts in cases in which the use of that power comes into conflict with personal liberties.

Police power-civil rights cases are fairly common. As courts decide them, they face a very difficult task: They must strike a balance between the needs of society on the one hand, and the rights of the individual, on the other.

[3]We looked at the key 1st Amendment cases in Chapter 5 and we shall look at those involving the 4th through the 8th Amendments over the next several pages in this chapter. As we shall see, the following provisions of the Bill of Rights have *not* been incorporated into the 14th Amendment's Due Process Clause: the 2nd and 3rd Amendments, the 5th Amendment's guarantee of grand jury, and the 7th Amendment's guarantee of jury trial in civil cases.

[4]As the National Government is a government of *delegated* powers, it does not have this broad police power. However, many laws are enacted by Congress under the commerce power and the postal power. Federal laws forbidding the shipment of such items as obscene materials, illicit drugs, and hand guns in interstate commerce or through the mails—are examples of what is sometimes called the "federal police power."

THE NATIONALIZATION OF THE BILL OF RIGHTS

Year	Amendment	Provision Held to be within Meaning of 14th Amendment's Due Process Clause	Case
1925	1st	Freedom of speech	*Gitlow v. New York*
1931	1st	Freedom of press	*Near v. Minnesota*
1937	1st	Freedom of assembly, petition	*DeJonge v. Oregon*
1940	1st	Freedom of religion	*Cantwell v. Connecticut*
1947	1st	Establishment Clause	*Everson v. Board of Education*
1961	4th	Protection from unreasonable searches, seizures	*Mapp v. Ohio*
1962	8th	Prohibition of cruel and unusual punishment	*Robinson v. California*
1963	6th	Right to counsel in criminal cases	*Gideon v. Wainwright*
1964	5th	Protection from self-incrimination	*Mallory v. Hogan*
1965	6th	Right to confront witnesses	*Pointer v. Texas*
1967	6th	Right to speedy trial	*Klopfer v. North Carolina*
1967	6th	Right to obtain witnesses	*Washington v. Texas*
1968	6th	Right to trial by jury in criminal cases	*Duncan v. Louisiana*
1969	5th	Prohibition of double jeopardy	*Benton v. Maryland*

Take, as an example, a matter often involved in drunk driving cases.

Driving while under the influence of intoxicating liquor is a crime in every State. And every State's laws allow the use of one or more tests to find out whether a person arrested and charged with the offense was in fact drunk at the time of the incident. Some of those tests are fairly simple (at least for most sober people)—for example, those in which the accused must walk a straight line or touch the tip of his or her nose. Some are more sophisticated, however—notably the "breathalyzer test" or the drawing of a blood sample to measure the level of alcohol in a person's system.

Question: Does the requirement that one submit to such a test violate that person's rights under the 14th Amendment? Does the test involve an unconstitutional search for and seizure of evidence? Does it amount to forcing a person to testify against himself/herself (unconstitutional compulsory self-incrimination)? Or is the requirement a proper use of the police power?

Time after time, both the State and federal courts have come down on the side of the police power here. They have consistently upheld the right of society to protect itself against the drunk driver and turned down the individual rights argument.

The leading case here is *Schmerber* v. *California,* 1966. The Supreme Court found no constitutional objection to a situation in which a police officer had directed a doctor to draw blood from a man he had arrested for drunk driving. The Court stressed these points: The blood sample was drawn in a hospital and in accord with accepted medical practice. The police officer had reasonable grounds to believe that the suspect was drunk. And, had the officer taken time to secure a search warrant, the evidence could very well have disappeared from the suspect's system.

Here are but a few more examples, to show the very large number of situations that involve a valid exercise of the police power:

To promote health, States have been permitted to forbid or limit the sale of intoxicants and dangerous drugs, forbid the practice of medicine or dentistry without a license, and require the compulsory vaccination of school children.

To promote safety, States have been permitted to forbid the carrying of concealed weapons, require adequate brakes, horns, lights, and shatter-proof glass on cars, and prohibit tall shrubs at street intersections.

To promote morals, States have been permitted to outlaw gambling, the sale of obscene materials, and prostitution, and forbid such establishments as taverns and adult book stores in certain locations.

To promote welfare, States have been permitted to enact minimum wage and maximum hours laws, hold public utilities to reasonable profits, and forbid the operation of certain businesses on Sundays.

Again, note the fact that though the States can regulate many activities through the police power, they cannot use that power in an unreasonable or unfair manner. Thus, a police officer may not use unnecessary force to make a person accused of drunk driving submit to a blood test. A city could not forbid a street demonstration by some group just because the mayor opposes its political aims. Nor could a State ban the operation of private schools or the sale of all foreign-made automobiles.

 FOR REVIEW

1. Why does the Constitution contain two Due Process Clauses?
2. At base, what does due process of law mean?
3. Distinguish between *procedural* and *substantive* due process.
4. What is the relationship between the Bill of Rights and the 14th Amendment's Due Process Clause?
5. What is a State's police power?

The Right to Freedom and Security of the Person

Slavery and Involuntary Servitude

The 13th Amendment was added to the Constitution in 1865. It brought to an end more than 200 years of Negro slavery in this country.

Section 1 of the Amendment states:

> Neither slavery nor involuntary servitude, except as a punishment for crime, whereof the party shall have been duly convicted, shall exist within the United States, or any place subject to their jurisdiction.

A Washington, D.C., fire inspector checks an apartment building for violations of city fire-prevention and fire-safety standards.

And, importantly, Section 2 gives Congress the expressed power "to enforce this article by appropriate legislation."

Until 1865, each State could decide for itself whether or not to allow slavery within its borders. With the 13th Amendment, that power was denied to them, of course—and to the National Government, as well.

Section 1 of the Amendment is self-executing. That is, no action by Congress was needed to make it effective. Nonetheless, Congress has passed several laws to implement it; and a violation of them can lead to a fine of up to $5000 and/or as much as five years in prison.

As a widespread practice, slavery disappeared nearly 120 years ago. There are still occasional cases of it, however. As recently as 1981, in fact, a federal court in North Carolina sentenced a leader of a small religious sect to 20 years in prison for the crime. Over a period of some four years, he had held eight teen-age members of his congregation as his slaves.

CIVIL RIGHTS GUARANTEES IN THE FEDERAL CONSTITUTION

Protections Against the National Government

—Writ of *habeas corpus* not to be suspended except during rebellion or invasion. *Article I, Section 9, Clause 2.*

—No bills of attainder. *Article I, Section 9, Clause 3.*

—No *ex post facto* laws. *Article I, Section 9, Clause 3.*

—Treason strictly defined and punishment limited. *Article III, Section 3.*

—No establishment of religion. *1st Amendment.*

—No interference with religious belief. *1st Amendment.*

—No abridgement of freedom of speech or press. *1st Amendment.*

—No interference with right of peaceable assembly or petition. *1st Amendment.*

—No interference with right of people to keep and bear arms. *2nd Amendment.*

—Soldiers not to be quartered in private homes in time of peace without owners' consent. *3rd Amendment.*

—No unreasonable searches, seizures; no warrants but upon probable cause. *4th Amendment.*

—No criminal prosecution but upon grand jury action. *5th Amendment.*

—No double jeopardy. *5th Amendment.*

—No compulsory self-incrimination. *5th Amendment.*

—No person to be deprived of life, liberty, property without due process of law. *5th Amendment.*

—Trials to be speedy, public. *6th Amendment.*

—Trial of crimes by impartial jury. *Article III, Section 2; 6th Amendment.*

—Persons accused of crime must be informed of charges, confronted with witnesses, have power to call witnesses, have assistance of counsel. *6th Amendment.*

—Jury trial of civil suits involving more than $20. *7th Amendment.*

—No excessive bail or fines. *8th Amendment.*

—No cruel and unusual punishment. *8th Amendment.*

—No slavery or involuntary servitude. *13th Amendment.*

Protections Against States (and Their Local Governments)

—No bills of attainder. *Article I, Section 10, Clause 1.*

—No *ex post facto* laws. *Article I, Section 10, Clause 1.*

—No slavery or involuntary servitude. *13th Amendment.*

—No denial or privileges and immunities to citizens of other States. *Article IV, Section 2, Clause 1; 14th Amendment.*

—No person to be deprived of life, liberty, property without due process of law. *14th Amendment.*

—No person to be denied equal protection of the laws. *14th Amendment.*

Most of the cases that have arisen under Section 1 have turned on the question of "involuntary servitude"— that is, forced labor. The Antipeonage Act of 1867 makes it a federal crime for any person to hold another in peonage— a condition of servitude in which a person is bound to work for another in order to fulfill a contract or satisfy a debt. It is still vigorously enforced.

Several times, the Supreme Court has struck down State laws making it a crime for any person to fail to work after having received money or other benefits by promising to do so. In destroying one of these State peonage laws, the Supreme Court said:

> The undoubted aim of the 13th Amendment as implemented by the Antipeonage Act was not merely to end slavery but to maintain a system of completely free and voluntary labor throughout the United States.[5]

The 13th Amendment does not forbid *all* forms of involuntary servitude, however. Thus, in 1918 the Court drew a distinction between "involuntary servitude" and "duty" in upholding the constitutionality of the selective service system (the draft).[6] Nor does imprisonment for crime violate the Amendment, as its own terms declare. And note that its guarantee, unlike any other in the Constitution, applies against *private* as well as public actions.

Section 2. Shortly after the Civil War, Congress passed several civil rights laws, based on the 13th Amendment and applicable to both public officials *and*

private parties. But in several cases (especially the *Civil Rights Cases*, 1883) the Supreme Court sharply narrowed the scope of federal authority. In effect, the Court held that racial discrimination against blacks by private persons did not place the "badge of slavery" on blacks nor keep them in servitude.

Congress soon repealed most of those laws; and federal enforcement of the few that remained was, at best, unimpressive. For years it was generally believed that Congress did not have the power under the 13th (or the 14th) Amendment to deal directly with private parties who practice racial discrimination.

In *Jones* v. *Mayer*, 1968, however, the Supreme Court breathed new life into the 13th Amendment. The case centered on one of the post-Civil War acts Congress had not repealed. Passed in 1866, that almost forgotten law provided in part that:

> All citizens of the United States shall have the same right in every State and Territory, as is enjoyed by white citizens thereof, to inherit, purchase, lease, sell, hold, and convey real and personal property.

Jones had sued because Mayer had refused to sell him a home in St. Louis County, Missouri, solely because he was black. Mayer contended that the 1866 law was unconstitutional, as it sought to prohibit *private* racial discrimination.

The Court, 7–2, decided for Jones. It upheld the law, declaring that the 13th Amendment abolished slavery *and* gives to Congress the power to abolish "the badges and the incidents of slavery," as well. Said the Court:

> At the very least, the freedom that Congress is empowered to secure under the 13th Amendment includes the freedom to buy whatever a white man can buy, the

---

[5] *Pollock* v. *Williams*, 1944; but note that the fact that a person cannot be forced to work in order to satisfy a debt does *not* relieve that person of the legal obligation to pay the debt.

[6] *Selective Draft Law Cases (Arver* v. *United States)*, 1918. The Court held military conscription to be a proper exercise of the power of Congress "to raise and support armies," Article I, Section 8, Clause 12.

A police officer does not need a warrant to search an individual believed to be carrying a concealed weapon in violation of the law.

The 4th Amendment also grew out of colonial practice. It was designed to prevent the use of **writs of assistance**—blanket search warrants, with which customs officials had gone into private homes to search for smuggled goods.

Unlike the 3rd Amendment, the 4th has proved a highly important guarantee. It reads:

> The right of the people to be secure in their persons, houses, papers, and effects, against unreasonable searches and seizures, shall not be violated, and no warrants shall issue, but upon probable cause, supported by oath or affirmation, and particularly describing the place to be searched, and the persons or things to be seized.

Each of the State Constitutions has a similar provision. Remember, too, the guarantee applies to the States through the 14th Amendment's Due Process Clause.

The general rule laid down by the 4th Amendment is this: Police must have a proper **warrant** (a court order) before they can make a search for or a seizure of evidence or persons.

But, notice, only *unreasonable* searches and seizures are prohibited by the 4th Amendment. There are some situations in which lawful searches and seizures may take place *without* a warrant.

For example: No warrant is necessary when police are in "hot pursuit" of a suspect. In *United States* v. *Santana,* 1976, the Supreme Court upheld the arrest, the search that was made, and the later conviction of a woman whom police had first spotted standing outside her home. The officers, who were there to arrest her on a heroin charge, pursued and caught her just inside. There they arrested her. In searching her, they found both heroin and the marked bills with which an undercover agent had only minutes earlier made a buy. Because all of this had taken place without a warrant, she argued that her arrest and the search conducted in her home was prohibited by the 4th Amendment.

An arrest is the "seizure" of a person. When a lawful one is made, officers do not need a warrant to search "the arrestee's person and the area within his immediate control"—that is, "the area within which he might gain possession of a weapon or destructible evidence."[8]

Nor do police need a warrant to search an automobile, a boat, an airplane, or other vehicle they have good reason to believe contains evidence of a crime or is being used to commit one—because such a "movable scene of crime" could disappear while the warrant was being sought.[9] *But*, notice, police cannot stop a motorist "at random." They must *first* have good reason to believe that a law is being broken, *Delaware* v. *Prouse*, 1979. Once they do stop a car in connection with a crime, however, they may search any container in that car that they think might contain evidence of the crime involved, *United States* v. *Ross*, 1982.

Nor is a warrant needed to seize evidence "in plain view"—for example, a bag of marijuana found during the routine inventory of a car's contents after it had been impounded for parking violations, *South Dakota* v. *Opperman*, 1976.

Look at a recent case to illustrate the line between warrantless searches which are lawful and those which are not. In *Michigan* v. *Tyler*, 1978, the Court set aside the arson convictions of two furniture dealers. Much of the evidence against them had come from two separate sets of warrantless searches. One set had taken place as the fire department fought a blaze in their store and immediately thereafter. The other searches were made some weeks later.

The Court found that a burning building presents an emergency situation—one in which a warrantless entry is clearly reasonable. And it held that the firefighters, once inside the store, could seize any evidence in plain view.

But it also held that the later searches, made *well after* the emergency, and also made without warrants, violated the 4th and 14th Amendments.

The Exclusionary Rule.   The real heart of the search and seizure guarantee lies in the answer to this question: *If an unlawful search or seizure does occur, what use can be made of the evidence that is found?*

If it can be used in court, the 4th Amendment's guarantee offers no real protection for one accused of crime. The officers who committed the illegal act might be punished. But that punishment would give no particular help to the person being tried on the basis of the evidence they had turned up.

To make the guarantee really effective, courts now follow the **exclusionary rule**, first laid down by the Supreme Court in *Weeks* v. *United States*, 1914. By that rule, any evidence gained from an unlawful search or seizure cannot be used in court.

In *Weeks* the Court held that evidence gained from an illegal search or seizure made by federal officers could not be used in the federal courts. For more than 40 years, however, it left the question of the use of such evidence in State courts for each of the States to decide for themselves. But, in a historic decision in 1961, *Mapp* v. *Ohio*, the Court extended the exclusionary rule against the States.

In the case, Cleveland police officers had gone to Dollree Mapp's home to search for gambling materials. They entered the house over her objections, forcibly, and without a warrant. Though they carried out a widespread search,

---

[8]The Supreme Court has had much trouble with setting the limits to which a search incident to a lawful arrest can be carried. The present rule, quoted here, was first laid down in *Chimel* v. *California*, 1969.

[9]But in the leading case on the point, *Carroll* v. *United States*, 1925, the Court emphasized that "where the securing of a warrant is reasonably practicable it must be used . . . In cases where seizure is impossible except without a warrant, the seizing officer acts unlawfully and at his peril unless he can show the court probable cause."

they turned up no gambling evidence. But they did find some obscene books, the possession of which Ohio law prohibited. Miss Mapp was later convicted of possession of the books and sentenced to jail. On appeal, the Court overturned her conviction—because the evidence against her had been found without a search warrant.

In short, the 4th and 14th Amendments generally forbid the use of evidence secured by any unlawful search or seizure in *any* court in the land.[10]

To apply all of this, look again at *Michigan* v. *Tyler*. There the Court ordered that the two furniture dealers be retried—and that, at their new trial, all evidence seized during the second set of searches not be presented.

Wiretapping. Wiretapping, electronic eavesdropping, videotaping, and other even more sophisticated means of "bugging" are now quite widely used. They present difficult search and seizure questions for the courts, questions that the framers of the 4th Amendment could not even begin to imagine.

In its first wiretapping case, in 1928, the Supreme Court held that intercepting telephone conversations without a warrant was not unreasonable search or seizure. In 1967 it reversed that decision, however, holding that such communications are within the 4th Amendment's protection.

The earlier case, <u>Olmstead v. United States</u>, 1928, involved a large ring of

Highly sophisticated equipment is needed in order to find out if a telephone is being tapped.

bootleggers operating out of Seattle. Federal agents had tapped Olmstead's telephone calls over several months. That bugging produced a mass of evidence that was then used to convict him and others in the ring. The Supreme Court upheld their convictions. It ruled that even though the agents had had no warrants they had not made any illegal searches or seizures. It found that there had been no "actual physical invasion" of Olmstead's home or office; the agents had tapped the lines *outside* those places.[11]

Congress reacted to the Court's decision in *Olmstead* in one part of the Federal Communications Act of 1934. Referring to radio, telegraph, and telephone communications, it prohibited any person to "intercept any communication and divulge or publish" its contents.

In several later cases the Supreme Court held that that law effectively banned the use of wiretap evidence in

---

[10]Of late, the Supreme Court has been narrowing the exclusionary rule, however. For example, it does not apply to federal grand jury proceedings, *United States* v. *Calandra*, 1974. Thus illegally obtained evidence that cannot be used at a person's trial could nonetheless have been presented to the grand jury (the body that indicted—brought the accusation against—that person and so caused the trial). The Court has also held that evidence against a defendant that was gained by an illegal search of *another* person's property is not "tainted"—i.e., can be used, *United States* v. *Payner*, 1980. Payner was convicted of tax evasion; an IRS agent had stolen some papers from a banker's briefcase, and those papers had led to the evidence of Payner's crime.

---

[11]In a vigorous dissent, Justice Oliver Wendell Holmes was strongly critical of "such dirty business"—federal agents acting without a warrant. He wrote: "For my part I think it is a less evil that some criminals should escape than that the government should play such an ignoble part."

the federal courts. (But note that what the 1934 law prohibited was to intercept *and* divulge; thus wiretapping could, and did, go on. In the eyes of many, that practice amounted to a most serious and unjustifiable invasion of privacy. That view was supported by the widespread bugging activities of the FBI and the CIA in the 1960s and early 1970s.)

The Supreme Court expressly overruled *Olmstead* in *Katz* v. *United States*, in 1967. Katz had been found guilty of transmitting betting information across State lines, from a public phone booth in Los Angeles to his contacts in Boston and Miami. Much of the evidence against him had come from an electronic listening and recording device FBI agents had placed on the outside of the booth. The Court of Appeals, using the *Olmstead* rule, held that there had been no need for a warrant because there had been "no physical entrance into the area occupied" by the defendant. (But the Court also noted that the 4th Amendment could be satisfied in such cases if law enforcement officers have a proper warrant *before* they install a listening device.)

But the Supreme Court reversed the conviction and, in doing so, overruled *Olmstead*. It held, 7–1, that the 4th Amendment protects *persons* and not just places. Though Katz was in a public, glass-enclosed booth, he was constitutionally entitled to the making of a *private* telephone call. Said the Court:

> What a person knowingly exposes to the public, even in his own home or office, is not a subject of 4th Amendment protection. . . . But what he seeks to preserve as private, even in an area accessible to the public, may be constitutionally protected.

Congress reacted to *Katz* in certain parts of the Omnibus Crime Control Act of 1968. Those parts amended the Communications Act of 1934. They make it illegal for any unauthorized person to tap telephone wires or use electronic bugging devices or sell those devices in interstate commerce.

The 1968 law does allow federal and State police agencies to search for and seize evidence by electronic means, however—under close court control. If officers can show **probable cause** (reliable evidence that a law is being violated), a federal or State judge may issue a warrant for a bugging operation.[12]

When it passed the 1968 law, Congress carefully avoided this knotty question: Does the President, acting under the inherent power to protect the nation against foreign attack and internal subversion, have the power to order the wiretapping or other bugging of suspected foreign agents or domestic subversives without a warrant? For many years, several Presidents had used the FBI, the CIA, and other federal police agencies in just that way.

However, the Supreme Court has since ruled that the President has no such power in cases of domestic subversion, *United States* v. *United States District Court*, 1972. And in the Foreign Intelligence Surveillance Act of 1978 Congress, for the first time, required a warrant even for the wiretapping or other electronic bugging of foreign agents in this country.[13]

---

[12]In certain "emergency" situations, especially those involving national security or organized crime, the Attorney General can authorize bugging operations by federal agents for up to 48 hours without a judge's approval—that is, without a warrant. A warrant must be sought during that period, however.

[13]The 1978 law set up a special federal court, the Foreign Intelligence Surveillance Court, with the power to issue such warrants. It is made up of seven U.S. District Court judges appointed by the Chief Justice and its proceedings are secret.

The law allows only one exception to its warrant requirement: The National Security Agency (the Defense Department's top-secret code-making and code-breaking agency) does not need a warrant to eavesdrop on the electronic communications of foreign governments.

A CASE IN POINT

GUN CONTROL: YES OR NO?

The mere mention of gun control laws—of measures to restrict or prohibit the ownership of firearms—sparks intense debate nearly everywhere today.

Suppose that you are a member of your city's council and now—at today's council meeting—you must vote on a gun control ordinance. Your six colleagues on the council are evenly divided on the question. Three of them are for the measure and the other three oppose it. Your vote will decide the matter.

The proposed ordinance has been carefully drawn. It would apply only to handguns. At base, it would outlaw the private possession, use, or sale of nearly all such weapons within the city. The only exceptions to the ban would be those handguns which are kept in gun collections or those used only for target-shooting purposes.

You have been bombarded by arguments, pro and con—at several long, crowded, and often stormy council sessions, in the newspapers, on television, and in many other places.

Most of those who support the ordinance have argued that its adoption would help to reduce violent crime in your city. They have built much of their case on the FBI's crime reports. They show that handguns are now used to commit more than 12,000 murders, 140,000 aggravated assaults, and 180,000 robberies in this country every year.

Many of those who want to see the ordinance passed have said that they are most deeply concerned about "Saturday-night specials"—that is, about those small, cheaply made, and easily concealed pistols which, they say, are the weapons most often used by criminals.

But most of them are deeply troubled by *all* handguns. They claim (again with FBI support) that there are now some 50 million handguns in circulation in the United States. That mind-boggling number, they say—the sheer, all-too-ready availability of those weapons—is itself a major cause of violent crime. As one of them put it at the last council meeting: "If you pass this ordinance, it will be much more difficult for the bad guys to get hold of guns; and it's a heckuva lot harder to rob a bank with a knife or a baseball bat than it is to do that job with a pistol."

The opponents of the measure have made a strong case, too. Nearly all of them have cited the 2nd Amendment and what they insist is the Constitution's guarantee of their right to keep and bear arms. But most of them have also developed a number of other points.

They have said that the anti-gun people are aiming at the wrong target: that *guns* don't kill people, *people* kill people. They have also argued that criminals will always find guns somewhere, even if they are outlawed, and that the only thing this law would do is make it more difficult for decent people to defend themselves against the criminals in your city.

And one of the measure's opponents took the FBI's statistics and turned them back on its proponents: "If you look closely at the FBI's data," he said, "you will see that the average American citizen can expect to live for at least 23,000 years before he or she is murdered."

There were other points made, on both sides. But these were the major ones, and now the debate is over. And now you must cast your vote. What will it be?

Right to Keep and Bear Arms

The 2nd Amendment reads this way: A well regulated militia being necessary to the security of a free state, the right of the people to keep and bear arms shall not be infringed.

Read those words again, and very carefully—because the 2nd Amendment is a very widely misunderstood part of the Bill of Rights. Its words were added to the Constitution *solely* to pro-

A billboard in Florida reminds people of the penalty for illegal possession of handguns. *Inset:* Some contend that such laws deny them 2nd-Amendment rights.

tect the right of each State to keep a militia. It was intended to preserve the concept of the citizen-solider—the "minuteman," as its text clearly suggests. It does not guarantee to any person the "right to keep and bear arms" free from any restriction by government; nor was it written to do so.

The Amendment has no real significance today—*except* for its propaganda weight in arguments over gun control.

The only important Supreme Court case dealing with the meaning of the 2nd Amendment was decided more than 40 years ago. In *United States* v. *Miller*, 1939, the Court upheld the constitutionality of a section of the National Firearms Act of 1934. That section of the law makes it a crime for any person to ship a sawed-off shotgun, a machine gun, or a silencer across State lines unless he or she has registered the weapon with the Treasury Department and paid a $200 tax on it. The Court said that it could find no reasonable relationship between the sawed-off shotgun involved in the case and "the preservation and efficiency of a well regulated militia."

The Court has never found the 2nd Amendment to be within the meaning of the 14th Amendment's Due Process Clause. Thus, each of the States may limit the right to keep and bear arms—and all of them do, in various ways.

Courtesy of *The Chicago Tribune*—New York News Syndicate, Inc.

"What we need is a strict club control law!"

☑ **FOR REVIEW**

1. Why does the 13th Amendment not forbid *all* forms of involuntary servitude?

2. Why is Section 2 of the Amendment so important?

3. How has the Supreme Court recently "breathed new life" into the Amendment?

4. Why is the 3rd Amendment of so little importance?

5. What does the 4th Amendment prohibit?

6. What is the exclusionary rule? Does it apply against the States?

7. Can evidence gained by wiretapping or other electronic bugging be used in court?

8. Why does the 2nd Amendment have much political but little legal significance today?

Rights of Persons Accused of Crime

The Federal Constitution and each of the State constitutions set out several guarantees of fair treatment for those persons who are accused of crime. As we look at these protections, keep these fundamentally important points in mind:

Crimes are legal wrongs, wrongs against the public. They are acts which the law prohibits, and for which the law provides punishment. Those persons who commit them harm *not only* their immediate victims; they do harm to *all* persons—to the people, as a whole. Criminals deserve to be punished; and society *must* punish them in order to preserve itself.

The law intends to protect *all* persons in criminal matters—*including* those persons who are suspected or accused of crime. Each of the protections to which we now turn are rooted in this historic concept: Any person who is suspected or accused of a crime must be presumed to be *innocent*—unless and until that person is *proved* guilty, by fair and lawful means.

Habeas Corpus

The **writ of habeas corpus**—sometimes called the "writ of liberty"—is intended to prevent unjust arrests and imprisonments.[14] It is a court order directed to an officer holding a prisoner. It commands that the prisoner be brought before the court and that the officer show **cause** (explain, with good reason) why the prisoner should not be released. If that cause cannot be shown, the court will then order that the prisoner be freed.

The right to seek a writ of *habeas corpus* is protected against the National Government in Article I, Section 9 of the Constitution. It is guaranteed against the States in each of their own constitutions.

The right to the writ cannot be suspended, says the Constitution, "unless when in cases of rebellion or invasion the public safety may require it." But the Constitution does not make clear if the right may be suspended throughout the country or, instead, only in those areas which are the actual scenes of rebellion or invasion.[15]

---

[14]The phrase *habeas corpus* comes from the Latin, meaning "you should have the body"—and those are the opening words of the writ. The writ is almost always directed to a public official—a sheriff, a jailer, or other such public officer; it may also be used in disputes between private parties, however.

[15]President Lincoln suspended the writ in 1861, early in the Civil War. His order covered various parts of the country, including several areas in which war was not then being waged. He issued the order on the basis of his military powers as Commander in Chief. Chief Justice Roger B. Taney sitting as a circuit judge, held Lincoln's action unconstitutional. Taney ruled that the Constitution gives the power to suspend the writ only to Congress, *Ex parte Merryman*, 1861. Congress then passed the Habeas Corpus Act of 1863; it gave the President the power to suspend the writ when and where in his judgment, that action was necessary.

Whether the writ may be suspended where there is no actual fighting, or not likely to be any, was considered by the Supreme Court in *Ex parte Milligan* in 1866. The full Court agreed that the President could not do so, and a majority of five justices also held that even Congress does not have that power.

The right to the writ has been suspended only once since the Civil War—in Hawaii during World War II. The Supreme Court later held that action illegal.[16]

Bills of Attainder

A bill of attainder is a legislative act which inflicts punishment without a court trial. Neither Congress nor the States can pass such measures.[17]

The ban on bills of attainder is both a protection of individual freedom *and* a part of the system of separation of powers. A legislative body may decide what conduct is criminal. That is, it may pass laws that define crime and set the penalties that may be imposed on those persons who are found to have broken those laws. But it *cannot* exercise the *judicial* function; it cannot decide that a person is guilty of a crime and then impose a punishment upon that person.

The Supreme Court has held that the prohibition is aimed at all legislative acts which apply "to named individuals or to easily ascertainable members of a group in such a way as to inflict punishment on them without a judicial trial," *United States* v. *Lovett*, 1946.

The Framers put the ban on bills of attainder in the Constitution because both Parliament and the colonial legislatures had passed many of them. They have been rare in our history, however.

United States v. *Brown* 1965, is one of the few cases, and the latest, in which the Court has struck down a law as a bill of attainder. There it overturned a part of the Landrum-Griffin Act of 1959 which made it a federal crime for a member of the Communist Party to serve as an officer of a labor union.

Ex Post Facto Laws

An *ex post facto law* has three features. It is (1) a *criminal* law, one defining a crime or providing for its punishment; (2) a law that is applied *retroactively*—that is, to an act committed *before* its passage; and (3) a law which works to the *disadvantage* of the accused. Neither Congress nor the State legislatures may pass such laws.[18]

For example, a law making it a crime to sell marijuana cannot be applied to one who sold it *before* that law was passed. (A person who sold it after the law was passed could be punished under it, of course.) Or, a law which changed the penalty for murder from life in prison to death could not be applied to a person who committed a murder before the punishment was changed; he/she has to be sentenced under the old law.

There are occasional *ex post facto* cases. The Supreme Court hears one every other year or so. In 1981, in *Weaver* v. *Graham*, it held that Florida ran afoul of the constitutional ban. The State had changed its rules for figuring the time off for good behavior to be subtracted from penitentiary terms and had then applied the new rules to prisoners doing time for crimes committed before the law was changed.

Retroactive civil laws are *not* forbidden. For example, a law raising income tax rates could be passed in November

---

[16]The Hawaiian Islands were put under martial law (military government) by the territorial governor immediately after the Japanese attack on Pearl Harbor, December 7, 1941. His order was issued with the approval of President Roosevelt. It suspended the writ of *habeas corpus* and also replaced all civilian courts with military tribunals.

In *Duncan* v. *Kohanamoku*, 1946, the Supreme Court held that the governor's order had been too sweeping. The Court's decision was not based on the constitutional provision, however. Instead, it found that in the Hawaiian Organic Act of 1900, under which the governor had acted, Congress had not intended to allow so great a subordination of civil to military authority.

[17]Article I, Sections 9 and 10.

[18]Article I, Sections 9 and 10. The phrase *ex post facto* is from the Latin, meaning "after the fact."

and made to apply to income earned through the whole year.

☑ FOR REVIEW

1. What is a crime? Why must society punish criminals?
2. What is a writ of *habeas corpus?* When may the right to the writ be suspended?
3. What is a bill of attainder? An *ex post facto* law? Who cannot make such laws?

The right to be represented by counsel is a fundamental part of the right to a fair trial. Here, a client meets with his lawyer.

Right to a Fair Trial

The Bill of Rights has several guarantees relating to fair trial in the federal courts.[19] A fair trial is guaranteed in the State courts by a State's own constitution and by the 14th Amendment's Due Process Clause.

Double Jeopardy. The 5th Amendment says, in part, that no person shall be "twice put in jeopardy of life or limb." The taking of a life or the cutting off of an arm, leg, ear, or some other "limb" was a common punishment in ancient times. The old English phrase "life or limb" was carried into our Constitution.

Today, the provision means, in plain language, that once a person has been tried for a crime he or she may not be tried again for that same crime. This needs some elaboration, however.

A single act may break both a national *and* a State law—such as kidnapping or peddling narcotics. The accused may be tried for the federal crime in a federal court and for the State crime in a State court.

A single act may also result in the commission of several different crimes. One who breaks into a store at night, steals liquor, and later sells it, can be tried on at least three separate counts—for illegal entry, theft, and selling liquor without a license.

In a trial in which a jury cannot agree on a verdict, there is no "jeopardy." It is as though no trial had been held, and the accused may be tried again. Nor is double jeopardy involved when a case is appealed to a higher court.[20]

Grand Jury. The 5th Amendment also provides that:

> No person shall be held to answer for a capital, or otherwise infamous, crime, unless on a presentment or indictment of a grand jury. . . .

[19]See the 5th, 6th, 7th, and 8th Amendments and also Article III, Section 2, Clause 3. The practice of excluding evidence obtained in violation of the 4th Amendment is also intended to guarantee a fair trial.

[20]The Organized Crime Control Act of 1970 allows federal prosecutors to appeal sentences they believe to be too lenient; they may seek stiffer punishments in the Court of Appeals. The Supreme Court has held that such appeals do not violate the double jeopardy guarantee, *United States* v. *DiFrancesco,* 1980. The case involved a "hardened habitual criminal" who had been sentenced to a total of 10 years for the crimes of arson-for-hire, fraud, and bombing a federal building.

The **grand jury** is, then, the formal device by which a person may be accused of a serious federal crime. It is a body of from 16 to 23 persons drawn from the area of the federal district court which it serves. The votes of at least 12 of the grand jurors are needed to return an indictment or make a presentment.[21] An **indictment** is a formal complaint laid before a grand jury by the prosecutor (the United States Attorney). It charges the accused with one or more federal crimes. If the grand jury finds that there is enough evidence for a trial, it returns a "true bill of indictment." The accused is then held for prosecution. If the grand jury does not make such a finding, the charge is dropped.

A **presentment** is a formal accusation brought by the grand jury on its own motion—rather than at the instance of the United States Attorney. It is little used in federal courts.

A grand jury's proceedings are not a trial, and since unfair harm could come if they were held in public, its sessions are secret. They are also one-sided (in the law: *ex parte*). That is, only the prosecution, not the defense, is present.

The 5th Amendment's grand jury provision is the only part of the Bill of Rights relating to criminal prosecution which the Supreme Court has not brought within the coverage of the 14th Amendment's Due Process Clause. In fact, the Court specifically rejected that notion in *Hurtado* v. *California*, in 1887. The States may use any fair method of accusation they choose.

The right to grand jury is intended as a protection against over-zealous prosecutors. But its use long has been the subject of criticism. Its critics say that it is too time-consuming, too expensive, and too likely to follow the dictates of the prosecutor. It has been abolished in England, where it began. In most of the States today most criminal charges are not brought by grand juries, but rather by an **information**—an affidavit in which the prosecutor swears that there is enough evidence to justify a trial; see page 565.

Speedy and Public Trial. The 6th Amendment commands that:

> In all criminal prosecutions, the accused shall enjoy the right to a speedy and public trial. . . .

The guarantee of a speedy trial is meant to insure that one accused of crime will be tried in a reasonable time, without undue delay. It seeks to prevent the accused from being forced to languish in jail while awaiting trial. It is also intended to prevent delays that could hinder the ability to mount an adequate defense.

The 6th Amendment's guarantee is of a prompt trial in *federal* cases. The Supreme Court first declared the right to apply against the States through the 14th Amendment in *Klopfer* v. *North Carolina*, 1967.

A trial must take place promptly, without undue delay. But how long a delay is too long? The Supreme Court has long recognized that there can be no pat answer to that question. No two cases are the same, and each must be looked at in its own light. In *Barker* v. *Wingo*, 1972, the Court did list four considerations which must be taken into account: the length of the delay; the reasons for it; whether the delay did in fact harm the defendant; and whether or not the defendant asked for a prompt trial. (Notice that a delay can work in *favor* of a defendant. For example, witnesses for the prosecution might die or

---

[21]Congress has provided that one may *waive* (put aside) the right to grand jury if he or she chooses. When, as increasingly, this happens, the trial goes forward on the basis of an accusation (an *information*) filed by the United States Attorney.

for some other reason become unavailable, or their memories might fade or become faulty.)

Congress has recently acted to make the speedy trial guarantee stronger. The Speedy Trial Act of 1974 sets a deadline for the start of a federal criminal trial. Since 1980, the time span between a person's arrest and the beginning of his or her trial cannot be more than 100 days. If that deadline is not met, the judge is to dismiss the case. (The law does allow certain exceptions—such as when the defendant must undergo a long mental examination, or the defendant or a key witness is ill.)

The 6th Amendment says that a "speedy" trial must also be a "public" trial. The right to be tried in public, not in secret, is an essential part of the 14th Amendment's guarantee of procedural due process. "The guarantee has always been recognized as a safeguard against any attempt to employ our courts as instruments of persecution," *In re Oliver*, 1948.

A trial must not be *too* speedy or *too* public, however. The Supreme Court threw out an Arkansas murder conviction in 1923 on just those grounds. In *Moore* v. *Dempsey*, five black men had been sentenced to death for the killing of a white man. Their trial had taken only 45 minutes, and it had been held in a courtroom packed by an angry and threatening mob.

Within reason, a judge may limit both the number and the kinds of spectators who may be present at a trial. The unruly, and especially those who seek to disrupt a courtroom, may be barred from it. And a courtroom may be cleared when testimony that may be embarassing to a witness or to someone else not a party to the case is to be given.

Many of the hard questions about how public a trial should be involve the news media. As we noted in Chapter 5,

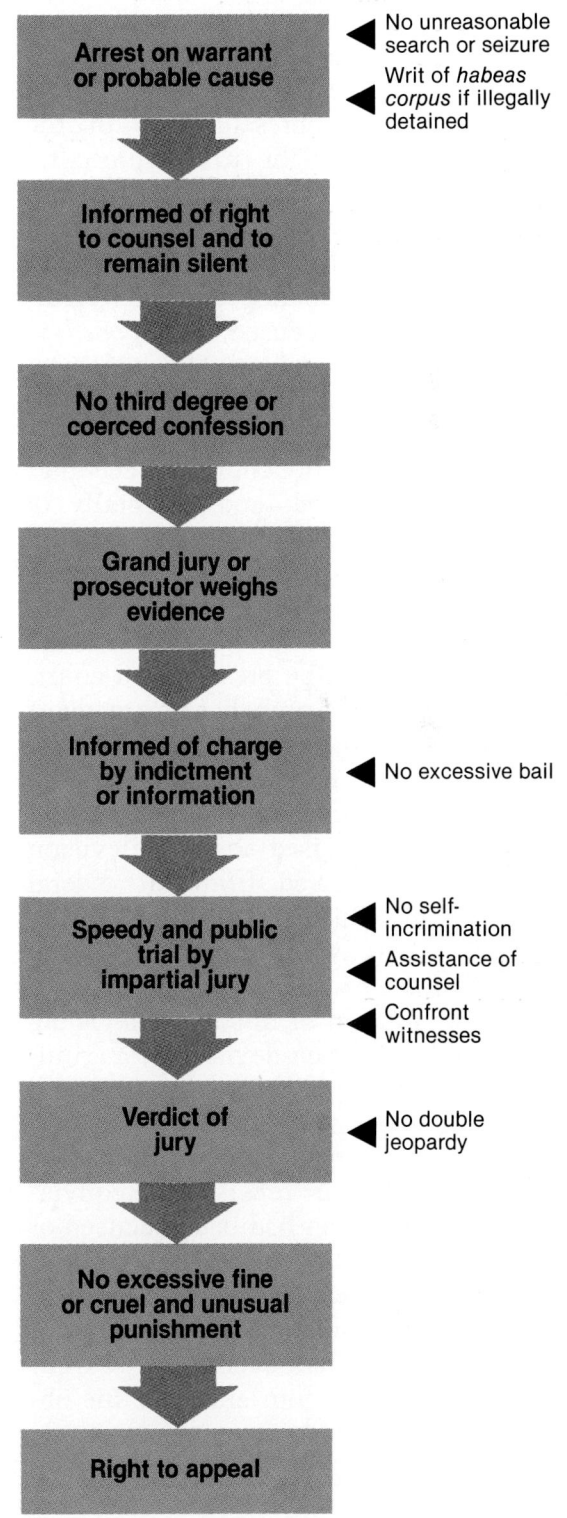

CONSTITUTIONAL PROTECTIONS FOR PERSONS ACCUSED OF CRIME

the guarantees of fair trial and of free press often come into conflict in the courts. When they do, judges face the very difficult task of finding a proper balance between them.

On the one hand: "A trial courtroom is a public place where the people generally—and representatives of the media—have a right to be present," *Richmond Newspapers, Inc.* v. *Virginia,* 1980. On the other, however: "Trial judges must take strong measures to ensure that the balance is never weighted against the accused," *Sheppard* v. *Maxwell,* 1966; see page 92.

Champions of the public's "right to know" hold that the broadest possible press coverage of court proceedings should be allowed—and especially of sensational criminal trials. The Supreme Court has often held, however, that newspaper, radio, and television reporters have only the *same* right as the general public to be present in a courtroom. That is, the press has no greater or special right to be there. In short, the right to a public trial belongs to the defendant, not to the news media.

What of televised trials? Television cameras are barred from all federal courtrooms. Until the mid-1970s the States generally followed the same rule.[22] More than half of the States now allow some form of in-court television, however. Does the televising of a criminal trial violate a defendant's 6th and 14th Amendment rights?

In an early major case on the point, the Supreme Court reversed the conviction of a man who had been accused of swindling on a massive, multibillion dollar scale, *Estes* v. *Texas,* 1965. It held that the radio and television reporting of his case, which had been allowed from within the courtroom and over his ob-

jections, had been so circus-like and disruptive that it denied Estes his constitutional rights to a fair trial.

The Court confined its ruling in *Estes* to that one case. It did not say that the Constitution bars any and all in-court televising of a criminal case.

Most recently, the Court has decided *Chandler* v. *Florida,* 1981. There it held that there is nothing in the Constitution to keep a State from allowing the televising of a criminal trial—so long as steps are taken to protect the defendant's rights. In that case, two Miami police officers had been convicted of burglary. Over their objections, their trial had been reported live on radio and television. On appeal, they held that that coverage had violated their rights to due process.

Their plea was turned down. The Court could find no evidence of the kinds of in-court distractions that would support their claim. However, the Court was careful to make this point: *Chandler* does not amount to a blanket endorsement of televised trials. Too much publicity—by television or otherwise—can threaten the fairness of a trial and so be constitutionally improper.

Trial by Jury. The 6th Amendment also says that a person accused of a federal crime must be tried "by an impartial jury."[23] This guarantee reinforces

---

[22]Except for Colorado, which has allowed television in its courtrooms since 1956.

[23]It adds that the members of the jury must be drawn from "the State and district wherein the crime shall have been committed, which district shall have been previously ascertained by law." This clause gives the defendant any benefit there may be in having a court and jury familiar with the people and problems of the area. It was also aimed at preventing what had been British colonial practice: Many colonists were forced to stand trial in England for crimes they were accused of having committed in America; see the Declaration of Independence, page 626.

A defendant may ask to be tried in another place (seek a "change of venue") on grounds that the people of the locality are so prejudiced in the case that an impartial jury cannot be drawn. The judge hearing the case must decide whether or not a change of venue is justified.

More than half of the States permit some form of in-court television coverage of trial proceedings. Here a trial is being televised in a Florida courtroom.

an earlier one set out in the Constitution—in Article III, Section 2.

The right to trial by jury is also binding on the States through the 14th Amendment's Due Process Clause, *Duncan* v. *Louisiana*, 1968.[24]

The trial jury is often called the "petit jury"—*petit,* from the French, "small." The term is used to distinguish it from the grand jury. We shall return to the role of the trial jury in Chapter 22. For now, however, these points:

The accused may *waive* (put aside, relinquish) the right to a jury trial. If the right is waived, a "bench trial" is held —the case is heard by the judge alone.

In federal practice a jury is made up of 12 persons, as it is in most of the States. Several States now provide for smaller juries, however—often with six members. A federal jury may convict only by unanimous vote; all 12 jurors must agree to a guilty verdict. Most of the States follow the same rule.[25]

In a long series of cases, dating from

Strauder v. *West Virginia,* 1880, the Supreme Court has held that a jury must be "drawn from a fair cross section of the community." A person is denied the right to an impartial jury if he or she is tried by a jury from which members of any groups "playing major roles in the community" have been excluded, *Taylor* v. *Louisiana,* 1975.

In short, no person may be kept off a jury on such grounds as race, color, religion, national origin, or sex. (Interestingly, the Court did not forbid the States to exclude women from jury service until as recently as 1975, in the Louisiana case just cited.)

Right to an Adequate Defense. Every person accused of crime has the right to offer the best possible defense that circumstances will allow. To that end, the 6th Amendment says that a defendant has the right: (1) "to be informed of the nature and cause of the

---

[24]The 7th Amendment also preserves the right to jury trial in civil cases "where the value in controversy shall exceed twenty dollars." This guarantee has not been incorporated into the 14th Amendment's Due Process Clause.

[25]The 14th Amendment does not dictate juries of no less than 12 members, *Williams* v. *Florida,* 1970; but it does not allow juries of less than six members, *Ballew* v. *Georgia,* 1978. Nor does it prevent a State from providing for a conviction on a less than unanimous jury vote, *Apadaca* v. *Oregon,* 1972; but if a jury has only six members it may convict only by a unanimous vote, *Burch* v. *Louisiana,* 1979.

accusation"; (2) "to be confronted with the witnesses against him" and question them in open court; (3) "to have compulsory process for obtaining witnesses in his favor"; and (4) "to have the assistance of counsel for his defence."

As parts of the Bill of Rights these key safeguards apply in the federal courts. But if a State fails to honor any of them in its own courts, a conviction may be appealed on grounds that the 14th Amendment's Due Process Clause has been violated (see pages 124–125).

These guarantees are intended to prevent the cards in the court contest from being stacked in favor of the prosecution. A well-known right-to-counsel case, *Escobedo* v. *Illinois*, 1964, illustrates the point.

Danny Escobedo was picked up by Chicago police for questioning in the death of his brother-in-law. On the way to the police station, and then while he was being questioned there, he asked several times to see his lawyer. These requests were refused—even though his lawyer was in the police station, was trying to see him, and the police knew that he was there. Through a long night of questioning by the police, and without the help of his lawyer, Escobedo made several damaging statements. Those statements were used in court and were a major part of the evidence that led to his conviction for murder.

The Supreme Court ordered Escobedo freed from prison four years later. It held that he had been improperly denied his right to counsel.

Self-Incrimination. The 5th Amendment says that no person can be

> compelled, in any criminal case, to be a witness against himself.

This protection must be honored in both the federal and State courts, *Malloy* v. *Hogan*, 1964.

In a criminal case, the defendant does not have to prove his or her innocence. Rather, the prosecution must show, if it can, that the criminal charge it has brought is true. The ban on self-incrimination prevents the prosecution from shifting the burden of proof to the defendant. As the Court put it in *Malloy* v. *Hogan*, the prosecution cannot force the accused to "prove the charge against" him "out of his own mouth."

The language of the 5th Amendment suggests that the guarantee applies only to criminal cases. In fact, it covers *any* governmental proceeding in which a person is legally compelled to answer any question which could lead to a criminal charge. A person may claim the right ("take the Fifth") in any number of situations, then—such as in a divorce proceeding (which is a *civil* case), or before a legislative committee, or in a hearing before a local school board.

The courts decide when the right may be properly invoked, not the individuals who claim it. If the plea of self-incrimination is pushed too far, a person may be held in **contempt.** That is, he or she may be punished by a court for the crime of obstructing the lawful processes of government.

The privilege against self-incrimination is a personal right. One can claim it only for himself or herself.[26] It cannot be invoked in someone else's behalf; a person *can* be forced to "rat" on another. Nor can it be used to protect such "artificial persons" as a corporation or a partnership.

The privilege covers only evidence given in compelled testimony—that is, in answers a person gives to lawful questions he or she must answer. It does not

---

[26]With this large exception: A husband may refuse to testify against his wife, or a wife against her husband; either one can testify against the other voluntarily, but neither can be compelled to do so, *Trammel* v. *United States*, 1980.

Editorial cartoon by Pat Oliphant. Copyright, *The Denver Post*. Reprinted with permission of Los Angeles Times Syndicate.

"Hey! I just killed 24 people—and you got that confession without advising me of my rights!"

From *Herblock Gallery* (Simon & Schuster, 1969)

"Of course I believe in the people's rights—but for the right people."

Two comments on the right of suspects to remain silent and the right to counsel when questioned by the police.

protect a person from being fingerprinted or photographed, submitting a handwriting sample, or appearing in a police lineup—or taking a blood test, as we saw in *Schmerber* v. *California*, on page 126.

A person cannot be forced to confess to a crime under duress—that is, as a result of torture or other physical or psychological force, or the threat of it. The Supreme Court has voided a number of State prosecutions based upon such "third degree" methods.

In *Ashcraft* v. *Tennessee*, 1944, for example, it threw out the conviction of a man accused of hiring another to murder his wife. The confession, on which his conviction rested, had been secured only after some 36 hours of continuous, abusive, and threatening interrogation. That questioning took place in a jail room under high-powered lights. It was conducted by police officers who worked in relays because, they said, they became so tired they had to rest.

The gulf between what the Constitution says and what in fact goes on in some police stations can be wide, in-

deed. For that reason, the Supreme Court has for the last several years come down hard in cases involving the protection against self-incrimination and the right to counsel.

Recall the Court's decision in *Escobedo* v. *Illinois*. There it held that a confession cannot be used against a defendant if it was obtained by police who refused to allow him to see his attorney and did not advise him of the right to refuse to answer their questions.

In a truly historic decision two years later, *Miranda* v. *Arizona*, 1966, the Court refined that holding. A mentally retarded man, Ernesto Miranda, had been convicted of kidnapping and rape. Ten days after the crime the victim picked him out of a police lineup. After two hours of questioning—during which the police did not tell him of his rights—he confessed. The Supreme Court struck down his conviction. Much more importantly, the Court said that, from that point on, it would not uphold convictions in any cases in which, before police questioning, suspects had not been told of their constitutional rights. It thus laid down what has since come to be called the **Miranda Rule.**

Today, under this rule, before police may question suspects, those persons must be:

(1) Told of their right to remain silent;
(2) Warned that anything they say can be used against them in court;
(3) Informed of their right to have an attorney present during questioning;
(4) Told that if they cannot afford to hire an attorney, one will be provided; and
(5) Told that they may bring any police questioning to an end at any time.

The Miranda precedent has been applied in several later cases. *Estelle* v. *Smith*, 1981, is but one of them. There the Court set aside the death penalty a Texas jury had imposed on Ernest Smith. The jury had convicted him of a murder that took place during an armed robbery. It then based its decision to sentence Smith to death on the results of a psychiatric examination. But Smith had not been told that he had a right to remain silent during that examination; nor had he been told that any statements he might make to the State's psychiatrist could be used against him in a court.

Many police officials, and others, criticise the Miranda Rule. They see it as a serious obstacle to effective law enforcement; and many of them say that it "puts criminals back onto the streets." Others applaud it, however. They hold that criminal law enforcement is most effective when it depends upon independently secured evidence, rather than confessions secured by questionable means and in the absence of counsel.

☑ FOR REVIEW

1. What does the protection against double jeopardy mean?
2. What is the basic function of a grand jury?
3. Why does the Constitution guarantee a speedy trial? A public trial?
4. Can criminal trials in federal courts be televised? In State courts?
5. Does the Constitution require that a person accused of crime must, in all cases, be tried by an impartial jury?
6. What are the 6th Amendment guarantees of the right to an adequate defense?
7. Why is compulsory self-incrimination forbidden?
8. What is the Miranda Rule?

Law enforcement officers are now required to issue warnings, of the sort shown here on a Miranda card, when making an arrest.

Before asking you any questions, it is my duty to advise you of your rights:
1. You have the right to remain silent;
2. If you choose to speak, anything you say may be used against you in a court of law or other proceeding;
3. You have the right to consult with a lawyer before answering any questions and you may have him present with you during questioning;
4. If you cannot afford a lawyer and you want one, a lawyer will be provided for you by the Commonwealth without cost to you;
5. Do you understand what I have told you;
6. You may also waive the right to counsel and your right to remain silent and you may answer any question or make any statement you wish. If you decide to answer questions you may stop at any time to consult with a lawyer;

Excessive Bail, Fines. The 8th Amendment says, in part:

> Excessive bail shall not be required, nor excessive fines imposed.

Each of the State constitutions sets out similar restrictions.

The general rule here is that the bail or fine in a case must bear a reasonable relationship to the seriousness of the crime involved.

Bail is a sum of money that the accused may be required to post (deposit with the court) as a guarantee that he or she will appear in court at the proper time. Its use is justified on two grounds: (1) A person is innocent until proved guilty and therefore should not be jailed unless and until guilt is established. And (2) a defendant is better able to prepare for trial *outside* of a jail.[27]

Bail is usually set on the basis of the nature of charge and the reputation and resources of the defendant. Because the poor often have trouble raising bail, the federal courts, and those of most States, now release many defendants "on their own recognizance"—*i.e.*, on their honor.

The leading case on bail in the federal courts is *Stack* v. *Boyle*, 1951. It involved the prosecution of a communist under the Smith Act (page 114). There the Court ruled that "bail set at a figure higher than the amount reasonable calculated" to guarantee that a defendant would appear at a trial "is 'excessive' under the 8th Amendment."

Cruel and Unusual Punishment. The 8th Amendment also forbids "cruel and unusual punishment." The 14th Amendment extends that prohibition against the States, *Robinson* v. *California*, 1962; and each of the State constitutions has a similar provision.

The Supreme Court decided its first cruel and unusual case just over 100 years ago. In *Wilkerson* v. *Utah*, 1879, a territorial court had sentenced a convicted murderer to death by a firing squad. The Court held that that punishment was not forbidden by the Constitution. The kinds of penalties the Constitution intended to prevent, said the Court, were such barbaric tortures as burning at the stake, crucifixion, drawing and quartering, "and all others in the same line of unnecessary cruelty."

Since then, the Court has heard only a small number of cruel and unusual cases—except for those relating to capital punishment, as we shall see in a moment. More often than not, the Court has come down on the side of the punishment. That is, it has usually rejected the cruel and unusual punishment claim.

Louisiana v. *Resweber*, 1947, is fairly typical. There the Court found that it was not unconstitutional to subject a convicted murderer to a second electrocution after the chair had failed to work properly on the first occasion.

So, too, is *Rummel* v. *Estelle*, 1980. In that case a man had been given a mandatory life sentence as an habitual criminal. A Texas court had imposed that punishment after his third conviction for fraud. The Supreme Court held that the punishment was not cruel and unusual—even though the crimes had all been relatively petty and non-violent, and had involved a total of only $230.

The Court has held some punishments to be cruel and unusual, of course. Thus, in *Trop* v. *Dulles*, 1958, it struck down denaturalization (the involuntary loss of citizenship) as the penalty for fleeing the country to avoid wartime military service. Denaturalization, it said, involves "no physical mistreatment, no primitive torture. There is instead the total destruction of the individual's status in organized society."

In *Robinson* v. *California*, 1962, it held that a State law that defined narcotics addiction as a crime to be punished,

---

[27]Bail is almost never allowed in **capital cases**—those involving crimes punishable by death. A defendant may appeal the denial of release on bail or the amount of the bail. If a person out on bail does not show up, the court may order the bail forfeited; "jumping bail" is itself a punishable crime.

rather than an illness to be treated, violated the 8th and 14th Amendments. And in *Estelle* v. *Gamble*, 1976, it ruled that a Texas prison inmate could not properly be denied needed medical care.

But, again, most cases have gone the other way. In *Rhodes* v. *Chapman*, 1981, the Court held that "double-celling"—putting two prisoners in a cell built for one—is not cruel and unusual punishment. In that Ohio case, the Court said that the Constitution "does not mandate comfortable prisons."

Capital Punishment.   Is the death penalty cruel and unusual and so forbidden by the Constitution? The Court was for years reluctant to face that highly charged issue. In fact, it did not give a direct answer to that question until 1976.[28]

The Court did meet the issue more or less directly in *Furman* v. *Georgia*, 1972. There it struck down all of the then existing State laws allowing the death penalty—but *not* because that penalty as *such* is cruel and unusual. Rather, they were voided because they gave too much discretion to judges or juries in deciding whether to impose it or not. The Court noted that of all those convicted of capital crimes, only "a random few," most of them black or poor or both, were "capriciously selected" for execution. The death penalty was "cruel and unusual in the same way that being struck by lightning is cruel and unusual."

Following that decision, 35 States passed new capital punishment laws—generally taking one of two forms:

Several States removed *all* discretion from the sentencing process. They made the death penalty *mandatory* for certain

[28]The Court avoided a direct ruling on the constitutionality of capital punishment laws in several earlier cases. It did hold that neither death by firing squad (*Wilkerson* v. *Utah*) nor by a second electrocution (*Louisiana* v. *Resweber*) are unconstitutional, as we have seen. But in neither of those cases, nor in others, did it deal with the question of the death penalty *as such*.

crimes—such as the killing of a police officer or murder done while committing rape, kidnap, or arson.

Others provided for a two-stage process in capital cases: *first*, a trial to settle the issue of guilt or innocence; then a *second*, separate hearing to decide whether the circumstances justify a sentence of death.

The Supreme Court has now (1983) considered scores of challenges to those newer laws—with these results:

The mandatory death penalty laws were found to be unconstitutional. They were "unduly harsh and rigidly unworkable," and simply attempts to "paper over" the decision in *Furman*, said the Court in *Woodson* v. *North Carolina*, 1976. Capital punishment laws "must allow for whatever mitigating circumstances" may be present in a case, *Roberts* v. *Louisiana*, 1977.

But the two-stage approach to capital punishment is constitutional. In *Gregg* v. *Georgia*, 1976, the Court held, for the first time, that the "punishment of death does not invariably violate the Constitution." And it ruled that well-drawn two-stage laws can practically eliminate "the risk that [the death penalty] will be inflicted in an arbitrary or capricious manner."

Treason.   Treason against the United States is the only crime which is defined in the Constitution. The Framers provided a specific definition of the crime because they knew that the charge of treason is a favorite weapon in the hands of tyrants. Examples of its use to do away with political opponents in recent times are not hard to find. It was a common practice in Nazi Germany, and it still is in several Latin American dictatorships and in the communist nations of Eastern Europe and Asia.

Treason, says Article III, Section 3, can consist of but two things: either (1) levying war against the United States or

(2) "adhering to their enemies, giving them aid and comfort." And, the Constitution adds, no person may be convicted of the crime "unless on the testimony of two witnesses to the same overt act, or on confession in open court." The penalty for treason can be imposed only on the traitors themselves; it may not be extended to their families.

The law of treason covers all American citizens, at home or abroad, and all permanent resident aliens. The maximum penalty for treason against the United States is death, but no person has ever been executed for the crime.

Note that treason may be committed only in wartime. But Congress has also made it a crime, in either peace or wartime, to commit espionage or sabotage, to attempt to overthrow the government by force, or to conspire to do any of these things; see pages 112–116.

Most of the State constitutions also provide for treason. John Brown was hanged as a traitor to Virginia after his raid on Harpers Ferry in 1859. He is believed to be the only person ever to be executed for treason against a State.

☑ FOR REVIEW

1. What is bail? What bail or fine is "excessive"?

2. What punishments do the 8th and 14th Amendments prohibit? Does the Constitution outlaw capital punishment?

3. Why does the Constitution set out a very specific definition of the crime of treason? What is that definition?

Equality Before the Law

Nothing—not even a constitutional command—can make all people equal in the literal sense, of course. People differ in strength, intelligence, height, weight, health, and countless other ways. But the democratic ideal demands that, insofar as government is concerned, all persons must be treated alike.

The Equal Protection Clause

The closest approach to a literal statement of equality is to be found in the 14th Amendment's Equal Protection Clause. It declares that

> No State shall . . . deny to any person within its jurisdiction the equal protection of the laws.

And the Supreme Court has often held that the Federal Government is also bound to provide "equal protection" by the 5th Amendment's Due Process Clause.

The Equal Protection Clause was originally intended to benefit the newly freed slaves. In practice, however—and especially in recent decades—it has become a much broader guarantee. In effect, it forbids State (and local governments) to draw *unreasonable* distinctions between different classes of persons.

Reasonable Classification. Government must have the power to classify—to draw distinctions between, to discriminate among persons and groups. Otherwise, it would be impossible for it to regulate any aspect of human behavior.

That is to say, the States may and do discriminate. Thus, those who rob banks fall into a special class and are subject to a special treatment by the law. This sort of discrimination is clearly reasonable. Or, the State may legally prohibit marriage by those under a certain age, or by those who are married to other persons. Again, these are reasonable discriminations (classifications).

But the States may not discriminate unreasonably. Every State now levies a sales tax on cigarettes—and so taxes

"Jim Crow" laws required segregation by race, even at public drinking fountains.

smokers, but not nonsmokers. But no State could lay a tax only upon *blonde* smokers or only upon *males* who buy cigarettes. Nor for example, may a State make *women* eligible for alimony in divorce actions but provide that *men* are not—as the Court ruled in a case from Alabama, *Orr* v. *Orr*, in 1979.

Ordinarily, when a State's law is challenged under the Equal Protection Clause, the Supreme Court upholds the law. This is especially true when the State can show some **rational basis** for the classification it has made—that is, that it has a reasonable relationship to some proper public purpose.

A recent California case, *Michael M.* v. *Superior Court*, 1981, illustrates the usual outcome. California law says that a man who has sexual relations with a girl who is under 18 and to whom he is not married can be prosecuted for statutory rape; but the girl cannot be charged with that crime, even if she is a willing partner. The Court found the law to be an appropriate means to a proper public end: preventing teen-age pregnancies. Justice Rehnquist wrote for the majority: "Because virtually all of the significantly harmful and inescapably identifiable consequences of teen-age pregnancy fall on the young female, a

legislature acts well within its authority when it elects to punish only the participant who, by nature, suffers few of the consequences of his conduct."

The Court does not always uphold the judgment a State legislature makes when it draws distinctions between persons or groups, however. This is especially true when a law deals with either of these matters: (1) Such "fundamental rights" as the right to vote, the right to travel between the States, or the rights guaranteed in the 1st Amendment; or (2) Such "suspect classifications" as those based upon race, sex, or national origins.

In these cases, the Court has said many times over in recent years that the *rational basis test* is not enough. Rather, such a law must meet a higher standard, the **strict scrutiny test**. To pass that stiffer check—to be upheld—the State must be able to show that some "compelling public interest" justifies the distinctions it has drawn in that law.

The alimony case we cited a moment ago *Orr* v. *Orr*, involved the use of the stricter test. The Alabama law was held unconstitutional, as a denial of equal protection. The Court found that need, not sex, is the factor upon which the award of alimony must hinge.

The Separate-but-Equal Doctrine. Beginning in the late 1800s nearly half of the States passed racial segregation laws. Most of these "Jim Crow" laws were aimed at blacks. Some of them were drawn to affect other groups, as well—Mexican-Americans, people of Oriental descent, and American Indians. In the main, they required segregation by race in the use of both public and private facilities—street cars, schools, parks and playgrounds, hotels, restaurants, and much else (even public drinking fountains).

In 1896, the Supreme Court provided a constitutional basis for these segregation laws—the **separate-but-equal doc-**

trine. In *Plessy* v. *Ferguson* it upheld a Louisiana law requiring the segregation of whites and blacks in rail coaches. It held that the law did not violate the Equal Protection Clause because the *separate* facilities for blacks were *equal* to those for whites.

The separate-but-equal doctrine soon became the constitutional justification for racial segregation in several other fields. And it stood for nearly 60 years. Indeed, until the late 1930s little real effort was made—by the courts or by any other arm of government—even to see that the separate accommodations for blacks were, in fact, equal to those reserved to whites. More often than not, they were not.

Brown v. Topeka Board of Education, 1954. The Supreme Court began to chip away at the doctrine in several cases in the late 1930s and the 1940s.

It did so for the first time in *Missouri ex rel. Gaines* v. *Canada* in 1938. Lloyd Gaines had applied for admission to the law school at the all-white State university. He was wholly qualified for admission, except for one thing: he was black. The State did not have a law school for blacks. However, it did offer to pay his tuition at a public law school in any of four neighboring States, where blacks were admitted on equal terms with whites. But Gaines insisted on a legal education in his home State.

The Supreme Court held that the separate-but-equal doctrine left the State of Missouri with but two choices here. It could either (1) admit Gaines to the State's law school or (2) establish a separate-but-equal one for him. Needless to say, the State gave in.

Over the next several years the Supreme Court took a sterner attitude toward the doctrine's requirement of equal facilities for blacks.

Finally, in a historic decision in 1954, the Court reversed *Plessy* v. *Fergu-* son. In *Brown* v. *Topeka Board of Education* it struck down the laws of four States requiring or allowing separate public schools for white and black students.[29]

Unanimously, the Supreme Court held that segregation by race in public education is unconstitutional:

> . . . Does segregation of children in public schools solely on the basis of race, even though the physical facilities and other "tangible" factors may be equal, deprive the children of the minority group of equal educational opportunities? We believe that it does.
>
> . . . To separate them from others of similar age and qualifications solely because of their race generates a feeling of inferiority as to their status in the community that may affect their hearts and minds in a way unlikely ever to be undone. . . . We conclude that in the field of public education the doctrine of "separate but equal" has no place. Separate educational facilities are inherently unequal.

How was its decision to be carried out? The Court recognized that that question presented "a problem of considerable complexity." (That observation proved to be a monumental understatement.) It held extensive hearings and in 1955, directed the States to make "a prompt and reasonable start" and to end school segregation "with all deliberate speed." Federal district courts were ordered to supervise the desegregation process.

A "reasonable start" was made in several places—Baltimore, Louisville, St. Louis, Washington, D.C., and elsewhere. In most of the Deep South, how-

---

[29]Kansas, Delaware, South Carolina, and Virginia. The Court also struck down racially segregated schools in the District of Columbia, under the 5th Amendment's Due Process Clause, *Bolling* v. *Sharpe*, 1954.

In 1963, Martin Luther King, Jr., gave his famous "I have a dream" speech to the thousands who took part in the "March on Washington."

ever, what came to be known as "massive resistance" soon developed. State legislatures passed a number of laws to block integration. Most of them were clearly unconstitutional; but the process of attacking them in the federal courts was both costly and slow. Many school boards, urged on by the white community, worked to bar progress. And, until the 1960s, neither Congress nor the President gave either support or leadership to integration efforts.

The pace of desegregation was speeded up after Congress passed the Civil Rights Act of 1964. Among its many provisions, that law forbids the use of federal funds to aid any State or local activity in which racial segregation is practiced.

It also gave the Justice Department power to file court suits to prompt desegregation actions.

The Supreme Court itself pushed that pace along in 1969. In a case from Mississippi it ruled that, after 15 years, the time for "all deliberate speed" had finally run out, *Alexander* v. *Holmes County Board of Education*. Said a unanimous Court: "The continued operation of segregated schools under a standard allowing for 'all deliberate speed' . . . is no longer constitutionally permissible."

De Jure and De Facto Segregation.[30] By the fall of 1970 *de jure* segregated school systems had been abolished throughout the country. What that statement means is that, by then, there was nowhere in the country a public school *legally* identified as one reserved either for whites or for blacks. The process of achieving a complete integration of the country's schools still goes on

[30] **De jure**—by law, with legal sanction; **de facto**—by fact, in reality.

today, of course—nearly 30 years after the Court's decision in *Brown*.[31]

For many years, segregation was seen by most as a problem peculiar to the South. Events of the past several years have shown that the problem is, and long has been, one of *nationwide* dimensions, however. Many of the more recent integration controversies have come in places where the schools have never been segregated by law. They have broken out instead, in communities where *de facto* segregation has long been present, and continues.

De facto segregation exists where, although no law required it, circumstances have in fact produced it. Housing patterns have most often been its major cause. The concentration of black populations in one or some sections of several cities inevitably led to local school systems in which some schools are largely black and others largely white. That condition is clearly apparent in many *northern* as well as southern communities.

Efforts to desegregate those school systems have taken several forms. School district lines have been redrawn; pupil assignment programs have been put in place; and the busing of students out of racially segregated neighborhoods has been tried. These efforts have often brought strong protests in many places and even violence in some.

The Supreme Court first sanctioned busing in a North Carolina case, *Swann v. Charlotte-Mecklenburg Board of Education*, 1971. There it held that "desegregation plans cannot be limited to walk-in schools." Since then, busing has been used to try to increase the racial mix in many school districts across the country—in some by court order, in others voluntarily.

The whole matter of school integration is packed with legal questions. It is just as clearly loaded with highly charged political and emotional issues. That point is sharply underlined by the ongoing national dispute over busing.

Segregation in Other Fields. A complete integration of the public schools has not yet been achieved. Legally-enforced racial segregation has been very largely eliminated in other areas of life, however. Many State laws and local ordinances have been repealed, and many have been struck down by the courts. The Supreme Court has found racial segregation in all other areas to be as unconstitutional as it is in education. Thus, it held that to be the case in public recreational facilities, in *Dawson* v. *Baltimore*, 1955; in local transportation, in *Gayle* v. *Browder*, 1956; in State prisons and local jails, in *Lee* v. *Washington*, 1968. And in *Loving* v. *Virginia*, 1967, it struck down all *miscegenation* laws—laws that barred interracial marriages.

Classification by Sex. In its many civil rights provisions, the Constitution speaks of "the people," "persons," and "citizens." Nowhere does it make its guarantees only to "men," or separately to "women."[32]

Sex has long been used as a basis of classification in the law, however. By and large, that practice reflected society's historic view of the "proper" role of women. Most often, those laws that treated men and women differently were seen as necessary to the protection of "the weaker sex." Over the years, the

---

[31]Most of the legal and political controversies surrounding desegregation have involved *public* schools. Some States, several school districts, and many parents and private groups have sought to block integration or avoid integrated schools through established or, often, newly-created *private* schools. But see page 130 and *Runyan* v. *McCrary*, 1976, where the Court held that private schools cannot refuse to admit students because of their race.

[32]The only reference to sex is in the 19th Amendment, which forbids the denial of the right to vote "on account of sex;" see page 192.

Supreme Court read that view into the 14th Amendment. It did not find *any* sex-based classification to be unconstitutional until as recently as 1971.

In the first case in which sex discrimination was challenged, the Court upheld a State law barring women from the practice of law, *Bradwell* v. *Illinois*, 1873. In that case, Justice Joseph P. Bradley wrote:

> The civil law, as well as nature itself, has always recognized a wide difference in the respective spheres and destinies of man and woman. Man is, or should be, woman's protector and defender. The natural and proper timidity and delicacy which belongs to the female sex evidently unfits it for many of the occupations of civil life.

Even in 1961, the Court could find nothing constitutionally wrong with a law which required men to serve on juries but gave women the choice of serving or not, *Hoyt* v. *Florida*.

Matters are far different today. In 1971 it struck down an Idaho law that required that fathers be given preference over mothers in the administration of their children's estates, *Reed* v. *Reed*.

Since then, it has found a number of sex-based distinctions to be unconstitutional. We have already noted some of them—for example, *Taylor* v. *Louisiana*, 1975, holding that the Equal Protection Clause forbids the States to exclude women from jury service. As other examples, it has struck down:

—A Utah law that said that sons are entitled to receive child support payments from their fathers until they reach age 21 but daughters only until age 18, *Stanton* v. *Stanton*, 1975.
—An Oklahoma law that prohibited the sale of beer to males under 21 and to females under 18, *Craig* v. *Boren*, 1976.
—A provision in the federal social security law giving widows higher benefits than widowers, *Califano* v. *Goldfarb*, 1977; and another giving benefits to families with unemployed fathers but not to those with unemployed mothers, *Califano* v. *Westcott*, 1979.
—A New York law that allowed an unwed mother, but not an unwed father, to block the adoption of their infant children, *Caban* v. *Mohammed*, 1979.

The court's present attitude was fairly well summed up by Justice William Brennan in a 1973 case:

> There can be no doubt that our nation has had a long and unfortunate history of sex discrimination. Traditionally, such discrimination was rationalized by an attitude of "romantic paternalism" which, in practical effect, put women, not on a pedestal, but in a cage.[33]

But not all sex-based distinctions are unconstitutional. The Court has upheld some of them in recent cases. We saw one example of this in *Michael M.* v. *Superior Court*, 1981, on page 150. And it has held that there was no denial of equal protection in:

—A Florida law that gives an extra property tax exemption to widows, but not to widowers, *Kahn* v. *Shevin*, 1974.
—An Alabama law that does not allow women to serve as prison guards in all-male penitentiaries, *Dothard* v. *Rawlinson*, 1977.
—The federal selective service law that requires men but not women to register for the draft (and also its provisions that exclude women from any future draft), *Rostker* v. *Goldberg*, 1981.

In effect, what all of these recent cases say is this: Classification by sex is not unconstitutional. *But* laws which treat men and women differently will not be upheld *unless:* (1) they are intend-

---

[33]*Frontiero* v. *Richardson*, 1973.

ed to serve an "important governmental objective" and (2) they are "substantially related" to achieving that goal.

Thus, in upholding the all-male draft, the Court found that Congress did have such an objective: to raise and support armies and, if necessary, to do so by "a draft of combat troops." "Since women are excluded from combat," said the Court, they may properly be excluded from the draft.

☑ FOR REVIEW————————

1. The Equal Protection Clause forbids what kinds of discrimination by the States?

2. What is the Supreme Court's rational basis test? Strict scrutiny test?

3. What was the separate-but-equal doctrine? What did the Court hold in *Brown* v. *Topeka Board of Education?* When was that case decided?

4. What is the difference between *de jure* and *de facto* segregation?

5. Does the Constitution forbid laws which treat men and women differently?

Federal Civil Rights Laws

From the 1870s to the late 1950s, Congress did not pass a single piece of meaningful civil rights legislation. We shall look at several reasons for that sorry fact later—especially in Chapter 8, when we consider the right to vote, and in Chapter 12, when we take a look at Congress in action.

That historic logjam was broken in 1957, however. Over the past 25 years Congress has passed a number of civil rights laws—most notably, the Civil Rights Acts of 1957, 1960, 1964, and

© 1981, Art Bimrose

1968 and the Voting Rights Acts of 1965, 1970, and 1975. Each of them is designed to carry out the Constitution's insistence upon the equality of all before the law.

The 1957 and 1960 laws set up modest safeguards for the right to vote.[34] Together with related provisions in the 1964 law and the much stronger Voting Rights Acts, we shall consider them in Chapter 8.

The Civil Rights Act of 1968 is often called the Open Housing Act. With minor exceptions, it forbids anyone to refuse to sell or rent a dwelling to any person on grounds of race, color, religion, or national origin. The law really has few teeth, however.

The Civil Rights Act of 1964 is a much broader law—and it has plenty of teeth. Beyond its voting rights provisions, it outlaws discrimination in a number of areas. With its several later amendments, its major sections now:

————————

[34]The 1957 law created the *Civil Rights Commission.* Its six members keep watch over the enforcement of the various civil rights laws, investigate cases of alleged discrimination, and report their findings and recommendations to the President, Congress, and the public.

ORGANIZING INFORMATION

PUTTING IT TOGETHER

Which tape deck is the better buy? Which candidate is more likely to support those public policies I do?

In personal and public life, there are many controversial issues and major decisions to be made. It is often difficult to keep track of all the information available to us. Making sense of the facts and conflicting viewpoints, remembering the most important ideas, and reaching informed decisions are important skills. One way to begin is by organizing information.

A useful way to organize information about a topic or issue is to sort the information into categories or groups of similar items such as events, people, objects, or ideas. Grouping bits and pieces of information in this way involves (1) identifying characteristics that the separate items have in common, (2) putting similar items together, and (3) giving each group a name or descriptive label. In organizing information about a controversial issue, for example, you might sort the available information and various viewpoints into categories such as *pro* (for) and *con* (against).

Grouping similar things together and labeling them makes them more meaningful and easier to remember. When you have organized information by grouping it, you also can easily add new information by deciding which category it belongs to. If new information does not fit any of the groups, additional ones can be created. Or, the information can be reorganized into new groups. Most information can be organized in more than one way. Which kind of grouping is best depends on your purpose. Thus, if you want to organize information about the constitutional rights of the American people, you might use these categories: the rights to free expression, the rights to freedom and security of the person, the rights of persons accused of crime, and the rights to equal treatment under the law. But if you want to organize information about the responsibilities of American citizenship, you would need different categories.

1. List the constitutional rights of persons accused of crime. Organize these rights into several subgroups, and give each subgroup a label. (Each right should fit into one of the subgroups.) Can you think of another way to group these rights?
2. List the arguments for and against some controversial public issue—for example, gun control or public aid for parochial schools.

(1)Provide that no person may be denied access to, or refused service in, various "public accommodations" on grounds of race, color, religion, or national origin (Title II).[35]

---

[35]Congress based this section of the law on the commerce power; see page 324. It covers those places in which lodgings are offered to transient guests and those where a significant portion of the things sold or the entertainment offered has moved in interstate commerce. These "public accommodations" include, for example, most restaurants, cafeterias, lunch counters, and other eating places; movie theatres, concert halls, and other auditoriums; gasoline stations; sports arenas and stadiums; and hotels, motels, and rooming houses (except owner-occupied units with less than six rooms for rent).

(2)Prohibit discrimination against any person on grounds of race, color, religion, national origin, sex, or physical handicap in any program which receives any federal funds (Title VI).

(3)Forbid employers and labor unions to discriminate against any person on grounds of race, color, religion, sex, physical handicap, or age (40 to 65) in hiring and all other job-related matters (Title VII).[36]

Affirmative Action. The several recent statutes and court decisions we have just reviewed all come down to this: Those discriminatory practices which are based on such factors as race, color, national origin, or sex are illegal.

But, what of the *present* and *continuing* effects of *past* discriminations? The fact that the law *now* prohibits discrimination does almost nothing to overcome the consequences of the discriminatory practices of the past.

As but one of many illustrations of the point, consider the black man who, for no reason of his own making, did not get a decent education and so today cannot get a decent job. Of what real help to him are all of those laws and court decisions which make illegal *today* what was done to him years ago?

So far, the Federal Government's chief answer to this troubling question has been a policy of **affirmative action**. It now requires that most employers take positive steps (affirmative action) to remedy the effects of past discriminations against women and members of various minority groups.

All public and private employers who receive federal funds must adopt affirm-

ative action programs. Thus, the policy covers most of the nation's major employers and many of its smaller ones. And it applies to *each* of them—including even those who have *never* engaged in discrimination.

In effect, these employers must strive to make their work forces reflect the general makeup of the population—with so many women, so many blacks, so many Latinos, and so on. Their affirmative action programs must include steps to correct (or prevent) inequalities in such job-related matters as pay, promotion, and fringe benefits. For most of them, this has meant that they must hire (and/or promote) more women and more persons from minority backgrounds. For most of them it has also meant that they must take these steps even when better qualified white males are available.

Affirmative action programs necessarily involve sex- and/or race-based classifications. Is this wise public policy? Are programs of this kind constitutional?

The supporters insist that some form of preferential treatment must be used to break down the long-standing patterns of discrimination against women and minorities in the job market. Its critics say that, however fine its goals, it amounts to **reverse discrimination**—that is, it demands that preference be given to females and/or non-whites, and solely on the basis of sex or race.

The Supreme Court has now decided three major affirmative action cases.

Regents of the University of California v. *Bakke,* 1978, involved the admissions policies of the University's medical school at Davis. The school had set a quota to make sure of minority representation in its student body; at least 16 of the 100 seats in each year's entering class were to be filled by nonwhites.

Allan Bakke, a white male, had twice

---

[36]The 1964 law also created the *Equal Employment Opportunities Commission.* The six-member EEOC's major charge is the enforcement of Title VII. It works to promote voluntary compliance with the law, but it can bring federal court suits to halt discriminatory practices and assure equal employment opportunities.

Allan Bakke, upon his graduation some three years after his admission to medical school of the University of California at Davis.

been denied admission. Both times, however, several nonwhite students, with admissions scores lower than his, had been accepted by the school.

Bakke sued, charging the University with reverse discrimination. The State supreme court agreed. It found that he had been denied admission because of his race and so had been denied his 14th Amendment right to equal protection. It ordered the school to admit him and directed the University not to use race as a factor in its admissions policy.

On appeal, the Supreme Court was very sharply divided. By one 5–4 majority it agreed with the California court that Bakke had been denied equal protection and so should be admitted to the medical school.

However, a differently composed 5–4 majority made the really important ruling in the case. That majority of the Court held this: While the Constitution does not allow race to be used as the *only* factor in the making of affirmative action decisions, both the Constitution and the 1964 Civil Rights Act do allow its use as *one among several* factors in such situations.

Kaiser Aluminum & Chemical Corporation v. *Weber*, 1979, involved an affirmative action plan agreed to by the company and the United Steelworkers in a labor contract. Kaiser and the union set up on-the-job training programs at 15 of the company's aluminum plants.

Those programs were designed to increase the number of skilled blacks in Kaiser's workforce. To that end, each training group was made up of an equal number of blacks and whites. The trainees were picked from each racial group—on a one-for-one basis, and by seniority (length of employment by the company).

Brian Weber, a white male working at Kaiser's plant in Gramercy, Louisiana, was turned down for training three times. Each time, several blacks with less seniority were selected, however.

Weber went to court. He claimed that the company and the union had subjected him to reverse discrimination —and so had violated Title VII of the 1964 law. The lower federal courts agreed. Both the company and the union appealed those decisions.

The Supreme Court then faced this question: Does Title VII forbid private parties (here the company and the union) to set up such affirmative action plans? (Notice the contrasts with *Bakke* —which had to do with Title VI and, because a State was involved, the 14th Amendment. *Weber* did not involve any public agency; and it called for the interpretation of a statute, not a provision in the Constitution.)

The Court ruled 5–2 for the company and the union. It held that a voluntarily adopted affirmative action program— even one containing quotas that give special preferences to black workers— does not automatically violate the law. It did admit that a literal reading of the law might suggest otherwise. But, said the Court, such a reading would contradict the very purpose of the law—"a law triggered by a nation's concern over centuries of racial injustice" and intended to speed "the integration of blacks into the mainstream of American society."

The Court did not hold that any and all job plans that give special preferences to blacks (or other minorities) are legal. But there are many plans very much like Kaiser's in force today; and they are conducted by hundreds of companies employing several millions of workers.

Fullilove v. *Klutznick*, 1980, centered on one section of the Public Employment Act of 1977. Congress had passed that law to combat unemployment in the construction industry. It authorized the Secretary of Commerce to make $4 billion in federal grants to State and local governments for public works projects.

What was at issue in the case was the law's "minority set-aside" provision. It directed that at least 10 percent of the grant monies be spent with (set aside for) minority businesses.

E. Earl Fullilove, a white contractor, challenged the set-asides. He said that they were quotas—and unconstitutional because they did not give to white contractors an equal chance to compete with black contractors for all of the available funds.

Fullilove lost in the lower federal courts and then in the Supreme Court. It found, 6–3, that Congress had properly exercised its constitutional powers to spend and to regulate interstate commerce. In short, it held that the law was a permissable attempt to overcome the effects of long-standing discrimination in the construction industry.

FOR REVIEW

1. What is the basic purpose of the several civil rights laws passed by Congress over the past 25 years?
2. What are the major provisions of the Civil Rights Act of 1964?
3. What are affirmative action programs? What is meant by the phrase "reverse discrimination"?

SUMMARY

There are two Due Process Clauses in the Constitution. One, in the 5th Amendment, restricts the National Government. The other, in the 14th Amendment, restricts the States and their local governments. These guarantees require that government, in all that it does, must act fairly (procedural due process) and must act under fair laws (substantive due process).

The Supreme Court has used the 14th Amendment's Due Process Clause to extend most of the guarantees of the Bill of Rights against the States. Each State has, among its many reserved powers, the broad police power—the power to protect the public health, safety, morals, and welfare. A State

law that can be justified as a valid use of the police powers does not violate the 14th Amendment's Due Process Clause.

All of the many constitutional guarantees to equal justice under law, set out in the Federal Constitution and in the several State constitutions, may be grouped and described in these terms: (1) The rights to freedom and security of the person; (2) The rights of persons accused of crime; and (3) The rights to equality under the law.

The many guarantees in the Federal Constitution are summarized in the table on page 128. All of them have been the subject of extensive interpretation and application by the United States Supreme Court.

CHAPTER REVIEW

Key Terms/Concepts

Affirmative action (157)
Bail (147)
Bill of attainder (138)
Capital punishment (148)
Classification (149)
Contempt (144)
Cruel and unusual punishment (147)
De facto, de jure segregation (152)
Discrimination (149)
Double jeopardy (139)
Due process of law (122)

Equal protection (149)
Excessive bail, fines (146)
Exclusionary rule (132)
Ex post facto law (138)
Grand jury (140)
Habeas corpus (137)
Indictment (140)
Information (140)
Jury (139)
Integration (152)
Involuntary servitude (129)
Miranda rule (146)
Peonage (129)
Police power (125)
Presentment (140)
Probable cause (134)

Procedural due process (123)
Public accommodations (156)
Rational basis test (150)
Reverse discrimination (157)
Right of confrontation (144)
Right to compel witnesses (144)
Right to counsel (144)
Right to keep and bear arms (135)
Segregation (151)
Self-incrimination (144)
Separate-but-equal doctrine (150)

Sex discrimination (153)
Slavery (127)
Speedy and public trial (140)
Strict scrutiny test (150)
Substantive due process (123)
Treason (148)
Trial by jury (142)
Unreasonable searches, seizures (131)
Warrant (131)
Wiretapping (133)
Writ (137)

Keynote Questions

1. What is the essential meaning of the phrase *due process of law*? What is the difference between procedural and substantive due process?

2. Why does the Constitution contain two Due Process Clauses?

3. What is the relationship between: (a) the Bill of Rights and the 14th Amendment's Due Process Clause? (b) each State's police powers and the 14th Amendment's Due Process Clause?

4. Does the 13th Amendment forbid all forms of involuntary servitude?

5. To what extent does the 2nd Amendment guarantee a right to keep and bear arms?

6. What searches and seizures does the Constitution prohibit? To whom

does that prohibition apply? What is the exclusionary rule?

7. Why *must* society punish those who commit crimes?

8. Why does the Constitution guarantee many different protections (rights) to persons suspected or accused of crime? Identify those several rights.

9. Does the 14th Amendment's Equal Protection Clause forbid the States to discriminate between or among different classes of persons?

10. Does the Constitution forbid laws which treat men and women differently?

11. Outline the major provisions of the several civil rights laws enacted by Congress over the past 25 years.

For Thought and Discussion

1. Now that you have read these two long chapters on civil rights, what is your reaction to the thoughts expressed by Judge Learned Hand, on page 90? And to these comments: "Liberty is advanced only by the rule of law"—Justice Robert H. Jackson. "The history of liberty is largely the history of the observances of procedural safeguards"—Justice Felix Frankfurter.

2. An informant tipped federal drug agents that a fugitive, Ricky Lyons, might be found at Gary Steagold's home in Atlanta. Armed with a warrant for Lyons' arrest, the agents went to Steagold's home. They entered the house and searched it for Lyons. That search, carried out without Steagold's consent, failed to turn up Lyons. However, during the search, one of the agents spotted what he thought might be cocaine. The agents then secured a search warrant, searched the house again, and found 43 pounds of cocaine. That evidence led to Steagold's conviction on federal narcotics charges.

   The Supreme Court overturned that conviction, in *Steagold* v. *United States*, 1981. On what grounds do you think that the Court, 7–2, did so? Do you think Steagold's conviction should have been thrown out? Why, or why not?

3. When the Supreme Court outlawed racial segregation in the public schools (*Brown* v. Topeka Board of Education, 1954), it did not order *immediate* desegregation. Why didn't it do so? Do you think it should have?

4. Many persons and groups favor a constitutional amendment that would prohibit court-ordered busing to bring about racial balance in public schools. Do you favor or oppose their efforts? Why?

5. On page 154 we noted the Supreme Court's recent and remarkable change of attitude toward those laws that treat men and women differently. What factors do you think brought the Court to come to its present position on those laws?

6. How would you describe, in your own words, the concept of reverse discrimination?

Suggested Activities

1. Read one or more of the many Supreme Court cases cited in this chapter, then prepare a descriptive and analytical report to the class. (A librarian can lead you to the volumes of the *United States Reports* or the *Supreme Court Reporter*.)

2. Ask several local police officers to comment on the Miranda Rule. Report your findings to the class.

3. List those situations (if any) in which you have recently seen instances of discrimination because of race, color, national origin, creed, or sex.

4. Discover and prepare a report on the affirmative action programs now in effect in your city, county, and/or local school district.

5. Stage a class debate or forum on one or more of the following topics: (a) *Resolved*, That a new Equal Rights Amendment be proposed; (b) *Resolved*, That the death penalty be (made legal/eliminated) in this State; (c) *Resolved*, That the laws of this State be amended to (allow/forbid) the live televising of criminal trials; (d) *Resolved*, That the Constitution be amended to include a positive guarantee of the right of each person to keep and bear arms; (e) *Resolved*, That the Selective Service law be amended to require that females register for the draft and, in the event of a draft, to allow their conscription into the armed forces.

UNIT THREE

The Politics of American Democracy

Perhaps the most important idea underlying the American governmental system is that of government by the people. The design of the system makes the people the *only* source of governmental authority in this country. The system exists to turn the people's beliefs and desires into public policy and to carry out that policy. In Unit Three we look at several of the ways in which this is done.

The term *politics* describes the conduct of public affairs. It includes all parts of the governing process: the making of public policy, the carrying out of that policy, the selection of the people who make and carry out policy, and everything else connected with government.

Politics can also be described as "the pursuit and exercise of power." That is, it can be viewed in terms of the ability of some persons and groups to gain and use the power to make policies and to set up rules that other persons and groups must follow.

Some people find politics distasteful, a "dirty business" with which "good people" should have as little as possible to do. It is true that the level of politics is not always all that it might be. It is also true, however, that at all times and in all places, the people themselves are responsible for the quality of the political atmosphere. And, most important of all, government cannot exist without politics.

In Unit Three we explore what Elihu Root, American statesman and Nobel Peace Prize winner, meant when he said that "Politics is the practical exercise of the art of self government, and somebody must attend to it if we are to have self-government." First we examine political parties. Then we consider the right to vote and the ways in which voters behave. We look at nominations and elections. And finally we discuss the roles of public opinion and pressure groups.

163

CHAPTER 7

Government by the People: Political Parties

CHAPTER OBJECTIVES

To help you to
Learn ▪ Know ▪ Understand

The nature of political parties.

The essential functions parties perform in American politics.

The American two-party system, its history, and the reasons for its existence and retention.

The nature and role of minor parties in American politics.

The organizational structure and composition of the two major parties.

No America without democracy, no democracy without politics, no politics without parties, no parties without compromise and moderation. . . .

Clinton Rossiter

Recall the derivation of the word *democracy.* As we noted in Chapter 1, it comes to us from two Greek words: *demos,* meaning "people," and *kratia,* meaning "rule" or "authority."

In a democracy the people rule. The people are sovereign. The people are the one and only source for any and all political authority. In a democracy, then, government must be "government by the people"—government by and with "the consent of the governed." To put it another way, a democratic government is one in which the people can and do participate.

In this chapter, and in the three to follow, we shall take a close look at that hallmark of democracy—that is, at popular participation. We shall study the ways in which people can and do take part in politics in this country—the ways in which they influence the actions of government and the means by which they give their consent for those actions.

In short, we'll deal with the point that government in the United States is, in fact, "government by the people."

164

The ideas of social diversity and popular participation in local politics are vividly portrayed in George Caleb Bingham's "On the Stump," painted in 1852. *Facing page:* A Whig Party coat button of 1840, one of the earliest of campaign buttons.

First, in this chapter, we look at political parties. And we do so because parties are one of the major vehicles of popular participation—a major means by which people take an active part in politics.

Nature and Functions of Parties

What Is a Party?

A **political party** may be defined as a group of persons who seek to control government through the winning of elections and the holding of public office.

This definition of party is a broad one, and it will fit *any* political party—including the two major parties in American politics, of course.

Another, more specific, definition may be used to describe *most* political parties, both here and abroad: A group of persons, joined together on the basis of certain common principles, who seek to control government in order to bring about the adoption of certain public policies and programs.

But this definition—with its emphasis on principles and public policy positions—will not fit the two major parties in the United States. Those two parties—the Republicans and the Democrats—are *not*, primarily principle-or issue-oriented groups. Rather, they are *election*-oriented. And they do for a number of reasons, as we shall see.

For now, our point can be put this way: Neither the Republicans nor the Democrats may be properly described as a group of like-minded persons. As a quick illustration of this, compare the public policy positions taken by various leading Republicans—or, for that matter, by various leading Democrats. Senators Barry Goldwater of Arizona and Mark Hatfield of Oregon are both Republicans. Yet they often take opposing sides in the Senate. And so do such other prominent Republicans as Jeremiah Denton of Alabama and Lowell Weicker of Connecticut, and Orrin Hatch of Utah and Charles Mathias of Maryland. Much the same can be said of many Democrats—for example, Senators Edward Kennedy of Massachusetts and John Stennis of Mississippi, or Gary Hart of Colorado and Russell Long of Louisiana.

Again, neither of the two major parties is a group of like-minded persons. Instead, as we shall see, each of them is composed of a great many persons who broadly speaking, share more or less similar views on many public questions.

What Do Parties Do?

We know from our own history—and from that of other peoples, as well—that political parties are essential to democratic government. In a word, they make democracy work. They are a vital link between the people and their government—between the governed and the governors. Indeed, many argue that they are *the* principal means by which the will of the people is made known to government and by which the government is held accountable to the people.

Parties serve the democratic ideal in another highly important way. They work to blunt conflict. Or, as it is often put, they are "power brokers." They bring conflicting groups together. They modify and compromise the contending views of different interests and groups— and so help to unify rather than divide the people. They soften the impact of extremists at both ends of the political spectrum.

Again, political parties are indispensable to American government—a fact underscored by a look at the major functions they perform.

The Nominating Function. The major function of a political party is to **nominate** (name) candidates for public office—to select them and then present them to the voters.

There must be some way to find—to recruit and choose—those candidates. And there must be some way to concentrate support (votes) for them. Parties are the best device we have yet found to do these jobs.

The nominating function is almost exclusively a party function in this country.[1] It is the one particular activity that most clearly sets political parties apart from all of the other groups operating in our politics.

The Informer-Stimulator Function. A party helps to inform the people and to stimulate their interest and participation in public affairs. It does so in many ways—most of all by campaigning for its candidates, taking stands on issue questions, and criticizing the candidates and stands of the opposition.

Of course, each party tries to inform the people as it thinks they should be informed—to the party's advantage. It conducts its "educational" process through pamphlets, signs, buttons, and stickers, advertisements in newspapers and magazines and on radio and television, speeches, rallies, and conventions, and by just about every other means available to it.

By taking at least *some* kind of stand on public issues, parties and their candidates offer the voters choices. But the major parties usually do not take *too* firm a stand on controversial questions. Remember, each party's chief aim is to win elections. And it attempts to do this by attracting as many votes as possible

---

[1]It is in fact, except in nonpartisan elections and in those rare instances in which an independent candidate enters a partisan contest. We deal with nominations, at length, in Chapter 9.

A tiny sampling of the kinds of devices that have been used by political parties and their candidates in conveying their "message" to the American voter.

while, at the same time, offending as few as possible.

The Bonding Agent Function. A party serves as a "bonding agent" to insure the good performance of its candidates and officeholders. In choosing its candidates it tries to see that they are men and women who are both qualified and of good character—or, at least, that they are not unqualified and that they have no serious blemishes on their records. And it also prompts its successful candidates to perform well in office. The very nature of the democratic process places this function on a party—whether it really wants to perform it or not. If it fails to do so, both it and its candidates may suffer the consequences in future elections—and, especially, where there is vigorous competition between the two major parties.

The Governmental Function. From several different points of view, government in the United States may be quite correctly described as government by party. Thus, public officeholders—those who govern—are regularly chosen on the basis of party. Congress and the State legislatures are organized and conduct much of their business on a partisan basis. Most appointments to executive offices, both federal and State, are made on that basis, too.

In yet another sense parties provide a basis for the conduct of government. Under our system of separation of powers the party is usually the major agent through which the executive and legislative branches cooperate with one another.

In this connection, remember our discussion of constitutional change by "informal amendment" (on pages 60–62). Political parties have played a large part in that process. As a leading illustration of that fact, the Constitution's cumbersome electoral college system works principally because political parties reshaped it in its early years and have made it work ever since.

The Watchdog Function. Parties act as a "watchdog" over the conduct of the public's business. This is particularly the function of the party out of power, of course. And it plays the role as it criticizes the policies and behavior of the party in power.[2] Its attacks tend to make the "ins" more careful of their public charge and more responsive to the wishes of the people. In short, the party out of power serves as "the loyal opposition."

 FOR REVIEW

1. Define *political party*.
2. What pivotal role do parties play in democratic government?
3. What more particular functions do parties have in our politics?
4. Which of those functions is the major one?

The Two-Party System

Two major parties dominate American politics. That is, we have a **two-party system** in this country. In the typical election, only the candidates of the Republican and/or the Democratic Parties have a reasonable chance of winning public office.

In some States, and in many communities, one of these two major parties may be overwhelmingly dominant, and for a long period of time—as, for example, the Democrats were throughout the South for decades. But, on the whole, and through most of our history, we have been a two-party nation.

There have been and are other parties —*minor* or *third parties*—in American politics, of course, and we shall look at them shortly. But only seldom does one of them make a serious bid for power, and then usually only at a local level.

Why a Two-Party System?

A number of factors help to explain why we have—and continue to have—a two-party system in this country. None of them, taken alone, offers a wholly satisfactory explanation for the phenomenon. But, taken together, they do stand as a quite persuasive answer.

The Historical Basis.   The two-party system is rooted in the beginnings of the nation itself. The Framers of the Constitution were opposed to political parties. As we saw in Chapter 2, however, their hope was a futile one.[3] The battle over the ratification of the Constitution saw the birth of our first two parties—the Federalists, led by Alexander Hamilton, and the Anti-Federalists, who followed Thomas Jefferson. In short, the American party system *began* as a two-party system.

The Force of Tradition.   Once established, human institutions are likely to be self-perpetuating—and so it has been with our party system. The very fact that we began with a two-party system has, in and of itself, been a leading reason for the retention of the arrangement. And it has become a more important—a self-reinforcing—reason over time.

Our point here can be made this way: Most Americans accept the idea of a two-party system simply because we've always had one. (And, notice, this inbred support for the arrangement is a

---

[2] In American politics the "party in power" is the party which controls the executive branch—*i.e.*, at the national level holds the Presidency, or at the State level the governorship.

[3] The Framers hoped to create a unified country; they sought to bring order out of the chaos of the Critical Period of the 1780's. To most of them, parties were "factions," leading to divisiveness and disunity. George Washington reflected this view when in his Farewell Address in 1796, he warned the new nation against "the baneful effect of the spirit of party." In this light, it is hardly surprising that the Constitution made no provision for political parties. The Founding Fathers could not foresee the ways in which the governmental system they set up would develop, of course. Thus, they could not possibly know that two major parties would emerge as prime instruments of government in the United States. Nor could they know that those two major parties would tend to be moderate, to choose middle-of-the-road positions, and so help to unify rather than divide the nation.

principal reason why challenges to it—minor party efforts—have made so little headway in our politics.)

The Electoral System. Several features of the American electoral system to promote the existence of but two major parties in American politics. That is to say, the basic shape and many of the details of the election process work in that direction.

Among the most prominent of these features is the *single-member district* arrangement. Nearly all elections in the United States—from the presidential contest on down to those at the most local level—are conducted on this basis. That is, they are **single-member district elections**—contests in which but one candidate is to be chosen to each office on the ballot. The winning candidate is the one who receives a **plurality** (the largest number) of the votes cast for the office he or she seeks.[4]

Where there are only two candidates for an office, one of them is bound to win an absolute plurality, a majority of the votes (barring the unlikely tie, of course). Practically, then, it has seemed wise to us to limit election contests to just two principal contenders. Put another way, the fact that our electoral map is dominated by single-member districts has been very persuasive to the establishment and the maintenance of a two-party system.

The single-member district pattern rather clearly works to discourage third-party efforts. Because only one winner can come out of each contest, voters usually face only two real choices: They can vote for the candidate of the party holding the office, or they can vote for

A Democratic headquarters in Austin, Texas

the candidate of the party with the best chance of replacing the incumbent. In short, most voters think of a vote for a third-party candidate as a "wasted" one.

Another very important aspect of the electoral system works to the same end: Much of American election law is quite purposefully written to discourage third parties and third-party candidates. Or, to put it the other way around, much of it is intentionally designed to preserve and protect the two major parties and the two-party system. Thus, for example, in most of the States it is much more difficult for minor parties to nominate their candidates—get them listed on the ballot—than it is for the major parties to do so.

The 1980 presidential election offers a striking illustration of the point. Both of the major party candidates, Ronald Reagan and Jimmy Carter, were on the ballots of all of the 50 States and the District of Columbia. But only two of the ten or more other, and serious, presidential hopefuls were also listed everywhere—only the Libertarian party nominee, Ed Clark, and independent candidate John Anderson.

---

[4]A candidate who wins a *plurality* of the votes wins more than does any other. A candidate who wins a **majority** wins more than half of all of the votes. Thus, a majority is always a plurality, but a plurality is not necessarily a majority.

Because of the shape of the laws in most States, both Clark and Anderson were forced to spend critical amounts of time, effort, and money in order to accomplish what was nearly automatic for the two major party nominees. This fact underscores our point here: By gaining the ballot everywhere, Clark and Anderson became the first two non-major party contenders to do so in more than 60 years—since the Socialist Party's candidate, Allan L. Benson, appeared on the ballots of all of the then 48 States in 1916.

The American Ideological Consensus.   Another leading reason for the two-party system can be seen in this profoundly important fact: We Americans are, on the whole, an *ideologically homogeneous* people. That is, over time, we have shared pretty much the same ideals, the same basic principles, the same patterns of belief. There is a broad consensus—a general agreement among us—in fundamental matters.

This is not to say that Americans have always agreed with one another, and in all matters. Far from it. We have been deeply divided at some times in our history, and over various questions —during the Civil War and in the years of the Great Depression, for example; and over such issues as racial discrimination and the war in Southeast Asia.

But it is to say that we have not been regularly plagued by sharp cleavages in our politics. We have not seen long-standing, bitter disputes based upon factors such as economic class, social status, religious tenets, or national origins.

Those conditions which could produce several strong rival parties simply do not exist in this country—unlike the situation in most other democracies. In short, the realities of American politics simply will not permit more than two major parties.

This fact of American life—the ideological consensus—has had another very important impact on our parties. It has given us two major parties which look very much alike. Both of them are moderate. They are built upon compromise; they tend to occupy "the middle of the road."

Both parties seek the same prize: the support (the votes) of a majority of the electorate. To do so, they must woo essentially the same voters. Inevitably, each of them takes policy stands very much like those taken by the other. Often—and for very good reason, then—the competition between them becomes a struggle between competing political personalities.

The Multi-Party Alternative

There are some who argue that the American two-party system should be scrapped. They would replace it with a **multi-party** arrangement—in which several major and many lesser parties would exist, as in most of the European democracies today.

In the typical multi-party system, the various parties are each based upon some distinctive interest, such as economic class, religious belief, sectional attachment, or political ideology.

Those who want such an arrangement here say that it would be more representative and more responsive to the will of the people. They insist that it would give voters a real choice among candidates and policy alternatives.

The practical effect of two of the factors we have just noted—*i.e.,* single-member districts and the American ideological consensus—seem to make such an arrangement impossible, however. Beyond that, a multi-party system tends to produce instability in government. One party is not often able to win the support of a majority of the voters. The power to govern must, therefore, be shared among a number of parties—by a coalition of them. Several of the multi-party nations of Western Europe have long been plagued by governmental crises and by frequent shifts in party control. Italy furnishes an almost nightmarish example: It has had a new government on the average of once every nine months ever since the end of World War II.

One-Party Systems

In most dictatorships, as in the Soviet Union and the People's Republic of China, only one political party—the party of the ruling clique— is allowed. For all practical purposes, it is quite accurate to say that in those circumstances a "no-party system "exists.

In quite another sense, several States and many local areas in this country can be described in "one-party" terms—either in the present or, more often, in the past tense. Thus, until as recently as the late-1950s, the Democrats almost completely dominated the politics of the South. And the GOP was almost always the winner in New England and in the upper Middle West.

But effective two-party competition has spread fairly rapidly in the past 20 years or so. Democrats have won many offices in every northern State. Republican candidates have become more and more successful throughout the once-solid South.[5]

Party Membership

Who are Republicans, and who Democrats? And who are independents in American politics? We shall take a long look at those questions in the next chap-

A campaign for major public office requires the willing help of many volunteer party workers.

ter. But, for now, this point: The answers to them can tell us much about both our parties and the party system.

Membership in either of the major parties is purely voluntary. A person is a Republican or a Democrat—or belongs to a minor party or is an independent—just because that's what he or she chooses to be.

As we have said, the two major parties are very broadly based. That is, they are multi-class in nature. They purposefully try to attract as much support from as many individuals and as many groups as they possibly can. Each of them has always been composed, in greater or lesser degree, of a cross-section of the nation's population. Each is made up of Protestants, Catholics, and Jews; whites, blacks, hispanics, and other minorities; professionals, farmers, employers, and union members. Each

A slogan used by the Republican Party for its presidential candidate in 1952 and 1956.

---

[5]Nevertheless, about a third of the States can still be said to have "modified one-party systems." That is, one or the other of the two major parties regularly wins elections in those States. Also, in most States, while there may be vigorous two-party competition at the Statewide level, there are many locales in which one party is overwhelmingly dominant.

A CASE IN POINT:

THE LOG CABIN CAMPAIGN

Before the coming of radio and then television, political candidates had to rely on other attention-getting devices to project their images. Just as candidates do today, they tried to create favorable images of themselves in the voters' minds.

However they went about it, most of them wanted to be seen as capable, hard-working, high-principled personalities dedicated to the public good. To that end, candidates have long used a variety of gimmicks, props, and other paraphenalia—from ribbons, flags, buttons, and bandannas to mugs, umbrellas, sunglasses, and peanuts—to grab the voter's attention.

The presidential contest of 1840 featured a classic example of campaign gimmickry. When the Whigs picked William Henry Harrison to run against President Martin Van Buren, a scornful Democrat said that all the 68-year-old hero of the War of 1812 really wanted to do was sit by his log cabin and swig hard cider.

Harrison's supporters quickly seized on that remark, using it to play up their candidate's humble beginnings. From that point on, Harrison campaigned from a log cabin—which he'd had build on top of a wagon, with a seemingly bottomless barrel of cider attached to it. The crowds loved it, and Harrison won handily.

1. Why did Harrison use this slogan in 1840: "Tippecanoe and Tyler, too"?
2. What unusual, out-of-the-ordinary campaign devices have you seen?
3. If you were to run for office, how would you try to create a favorable public image?

A hand-sewn Harrison emblem

numbers the young, the middle-aged, and the elderly; city-dwellers, suburbanites, and small-town and rural residents among its members. These and all of the others groupings that make up American society are to be found in both Republican and Democratic ranks.

It is true that the members of certain segments of the electorate tend to align themselves more solidly with one or the other of the major parties, at least for a time. Thus, blacks, Catholics and Jews, and labor union members have voted far more often for Democrats than for Republicans in recent decades. In the same way, white males, Protestants, and those from the business community have been inclined to back the GOP. Yet, never have all of the members of any race, or creed, or economic or social group tied themselves permanently, or indivisibly, to either of the parties.

Individuals identify themselves with a party for many reasons. Family is almost certainly the most important among them. Many studies of voter behavior show that about two out of every three Americans follow the party allegiance of their parents. That is, most of us inherit our party preferences.

Major events can have a decided influence on party choice. Of these, the Civil War and the Depression of the 1930s have been the most significant in American political history, as we shall see in a moment.

Economic status is also important. Generalizations are quite risky here—as they are in all other matters. But it is clear that those in higher income groups are likely to think of themselves as Republicans and for those with lower incomes to be Democrats.

Several other factors also feed into the mix of both party choice and voting behavior—including, for example, age, level of education, place of residence, and the work environment. And some of those factors may conflict with one another in the case of any individual—and, in fact, they often do.

Again, we shall return to this whole matter of partisan preference and voting behavior in Chapter 8.

☑ FOR REVIEW

1. Why do we have a two-party system in the United States?
2. Define: (a) single-member districts, (b) the American ideological consensus.
3. What is a multi-party system? A one-party system?
4. How does one become a member of either of the major parties?

The Evolution of the Two-Party System

The Nation's First Parties

Today is the product of yesterday—with political parties as with all else. As we have seen, the beginnings of the American two-party system can be traced to the battle over the ratification of the Constitution.

The Federalist Party was the first to appear. It formed around Alexander Hamilton, who had become Secretary of the Treasury in the new government organized by George Washington. The Federalists were, by and large, the party of "the rich and the well-born." Most of them had supported the Constitution. Now, led by Hamilton, they worked to make a stronger national government a reality. Their program was particularly beneficial to financial, manufacturing, and commercial interests. And, to reach their goals, they urged a liberal interpretation of the Constitution.

Thomas Jefferson, while serving as Secretary of State, led the opposition to Hamilton and his Federalists.[6] Jefferson and his followers were more sympathetic to the "common man." They favored a limited role for the new government. In their view, Congress should dominate that government and its policies should help the nation's small shopkeepers, laborers, farmers, and planters. And, they insisted upon a strict construction of the provisions of the Constitution.

Jefferson resigned from Washington's Cabinet in 1793 to give his time to the organization of his party. Originally, the new party took the name Anti-Federalist; then it was known as the Jeffersonian Republicans or the Democratic-Republicans, and finally (by 1828) as the Democratic Party.

These first two parties clashed in the elections of 1796. John Adams, the Federalists' candidate to succeed Washington as President, defeated Jefferson by just three votes in the electoral college. Over the next four years Jefferson and James Madison worked tirelessly to build the Democratic-Republicans. Their work paid large dividends in the elections of 1800. Jefferson defeated the incumbent President Adams and his party also won control of Congress. The Federalists never returned to power.

The Eras of One-Party Domination

The history of the American party system since 1800 may be fairly neatly divided into three major periods. During each of them, one or the other of two major parties has regularly held the Presidency, and, with it, usually both houses of Congress, as well.

In the first of these periods, from

---

[6]Given his opposition to the rise of parties, President Washington named arch foes Hamilton and Jefferson to his new Cabinet to get them to work together—*i.e.,* in an (unsuccessful) attempt to avoid the creation of formally organized and opposing groups.

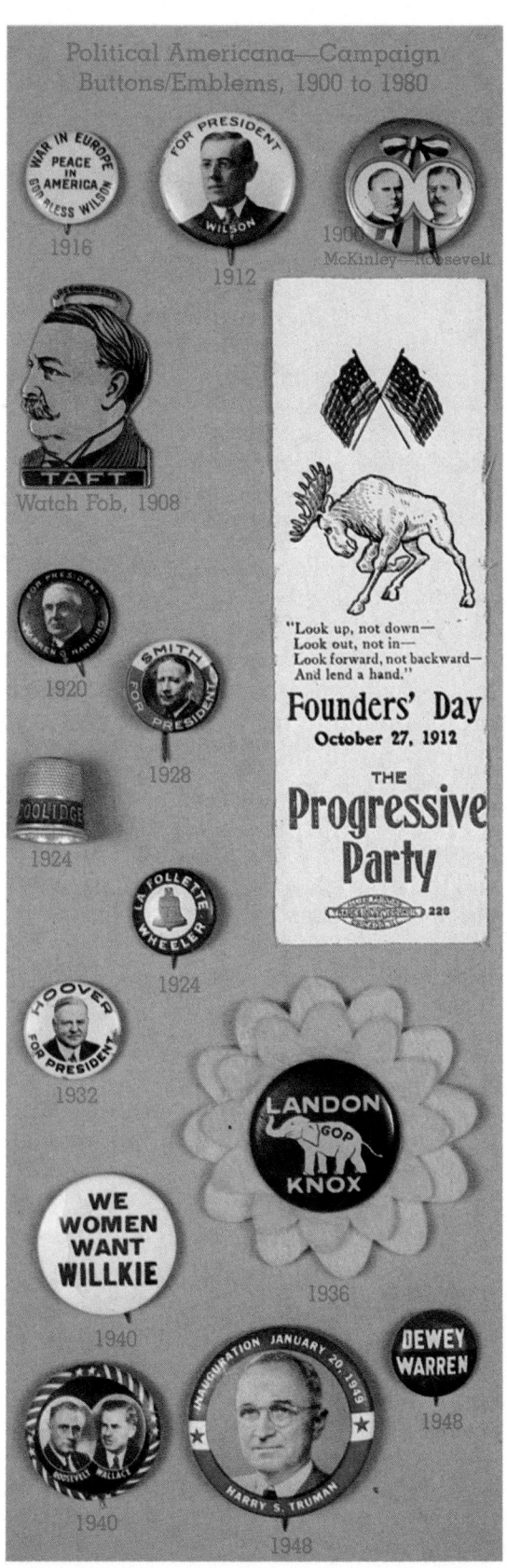

Political Americana—Campaign Buttons/Emblems, 1900 to 1980

1800 to 1860, the Democrats won 13 of 15 presidential elections; they lost the office only in the elections of 1840 and 1848. In the second era, from 1860 to 1932, the Republicans were in control. They won 14 of 18 elections, losing only in 1884, 1892, 1912, and 1916.

The third period came with Franklin Roosevelt's first election as President in 1932. Since then, the Republicans have been able to win the White House with but three of their candidates: Dwight Eisenhower in 1952 and 1956; Richard Nixon in 1968 and 1972; and Ronald Reagan in 1980.

The Era of the Democrats, 1800–1860. Jefferson's election in 1800 marked the beginning of a period of Democratic domination that was to last until the Civil War. (The Federalists, shattered in 1800, had disappeared altogether by 1816.)

For a time, through the Era of Good Feeling, the Democratic-Republicans were unopposed in national politics. They had split into factions by the mid-1820s, however. By Andrew Jackson's administration (1829–1837) a potent National Republican (Whig) Party had arisen to challenge the Democrats. The major issues of the day—conflicts over public lands, the Second Bank of the United States, high tariffs, and the slave question—all had made new party alignments inevitable.

The Democrats, led by Jackson, were a coalition of small farmers, debtors, frontiersmen, and slaveholders. Their main strength lay in the South and West. The years of Jacksonian democracy saw the coming of universal white male voting, a large increase in the number of elective offices around the country, and the spread of the spoils system.

The Whig Party was led by the widely popular Henry Clay and the great orator, Daniel Webster. It was a loose coalition of eastern bankers, merchants, and industrialists, and southern planters —all opposed to the precepts of Jacksonian democracy and dedicated to the high tariff. The Whigs' victories were few. As the other major party from the mid-1830s to the 1850s, they were able to elect only two Presidents, both of them war heroes—William Henry Harrison in 1840 and Zachary Taylor in 1848.

By the 1850s the growing crisis over slavery split both major parties. Left without a leader by the deaths of Clay and Webster, the Whig coalition fell apart. The Democrats split into two sharply divided camps, North and South. Through the decade the nation drifted toward civil war.

Of the several groupings which arose to compete for supporters, the Republican Party was the most successful. Born in 1854, it drew many Whigs and anti-slavery Democrats. The Republicans nominated their first presidential candidate, John C. Fremont, in 1856 and elected their first President, Abraham Lincoln, in 1860. The Republican Party thus became the only party in the history of our politics to make the jump from third-party to major-party status.

The Era of the Republicans, 1860– 1932.   The Civil War began the second era. For nearly 75 years, the Republicans —supported by business and financial interests, and by farmers, laborers, and newly-freed blacks—were to dominate the national scene.

The Democrats, crippled by the war, were able to survive mainly through their hold on the Solid South. For the remaining years of the century they slowly rebuilt their electoral base. In all of that time they were able to place only one of their candidates in the White House—Grover Cleveland in 1884 and again in 1892. Those elections marked only short breaks in Republican supremacy, however. Riding the crest of both popular acceptance and unprecedented prosperity, the GOP remained the dominant party well into the 20th century.

The election of 1896 was especially important in the development of the party system. It climaxed years of protest by small businessmen, farmers, and the emerging labor unions against big business and financial monopolies and the railroads. The Republicans regained the Presidency with William McKinley and, in so doing, they were able to gather new support from several segments of the electorate—new strength that allowed them to keep their majority role in national politics for another 36 years. Although the Democratic nominee, William Jennings Bryan, lost, he championed the "little man"—and so helped to push the nation's party politics back toward the economic arena, and away from the divisions of sectionalism.

The Republicans suffered their worst setback of the era in 1912, when they renominated incumbent President William Howard Taft. Former President

An 1896 William Jennings Bryan campaign button. The Democrat's candidate for President, he ran on a "free silver" platform, one demanding the free and unlimited coinage of silver.

AMERICAN POLITICAL PARTIES

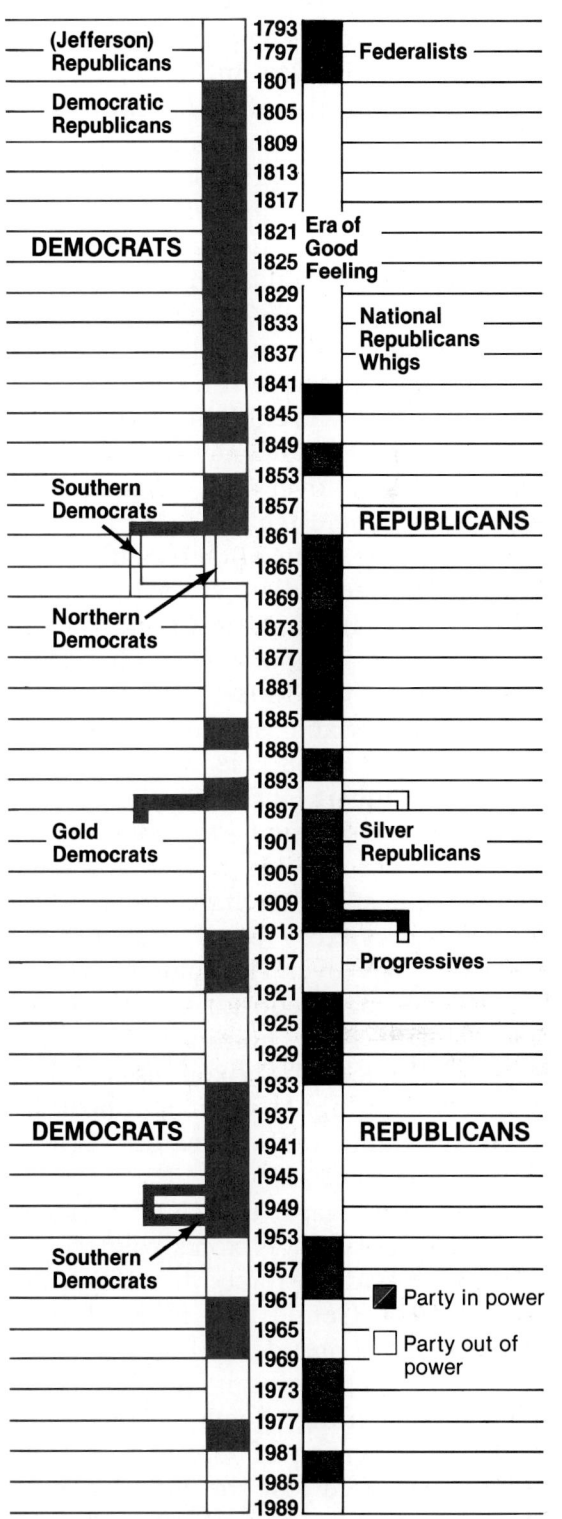

(Jefferson) Republicans — 1793, 1797 — **Federalists**

1801, 1805, 1809, 1813, 1817

Democratic Republicans

1821, 1825 — **Era of Good Feeling**

DEMOCRATS

1829, 1833, 1837 — **National Republicans Whigs**

1841, 1845, 1849, 1853

Southern Democrats

1857, 1861 — **REPUBLICANS**

1865, 1869

Northern Democrats

1873, 1877, 1881, 1885, 1889, 1893, 1897

Gold Democrats

1901 — **Silver Republicans**

1905, 1909, 1913 — **Progressives**

1917, 1921, 1925, 1929, 1933

DEMOCRATS 1937, 1941 **REPUBLICANS**

1945, 1949, 1953

Southern Democrats

1957, 1961, 1965, 1969, 1973, 1977, 1981, 1985, 1989

■ Party in power
□ Party out of power

Source: Historical Statistics of the U.S.; Statistical Abstract

The 1876 Republican National Convention, held in Cincinnati, nominated Rutherford B. Hayes for President.

SOME SIGNIFICANT MINOR PARTIES

Party	First Appearance in National Election	Latest Appearance in National Election
Anti-Masonic	1832	1832
Liberty	1840	1844
Free Soil	1848	1852
Know Nothing (American)	1856	1856
Constitutional Union	1860	1860
Labor Reform	1872	1872
Prohibition	1872	1984
Greenback	1876	1884
Union Labor	1888	1888
Socialist-Labor	1892	1984
People's (Populists)	1892	1908
Socialist	1900	1984
Progressive:		
T.R. Roosevelt	1912	1912
R.M. La Follette	1924	1924
H. Wallace	1948	1948
Farmer-Labor	1920	1932
Communist	1924	1984
States' Rights	1948	1948
American Independent	1968	1984
Libertarian	1972	1984
Citizens	1980	1984

Theodore Roosevelt, denied the nomination, left the party to become the candidate of his "Bull Moose" Progressive Party. With Republican support divided between Taft and Roosevelt, the Democratic nominee, Woodrow Wilson, took the Presidency. He was kept in office by a very narrow margin four years later.

But, again, the Democratic successes of 1912 and 1916 proved only an interlude. The Republicans won each of the next three presidential elections—with Warren Harding in 1920, Calvin Coolidge in 1924, and Herbert Hoover in 1928.

The Return of the Democrats, 1932 to ???.   The Great Depression, which began in 1929, had a massive impact upon nearly all aspects of American life and politics. The landmark election of 1932 brought Franklin D. Roosevelt to the Presidency and the Democrats back into power at the national level. A Democratic reign was begun—a reign which lasted, almost uninterrupted, on to the 1980s. And, of fundamental importance, that 1932 election marked a basic shift in the American people's feelings about the part government should play in economic and social matters.

Franklin Roosevelt and the Democrats engineered their victory in 1932 with a new coalition of electoral support. It was built very largely of southerners, small farmers, organized labor, and big city political organizations. The economic and social welfare programs, which formed the heart of the New Deal of the 1930s, strengthened that coalition; and it soon brought increasing support from blacks and other minorities in the electorate.

President Roosevelt won overwhelming reelection in 1936. And he secured an unprecedented third term in 1940 and yet another term in 1944, both times by heavy majorities. Harry S Truman completed the fourth term following FDR's death in 1945. Mr. Truman then earned a full term of his own, turning back the Republican challenge of Thomas E. Dewey, in 1948.

Since 1932, the GOP has won only five presidential elections. They returned to the White House, for the first time in 20 years, in 1952, marching behind World War II hero Dwight D. Eisenhower. General Eisenhower repeated his triumph in 1956. In both elections he defeated Democrat Adlai Stevenson.

The Republican return to power was short-lived, however. John F. Kennedy recaptured the Presidency with a razor-thin plurality over the Republicans' Vice President Richard M. Nixon in 1960. Lyndon Johnson took office following President Kennedy's assassination in 1963. In 1964, he virtually annihilated his Republican opponent, Senator Barry Goldwater.

Richard Nixon staged a dramatic comeback in 1968. He defeated Vice President Hubert Humphrey, the candidate of a Democratic Party badly torn by conflicts over the war in Vietnam, civil rights, and social welfare issues. The Republican victory came with only a bare plurality over Humphrey and the strong third-party effort of the American Independent Party nominee, Governor George Wallace. Mr. Nixon remained in power by routing the choice of the still-divided Democrats, Senator George McGovern, in 1972.

But, once again, the GOP hold did not last. President Nixon's role in the Watergate scandal forced him from office in 1974. Gerald Ford filled out the balance of the presidential term.

Beset by problems in the economy, by the continuing effects of Watergate, and by his pardon of former President Nixon, Mr. Ford lost the Presidency to Jimmy Carter and the resurgent Democrats in 1976.

A steadily worsening economy and his own inability to establish himself as an effective President spelled defeat for Mr. Carter in 1980, however. Led by Ronald Reagan, the Republicans scored a landslide victory in the most recent presidential election.

Did the elections of 1980 mark the beginning of yet another era in our politics? We must wait and see.

The Minor Parties

Two major parties dominate American politics. But that fact should not blind us to the existence, nor to the importance, of the several minor or third parties. Only a few have gained any permanence—for example, the Prohibition Party, founded in 1869. But all of them have left a continuing imprint on the American political system.

Types of Minor Parties

The number and variety of these parties makes it rather hard to describe and classify them. Still, four quite distinct types can be seen:

(1) The **ideological parties**—those based upon a particular set of beliefs, some comprehensive view of social, economic, and political matters. Most of these minor parties have been built on some shade of Marxist thought—for example, the Socialist, Socialist Labor, Socialist Worker, and Communist Parties. Some have had a quite different color, however—especially, the Libertarian Party of today, which emphasizes individualism and calls for doing away with most of government's present functions and programs.

The ideological parties have not often been able to win many votes. But, as a rule, they have been long-lived.

(2) The **single-issue parties**—those concentrating on a single public policy

The finishing touches are put to a Reagan sign before its use during the Republican National Convention, held in Detroit in 1980.

matter. Their names have usually indicated their primary concern—for example, the Free Soil Party, opposed to the spread of slavery in the 1840s and 1850s; the American Party (the "Know Nothings"), opposed to Irish Catholic immigration in the 1850s; and the Right to Life Party, opposed to abortion today.

Most of the single-issue parties have faded into history as events have passed them by, or as their theme has not brought voters flocking to the polls, or as one or both of the major parties has taken their key issue as its own.

(3) The **economic protest parties**—those rooted in periods of economic discontent. Unlike the socialist parties, these groups have not had any clear-cut ideological base. Most often, they have been sectional parties, drawing their strength from the agricultural South and West. Thus, the Greenback Party tried to

organize agrarian discontent from 1876 through 1884. It called for the free coinage of silver, federal regulation of the railroads, an income tax, and labor legislation. Its descendant, the Populist Party of the 1890s, added demands for public ownership of railroad, telephone and telegraph companies, lower tariffs, and the adoption of the initiative and referendum (see page 533).

Each of these economic protest parties has disappeared as the nation has climbed out of the difficult economic period in which that party was born.

(4) The **splinter parties**—those which have split away from one or the other of the major parties. Most of the more important minor parties in our politics have been of this kind. Among the leading groups which have split away from the Republicans are: Theodore Roosevelt's "Bull Moose" Progressive Party of 1912, and Robert LaFollette's Progressive Party of 1924. And from the Democrats: Henry Wallace's Progressive Party and the States' Rights (Dixiecrat) Party, both of 1948, and George Wallace's American Independent Party of 1968.

Most splinter parties have formed around some strong personality—most often one who has failed to win his major party's presidential nomination. They have faded or collapsed when

CASE STUDY

THE WINLESS WONDERS

Well over a hundred minor parties have appeared over the course of our political history—and most of them have soon disappeared.

Measured in terms of winning public office, these parties have been notably unsuccessful. Still, a number of them have had a substantial impact on the political system—and we illustrate that point on nearby pages.

On occasion, minor parties have played a significant role in some of the States. And a few do so today. In New York, for example, both the Liberal Party and the Conservative Party sometimes hold the balance of power in elections in that State.

But many minor parties have been unusual, to say the least. The Poor Man's Party was certainly one of them. Formed in 1952, it was as often as not called the Pig Party—after its presidential candidate Henry Krajewski, who raised pigs at his home in New Jersey.

Among other things, its platform advocated the annexation of Canada and a mandatory year of farm work for every teenager in this country. (Henry was on the ballot only in New Jersey and only in 1952, when he won 4,203 votes for President.)

And there have been others, like the Vegetarian Party. It wanted to outlaw the eating of meat in the United States. John Maxwell, one of its founders and a New York restaurant owner, ran as its presidential candidate in 1948, 1952, and 1956 (but didn't make the ballot in any of the States).

1. Why can it be said that the American electoral system may keep minor parties from winning but it does not prevent them from forming?

2. Why is it curious *not* that we have had so many minor parties but, rather, that we have not had *more* of them?

that leader has stepped aside.

A few of the minor parties have been successful at the State or local level. Some have elected a few members of Congress. A minor party has occasionally won some electoral votes, but none has ever won the Presidency.

Importance of Minor Parties

Most Americans do not support them, but minor parties still have had several impacts upon our politics and upon the major parties. It was a minor party, the Anti-Masons in 1831, that first used a national convention to nominate a presidential candidate. The Democrats and then the Whigs followed suit for the elections of 1832. Ever since the national convention has been the means by which the major parties have picked their presidential tickets.

A strong third-party candidacy can play a decisive role—often a "spoiler" role—in an election. The point was dramatically illustrated in the presidential election of 1912. A split in the Republican Party and the resulting third-party candidacy of Theodore Roosevelt that year produced these results:

Party and Candidate	Popular Vote	%	Electoral Vote
Democrat— Woodrow Wilson	6,293,152	41.8	435
Progressive— Theodore Roosevelt	4,119,207	27.4	88
Republican— William H. Taft	3,486,333	23.2	8
Socialist— Eugene V. Debs	900,369	6.0	—
Prohibition— Eugene Chafin	207,972	1.4	—

Almost certainly, had not TR quit the Republican Party, Woodrow Wilson would not have become President.

Historically, the most important

roles of the minor parties have been those of critic and innovator. Unlike the major parties, they have been ready, willing, and able to take quite clear-cut stands on the controversial issues of their day.

Over the years, many of the more important issues of American politics were first brought to the public attention by a minor party—for example, the

SIGNIFICANT MINOR PARTIES IN PRESIDENTIAL ELECTIONS, 1880–1980*

Year	Party and Candidate	Percent of Popular Vote	Electoral Votes
1880	Greenback James B. Weaver	3.72	—
1888	Prohibition Clinton B. Fisk	2.19	—
1892	Populist James B. Weaver	8.50	22
	Prohibition John Bidwell	2.25	—
1904	Socialist Eugene V. Debs	2.98	—
1908	Socialist Eugene V. Debs	2.82	—
1912	Progressive (Bull Moose) Theodore Roosevelt	27.39	88
	Socialist Eugene V. Debs	5.99	—
1916	Socialist Allan L. Benson	3.18	—
1920	Socialist Eugene V. Debs	3.42	—
1924	Progressive Robert M. LaFollette	16.56	13
1932	Socialist Norman M. Thomas	2.22	—
1948	States' Rights (Dixiecrat) Strom Thurmond	2.40	39
	Progressive Henry A. Wallace	2.38	—
1968	American Independent George C. Wallace	13.53	46

*Includes all minor parties that polled at least 2% of the popular vote. No minor party did so in the years not shown—including 1972, 1976, and 1980.

In 1976 independent (non-party) candidate Eugene J. McCarthy won 0.8% of the popular vote, and in 1980 independent John B. Anderson won 6.61%; neither McCarthy nor Anderson received any electoral votes.

progressive income tax, woman suffrage, railroad and banking regulation, old-age pensions, and farm relief programs. When their proposals have gained any real degree of popular support, one and then shortly both of the major parties have taken them over and presented them as their own. The late Norman Thomas, six times the Socialist Party's candidate for President, often complained that "the major parties are stealing from my platform."

The presidential candidates of at least 10 minor parties appeared on the ballots of different States in 1980—and there will likely be at least that many in 1984. Then, too, there was the very active independent effort made by Congressman John Anderson of Illinois. Some 300 minor party nominees ran for seats in Congress, as well.

☑ FOR REVIEW

1. Out of what circumstances did the nation's first two parties arise? Identify and contrast them.

2. Since 1800 the history of the American party system can be divided into what three major eras?

3. Describe the four types of minor parties in American politics. What important roles have these parties played in our politics?

Party Organization

The Major Parties Are Highly Decentralized

We often speak of the two major parties in terms that suggest that they are highly organized, close-knit, well-disciplined groups. Even though they look that way "on paper," neither is anything of the sort. Rather, both are highly decentralized—fragmented, and often torn by internal strife.

Federalism is a leading cause for this condition. Remember, the basic goal of the major parties is to gain control of government, and they try to do this by winning elective offices. In the American federal system those offices are scattered over a broad political landscape. They are widely distributed at the national, the State, and the local levels. In short, because the governmental system is decentralized, so, too, is the structure of each of the major parties.

The *nominating process* is another major factor here. Two aspects of that process have a large impact on the shape of both major parties.

(1) Candidate selection is an *intra-party* process. That is, nominations are made within the party. (2) That process can be (and often is) a *divisive* one. When there is a fight over a nomination, it pits members of the same party against one another—Republicans compete with Republicans, Democrats do battle with Democrats.

Again, both major parties are highly decentralized. It is quite misleading to think of them in terms of a cohesive or disciplined organizational pattern. Each of the State party organizations is only loosely tied to the party's national structure. And, too, local party organs are often quite independent of their parent State organizations. The party units regularly cooperate with one another, of course—but they don't always do so.

The President's party is usually more solidly united, more cohesively organized, than is the opposition. The President is automatically the party leader. There are a number of weapons with which that leadership can be asserted—such as the President's own popularity and the power to make appointments to federal office and dispense other favors.

The other party, the party out of power, has no one in an even faintly comparable position. Indeed, in our

PARTY ORGANIZATION

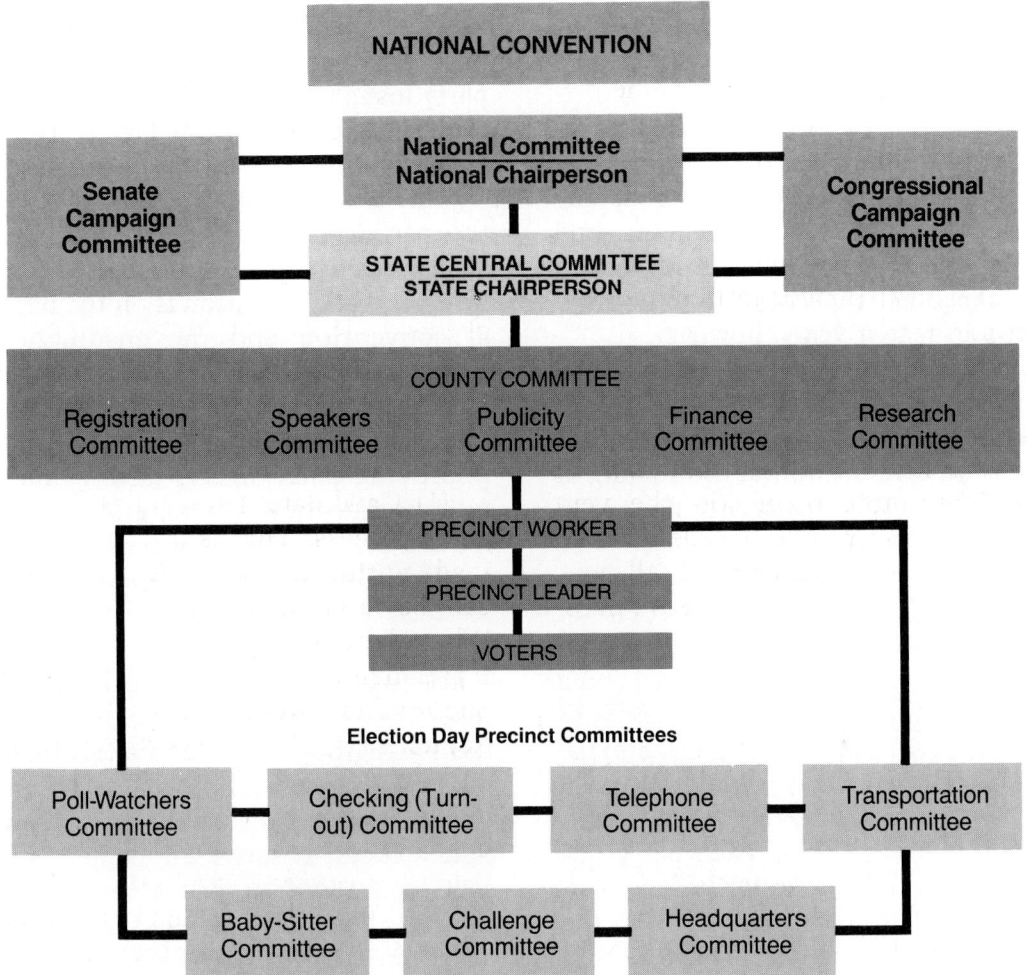

party system there is almost never any one personality in that party who can be called, in fact, its leader.[7]

National Party Machinery

There are four major elements in the structure of both major parties at the national level.

The National Convention. The national convention is often described as the party's national voice. It meets only every fourth year, in the summer.[8] The convention nominates the party's presidential and vice-presidential candidates, of course. It does perform some other functions, including the adoption of the party's rules and the making of its platform. Beyond that, it has little or no real authority, however. It has no control over the selection of the party's candidates for other offices nor over the policy stands those nominees take.

---

[7]Except the party's presidential candidate from the time of nomination on through the campaign period. A defeated presidential candidate is often called the "titular leader" of the party. That label is really very descriptive—the losing candidate is the party's leader in title, by custom, but not in fact.

[8]First in 1974 and again in 1978 and 1982, the Democrats held a mid-term convention—a "mini-convention," between presidential elections. They met to discuss issues and consider party rules changes; and they will likely do so again in 1986. To this point, the GOP has not seriously considered such a meeting.

The National Committee. Between conventions, the party's affairs are handled, at least in theory, by the national committee and by the national chairperson.

For years, each party's national committee was composed of a committeeman and a committeewoman chosen by the party organization in each State and several of the territories. Both parties have expanded the committee's membership in recent years, however.

On paper, the national committee appears to be a powerful organ. In fact, it does not have a great deal of clout. Most of its work centers around the staging of the party's national conventions.

The National Chairperson. The national chairperson heads up the national committee in both parties. In form, he or she is chosen to a four-year term by the national committee, at a meeting right after the national convention adjourns. In fact, the choice is made by the presidential candidate and is then ratified by the committee.

To this point (1984), each party has picked only one woman for its top post. Jean Westwood of Utah chaired the Democratic National Committee from the 1972 convention until early 1973; and Mary Louise Smith of Iowa headed the RNC from 1974 to early 1977. Each of them was replaced soon after her party lost a presidential election; that is, each suffered the usual fate of the national chairperson in the losing party.

The chairperson directs the work of the party's headquarters and its small staff in Washington. In presidential election years the attention is on the national convention and the ensuing campaign. In between, the chairperson and the national committee work to strengthen the party and its fortunes—improving party unity, raising money, rounding up new voters, and preparing for the next presidential season.

The Congressional Campaign Committees. Each party also has a campaign committee in each house of Congress—a Congressional Campaign Committee and a Senatorial Campaign Committee. Each group works to re-elect incumbents and to save the seats being given up by retiring party members. They also take a hand in some campaigns to unseat incumbents in the other party—at least in those races where the prospects seem to justify such efforts.

Every fourth year, each major party holds a national convention to nominate the party's presidential and vice-presidential candidates. Here, delegates from each of the States stand in prayer as the 31st Democratic National Convention opened in Chicago in 1952. In that year, Adlai Stevenson won the Democratic nomination, but lost the presidential election to Dwight Eisenhower, the Republican candidate.

In both parties, and in both houses, the members of these campaign committees are chosen by their colleagues. They serve for two years—that is, for a term of Congress.

State and Local Party Machinery. National party organization is largely the product of custom and the rules adopted by successive national conventions. At the State and local levels, however, party structure is very largely set by State law.

The State Organization. At the State level, party machinery is built around a State central committee, headed by a State chairperson. The members of the central committee most often come from the party's county organizations; and they usually pick the chairperson.

The chairperson may be an important figure in his/her own right. But, more often, her or she fronts for the governor, a U.S. Senator, or some other powerful leader or group in the politics of the State.

Together, the chairperson and the central committees are expected to further the party's interests in the State. Most of the time they do so, with more or less success—building an effective organization and party unity, finding candidates and campaign funds, and so on. But, remember, both of the major parties are highly decentralized—fragmented, and sometimes torn by struggles for power within their own ranks.

Local Organization. Local party structures vary so widely that they nearly defy brief description. Generally, they follow the electoral map of the State, with a party unit for each constituency (each district) in which elective offices are to be filled—congressional and legislative districts, counties, cities and towns, wards and precincts.

In some places, local party organizations are active year-round; but, most often, they are lifeless except for those few hectic months before an election.

The Three Basic Elements of the Party

Look at the structure of the two major parties from another angle—the roles of their members, rather than their tables of organization. From this vantage point, they are made up of three basic elements:

(1) **The Party Organization**—the leaders, the activists, and the hangers-on who control and run the party machinery: "all those who give their time, money, and skills to the party, whether as leaders or followers."[9]

(2) **The Party in the Electorate**—the party's voters, its loyalists who vote the straight party ticket and those other voters who call themselves party members and usually vote for its candidates.

(3) **The Party in Government**—the party's officeholders, those who hold elective and appointive offices in the executive, legislative, and judicial branches of the Federal, State, and local governments.

We have taken a quick look at the party organization here. We shall consider the party in the electorate in the next chapter, and the party in government in several later chapters.

Parties and the Future

Political parties have never been very widely respected nor even very much admired in the United States. Rather, over time, most Americans have had very mixed feelings about them. Most of us have accepted them as quite necessary institutions, yes; but, at the same time, we have felt that they should be closely watched and sternly controlled. To many they have seemed little better

---

[9]Frank J. Sorauf, *Party Politics in America.* Little, Brown, 4th ed., 1980, p. 8.

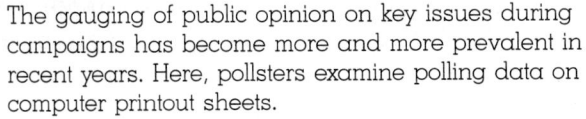

The gauging of public opinion on key issues during campaigns has become more and more prevalent in recent years. Here, pollsters examine polling data on computer printout sheets.

than necessary evils. There has always been a strong anti-party feeling in this country.[10]

Clearly, political parties are not very popular institutions today. In fact, they have been in a period of decline for the past several years. (And their decline has even led some analysts to this very disturbing conclusion: Not only are the parties in serious trouble, the party system itself may be on the point of collapse.)

---

[10]Recall that George Washington warned the new nation of "the baneful effect of the spirit of party" in 1796 (page 169). That sentiment has been echoed often and by many prominent figures ever since. Thus, in 1844 Ralph Waldo Emerson wrote: "Our parties are parties of circumstance, and not of principle . . . [Both] are perpetually corrupted by personality . . . [and] the only safe rule is always to believe that the worst will be done."

The present, weakened state of the parties can be traced to several factors, and the evidences of it are not hard to find. They include:

A sharp drop in the number of voters willing to identify themselves as Republicans or Democrats, and a growing number who look at themselves as independents.

A big increase in *split-ticket voting* (voting for candidates of *both* parties for the different offices at the same election).

Various structural changes and "reforms"—from the introduction of the direct primary early in the 1900s to the more recent and far-reaching changes in campaign finance laws—which have made the parties more "open" but have also led to greater internal conflict and disorganization.

More and more changes in the technology of campaigning for office—especially the heavy use of television and of such other devices as professional campaign managers and direct-mail advertising—which have made candidates much less dependent upon party organizations.

The growth, in both numbers and impact, of *single-issue organizations* in our politics—groups which take sides for or against candidates based on their own closely defined views in some specific area of public policy (abortion, gun control, or nuclear power development, for example), rather than on the candidates' stands on the whole slate of public policy questions.

We shall look at these and at several other matters affecting the condition of the parties over the course of the next three chapters. As we do so, bear in mind much of what we have said in this chapter. In particular, remember these points: Political parties are indispensable to democratic government—and so, then, to American government. Our present-day major parties have existed for a far longer period of time than have any other parties anywhere in the world. And, as we have seen, they perform a number of necessary functions.

In short, the reports of their passing may not only be premature; they may in fact be quite far-fetched.

☑ FOR REVIEW

1. Why are federalism and the nominating process significant causes for the decentralized character of the two major parties?
2. What are the four major elements of major party organization at the national level?
3. What is the basic shape of party organization at the State level? At the local level?
4. Viewing the major parties from the standpoint of the roles of their members rather than their organizational structure, each of them is made up of what three elements?
5. Over time, how have most Americans viewed political parties?
6. What is the present state of the major parties?

S U M M A R Y

Political parties are indispensable to democratic government. They are a necessary link between the people and their government and work to blunt conflict.

With particular reference to our two major parties, a political party is a group of persons who seek to control government through the winning of elections and the holding of public office. The major parties carry out five important functions in American politics. They (1) nominate candidates and present them to the electorate; (2) inform voters and stimulate their interest in public affairs; (3) act as bonding agents to insure the good performance of their candidates and officeholders; (4) provide a basis for the conduct of government; and (5) act as watchdogs over the conduct of the public's business.

Our two-party system is mostly the result of historical factors, the continuing force of tradition, several features of the electoral process, and the American ideological consensus. Membership in the two major parties is purely voluntary and multi-class in nature. Many factors—including family, economic status, and place of residence—influence each person's choice of party.

From its beginnings with the Federalists and the Anti-Federalists, the history of American political parties may be traced through three broad periods: The era of the Democrats, 1800–1860; the era of the Republicans, 1860–1932; and the return of the Democrats, 1932 to ???

Minor (or third) parties have also played an important part in American politics, especially in getting the two major parties to move on issue questions. They may be separated into: (1) ideological, (2) single-issue, (3) economic protest, and (4) splinter parties.

Each of the major parties is highly decentralized, largely as the result of federal-

ism and the potentially divisive nature of the nominating process. At the national level, both are organized around four principal elements: the national convention, the national committee, the national chairperson, and the congressional campaign committees. State and local party organization is generally built along geographic-electoral lines. Each of the major parties may also be viewed as a three-part structure: the party as an organization, the party in the electorate, and the party in government.

Political parties have never been widely popular in the United States. And they most certainly are not today. However, they remain a very necessary part of the American governmental system.

CHAPTER REVIEW

Key Terms/Concepts

American ideological consensus (170)
Bonding agent function (167)
Economic protest parties (179)
Governmental function (167)
Ideological consensus (170)
Ideological parties (179)
Informer-stimulator function (166)
Major party (168)
Majority (169)
Minor party (179)
Multi-party system (170)
National committee (184)
National convention (183)

Nominating function (166)
One-party system (171)
Party in government (185)
Party in power (168)
Party in the electorate (185)
Party membership (171)
Party organization (185)
Party out of power (167)
Plurality (169)
Political party (165)
Single-issue parties (179)
Single-member district (169)

Splinter parties (180)
Third party (179)
Two-party system (168)

Watchdog function (167)

Keynote Questions

1. Define the term political party in a way that will accommodate our two major parties.
2. What functions do parties perform in American politics?
3. Why do we have a two-party system in the United States?
4. Why did the Framers of the Constitution make no provision for political parties?
5. The history of the American party system since 1800 can be divided into what three major eras?
6. Describe the various types of minor parties in American politics. What important roles have those parties played over time?

7. Why are both federalism and the nominating process significant causes for the decentralized character of our two major parties?

8. Describe the basic shape of party organization at the national and the State and local levels.

9. From the standpoint of their membership, each of the major parties is composed of what three elements?

10. Over time, how have most Americans viewed political parties?

11. What is the present condition of the two major parties? Why?

For Thought and Discussion

1. What advice would you give to a friend who wants to make politics his or her career?

2. In British politics the party out of power is known as "Her Majesty's Loyal Opposition." Why has it been said that that phrase is "one of the most illustrative of terms in the democratic dictionary"?

3. Based upon presidential, congressional, gubernatorial, and legislative election results over the past 40 years, how would you classify your State: as one-party, modified one-party, or two-party? (The necessary data can be found in several sources, probably most readily in successive editions of your State's *Manual* or *Blue Book.*)

4. Regardless of your own view of the matter, put together the strongest argument you can in favor of straight-ticket as opposed to split-ticket voting.

5. We have said that political parties have been a principal agent in the process of informal amendment of the Constitution, and also that government in the United States is in many ways government by party (on pages 61 and 167). Give at least five illustrations of these comments.

Suggested Activities

1. Look into the structure and functions of party organizations in your area. Interview local party leaders and elected officeholders (and, if possible, invite them to speak to the class). How do they describe political parties? What functions do they see the party performing? What changes in party structure (if any) would they like to see?

2. Stage a class forum or debate on this question: *Resolved*, That the American two-party system be restructured to produce two quite different major parties, one clearly identifiable as the conservative party and the other as the liberal party.

3. Secure copies of the latest national platforms of the Republican and Democratic Parties. (They should be readily available in the school and/or local libraries, and from the respective State party organizations.) Outline each of those documents, and compare them in terms of their differences, their similarities, and their vague and their specific planks.

4. Prepare a bulletin board display showing the principal functions performed by the two major parties in American politics.

8

Government by the People: Voters and Voter Behavior

CHAPTER OBJECTIVES

To help you to
Learn ▪ Know ▪ Understand

The historical development of the right to vote in the United States.

The present-day shape of the right to vote.

The several recent federal voting rights statutes.

Voter turnout and non-voting in American elections.

The complex of factors affecting the behavior of the American voter.

I often think it's comical—
    Fal, lal, la!
How Nature does contrive—
    Fal, lal, la!
That every boy and every gal
That's born into the world alive
Is either a little Liberal
Or else a little Conservative!

Gilbert and Sullivan,
Iolanthe

We have noted several times that democratic government is, for us, representative government. It is "government by the people"—self-government conducted through the medium of elected representatives. Those representatives are the agents of the people. They are chosen by the people to act for the people.

Those representatives, those who hold public office, are held accountable to the people at periodic elections. It is by voting at those elections that the typical citizen can most directly take part in the governing process in this country.

Clearly, then, **suffrage**[1]—the right to vote—lies at the very heart of the democratic notion.

Suffrage a Political Right

The use of the word "right" in the phrase "right to vote" should be clearly understood. No one has the right to vote

---

[1]The word comes from the Latin *suffragium*— literally, "a vote." The word *franchise* (from the French, *franchir*) has the same meaning—*i.e.*, the right to vote.

Throughout the early 1900s, there was strong opposition to a constitutional amendment that would allow women to vote.

in quite the same sense as he or she has the right to free speech, to a fair trial, or to any of the other *civil* rights guaranteed by the Constitution. The right to vote is *not* a civil right—one belonging to all persons. Rather, it is a *political* right—one belonging to all those who qualify, all those who can meet certain requirements set by law.

In this chapter we first take up the matter of suffrage qualifications—*who* has the right to vote in elections in the United States. Then we turn to non-voting—to the fact that, and the reasons why, millions of potential voters do *not* go to the polls in this country. Finally, we look at voter behavior—at *how* and *why* the many millions more who *do* vote cast their ballots in elections.

Suffrage and the Constitution

The overall size of the American electorate is truly impressive. More than 170 million persons—just about all of our citizens who are at least 18 years of age—can qualify to vote.

That huge number—the size of the **electorate**, the potential voting population—is a direct result of the legal definition of the right to vote. That is, it is the product of those laws by which suffrage qualifications have been set, those laws which determine who may (and who may not) vote. It is also the product of some two hundred years of continuing, often contentious, and sometimes violent struggle.

A polling place in New Hampshire during a presidential primary election.

Historical Development of the Suffrage

Largely because the Framers could not agree upon specific requirements, the Constitution left the power to set suffrage qualifications to the States.[2]

When the Constitution became effective in 1789 probably not one man in 15 could vote in elections in the different States. The long history of the development of the suffrage since then has been marked by two long-term trends:

First, by the elimination of a number of restrictive requirements based upon such arbitrary factors as religious belief, property ownership, tax payment, race, and sex; and

Second, by the transfer of more and more authority over the suffrage from the States to the Federal Government.

The historical development of the electorate has taken place in five fairly distinct stages—and those two trends have been woven through them.

The Five Historical Stages. The first stage of the struggle to extend voting rights came in the early part of the 1800s. Religious qualifications, born in the colonies, rather quickly disappeared; no State has had a religious test since 1810. Property ownership and tax payment qualifications then began to fall, one by one, among the States. By mid-century, universal white adult male suffrage was very largely fact.

The second major effort to broaden the electorate followed the Civil War. The 15th Amendment, ratified in 1870, was intended to protect any citizen from being denied the right to vote because of race or color. (Despite that amendment, black Americans have, until quite recently, made up the largest single group of disfranchised citizens.)

The third expansion was marked by the ratification of the 19th Amendment in 1920. That amendment prohibited the denial of the right to vote on account of sex. Wyoming, while still a territory, first gave women the right to vote in 1869. By 1920 more than half of the States had followed that lead.

A fourth major extension took place during the 1960s—as federal legislation and court decisions centered on securing to blacks a full role in the electoral process in all States. With the passing and then the strong enforcement of several civil rights acts, racial equality finally became a fact in polling booths throughout the country.[3] The 23rd Amendment, added in 1961, included the voters of the District of Columbia in the presidential electorate. And the 24th Amendment, ratified in 1964, did away with the poll tax, and any other tax, as a condition for voting in federal elections.

---

[2]Originally, the Constitution had only two provisions relating to the right to vote: (1) Article I, Section 2, Clause 1 requires each State to allow those persons qualified to vote for members of "the most numerous branch" of its own legislature to vote as well for members of the national House of Representatives. And (2) Article II, Section I, Clause 2 provides that presidential electors be chosen in each State "in such manner as the legislature thereof may direct."

The fifth and latest expansion of the electorate came with the adoption of the 26th Amendment in 1971. It set the minimum age for voting in all elections in the United States at 18.

Power to Establish Voting Qualifications

The Constitution does not give to the Federal Government the power to set suffrage qualifications. Rather, that matter is reserved to the States. *But* the Constitution does place five particular restrictions on the States in the use of that power:

(1) Any person whom a State allows to vote for members of the "most numerous branch" of its own legislature must also be allowed to vote for Representatives and Senators in Congress.[3] This restriction is of little real meaning today. With only minor exceptions, each of the States allows the same voters to vote in *all* elections within the State.

(2) No State may deprive any person of the right to vote "on account of race, color, or previous condition of servitude."[4]

(3) No State may deprive any person of the right to vote on account of sex.[5]

(4) No State may require the payment of any tax as condition for taking part in the nomination or election of any federal officeholder. That is, no State

---

[3]Article I, Section 2, Clause 1; 17th Amendment.

[4]15th Amendment. The phrase "previous condition of servitude" refers to slavery, of course. Note that this amendment does *not* guarantee the right to vote to blacks, or to anyone else. Instead, it forbids the States to discriminate against any person on these grounds in the setting of suffrage qualifications.

[5]19th Amendment. Note that this amendment does *not* guarantee the right to vote to females, as such. Technically, it forbids States the power to discriminate against either males *or* females in setting suffrage qualifications.

[6]24th Amendment.

[7]26th Amendment. Note that this amendment does not prevent any State from allowing persons *younger* than the age 18 to vote. But it does prohibit a State the power to set a *maximum* age for voting.

may do so in any process connected with selecting the President, Vice President, or members of Congress. [6]

(5) No State may deprive any person who is at least 18 years of age the right to vote on account of age. [7]

Again, no State may violate any of these five restrictions—each of them relating expressly to the right to vote. Beyond that, remember, no State may violate any other provision in the Constitution—in the setting of suffrage qualifications or in anything else that it does.

A case decided by the Supreme Court in 1975, *Hill* v. *Stone*, deals with the point. There the Court struck down a section of the Texas constitution. That provision declared that only those persons who owned taxable property could vote in city bond elections. The Court found the drawing of such a distinction for voting purposes—between those who do and those who do not own taxable property—to be an unreasonable classification, prohibited by the 14th Amendment's Equal Protection Clause.

But, notice, so long as a State does not violate any provision in the Constitution of the United States, it may set voting qualifications as it chooses.

☑ FOR REVIEW

1. Distinguish a *political* from a *civil* right.

2. What is the size of the American electorate today?

3. What two long-term trends have marked the development of the right to vote in the United States?

4. What specific restrictions does the Constitution place upon the States in the setting of suffrage qualifications?

5. Does the Constitution guarantee the right to vote to any group?

Voter Qualifications Among the States

Citizenship and Residence

Each of the States requires all voters to meet qualifications based on two factors today: citizenship and residence.

Citizenship.   No alien may vote legally in any public election held anywhere in the United States. Still, nothing in the Constitution says that aliens cannot vote, and any State could allow them to do so if it chose.[7a]

Only one State now draws any distinction between native-born and naturalized citizens with regard to the suffrage. The Minnesota constitution requires a person to have been an American citizen for at least three months.

In practice, a few aliens do vote—though in what number no one knows. Those who do so either wrongly believe that they are citizens or unlawfully pass themselves off as citizens.

Residence.   Each State requires that a person live within the State for at least some period of time in order to qualify to vote.

The residence requirement rests on two principal justifications, one historical and the other of continuing significance. The first one: to keep a political machine from importing (bribing) enough outsiders to affect the outcome of local elections. The adoption and enforcement of residence qualifications dried up that once common practice. The second: to make sure that every voter has had at least some time in which to learn something about the candidates and issues in an election.

The period of time that a voter must have lived in the State is now quite brief. The details vary somewhat—but only slightly—among the 50 States. And the fact that the residence requirement is a fairly uniform one today is a direct result of a 1972 decision by the Supreme Court. We shall see why in a moment.

Today in 18 States voters must live within the State for at least 30 days before an election.[8] In two others the minimum period is slightly longer: 32 days in Colorado and 50 days in Arizona.

Nine States have shorter periods: 29 days in West Virginia; 28 days in Massachusetts; 20 days in Kansas, Minnesota, Oregon, and Tennessee; and 10 days in Alabama, New Hampshire, and Wisconsin.

The other 21 States[9] require no fixed number of days and only demand that a voter be a legal resident of the State.

Until recently, every State required a much longer period—typically, a year in the State, 60 or 90 days in the county, and 30 days in the local ward or precinct.[10] But in the Voting Rights Act Amendments of 1970 Congress prohibited any requirement of longer than 30 days for voting in presidential elections. And, in _Dunn_ v. _Blumstein_, 1972, the Supreme Court found Tennessee's requirement—at the time, a year in the State and 90 days in the county—unconstitutional. It held such a lengthy requirement to be an unsupportable discrimination against new residents and so in conflict with the 14th Amend-

---

[7a]At one time about a fourth of the States permitted those aliens who had applied for naturalization to vote. Typically, the western States did so, to help attract settlers. Arkansas was the last State in which aliens could vote, and it adopted a citizenship requirement in 1926.

[8]Alaska, Illinois, Indiana, Kentucky, Michigan, Mississippi, Montana, Nevada, New Jersey, New York, North Carolina, North Dakota, Ohio, Pennsylvania, Rhode Island, Texas, Utah, Washington.

[9]Arkansas, California, Connecticut, Delaware, Florida, Georgia, Hawaii, Idaho, Iowa, Louisiana, Maine, Maryland, Missouri, Nebraska, New Mexico, Oklahoma, South Carolina, South Dakota, Vermont, Virginia, Wyoming.

[10]The **precinct** is the basic, smallest unit of election administration; for each precinct there is a polling place. It is also the basic unit of party organization; see page 185. The **ward** is a unit into which cities are often divided for the election of members of the city council.

ment's Equal Protection Clause. While the Court did not state just how lengthy an acceptable period might be, it did say that "30 days appears to be an ample period of time." Election law and practice among the 50 States quickly accepted that standard.

As we've just noted, Congress acted in 1970 against lengthy residence requirements for voting in presidential elections. The 30-day lid that it had placed on those elections was upheld by the Supreme Court on *Oregon* v. *Mitchell* in 1970. Speaking for the Court, Justice Hugo Black said:

> Acting under its broad authority to create and maintain a national government, Congress unquestionably has power under the Constitution to regulate federal elections. The Framers of our Constitution were vitally concerned with setting up a national government that could survive.
>
> Essential to the survival and the growth of our national government is its power to fill its elective offices and to ensure that the officials who fill these offices are as responsive as possible to the will of the people whom they represent.

Nearly every State does prohibit **transients**—persons in the State only for a short time and for a specific purpose—from gaining a legal residence there. Thus, a traveling sales agent, a member of one of the armed services, or an out-of-State college student usually cannot vote in a State where he or she has only a temporary, *physical* residence.

In several States, however, the courts have now held that college students who claim the campus community as their legal residence, must be allowed to vote there. And they have held this to be so no matter where a student's parents may live or where his or her "permanent" home may be.

Age. Recall, the 26th Amendment sets 18 as the minimum age for voting in all elections. Prior to its adoption in 1971, 21 was the generally accepted standard.

In fact, up to 1970 only four of the States had put the voting age at less than 21. Georgia first allowed 18-year-olds to vote in 1943 and then Kentucky did so in 1955. Alaska entered the Union in 1959 with the age set at 19, and Hawaii do so later that same year with the age floor at 20. (Both Alaska and Hawaii set the age above 18 but below 21 to avoid any problems that might be caused by high school students voting in local school district elections. But, whatever the fears on that score, they have not been borne out by the behavior of high school age voters since the adoption of the 26th Amendment.)

Other Qualifications

A few other qualifications are imposed by several of the States.

Registration. Forty-nine States—

I'm what you'd call politically flexible: Republican when I'm working, Democrat when I ain't.

Clyde Peterson in *Houston Chronicle*

all except North Dakota—require that all voters, or at least most of them, be *registered* to vote. At base, registration gives election officials a list of those persons who may legally vote in an election.[11] (In a few States the voter registration process is known, instead, as "enrollment.")

Most States require *all* voters to register. But in a few—Wisconsin, for example,—only those in urban areas must do so. Typically, a prospective voter must "register" his or her name, age, place of birth, present address, length of residence and similar pertinent facts with a local registration officer.[12]

Every State (except North Dakota) now has some form of *permanent* registration. Typically, a voter remains registered unless or until he or she moves, dies, is convicted of a serious crime, is placed in a mental institution, or fails to vote for a certain number of years or elections.

The registration requirement has become somewhat controversial in recent years. Some argue that it should be done away with. They see it as a serious bar to voter turnout, especially among the poor and the less educated.

Others favor keeping registration but making it easier. To that end, two states (Maine and Oregon) now allow voters to register at any time, including election day. But, elsewhere, one must register at some time before an election is to be held—usually at least 30 days. (Nearly

Copyright ©, 1962, *St. Louis Post-Dispatch,* reproduced by courtesy of Bill Mauldin.

"By the way, what's that big word?"

half of the States now permit voters to register by mail.)

Literacy.   In the Voting Rights Act Amendments of 1970 Congress suspended for five years the use of any literacy requirement as a voting qualification anywhere in the United States. It made that ban a permanent one in 1975.

Until 1970 some form of a literacy requirement was found in 18 States. In some, just being able to read was required; in others, to read and write. In still others, the ability to read, write, and "understand" a piece of printed material was required—usually a passage from the State Constitution or the National Constitution.

The first literacy qualifications were adopted in Connecticut in 1855 and then in Massachusetts in 1857. They were aimed at Irish Catholic immigrants. Mississippi adopted a literacy requirement in 1890 and, shortly, most of the other southern States followed suit, usually with an "understanding clause."[13]

---

[11]Several States also use their voter registration to identify voters in terms of their party preference and, hence, their eligibility to take part in *closed primaries;* page 221. In most States one must be registered in order to vote in any election held within the State; but a few do not impose the requirement for *all* elections—e.g., registration is not required for some school district elections in Minnesota.

[12]Most often with an officer known as the *registrar of elections,* or with the county clerk. In a few States party officials and even candidates are allowed to register new voters.

SUMMARIZING

IN A FEW WORDS

What was the movie about? What happened in class? How was the game?

When we ask, or are asked, questions such as these, only a brief answer is expected. The questioner wants to know the highlights or major points and perhaps a few of the more interesting details—in other words, a *summary*.

In and out of school, we often encounter situations where summarizing information is called for. Summarizing helps us to remember important information, to compare information from several sources, and to share information with other people. Since few of us have photographic memories, we cannot keep track of everything and, therefore, depend on summaries.

To **summarize**, then, means to sum up, to state concisely, to present the general theme or major points in a brief form. A useful summary includes (1) the main ideas and (2) a few important details or examples to illustrate or explain the main ideas. A written summary might take the form of a list, an outline, or one or more paragraphs.

Here are some guidelines for making your own summaries:

1. Identify the main ideas.
2. Use category names and a few examples instead of longer lists of examples. For instance, say "civil rights legislation such as the Voting Rights Act of 1965" instead of "the Civil Rights Act of 1957, the Civil Rights Act of 1960, the Civil Rights Act of 1964, the Voting Rights Act of 1965," etc.
3. Eliminate trivial (less important) information.
4. Eliminate redundant (superfluous, unnecessary) information.

Now, see how well you can summarize information. Assume that someone asked you, "What seems to influence how people vote in the United States?" To answer the question, write a summary of the section in this chapter entitled "Voting Behavior." You might then exchange summaries with another member of the class and then compare and critique one another's summary.

A number of States outside the South also adopted literacy qualifications of various sorts. Wyoming did so in 1889,

[13] A "grandfather clause" was added to the Louisiana constitution in 1895, and six other States (Alabama, Georgia, Maryland, North Carolina, Oklahoma, and Virginia) soon added them, as well. These clauses stated that any person, or his male descendants, who had voted in the State at some time before the adoption of the 15th Amendment (1870) could become a legal voter without regard to any literacy or taxpaying qualifications. Those qualifications were specifically aimed at disfranchising blacks, and the grandfather clauses were designed to enfranchise those whites who would otherwise be disqualified by them. The Supreme Court found the Oklahoma provision, the last to be adopted (in 1910), in conflict with the 15th Amendment in *Guinn v. United States* in 1915.

California in 1894, Washington in 1896, New Hampshire in 1902, Arizona in 1913, New York in 1921, Oregon in 1924, and Alaska in 1949.

The literacy requirement could be —and in many places was—used to make sure that a qualified voter had at least some capacity to cast an informed ballot. But it could also be—and in many places was—used unfairly, to prevent or discourage certain groups from voting. The device was used in just that way for many years in many parts of the South.

Its unfair use finally led Congress to

destroy literacy as a suffrage qualification. The Supreme Court agreed with that ban in *Oregon* v. *Mitchell*, 1970:

> In enacting the literacy ban . . . Congress had before it a long history of discriminatory use of literacy tests to disfranchise voters on account of their race.

Tax Payment. Property ownership —as proved by the payment of property taxes—was once a common suffrage requirement. It has now all but disappeared. In the few States where it is still found it is used only as a prerequisite to voting on some bond issues or special assessments. It is of very doubtful constitutionality today; see page 193.

The poll tax, once found everywhere in the South, has now disappeared altogether as a voting qualification. Beginning with Florida in 1889, each of the 11 southern States had adopted it as part of an effort to disfranchise the Negro. The device proved to be of only limited effect, however. That fact, together with opposition to its use (from within the South as well as elsewhere) led most of those States to abandon it.[14]

The 24th Amendment, ratified in 1964, outlawed the poll tax—or any other tax—as a condition for voting in any federal election. But, remember, it does not apply to State and local elections.

The Supreme Court finally destroyed the poll tax as a qualification for voting in *all* elections in 1966. In *Harper* v. *Virginia State Board of Elections*, the Court held the Virginia tax to be in conflict with the 14th Amendment's Equal Protection Clause.

[14]By 1966, the final year of its life, the poll tax was still in use in but four States: Alabama, Mississippi, Texas, and Virginia. It had been abolished in North Carolina (in 1924), Louisiana (1934), Florida (1937), Georgia (1945), South Carolina (1950), Tennessee (1951), and Arkansas (1964, shortly after the ratification of the 24th Amendment).

Suffrage Disqualifications

Every State bars certain groups from voting. Thus, no State allows the inmates of mental institutions, or any other persons who have been legally found to be mentally incompetent, to vote. Nearly all of the States also disqualify those who have been convicted of serious crimes (including election offenses). A few States also do not allow anyone dishonorably discharged from the armed forces to vote. In some a few odd groups like duelists, vagrants, or polygamists are also disqualified.

FOR REVIEW

1. On what two bases does each State now set voter qualifications?
2. How was the residence requirement affected by the Voting Rights Act Amendments of 1970? By the Supreme Court's decision in *Dunn* v. *Blumstein*, 1972?
3. What amendment to the Constitution lowered the voting age to 18?
4. What is the essential purpose of a voter registration requirement? Why do some urge its elimination?
5. Why, and on what constitutional grounds has Congress said that literacy cannot be used as a voting qualification?
6. Why may no State now set a poll tax as a voting qualification?

Civil Rights Laws and the Suffrage

The 15th Amendment was ratified in 1870. It states that the right to vote cannot be denied on grounds of race, color, or previous condition of servitude. The Amendment is not self-executing, however; to make it effective, Congress had to act. And for almost 90 years the Federal Government paid little attention to the problem of black voting.

Over that period, blacks were quite generally and systematically kept from the polls in much of the South. White supremacists employed a number of tactics to that end. Violence and threats of it were a major weapon. So, too, were more subtle intimidations and social pressures—such as firing a black man who did try to register or vote, or not giving his family credit at local stores.

More formal—"legal"—devices were used, as well. Of these, the most effective were the literacy tests, which we considered on page 196. They were regularly manipulated by white election officials to disfranchise black citizens.

Registration requirements often served the same end. On their face, those requirements applied to all potential voters, black or white. In practice, however, they were often administered to keep blacks from qualifying to vote. Poll taxes, gerrymandering, "white primaries," and several other devices were used to that end, too.[15]

Led by decisions of the Supreme Court, the lower federal courts began to strike down many of these practices in

the 1940s and 1950s. But those courts could act only when suits were filed by those who claimed to be the victims of discrimination; and that case-by-case approach was, at best, agonizingly slow.

Finally, Congress was moved to act—and very largely in response to the civil rights movement led by Dr. Martin Luther King, Jr. It has passed several civil rights measures since the late 1950s.

The first of them, the *Civil Rights Act of 1957*, set up the United States Civil Rights Commission (page 155). One of its major duties is to inquire into claims of voter discrimination. It reports its findings to Congress and the President and, through the media, to the public at large. The Act also gave to the Attorney General the power to seek federal court orders *(injunctions)* to prevent interferences with any person's right to vote in federal elections.

The *Civil Rights Act of 1960* added

The Voting Rights Act, first passed by Congress in 1965, has now been extended three times—most recently in 1982.

---

[15]**Gerrymandering** is the practice of drawing electoral district lines to the advantage of a particular party or faction; see page 280. The Supreme Court finally outlawed gerrymandering when used for racial discrimination in a case from Alabama, *Gomillion* v. *Lightfoot*, in 1960.

The *white primary* arose out of the near-complete and decades-long Democratic Party domination of the politics of the South. Almost always, only the Democrats nominated candidates for office—and generally in primaries. In several southern States, political parties were defined by law as "private associations." As such, they could admit members as they chose; and the Democrats regularly refused to admit blacks. Because only party members could vote in the party's primary, blacks were then excluded from *the* critical step in the public election process. The Supreme Court finally outlawed the white primary in a case from Texas, *Smith* v. *Allwright*, 1944. There it held that because nominations are an integral part of the election process, when a political party holds a primary it is performing a *public* function and its operations are bound by the 15th Amendment.

another safeguard. It provided for the appointment of federal voting referees. These officers were to serve anywhere a federal court found that voter discrimination was present. They were given the power to help qualified persons to register and to vote in federal elections.

The *Civil Rights Act of 1964* is a much broader measure than either of the two earlier ones—a point we noted on page 155. With regard to voting rights, its most important section forbids the use of any registration requirement in an unfair or discriminatory manner.

The 1964 law continued a pattern set in the earlier laws. In the main, it relied on judicial action to overcome racial barriers. It emphasized the use of federal court orders—injunctions, backed by the power of the courts to punish for contempt any public official or any other person who refused to obey those court orders.

Dramatic events in Selma, Alabama, soon pointed up the shortcomings of this approach, however. Dr. King had mounted a voter registration drive in that city in early 1965. He and his supporters hoped that they could center national attention on the issue of black voting rights—and they most certainly did. Their registration efforts were met with unbridled abuse and violence—by local whites, by city and county police, and then by State troopers. The nation saw much of the drama on television and was shocked. An outraged President Johnson urged Congress to pass new and stronger legislation to ensure the voting rights of black Americans. And Congress acted, quickly.

The *Voting Rights Act of 1965* made the 15th Amendment, at long last, a truly effective part of the Constitution. Unlike its predecessors, it applies to *all* elections held anywhere in this country —State and local as well as federal.

Protesting voter discrimination, Martin Luther King leads civil rights demonstrators on a Selma-to-Montgomery march in March of 1965.

The law has now been extended three times—in the Voting Rights Act Amendments of 1970, 1975, and 1982.

The 1965 law directed the Attorney General to attack the constitutionality of the remaining State poll tax laws—and that provision led directly to *Harper* v. *Virginia State Board of Elections*, in 1966 (see page 198).

It also suspended the use of any literacy test or similar device in any State or county where less than half of the population of voting age had been registered or had voted in the 1964 elections. The Attorney General was authorized to appoint voting examiners to serve in any of those States or counties; and these federal officers were given the power to register voters and otherwise oversee the conduct of elections in those areas.

The 1965 law also declared that no new election laws can go into force in any of those States unless first approved (given "pre-clearance") by the Department of Justice.

Under the law's "bail-out" process, any State or county subject to its voter examiner and pre-clearance provisions can be removed from their coverage. That relief can come if the State can show a three-judge panel of the United States District Court in the District of Columbia that it has not applied any of its voting procedures in any discriminatory way for at least the past 10 years.

The law's triggering formula made the voter examiner and pre-clearance provisions apply to six entire States—Alabama, Georgia, Louisiana, Mississippi, South Carolina, and Virginia, and to 40 North Carolina counties, too.

The constitutionality of the Voting Rights Act was upheld by the Supreme Court in 1966. In *South Carolina* v. *Katzenbach* the Court ruled that Congress had chosen both "rational and appropriate" means to implement the 15th Amendment.

The 1970 Amendments extended the law for another five years. The 1968 elections were added to its triggering formula—and so several counties in six more States (Alaska, Arizona, California, Idaho, New Mexico, and Oregon) were added to its coverage.

The 1970 law also provided that, for five years, none of the States could use literacy as the basis for any voting requirement. That temporary ban, and the

law's residence provisions, were upheld by the Court in *Oregon* v. *Mitchell* in 1970 (see pages 195 and 198).

The law was extended again in 1975, this time for seven years. The five-year ban on literacy tests became a permanent one. And the law's voter examiner and pre-clearance provisions were broadened. Since 1975 they have also covered any State or county where more than five percent of the voting-age population belongs to certain "language minorities." These groups are defined to include all persons of Spanish heritage, American Indians, Asian Americans, and Alaskan Natives. This addition spread the law's coverage to all of Alaska and Texas and to several counties in 24 other States, as well. In each of these language-minority areas, all ballots and all other official election materials must be printed both in English and in the language of the minority (or minorities) involved.

The 1982 Amendments extended the basic features of the Voting Rights Act for another 25 years (with this major exception: its language-minority provisions are to remain in effect only until 1992).

BLACK VOTER REGISTRATION
(in 11 Southern States)

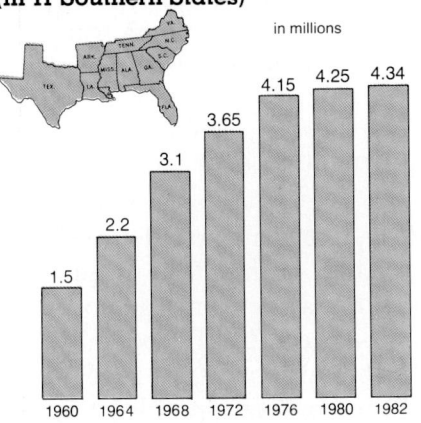

in millions: 1960 – 1.5; 1964 – 2.2; 1968 – 3.1; 1972 – 3.65; 1976 – 4.15; 1980 – 4.25; 1982 – 4.34

ELECTED BLACK OFFICIALS

	U.S. Congress 1970	U.S. Congress 1980	State Legislature '70	State Legislature '80	City &County Offices '70	City &County Offices '80	Law Component '70	Law Component '80	Education '70	Education '80	Total '70	Total '80
Ala				15	52	157	27	40	7	26	86	238
Ark				4	14	136	4	1	37	86	55	277
Fla			1	4	31	87	2	6	2	12	36	109
Ga			14	23	18	173	1	8	7	45	40	249
La			1	12	34	217	20	42	9	92	64	363
Miss			1	17	57	218	18	78	5	74	81	387
N Car			1	5	50	172	1	8	10	62	62	247
S Car				14	32	138	4	20	2	66	38	238
Tenn	1		8	12	9	78	17	7	4	14	38	112
Texas	1		3	13	16	82		21	10	79	29	196
Va			3	5	27	82	6	4			36	91
TOTALS	**0**	**2**	**32**	**124**	**340**	**1,540**	**100**	**235**	**93**	**556**	**565**	**2,457**

Sources: Voter Education Project, Inc.; Joint Center for Political Studies

1. Identify the major civil rights laws enacted by Congress over the past 20 years. Outline their voting rights provisions.
2. Why did Congress pass those laws? Who (what person) played a leading part in prompting Congress to act?

Non-Voting

We began this chapter by pointing out the critical relationship between voting and democratic government. That relationship is clearly a most important one; yet there are millions of persons who, for one reason or another, do not vote in this country.

Scope of the Problem

The table on page 203 lays out the major facts of the non-voter problem in American elections. Notice that on election day in 1980 there were an estimated 164,381,000 persons of voting age in the United States. But only some 86.5 million persons—less than 53 percent of them—actually voted in the presidential election. That is, some 75 million—very nearly half—did not vote.

And in 1980 there were some 78 million votes—47.5 percent—cast in the elections held across the country to fill the 435 seats in the House of Representatives. That is, more than half of the potential electorate did not vote in the congressional elections of 1980.

Little-Recognized Aspects of the Problem. The fact that we do have a non-voter problem of considerable proportions is widely recognized, of course.

But there are several aspects of the problem which are *not* widely known—even by many who are very much concerned about it. For example, this: there are millions of non-voters *among those who vote.* Look again at the 1980 figures. More than 8 million persons who *did* vote in the presidential election did *not* vote, at that same election, for a candidate for a seat in the House of Representatives.

This "non-voting voter" aspect of the problem is a much larger one at the State and local levels. As a general rule, the further down the ballot an office is, the fewer the number of votes that will be cast for it. This phenomenon is sometimes called "ballot fatigue." The expression suggests that many voters exhaust themselves (and/or their patience and/or their knowledge) as they work their way down the list of offices.

Some quick illustrations of the point: More votes are regularly cast in the presidential election than in the gubernatorial election in every State. And more votes are generally cast for the governorship than for such other Statewide offices as lieutenant governor and secretary of state, and so on.

There are other little-recognized sides to the non-voter problem, too. Thus, the figures in the table show that the voter turnout in congressional elections is consistently higher in the presidential years than it is in the "off-years." The same pattern holds true among the States when comparing voter turnout in general elections, primaries, and special elections.

Reasons for Non-Voting

Why do we have so many non-voters? Why, even in a presidential election, do nearly half of all those who could vote stay away from the polls?

"Cannot-Voters." To begin with, look at another of those little-recognized aspects of the non-voter problem: Several million persons who are generally identified as "non-voters" can be much more accurately described as "cannot-voters." That is, although it is true that they do not vote, the fact of the matter is that they *cannot* do so.

The 1980 data we have just looked at can be used to make the point. In that figure of some 75 million persons of voting age who did not vote in the last presidential election are some 4 million resident aliens—and, remember, they are barred from the polls in every State. Also there are 5 to 6 million citizens

who were so ill or otherwise physically handicapped that they simply could not do such things as vote. There are another 2 or 3 million persons who were traveling, suddenly and unexpectedly, and so were away from their home precincts on election day.

That figure counts several other groups of "cannot-voters," too—as some 500,000 persons confined to mental care facilities or under some other form of legal restraint because of their mental

VOTER TURNOUT, 1932–1982

	Population of Voting Age[a]	Votes Cast for President		Votes Cast for U.S. Representatives	
	(in millions)	(in millions)	(percent)	(in millions)	(percent)
1932	75.768	39.732	52.4	37.657	49.7
1934	77.997	—	—	32.256	41.4
1936	80.174	45.643	56.9	42.886	53.5
1938	82.354	—	—	36.236	44.0
1940	84.728	49.900	58.9	46.951	55.4
1942	86.465	—	—	28.074	32.5
1944	85.654	47.977	56.0	45.103	52.7
1946	92.659	—	—	34.398	37.1
1948	95.573	48.794	51.1	45.933	48.1
1950	98.134	—	—	40.342	41.1
1952	99.929	61.551	61.6	57.571	57.6
1954	102.075	—	—	42.580	41.7
1956	104.515	62.027	59.3	58.426	55.9
1958	106.447	—	—	45.818	43.0
1960	109.672	68.838	62.8	64.133	58.5
1962	112.952	—	—	51.267	45.4
1964	114.090	70.645	61.9	65.895	57.8
1966	116.638	—	—	52.908	45.4
1968	120.285	73.212	60.9	66.288	55.1
1970	124.498	—	—	54.173	43.5
1972	140.777	77.625	55.1	71.348	50.7
1974	146.338	—	—	52.418	35.8
1976	152.308	81.603	53.6	74.419	48.9
1978	158.369	—	—	54.680	34.5
1980	164.381	86.497	52.6	78.025	47.5
1982	169.342	—	—	63.853	37.7

[a]As estimated by Census Bureau. Population 18 years of age and over since ratification of 26th Amendment in 1971; prior to 1971, 21 years and over in all States, except: 18 years and over in Georgia since 1943 and Kentucky since 1955, 19 years and over in Alaska and 20 and over in Hawaii since 1959.
Source: Census Bureau, *Statistical Abstract of the United States.*

condition; some 400,000 or so in jails and prisons; and perhaps as many as 100,000 who do not (cannot) vote because of their religious beliefs.

Discrimination still plays a part here, too. An estimated 5 million persons could not vote in 1980 because of: (1) the purposeful administration of election laws to keep them from doing so, and/or (2) "informal" local pressures applied to that same end.

In short, that figure of about 75 million non-voters in 1980 counts at least 20 million persons who, in fact, really should not be included in that number.[16]

Actual Non-Voters.   Even so, there are millions of *actual* non-voters in the United States. Thus, in 1980 some 55 million Americans *could* have voted in the presidential election but did not.

There are any number of reasons for that behavior. As a leading example: Many do not go to the polls because they are convinced that it makes little real difference who wins a certain election.

But, notice, that large group includes two quite different categories of non-voters. On the one hand, there are those who approve of the way in which the public's business is being managed. They believe that, no matter who wins, things will continue to go well for themselves and for the country.

On the other hand, that group also includes many who feel **alienated**— many who deliberately refuse to vote because they don't trust political institutions and processes, many who fear or scorn "the system." To them, elections are meaningless, choiceless exercises.

Another large group of non-voters is

---

[16]Essentially, this counting (or miscounting) problem arises out of the standard upon which it is based— *i.e.*, the yardstick regularly used to measure rates of voter participation. That standard is the Census Bureau's estimate of the population of voting age at the time a given election is held. Quite clearly, that estimate includes many persons who are *old enough* to vote but cannot do so for reasons *other than* age.

AMERICAN VOTING RECORDS

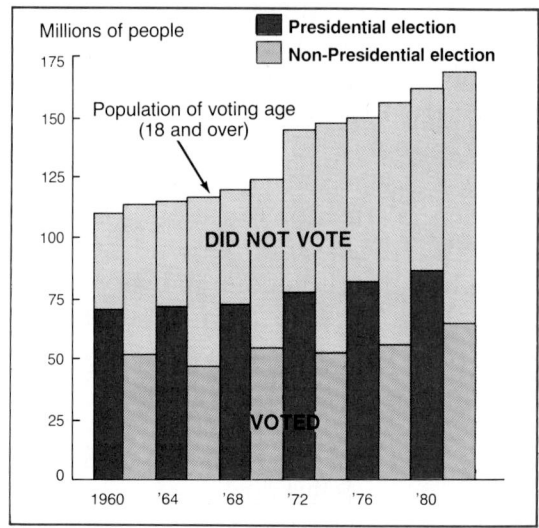

Source: U.S. Bureau of the Census

made up of those persons who have no sense of **political efficacy.** That is, they lack any feeling of influence or effectiveness in politics. They simply do not believe that they (or their votes) can have an impact on how government is run or what government does.

Cumbersome election procedures are another factor here—for example, inconvenient registration requirements, long ballots, and long lines at polling places. And such other things as bad weather tend to discourage turnout, too.

But, of all the reasons given, the *chief* cause for non-voting is—purely and simply—a *lack of interest.*

Those who lack sufficient interest— who are indifferent and apathetic, who just can't be bothered—are usually uninformed. They often do not know even the simplest facts about an election.

The fact that those persons don't very often vote might well be counted among our blessings. Surely, elections are not intended to be polls of the indifferent, lazy, apathetic, or ignorant.

The accompanying table sets out a number of factors connected with voter

---

TO VOTE OR NOT TO VOTE? FACTORS AFFECTING TURNOUT

A person is *more likely* to vote if:	A person is *less likely* to vote if:
Higher level of income	Lower level of income
Higher level of education	Lower level of education
White	Non-white
35 years of age or older	Younger than age 35
Married	Not married
Catholic or Jew	Protestant
Occupation:	Occupation:
Business or profession	Unskilled
White-collar	Blue-collar
Union member	Non-union member
Residence:	Residence:
Urban, suburban	Rural
Northeast, Middle West, West	South
Long-term in locale	Newcomer to locale
Homeowner	Renter
Member of civic groups	Isolated individual
Strong party identification in family	Weak or no party identification in family
Strong supporter of party	Weak partisan or independent
High sense of political efficacy	Little, no sense of political efficacy
High sense of civic duty	Little, no sense of civic duty
Much political interest in work group	Little, no political interest in work group
Perceives personal stake in election	Perceives no personal stake in election
Subject to few cross-pressures	Subject to many cross-pressures
Crisis political situation	Normal political situation
Absence of cumbersome registration, other election procedures	Restrictive, cumbersome election procedures
Vigorous two-party competition	One-party constituency
Lack of community pressures against participation	Community pressures work to discourage participation

---

turnout. As you can see, those persons who are most likely to vote display such characteristics as higher levels of income and education, and of occupational and ethnic status. Those persons are usually well integrated into community life—that is, long-time residents who are active in or at least comfortable with their surroundings. They are likely to have a strong sense of party identification, believe that voting is an important act, and are subject to few cross-pressures that would discourage their

participation. They also are likely to live in those States and locales where laws, customs, and interparty competition all work to promote turnout. The opposite characteristics give a profile of those who are least likely to vote, of course.

A few of the factors in the table are so important that they influence turnout even when they are not supported by, or are in conflict with, other factors. Thus, those persons with a high sense of political efficacy are very likely to vote —no matter what their income, education, age, race, and so on may be. The degree of two-party competition has much the same kind of across-the-board effect. That is, the greater (or lesser) the competition between candidates, the higher (or lower) the voter turnout will be, regardless of other factors.

Despite the greater weight of some factors, however, notice this important point: It is the *combined* effect of several of them, rather than the force of one of them alone, that prompts the individual's decision to vote or not.

☑ **F O R   R E V I E W**

1. How many votes were cast in the last presidential election? Congressional elections of that year?
2. About how many potential voters did not vote in the last presidential election?
3. What does "non-voting by voters" refer to?
4. Identify the causes for non-voting. Which is the major one? Who are the "cannot voters"?

A   C A S E   I N   P O I N T

GET-OUT-THE-VOTE DRIVES

The latter stages of every election season are marked by get-out-the-vote drives—by the vigorous efforts of many civic groups and the media to get people to the polls on election day.

Their message—VOTE!—appears nearly everywhere. We see it in newspapers and magazines and on posters, billboards, shopping bags, and sidewalks. It comes over the telephone, by radio and television, and so on.

Those who conduct these drives do so for an altogether laudable reason, of course. They want to help make democracy work, by stimulating the largest possible turnout at the polls.

But some think that those public-spirited efforts are wrong-headed—that they do not in fact serve the best interests of democracy.

Those critics build their case on this question: Who are the real targets of those campaigns? That is, who goes to the polls because of those efforts?

The critics insist that those drives are (can only be) aimed at people who would not otherwise vote. (Clearly, it makes no sense to urge those people to vote who are going to vote anyway.) And who are those who would not otherwise go to the polls? They are, say the critics, the classic non-voters—the uninterested and the uninformed.

In short, these critics argue that the targets of those drives really serve democracy best by staying home on election day—and should be left alone.
—What do you think of this view of civic-minded get-out-the-vote drives?

There are other vote drives which are quite different from those public-spirited ones. They are the ones conducted by various special interest groups—by the AFL-CIO, the National Rifle Association, the National Right-to-Life Committee, and so on. Those campaigns are much more narrowly targeted, aimed at some specific part of the electorate—at union members or gun-owners or opponents of abortion and so on.
—Why can't the same argument (the one against the civic-minded efforts) be made against these other campaigns?

Voting Behavior

Several million potential voters do not go to the polls, but many millions more do. How do those who do vote behave? Why do they vote as they do?

We do not know *exactly* why voters behave as they do. But voting has been studied more closely than any other form of political participation in the United States.[17] That research has produced a huge amount of information about why people *tend* to vote as they do.

Most of what we know about voter behavior comes from studies based on data from three sources:

(1) The most obvious source—the *results of particular elections.* As a quick illustration: The careful study of the returns from areas populated largely by blacks or by Catholics or by high income families will show how those groups voted in a given election.

(2) The field of **survey research**—the polling (questioning, interviewing) of scientifically-drawn samples (cross-sections) of the population. It is the method by which public opinion is most often identified and measured. The American Institute of Public Opinion (the Gallup Poll) is perhaps the best known survey-research organization today.

(3) Studies of **political socialization**—the process by which people gain their political attitudes and opinions. That very complex process begins in early childhood and continues on through each person's life. It involves all of the experiences and relationships that lead each of us to see the political world, and to act in it, as we do.

---

[17]It has because of the importance of the topic, of course, and because of the almost unlimited amount of data available (innumerable elections in which millions of voters have cast billions of votes). Much of the most useful research on voter behavior is done by the Center for Political Studies at the University of Michigan.

Factors Affecting Voter Behavior

There is still much to be learned about voter behavior, but it is quite clear that the ways in which people vote are heavily influenced by a number of *sociological* and *psychological factors.*

The **sociological** factors at work here are really the many pieces of a voter's social and economic life. Those pieces are of two broad kinds: (1) a voter's personal characteristics—age, race, income, occupation, education, religion, and so on and (2) a voter's group affiliations—family, co-workers, friends, and the like.

The **psychological** factors in the voting mix are a voter's perceptions of politics—that is, how he or she sees the parties, the candidates, and the issues in an election.

The differences between these two kinds of influences are not so great as they might seem. In fact, they are quite closely related. And they constantly interact upon (work in combination with) one another. How voters look at parties, candidates, or issues is very often shaped by their social and economic backgrounds. Or, to put it another way, all of us are likely to look at politics through the glasses of our own lives.

The Sociological Factors. From the table on page 209, you can see that it is possible to draw a composite picture of the American voter in terms of a number of sociological factors.

But a large word of caution here: Do not make too much of any one of these factors. The table reports how voters, grouped by a *single* characteristic, voted in each of eight successive presidential elections. But, remember, *each* voter has *several* of the characteristics shown.

To make the point here, consider this: College graduates are more likely to vote Republican. So are persons over 50 years of age. Catholics are more likely to vote for Democrats. So are members of labor unions. What, then, of a 55-year-old college-educated Catholic who belongs to the AFL-CIO?

Income, Occupation.   Voters in the middle-to-upper income brackets are more likely to be Republicans. Voters with lower incomes tend to be Democrats. This pattern has held up over time—and it showed up even in the presidential election landslide of 1980. Those with family incomes above $35,000 voted for Ronald Reagan by better than 2 to 1; a majority of those with incomes of less than $15,000 voted for Jimmy Carter.

Most often, how much one earns (income) and what one does for a living (occupation) are closely related matters. Professional and business people, and others with higher incomes, tend to vote for Republican candidates. Manual workers, and others from lower income groups, are more likely to vote for Democrats. Thus, with the single exception of 1964, professional and business people voted heavily Republican in the eight presidential elections from 1952 through 1980.

Education.   A number of studies of voter behavior show that college graduates vote for Republicans in higher percentages than do high school graduates. They also show that high school graduates vote more often Republican than do those who have only gone through grade school.

Sex, Age.   On the whole, sex does not appear to be a major factor in partisan voting behavior. That is, men are no more or less likely to favor one party and its candidates than are women. A number, of studies, however, do suggest this: Men and women do vote in measurably different ways when issues related to war and national defense or human rights are prominent in an election.

Age is another matter, however. Younger voters are much more likely to be Democrats than Republicans. Older voters are likely to find the GOP and its candidates more attractive. So it is that in every presidential election from 1952 through 1980, the Democratic candidate received a larger percentage of the votes cast by the under-30 age group than of those cast by voters age 50 and over.

Religious, Ethnic Background.   A majority of northern Protestants prefer the GOP. Catholics and Jews are much more likely to be Democrats.

Historical factors account for much of this pattern. Most of those who first settled this country were of English stock, and Protestant. The later tides of immigration, from Southern and Eastern Europe, brought many Catholics and Jews to the United States. Those later immigrants were often treated as minority groups by the largely Protestant establishment. And they most often settled in the larger cities, where local Democratic Party organizations helped them to become citizens and voters. From the New Deal period of the 1930s on, social welfare programs have strengthened the ties of most minority groups to the Democratic Party.

In 1960 John Kennedy became the first Roman Catholic to win the Presidency. His election was marked by a sharper split between Catholics and Protestants than in any of the other elections covered by the table on the next page.

Nonwhites support the Democratic Party—consistently and massively. Notice that they form the *only* group that has given the Democratic candidate a clear majority in *every* presidential election since 1952.

Black Americans make up the single most important racial minority in the country. Northern blacks generally voted Republican until the 1930s. They moved away from the party of Abraham Lincoln with the coming of the New

VOTING BY GROUPS IN PRESIDENTIAL ELECTIONS, 1952–1980
(By Percent of Votes Reported Cast)

	1952		1956		1960		1964		1968			1972		1976			1980		
	D	R	D	R	D	R	D	R	D	R	AIP	D	R	D	R	I	D	R	I
	44.6	55.4	42.2	57.8	50.1	49.9	61.3	38.7	43.0	43.4	13.6	37.5	60.7	50	48	1	41	50.7	6.6
National																			
Men	47	53	45	55	52	48	60	40	41	43	16	37	63	53	45	1	38	53	7
Women	42	58	39	61	49	51	62	38	45	43	12	38	62	48	51	*	44	49	6
Race																			
White	43	57	41	59	49	51	59	41	38	47	15	32	68	46	52	1	36	56	7
non-white	79	21	61	39	68	32	94	6	85	12	3	87	13	85	15	*	86	10	2
Education																			
College	34	66	31	69	39	61	52	48	37	54	9	37	63	42	55	2	35	53	10
High school	45	55	42	58	52	48	62	38	42	43	15	34	66	54	46	*	43	51	5
Grade school	52	48	50	50	55	45	66	34	52	33	15	49	51	58	41	1	54	42	3
Occupation																			
Professional and business	36	64	32	68	42	58	54	46	34	56	10	31	69	42	56	1	33	55	10
White-collar	40	60	37	63	48	52	57	43	41	47	12	36	64	50	48	2	40	51	9
Manual	55	45	50	50	60	40	71	29	50	35	15	43	57	58	41	1	48	46	5
Members of labor union families	61	39	57	43	65	35	73	27	56	29	15	46	54	63	36	1	50	43	5
Age																			
Under 30 years	51	49	43	57	54	46	64	36	47	38	15	48	52	53	45	1	47	41	11
30–49 years	47	53	45	55	54	46	63	37	44	41	15	33	67	48	49	2	38	52	8
50 years or older	39	61	39	61	46	54	59	41	41	47	12	36	64	52	48	*	41	54	4
Religion																			
Protestants	37	63	37	63	38	62	55	45	35	49	16	30	70	46	53	*	39	54	6
Catholics	56	44	51	49	78	22	76	24	59	33	8	48	52	57	42	1	46	47	6
Politics																			
Republicans	8	92	4	96	5	95	20	80	9	86	5	5	95	9	91	*	8	86	5
Democrats	77	23	85	15	84	16	87	13	74	12	14	67	33	82	18	*	69	26	4
Independents	35	65	30	70	43	57	56	44	31	44	25	31	69	38	57	4	29	55	14
Region																			
East	45	55	40	60	53	47	68	32	50	43	7	42	58	51	47	1	43	47	9
Midwest	42	58	41	59	48	52	61	39	44	47	9	40	60	48	50	1	41	51	7
South	51	49	49	51	51	49	52	48	31	36	33	29	71	54	45	*	44	52	3
West	42	58	43	57	49	51	60	40	44	49	7	41	59	46	51	1	35	54	9

D = Democratic candidate; R = Republican; AIP = American Independent Party Candidate (George Wallace, 1968); I = Independent candidate (Eugene McCarthy, 1976; John B. Anderson, 1980). Figures do not add to 100% in some groups because of rounding and/or minor party votes. *Less than 1%
Source: *The Gallup Opinion Index*, Report No. 183, December 1980.

Deal, however. The civil rights movement of the 1960s led to greater black participation in the South—and there, too, blacks now vote overwhelmingly Democratic.

Geography.   Geography—the part of the country, the State, and/or the locale in which a person lives—has an impact on voter behavior.

After the Civil War, the States of the old Confederacy voted so consistently Democractic that the entire southeast quarter of the nation became known as the Solid South. For more than a hundred years now, most southerners—regardless of income, occupation, education, or any other factor—have been Democrats. The Solid South has disappeared in terms of presidential elections, but the Democrats still dominate the politics in most of the South.

Over time, the strongest and most consistent support for the Republicans by States can be found in Maine and Vermont in the Northeast and in Kansas, Nebraska, and the Dakotas in the Midwest. Lately, there has been much speculation about present and future voting patterns in the "Sunbelt"—that area stretching from the southeastern States westward to California. Some pundits see the region as a base for increased conservatism and new strength for the Republican Party in national politics.

Voters' attitudes also vary in terms of the size of the communities in which they live—larger cities, suburban areas, smaller cities, or rural areas. In general, the Democrats draw strength from the big cities of the North and East. Many white Democrats have moved from the central cities and taken their political preferences with them, but Republican voters still dominate much of suburban America. Outside the South, voters in the smaller cities and rural areas are likely to be Republicans.

Family, Other Group Affiliations. Typically, the members of a family vote in strikingly similar ways. Nine out of ten married couples have the same partisan leanings; regularly, a husband and wife vote almost exactly alike. To the same point, as many as two out of every three voters follow the political attachments of their parents.

Those who work together and circles of friends vote very much alike.

The like-mindedness of these groups is hardly surprising. People with similar social and economic backgrounds tend to associate with one another. In short, group associations often simply reinforce a voter's already-held opinions.

The Psychological Factors.   Again, it would be wrong to give too much weight to the sociological factors in the voting mix. They are clearly important. But they are also fairly static. That is, they tend to change only very gradually and over a period of time. (The percentage of Catholics or Jews or Protestants in the population remains fairly steady, for example.) Yet, the electorate sometimes behaves very differently from one election to the next. (Thus, Jimmy Carter won the Presidency with just over 50 percent of the popular vote in 1976; but he received only 41 percent of that vote and lost the office to Ronald Reagan in 1980.)

So, in order to understand the voting process, we must look beyond such factors as occupation, level of education, ethnic background, and place of residence. We must also take into account a number of psychological factors. That is, we must look at the voters' *perceptions* of politics—how they see, how they react to, the parties, the candidates, and the issues in an election.

Party Identification.   Most Americans identify themselves with one or the other of the two major parties early in life. Many never change. They support

SELECTED PRESIDENTIAL ELECTIONS

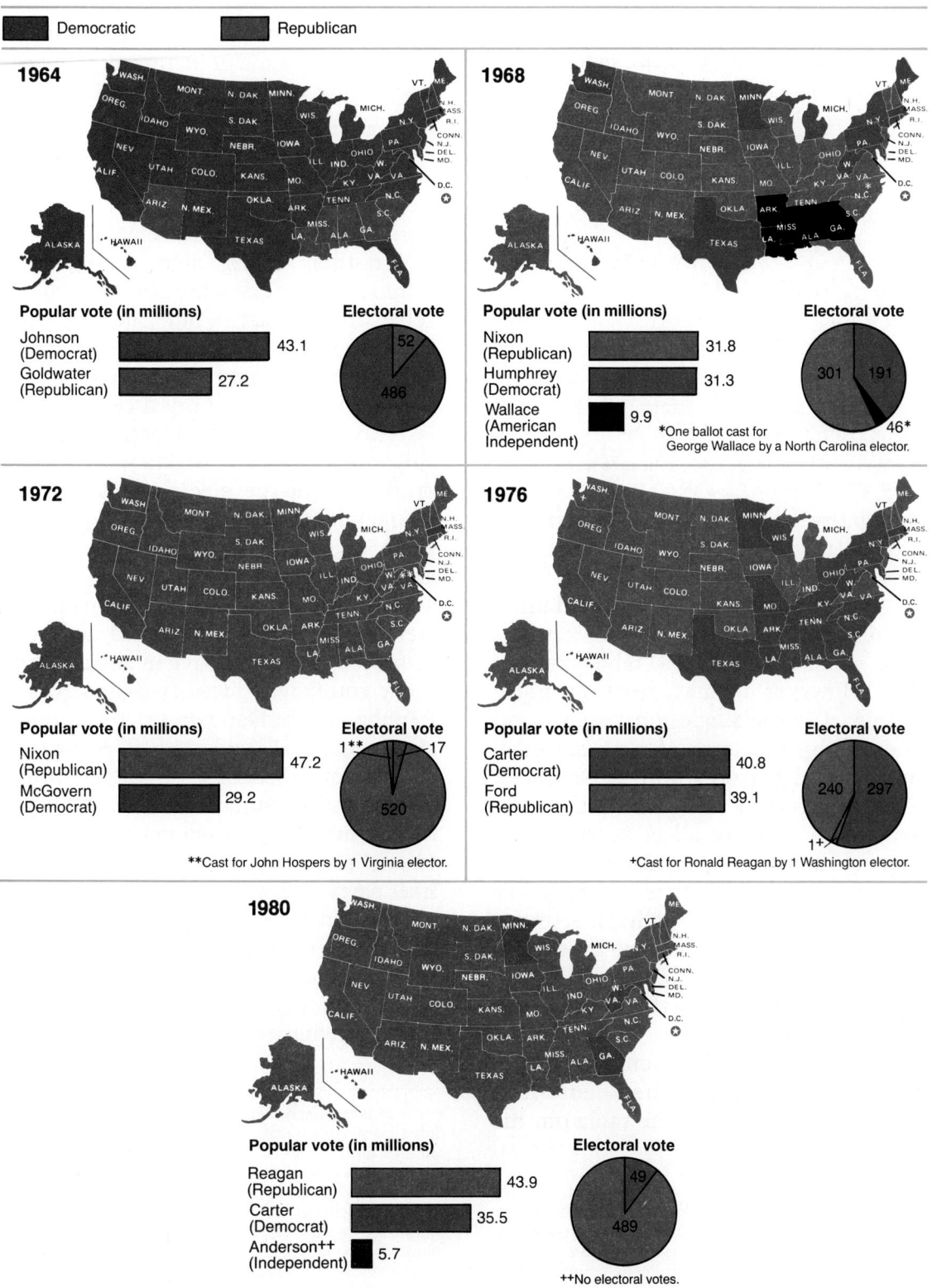

■ Democratic   ■ Republican

1964

Popular vote (in millions)
Johnson (Democrat) 43.1
Goldwater (Republican) 27.2

Electoral vote 52 / 486

1968

Popular vote (in millions)
Nixon (Republican) 31.8
Humphrey (Democrat) 31.3
Wallace (American Independent) 9.9

Electoral vote 301 / 191 / 46*

*One ballot cast for George Wallace by a North Carolina elector.

1972

Popular vote (in millions)
Nixon (Republican) 47.2
McGovern (Democrat) 29.2

Electoral vote 1** / 17 / 520

**Cast for John Hospers by 1 Virginia elector.

1976

Popular vote (in millions)
Carter (Democrat) 40.8
Ford (Republican) 39.1

Electoral vote 240 / 297 / 1+

+Cast for Ronald Reagan by 1 Washington elector.

1980

Popular vote (in millions)
Reagan (Republican) 43.9
Carter (Democrat) 35.5
Anderson++ (Independent) 5.7

Electoral vote 49 / 489

++No electoral votes.

PARTY IDENTIFICATION IN THE
AMERICAN ELECTORATE, 1940–1982

	Democrat	Republican	Independent
1982	48%	26%	26%
1980	43	26	31
1978	46	23	31
1976	46	22	32
1974	44	24	33
1972	43	28	29
1970	45	29	26
1968	46	27	27
1964	53	25	22
1960	47	30	23
1950	45	33	22
1940	42	38	20

Source: The Gallup Poll Report, Report No. 202, July, 1982. (The question: "In politics, as of today, do you consider yourself a Republican, a Democrat, or an Independent?")

that party, election after election, and with little or no regard for either the candidates or the issues.

The hefty impact of **party identification**—party loyalty—on how people vote can be seen in the table on page 209. However it may have been acquired, it is the single most significant and lasting predictor of how a person will vote. A person who is a Democrat (or a Republican) will, for that reason, very likely vote for all or most of that party's candidates in an election.[18]

Party identification is, then, a key factor in American politics. Among many other things, it means that each of the major parties can count upon the votes of millions of faithful supporters in every election.

The Democrats have enjoyed a substantial advantage over the Republicans in this matter. And, as the table on this page shows, that has been the case since 1940.

Several signs suggest that, while it remains a major factor, party identification has lost some of its impact in recent years. One of those signs is the weakened condition of the parties themselves (see pages 185–187). Another is the marked increase since the 1960s in **split-ticket voting**—voting for candidates of *both* parties at the same election.

Another telling sign is the large number of voters who now call themselves *independents*. But "independent" is a very tricky term.[19] Many who claim to be independents really support one or the other of the major parties regularly.

The loose nature of party membership makes it hard to know just what proportion of the electorate is, in fact, independent. The best guesses put that share at somewhere between a fourth and a third of all voters today.

Until fairly recently, independents were generally less concerned, less well informed, and less active in politics than those voters who identify themselves as Republicans or Democrats. A new breed appeared in the 1960s and 1970s, however. Largely because of the political events and personalities of that period, these "new" independents do not wish to join either major party. But they are like party identifiers in many ways—except that they are likely to be younger and to be above average in education, income, and occupational status.

Candidates and Issues. From much of what we have said about party

---

[18]The practice of voting for the candidates of but one party in an election is known as **straight-ticket voting.** That behavior may or may not be an unthinking, irrational act. It frequently is. But a voter may have come to the conscious, thoughtful conclusion that that party best serves his or her own particular interests.

[19]It is regularly used to identify those voters who have no partisan affiliation—voters who are independent of both the Republicans and the Democrats. But, notice, it is also sometimes *mistakenly* used in ways that suggest that independents form a more or less cohesive group in politics, and one that can be readily compared with Republicans and/or Democrats. In short, independents are not only independent of Republicans and Democrats; independents are also independent of all other independents.

identification, one might very well ask this question: How does the Republican Party ever win a presidential election? A very large part of the answer can be put in these terms: candidates and issues.

Party identification is a *long-term* factor. Most voters identify with one or the other of the major parties; and, over time, they most often support its candidates. But they don't *always* vote that way. One or more *short-term* factors may cause them to switch sides in a given election—or, at the least, to vote a split ticket. Look again at the table on page 209. Note that one out of every three voters who normally vote Democratic did not vote for Carter in 1980.

The most important of these short-term factors are the candidates and the issues in an election. Clearly, the impressions a candidate makes on the voters can have an impact on how they vote. What "image" does a candidate project? How is he or she seen in terms of personality, character, style, appearance, past record, abilities, and so on?

Just as clearly, issues can also have a large impact on voter behavior. Their role varies from election to election, however—depending on such things as the emotional content of the issues themselves, the voters' awareness of them, and the ways in which they are presented to the electorate.

Several studies show that issues now play a larger part in voter decisions than was true as recently as the early 1960s. The tumultuous nature of American politics over the past 20 years—highlighted by the civil rights movement, the Vietnam War, the Watergate scandal, and mounting economic problems—are almost certainly responsible for the upsurge in issue concern.

✓ FOR REVIEW

1. Identify the sociological factors that affect voting behavior.
2. Why should no one of them be given too much weight in analyzing that behavior?
3. Identify the psychological factors that affect voting behavior.
4. What is the single most significant, lasting indicator of an individual's voting behavior?

Six days before election day in 1980, the two major party candidates for President engaged in a televised debate in Cleveland. Their comments and views on such matters as foreign affairs, the economy, taxes, and defense were heard by an estimated 100 million TV viewers.

S U M M A R Y

More than 170 million persons—just about every American citizen who is at least 18 years of age—can qualify to vote. The history of the right to vote in this country has been marked by two long-term trends: (1) the gradual elimination of such restrictive requirements as those based on property, race, and sex, and (2) more and more federal control over the matter.

Voting qualifications are set by the States, subject to the limits set by the Constitution—most importantly the 15th, 19th, and 26th Amendments. All States now impose qualifications based upon citizenship and residence; and the 26th Amendment sets 18 as the minimum voting age in all elections. Every State, except North Dakota, has a voter registration system, intended to prevent fraudulent voting. Mental imcompetents, felons, and some others are commonly barred from voting by the States.

Congress has passed several laws in recent years to implement the 15th Amendment's guarantee: the Civil Rights Acts of 1957, 1960, and 1964, and the Voting Rights Act of 1965 and its substantial Amendments in 1970, 1975, and 1982.

Millions of potential voters fail to vote for a number of reasons—but, chiefly, out of a lack of interest. (About a third of the non-voter population can be much more accurately called "cannot-voters," however.)

Extensive studies of voter behavior indicate that how people vote is heavily influenced by a number of (1) sociological factors —such characteristics as a voter's income, occupation, education, age, race, and so on, and his or her primary group affiliations— especially family, co-workers, and friends, and (2) psychological factors—how the voter sees the parties, candidates, and issues in an election. Of these factors, the single most important and lasting predictor of a person's voting behavior is party identification.

C H A P T E R   R E V I E W

Key Terms/Concepts

Age qualification (195)
Alienation (204)
Ballot fatigue (202)
"Cannot-voters" (202)
Citizenship qualification (194)
Civil Rights Acts of 1957, 1960, 1964 (199,200)
Electorate (191)

Group affiliations (207)
Independents (212)
Literacy qualification (196)
Non-voting (202)
Party identification (210)
Political efficacy (204)
Political right (190)
Political

socialization (206)
Poll tax (198)
Psychological factors (207)
Registration (196)
Residence qualification (194)
Sociological factors (207)
Split-ticket voting (212)
Straight-ticket voting (212)

Suffrage (190)
Survey research (207)
Turnout (203)
Voter behavior (207)
Voting Rights Act of 1965 (200)
Voting Rights Act Amendments of 1970, 1975, 1982 (200)

Keynote Questions

1. What two long-term trends have marked the development of the right to vote in the United States?
2. What specific restrictions does the Constitution place upon the States in setting suffrage qualifications?
3. Each State now requires voters to meet qualifications based upon what two factors?
4. What is the essential purpose of a voter registration system?
5. Why can no State impose a literacy requirement as a voting qualification? A poll tax?
6. Outline the major voting rights provisions contained in the several civil rights laws enacted by Congress in recent years.
7. What are the leading causes for nonvoting in American elections? Which of them is the major cause? What are "cannot-voters"?
8. Most of what we know about voter behavior comes from studies which draw their data from what three sources?
9. What are the principal sociological factors which influence the ways in which people vote? The principal psychological factors?
10. What is the single most reliable indicator of a typical voter's voting behavior?

For Thought and Discussion

1. What are the voter qualifications set out in your State's constitution and election laws? What qualifications do you think should be added? Made more, or less, stringent? Deleted?
2. What are the provisions of your State's registration law? Does it make registration easy or difficult? What changes, if any, do you think should be made in that law?
3. Would you be for or against a compulsory voting law? Why, or why not?

4. Some criticize the American election system for placing more emphasis upon the *quantity* of voter turnout than on the *quality* of that participation. Is this a valid criticism?
5. How do you explain this apparent paradox? Over the past two decades, many of the changes in American election law have been designed to make it *easier* for many more people to vote (*e.g.*, the 26th Amendment, civil rights statutes, reduced residence qualifications, and the easing of registration requirements). Yet, over this same 20-year period, the rate of voter turnout has in fact *declined*.

Suggested Activities

1. Invite the registrar, county clerk, or other local election official to discuss your State's voting qualifications and voter registration process.
2. Stage a debate or class forum on one or more of the following questions: (a) *Resolved*, That the voting age in all States be raised to 21; (b) *Resolved*, That this State's voter registration law be repealed; (c) *Resolved*, That voting qualifications be made uniform throughout the United States.
3. Look up the returns for the most recent general election in your State (usually readily available in the State's manual or bluebook or from the secretary of state's office). Analyze those data in terms of the text's discussion of voter turnout and nonvoting (pages 202–206) and/or the various factors affecting voter behavior (pages 207–213).
4. Write an editorial or other comment on this point: Our word "idiot" comes from the Greek word *idiotes*—a term that was used for those citizens who did not take an active part in public affairs.

CHAPTER  9

Government by the People: The Electoral Process

CHAPTER OBJECTIVES

To help you to
Learn ▪ Know ▪ Understand

The critical role of the electoral process, and its two basic stages, in democratic government.

The evolution and the present-day shape of the nominating and the election process in American politics.

The place of money and its regulation in American politics.

As citizens of this democracy, you are the rulers and the ruled, the lawgivers and the law-abiding, the beginning and the end.

Adlai Stevenson

In a representative democracy there must be some means by which the people can choose those who govern—those who represent the people in the conduct of the people's business. There must also be some method by which those who govern with the consent of the people can be held accountable to the people. Popular election is the only technique we know that meets both of these democratic needs.

In the United States we elect far more public officeholders than most people realize—*more than 490,000* of them, in fact. We vote more often—hold far more elections—than most realize, too. Indeed, Sundays and holidays are about the only days in any year on which people do not go to the polls somewhere in this country.

In this chapter we deal with the two basic stages of the electoral process: (1) the nomination of candidates for public office and (2) the final election of officeholders from among those who have been nominated. We shall also look at the very complex and troublesome matter of money in the electoral process.

HARRISONIAN

BALL ROLLING.

WILLIAM HENRY HARRISON THE FARMER OF NORTH BEND.

KEEP THE

RALLY!

216

A scene from the 1980 Republican National Convention, in which Ronald Reagan won his party's presidential nomination. *Facing page:* An 1840 campaign poster.

The Nominating Process

The nominating process is the process of candidate selection—the picking (naming) of those who will seek office in an election.

Candidates are nominated in a number of different ways in American politics. But, first this crucial point: The making of nominations, whatever the details of the process, is a very significant matter—and from a number of standpoints.

We have already seen two important illustrations of this. In Chapter 7, recall, we discussed the making of nominations (1) as a prime function of political parties in the United States (page 166) and (2) as a leading reason for the decentralized character of the major parties in the American two-party system (page 182).

The nominating process has a very real impact on the exercise of the right to vote. In the typical election in this country, voters can make one of two choices for each office: They can vote for the Republican candidate or they can vote for the Democratic candidate.[1] As we have said before, this is another way of saying that we have two-party system in the United States. It is also another way to say that the nominating process is critically important: Those who make nominations place very real—very practical—limits on the choices that voters can make in an election.

---

[1]Except for nonpartisan elections; see page 222. Other choices are sometimes listed, of course — minor party or, once in a while, independent nominees. But these are not often meaningful alternatives; most voters choose not to "waste" their votes; see page 169. In 1980, for example, the very substantial campaign for independent candidate John B. Anderson produced only 6.6% (only one of every 16) of the votes cast in the presidential election.

In **one-party constituencies** — those places where one party regularly wins elections—the nominating stage is the only point at which there is usually any real contest for a public office. Once the dominant party has made its nominations the general election is little more than a formality.

Dictatorial regimes underscore the importance of the nominating process. In the Soviet Union, for example, general elections are held in much the same manner as they are in the United States. The comparison ends there, however. In Soviet elections, only candidates who are acceptable to the Commusist Party can be nominated. Typically, the ballot lists only one candidate for each office. It is hardly surprising that the candidates who do win office in the Soviet Union regularly win with 98 to 100 percent of the votes.

The several methods used to nominate candidates in this country fall into five broad categories: (1) *self-announcement*; (2) *caucus*; (3) *convention*; (4) *direct primary*; and (5) *petition*.

Self-announcement

Self-announcement is the oldest form of the nominating process in American politics. It was first used in colonial times and is still often found at the small town and rural levels in many parts of the country.

The process is quite simple. A person who wishes to run for an office simply announces that fact. Modesty or local custom may dictate that someone else make the candidate's announcement, but even so the process amounts to the same thing.

The process is sometimes used by someone who tried for but failed to win a regular party nomination, or by someone who is not happy with the party's choice. Note that whenever a "write-in" candidate appears in an election the self-announcement process has been used.

Three prominent presidential contenders have made use of that process in recent years: George Wallace, the American Independent Party's nominee in 1968, and independent candidates Eugene McCarthy in 1976 and John Anderson in 1980.

The Caucus

As a nominating device,[2] a **caucus** is a group of like-minded persons who meet to select the candidates they will support in an upcoming election.

The first caucus nominations were made toward the end of the colonial period, probably in Boston in the mid-1720s. One of the earliest descriptions of the device can be found in John Adams' diary, in an entry February of 1763:

> This day learned that the Caucus club meets at certain times in the garret of Tom Dawes, the Adjutant of the Boston regiment. He has a large house, and he has a movable partition which he takes down, and the whole club meets in one room. There they smoke tobacco until you cannot see from one end of the garret to the other. There they drink flip, I suppose, and they choose a moderator who puts questions to the vote regularly; and selectmen, assessors, collectors, fire-wards, and representatives are regularly chosen before they are chosen in the town.[3]

---

[2]Generally, the term *caucus* is used to describe any private meeting at which party members decide upon some course of political action. Most often, it is used in connection with a legislative body today. The **legislative caucus** is now a meeting of a party's members in the legislature to decide upon matters of legislative organization, committee assignments, the party's position on bills, and the like; see page 297.

[3]Charles Francis Adams (ed.), *The Works of John Adams* (Boston: Little, Brown, 1856), Vol. II, p. 144. The origin of the term *caucus* is not clear. Most authorities suggest that it comes from the word *caulkers*, because the Boston caucus club met at times in a room formerly used as a meeting place by the caulkers in the Boston shipyards.

In its earliest form, the caucus was a private meeting, a gathering of the select few in a locale. As parties appeared, they soon took over the device and began to broaden its membership.

The coming of Independence brought the need to nominate candidates for governor, lieutenant governor, and other offices above the local level. That need was met rather quickly in most of the new States. The *legislative caucus*, a meeting of a party's members in the State legislature, took on the job. By 1800 both the Federalists and the Democratic-Republicans in Congress were choosing their presidential and vice-presidential candidates through the *congressional caucus*.

The legislative and congressional caucuses were quite practical in their day. Transportation and communication were difficult at best, and legislators regularly came together in a central place. The spread of democracy, especially in the newer States on the frontier, spurred opposition to them, however. More and more, the legislative and congressional caucuses were condemned for their closed and unrepresentative character.

Criticism of the caucus reached its peak in the early 1820s. The supporters of three of the leading contenders for the Presidency in 1824—Andrew Jackson, Henry Clay, and John Quincy Adams—boycotted the Democratic-Republicans' congressional caucus that year. In fact, Jackson and his people made "King Caucus" a leading campaign issue. The other major aspirant, William H. Crawford of Georgia, became the caucus nominee—at a meeting attended by fewer than a third of the party's members in Congress.

Crawford ran a poor third in the electoral college balloting in 1824, and the reign of "King Caucus" at the national level was ended. With its death in Presidential politics, the caucus system soon withered at the State and local levels, as well.

The caucus is still used to make local nominations in some places—especially in New England, where its meetings are open to all of the members of a party and it looks only faintly like the original form.

The Convention

As the caucus method collapsed, its place was taken by the convention. The first national convention, to nominate a presidential candidate, was held by a minor party—the Anti-Masons, meeting in Baltimore in 1831. Both the Democrats and newly-formed Whigs picked up the practice in 1832—and all major party presidential nominees have been chosen by conventions ever since. By the 1840s conventions had become the major means for the making of nominations at every level in American politics.

On paper, the convention process seems ideally suited to representative government. A party's members meet in a local caucus to pick candidates for local offices and, at the same time, to select delegates to represent them at a county convention.[4] At the county convention, the delegates nominate candidates for county offices and also select delegates to the next rung on the convention ladder, usually the State convention. There, the delegates from the county conventions pick the party's nominees for governor and other State-wide offices. State conventions also send delegates to the party's national convention—where its presidential and vice-presidential candidates are to be chosen.

In the theory of the convention sys-

---

[4]The meetings at which delegates to local conventions are chosen are still often called *caucuses*. Earlier, they were also known as *primaries*—that is, first meetings. The use of that name gave rise to the term *direct primary*, to distinguish that newer nominating method from the convention process; see next page.

NEW ENGLAND CONVENTION
BUNKER HILL.

TIPPECANOE

WILLIAM HENRY HARRISON

SEPTEMBER 10th
1840.

By the 1840s, conventions had largely replaced the caucus in the making of nominations.

tem, the will of the party's rank and file membership is passed on up through each of its representative levels. Practice soon pointed up the weaknesses of the theory, however, as party bosses found ways to manipulate the new process. By playing with the selection of delegates, mostly at the local and county levels, regularly they were able to dominate the entire system.

The caliber of most conventions, at all levels, declined, especially in the late 1800s. How low some of them fell can be seen in this description of a Cook County (Chicago) convention in 1896:

> Of [723] delegates, those who had been on trial for murder numbered 17; sentenced to the penitentiary for murder or manslaughter and served sentence, 7; served terms in the penitentiary for burglary, 36; served terms in the penitentiary for picking pockets, 2; served terms in the penitentiary for arson, 1; . . . jailbirds identified by detectives, 84; keepers of gambling houses, 7; keepers of houses of ill-fame, 2; convicted by mayhem, 3; ex-prize fighters, 11; poolroom operators, 2; saloon keepers, 265; . . . political employees, 148; . . . no occupation, 71; . . .[5]

Many had hailed the change from caucus to convention as a major change for the better, as a big step forward for democracy in the nominating process. The abuses of the newer device soon dashed that view, however. More and more, the convention system was attacked as itself a chief source of evil in American politics. Little by little, and finally by the 1910s, it was replaced by the direct primary as the nation's principal nominating method.

The primary is now used for all or at least most nominations in most States. The convention is still used in some, however—in Connecticut, Michigan, Utah, and Virginia, for example, where it is closely regulated by State law. And no adequate substitute for it has yet been found at the presidential level—as we shall see when we take a closer look at the major parties' national conventions in Chapter 14.

✓ **FOR REVIEW**

1. What is the nominating process?
2. Why are nominations such an important part of the electoral process?
3. Which is the oldest of the several nominating methods used in American politics?
4. Why was the use of the caucus as a nominating device very largely abandoned in early 1800s?
5. Why may it be said that in theory the convention method seems ideally suited to representative government?

---

[5]R.M. Easley, "The Sine-qua Non of Caucus Reform," *Review of Reviews*, September, 1897, p. 322.

The Direct Primary

The **direct primary** is an election held *within* the party at which those who vote choose the party's candidates for public office.

Its origins are not clear, but the first direct primary was probably held by the Democrats in Crawford County, Pennsylvania, in 1842. Its use spread to other parts of the country through the latter decades of the 1800s. Wisconsin adopted the first Statewide direct primary law in 1903, and other States soon followed.

Today every State makes some provision for its use. In most of them, State law requires that the major parties use the primary to choose their candidates for the United States Senate and House, for the governorship and all other State offices, and for most local offices, as well. In a few, however, different combinations of convention and primary are used to pick candidates for the top offices. In Indiana and Michigan, for example, the major parties must select their candidates for the U.S. Senate and House and for governor and lieutenant governor in primaries; nominees for other state offices are picked in conventions.

Although a primary is a party nominating election, it is closely regulated by law in most States. The State usually sets the date on which primaries are to be held. It conducts them, as well, providing ballots and election officials, using its official registration lists, and otherwise policing the process.

Two basic forms of the direct primary are used today: (1) the *closed primary* and (2) the *open primary*.

The Closed Primary. Thirty-eight States[7] now use the **closed primary**—a party nominating election in which *only* declared party members may vote. It is *closed* to all others.

Small Society   By Brickman

©King Features Syndicate

In most of the closed primary States, party membership is established by registration (see page 196). When voters appear at the polling places on primary election day, their names are checked against the poll books (the lists of registered voters for each precinct). Each of them is then handed the ballot of the party in which he or she is registered.

In the other closed primary States, voters simply declare their party preference at the polling place. In some of them, that settles the matter; the person may vote in that party's primary. In others, however, that person may be challenged by a party's poll watcher. If that happens, the voter is most often required to take an oath of party loyalty —swearing that he or she has supported that party and its candidates in the past and/or now does so.

The Open Primary. Although it is the form the direct primary first took, the open primary is now found in only 12 of the States.[8] The **open primary** is a party nominating election in which *any* qualified voter may take part. That is, it is *open* to any such person. No one has to declare a party preference at registration or at any other time.

When voters appear at the polling place they are handed either the ballots of all of the parties holding primaries or one large ballot containing the separate

---

[7]All of the States except those listed in note 8; the District of Columbia also uses the closed primary.

[8]Alaska, Hawaii, Idaho, Louisiana, Michigan, Minnesota, Montana, North Dakota, Utah, Vermont, Washington, Wisconsin. But see the text comments on Alaska, Louisiana, and Washington.

---

ballots of the various parties. Voters then pick the particular party primary in which they wish to vote, and mark that ballot.

A different version of the open primary is used in Alaska and Washington—where it is known as the "wide open" or "blanket" primary. In each of those States the voter receives a single large ballot listing each party's contenders for each nomination. The voter can vote in a single party's primary, as in the typical open primary. *Or* the voter can vote to nominate a Democrat for one office, a Republican for another, and so on.

Louisiana adopted yet another form of the open primary in 1975. Its unique "open election" law provides for what amounts to a combination primary and election. The names of *all* persons who seek nominations are listed (by office) on a single primary ballot.[9] A contender who wins a majority of the votes cast in the primary then runs unopposed for that office in the general election. This really means that he or she is elected at the primary. Otherwise, the two top vote-getters in each primary race—regardless of party—run against one another in the general election.

Pro and Con: The Closed v. the Open Primary. Those who favor the closed primary regularly make three arguments for it: (1) That it keeps the members of one party from "raiding" the other's primary, in the hope of nominating weaker candidates in the other party.[10] (2) That it helps to make candidates more responsive and responsible to the party, its platform, and its members. And (3) that it helps to make voters more thoughtful, because they must choose between the parties in order to vote in the primaries.

The critics of the closed primary make two principal arguments against it. They claim that it: (1) compromises the secrecy of the ballot, because it forces voters to make their party preferences known in public, and (2) tends to exclude independent voters from the partisan nomination process.

The Runoff Primary. In most States candidates need to win only a *plurality* of the votes in the primary to win their party's nomination.[11]

In 10 States,[12] however, an absolute majority is needed. If no one wins a majority in a race, a second contest—a **runoff primary**—is held a few weeks later. In the runoff, the two top contenders in the first race face one another; and the winner becomes the nominee.

The Nonpartisan Primary. In most States all or nearly all of the elective school and municipal offices are filled in **nonpartisan elections**—elections in which candidates are not identified by party labels.[13]

---

[9]Each aspirant's name is listed with or without a party label—as he or she chooses.

[10]Raiding the opposition primary became so common in the early years of the direct primary that the closed form was developed to prevent it. The tactic is still found in some open-primary States today.

[11]Recall, a *plurality* is a greater number of votes than the number received by any other candidate, whether a *majority* or not. Iowa and South Dakota require a candidate to win at least 35 percent of the votes cast in a primary contest; if no aspirant wins that vote in a given race, the party must then nominate its candidate for that office by convention.

[12]Alabama, Arkansas, Florida, Georgia, Mississippi, North Carolina, Oklahoma, South Carolina, Texas—and Louisiana under its unique "open election" law.

[13]A small segment of the progressive reform movement of the early 1900s hoped to do away with public corruption by doing away with both parties and partisan elections from all of American politics. Many of those reformers focused their nonpartisan efforts at the local level, however—and especially in the bigger cities. Nonpartisanship remains an article of faith for many who favor local governmental reforms in many parts of the country today.

Many opponents of nonpartisanship insist that that label is often more apparent than real. They argue that nonpartisan candidates and officeholders are frequently known by their partisan attachments, and eliminating party labels from the local election process cannot hide that fact.

The ongoing spread of nonpartisanship at the local level (especially in cities) has weakened the two major parties, at least to some extent—by severing some of their grass-roots strength. It is, then, one of the several factors in their continuing decline in American politics; see pages 185–187.

CASE STUDY

VOTING RIGHTS
17-YEAR-OLD VOTERS IN THE PRIMARIES?

If you read the 26th Amendment carefully, you will see this point: It does *not* say that a person who is less than 18 years of age cannot be allowed to vote. Rather, it says that no State can deny the vote to anyone who is at least 18 years old and is otherwise qualified.

In short, any State can permit those who are less than 18 to vote, if it chooses to do so.

Given that fact, look at this question: Should a person whose 18th birthday falls *after* the primaries but *before* the general elections are held in November be allowed to vote in the earlier primaries as well as in the November elections?

Students at San Rafael High School in California felt that the answer to that question should be a loud "Yes." So, with their teacher, Dr. Virginia Franklin, they set out to change the situation in their State in 1976.

They began by researching the history of voting rights and studying the ins and outs of the legislative process. They received lobbying tips from several groups, including the American Civil Liberties Union and the National Education Association. They wrote to a number of public officials at both the State and federal levels and also prepared information packets for the members of the State legislature.

Their efforts, and those of students who have come after them, have led to the introduction of several bills in both the California legislature and in Congress—measures that would allow anyone who will be old enough to vote in November to vote in the earlier primaries, as well.

To this point, none of their bills has been passed, either in Sacramento or in Washington. But the students are far from discouraged. They continue to hope that what they see as a real inequity in voting rights will be overcome. They agree with the late Representative Leo Ryan who, when he sponsored one of their bills in the House in 1978, said that "voting is the ultimate field trip for students."

1. Do you think that 17-year-olds should be able to vote in the circumstances involved here? Why, or why not?

2. A few States do in fact allow 17-year-olds to vote in these circumstances. Can you discover which ones now do so?

Representative Barbara Boxer (D., Calif.), second from right, meets with San Rafael students to discuss their primary-vote project.

About half of all State judges are chosen on nonpartisan ballots, as well.

The nomination of candidates for these offices takes place on a nonpartisan basis, too—often in nonpartisan primaries.

Typically, a contender who wins a clear majority in a nonpartisan primary then runs unopposed in the general election—but subject to write-in opposition, of course. In many States, however, a candidate who wins a majority in the primary is declared elected at that point. If there is no majority winner, the names of the two top contenders are placed on the general election ballot.

The direct primary first appeared as a partisan nominating device, as we have seen. Many have long argued that it is really not very well suited for use in nonpartisan election situations. They favor, instead, the petition method, to which we shall turn in a moment.

Evaluation of the Primary.   The direct primary, open or closed, is an *intraparty nominating election*. It came about as a reaction to the boss-dominated convention system. It was intended to take the nominating function away from the party organization and put it in the hands of the party's membership.

But these basic facts about the primary have never been very well understood by most voters. Thus, many resent having to declare their party choice in closed primary States. And, where the typical open primary is used, many are upset because they cannot nominate in more than one party. Many voters are also annoyed by the "bed-sheet ballot," not understanding that the use of the primary almost automatically dictates a long ballot.

It is fairly clear, too, that a large part of the electorate does not see the critical importance of the nominating stage. Thus, the turnout in the primaries in most States is usually less than half of that in the general elections.

The fact that turnout is usually much lower in primary elections leads to this little-recognized point: There are often two quite different electorates involved in the electoral process. One of them (the smaller of the two) is that group of voters who vote in the primaries—and, clearly, it is made up mostly of those persons who are most likely to vote. The other (and larger) one is that group of voters who take part in the general election. To really grasp this point, look again at the table of those factors that affect voter turnout on page 205.

When nominations are contested, primary campaigns can be quite expensive. The fact that successful contenders must mount (and find the money for) yet another campaign (for the general election) adds to the money problems. It is unfortunately true that the financial facts of political life mean that some well-qualified people will not seek public office; see pages 232–238.

The nominating process, whatever its form, can have a very divisive effect on a party. It takes place *within* the party. So, when there are conflicts, that's where they occur—among the members of the *same* party. The direct primary magnifies this aspect of the nominating process—because primaries are so *public* in nature. A bitter contest in the primaries can so wound and divide a party that it cannot be healed and united in time for the general election. Many a primary fight has cost a party an election.

Because many voters are not very well informed, the primary places a premium on "name-familiarity." That is, it often gives an edge to a contender who has a well-known name, or has a name that sounds much like that of another person who is well-known to the public. And, notice, the fact of name-familiarity

A VETERAN OF MANY CAMPAIGNS

Drawing by P. Steiner; © 1981 The New Yorker Magazine, Inc.

may have little or nothing to do with a contender's qualifications.

Clearly, the direct primary is not without its problems—nor is any other nominating device. Still, it does give a party's members the opportunity to participate, in a very meaningful way, at the very core of the political process.

The Presidential Primary

The presidential primary developed as an off-shoot of the direct primary. It is *not* a nominating device, however. It is, rather, an *election*—held as a part of the presidential nominating process.

The presidential primary is a very complex device. It is one or both of two things, depending upon the State involved. It is a process in which a party's voters elect some or all of a State party organization's delegates to that party's national convention. *And/or* it is a preference election in which voters may choose (vote their preference) among various contenders for a party's presidential nomination.

Much of what happens in presidential politics in the early months of every fourth year—including 1984—centers around the very complicated presidential primary process. (This process will be closely examined in chapter 14, when we look at presidential selection.)

Petition

One other nominating method is fairly widely used in American politics today—nomination by **petition**. Here, candidates are nominated by petitions signed by a certain number of qualified voters in the election district.[15]

Nomination by petition is found most widely at the local level—and there chiefly for nonpartisan school posts and municipal offices in middle-sized and smaller communities. It is also the process usually required by State law for the nomination of minor party and independent candidates—and, as we noted on page 169, the States frequently make the process purposefully difficult for them.

The details of the petition process vary widely from State to State, and even from one city to the next in many of them. As a general rule, however, the higher the office and/or the larger the size of the constituency involved, the greater the number of signatures needed for nomination.

☑ FOR REVIEW

1. What is a direct primary?
2. How do the open and closed forms of the primary differ?
3. What are the major arguments for and against the closed primary? What is the wide-open primary?
4. Which form of the primary is used in your State?
5. What is a runoff primary? A nonpartisan primary? A presidential primary?

---

[15]The petition device is also used in several other aspects of the electoral process. Thus, it (and/or a filing fee) is generally the method by which an aspirant's name is placed on the direct primary ballot. It is also an important part of the recall (page 541) and the initiative and the referendum processes (pages 533–536).

A polling place during election day in a town in Mississippi.

Elections

Once candidates have been nominated they must face their opponents, and the voters, in the general election—in what H. G. Wells once called democracy's "feast, its great function."

There are elections in which the outcome is never in question. Most often and in most places this is not the case. But it is so in one-party constituencies—in those areas where one party is so dominant, so regularly and heavily supported by the voters, that its candidates are just about certain of election. There, as we noted on page 218, the nominating stage is far more important than final election.

The Administration of Elections

Democratic government cannot succeed unless elections are free, honest, and accurate exercises. Too many look at the details of the election process as too complicated, too legalistic—too dry and boring—to worry about. But those who do miss the vital part those details play in making democracy work.

How something *can* be done regularly has a marked effect on what *is* done—and this is as true in politics as it is in other matters. The often lengthy and often closely detailed provisions of election law are usually designed to protect the integrity of that process. And they often have a telling effect upon the outcome of elections, as well.

We've seen the point demonstrated several times, of course—in terms of *who* can vote and *how* candidates can get on the ballot, for example, and in many other ways.

The Extent of Federal Control

Nearly all elections in this country are held to choose the more than 490,000 persons who hold public offices in the more than 80,000 units of government at the State and local levels. It is quite understandable, then, that the greatest bulk of election law in the United States is *State* law.

There is a body of federal election law, however. The Constitution gives to Congress the power to fix "the times, places, and manner of holding elections" of members of Congress.[16] Congress also has the power to set the time for choosing the presidential electors, to set the date for casting their electoral votes, and to regulate other aspects of the presidential election process.[17]

Congress has set the date for holding congressional elections as the first Tuesday following the first Monday in November of every even-numbered year. It has set the same date every fourth year for the presidential elections. Thus, the next (off-year) congressional elections will be held on November 4, 1986, and this year's presidential election falls on November 6.[18]

[16]Article I, Section 4, Clause 1; 17th Amendment; see pages 279–283.

[17]Article II, Section 1, Clause 4; 12th Amendment; see pages 367–368.

Congress has required the use of secret ballots and allowed the use of voting machines in federal elections. It has passed several laws to protect the right to vote in all elections, as we saw on pages 198–201. And it has prohibited various corrupt practices and regulated the financing of campaigns for federal office, as we shall see on pages 232–238.

All other matters relating to national elections are dealt with in the laws of the individual States.

When Elections Are Held. Most of the States hold their elections to fill State offices on the same date Congress has set for national elections—in November of every even-numbered year.[19]

Some States do fix other dates, however, for at least some offices. Thus, Mississippi, New Jersey, and Virginia elect the governor, other executive officers, and State legislators in November of the *odd*-numbered year—and Louisiana, in December of those years. City, county, and other local election dates vary from State to State. Where those elections are not held in November, they generally take place in the spring.

The Coattail Effect. Strong candidates running for top offices on the ballot can produce a "coattail effect." Those candidates, with their broad appeal, can help to pull voters to other candidates on the party's ticket. In effect, the lesser-known office-seekers "ride the coattails" of the more prestigious personalities.

The coattail effect is usually most apparent in presidential elections. But a popular candidate for senator or gover-

nor can have the same kind of pulling power. (There can be a *reverse* coattail effect, too. It comes when a candidate for high office is less-than-popular with many voters—for example, Barry Goldwater as the Republican presidential nominee in 1964, and George McGovern for the Democrats in 1972. Ronald Reagan's coattails helped many Republican candidates in 1980; Jimmy Carter's were of the reverse variety that year.)

Some have long held that all State and local elections should take place on dates other than those set for federal elections. This, they say, would help make voters pay more attention to State and local candidates and issues—be less subject to the coattail effect.

Precincts and Polling Places

Precincts are voting districts. They are the basic (smallest) geographic units for the conduct of elections. State law regularly restricts their size—generally to an area with no more than 500 or 1000 or so qualified voters. A **polling place**—where the voters who live in that precinct may vote—is located somewhere in each of them.

A precinct election board usually supervises the polling place and the voting process in each precinct. (Typically, the county clerk or county board of elections draws precinct lines, fixes the location of each polling place, and picks the members of the precinct boards.)

The precinct board opens and closes the polls at the times set by State law. In most States, the polls are open from 7 or 8 A.M. to 7 or 8 P.M.

The board also has several other and important tasks. It must see that ballots and ballot boxes, or voting machines, are available. It must make certain that only qualified voters cast ballots in the pre-

---

[18]Up to 1960, Maine was allowed to hold its congressional elections in early September; the practice gave rise to the oft-quoted, but not-too-often accurate, saying: "As Maine goes, so goes the nation."

[19]The formula-like "Tuesday-after-the-first-Monday" is purposeful. It prevents election day from falling (1) on Sundays, to maintain the principle of separation of church and state, and (2) on the first day of the month, which is often payday and so peculiarly subject to campaign pressures.

cinct. And it must count the votes and certify the results to the proper place— usually to the county clerk or board of elections.

"Poll watchers," one from each party, are allowed at each polling place. They may challenge any person they have reason to believe is not qualified to vote, see that as many as possible of their own party's supporters do vote, and watch the whole process (including the counting of the ballots) to insure its fairness.

The Ballot

The **ballot** is the device by which a voter registers a choice in an election.[20] It can take a number of different forms. But, whatever its form, it is clearly an important and sensitive part of the electoral process.

Each of the States now provides for a **secret ballot**. That is, each requires that ballots be cast in such manner that others cannot know how a voter has voted—unless, of course, the voter wants to give out that information.

Voting was a public process through much of our earlier history. Paper ballots were used in some colonial elections, but voting was commonly by voice (*viva voce*). Voters simply stated their choices to election officials. With suffrage limited to the privileged few, oral voting was often defended as the only "manly" way in which to participate. Whatever the merits of that view, the expansion of the electorate brought with it intimidation, vote-buying, and other corruptions of the voting process.

Paper ballots came into general use in the middle years of the 19th century. The first ones were unofficial—slips of

paper that voters prepared themselves and dropped in the ballot box. Soon candidates and parties began to prepare ballots and hand them to voters to cast —sometimes paying them to do so. Those party ballots were often printed on distinctively colored paper and anyone watching could tell for whom voters were actually voting.

Political machines, reaping their harvest from the unofficial ballots, fought all attempts to make voting a more secure process. The corruption of the post-Civil War years brought widespread demand for ballot reforms, however.

The Australian Ballot. A new voting arrangement was devised in Australia, where it was first used in an election in Victoria in 1856. Its successes there led to its use in other countries. By 1900 nearly all of the States were using it, and it remains the basic form of the ballot in all of them today.

The **Australian ballot** has four essential features: (1) It is printed at public expense. (2) It lists the names of all of the candidates in an election. (3) It is given out only at the polls, one to each qualified voter. And (4) it is voted in secret.

Two basic varieties of the Australian ballot have developed over the years. In nearly half of the States the *office-group* version is used, and in a little more than half of them the *party-column* ballot.

The Office-Group Ballot. The office-group ballot is the original form of the Australian ballot. It is also sometimes called the Massachusetts ballot, because of its early (1888) use there. On it, the candidates for each office are listed (grouped) together. At first, the names of the candidates were listed in alphabetical order. In most States using the form, the names are now rotated—so that each candidate will have any psychological advantage that may come having his or her name at the top of the list.

---

[20]The word comes from the Italian *balla*—"ball" (or, more exactly, *ballota*—"little ball"), and reflects the practice of dropping tokens (commonly black or white balls) into a box to indicate a choice. The term "blackball" comes from the same practice.

IT IS A CRIME TO FALSIFY THIS BALLOT OR TO VIOLATE INDIANA ELECTION LAWS

SAMPLE NATIONAL BALLOT

Democratic Ticket	Republican Ticket	American Party of Indiana Ticket	Libertarian Party Ticket	Communist Party U.S.A. Ticket	Socialist Workers Party Ticket	Independent Ticket	The Citizens' Party Ticket
FOR PRESIDENTIAL ELECTORS	FOR PRESIDENTIAL ELECTORS	FOR PRESIDENTIAL ELECTORS	FOR PRESIDENTIAL ELECTORS	FOR PRESIDENTIAL ELECTORS	FOR PRESIDENTIAL ELECTORS	FOR PRESIDENTIAL ELECTORS	FOR PRESIDENTIAL ELECTORS

A portion of an Indiana ballot in 1980. Note that the candidates are listed under their respective parties' names in this sample ballot.

The Party-Column Ballot. The party-column ballot is also known as the Indiana ballot—from its early (1889) use in that State. It lists each party's candidates in a column under the party's name. Often there is a square or circle at the top of each party's column where, with a single X, the voter can vote for all of that party's candidates.

Professional politicians tend to favor the party-column ballot. It encourages "straight-ticket" voting—especially if the party has a strong candidate at the head of the ticket. Most students of the political process favor the office-group form—because it encourages voter judgment and "split-ticket" voting.

Sample Ballots. Sample ballots, clearly marked as such, are available in most States. In some they are mailed to all voters before an election, and they apear in most newspapers. They cannot be cast, of course—but they can help voters prepare for an election.[21]

The Long and the Short of It. The ballot in the typical American election is a lengthy one—often and aptly called a "bed-sheet ballot." It often lists so many offices, and so many candidates, and so many measures that even the most conscientious and well-informed voters have a difficult time marking it intelligently.

The long ballot came to American politics in the era of Jacksonian Democracy in the 1830s. Many held the view at

A part of an office-group ballot used in Massachusetts in the 1982 primary elections.

SENATOR IN CONGRESS

Vote for ONE

EDWARD M. KENNEDY - Squaw Island, Barnstable · · · · · · · · · · · · · · · 3 ▶
Present United States Senator

GOVERNOR

Vote for ONE

EDWARD J. KING - 20 Dix Street, Winthrop · · · · · · · · · · · · · · · 7 ▶
Present Governor

MICHAEL S. DUKAKIS - 85 Perry Street, Brookline · · · · · · · · · · · · · · · 8 ▶

LIEUTENANT GOVERNOR

Vote for ONE

JOHN F. KERRY - 206 Chestnut Hill Road, Newton · · · · · · · · · · · · · · · 13 ▶
Former First Assistant District Attorney, Middlesex County; Veteran

EVELYN MURPHY - 148 Fuller Street, Brookline · · · · · · · · · · · · · · · 14 ▶
Former Secretary of Environmental Affairs, Commonwealth of Massachusetts

LOU NICKINELLO - 6 Pryor Road, Natick · · · · · · · · · · · · · · · 15 ▶
State Representative; Chairman, Transportation Committee

LOIS G. PINES - 40 Helene Road, Newton · · · · · · · · · · · · · · · 16 ▶
Former Representative; former Regional Director, Federal Trade Commission

SAMUEL ROTONDI - 54 Sunset Road, Winchester · · · · · · · · · · · · · · · 17 ▶
Present State Senator; Veteran

---

[21]First in Oregon (1907), and now in several States, an official Voter's Pamphlet is mailed to all voters before an election. It lists all candidates and measures that will appear on the ballot. In Oregon each candidate is allowed space to present his or her qualifications and issue stands, and supporters and opponents of measures are allowed space to present their arguments, as well.

that time that the greater the number of elective offices the more democratic the governmental system. The idea remains widely accepted today.

Generally, the longest ballots are found at the local level, and especially among the nation's 3000-odd counties. In most counties, throughout the country, it is not at all unusual to find a large number of elected officials—including several commissioners, a clerk, a sheriff, one or more judges, a prosecutor, a coroner, a treasurer, an assessor, a surveyor, a school superintendent, an engineer, a sanitarian, and, in some places, even the proverbial dog-catcher.

Critics of the long ballot do not accept the argument that the more you elect the more democratic you are. They believe that quite the reverse is true— that, with a smaller number of elected offices to fill, the voter can better know the candidates and their qualifications. They also point to "ballot fatigue"—the drop-off in voting that can run as high as 20 to 30 percent at or near the bottom of the ballot (see page 202).

There seems little, if any, good reason to elect such local officials as clerks, coroners, surveyors, and engineers. Their jobs, and many others filled by the voters, do not carry basic policy-making responsibilities. Rather, they carry out policies made by others. For good government, the rule should be: *Elect* those who make public policies; *appoint* those who only administer them.

Voting Machines

Thomas Edison took out the first American patent for a voting machine. His invention was first used in an election in Lockport, New York, in 1892. The use of similar devices has long since spread to the point where their use is now allowed under the laws of every State.

Only a handful of States make the use of voting machines mandatory. The machines are most often used in some (and usually the more populous) areas but not in others within the same State. All told, however, more than half of all of the votes in national elections today are cast on some form of the machine.

The typical voting machine serves as its own booth. By pulling a lever, the voter: (1) encloses himself/herself within a three-sided curtain (the machine itself becomes the fourth side of the voting booth) and (2) unlocks the machine. The ballot appears on the face of

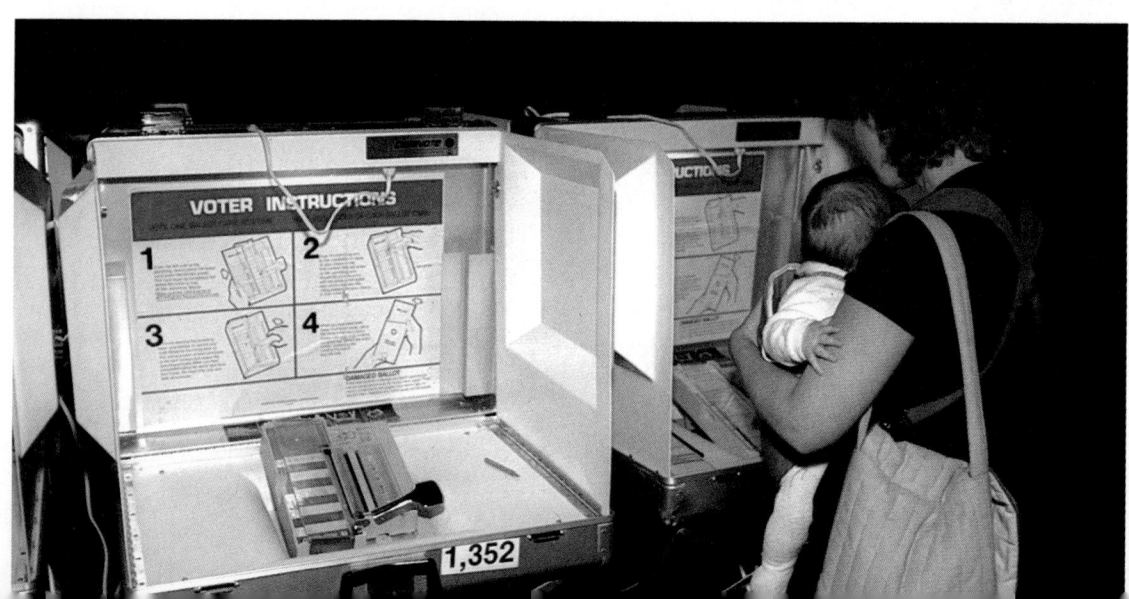

VOTER INSTRUCTIONS

1   2

3   4

1,352

the machine, and the voter makes his or her choices by pulling down the small levers over the names of the candidates he or she favors. In most of the States using the party-column ballot the voter may pull a master lever to vote a straight ticket.

The machine has space for measures, as well as candidates, with *yes* and *no* levers for each. It is programmed so that a voter can cast only one vote per contest. Once all of the levers are in their desired positions, the voter opens the curtain. That action records the votes and at the same time clears the machine for the next voter.

The use of voting machines does away with the need (and time) for manual vote counting, reduces the number of persons needed to administer elections, and speeds the voting process. It also increases the number of voters who can be handled per precinct, makes ballot spoilage impossible, and minimizes fraud and counting errors.

The machines in common use today are rather expensive, costing several thousand dollars apiece. Then, too, they are quite large and present storage, moving, and maintenance problems. Some voters, often older ones and rural residents, complain that the machines are too complicated and confusing. Clearly, they are most useful in the more densely populated areas.

Electronic Vote Counting. Electronic data processing techniques have been applied to the voting process in recent years—first in California and Oregon and now, to at least some degree, in two-thirds of the States.

To date, EDP applications have followed two general lines. The most widely used adaptation involves punch-card ballots which are counted by high-speed computers. The other involves paper ballots marked with sensitized ink and counted by optical scanners.

By pulling a lever on a voting machine, the voter is surrounded by a curtain that forms a secret voting booth.

☑ FOR REVIEW

1. Why are the details of the electoral process vital to the success of democratic government?

2. Why is most election law in this country State rather than federal law?

3. When are national elections held? Most State general elections? Why do some favor separate dates for national and for State and local elections?

4. What is the Australian ballot? How do the office-group and party-column forms of the ballot differ?

5. Why is the typical ballot used in American elections so lengthy? Consequences?

Money in Elections

Political activities, especially campaigns for public office, cost money—and often a great deal of it. That fact gives rise to some of the most difficult of all of the many problems in American politics.

There is ever present the threat that some candidates will try to buy their way into public office. And there is always the possibility that some special interests will try to buy favors from those who are elected to office.

Certainly, government by the people must be guarded against these dangers. But how? Parties and their candidates *must* have money. Without it, they can't campaign—they can't take steps to inform the voters and attract their support. In short, dollars are an absolutely necessary campaign resource. Yet, their getting, and their spending, can corrupt the entire political process.

From Herblock's *On All Fronts*
(New American Library, 1980)

How Much?

No one really knows how much money is spent on elections in the United States. Reliable *estimates* of total campaign spending in recent presidential election years—for all offices at all levels, including nominations and general elections—show this:

	Estimated Spending	Vote Cast for President	Cost per Voter
1952	$140 million	61.6 million	$2.28
1956	155 million	62.0 million	2.50
1960	175 million	68.8 million	2.54
1964	200 million	70.6 million	2.83
1968	300 million	73.2 million	4.10
1972	425 million	77.7 million	5.47
1976	540 million	81.6 million	6.62
1980	900 million	86.5 million	10.40

The presidential election eats up by far the largest share of campaign dollars. For 1980, total spending — for all of the pre-convention primaries, the national party conventions, the campaign itself, and for all minor party and independent efforts—was at least $250 million. The comparable figure for 1976 was $160 million, and it will almost certainly top $300 million for 1984.

The totals for all the U.S. Senate and House races in 1980 reached $239 million, (up from $192 million for 1978), and climbed past $342 million in 1982.[22]

Radio and especially television time, paper, printing, newspaper advertisements, pamphlets, buttons, posters, and bumper strips, office rent, furniture and equipment, mass mailings, travel—these and a host of other items make up the huge sums spent in campaigns. Television is by far the largest item in a typical campaign budget today. A single half hour of network TV time can run as

[22]Principal sources for the data in this section are: Herbert E. Alexander, Citizens' Research Foundation; *Congressional Quarterly*; and the Census Bureau.

much as $300,000 and a one-minute spot in prime time can cost $150,000. As Will Rogers put it years ago: "You have to be loaded just to get beat."

The dollars spent on particular races vary, of course—and widely. More, or less, is spent depending on many factors, among them: the office envolved, the size of the constituency, the candidate (and whether he or she is the incumbent), the opposition, and (not least) the availability of campaign funds.

Who Gives and Why?

In the broadest sense, parties and their candidates draw their money from two sources: private contributions and the public treasury. Recent campaign finance laws have had a major impact on both of these sources, as we shall see in a moment. But, first, a more specific cataloging of that first one—for private contributions have been and still are the major source of campaign monies in American politics.

Clearly, the democratic ideal would best be served if political campaigns were entirely supported by (1) small contributions made by millions of Americans. But only about one in every 10 persons of voting age ever makes such gifts. Because of this, parties and their candidates have had to look to other places for much of their funding.

They have had to depend upon: (2) wealthier persons and families—the so-called "angels" or "fat-cats"; (3) the candidates themselves, incumbents, and those who hold appointive public offices; (4) non-party private organizations —special interest groups with a major stake in the making and content of public policy, most notably organized labor and business groups; (5) *ad hoc* committees formed for the immediate purposes of a campaign, including fund-raising— for example, Kansans for Carter-Mondale or the Fund for a Conservative

Fund raising at a political rally.

Majority (pro-Reagan, 1980); and (6) special fund-raising events—including telethons, direct-mail campaigns, and such social-electioneering affairs as $25-, or $100-, or $1000-a-plate dinners, picnics, concerts, receptions, cocktail parties, and rallies.

To these traditional sources a newer one—**public subsidies**, funding from federal and/or State treasuries—has lately been added. To this point, at least, it has been most important at the presidential level, as we shall see.[23]

---

[23]Public funds for presidential campaigns come from the federal treasury. Several States now also have some form of public financing for parties and/or candidates.

Campaign donations are a form of political participation, and those who make them do so for a number of reasons. Many small contributors give simply because they believe in a party or a candidate. But most who give want something in return. They want access to government, and they hope to get it by helping their "friends" win elections.[24]

Some big donors want appointments to public office, and others want to keep the ones they have. Some long for social recognition —and for them dinner at the White House or knowing the governor on a first-name basis may be enough. Organized labor, business, professional, and various other groups almost always have particular policy aims. They want certain laws passed, or changed, or repealed, or certain appropriations made, or certain administrative actions taken.[25]

Campaign Finance Regulation

Congress first began to regulate the use of money in the federal election process in 1907. In that year it became unlawful for any corporation or national bank to make "a money contribution in any election" of candidates for federal office. Since then, Congress has passed several laws to regulate the use of money in presidential and congressional campaigns.

Today, these regulations are found in three very detailed laws: the Federal Election Campaign Act of 1971, the FECA Amendments of 1974, and the FECA Amendments of 1976.[26]

The Federal Election Commission. All federal law dealing with campaign finance is administered by the Federal Election Commission. The FEC was set up by Congress in 1974. It is an independent agency in the executive branch and its six members are appointed by the President, with Senate confirmation.[27]

The laws which the Commission enforces cover four broad areas. They (1) require the timely disclosure of campaign finance data; (2) place limits on campaign contributions; (3) place limits on campaign expenditures; and (4) provide public funding for several parts of the presidential election process.

Disclosure Requirements. Congress first required the reporting of certain campaign finance information in 1910. Today, the disclosure requirements are very detailed—to spotlight the place of money in federal campaigns. In fact, the several reports that must be filed with the FEC are so comprehensive

---

[24]One of the better demonstrations of the point can be seen in the fact that some contributors give to *competing* candidates. They hedge their bets; heads they win and tails they still win.

[25]Among those "various other groups" is organized crime—which has an obvious stake in public policy and so in public policy-makers. Large-scale operations in narcotics, prostitution, gambling, loan-sharking, and other illegal activities cannot survive without close ties to at least some public officials. The profits of organized crime are huge, untold—and untaxed—billions. Campaign contributions can be a cheap form of insurance.

[26]The earlier federal laws were often called "more loophole than law"; they were loosely drawn, not often obeyed, and almost never enforced. The 1971 law, which became effective in 1972, replaced them. The 1974 law marked the major legislative response to the Watergate scandal; it made many of the provisions of the 1971 law tighter and the coverage broader. The 1976 law was passed in direct response to the Supreme Court's decision in *Buckley* v. *Valeo*, 1976. A number of minor changes were made in these laws in 1980.

Congress does not have the constitutional power to regulate the use of money in State and local elections. Every State now does regulate at least some aspects of campaign finance. Several do so quite extensively; but, unfortunately, some do so very inadequately.

[27]The FEC was originally made up of two members appointed by the President, two by the Speaker of the House, and two by the President *Pro Tem* of the Senate, with the Clerk of the House and the Secretary of the Senate as *ex officio* members. However, the Supreme Court found this structure unconstitutional in *Buckley* v. *Valeo*, 1976. It held that, because the FEC is an *executive* agency, both the doctrine of separation of powers and Article II, Section 2 (giving the appointing power to the President), require that *all* of its members be appointed by the President. Congress restructured the FEC in 1976. The Clerk of the House and the Secretary of the Senate remain as *ex officio* (by virtue of office), non-voting members of the Commission.

WE'RE GOING WITH A $400,000 PRINT CAMPAIGN, $650,000 FOR RADIO AND A HALF-MILLION FOR DIRECT MAIL. AND IF **THAT** DOESN'T GET THE MESSAGE ACROSS THAT YOUR OPPONENT'S A BIG SPENDER, WE'VE SAVED A MILLION FOR A LAST-MINUTE TV BLITZ.

©1980. Reprinted by permission of NEA, Inc.

that nearly all candidates for federal office find that their campaign organization must include at least one certified public accountant.

All contributions to a candidate for federal office must be made through a single campaign committee. Only that committee can spend that candidate's campaign money. Any and all of those contributions, and spendings, must be closely accounted for by that one committee. Any contribution, including any loan, of more than $200 must be identified by source and by date. So, too, must any spending over $200—by the name of the person or firm to whom payment was made, by date and by purpose.

Any contribution of more than $5000 must be reported to the FEC no later than 48 hours after it is received. So, too, must any sum of $1000 or more received in the last 20 days of a campaign. A cash contribution of more than $100 cannot be accepted under any circumstances.

Any "independent committee" (or person) spending more than $100 for a candidate, on its own—outside of that candidate's organization, must also file

with the FEC. It must report the financial details of its operations and must swear, subject to perjury, that none of its activities was carried on in collusion with that candidate or his or her organization.

All reports must be filed with the FEC in timely fashion. Their due dates fall at the end of each calendar quarter and also 12 days before and again not more than 30 days after an election.

Limits on Contributions. Congress first began to regulate campaign contributions in 1907—when, as we noted, it outlawed donations by corporations and national banks. A similar ban was first applied to labor unions in 1943. Individual contributions first became subject to regulation in 1939.

Today, no person may give more than $1000 to any federal candidate in a primary election, and no more than $1000 to any federal candidate's general election campaign. Also, no person may give more than $5000 in any year to a political action committee, or $20,000 to a national party committee. The *total* of any person's contributions to federal candidates and committees cannot be more than $25,000 in any one year.

These limits have now been in place since 1976. And, clearly, they have finally curbed the long-standing and very substantial impact of the "fat-cats" in *federal* elections.[27] (But, remember, they do *not* apply to campaigns for State and local offices.)

Neither corporations nor labor unions may themselves make campaign contributions. But their **political action**

[28]The limits may seem generous; in fact, they are very tight. Before 1976, many wealthy persons made contributions far larger than those amounts. In 1972, W. Clement Stone, a Chicago insurance executive, gave more than $2 million and Richard Mellon Scaife, heir to oil, aluminum, and banking fortunes, gave more than $1 million to President Nixon's reelection campaign. In all, the top ten individual contributors gave at least $7.4 million to federal candidates in 1972, most of it to the major party presidential nominees.

THE GROWTH OF PAC'S (Political Action Committees)

Number of committees (in thousands)

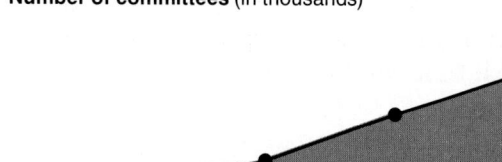

1974   1976   1978   1980   1982

Source: Common Cause

Contributions (in millions of dollars)

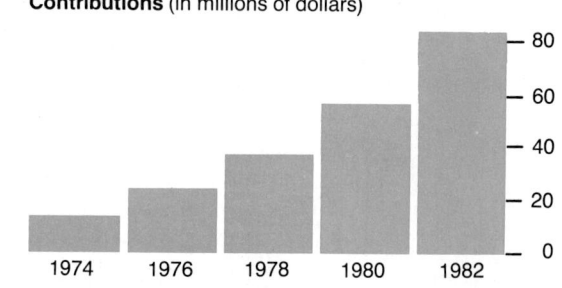

1974   1976   1978   1980   1982

committees (**PACs**) can—and do. A PAC is the political arm of a business, labor, professional or other special interest group. Examples of such groups include BIPAC (the Business-Industry Political Action Committee), COPE (the AFL-CIO's Committee on Political Education), and AMPAC (the American Medical Association's national political organization). PACs fill their political war chests with voluntary contributions from their members—from the executives, stockholders, and employees of a corporation, from union members, from doctors or dentists or teachers, or from those who are for or against gun-control laws, and so on. They distribute their money to favored parties and candidates, of course.

There were fewer than 1000 PACs in 1974; by 1984 their number had grown to nearly 3500. They put close to $60 million into presidential and, especially, congressional campaign coffers in 1980.

No PAC may give more than $5000 to any one federal candidate. But there is no overall limit on PAC giving. Each of them may contribute up to the $5000 ceiling to as many different candidates as it chooses.

No contribution may be made by any person or group in the name of another. Cash gifts of more than $100 are absolutely prohibited. So, too, are contribu-

tions from any foreign source. All newspaper, radio, and television ads, circulars, and all other materials promoting a candidate for a federal office must carry the name of the persons or groups which sponsor them.

Limits on Expenditures. Congress first began to limit federal campaign spending in 1925. Most of the limitations now in the law apply only to the presidential election process.[29]

Those presidential contenders who accept federal campaign subsidies are subject to limits on their campaign spending—in both the pre-convention primaries and in the general election campaign.[30]

---

[29]In *Buckley* v. *Valeo*, 1976, the Supreme Court struck down several restrictions the 1974 law put on spending in federal campaigns. The Court held each of them to be contrary to the 1st Amendment's guarantees of freedom of expression. In effect, said the Court, in politics "money is speech." The voided provisions: (1) placed strict limits on House and Senate campaign expenditures; (2) placed strict limits on how much of their own money candidates could put into their own campaigns; and (3) said no person or group (independent committees) could spend more than $1000 in behalf of a candidate without his or her authorization. The Court also struck down limits on presidential campaign spending—*except* for candidates who accept FEC subsidies for their campaigns. To this point, Congress has not found any constitutionally acceptable way to reimpose those limits.

[30]The limits go along with the subsidies, as a part of the bargain. So far (1976 and 1980), only one major party aspirant has not accepted federal funds — former Governor John B. Connally of Texas; he raised and spent some $12 million in private funds in his unsuccessful bid for the Republican presidential nomination in 1980.

Ronald Reagan and George Bush shake hands with well-wishers as they campaign in Washington, D.C.

For 1980, no contender could spend more than $14.7 million in the pre-convention period. After the conventions, the Carter and Reagan campaigns could each spend up to $29.4 million. And each of the major parties was allowed to spend only $2.9 million for its 1980 national convention.[31]

Public Funding of Presidential Campaigns. Congress first began to provide for the public funding of presidential campaigns in the Revenue Act of 1971. It broadened sections of that law in 1974 and again in 1976.

The 1971 law set up the Presidential Election Campaign Fund. It also provided that each person who files a federal income tax return may "check off" $1 of his or her tax payment (or $2 on a joint return) to go to the Fund.

As the law now stands, the monies in the Fund are to be used to pay for public subsidies for presidential primary campaigns, presidential nominating conventions, and presidential election campaigns.[31] The FEC administers the subsidy process.

Presidential Primaries. Presidential primary campaigns are now supported by the private contributions a candidate raises *plus* the public money he or she receives from the Federal Election Commission.

To be eligible for the public funds, a presidential hopeful must first get past a rather complicated barrier. He or she must raise at least $100,000 from private sources. That amount must be gathered in $5000 lots in each of at least 20 States, with each of those lots built from individual donations of not more than $250. This tangled requirement is meant to discourage both hopeless and frivolous candidates.

---

[31]The 1974 law set these three limits at $10 million, $20 million, and $2 million, respectively. However, the law took inflation into account and authorized the FEC to adjust the amounts for each presidential year. For 1976, these three limits were $10.9 million, $21.8 million, and $2.1 million—and they will be considerably higher in 1984.

[32]The Revenue Act of 1971 also tried to stimulate and broaden the base of campaign giving. As amended in 1978, it allows an income taxpayer to take a *credit* (a subtraction from the total tax due) of up to $50, or $100 on a joint return, for political contributions. The tax laws of several States now include similar provisions.

For each contender who passes that test, the FEC matches the first $250 of each of the additional private contributions he or she can raise—up to a total of half of the overall on primary spending. That is, up to as much as $7.35 million in 1980 when, remember, that ceiling was $14.7 million for each candidate.

These primary subsidies had a number of significant effects on the nominating process in 1976 and again in 1980. Their impact was felt in both major parties. Just the fact that there was public money to be had caused a much larger than usual number of presidential hopefuls to enter the pre-convention battle—in both of the major parties and in both election years.

In 1980, all presidential hopefuls, combined, spent about $129 million in the pre-convention period—including nearly $31 million the FEC gave to six GOP and four Democratic contenders.

National Conventions. If a major party applies for the money—and both did in 1976 and 1980—it automatically receives a grant to defray the costs of its national convention. The Republicans and the Democrats each got $2.9 million for their convention in 1980. And, recall, that is all the law permitted them to spend for that purpose.

Presidential Campaigns. Each major party presidential nominee automatically qualifies for a public subsidy to cover the costs of the general election campaign. For 1980, the Reagan and the Carter organizations each received $29.4 million from the FEC.

In addition, each major party's national committee received $4.6 million for its presidential campaign efforts. All told, then, each of the major party campaigns was financed with $34 million in public funds in 1980.

A party's candidate, or its national committee, can refuse to accept the public money. If either does so, it can then raise however much it is able to from private sources.

Both the Republican and the Democratic candidates, and their national committees, took the public money in both 1976 and 1980. By doing so, each of them automatically: (1) could spend no more than the amount of the subsidy for the presidential campaign, and (2) could not accept campaign funds from any other source.

A minor party candidate may also qualify for public funding — but not automatically. To be eligible, the minor party must either: (1) have won at least five percent of the popular vote in the last presidential election or (2) win at least that much of the vote in the current election.[33]

CAMPAIGN SPENDING, MAJOR
PARTY PRESIDENTIAL
CANDIDATES, 1952–1980

(in millions of dollars)

Year		Republican		Democrat
1952	$ 6.61	Eisenhower*	$ 5.03	Stevenson
1956	7.78	Eisenhower*	5.11	Stevenson
1960	10.13	Nixon	9.80	Kennedy*
1964	16.03	Goldwater	8.76	Johnson*
1968	25.40	Nixon*	11.60	Humphrey
1972	61.40	Nixon*	30.00	McGovern
1976	21.79	Ford	21.80	Carter*
1980	29.40	Reagan*	29.40	Carter

*Indicates winner of presidential election.
Source: Adapted from Herbert E. Alexander, *Financing Politics: Money, Elections and Reform* (Washington, D.C.: Congressional Quarterly Press, 2nd ed., 1980), p. 5; 1980 data from Federal Election Commission.

---

[33]In which case the public money would be received *after* the election and could not possibly help the candidate in that election. Again, as we noted on page 169, many provisions of election law are purposely drawn to discourage minor party efforts. No minor party candidate received five percent of the presidential vote in 1976 or in 1980. But independent candidate John Anderson won 6.6 percent in 1980; he received $4.2 million in post-election funds from the FEC and, presumably, is eligible for public funding in 1984.

1. Why must campaign finances be regulated by law?
2. What are the major sources of campaign contributions in American politics?
3. Why do most who make campaign contributions do so?
4. What is the Federal Election Commission?
5. With what four major areas of campaign finance do federal laws now deal?

Three presidential campaign devices of the last century; (top) McKinley-Roosevelt umbrella, 1900; (left) Polk-Dallas flag, 1844; (lower right) Garfield-Arthur bandanna, 1880.

SUMMARY

Both the nomination and the election process are fundamental to democracy.

Five different methods have been and are used to make nominations in American politics. In order of their historical appearance, they are: (1) self-announcement, (2) the caucus, (3) the delegate convention, (4) the direct primary, and (5) petition.

The direct primary, which developed at the turn of the century in reaction to the ills of the convention system, is the most widely used nominating method today. It is an intra-party nominating election. It now takes two forms among the States: (1) the closed primary, in which only party members may vote, and (2) the *open primary*, in which any qualified voter may take part. *Runoff primaries* are widely used in southern States, where a nominee must have a majority of the primary vote in order to win party nomination. *Nonpartisan primaries* are often used to nominate candidates for nonpartisan offices. *Presidential primaries*, now found in nearly three-fourths of the States, are not nominating devices; rather, they are elections held as a part of the presidential candidate selection process.

There is only a limited amount of federal control over the election process. It is very largely regulated by State law.

Presidential and congressional elections are held on the Tuesday following the first Monday in November in even-numbered years. Most States hold their general elections at the same time; local elections are generally held then, too, or in the spring. The elections take place in precincts (voting districts), each of which has a polling place.

In all States today voters cast the Australian ballot which is either of the office-group or the party-column type. Voting machines and/or electronic data processing to count ballots are now found in most places where there is a heavy population. Most ballots used in American elections are much too long, are likely to confuse and discourage voters, and often lead to blind voting.

Money plays a key part in politics and presents serious problems for democratic government. The major sources of campaign funds are: (1) small individual contributors, (2) large individual donors, "fat-cats," (3) officeholders and office seekers, (4) nonparty private organizations—special interest groups and their political action committees (PACs), (5) temporary party campaign committees, (6) party fund-raising events, and, now, (7) public subsidies. Most who give political money want something in return.

The several recently-enacted federal campaign finance laws are administered by the Federal Election Commission. They apply only to presidential and congressional elections, not to State and local contests. Generally, these laws: (1) require the disclosure of campaign finance data; (2) place limits on contributions, (3) place limits on expenditures, and (4) provide for public funding of several aspects of the presidential election process.

CHAPTER REVIEW

Key Terms/Concepts

Ballot (228)
Blanket primary (222)
Campaign finance (232)

Caucus (218)
Closed primary (221)
Coattail effect (227)

Convention (219)
Direct primary (221)
Legislative caucus (219)

Name familiarity (225)
Nomination (217)
Nonpartisan primary (222)

Open primary (221)
Petition (225)
Political action committee (236)
Polling place (227)
Precinct (227)
Public funding (237)
Presidential primary (225)
Public subsidy (234)
Run-off primary (222)
Self-announcement (218)

Keynote Questions

1. Why is the nominating stage such a critically important part of the electoral process?
2. Identify the five major methods used for the making of nominations in American politics. Which of them was the first to be used? Which is most widely used today?
3. What is a direct primary? Distinguish between the open and the closed forms of the primary. What are the major arguments made for and against each of those forms?
4. Why are the specific details of the electoral process such vitally important matters?
5. Why is nearly all election law in this country State law?
6. What is the Australian ballot? Identify and distinguish the two basic forms of it now used in American elections.
7. Why is the long ballot so widely found in American elections?
8. Why must campaign finances be regulated by law?
9. What are the major sources of campaign contributions in American politics? Why do most who make campaign contributions do so?
10. With what four broad areas do federal campaign finance laws now deal?

For Thought and Discussion

1. What do you think Adlai Stevenson meant when he said: "Your public servants serve you right"?
2. What arguments can you present in opposition to the author's contention (page 230): "For good government, the rule should be: *Elect* those who make public policies; *appoint* those who only administer them."
3. Outline the provisions of your State's campaign finance laws. What changes, if any, do you think should be made in them?
4. Why do you suppose that, despite the urgings of many, Congress has not provided for some form of public financing of the congressional election process?

Suggested Activities

1. Prepare a bulletin board display of sample ballots and other materials from recent elections in your State. (You can usually get ballots from local election officials, party groups, or the Secretary of State's office.)
2. Invite the county clerk or other election official to speak to the class about the way elections are run in your locale.
3. From your State's election code, draw a flow chart of the steps that are taken in the casting and counting of ballots in an election.
4. Invite a recent candidate (either successful or unsuccessful) to describe his/her campaign experiences to the class.
5. Stage a debate or class forum on one or more of the following topics: (a) *Resolved*, That this State (abandon/adopt) the direct primary as its basic nominating device; (b) *Resolved*, That this State adopt the (open/closed) form of the direct primary; (c) *Resolved*, That this State change to the use of the (office-group/party-column) ballot in all partisan elections; (d) *Resolved*, That all campaigns for public office be financed entirely with public funds.

10

Government by the People: Public Opinion and Pressure Groups

CHAPTER OBJECTIVES

To help you to
Learn ▪ Know ▪ Understand

Public opinion and its role in American politics.

The complex process out of which opinions are formed.

The means by which opinions are expressed and may be measured.

Public opinion polls and the scientific polling process.

Pressure groups and:
—their role in politics
—how they differ from political parties
—bases upon which they are formed
—varied tactics used by them.

The common sense of the common people is the greatest and soundest force on earth.

Thomas Jefferson

American government is democratic government. It is, then, self-government—government by the people through their elected representatives. Above all else, its aim is to translate the public will into public policy. Somehow, says the American theory of democracy, the will of the people is supposed to become law in the United States.

A very wise Englishman once said all of this in several fewer words. Government in the United States, wrote Lord Bryce nearly 100 years ago, is "government by public opinion."[1]

To this point, we have taken a close look at three of the major instruments of democratic government in this country: political parties, voting, and elections. In this chapter we shall look first at public opinion and its place in American politics and then at another of those vital instruments of democracy: pressure groups.

[1] James Bryce, *The American Commonwealth* (New York: Macmillan, 1888), vol. II, page 251.

Marchers observe the 20th anniversary of Martin Luther King Jr.'s "March on Washington" in August of 1983. *Facing page:* Maggie Kuhn leader of the Gray Panthers, a group organized to advance the rights of the aged.

Public Opinion

What Is Public Opinion?

Few terms are more widely used—and, at the same time, less well understood—in American politics than "public opinion." It appears regularly in newspapers and magazines, and we frequently hear it on both radio and television.

Quite often, the phrase is used in a way that suggests that all or at least most of the American people hold the same view on some public matter. Thus, time and again, politicians say that "the people" want such and such, television commentators tell us that "the public" favors this or opposes that, and so on.

In fact, however, there are very few matters in which all or nearly all of "the people" think alike. The "public" holds many different and often conflicting views on nearly every public question.

So, to understand what public opinion is, and what that phrase means, we must recognize this important point: Public opinion is a complex collection of the opinions of many different persons and groups. It is an aggregate—the sum total—of all of their views. It is *not* the single and undivided view of some mass mind.

In short, public opinion is made up of publics and their opinions.

There are *many* publics in the United States—in fact, an uncountable number of them. Each one of them is made up of all of those persons who hold the same view on some particular public question. Each of them is a separate public with regard to that matter. The view that its members share sets each one of them apart from all of the other publics in our politics.

To illustrate: All of those persons who think that public employees should not be allowed to strike belong to the public which holds that view. All of those who believe that Ronald Reagan is doing an excellent job as President, or that capital punishment should be abolished, or that prayers should be offered in the public schools, or that marijuana should be legalized are members of the separate publics with those particular opinions. And note this: Many persons belong to more than one of these publics; but almost certainly only a very few (and perhaps even none) belong to all five of them.[2]

In its proper sense, public opinion includes *only* those opinions that are clearly *public*. That is, it is made up only of those views that relate to matters of government—to politics, to public issues, and to the making of public policies.

To put this the other way, public opinion does *not* include views on matters of private concern. Many people think that they are too tall or too short, or that their feet are too big. But these opinions are generally of little or no interest to anyone else. To be an opinion in the public sense, a view must involve something of general concern, something of interest to a significant portion of the people as a whole.

Of course, the people as a whole are interested in a great many things—in rock groups and symphony orchestras,

the New York Yankees and the Dallas Cowboys, candy bars and green vegetables, and a great deal more. And people have opinions on each of these things— views that are sometimes loosely called "public opinion."

But, again, and in its proper sense, public opinion involves only those views that people hold on such things as parties and candidates, taxes, unemployment, welfare programs, national defense, foreign policy, and so on.

Definition.   Clearly, the thing that we call public opinion is so complex that it cannot be readily defined. But, with what we have said about it, it may be described this way: *Those attitudes held by a significant number of persons on matters of government and politics.*

As we have suggested, the term can be better understood in the plural—that is, as public opinions, the opinions of publics. Or, to put it another way, public opinion is made up of expressed group attitudes.[3]

 FOR REVIEW

1. How and why is the phrase "public opinion" often misused?
2. Why is the meaning of public opinion best understood in terms of the opinions of publics?
3. How many publics are there? How do they differ from one another?
4. Views held on what matters are properly part of public opinion?
5. Define public opinion.

The Formation of Public Opinion

None of us is *born* with a set of attitudes about government and poli-

[2]There are as many different publics on any given issue as there are sides to that question. For example, on the public employees strike question one public holds the view that *no one* who works for government should be allowed to strike. Another thinks that *all* who do so should have that right. Yet another believes that all *except* those whose jobs have a direct bearing on the public's safety (police and fire for example) should be able to strike; and so on. Students of public opinion often identify the several publics with differing views on the same issue as "sub-publics."

[3]Clearly, unless an opinion is expressed in some way it cannot be known by others; and if it cannot be known, it cannot be identified with any public.

tics, of course. Instead, we *learn* our political opinions—and we do so in a life-long "classroom" and from many different "teachers."

In other words, public opinion—which is the sum total of all of the political attitudes that all of us hold—is formed out of a very complex process, and the factors involved in it are almost without number.

We have already said much of this—in Chapter 8, when we talked about voting behavior. In effect, that extensive look at why people vote as they do amounted to an extensive look at how public opinion is formed.

There, remember, we described the process by which each of us acquires our political opinions as the process of **political socialization.** As we said at the time, that very complex process begins in early childhood and continues on through a person's lifetime. It involves all of the means—all of the experiences and relationships—that lead each of us to see the political world, and to act in it, as we do.[4]

There are many different agents of political socialization—a large number of factors (influences) at work in the opinion-shaping process. Again, we looked at these agents at some length in Chapter 8—age, race, income, occupation, residence, group affiliations, and many others. But two of them—the family and education—have such a vital impact that we must take another (and slightly different) look at them here.

The Family.   Most parents do not think of themselves as agents of political socialization—nor do the other members of most families. They are, nonetheless, and very importantly so.

"Full Disclosure," by Auth & Szep.
© 1983 The Washington Post Co.

Children first see the political world from within the family and through the family's eyes. They begin to learn about it much as they begin to learn about most other things—from what their parents have to say, from the stories that their older brothers and sisters bring home from school, from watching the family's television set, and so on.

Most of what smaller children learn in the family setting cannot really be called political opinions. Clearly, they are not concerned with the wisdom of spending billions of dollars on an MX missile system or the pros and cons of the tight money policies of the Federal Reserve Board. They do pick up some basic attitudes, however—and with them a basic slant toward such things as authority and rules of behavior, property, neighbors, people of other racial or religious groups, and the like. In short, they lay some very important foundations upon which their political opinions will be built.

A large number of scholarly studies report what common sense also tells us: The strong influence that the family has on the development of political opinions is due very largely to the near monopoly

---

[4]The concept of *socialization* comes from the fields of sociology and psychology. Socialization is the multisided, life-long process in which people come to know, accept, and follow the beliefs and practices of their society. *Political* socialization is a part of that much broader process, of course.

it has on the child in his or her earliest, formative, most impressionable years. They also show that:

> The orientations acquired in early childhood tend to be the most intensely and permanently held of all political views. They serve as the base on which all later political learning is built. . . . Adult political behavior is the logical extension of values, knowledge, and identification formed during childhood and youth.[5]

The Schools.   The start of formal schooling marks the first break in the force of family influence. For the first time children become regularly involved in activities outside the home.

From the very first day, schools teach children the values of the American political system. They very purposefully work to indoctrinate the young, to train them to become "good citizens." Schoolchildren salute the flag, recite the pledge of allegiance, and sing patriotic songs. They learn about George Washington and Abraham Lincoln and other great figures of the American past. From the early grades on, they pick up growing amounts of more specific political knowledge and they begin to form their political opinions. And, as high school students, they are often required to take a course in American government and even to read books like this one.[6]

No one factor, by itself—family or school or any other—shapes any person's opinion on any matter. Some do play a larger role than others, however.

Thus, in addition to family and education, occupation and race are usually much more significant than, say, sex or place of residence.

But this is not *always* the case. On the question of public employee strikes, for example, the kind of job a person has (whether public or private, professional, white-collar or blue-collar, union or non-union, and so on) will almost certainly have a greater impact on that person's view than will his or her sex or where he or she happens to live. On the other hand, if the question involves something like equal pay for women, or flood control projects in the Ohio River Valley, then sex, or place of residence, will almost certainly loom much larger in the opinion-making mix. In short, the relative weight of each of the many factors that influence public opinion depends a great deal upon the nature of the particular issue involved.

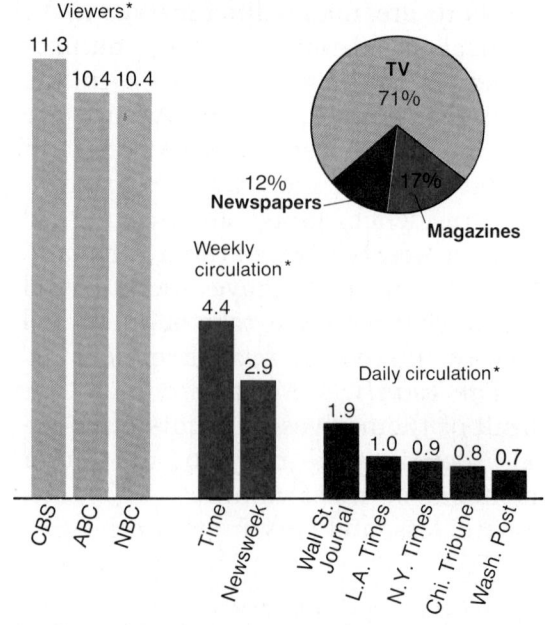

AUDIENCES REACHED BY LEADING MEDIA (in millions)

Viewers*

TV 71%

12% Newspapers

17% Magazines

Weekly circulation*

Daily circulation*

CBS 11.3
ABC 10.4
NBC 10.4
Time 4.4
Newsweek 2.9
Wall St. Journal 1.9
L.A. Times 1.0
N.Y. Times 0.9
Chi. Tribune 0.8
Wash. Post 0.7

*All data is average for latest 6 month period available

Source: Ayer Directory of Publications, 1982; CBS Television Network

---

[5]Richard Dawson, Kenneth Previtt, and Karen Dawson, *Political Socialization* (Boston. Little, Brown, 2nd ed., 1977), pg. 48.

[6]In fact, the schools may be even more significant than the family here. Much recent research on opinion formulation supports this finding: "The public schools appear to be the most important and effective instruments of political socialization in the United States." Robert Hess and Judith Torney, *The Development of Political Attitudes in Children* (Garden City, N.Y.: Doubleday, 1968), page 120.

Opinion Leaders. The views expressed by certain people—opinion leaders—also bear heavily on public opinion. An **opinion leader** is any person who, for any reason, has a more than usual influence on the views of others.

These opinion-shapers are a distinct minority in the total population, of course, but they are to be found everywhere. Many of them hold public offices. Some write for newspapers or magazines or broadcast their opinions on radio or television. Others are prominent in business, labor, agriculture, civic organizations, and so on. Many are in professional occupations—as doctors, lawyers, teachers, ministers, and the like, who have contact with fairly large numbers of people on a regular basis.

Whoever they may be, these opinion leaders are persons to whom others listen and from whom others draw ideas and convictions. Whatever their political, economic, or social standing or outlook may be, they play a very significant role in the formation of public opinion.

The Mass Media. Who really needs to be told that the **mass media**—newspapers, magazines, radio, and especially television—also have a large impact on public opinion in this country? Every day Americans buy more than 60 million daily newspapers. The three major newsmagazines *(Time, Newsweek,* and *U.S. News)* sell nearly 10 million copies every week. Some 60 million Americans watch the nightly news programs on CBS, ABC, and NBC; and tens of millions also hear reports and commentaries on radio, too.

Clearly, the media do play a significant role in the shaping of public attitudes. But *how much* of a role is the subject of long, unsettled argument.

Whatever its weight, the media's influence can be seen in any number of situations. It is most often visible— most often has its greatest weight—in two of them in particular, however: (1) in the level of the public's interest in certain issues at any given time and (2) in the voters' reactions to candidates in an election.

Interest in Issues. Much of the media's impact on public attitudes stems from the fact that they are a major source for the public's information about public affairs. Most of what most of us know about current events we learn from the media. (Television, newspapers, radio, and magazines are, in that order, the leading sources of political information for most people.)

Very largely, then, the media shape the public agenda. That is, as they report and comment on the issues of the day, they have a considerable effect on the public's sense of the relative importance of the many items they cover. A quick look at any issue of most daily newspapers, or a quick review of the content of any half-hour network news program, will demonstrate the point.

Reactions to Candidates. As we've seen, how voters see a candidate— the impressions they have of that candidate's personality, character, abilities, and so on—is one of the major factors that influence voting behavior. The kind of "image" a candidate projects—often on television but also and very often in the other media—can have a telling effect on the outcome of an election.

Limits on Media Influence. It is all too easy to overstate the media's role, however. There are a number of built-in factors that work to limit media impact.

For one thing, not very many people follow political events of any sort very closely—whether at the international level, in Washington or elsewhere in the country at large, or even in their own communities. Many studies of voting behavior show, for example, that in the typical election only about 10 percent of all of those who can vote, and only about 15 percent of all of those who do vote, can be said to be well informed on the candidates and issues. In short, only a very small part of the public takes in very much of what the media have to say about public affairs.

Moreover, most of those who do pay at least some attention to public affairs are likely to be selective about it. That is, they most often watch, listen to, and read those presentations that generally agree with their own viewpoints; they regularly ignore those that disagree. Thus, for example, many Democrats don't watch the televised speeches of Republican candidates, and many Republicans don't read the newspaper advertisements by Democrats.

Another important limit on the media's impact can be seen in the content of much of what they carry. This is especially true of radio and television. Most television programs, for example, have little or nothing to do with public affairs.[7] Advertisers, who pay the high costs of air time, want to reach the largest possible audience. So, because most people are far more interested in being entertained than they are in being informed, we find very few public affairs programs aired in prime time. (There are a few exceptions—"60 Minutes" on CBS, ABC's "20/20," and NBC's occasional "White Papers," for example; but they are just that—exceptions.)

Radio and television mostly "skim" the news. They report only what their news editors consider to be the most important events of the day. Even on the widely-watched evening news programs, most stories are presented in 60- to 90-second time slots. In short, the broadcast media (or at least most of it) seldom give the kind of in-depth coverage that a good newspaper can supply.

Newspapers are not so hampered in their ability to cover public affairs. Still, much of the content of most papers is nonpolitical. Or, to put it another way, most newspaper readers are more interested in the comics, the sports pages, or the social or travel-movies-television sections of a paper than they are in its news and editorial pages.

All of this is not meant to say that there is no in-depth coverage of public affairs in the media. There is, to those who want it. There are a number of good newspapers around the country; and it can also be found on a number of radio and television stations—including public broadcast outlets. But, remember, there is nothing about democracy that guarantees an alert and informed public. Like voting and other forms of political participation, being an informed citizen does require some effort.

☑ FOR REVIEW

1. Out of what factors is public opinion formed?
2. What is political socialization?
3. Why are the family and schools especially important agents in that process?
4. Who are opinion leaders?
5. What are the mass media? In what two matters do they usually have their greatest impact on public opinion? What factors work to limit media impact?

---

[7]At least not directly. A number of popular programs do relate to public affairs indirectly, however. Thus, many of them are "crime shows"—and crime is certainly a matter of public concern. Many of them also carry a political message, telling us, for example, that police officers are hard-working public servants and that most of them are very decent human beings.

The Measurement of Public Opinion

If public policy is to be based on public opinion, it must be possible to find the answers to these questions: What is the content of public opinion on

The nearly 1750 daily newspapers published today have a circulation of more than 60 million copies per issue; more than 1000 television stations air programs that can be viewed on an estimated 150 million TV sets.

a certain issue? How many persons share a given view on that matter? How firmly do they hold that view? That is to say, it must be possible to "measure" public opinion.

Means of Expression. The general content of public opinion on some matter—what different groups of people say they think about it—can be found in a very obvious way: By consulting the means by which opinions are usually expressed in our society. Those means include voting, lobbying, books, pamphlets, magazine and newspaper articles, editorial comments in the press and on radio and television, paid advertisements, letters to editors, and public officials, and so on.

But, usually, the *means* by which a view is expressed tell little—and often nothing reliable—about the *size* of the group that holds that opinion or how *strongly* it is held.

Measurement Through Elections. In a democracy the voice of the people is supposed to be heard through the ballot box. Election results are very often said to be indicators of public opinion. The votes cast for rival candidates are regularly taken as evidences of the people's approval or rejection of the stands taken by those candidates and their parties. A party and its victorious candidates regularly claim to have been given a "mandate" to carry out their campaign promises.[8]

In fact, however, election results are not often an *accurate* measure of public opinion. Voters make the choices they do in elections for any of several reasons, as we have seen. Very often, those choices have little or nothing to do with the candidates' stands on public questions. Then, too, candidates often disagree with some of the planks of their party's platform.

---

[8]The term *mandate* comes from the Latin, *mandare*—literally, to place in one's hand or to commit to one's charge. In American politics it refers to the instructions or commands a constituency gives to its elected officials.

In short, much of what we have said about voting behavior—and about the nature of parties, too—adds up to this: Elections are, at best, only useful indicators of public opinion. To call the typical election a "mandate" for much of anything more than a general direction in public policy is to be on very shaky ground.[9]

Measurement Through Pressure Groups. We shall turn to pressure groups at some length in a moment. But, for now, notice that **pressure groups** are private organizations whose members share certain views and objectives and which actively work to influence the making and content of public policy.

As such, they serve as a chief means by which public opinion is made known. They present their views (exert their pressures) through their lobbyists, by letters, telephone calls, and wires, in political campaigns, and by a number of other methods. In dealing with them, public officials often find it very difficult to determine two things, however: Whatever its claims, how many people does a group really represent? And just how strongly do those people hold the views that the organization says they do?

Measurement through the Media. A few moments ago we looked at some very impressive numbers that help to describe the place of the mass media in the opinion process. Here are some more of those statistics:

More than 9600 newspapers are published in the United States today—including nearly 1750 dailies, more than 7000 weeklies, and several hundred foreign-language newspapers. They have

a combined circulation of more than 150 million copies per issue.

There are now more than 1000 television stations—including more than 700 commercial outlets and nearly 300 public broadcasters. Their programs can be seen on some 150 million television sets. No one knows how many hundreds of millions of radios there are—in homes, cars, offices, backpacks, and other places; but they can pick up some 6000 stations on the AM and FM dials.

There is at least one television set in nearly every home in the country—according to the Census Bureau, in more than 98 percent of the nation's 84 million households. There are two or more sets in millions of homes, and millions more in many other places. Most of them are turned on for at least six hours every day—for a mind-boggling total of nearly a billion hours a day.

All of these facts, and many more like them, tell us that the mass media are mass, indeed. They have also led many to describe the media as "mirrors" as well as "molders" of the public's attitudes. That is, it is often said that the views put forth in newspaper editorials, syndicated columns, newsmagazines, television commentaries, and so on are fairly good indicators of public opinion.

They are *not* very good reflectors, however. In fact, they cannot be. Remember, as we noted on page 243, public opinion is made up of the many different opinions of many different publics.

Look at just one more illustration of that point: Most of the nation's daily newspapers almost always support the Republican Party's candidate for President. The large majority of them gave their editorial endorsements to the GOP candidate in all but one of the 13 presidential elections from 1932 through 1980. Yet, the Democrats won the Presi-

---

[9]Initiative and referendum elections—at which voters approve or reject measures—*are* elections in which public opinion is registered much more directly on public policy questions, of course; see pages 533–536. Still, their accuracy depends in large part on the rate of voter turnout.

dency in eight of those elections, and the Republicans took the office in only five of them.[10]

Measurement through Personal Contacts. Most public officials have frequent and wide-ranging contacts with large numbers of people—in many different forms and in any number of situations. In all of them they try to read the public's mind. In fact, their jobs demand that they do so.

Members of Congress receive bags of mail, stacks of telegrams, hundreds of phone calls; many of them make frequent trips "to keep in touch with the folks back home." Cabinet officers and other top administration figures are often on the road, selling the President's programs and sensing the people's reactions. Even the President does some of this, with speaking trips and other visits to different parts of the country.

Governors, State legislators, mayors, and other officials have any number of contacts with the public, too: in their offices, in public meetings, at social gatherings, at ball games, and so on.

Can public officials find "the voice of the people" in all of those contacts? Many can and do, and often with surprising accuracy. But some cannot. They fall into an ever-present trap: They find only what they *want* to find, only those views that support and agree with their own.

Measurement through Public Opinion Polls. The public's opinions are best measured by public opinion polls—or, more accurately, by those polls which are based on scientific polling techniques.

---

[10]We cite only the last 13 elections here because the magazine *Editor & Publisher*, which polls daily papers on this point every four years, first did so in 1932. The one exception in the last 13 elections is 1964, when 56 percent of the daily papers supported President Lyndon Johnson over the Republican candidate Barry Goldwater. In 1980 Ronald Reagan was endorsed by 74 percent of them, then-President Jimmy Carter by 20 percent, and John Anderson by 6 percent.

President Truman grins over his victory in 1948 that upset pollsters, and others, who predicted a landslide victory for Thomas E. Dewey.

© 1980. Reprinted by permission of United Features Syndicate.

Public opinion polls have been used in this country for far more than a century. Until the 1930s, however, they were far from scientific. Most earlier polling efforts were of the "straw vote" variety. That is, they were polls which sought to read the public's mind simply by asking the same question of a large number of people. Straw votes are still fairly common. Newspapers often run "clip-out and mail-in" ballots; radio talk-shows ask listeners to respond to questions with phone calls; and so on.

The straw-vote technique is highly unreliable, however. It rests on the false assumption that a relatively large number of responses will give a fairly accurate picture of the public's views on a given question. But nothing in the process ensures that those who do respond—

DICTIONARIES, OTHER LEXICONS

KNOW HOW TO LEARN

As any good dictionary will tell you, the word *poll* comes from the old Middle English word "polle," meaning the top or back of the head.

A good dictionary will also tell you that *poll* (like many other words) has a number of different meanings—and most of them have little or nothing to do with politics.

We use *poll* in several places in this book—in its political context, to refer to several aspects of the electoral (head-counting) process. And, notice, that phrase "several aspects of" says that *poll* has more than one meaning.

There are several dictionaries and other lexicons in your school library—and in other nearby places, as well. Those epistemic volumes are a truly indispensable part of the knowledge-gathering and -using processes. (Take a lesson from Henry Adams: "He knows enough who knows to learn.")

Where can you find the several and specific meanings of *poll* as a political term? One of those good dictionaries would be a good place to start, of course. But most dictionaries give only very brief definitions, and many of them do not list all of the definitions of many terms.

There are several dictionary-like volumes devoted to politics; and most of them will tell you much more about *poll*, and other political terms, than any standard dictionary can. One very useful (and witty) one is by William Safire, *Safire's Political Dictionary* (Random House, 1978); another, by Jack Plano and Milton Greenberg, *The American Political Dictionary* (Holt, Rinehart and Winston, 6th ed., 1982).

1. What dictionaries and similar epistemic volumes are in your school's library? What does "epistemic" mean?
2. What are the several meanings of *poll*, both as a political term and in its other usages?

no matter how many—will in fact represent a reasonably accurate cross-section (sample) of the total population. It emphasizes the *quantity* rather than the *quality* of the sample to which its question is posed.

The most famous of all straw-polling snafus took place in 1936. The *Literary Digest* mailed postcard ballots to more than 10 million people and received answers from more than 2,376,000 of them. Based on that huge return, the magazine confidently predicted the outcome of the presidential election that year. It said that Governor Alfred Landon, the Republican nominee, would easily defeat incumbent President Franklin Roosevelt. Instead, Roosevelt won in a landslide. He captured more than 60 percent of the popular vote and carried every State but two. Landon was able to win only in Maine and Vermont.

The *Digest* had drawn its sample on an altogether faulty basis: from automobile registration lists and from telephone directories. But in the mid-Depression year of 1936 millions of people could not afford to own cars, and most private telephones were to be found in upper and middle class homes. In short, its poll failed to reach most of the poor and the unemployed, millions of blue-collar workers, and most of the ethnic minorities—and those were the very segments of the population from which FDR and the Democrats drew their greatest support.[11]

Scientific Polling. Serious efforts to take the public's pulse on a scientific basis date from the mid-1930s. They began with the pioneering work of such early pollsters as George Gallup and Elmo Roper. The techniques that they and others have developed since then have reached a highly sophisticated level.

There are now more than 1000 national and regional polling organizations in this country. Many of them do mostly commercial work. They tap the public's preferences on everything from toothpastes and headache remedies to television shows and thousands of other things. At least 200 of them poll the political preferences of the American people, however. Certainly, among the best known of the national pollsters today are the American Institute of Public Opinion (the Gallup Poll) and Louis Harris and Associates (the Harris Survey).

At best, we can only hope to outline the major features of scientific poll-taking. To that end, that whole and complex process can be described in five basic steps. Pollsters must:

1. Define the **universe** to be surveyed—that is, the whole population to be measured, the group whose opinions the poll will seek to discover. That universe can be all voters in Chicago, or every high school student in North Carolina, or all Republicans in New England, or all Catholic women over age 35 in the United States, and so on.

---

[11]The magazine had predicted the winner of each of the three previous presidential elections; but its failure to do so in 1936 was so colossal that it stopped publication almost immediately afterwards.

2. Construct a *sample*. If a total universe is made up of the 35 members of a high school class, the best way to find out what they think about some issue would be to poll every one of them. In most cases, however, it is not possible to interview a complete universe; there are simply too many people to talk to. So, a **sample**—a representative slice of the total universe—must be selected.

Most professional pollsters now draw a *random sample* (also called a *probability sample*). In a **random sample** a certain number of randomly selected people who live in a certain number of randomly selected places are picked to be interviewed. (Here, "random" means that each member of the universe and each geographic area within it have a mathematically equal chance of being included within the sample.)

Most major national polls interview about 1500 people to represent the nation's adult population of some 160 million people. The composition of the Gallup Poll's sample, and Dr. Gallup's description of its design, are set out on page 255.

How can the views of so few people represent the opinions of so many? At base, the answer to that question lies in something which most people, though they may have to be reminded of it, know quite well: the mathematical law of probability. Flip a coin 1000 times. The law of probability says that, given an honest coin and an honest flip, heads will come up 500 times.

In short, if the sample is of sufficient size and is properly selected at random from the entire universe, the law of probability says that the result will be quite accurate—to within a very small margin of error.

Mathematicians tell us that a properly drawn random sample of 1500 people will reflect the opinions of all of the nation's population that will be accurate to within a margin of plus or minus (±) 3 percent.[12]

Some pollsters do use a less complicated, but less reliable, sampling method. They draw a **quota sample**, a sample which is deliberately constructed to reflect several of the major characteristics of the universe. For example, if 51.3 percent of that overall group is female, 17.5 percent of it is black, and so on, then the sample will be made up of 51.3 percent females, 17.5 percent blacks, and so on.

3. Prepare valid questions. The way in which questions are worded is a very important matter. Clearly, it can affect the reliability of any poll. For example, most people will probably say "yes" to a question put this way: "Should local taxes be reduced?" But many of those same persons will also give the same answer to this question: "Should the city's police force be increased to fight the rising tide of crime in our community?" Yet, expanding the police force would almost certainly require more local tax dollars.

Responsible pollsters phrase their questions very carefully. They purposefully try not to use loaded words, terms that are difficult to understand, and questions that may prejudice the answers that will be given to them.

4. Select and control the means by which the poll will be taken. In part, this point relates to how the poll-takers communicate with the sample. Most polls are taken face-to-face; the interviewers question the respondents in person. Some surveys are conducted by telephone, however, and others by mail. Professional pollsters see both advantages and drawbacks in each of these approaches; but they all agree that only one method, the same technique, must be used in the questioning of all of the respondents in a sample.

The interview itself is a very sensitive point in the process. The poll-taker's appearance, dress, apparent attitude, or tone of voice in asking questions may influence the replies he or she receives. Some of those replies may be snap judgments or emotional reactions. Others may be of the sort that the person being interviewed thinks "ought" to be given; or they may be answers that the respondent thinks will please (or offend) the interviewer. To avoid such pitfalls, polling organizations try to hire and then carefully train the most competent interviewing staff they can.

5. Report their findings. Polls, whether they are scientific or not, try to measure the attitudes of people. To be of

The quality, reliability, and use of opinion polling has increased greatly since the 1930s and '40s.

---

[12]To bring the sampling error down from ± 3 percent to ± 1 percent, the size of the sample would have to be 9500 people. Both the time and the money that would be needed to interview a sample of that size make that a practical impossibility.

THE GALLUP POLL'S NATIONAL SAMPLE

Size of the Sample

The following table provides the approximate number of persons interviewed in each group for any single survey. These sample sizes apply to all surveys unless otherwise noted.

Sex		Household		Occupation	
Male	750	**Income**		Professional	
Female	750	$25,000 & over	465	& business	475
Race		$20,000 - $24,999	160	Clerical & sales	115
White	1295	$15,000 - $19,999	230	Manual workers	605
Non-white	205	$10,000 - $14,999	265	Farmers	55
Education		$ 5,000 - $ 9,999	245	Non-labor force	250
College	540	Under $5,000	135	**City Size**	
High school	805	**Politics**		1,000,000 & over*	300
Grade school	155	Republican	410	500,000 - 999,999*	195
Region		Democrat	685	50,000 - 499,999*	385
East	415	Independent	405	2,500 - 49,999	215
Midwest	400	**Religion**		Under 2,500, rural	405
South	415	Protestant	885	**Labor Union**	
West	270	Catholic	425	Labor union families	295
Age		Jewish	30	Non-labor union	
18–24 years	215	Other	160	families	1205
25–29 years	165			*Including urbanized areas around the central city.	
30–49 years	515				
50 & older	605				

Design of the Sample

The design of the sample is that of a replicated probability sample down to the block level in urban areas and to segments of townships in rural areas.

After stratifying the population geographically and by size of community in order to insure conformity of the sample with the latest available estimates by the Census Bureau of the distribution of the adult population, over 350 different sampling locations or areas are selected on a mathematical random basis. . . . The interviewers have no choice whatsoever concerning the part of the city or county in which interviews are conducted.

Approximately five interviews are conducted in each such randomly selected sampling point. Interviewers are given maps of the area to which they are assigned, with a starting point indicated; they are required to follow a specified direction. At each occupied dwelling unit, interviewers are instructed to select respondents by following a prescribed systematic method and by a male-female assignment. This procedure is followed until the assigned number of interviews has been completed.

Since this sampling procedure is designed to produce a sample which approximates the adult civilian population (18 and older) living in private households in the United States (that is, excluding those in prisons and hospitals, hotels, religious and educational institutions, and on military reservations), the survey results can be applied to this population for the purpose of projecting percentages into number of people. The manner in which the sample is drawn also produces a sample which approximates the population of private households in the United States. Therefore, survey results can also be projected in terms of numbers of households when appropriate.

Source: The Gallup Poll Report

Reprinted by permission of the *Chicago Tribune*–New York News Syndicate, Inc.

"Put me down for 'no comment' on that one . . . I really haven't read enough polls on the subject to form an opinion!"

any real value, however, their results must be analyzed and reported. Scientific pollsters collect huge amounts of raw data today. So, in order to handle this data, computers and other electronic hardware have become routine parts of the processes by which they tabulate and then interpret their data, draw their conclusions, and then publish their findings.

How good are the polls? On balance, the major national polls are fairly reliable. So, too, are most of the regional surveys around the country. Still, they are far from perfect. Fortunately, most pollsters themselves are quite aware of that fact, and many of them are involved in continuing efforts to refine every aspect of the polling process.

For example, pollsters know that they have difficulty measuring these qualities of the opinions they report: The intensity—the strength of feeling—with which an opinion is held. Its stability or fluidity—that is, the relative permanence or changeableness of an opinion. Its relevance or salience—that is, how important a given opinion is to the person who holds it.

Polls and pollsters are sometimes said to shape the opinions they are supposed to measure. Some critics of the polls say that in an election, for example, they often create a "bandwagon effect"—that is, some voters, wanting to be with the winner, jump on the bandwagon of the candidate who is ahead in the polls. The charge is most often levelled against those polls that appear as syndicated columns in many newspapers.

Even so, it is clear that scientific polls are the most useful tools we have in the difficult task of measuring public opinion. Though they may not be always or precisely accurate, they do offer reasonably reliable guides to public thought. Moreover, they have another large value: They help to focus attention on public questions and to stimulate discussion of them.

☑ FOR REVIEW

1. Why must public opinion be measured?

2. How can its general content be found?

3. How useful are elections as measurements of opinion? Pressure groups? The mass media? Citizen contacts with public officials?

4. By what device can the public's opinions be best measured? What is a straw vote?

5. What is scientific polling? A universe? A sample?

6. What is a random sample? On what mathematical law is it based? A quota sample?

7. Why is question-wording a critically important step in the polling process? The interview step?

8. Identify two shortcomings or criticisms of current scientific polling operations.

Limits on the Force of Public Opinion

One last word here, before we turn to pressure groups. Government in the United States *is* "government by public opinion." That is, it is *if* that description is understood to mean that public opinion is the *major*—but not the only—influence on public policy in this country. Its force is tempered by a number of other factors—and we are going to look at some of them in a moment.

Most importantly, however, remember this: Our system of constitutional government is *not* designed to give free and unrestricted play to public opinion —and especially not to *majority* opinion. In particular, the doctrines of separation of powers and of checks and balances and the constitutional guarantees of civil rights are intended to protect minority interests against the excesses of majority views and actions.

Pressure Groups

One of the major ways in which Americans try to get government to respond to their individual opinions is to join with others who hold the same views. That is, they form *pressure groups*—organizations whose members are linked by a common opinion on some political question. Those who oppose nuclear power join with others who also oppose it. Those who favor prayer in the public schools join with others who share that view; and so on.

Pressure groups are also called *interest groups* or *special interest groups*. By definition, they are private organizations that try to persuade government to respond to the shared attitudes of their members. Committees, associations, unions, leagues, or clubs—whatever they call themselves, they seek their ends by attempting to influence the making and content of public policy.

Organized efforts to promote group interests—to advance the shared concerns of people—are a fundamental part of the democratic process. The right to do so is protected by the Constitution. Remember, as we noted in Chapter 5, the 1st Amendment guarantees "the right of the people peaceably to assemble, and to petition the government for a redress of grievances."

Political Parties and Pressure Groups

Both parties and pressure groups are political organizations—and so they share several characteristics. They differ from one another in three very striking ways, however:

Nominations. Parties nominate candidates for public office; pressure groups do not. Remember, the making of nominations is a major function of parties. If a pressure group were to nominate candidates, it would, in effect, become a political party.

Primary Interest. Political parties are chiefly interested in winning elections and controlling government. Pressure groups are primarily concerned with controlling or influencing the policies of government. That is, parties are mostly interested in the *who* and pressure groups in the *what* of government.

Scope of Interest. Parties are (and must be) concerned with the whole range of public affairs. Pressure groups are almost always interested only in those questions that directly affect the interests of their members.

Functions of Pressure Groups

Pressure groups perform several valuable functions in American politics.

First, they help to stir up public interest in and discussion of public affairs. Most importantly, they do so by developing and pushing those policies they favor and by opposing those policies they see as threats to their interests.

Second, these groups represent their members on the basis of shared attitudes rather than on the basis of geography—by what their members think as opposed to where they happen to live. Public officials are elected from districts drawn on maps. But many of the interests that unite people today have at least as much to do with *how* they make a living as with *where* they live. A labor union member who lives in Chicago may have much more in common with someone who does the same kind of work in Seattle than he or she does with someone who owns a business in Chicago or runs a farm in another part of Illinois.

Third, organized interests often give useful, specialized, and detailed information to government. This data can be important to the making of public policy and often cannot be obtained from any other source. This process is a two-way street, however; organized groups often get information from public agencies and pass it along to their members.

Fourth, these groups add another element to the check-and-balance features of the political process. When, for example, one pressure group makes an extreme or unreasonable demand on government, other groups are very likely to oppose it. Many pressure groups also keep fairly close track of public officials —and help to make sure that those officials carry out their tasks in a responsible fashion.

Criticisms of Pressure Groups

Certainly, we do not mean to suggest that all of these groups have no failings. They can be and have been criticized on several counts.

First of all, some groups have an influence on government far out of proportion to their size—or, for that matter, their importance or contribution to the public good. Thus, the struggle over "who gets what, when, and how" is not always a fair fight. The more highly organized and better-financed groups often have a decided advantage in that struggle.

Second, it is sometimes very hard to tell just who or how many people a group really represents. Some groups, which call themselves such things as "The American Citizens Committee for . . ." or "The People United Against . . ." are in fact only "fronts" for a very few persons with very narrow interests.

Third, many groups do not in fact represent the views of all of the people for whom they claim to speak. Very often, an organization is dominated by an active minority who conduct its affairs and make its policy decisions. To put this another way, many groups do not have to answer to anyone—except perhaps to their members, and not always to them.

Fourth, some groups use tactics which, if they were to become widespread, would undermine the whole political system. These practices— including bribery and other heavy-handed uses of money, crude threats of revenge, and so on—are not very common, but the danger is certainly there.

Types of Pressure Groups

The United States has often been called "a nation of joiners." "In no country in the world has the principle of association been more successfully used, or more unsparingly applied to a multitude of different objects, than in America," wrote Alexis de Tocqueville in the 1830s.[13] "Americans of all ages, all conditions, and all descriptions constantly form associations . . . not only

---

[13]Alexis de Tocqueville, *Democracy in America*, Henry Reeve, trans. (New York: Schocken Books, 1961), vol. I, p. 216.

commercial and manufacturing . . . but . . . of a thousand different kinds—religious, moral, serious, futile, extensive or restricted, enormous or diminutive."[14]

Tocqueville's comments, accurate when they were made, have become more and still more so over time. No one really knows how many associations (organizations) Americans belong to today. There are thousands upon thousands of them. Each and every one of them, remember, is a pressure group whenever it tries to influence the actions of government.

Pressure groups come in all shapes and sizes. They may have thousands or even millions of members, or only a handful. They may be well- or little-known, long-established or new and even temporary, highly structured or quite loose and informal, wealthy or with few resources, and so on. But, no matter what their characteristics, they are found in every field of human activity in this country.

The largest number of pressure groups have been founded on the basis of an economic (occupational) interest—and especially on the bases of business, labor, agricultural, and professional interests. Many are founded on other bases, however. Some, for example, are grounded on a geographic area—like the South, the Columbia River Basin, or the State of Ohio. Others have been born out of a cause or an idea, such as prohibition, environmental protection, women's rights, or gun control. Still others live to promote the welfare of certain groups of people—veterans, the aged, a racial minority, the handicapped, and so on.

Pressure groups often share members. A car dealer, for example, may be a member of the local Chamber of Com-

A 350-foot petition, signed by 10,000 of his constituents opposed to ratification of the Panama Canal treaties, is displayed by then-Senator Dewey Bartlett of Oklahoma.

merce, a car dealers' association, the American Legion, a local taxpayers' league, a garden club, a church, the PTA, the American Cancer Society, the National Wildlife Federation, and several other local, regional, or national groups. All of these are, to one degree or another, pressure groups—including the church and the garden club, even though the car dealer may never think of them in that light.[15]

Also, many people belong to groups that take conflicting stands on political issues. A program to improve the city's streets may be backed by the local Chamber and the car dealers' association but opposed by the taxpayers' league, and so on.

---

[14]*Ibid.*, vol. II, p. 128.

[15]Churches often take stands on such public issues as drinking, curfew ordinances, legalized gambling, and so on; and they often try to influence public policy in those matters. Garden clubs often try to persuade cities to do such things as improve public parks, beautify downtown areas, and the like.

Members of the National Farmers Organization dramatize the farmers' high-costs/low prices problem in Washington, D.C.

Groups Based on Economic Interests. Most pressure groups are formed on economic interests. That is, they are based on the manner in which people make their livings. Among them, the most active, and certainly the most effective, are those representing business, labor, agriculture, and at least certain professions.

Business Groups. Business has long looked to government to promote and protect its interests. As we have seen, it was merchants, creditors, and property owners who were most responsible for the calling of the Constitutional Convention in 1787. The idea of the

protective tariff was fought for and won in the very early years of the Republic; and business interests have worked to maintain it ever since.

Hundreds of business groups now operate in Washington, in the 50 State capitols, and at the local level across the country. The two best-known overall business organizations today are the National Association of Manufacturers (the NAM) and the Chamber of Commerce of the United States. The NAM was formed in 1895 and now represents some 12,000 firms. It generally speaks for "big business" in public affairs. The Chamber of Commerce was founded in 1912. Over the years, it has become a major voice for the nation's thousands of smaller businesses. It has more than 2500 local chambers and now counts over 100,000 business and professional firms and some 5 million individuals among its members. Another major group, the Business Roundtable, has also taken a large role in promoting and defending the business community in recent years. The Roundtable was set up in 1972 and is composed of the chief executive officers of some 200 of the nation's largest, most prestigious corporations.

Most segments of the business community also have their own pressure groups, often called trade associations. They number in the hundreds—the American Trucking Association, the Association of American Railroads, the American Bankers Association, the National Association of Retail Grocers, and many, many more.

Despite a common impression, business groups do not always present a solid front as they try to influence public policy. The trucking industry, for example, does its best to get as much federal aid as possible for highway construction. But the railroads are less than happy with what they see as "special favors" for their competition. At the same time, the railroads see federal taxes on gasoline, oil, tires, and other "highway users fees" as quite legitimate and necessary sources of federal income. But the truckers take quite another view, of course.

Labor Groups. The interests of organized labor are also represented by a host of groups. The largest, in both size and political power, is the AFL-CIO (the American Federation of Labor-Congress of Industrial Organizations).[16] It is now made up of some 95 separate unions—such as the Retail Clerks International Union, the International Association of Machinists and Aerospace Workers, the Postal Workers Union, and the American Federation of Musicians. With all its unions, the AFL-CIO, has about 15 million members; and each union, like the AFL-CIO itself, is organized on a national, State, and local basis.

There are also a number of independent unions—that is, unions not affiliated with the AFL-CIO. The largest and most powerful of them include such groups as the International Brotherhood of Teamsters, the United Mine Workers, and the International Longshoremen's and Warehousemen's Union.

Organized labor generally speaks with one voice on such social welfare and job-related matters as social security programs, minimum wages, and the fight against unemployment. But labor sometimes opposes labor. White-collar and blue-collar workers, for example, do not always share the same interests. Then, too, such factors as sectional interests (East-West, North-South, urban-rural, and so on) and production interests (trucks versus railroads versus airplanes, for example) sometimes divide labor's forces.

Also, organized labor cannot possibly speak for all workers in the United States. The nation's labor force now numbers about 113 million persons; only a fifth of that number—some 21 million—belong to labor unions today.

Agricultural Groups. Several powerful associations serve the interests of agriculture. The most prominent farm groups are the National Grange, the American Farm Bureau Federation, and the National Farmers Union. The Grange, established in 1867, is the oldest and generally the most conservative of them. Over the years, it has been as much a social as a political organization, concerned about the welfare of farm families. Some 450,000 farm families are now members and much of its strength is centered in the Northeast and the Mid-Atlantic States.

The Farm Bureau is the largest and generally the most effective of the three. It was formed in 1920 and soon developed a close working relationship with the Department of Agriculture. It has some 3.5 million farm-family members and is especially strong in the Midwest. The Farm Bureau generally supports federal programs to promote agriculture; but it opposes most government regulation of agriculture and favors the free market economy.

The smaller Farmers Union draws its strength from smaller and less prosperous farmers. It now has some 300,000 farm-family members, most of them in the Upper Midwest and West. The Farm-

---

[16]The AFL was formed in 1886, as a federation of *craft* unions. (A **craft union** is one made up only of those workers who have the same craft or skill—for example, a carpenters, plumbers, or electricians union.) The growth of mass production created a large class of industrial workers not skilled in any particular craft, however. Many of them are organized in **industrial unions**—unions made up of workers, skilled or unskilled, in a single major industry (such as the Textile Workers Union and the United Steel Workers). The AFL found it hard to organize workers in the new mass production industries. Many of its craft unions were against having unions of unskilled workers in the AFL. After years of bitter fights over craft versus industrial unionism, a group led by John L. Lewis of the United Mine Workers was expelled from the AFL in 1935. They formed the CIO in 1938. The rivalries between these two major national unions cooled down to the point where merger, as the AFL-CIO, took place in 1955.

ers Union often calls itself the champion of the dirt farmer and it often disagrees with the other two major organizations. It generally favors high levels of federal price supports for crops and livestock and other programs to regulate the production and marketing of farm commodities.

Another group, the National Farmer's Organization, came to the fore in the 1970s. The NFO calls for efforts to withhold produce from the market in order to raise the prices paid to farmers. It has sponsored "tractorcades" to Washington and other cities to dramatize the farmers' high-costs/low-prices problems.

Many other groups speak for the producers of specific farm commodities—dairy products, grain, fruit, peanuts, livestock, cotton, wool, corn, soybeans, and so on.

Like business and labor groups, farm organizations sometimes find themselves at odds with one another. Thus, dairy, corn, soybean, and cotton groups compete as each of them tries to influence State laws regulating the production and sale of such products as margarine and yogurt. California and Florida citrus growers are sometimes pitted against one another; and so on.

Professional Groups.   The professions are generally organized for political purposes, too. Most of them are not nearly so large, well-organized, well-financed, or effective as most business, labor, and farm groups. Three major groups stand as large exceptions, however: the American Medical Association, the American Bar Association, and the National Education Association.

There are dozens of less well-known, and less politically active, professional groups—the American Society of Civil Engineers, the American Library Association, the American Political Science Association, and a great many more.

Much of their effort is given over to such matters as the standards of the profession, the holding of professional meetings, and the publishing of scholarly journals. Still, each of them acts in some ways as a pressure group, bent on promoting the welfare of the profession and its members.

The Maze of Other Groups.   As we have said, pressure groups come in all shapes and sizes, and they can be found in every field of human activity in this country. Most are based on economic interests. But there are hundreds that were formed for other reasons, and many of them have a good deal of political clout.

A large number of these other groups exist to promote a *cause* or an *idea*. In fact, it would take several pages just to list them here, and so we can mention only a few of the more important ones. The Women's Christian Temperance Union (the WCTU) has long sought prohibition. The American Civil Liberties Union (the ACLU) fights in and out of court to protect civil and political rights. Common Cause works for major reforms in the political process and calls itself "the citizen's lobby." The League of Women Voters of the United States and its many local leagues are dedicated to stimulating participation in and greater knowledge about public affairs.

The list of cause groups goes on and on. Many women's rights groups—the National Organization for Women (NOW), the National Women's Political Caucus, and several others—carry that banner. Several, including the National Wildlife Federation, the Sierra Club, the Wilderness Society, and Friends of the Earth, are pledged to conservation and environmental protection. The National Right-to-Life Committee and other groups oppose abortion; they are countered by the National Abortion Rights Action League and its allies. The Na-

Even though the Equal Rights Amendment (ERA) failed ratification in 1982, its supporters and opponents continue to keep the issue before the public.

tional Rifle Association fights gun control legislation; Handgun Control, Inc. works for it. And, again, the list goes on and on . . . .

A number of groups seek to promote the *welfare* of certain segments of the population. Among the best-known and most powerful of them are the American Legion and the Veterans of Foreign Wars; they work to advance the interests of the country's veterans. Groups like Older American, Inc. and the American Association of Retired Persons are very active in such areas as old-age pensions and medical care for the aged. Several organizations—notably the National Association for the Advancement of Colored People (the NAACP), the National Urban League, and People United to Save Humanity (PUSH)—are closely concerned with public policies of special interests to blacks. And again, the list goes on and on . . . .

Many church-related organizations also try to influence public policy in several important areas. Thus, many individual Protestants and their local and national churches do so through the National Council of Churches. Roman Catholics do so through the National Catholic Welfare Council; and Jewish communicants, through the American Jewish Congress and B'nai B'rith's Anti-Defamation League. And, yet again, the list goes on . . . .

Public-Interest Groups. As we have said, pressure groups are *private* groups. Most of them represent some special interest—business, labor, agriculture, veterans, teachers, and so on. They seek public policies of special benefit to their members, and they work against policies that threaten their own interests.

There are some groups—often called *public-interest groups*—with a broader goal, however. They work for the "public good." That is, a **public-interest group** is a pressure group that seeks certain public policies of benefit to *all* of the people, whether they belong to or support that organization or not. (Of course, nearly all pressure groups claim that the "public good" is really their basic aim. Thus, for example, the NAM says that lower taxes on business will stimulate the economy and so help everyone; and the AFL-CIO says the same thing about spending more public dollars for more public works programs.)

Unlike most pressure groups, the public-interest groups are based on roles that all Americans share. That is, they are set up to represent people as citizens, as consumers, as breathers of air, as drinkers of water, and so on. They have become quite visible over the past 10 years or so. Among the best-known and most active of them today are Common Cause and the several organizations that make up Ralph Nader's Public Citizen, Inc. Some of them have been with us for a much longer time, however—for example, the League of Women Voters. The League, founded in 1920, has roots that reach deep into the long history of the women's suffrage movement.

☑ F O R   R E V I E W————

1. What is a pressure group? By what other names are they known?
2. What are the basic differences between pressure groups and political parties?
3. What four important functions do pressure groups perform? List four major criticisms of them.
4. The largest number of these groups is formed on the basis of what particular kind of interest? List several examples. On what other bases do they rest?
5. What are public-interest groups?

Pressure Group Tactics

Pressure groups exist to influence public policies, and they operate wherever those policies are made or can be influenced. That is, they operate at *all* levels of government in the United States. And the fact that there are so many places in the American political system where decisions are made is a major reason why many of these groups are able to realize many of their goals. In short, we can still agree with Lord Bryce's somewhat indelicate comment: "Where the body is, there will the vultures be gathered."

Propaganda and Public Opinion. As hard as it may be to define, public opinion is the most significant long-term force in American politics. Over the long run, no public policy can be followed successfully without the support of a goodly portion of the population. Pressure groups know this, of course. They regularly court the public's opinions.

Pressure groups try to create the public attitudes they want with **propaganda.**[17] Propaganda, much like public opinion, is a vague and somewhat inexact term. Its goal is to create a particular popular belief. That belief may be in something "good" or "bad," depending on who makes that judgment. It may be completely true or false, or it may lie somewhere between those extremes. But, as a *technique*, it is neither moral nor immoral; it is amoral. It does not use objective logic; rather it begins with a conclusion and then brings together evidences to support it. Propaganda and objective analysis sometimes agree in their conclusions, but their methods are quite different. In short, propagandists are not teachers; they are advertisers, persuaders, brainwashers.

Propaganda techniques have been brought to a high level in this country—first in the field of commercial advertising and more recently in politics. The major techniques propagandists use are outlined in the chart on the next page.

Talented propagandists almost never attack the logic of some policy they

_____

[17]The term has been a widely used part of the American political vocabulary since the 1930s. It comes from the Latin verb *propagare*—to propagate, spread, disseminate.

PROPAGANDA TECHNIQUES

Plain Folks

Pretend to be one of the common people
"I'm the workingman's friend"

Bandwagon

Follow the crowd, be with the majority
"A is voting for X; so are B, C, and D. Why not you, too?"

Glittering Generalities

Broad and vague statements
"In the interest of Peace and Prosperity"

Name Calling

Do not discuss facts. Just give it a bad name.
"Un-American"

Testimonial

Endorsement by a celebrity
"Mr. Big says, 'Vote for X, he's my choice'."

Transfer

Use symbols to accomplish purposes for which they were not intended
"Uncle Sam"

Card Stacking

Present only one side of an issue through the distortion and juggling of facts
"2 + 2 = 22"

oppose. Instead, they often attack it with name-calling—painting it with such labels as "communist," "fascist," "ultra-liberal," "ultra-conservative," "pie-in-the-sky," "greedy," and so on. Or they try to do the same thing by card-stacking—that is, presenting only material that will make something appear to be that which in fact it is not.

Policies they support are given labels that will produce favorable reactions—such glittering generalities as "American," "sound," "fair," and "just." Symbols are often used to transfer those reactions, too: Uncle Sam and the flag are favorites. So, too, are testimonials—endorsements, supporting statements from well-known television stars, professional athletes, and the like. And both the bandwagon and the plain-folks approaches get heavy use, as well.

Propaganda is spread through newspapers, radio, television, movies, billboards, books, magazines, pamphlets, posters, speeches—in fact, every form of mass communication. Pressure groups use them all.

Parties and Elections. We know that pressure groups and political parties are very different creatures (page 257). They do live in the same environment, however; and their paths cross often and in several places.

For their part, pressure groups know that the parties play a central role in selecting those people who make public policy decisions. They are quite aware, too, of the fact that much of government's policy-making machinery is organized by and through parties.[18] In short, many pressure groups are closely involved with efforts to elect their friends and defeat their enemies.

Pressure groups try to influence the behavior of political parties in a number of ways. Some keep close ties with one

---

[18]We have the two major parties in mind here, of course; remember, many minor parties can be much more readily compared with pressure groups than they can with the major parties; see page 179.

or the other of the major parties. Most hope to secure the support of both of them, however. Several urge their members to become active in party affairs and try to win posts in party organizations.

As we've seen, campaigns for public office cost money—and sometimes large amounts of it. Pressure groups know this, too—and they and their members are a major source of campaign contributions today. Much of their financial help now goes to parties and their candidates through political action committees (PACs), as we saw in Chapter 9.

The number of PACs has grown very fast in the past few years, as we noted on page 236. One particular variety of them has grown most rapidly, however. These organizations are often called **single-interest groups**. They are PACs that concentrate their efforts on *one* issue—for example, abortion, gun control, nuclear power development, or women's rights. They work for or (more often) against a candidate *solely* on the basis of that candidate's stand on that *one* issue. For them, all other considerations—the candidate's record on other questions, his or her party identification or political experience, and so on—are altogether unimportant.

A pressure group's election tactics often have to involve some very finely-tuned decisions. If, for example, it supports the Democratic candidate for a seat in the U.S. Senate, it may not want to help the campaign by attacking the Republican candidate for that post. The Republican might stand a good chance of winning—and then what? Or a Republican candidate who won a seat in the House or some other office might be offended by attacks on a party colleague, even if he or she agrees with the group's policy aims. Most pressure groups try to remember that their *first* concern is with the making of public policy; any part they play in the election process is only secondary to that objective. (Notice that the single-interest groups do not follow this rule, however.)

Lobbying. *Lobbying* is usually defined as those activities by which group pressures are brought to bear on legislators and the legislative process. Certainly, it is that—but it is also much more. Realistically, **lobbying** includes all of the means by which group pressures are brought to bear on *all* aspects of the public policy-making process. Lobbying takes place in legislative bodies, of course; and it often has important effects there. But it is also often directed at administrative agencies, and at times even at the courts.

What happens in a legislative body is often of deep concern to several different —and competing—interests. A bill to regulate the sale of firearms, for example, excites the interest of many persons and groups. Those companies which make guns, those which sell them, and those which produce or sell ammunition, targets, scopes, hunting jackets, sleeping bags, and a host of other things have a clear stake in that bill's contents and its fate. So, too, do law enforcement agencies, hunters, wildlife conservationists, such groups as the National Rifle Association and the American Civil Liberties Union, and many others.

But, notice, public policy is made by much more than the words in a statute. What happens *after* a law has been passed is often of real concern to organized interests, too. How is a law interpreted and how vigorously is it applied by the agency that enforces it? And what attitude do the courts take if the law is challenged on some legal ground? These questions point up the fact that pressure groups often have to carry their lobbying efforts beyond the legislative arena— into one and sometimes several agencies in the executive branch and sometimes into the courts, as well.

"So far, my mail
is running three to one
in favor of my position."

Nearly all of the more important organized interests in the country—business groups, labor unions, farm organization, the professions, veterans, the aged, churches, and many more—maintain *lobbyists* in Washington.[19]

Lobbyists themselves would often rather be known by some other title—"legislative counsel," or "public representative," for example. But, whatever they call themselves, their major task is to work for those matters of benefit to their clients and against those that may harm them.

The competent lobbyist is thoroughly familiar with government and its ways, with the facts of current political life, and with the techniques of "polite" persuasion. Some have been members of Congress (or the State legislature). They know the "legislative ropes" and have many close contacts among present-day members. Many others are lawyers, former journalists, or men and women who have come into lobbying from the closely related field of public relations.

---

[19]Of course, many lobbyists are also stationed in the 50 State capitols, and their number grows whenever the State's legislature is in session. The "lobby" is actually an ante-room or a main corridor or some other part of a capitol building to which the general public is admitted. The term "lobby-agent" was being used to identify favor-seekers at sessions of the New York State legislature in Albany by the late 1820s. By the 1830s it had been shortened to "lobbyist" and was in wide use in Washington and elsewhere.

Lobbyists at work use a number of techniques as they try to bring legislators and other policy-makers around to their points of view. They see that articles, reports, and all sorts of other information reach those officeholders. Many testify before legislative committees. If the House Committee on the Judiciary is considering a gun control bill, for example, then representatives of all of those groups we mentioned a moment ago are certain to be invited, or to ask for the opportunity, to present their views. The testimony that lobbyists give is usually "expert"; but, of course, it is also couched in terms favorable to the interests they represent.

Most lobbyists also know how to bring "grass-roots" pressures to bear. The groups they speak for can mount campaigns by letter, phone, and wire from "the folks back home"—and often on short notice. Favorable news stories, magazine articles, advertisements, radio and television appeals, endorsements by noted personalities—these and the many other weapons of publicity are within the arsenal of the good lobbyist.

The typical lobbyist of today is a far cry from those of yesterday. The once fairly common practice of bribery and the heavy-handed use of "wine, women, and song" are almost unknown. Most present-day lobbyists work in the open, and their major techniques come under the headings of friendliness, persuasion, and helpfulness.

Lobbyists are ready to do such things as buy lunches and dinners, provide information, write speeches, and prepare bills in proper form. The food is good, the information is usually quite accurate, the speeches forceful, and the bills well drawn. Most lobbyists know that if they were to behave otherwise—give false information, for example—they would damage, if not destroy, their credibility and so their effectiveness.

Lobbyists work hard to influence committee action, floor debate, and the final vote in a legislative body. If they fail in one house they carry their fight to the other. If they lose there, too, they may turn to the executive branch[20] and, perhaps to the courts, as well.

Lobby Regulation.   Lobbying abuses do occur now and then, of course. False or misleading testimony, bribery, and other unethical pressures are not at all common; but they are not unknown either.

To try to keep lobbying within bounds, Congress passed the Federal Regulation of Lobbying Act in 1946. Each of the States now has a somewhat similar law.

The federal law requires lobbyists to register with the Clerk of the House and the Secretary of the Senate. More exactly, it requires individuals and groups to register if they collect or spend money or any other thing of value for the "principal purpose" of influencing legislation.

The Supreme Court narrowed the scope of the law somewhat in 1954. In _United States_ v. _Harris_, it upheld the law against 1st Amendment attacks on its constitutionality. But it also held that its registration provisions apply only to lobbying efforts aimed at Congress, not to those aimed at the public at large.

The law has proved to be quite inadequate over the past 35 years—and Congress has not seen fit to strengthen it. Its vague phrase "principal purpose" is a huge loophole through which many active groups avoid registration. They do so on grounds that lobbying is only "incidental" to their main objectives or that their monies are spent for "research" and "public information." Most estimates put the number of people who now earn at least part of their living by lobbying Congress at about 20,000; yet only some 5500 persons are registered under the law—and that number includes many multiple filings by persons who lobby for several different groups. The law does have penalties for its violation but it has no enforcement provi-

Drawing by Weber; ©1981 The New Yorker Magazine, Inc.

"I'm peddling influence. Would you be interested?"

---

[20]Notice that various government agencies often act much like pressure groups in their relations with Congress or with a State's legislature—for example, when they ask for funds or when they argue for or against some bill in committee.

sions. Also, it does not apply to lobbying aimed at the executive branch nor does it cover testifying before congressional committees.

✓ FOR REVIEW

1. Where do pressure groups try to influence public policy? Why?
2. What is propaganda? What are four of the major techniques of propagandists?
3. Why do pressure groups take part in the election process? How?
4. What is a PAC? A single-interest group?
5. What is lobbying?
6. Describe the techniques most lobbyists use. How effective is the law that regulates lobbying?

SUMMARY

Democratic government—and so American government—may be described as "government by public opinion." That is, it is a system of government in which public officials are expected to translate the will of the people into public policy. Though the importance of public opinion is well understood, the term itself is not and is in fact very difficult to define. It is made up of all of those attitudes that people hold on matters of government and politics. Its meaning is best understood in the plural—that is, as public opinions, the opinions of publics.

Political socialization is the very complex, life-long process by which each of us acquires our political opinions. It involves all of the uncountable factors that lead each of us to see the political world, and to act in it, as we do. The family and formal education play a leading part in that process. So do many other agents—age, race, income, occupation, opinion leaders, the mass media, and many others.

The overall content of public opinion can be seen, and to some extent measured, in the varied means by which it is expressed, especially: elections, the competing claims of organized groups, the mass media, and citizen contacts with public officials. Scientific public opinion polls are the most reliable devices for the measurement of the public's attitudes, however. Most of them measure opinion by taking a random sample of a larger population (universe). Because of the mathematical law of probability, their findings generally reflect the opinions of the larger group.

Pressure groups are private organizations that work to persuade government to respond to the shared attitudes of their members. They are also known as interest groups or special interest groups. They seek to influence both the making and the content of public policies—wherever those policies are made or can be influenced. They overlap with political parties in a number of ways but are a significantly different type of political organization. They are subject to many criticisms, but they do perform several valuable functions in American politics.

Most pressure groups arise out of economic interests; among the most influential of them are those representing business, labor, agriculture, and the professions. Many rest on a variety of other bases, however—including such interests as sectionalism, a cause or an idea, or the welfare of a certain segment of the population. Public-interest groups, unlike other pressure groups, work for policies for the "public good."

Organized interests apply their pressures to government through all of the means available to them—with the techniques of propaganda, through parties, their candidates, and elections, and by lobbying.

C H A P T E R   R E V I E W

Key Terms/Concepts

Interest group (257)

Lobby, lobbyist (266, 267)

Mandate (249)

Mass media (247)

Opinion (243)

Opinion leader (247)

Political action committee (PAC) (266)

Political socialization (243)

Poll (251)

Pressure group (257)

Probability sample (253)

Propaganda (264)

Public-interest group (263)

Public opinion (244)

Publics (243)

Quota sample (254)

Random sample (253)

Scientific polling (253)

Single-interest group (266)

Special interest group (257)

Straw vote (251)

Universe (253)

Keynote Questions

1. Define public opinion. Why can that term be better understood in the plural-*i.e.*, public opinions, the opinions of publics?
2. What is the process of political socialization? Why are the family and the school such important agents in that process?
3. In what two particular matters can the mass media's influence on political attitudes be most readily seen? What factors tend to limit media impact on public opinion?
4. In what various ways can public opinion be measured? What are the five basic steps involved in scientific polling?
5. What is a pressure group?
6. In what three significant ways do pressure groups and political parties differ from one another?
7. What major functions do pressure groups perform? On what bases are they often criticized?
8. On what particular basis is the largest number of pressure groups founded? On what other bases do they exist? What are public-interest groups?
9. By what various means do pressure

groups attempt to influence public policies?
10. What is propaganda? What are PACs? Single-interest groups?

For Thought and Discussion

1. In a dictatorship, both freedom of expression—the rights of free speech, free press, assembly, and petition—and the means of expression—newspapers, radio, television, and others—are sharply restricted and closely controlled. Why? Was Alexander Hamilton correct when he wrote: "All governments, even the most despotic, depend, in a great degree, on public opinion"?
2. Can such television news personalities as Mike Wallace, Dan Rather, John Chancellor, David Brinkley, Peter Jennings, and Ted Koppel be properly described as "a tiny, enclosed fraternity of privileged men" and "self-annointed, supercilious, electronic barons of opinion"? (As Vice President, Spiro Agnew applied those descriptions, and many others like them, to television news commentators as a class. Why did Agnew attack them, and other media com-

mentators, as well? Why did many of them return the favor?)

3. Several studies show that by the time most students are seniors in high school they have spent more time sitting in front of the television screen than they have in the classroom. Is this an accurate description of your own experience? How much and what kind of a role does television play in your life? Is television, in fact, the "boob tube"? Who or what is really the "boob" in that phrase?

4. In what particular ways can the average citizen best go about the business of becoming as fully informed as possible about public affairs?

5. How does the structure of the American system of government contribute to the strength and importance of pressure groups in our politics? Explain this comment by Fred R. Harris: "A fragmented system of power protects against a strong minority or a runaway majority. But it also results in a highly complicated system, which ordinary citizens may find confusing and difficult to influence. Hence, fragmentation of power is an important cause of the formation and influence of interest groups in America." *Americas' Democracy: The Ideal and the Reality* (Glenview, Ill.: Scott, Foresman, 1980), page 238. Who is Fred Harris?

6. Horatio Seymour wrote this in the *North American Review* in 1878: "It is necessary for those who have charge of public affairs to learn what men have in their minds, what views they hold, at what ends they aim . . . . The follies of fanatics frequently teach wisdom better than the words of the wise." How appropriate are his comments today? Why might the members of an organization like NOW not find them wholly acceptable? Who was Horatio Seymour?

Suggested Activities

1. Ask a newspaper editor or the manager of a television station to talk with the class about the role of the mass media in public affairs and their impact on public opinion.

2. Tape a typical five-minute, on-the-hour network radio news broadcast. Analyze its contents from such standpoints as these: How much time given to news items? How much to advertising? How much to "hard news"—that is, matters of international and domestic politics? How much to other items—such as the weather, sports, human-interest stories, and the like? Do you find any editorial biases in the presentation? (It would be much less convenient, but nevertheless worthwhile, to take the same kind of look at a typical television news program.)

3. Conduct an opinion poll on some current local issue, using the sampling and other techniques of scientific polling as best you can.

4. Ask a representative of a local pressure group to describe that group's basic aims, its membership, its organization and financing, and the methods it uses to realize its goals.

5. Invite a lobbyist, a legislator or other knowledgeable person to discuss the subject of group pressures in the political process.

6. Select an important national, regional, or local issue of the day—preferably one you are concerned about. List as many pressure groups as you can find involved in the consideration of that question. Identify the reasons for their interests in the issue and their respective positions on it.

7. Draw up a list of those public-interest groups and those single-interest groups that now operate in your State and/or community.

UNIT FOUR

Congress:
The First Branch

One of the most distinctive features of the American governmental system is the separation of the powers of government into three distinct branches: legislative, executive, and judicial. Unit Four of this book examines the first of these branches, the legislative.

In the American system, the legislative branch of the National Government consists of the two houses of Congress, the Senate and the House of Representatives. They are referred to here as "the first branch" both because the legislative is the branch of the National Government for which the Constitution first provides and because the Congress is the central institution of our representative democracy. It is the branch closest to the people and the one to which the Constitution gives the bulk of the powers held by the National Government.

"Any one who is unfamiliar with what Congress actually does and how it does it" wrote Woodrow Wilson, " . . . is very far from a knowledge of the constitutional system in which we live." In the next three chapters, we explore "what Congress actually does and how it does it." We look first at its structure—the size of each house, the terms of its members, their qualifications, and so on. Then we examine how the two houses operate and how a bill introduced in either house eventually becomes (or does not become) a law. Finally we consider the powers of the Congress, both those expressed, spelled out, in the Constitution, and those implied, that is, reasonably deduced from the expressed powers.

Congress, the first branch "is too complex to be understood without . . . a careful and systematic process of analysis," President Wilson said. Unit Four is designed to encourage and facilitate that process.

The nation's Capitol at night

11

The Congress

Congress is neither as doltish as the cartoonists portray it nor as noble as it portrays itself. While it has its quota of knaves and fools it also has its fair share of knights. And sandwiched between these upper and nether crusts is a broad and representative slice of upper-middle class America.

Cabell Phillips

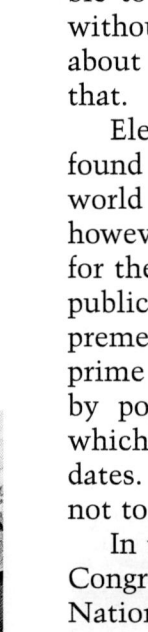

A responsible, responsive, and effective legislative body is absolutely indispensible to democratic government. Indeed, without such an agency, any "talk" about democratic government is only that.

Elected assemblies of some kind are found in nearly all governments in the world today. Many of them are shams, however. They are false fronts, masks for the real location and exercise of the public policy-making power. The Supreme Soviet in the USSR stands as a prime example. Its members are chosen by popular vote, but in elections in which there are no opposition candidates. It meets to be told and to agree—not to propose, debate, and decide.

In the American democratic system, Congress is the legislative branch of the National Government. Its major function is to make law. It, then, is charged with *the* basic governmental function in a democratic system: that of translating the public will into public policy in the form of law.

Bicameralism

Immediately, the Constitution establishes a *bicameral* Congress—that is,

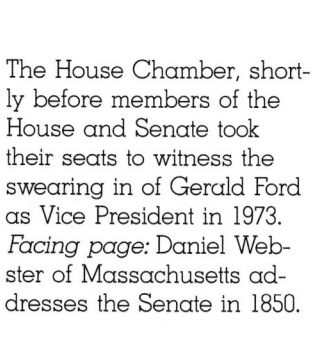

The House Chamber, shortly before members of the House and Senate took their seats to witness the swearing in of Gerald Ford as Vice President in 1973. *Facing page:* Daniel Webster of Massachusetts addresses the Senate in 1850.

one made up of two houses. It does so for a number of reasons:

Historically, the British Parliament, which the Framers and most other Americans knew quite well, had consisted of two houses since the 1300s. Most of the colonial assemblies, and all but two of the State legislatures in 1787, were also bicameral; see page 519.

Practically, a two-chambered body had to be created to settle the conflict between the Virginia and the New Jersey Plans at Philadelphia in 1787; see pages 40-42. And, notice, bicameralism is also a reflection of federalism: Each State is equally represented in the Senate and in accord with its respective populations in the House.

Theoretically, the Framers favored a bicameral Congress in order that one house might act as a check on the other. A leading constitutional historian reports:

Thomas Jefferson, who possessed great faith in "the voice of the people," was in France when the Constitution was framed. Upon his return, while taking breakfast with Washington, he opposed the two-body form of legislature, and was disposed to twit Washington about it. At this time Jefferson poured his coffee from his cup into his saucer. Washington asked him why he did so. "To cool it," he answered. "So," said Washington, "we will pour legislation into the Senatorial saucer to cool it."[1]

Some say that the equal representation of the States in the Senate should be scrapped as undemocratic.[2] They often

---

[1]Max Farrand, *The Framing of the Constitution.* New Haven: Yale University Press, 1913, p. 74.

[2]The prospects for any such change are so slim as to be nonexestent. Article V of the Constitution provides, in part, that "no State, without its consent, shall be deprived of its equal suffrage in the Senate."

point to the two extremes to make their case: The State with the least population, Alaska, has only some 420,000 residents; the largest State, California, has more than 23.5 million; yet each of these States has two Senators.

Those who argue against State equality in the Senate ignore this vital fact: The Senate was purposefully created as a body in which the States would be represented as co-equal members and partners in the Federal Union. And, recall, had the States not been equally represented in the upper house, there might well never have been a Constitution.

Terms of Congress

Each **term** of Congress lasts for two years[3] and is numbered consecutively from the first term, which began on March 4, 1789.

The date for the start of each term was changed by the 20th Amendment in 1933. It is now "noon on the 3d day of January" of every odd-numbered year. Thus the term of the 98th Congress began at noon on January 3, 1983; and it will end at noon on January 3, 1985.

Sessions of Congress

There are two **regular sessions** to each term of Congress—one each year. Section 2 of the 20th Amendment states

> The Congress shall assemble at least once in every year, and such meeting shall begin at noon on the 3d day of January. . . .

Congress adjourns each session as it sees fit. Until World War II a session might run for perhaps four or five months. But the many and pressing issues since then have forced it to remain in session through most of each year.

Neither house may adjourn—end a session—without the consent of the other. Article I, Section 5, Clause 4 provides that:

> Neither House . . . shall, without the consent of the other, adjourn for more than three days, nor to any other place than that in which the two Houses shall be sitting.[4]

Special Sessions

Only the President may call a **special session** of Congress.[5] Only 26 such sessions have ever been held. The last one was called by President Truman in 1948 —to consider a number of anti-inflation and welfare measures. The fact that Congress now meets nearly year-round clearly cuts down the likelihood of special sessions. (And that fact also lessens the importance of the President's power to call one.)

☑ FOR REVIEW

1. Why is a representative legislative body indispensable to democratic government?
2. Why is Congress bicameral?
3. What is the difference between a *term* and a *session* of Congress.
4. Who may call a special session of Congress?

---

[3]Article I, Section 2, Clause 1 dictates a two-year term for Congress by providing that Representatives "shall be chosen . . . every second year."

[4]Article II, Section 3 gives the President power to adjourn (*prorogue*) a session, but only when the two houses cannot agree upon a date for adjournment. No President has ever had to use this power. The Legislative Reorganization Act of 1946 requires each regular session to adjourn no later than July 31—unless Congress should decide otherwise or a national emergency exists. But Congress has met this self-imposed deadline only twice, in 1952 and 1956. Both houses recess for short periods during a session.

[5]Article II, Section 3 provides that the President may "convene both Houses, or either of them," in a special session. The Senate has been called into special session alone on 46 occasions, to consider treaties and appointments (but not since 1933). The House has never been called alone.

COMPOSITION OF CONGRESS

Party Strength at Beginning of 1984

House of Representatives—435 members **Senate—100 members**

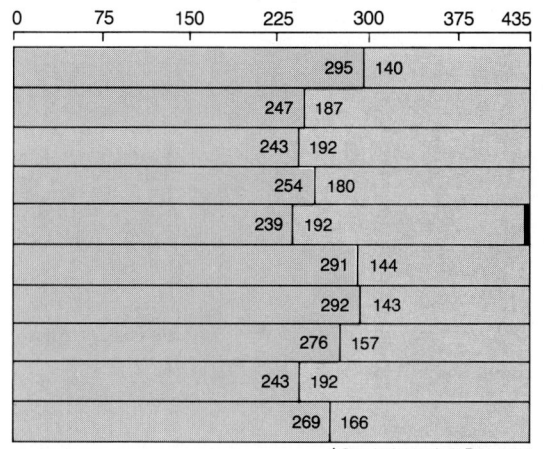

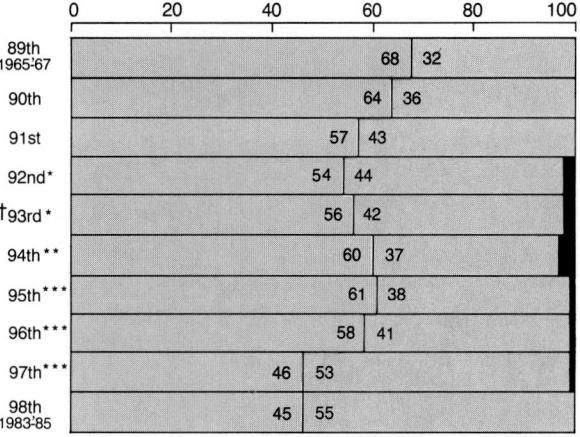

Congress	House D	House R	Senate D	Senate R
89th 1965-'67	295	140	68	32
90th	247	187	64	36
91st	243	192	57	43
92nd*	254	180	54	44
†93rd*	239	192	56	42
94th**	291	144	60	37
95th***	292	143	61	38
96th***	276	157	58	41
97th***	243	192	46	53
98th 1983-'85	269	166	45	55

†One Independent-Democrat

Democrats   Republicans   Other

*One Independent, one Conservative-Republican
**One Independent, one Conservative-Republican and one undecided (New Hampshire)
***One Independent

Source: U.S. Congress, *Congressional Directory*

Representation by State, 1984

State	House D	House R	Senate D	Senate R
Alabama	5	2	1	1
Alaska	—	1	—	2
Arizona	2	3	1	1
Arkansas	2	2	2	—
California	28	17	1	1
Colorado	3	3	1	1
Connecticut	4	2	1	1
Delaware	1	—	1	1
Florida	13	6	1	1
Georgia	9	1	1	1
Hawaii	2	—	2	—
Idaho	—	2	—	2
Illinois	12	10	1	1
Indiana	5	5	—	2
Iowa	3	3	—	2
Kansas	2	3	—	2
Kentucky	4	3	2	—
Louisiana	6	2	2	—
Maine	—	2	1	1
Maryland	7	1	1	1
Massachusetts	10	1	2	—
Michigan	12	6	2	—
Minnesota	5	3	—	2
Mississippi	3	2	1	1
Missouri	6	3	1	1
Montana	1	1	2	—
Nebraska	—	3	2	—
Nevada	1	1	—	2
New Hampshire	1	1	—	2
New Jersey	9	5	2	—
New Mexico	1	2	1	1
New York	20	14	1	1
North Carolina	9	2	—	2
North Dakota	1	—	1	1
Ohio	10	11	2	—
Oklahoma	5	1	1	1
Oregon	3	2	—	2
Pennsylvania	13	10	—	2
Rhode Island	1	1	1	1
South Carolina	3	3	1	1
South Dakota	1	—	—	2
Tennessee	6	3	1	1
Texas	21	6	1	1
Utah	—	3	—	2
Vermont	—	1	1	1
Virginia	4	6	—	2
Washington	5	3	1	1
West Virginia	4	—	2	—
Wisconsin	5	4	1	1
Wyoming	—	1	—	2

The House of Representatives

Size

The House is the larger of the two chambers of Congress. The Constitution provides that the total number of seats—today, 435—shall be *apportioned* (distributed) among the States. The apportionment is to be based on their respective populations.[6]

Each State is guaranteed at least one seat in the House, no matter what its population. Today, six States—Alaska, Delaware, North Dakota, South Dakota, Vermont, and Wyoming—have only one Representative apiece. (The District of

---

[6]Article I, Section 2, Clause 3.

CONGRESSIONAL APPORTIONMENT, 1983-1993

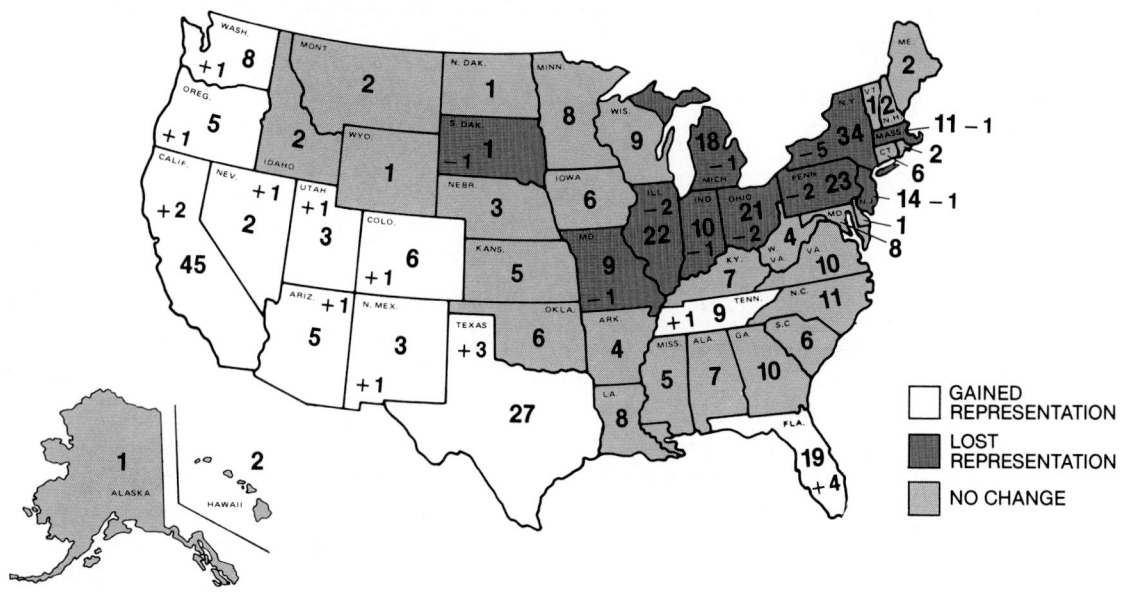

This map shows the changes in State representation due to the reapportionment of the House after the 1980 Census, and effective from January 3, 1983 to January 3, 1993. Large numbers = State's seats in the House; small numbers = seats gained or lost. The next apportionment, following the 1990 Census, will occur in 1991 and become effective with the congressional elections in 1992.

Columbia, Guam, the Virgin Islands, and American Samoa are represented by a Delegate, and Puerto Rico by a Resident Commissioner—but they are not, in fact, *members* of the House.)

Terms

The Constitution provides that "Representatives shall be . . . chosen every second year"[7]—that is, for two-year terms. This rather short term is intended to make the House more immediately responsive to popular pressures than the Senate.

Reapportionment

The Constitution directs Congress to **reapportion** (redistribute) the seats in the House after each decennial census.[8] Until a first census could be taken, it set

the size of the House at 65 seats—and there were that many in the 1st and 2nd Congresses (1789–1793). The Census of 1790 showed a national population of 3,929,214 persons, and in 1792 the number of House seats was increased by 41 to 106.

As the nation's population grew, and as the number of States increased, so did the size of the House. By 1912, following the Census of 1910 and the admissions of Arizona and New Mexico, the House had grown to 435 seats.

With the Census of 1920, Congress faced an extraordinary dilemma. The House had long since grown too large for effective floor action. But, to reapportion without adding more seats had to mean that some of the States would lose seats if every State was to be represented on the basis of its population.

Congress met the problem by doing nothing. So, despite the Constitution's

---

[7]Article I, Section 2, Clause 1.
[8]Article I, Section 2, Clause 3.

command, there was no reapportionment on the basis of the 1920 census.

The Reapportionment Act of 1929. Faced with the 1930 Census, Congress moved to avoid repeating its earlier lapse—with the Reapportionment Act of 1929. That law, still on the books, sets up what is often called an "automatic reapportionment." It provides that:

(1) The "permanent" size of the House is 435 members. Of course, that figure is permanent only so long as Congress does not decide to change it.

(2) Following each census, the Census Bureau is to determine the number of seats each State should have.

(3) When the Bureau's plan is ready, the President must send it to Congress.

(4) If, within 60 days of receiving it, neither house rejects the Census Bureau's plan, it becomes effective.

The scheme set out in the 1929 law has worked quite well through now six reapportionments—most recently in 1981. It leaves to Congress its constitutional responsibility to reapportion the House—but it gives to the Census Bureau the mechanical chores (and political heat) that go with that task.

Today each seat in the House represents an average of 540,000 persons.

Election

According to the Constitution, any person a State allows to vote for members of "the most numerous branch" of its own legislature is qualified to vote in congressional elections.[9] And the Constitution also declares that:

> The times, places, and manner of holding [congressional] elections . . . shall be prescribed in each State by the legislature thereof; but the Congress may at any time, by law, make or alter such regulations . . .[10]

Date. Congressional elections are held on the same day in every State. Since 1872 Congress has required that those elections be held on the Tuesday following the first Monday in November of each even-numbered year.[11] In the same law it directed that Representatives be chosen by written or printed ballots. The use of voting machines was sanctioned in 1899.

Districts. The 435 members of the House are chosen by the voters in 435 separate congressional districts across the country.[12]

The Constitution does not speak of congressional districts. For more than half a century, Congress allowed each State to decide whether to elect its members by a *general ticket* system or on a *single-member district* basis.

Most of the States quickly set up congressional districts—with the voters in each district electing one of the State's Representatives. Several States used the general ticket system, however. Under that arrangement, all of the State's seats were filled from the State **at-large**—that is, from the State as a whole, by all of the voters of the State.

At-large elections proved grossly unfair. A party with a plurality of the votes in a State, no matter how small, could win all of the State's seats in the House. Congress finally did away with the general ticket system in 1842. It did so by requiring that, thereafter, all of the seats in the House be filled from districts within each State.

The 1842 law made each of the State legislatures responsible for the drawing of the congressional districts within its

---

[9]Article I, Section 2, Clause 1.
[10]Article I, Section 4, Clause 1; see page 226.

[11]On the formula fixing the election date, see page 227.
[12]The Constitution allows only one method for filling a vacancy in the House. This is by a special election, which may be called only by the governor of the State involved. Article I, Section 2, Clause 4.

THE GERRY-MANDER!

ALL that we can learn of the natural history of this remarkable animal, is contained in the following learned treatise, published in the newspapers of March, 1812, embellished by a drawing, which is pronounced by all competent judges, to be a most accurate likeness.

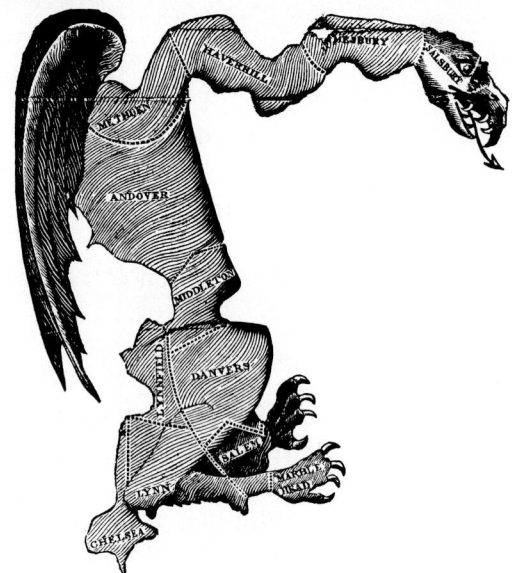

Gerrymandering takes its name from Elbridge Gerry (1744-1814). In 1812, while Gerry was governor of Massachusetts, his supporters in the legislature redrew the State's legislative districts to favor the Democratic-Republicans. It is said that the noted painter Gilbert Stuart added a head, wings, and claws to Essex County on a district map hanging over the desk of a Federalist newspaper editor. "That," he said, "will do for a salamander." "Better say Gerrymander," growled the editor.

own State.[13] It also required that each of the districts be made up of "contiguous territory." In 1872 Congress added the command that the districts within each State have "as nearly as practicable an equal number of inhabitants." In 1901 it further directed that all the districts be of "compact territory."

These requirements of contiguity, population equality, and compactness were often disregarded by the State legislatures; and Congress made no real effort to enforce them. They were left out of the Reapportionment Act of 1929; and in 1932 the Supreme Court held (in *Wood* v. *Broom*) that they had therefore

been repealed. For years, then, many districts were of very odd geographic shape. In many States they were also of widely differing populations.

Gerrymandering. Districts which on a map appear much like a shoestring, a dumbbell, the letter Y, or take some other odd form, have usually been **gerrymandered.** That is, they have been drawn to the advantage of the party or faction in power.

The practice of gerrymandering is both ancient and modern. It is also widespread. It can be found in most places where lines are drawn for the election of public officeholders—at the State and the local as well as at the congressional level. Most often it takes one of two forms. Either the lines are drawn: (1) to concentrate the opposition's voters in one or a few districts, or (2) to spread the opposition as thinly as possible among several districts.

For decades, gerrymandering produced congressional districts of widely different populations. Clearly, the State legislatures were responsible for this situation. A number of them regularly drew the district lines on a strictly partisan basis—with the Republicans gouging the Democrats in some States and the Democrats only too willing to return the favor in others. (And, in fact, that is still the case in several States today.)

Historically, however, most of the States were carved up on a rural versus urban basis—for, until recently, the typical State legislature was dominated by the less-populated, over-represented rural areas of the State.[14]

---

[13]Except, of course, in States with only one Representative; in those States the one seat is filled at-large.

[14]The long-standing pattern of rural-over-representation and urban under-representation in the State legislatures has now all but disappeared—as a direct consequence of the Supreme Court's several "one-man, one-vote" decisions of the 1960s and 1970s. In the leading case, *Reynolds* v. *Sims* (1964), the Court held that the seats in both houses of a State's legislature must be apportioned (districted) on the basis of population equality. See pages 521-522.

CONGRESSIONAL REDISTRICTING*

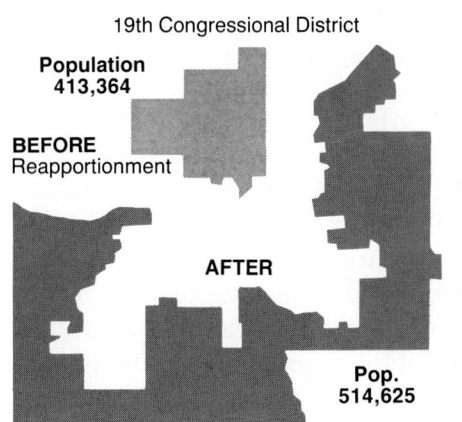

19th Congressional District

Population 413,364

BEFORE Reapportionment

AFTER

Pop. 514,625

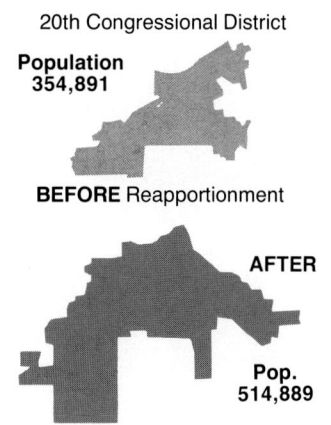

20th Congressional District

Population 354,891

BEFORE Reapportionment

AFTER

Pop. 514,889

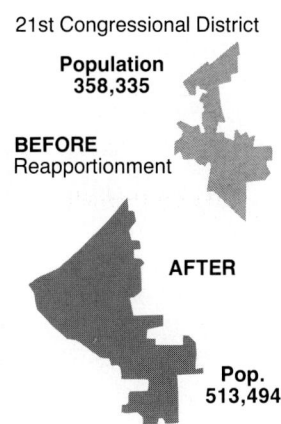

21st Congressional District

Population 358,335

BEFORE Reapportionment

AFTER

Pop. 513,494

*These maps show how the State legislature redrew the three congressional districts in and around Cleveland, Ohio, after the 1980 Census. (Notice that the three districts fit together, much like a jigsaw puzzle. Thus, what are now the 20th and 21st Districts are actually located within the "U" formed by the present 19th District.)

Wesberry v. Sanders, 1964. Suddenly, and quite dramatically, the long-standing patterns of wide population variation and of rural over-representation came to an end in the late 1960s. In State after State congressional district lines were redrawn to produce districts of approximately equal populations.

These abrupt changes were the direct result of an historic decision by the Supreme Court in 1964. In *Wesberry* v. *Sanders* the Court held that the population differences among Georgia's congressional districts were so great as to violate the Constitution.

In reaching its historic decision, the Court noted that Article I, Section 2 declares that Representatives shall be chosen "by the people of the several States" and shall be "apportioned among the several States . . . according to their respective numbers." These words, the Court held, especially when viewed in light of what the Framers intended, mean that

. . . as nearly as practicable one man's vote in a congressional election is to be worth as much as another's.

And, the Court added

While it may not be possible to draw congressional districts with mathematical precision, that is no excuse for ignoring our Constitution's plain objective of making equal representation for equal numbers of people the fundamental goal of the House of Representatives. That is the high standard of justice and common sense which the Founders set for us.

It is hard to overstate the importance of *Wesberry* and the Court's later "one-man, one-vote" decisions. They have had an extraordinary impact on the make-up of the House, on the content of public policy, and on electoral politics in general. The nation's cities and suburbs now speak with a much larger voice in Congress than ever before.

But notice this: It is still quite possible to draw congressional (and other) district lines in keeping with the "one-man, one vote" rule and, at the same time, gerrymander those districts.[15]

Qualifications

A member of the House must be at least 25 years of age, must have been a citizen for at least seven years, and must be an inhabitant of the State from which he or she is chosen.[16]

Long-standing custom, not the Constitution, also requires that a Representative must live in the district he or she represents. The custom is based on the feeling that the legislator should know thoroughly the locale, its people, and its problems. Whatever the merits of the custom, it is rare that one who does not live in a district is chosen to represent it.

The Constitution makes the House "the judge of the elections, returns, and qualifications of its own members."[17] Thus when the right of a member-elect to be seated is challenged, the House itself has the power to decide the matter. Very few challenges are successful.

The House may refuse to seat (exclude) a member-elect by majority vote. It may also "punish its own members for disorderly behavior" by majority vote, and "with the concurrence of two-thirds, expel a member."[18]

Historically, the House viewed its power to judge the qualifications of any member-elect as the power to impose additional, informal qualifications. In *Powell* v. *McCormack*, 1969, however,

the Supreme Court held that it could not exclude any member-elect who meets the Constitution's standards of age, citizenship, and residence.[19]

In nearly 200 years, the House has expelled only four of its members. Three were ousted in 1861, for their "support of rebellion." More recently, Michael Myers (D., Pennsylvania) was expelled in 1980, for corruption. Myers had been caught up in the Abscam probe—an undercover FBI investigation of corruption among public officials. Two FBI agents, pretending to represent an oil-rich Arab sheikh, had given him $50,000; in return, he had promised to introduce a bill to allow their supposed employer to enter the country as a permanent resident. For taking the money, Myers was convicted in court for bribery.[20]

The House has not often punished a member for "disorderly behavior," but such actions are not nearly so rare as expulsions. The most recent case came in 1983, when the House voted to "censure" two members: Daniel B. Crane (R., Ill.) and Gerry E. Studds (D., Mass.). Both were punished for having had sexual relations with teen-age congressional pages. (The House Committee on Stan-

---

[15]Except for gerrymandering based upon race, a violation of the 14th Amendment's Equal Protection Clause, *Gomillion* v. *Lightfoot*, 1960; see page 199.

[16]Article I, Section 2, Clause 2. The Constitution also provides that neither a Representative nor a Senator "shall during the time for which he was elected, be appointed to any civil office under the authority of the United States, which shall have been created, or the emoluments whereof shall have been increased, during such time; and no person holding any office under the United States shall be a member of either House during his continuance in office." Article I, Section 6, Clause 2.

[17]Article I, Section 5, Clause 1

[18]Article I, Section 5, Clause 2.

---

[19]Until then the House had excluded several members-elect on extra-constitutional grounds. Thus, in 1900 it refused to seat Brigham H. Roberts of Utah because he was a practicing polygamist. The late Representative Adam Clayton Powell of New York, re-elected to a 12th term in 1966, was barred in 1967. A special committee had recommended that Powell be seated but then be censured for "gross misconduct." It found that he had misused public funds, defied the courts of his State, and been "contemptuous" in refusing to cooperate with its investigation of him. The House voted instead to exclude him. The Court held that, as Powell had been "duly elected by the voters of the 18th Congressional District of New York and was not ineligible to serve under any provision of the Constitution, the House was without power to exclude him from its membership." The House has not excluded a member-elect since the *Powell* case.

[20]A few other members have resigned their seats rather than face the possibility of expulsion—most recent, John W. Jenrette (D., South Carolina) in 1980 and Raymond F. Lederer (D., Pennsylvania) in 1981. Both Jenrette and Lederer had also been convicted in Abscam bribery cases.

dards of Official Conduct had recommended that each of them receive a "reprimand"—the least severe form of punishment the House can impose. A censured member must appear before the House to hear the charges read against him or her.)

☑ **FOR REVIEW**

1. What is the present size of the House? How is that number fixed?

2. The Constitution directs what body to reapportion the House after each census? How has that constitutional responsibility been met since 1929?

3. What are congressional districts? By whom are they drawn? What is gerrymandering?

4. What did the Supreme Court hold in *Wesberry* v. *Sanders*, 1964? Why is that case, and related ones, so important?

5. For what term are members of the House elected? What qualifications must they have? What powers does the House have over the election and qualifications of its members?

Representative Romano L. Mazzoli (D., Kentucky), a member of the House Committee on Small Business, talks with constituents of his district.

The Senate

Size

The Senate is a much smaller body than the House. It "shall be composed of two Senators from each State," says the Constitution.[21] As there are now 50 States, there are, of course, 100 Senators.

Election

Until the adoption of the 17th Amendment in 1913, Senators were chosen by the several State legislatures.

But, from 1914 on, they have been chosen by the people at the regular November elections.[22]

Each Senator is elected from the State at-large. The 17th Amendment declares that all persons whom the State allows to vote for members of "the most numerous branch" of its legislature are qualified to vote for candidates for the United States Senate.

Terms

Senators are chosen for six-year terms—three times the length for which members of the lower house are chosen.[23] The terms are staggered. Only

---

[21]Article I, Section 3, Clause 1; 17th Amendment.

[22]Only one Senator is elected from a State at any given election, except when the other seat has been vacated by death, resignation, or expulsion. The 17th Amendent gives each State a choice of methods for the filling of a vacancy in the Senate. A State may (1) fill the seat at a special election called by the governor, or (2) allow the governor to appoint someone to serve until the voters fill the vacancy at such a special election or at the next regular (November) election. Most States use the appointment/special election method.

[23]Article I, Section 3, Clause 1.

a third of them—33 or 34—expire every two years. Unlike the House, all of its seats are never up for election at the same time.

The six-year term makes Senators less subject to the pressures of public opinion, and to the pleas of special interests, than their colleagues in the House. Also, the larger size and the geographic scope of their constituencies have much the same effect.

Qualifications

A Senator must meet a higher set of qualifications than those the Constitution sets for a Representative. He or she must be at least 30 years of age, must have been a citizen for at least nine years, and must be an inhabitant of the State from which elected.[24]

The Senate, like the House, may judge the qualifications of its members and may exclude a member-elect by a majority vote.[25] And it may also "punish its members for disorderly behavior" by majority vote, and "with the concurrence of two-thirds, expel a member."[26]

Fifteen members of the Senate have been expelled by that body—one in 1797 and 14 during the Civil War.[27]

The punishing of a Senator for "disorderly behavior" has also been rare.

---

[24]Article I, Section 3, Clause 3. Under the inhabitant qualification, a Senator need not have lived in the State for any prescribed time. Most often, of course, Senators have been long-term residents of their States.

[25]Article I, Section 3, Clause 1. As has the House, the Senate has at times refused to seat a member-elect. Presumably, the Court's holding in *Powell* v. *McCormack* applies with equal force to the Senate.

[26]Article I, Section 5, Clause 2.

[27]Senator William Blount of Tennessee was expelled in 1797 for conspiring to lead two Indian tribes, supported by British warships, in attacks on Spanish Florida and Louisiana. The 14 Senators ousted in 1861 and 1862 were all from States of the Confederacy and were expelled for supporting secession. In 1982 Senator Harrison Williams (D., New Jersey) resigned to avoid expulsion by the Senate. He had been the only Senator caught up in the FBI's Abscam operation and was convicted of bribery in 1981. Following his trial, the Senate Ethics Committee had unanimously recommended that he be expelled.

MAJOR DIFFERENCES BETWEEN HOUSE AND SENATE

House	Senate
Larger body (435 members)	Smaller body (100 members)
Shorter term (2 years)	Longer term (6 years)
Smaller constituencies (elected from districts within States)	Larger constituencies (elected from entire State)
Younger membership	Older membership
Less prestige	More prestige
Lower visibility in news media	Higher visibility in news media
More rigid rules	More flexible rules
More committees	Fewer committees
Strict leadership control of floor proceedings	Less leadership control of floor proceedings

The most recent case was in 1979, however. Then, the Senate voted to "denounce" one of its senior members, Herman Talmadge (D., Georgia). The Senate Ethics Committee found that he had mishandled thousands of dollars in Senate expense monies and campaign contributions. On the committee's recommendation, the Senate declared his conduct "reprehensible," tending "to bring the Senate into dishonor and disrepute." (Senator Talmadge, first elected to the Senate in 1956, was defeated for reelection in 1980.)

☑ FOR REVIEW

1. What is the size of the Senate? How is that number fixed?
2. By whom are Senators chosen? For what term? Why is the Senate a "continuous body"?
3. Senators must meet what constitutional qualifications?
4. What powers does the Senate have with regard to the election and qualifications of its members?

The Members and Their Job

The Members

Whatever else they may be, the 535 members of Congress are *not* a representative cross-section of the American people.

Rather, the "average" member is a white male in his latter 40's. The median age of the members of the House is now just over 46 and of the Senate, 54. There are only 24 women in Congress: 22 in the House and two—Nancy Landon Kassebaum (R., Kansas) and Paula Hawkins (R., Florida)—in the Senate. And there are only 21 blacks and 11 Hispanics in Congress. All of them sit in the House of Representatives.

Nearly all members of Congress are married, a few are divorced, and they have, on the average, two children. Only a very few say they have no church affil-

Jeannette Rankin (R., Montana), the first woman to serve in Congress, was elected to the House in 1916 and again in 1940.

Hiram Rhodes Revels (R., Mississippi), the first black to sit in the Senate, represented his State for a partial term, 1870–1871.

iation. Just over two-thirds of them are Protestants, a fourth are Roman Catholics, and nearly seven percent are Jewish.

More than half of the members of each house are lawyers. Most of the others come from these major occupational backgrounds: business and banking, education, agriculture, journalism, and public service/politics. Nearly all of them went to college. Better than four out of five have a college degree and a number have several.

Most Senators and Representatives were born in the States they represent. Only a bare handful were born outside of the United States. Sprinkled among them are several millionaires. A surprisingly large number of them, however, depend upon their official salaries as their major source of income.

Most members of Congress have had considerable political experience. The average Senator is now in a second term in the Senate, and the average Representative has served four terms in the House. Nearly a third of the Senate once sat in the House; several Senators are former governors; and a few of them have held Cabinet or other high posts in the executive branch. The House has a large number of former State legislators and prosecuting attorneys.

Again, Congress is not an accurate cross-section of the nation's population. Rather, it is made up of upper-middle class Americans who, on the whole, are quite able and hard-working people.

Their Job

The major job of the 535 members of Congress is to make law, of course. That is to say, they are legislators.

As legislators, they play several closely related and vital roles. They do (1) make law. But they also serve (2) as representatives of their constituents, (3) as servants of their constituents, (4) as committee members, and (5) necessarily, as politicians.

We've looked at some aspects of these roles, in this and in earlier chapters; and we shall consider other pieces of them in the next two chapters. But, for now, ponder this job description, offered only half-jokingly by former Representative Luther Patrick of Alabama:

A Congressman has become an expanded messenger boy, an employment agency, getter-outer of the Navy, Army, Marines, ward heeler, wound healer, trouble shooter, law explainer, bill finder, issue translator, resolution interpreter, controversy oil pourer, gladhand extender, business promoter, convention goer, civil ills skirmisher, veterans' affairs adjuster, ex-serviceman's champion, watchdog for the underdog, sympathizer with the upper dog, namer and kisser of babies, recoverer of lost luggage, sober-

er of delegates, adjuster for traffic violators, voters straying into Washington and into toils of the law, binder up of broken hearts, financial wet nurse, good samaritan, contributor to good causes—there are so many good causes—cornerstone layer, public building and bridge dedicator, ship christener—to be sure he does get in a little flag waving—and a little constitutional hoisting and spread-eagle work, but it is getting harder every day to find time to properly study legislation—the very business we are primarily here to discharge, and that must be done above all things.

Members of Congress are elected to represent their **constituents**—the people of their State or district. But some of those people take this to mean that their Senators and Representatives are in Washington most of all to do favors for them. The average member of Congress is swamped by their requests—as Mr. Patrick points out—from the moment he or she takes office. Most members of Congress know that to refuse—or at least not to respond in some way to most of these requests—would mean to lose votes at the next election.

Compensation

The members of both houses are now paid an annual salary of $69,800.[28]

The Speaker of the House receives the same pay as the Vice President, today $91,000 a year. The Senate's President *pro tem* and the majority and the minority floor leaders in each house now make $78,900 a year.

---

[28]The Constitution gives Congress the power to set its own pay, Article I, Section 6, Clause 1. By law, the fees a Senator may receive for articles and speeches or other public appearances cannot exceed 30 percent ($20,940) of his/her congressional pay each year. A House rule provides that a Representative cannot earn more than 30 percent of the annual salary from all outside sources, including whatever amounts he or she may be paid for articles and speeches or other appearances.

ELECTION STUDY

TURNING THE TABLES:
THE OFF-YEAR ELECTIONS

Congressional elections are held every two years—on the Tuesday after the first Monday in November of every even-numbered year. On each of those occasions, all 435 seats in the House and one-third of the seats in the Senate (33 or 34) are up for election.

Those congressional elections which occur in the non-presidential years— that is, between presidential elections— are regularly called the "off-year elections." The most recent ones were held in 1982, of course; and the next ones will come in 1986.

Quite consistently, the party in power —the party which holds the Presidency —loses seats in the off-year elections. The table below illustrates that point. It sets out the House and Senate seats

gained (+) or lost (−) by the President's party in the 16 off-year elections over the past 60 years (1922 through 1982).

Year	Party in Power	House Seats	Senate Seats
1922	R	−75	−8
1926	R	−10	−6
1930	R	−49	−8
1934	D	+9	+10
1938	D	−71	−6
1942	D	−45	−9
1946	D	−55	−12
1950	D	−29	−6
1954	R	−18	−1
1958	R	−47	−13
1962	D	−4	+4
1966	D	−47	−3
1970	R	−12	+2
1974	R	−43	−3
1978	D	−11	−3
1982	R	−26	0

1. Why does the party in power usually lose seats in both houses in the off-year elections?

2. In which one of these 16 elections was the usual pattern *not* reflected by the results of both the House and the Senate contests? Why do you think that that election proved to be an exception to the general rule?

3. Why do the results of the Senate elections not follow the usual pattern quite as closely as do House elections?

4. Over time, many have suggested that the terms of members of the House be increased to four years. A constitutional amendment would be necessary to accomplish that, of course. If that change were made, would it have any impact on the historic pattern of off-year election results? Why have most members of the Senate regularly opposed such a change?

5. Over time, many have also proposed that the Constitution be amended to provide a single six-year term for the President. If that change were made, would it have any impact on that historic pattern?

Other Compensation.   Each member also receives a number of "fringe benefits," and some of them are quite substantial. Each is allowed a tax deduction to help keep up two residences, one at home and another in Washington. Liberal travel allowances cover the costs of several round trips between the home State and the capital each year.

Each member pays only small amounts for a $45,000 life insurance policy and for health insurance. A medical staff offers free care at the Capitol and full care can be had, at very low rates, at any military hospital. Also, there is a generous pension plan (to which members contribute). The plan is based on years of service and can lead to a retirement income of as much as $48,530 a year.

Each member also has a suite of offices in one of the Senate or House office buildings and allowances for offices in the home State or district. Then, too, each is allowed funds for hiring staff and other office assistants, for stationery, office equipment and furnishings, and for telephone and telegraph services and special delivery postage. All of a member's official mail goes free under the "franking privilege."

Beyond all that, there is free printing and distribution of speeches, newsletters, and much other material, and radio and television tapes at sharply reduced cost. Each member also has the right to free parking, plants for the office, the research help of the Library of Congress, and still more—as the use of several fine restaurants and two first-rate gymnasiums (with swimming pools and saunas).

With the salary and all of the many allowances, the typical member's compensation amounts to well over $100,000 a year. Even so, it doesn't seem reasonable to argue that members of Congress are overpaid. Their responsibilities are so great and the demands made upon them so many and varied as to defeat any attempt to fix an "adequate" salary.

In fact, many Senators and Representatives insist that their "day-to-day expenses" are regularly more than their allowances. Senator Bob Packwood (R., Oregon) estimates that just two items—trips to his home State and newsletters to his constituents—push his expenses some $40,000 above his allowances each year. Add such items as the high cost of living in and around Washington, the need to maintain two homes, campaign costs, and coping with all of the other "extras" imposed by the office, and it is easy to appreciate the point.

The fear—and certainty—of political repercussions has always made members of Congress reluctant to raise their own salaries. They have more often chosen to give themselves such fringe benefits as a special tax deduction, a generous pension plan, and other "perks" which are much less apparent to the voters.

Congress has tried to avoid the pitfalls of a pay increase in recent years—but not very successfully. Since 1967, it has provided that a panel of private citizens should recommend to the President the appropriate salaries for members of Congress, top-level executive officials, and all federal judges. After reviewing the panel's report, the President makes salary recommendations to Congress. Those recommendations then become law if neither house rejects them within 30 days. The present congressional salary figure was fixed in this way in 1982 an again in 1983; but it was done with a great deal of controversy and criticism.

Higher salaries, alone, will not bring the most able men and women to Congress, or to any other public offices. But, certainly, they can make public service much more appealing.

Privileges of Members

The Constitution commands that Senators and Representatives

> shall, in all cases, except treason, felony, and breach of the peace, be privileged from arrest during their attendance at the session of their respective Houses, and in going to and returning from the same. . . .[29]

The first responsibility of the Library of Congress is service to Congress. Its Congressional Research Service has the sole function furnishing information bearing on legislation to members of Congress.

The provision dates from English and colonial practice, when the King's officers often harassed legislators on petty grounds. It has been of little importance in our national history.[30]

Another and much more important privilege is set out in the same place in the Constitution. The Speech and Debate Clause declares

> . . . and for any speech or debate in either House, they shall not be questioned in any other place.

The words "any other place" refer to the courts.

The privilege is intended to "throw a cloak of legislative immunity" about members of Congress. It protects them from suits for libel or slander arising out of their official conduct. The Supreme Court has held that the immunity applies "to things generally done in a session of the House [or Senate] by one of its members in relation to the business before it."[31] The protection goes, then, beyond floor debate—to include work in committees and all of the other things generally done by members of Congress in relation to congressional business. But a member is not free to defame another person in a public speech, an article, a conversation, or otherwise. The very important and necessary goal of the provision is to protect freedom of legislative debate.

 FOR REVIEW

1. Is Congress an accurate reflection of the nation's population?
2. Members of Congress must play what five principal roles?
3. Who sets the salary of members of Congress? How much is that pay today? Is that all of the compensation they receive?
4. For what does the Speech and Debate Clause provide? Why?

---

[29]Article I, Section 6, Clause 1.

[30]The courts have regularly held that the words "breach of the peace" cover all criminal offenses—misdemeanors (minor crimes) as well as felonies. So the protection covers only arrest for civil (non-criminal) offenses while engaged in congressional business.

[31]The leading case is *Kilburn* v. *Thompson*, 1881; the holding has been affirmed many times since. In *Hutchinson* v. *Proxmire*, 1979, however, the Court held that members of Congress may be sued for libel for statements they make in news releases or in newsletters.

S U M M A R Y

Congress is the legislative (lawmaking) branch of the National Government. It is made up of two houses—the House of Representatives and the Senate. Congress is bicameral for several reasons: because the Framers were familiar with two-chambered legislatures in British, colonial, and early State practice; the Connecticut Compromise; and the desire to have one house act as a check on the other.

A term of Congress lasts for two years. There are two regular sessions to each term, one a year. Special sessions may be called only by the President.

Members of the House serve a two-year term and are popularly elected. The Congress reapportions the seats in the House among the States based on their respective populations after each decennial census, but each State is entitled to at least one Representative. The House now has 435 members elected from districts drawn by the legislature in each State. The districts must contain about equal populations, but they may be (and often are) gerrymandered.

A Representative must be at least 25 years old, seven years a citizen, and an inhabitant of the State from which chosen. Each house has the power to decide contests over the seating of its members-elect, and each has the power to refuse to seat a member-elect. Each house may also discipline (censure or expel) any of its members.

Each State has two seats in the 100-member Senate. Senators serve six-year terms. One-third of those terms end every two years. Since 1913 (the 17th Amendment), Senators have been popularly elected. They must be at least 30 years old, nine years a citizen, and an inhabitant of the State from which chosen.

Congress is not an accurate cross-section of the American people. Rather, the "average" member is a white male over 45.

As legislators, the members of Congress make law, of course. They also serve as representatives and as servants of their constituents, as committee members, and as politicians. They fix their own salaries by law. and provide themselves with a number of other (rather generous) compensations. They also enjoy freedom from petty (harassing) arrest during sessions and immunity in debate and other official conduct.

C H A P T E R   R E V I E W

Key Terms/Concepts

Adjournment (276)
At-large (279)
Apportionment (277)
Bicameral (274)
Congress (274)
Congressional district (279)
Constituent (286)

Decennial census (278)
District (279)
Franking privilege (288)
Gerrymander (280)
House of Representatives (277)

Legislative immunity (289)
"One-man, one vote" (281)
Reapportionment (278)
Redistricting (278)
Senate (283)

Session (276)
Special session (276)
Term (276)

Keynote Questions

1. Why did the Framers of the Constitution provide for a bicameral Congress?
2. How long is a term of Congress? How long does a session last? Who may call a special session?
3. What is the current size of the House? The Senate? On what basis is the size of each house fixed?
4. What body has the constitutional responsibility to reapportion the seats in the House after each census? On what basis? How has that responsibility been met since 1929?
5. What are congressional districts? By whom are they drawn? What is gerrymandering?
6. For what term are Representatives elected? Senators? What qualifications must they meet? Why is the Senate a "continuous body"?
7. What five closely related roles do the members of Congress play?
8. What salary and other compensation do members of Congress receive?
9. For what does the Speech and Debate Clause provide? Why?

For Thought and Discussion

1. Why did James Madison speak of Congress as "the First Branch"?
2. Members of Congress are sometimes pictured as overpaid, underworked, and ineffective. Will Rogers was not the first, and far from the last, to make this sort of comment: "Suppose you were an idiot. And suppose you were a Congressman. But I repeat myself." Similar assessments can be found in many places—for example, in editorial cartoons. Yet, on page 286, the author of this book says that members of Congress are "on the whole, . . . able and hard-working people." And that judgment is supported by any number of academic, journalistic, and other studies and commentaries. Can you explain the apparent contradiction here?
3. Would you favor or oppose a constitutional amendment to lengthen (or shorten) the elected term of Representatives? Of Senators? Why?
4. Are the congressional districts in your State gerrymandered? If so, how and to whose benefit? Should Congress enact a law to end the practice? How else might it be prevented?

Suggested Activities

1. Invite one of your members of Congress to speak to the class (or to the entire student body) on his/her role as a legislator. (Or on another topic of his/her choosing).
2. Prepare a biographical study of your Representative and Senators. Use such sources as *The Congressional Directory* and *The Almanac of American Politics.*)
3. Stage a debate or class forum on one or more of these questions: (a) *Resolved,* That former Presidents should automatically become lifetime members of the Senate; (b) *Resolved,* That Senators should receive a higher salary than that paid to Representatives; (c) *Resolved,* That no member of either house should be allowed to serve more than three consecutive terms in office.

The bronze Statue of Freedom towers above the Capitol Dome.

12

Congress in Action

To help you to
Learn ▪ **Know** ▪ **Understand**

The formal and the party organizational structure in both houses of Congress.

The committee system in Congress and the different types of committees to be found in both houses.

The overall shape and the several steps of the legislative process in both houses of Congress.

For this reason the laws are made: That the strong shall not have the power to do all that they please.
Ovid

We have just studied the overall structure of the Congress. We have looked at its bicameral character, the selection and terms of its members, and the shape of the different roles its members play. Now we turn to Congress at work—to its internal organization, procedures, and practices. With what machinery and in what ways does it play its pivotal part in our governmental system?

The answers to these questions are of great importance. They are, of course, because of the place of the lawmaking function at the center of the democratic process. They are, as well, because they determine how power is distributed within Congress, in each of its houses. They point to who has and can exercise major influence and control over the making of law, and who then gets "what, when, and how."

Woodrow Wilson once said that "the making of law is a very practical matter." It is; and it is also a very complicated matter, as we shall see.

Congress Convenes

As we know, a new Congress meets every two years. That is, it convenes (begins a new term) on the 3rd of January in every odd-numbered year, following the regular November elections.

Members of the House of Representatives take the oath of office as Congress begins a new term. *Facing page:* Henry Clay addresses the Senate in 1850.

Opening Day in the House

When the 435 men and women who have been elected to the House come together at the Capitol on January 3rd, they are, in effect, just so many Representatives-elect. Because all 435 of its seats are filled by the voters every two years, the House has no sworn members, no rules, no organization until its opening day ceremonies are held.

The Clerk of the House in the preceding term presides at the beginning of the first day's session.[1] He calls the chamber to order and checks the roll of Representatives-elect. Those members-to-be then choose a Speaker as their permanent presiding officer.

The Speaker is always a senior member of the majority party, and election on the floor is only a formality. The majority party *caucus* (conference of party members in the House) has settled the matter beforehand.

The Speaker then takes the oath of office. It is administered by the "Dean of the House," the member-elect with the longest record of service in the House of Representatives.[2] With that accomplished, the Speaker swears in the rest of the members, as a body. The Democrats take their seats to the right of the center aisle, the Republicans to the left.

Next, the House elects its Clerk, Sergeant at Arms, Doorkeeper, Postmas-

---

[1]The Clerk is a non-member officer, chosen by the House. He serves as that body's chief administrative officer. No woman has as yet (1789–1984) held the post.

[2]Today (1984), Representative Jamie L. Whitten (D., Mississippi), who has been a member of the House since November 4, 1941.

ter, and Chaplain. Their choices are also a formality; the majority caucus has already decided who they will be.

Then the House adopts the rules that will govern its proceedings through the term. The rules of the House have been developing for more than 190 years now, and they are contained in a volume of several hundred pages. They are regularly re-adopted, with little or no change, at the beginning of each term.

Finally, the members of the 22 permanent committees of the House are appointed by a floor vote and the House of Representatives is organized.

Opening Day in the Senate

The Senate is a continuous body. That is, it has been uninterruptedly organized since its first session in 1789. Recall, only one-third of the seats are up for election every two years. From one term to the next, then, there is a carryover of two-thirds of its membership.

The Senate does not face the large organizational problems the House does at the beginning of a new term. Its first-day session is nearly always quite short and routine—even when (as in 1981) the most recent elections have brought a change in party control. Newly elected and reelected members must be sworn in, vacancies in its organization and on committees must be filled, and a few other details attended to.

The President's State of the Union Message

When the Senate is notified that the House is organized, a joint committee of the two is appointed and instructed:

> . . . to wait upon the President of the United States and inform him that a quorum of each House is assembled and that the Congress is ready to receive any communication he may be pleased to make.

Within a few days the President delivers his annual State of the Union Message. From Woodrow Wilson's first one in 1913, each President has usually made these speeches in person. The members of both houses, together with the members of the Cabinet, the Supreme Court, the foreign diplomatic corps, and other dignitaries assemble in the House chamber to receive him.

In his address, the Chief Executive reports on the state of the nation in all of its concerns, foreign and domestic; and his speech often includes a number of specific (and sometimes controversial) legislative recommendations, as well.

The message is followed very closely, both here and abroad—for in it the President lays out the broad shape of the policies his administration will follow and the course he has charted for the nation.

With the conclusion of the President's speech, the joint session is adjourned and each house returns to the mass of legislative business before it.

The Organization of Congress

The national legislature is a far larger operation than most realize. Congress has appropriated some $1.4 billion to pay its bills in the current fiscal year. Of that huge sum, only $37,333,000—less than three percent—is spent to pay the salaries of the 535 members. Nearly $300 million now goes to hire staff assistants for members, and the yearly postage ("franking") bill runs to well over $50 million a year.

There are, all told, some 38,000 congressional employees. There are hundreds of committee aides, legislative and administrative assistants, office clerks, secretaries, guards, maintenance personnel, and so on. Each is important to the workings of Congress.

A CASE IN POINT

SENIORITY = CLOUT:

Now serving his 21st term in Congress, is "Dean of the House" Jamie L. Whitten (D., Miss.)

THOSE WHO HAVE, GET. . . .

This very practical and very important point can be seen time and again in this chapter: How long a Representative or a Senator has been in office—*i.e.*, that member's "seniority"—has much to do with his/her place in the power structure of the House or the Senate. In short, this is most often the case: The longer the record of service, the greater the clout.

Seniority is built out of a continuing success at the polls, of course—out of repeated reelection. And, as the tables show, most members of Congress who do seek reelection do so successfully.

SENATE

Year	Sought Reelection	Defeated Primary	Defeated General	Percent Reelected
1962	35	1	5	82.9
1964	33	1	4	84.8
1966	32	3	1	87.5
1968	28	4	4	71.4
1970	31	1	6	77.4
1972	27	2	5	74.1
1974	27	2	2	85.2
1976	25	0	9	64.0
1978	25	3	7	60.0
1980	29	4	9	55.1
1982	30	0	2	93.3

HOUSE

Year	Sought Reelection	Defeated Primary	Defeated General	Percent Reelected
1962	402	12	22	91.5
1964	397	8	45	86.6
1966	411	8	41	88.1
1968	409	4	9	96.8
1970	401	10	12	94.5
1972	390	12	13	93.6
1974	391	8	40	87.7
1976	384	3	13	95.8
1978	382	5	19	93.7
1980	392	6	31	90.6
1982	380	4	29	91.3

1. Among several other things, the table suggests that Senators tend to be more vulnerable at the polls than do Representatives. Look again at the chart on page 284. Which of the various comparisons we made there also seem to support this view?

2. How does the "seniority=clout" formula test out with regard to the Representative from your congressional district? Each of the two Senators from your State?

The Presiding Officers

The Constitution provides for the presiding officers of each house.

The **Speaker of the House** is by far the most important and influential member of the House of Representatives. The Speakership was created by the Constitution and, as that document commands, the post is filled by a vote of the House at the beginning of each of its two-year terms.[3] In practical fact, the Speaker is the leader of the majority party in the House—and so is actually chosen by the members of that party.

Although neither the Constitution nor its own rules require it, the House has always chosen the Speaker from among its own members. Usually, the Speaker is a long-time member who has risen in stature and influence through years of service.

The present incumbent, Thomas P.

---

[3]Article I, Section 2, Clause 5.

"Tip" O'Neill (D., Mass.), has been in the House since 1953 and became Speaker in 1977.[4]

At base, the immense power held by the Speaker arises from this fact: The Speaker is, at one and the same time, the elected presiding officer of the House *and* the acknowledged leader of its majority party. Speakers are expected to preside in a fair and judicial manner, and they regularly do so. But they are also expected to aid the fortunes of their own party and their party's legislative goals —and they regularly do that, too.

Nearly all the Speaker's specific powers revolve about two duties: to preside and to keep order. The Speaker presides over all sessions of the House, or appoints a temporary presiding officer to do so. No member may speak until "recognized" by the Speaker. The Speaker interprets and applies the rules, refers bills to the standing committees, rules on points of order (questions of procedure raised by members), puts questions to a vote, and determines the outcome of most of the votes taken.[5] The Speaker also names the members of all special committees and signs all bills and resolutions passed by the House.

As a member, the Speaker may debate and vote on any matter before the House; but to do so, a temporary presiding officer must be appointed and the chair vacated by the Speaker. The House rules *require* that the Speaker vote only to break a tie. (A tie vote defeats a question; thus the Speaker can *cause* a tie and so defeat a proposal.)

The **President of the Senate** is not a member of the Senate. The Constitution assigns that office to the Vice President of the United States.[6] Largely because of this, the President of the Senate occupies a much less powerful chair than that of the Speaker in the House. The Vice President does not become the Senate's presiding officer out of long service in that body. In fact, the President of the Senate is sometimes not even a member of the party with a majority of seats in the upper house.

The President of the Senate does have the usual powers of a presiding officer—to recognize members, put questions to a vote, and so on. But the Vice President cannot take the floor to speak or debate and may vote *only* to break a tie.

The influence a Vice President may have in the Senate is largely the result of personal abilities. Several of the more recent Vice Presidents came to that office from the Senate: Harry Truman, Alben Barkley, Richard Nixon, Lyndon Johnson, Hubert Humphrey, and Walter Mondale. Each of them was able to build some power into the position out of that earlier experience.

The Senate does have another presiding officer, the **President *pro tempore*,** who serves in the Vice President's absence. The President *pro tem* is elected by the Senate itself and is always a leading member of the majority party. Today (1984) the Senate's President *pro tem* is Senator Strom Thurmond (R., South Carolina). He was first elected to the Senate in 1954 and became its President *pro tem* in 1981.

Other members of the Senate also preside over the chamber, on a temporary basis; newly-elected Senators are regularly given this "honor" early in their terms.

---

[4]Speaker O'Neill is the 47th person to serve in the post. The first Speaker, elected at the first session in 1789, was Frederick A. C. Muhlenburg, a Federalist from Pennsylvania. Sam Rayburn (D., Texas) held the office for a record 17 years, 62 days. Except for two terms in which the Republicans controlled the House (1947-1948, 1953-54), "Mr. Sam" was the Speaker from September 16, 1940 until his death November 16, 1961.

[5]On most matters the House takes a voice vote; see page 309.

[6]Article I, Section 3, Clause 4.

Floor Leaders and Other Party Officers

Congress is distinctly a *political* body. It is for two leading reasons: *first,* because it is the nation's central *policy-making* organ; and, *secondly,* because of its *partisan* make-up. And, reflecting its political complexion, both houses are organized along party lines.

The Floor Leaders. Next to the Speaker, the most important officers in Congress are the **majority and minority floor leaders** in the House and Senate. These officers are the managers of their party's interests on the floor in each chamber. They do not hold *official* posts in either house; rather, they are *party* officers chosen by their party caucuses.

The floor leaders are their party's legislative strategists. They try to steer floor action to the party's benefit. To do so, they must keep in close touch with the party's members as a whole, with key committee members, and with the leaders of the various State delegations. They must also keep in close touch with such unofficial but pivotal coalitions as the Black Caucus or the Democratic Study Group.

The majority leader's post is the more important of the two in each house—for the obvious reason that the majority party has more seats (more votes) than does the minority leader's. Together with the presiding officer and the minority leader, the majority leader plans the order of business on the floor.

The two floor leaders are assisted by party whips in each house. The whips really serve as assistant floor leaders. They are chosen by the party caucus, usually recommended by the floor leader. There are also several assistant whips in each party in both houses.

The whips check with party members and advise the floor leader of the number of votes that can be counted upon in any particular matter. Of course, they attempt to see that mem-

At right/front is House Majority Leader James Wright, Jr. (D., Texas) as he meets with Democratic floor leaders and party whips.

bers vote with the party leadership and that they are present when important votes are to be taken. (If a member must be absent for some reason, the whip sees that that member is "paired" with a member of the other party—one who is also absent or who agrees not to vote on certain measures.)

The party caucus is a closed meeting of the members of each party in each house. It meets just before Congress convenes in January and sometimes during a session. In recent years the Republicans have called their caucus in each house the *party conference,* and the Democrats now use this term in the Senate, too.

The caucus deals mostly with matters of party organization—the selection of the party's floor leaders, questions of committee membership, and the like. It also works for united party action on certain measures. But neither party tries to force its members to follow its caucus decisions—nor can it. The policy committee, composed of the party's top leadership, acts as an executive committee for the caucus.

Committee Chairmen[7]

The large bulk of the work of Congress—especially in the House—is really done in committee. Thus, those members who head the standing committees in each chamber—the **committee chairmen**—also hold very strategic posts. The chairman of each of these permanent committees is chosen by the majority party caucus and is a ranking member of that party.

Committee chairmen regularly decide when their committees will meet, which bills they will take up, whether public hearings are to be held, and what witnesses are to be called. And when a committee's bill has been reported to the floor, they manage the debate and try to steer it to final passage.

We shall turn to the committees, and return to the role of the chairmen, in a moment. But, first, we must look at the *seniority rule.*

The seniority rule is, in fact, an *unwritten custom.* It first appeared in congressional practice in the late 1800s and is still closely followed, in both houses, today. It provides that the most important posts in both the formal and the party organization in each chamber will be held by the "ranking members"— that is, by those members of the party with the longest records of service in Congress.

The rule is applied most strictly to the choice of commitee chairman. The head of each committee is almost always the member of the majority party who has served for the longest period of time on that particular committee.

---

[7]We use the title chairman, rather than *chairperson,* advisedly: first, because this is the form used in both houses of Congress, both officially and informally; and secondly, because no woman now (1984) chairs a standing committee in either house. Only three women have ever done so; the most recent, Leonor K. Sullivan (D., Missouri), chaired the House Merchant Marine and Fisheries Committee from 1973 until her retirement from the House in 1977.

Critics of the rule are legion, and they do make a strong case. They insist that it ignores ability, puts a high value on mere length of service, and discourages younger members. They also note that the rule means that a committee head almost always comes from a "safe" constituency—from a State or district in which, election after election, one party regularly wins. They say that, with no play of fresh and contending forces in those places, the chairman of a committee is often out of touch with current public opinion.

Defenders of the rule argue that it means that a powerful and experienced member will head each committee, that it is easy to apply, and that it very nearly eliminates the possibility of intraparty fights.

Critics of the rule have scored a few points in recent years. But there is little chance that it will be eliminated. Those members with the real power to abolish the practice are the ones who reap the largest benefits from its operation.

✔ FOR REVIEW

1. Why is the first daily session of a term simpler and more routine in the Senate than in the House?
2. Who presides over the House? How is that officer chosen?
3. Who presides over the Senate? How is that officer chosen?
4. Who is the Senate's alternate presiding officer? Why does that post exist?
5. Who selects the floor leaders in each house? The whips? What are their functions?
6. How are committee chairmen chosen? Why are they so powerful? What is the seniority rule?

STANDING COMMITTEES OF CONGRESS

House Committees

Agriculture
Appropriations
Armed Services
Banking, Finance and
    Urban Affairs
Budget
District of Columbia
Education and Labor
Energy and Commerce
Foreign Affairs

Government Operations
House Administration
Interior and Insular Affairs
Judiciary
Merchant Marine and Fisheries
Post Office and Civil Service

Public Works and
    Transportation
Rules
Science and Technology
Small Business
Standards of Official
    Conduct
Veterans' Affairs
Ways and Means

Senate Committees

Agriculture, Nutrition, and
    Forestry
Appropriations
Armed Services
Banking, Housing, and
    Urban Affairs
Budget

Commerce, Science, and
    Transportation
Energy and Natural Resources
Environment and Public
    Works
Finance

Foreign Relations
Governmental Affairs
Judiciary
Labor and Human
    Resources
Rules and Administration
Small Business
Veterans' Affairs

The Committee System

Both the House and the Senate are so large and the volume of their business is so great that each depends heavily upon its committee system.

Standing Committees

In 1789 the House and Senate each adopted the practice of naming a special committee to consider each bill as it was introduced. By 1794 there were more than 300 committees in each chamber. Each house then began to set up permanent groups—**standing committees**—to which all similar bills could be sent.

The number of these committees has varied in each house over the years. Today there are 22 standing committees in the House and 16 in the Senate. Each committee has from 12 to as many as 57 members in the lower house and from 12 to 29 in the upper chamber. The rules of the House limit Representatives to

service on one major committee, and the Senate allows its members to serve on only two.

When a bill is introduced in either house the Speaker or the President of the Senate refers the measure to the proper standing committee. For instance, the Speaker sends all tax measures to the House Ways and Means Committee and in the Senate they go to the Finance Committee. A bill dealing with enlistments in the Navy is sent to the Armed Services Committee in either chamber, and so on.

We have already seen how the chairman of each of the standing committees is chosen according to the seniority rule. That rule is also applied quite closely in each house when it elects the other members of each of its committees.[8]

[8]In *form*, the members of each standing committee are elected by a floor vote at the beginning of each term of Congress. In *fact*, each party draws up its own committee roster, and those party decisions are then ratified on the floor.

The majority party controls each of the committees.[9] That is, it always holds a majority of the seats on each of them. But the other party is always well represented, too. In fact, party membership on each committee is more or less in line with party strength in each house. Thus, if the Democrats hold 240 seats in the House and the Republicans 195, the party split on, say, a 25-member committee will likely be 14 Democrats and 11 Republicans.

Except for the House Committee on Rules and the Senate Committee on Rules and Administration, each of the standing committees is a "subject-matter committee." Each deals with bills on certain subjects, as: the House Committee on Veterans' Affairs or the Senate Committee on the Judiciary.

We shall look at the strategic role of these committees in the legislative processs shortly. But, first, we must take special note of one of them.

The House Rules Committee. The House Committee on Rules is sometimes called the "traffic cop" in the legislative process in the lower house.

So many measures are introduced in the House each term—as many as 10,000 now—that some sort of screening is clearly necessary. The standing committees carry out that chore. Most bills die in the committees to which they are referred. Still, several hundred of them are reported out every year. So, before most bills can reach the floor, they must also clear the Rules Committee.

This powerful 13-member committee usually (but not always) works in close cooperation with the House leadership. It manages the flow of bills for action by the full House. Normally, a bill cannot be brought to the floor unless it has been "granted a rule"—that is, scheduled for consideration—by the Rules Committee. That committee decides (1) whether or not and (2) if so, under what conditions a bill will be taken up. In short, the Rules Committee can hasten, delay, or even prevent House consideration of a measure.

In the smaller Senate, where the lawmaking process is not so strictly regulated, the Committee on Rules and Administration is only a pale shadow of its counterpart in the lower house.

Select Committees

At times, each house finds need for a *select committee*—that is, a special group set up for some specific purpose and (most often) for a limited time. The members of these special committees are appointed by the Speaker or the President of the Senate, with the advice of majority and minority floor leaders.

Most select committees are formed to investigate some particular and current matter.

The congressional power to investigate is an essential part of the lawmaking function. Congress must have the power to inform itself on matters before it. It must decide on the the need for new laws, and the adequacy of laws it has already passed. It must also exercise its "oversight" function. That is, Congress must determine whether executive agencies are working effectively and in line with the policies Congress has set by law. Also, Congress sometimes carries out an investigation in order to center public attention on some topic.

Most congressional investigations—the usual and routine, as well as the ones that capture the headlines—are conducted by standing committees, or their subcommittees.

Select committees are also some-

---

[9]The only exception here is the House Committee on Standards of Official Conduct, with six Democrats and six Republicans. It investigates allegations of misconduct by House members and makes recommendations to the full chamber. (In the Senate, a six-member bipartisan group, the Select Committee on Ethics, plays a similar role.)

times used for that work, however. Thus, over the past several years both houses have created, and re-created, a Select Committee on Aging. Each of those bodies is very much concerned with the many different problems faced by the elderly in our society. They hold hearings in Washington and elsewhere in the country, issue committee reports, and prompt public and governmental attention to those problems.

At times, a select committee becomes a spectacularly important body. This happened, for example, to the Sen-

ate's Select Committee on Presidential Campaign Activities, also known as the Senate Watergate Committee. As the Watergate scandal began to unfold in 1973, the Senate created that committee. Chaired by Senator Sam Ervin (D., North Carolina), its job was to investigate "the extent, if any, to which illegal, improper, or unethical activities were engaged in by any persons . . . in the presidential election of 1972." Its lengthy, often televised, and frequently sensational hearings fascinated the nation for months. They were a major link

HOUSE LEADERSHIP, 1984

Position	Name	Age*	Year Entered House	State
Leadership				
Speaker	Thomas P. O'Neill, Jr.	72	1953	Massachusetts
Majority Leader	James C. Wright, Jr.	62	1955	Texas
Majority Whip	Thomas S. Foley	55	1965	Washington
Minority Leader	Robert H. Michel	61	1957	Illinois
Minority Whip	Trent Lott	43	1973	Mississippi
Committee Chairmen				
Agriculture	E (Kika) de la Garza	57	1965	Texas
Appropriations	Jamie L. Whitten	74	1941	Mississippi
Armed Services	Melvin Price	79	1945	Illinois
Banking, Finance and Urban Affairs	Fernand J. St. Germain	56	1961	Rhode Island
Budget	James R. Jones	45	1973	Oklahoma
District of Columbia	Ronald V. Dellums	49	1971	California
Education and Labor	Carl D. Perkins	72	1949	Kentucky
Energy and Commerce	John D. Dingell	72	1956	Michigan
Foreign Affairs	Dante Fascell	67	1955	Florida
Government Operations	Jack Brooks	77	1953	Texas
House Administration	Augustus F. Hawkins	62	1963	California
Interior and Insular Affairs	Morris K. Udall	58	1961	Arizona
Judiciary	Peter W. Rodino, Jr.	75	1949	New Jersey
Merchant Marine and Fisheries	Walter B. Jones	71	1966	North Carolina
Post Office and Civil Service	William D. Ford	57	1965	Michigan
Public Works and Transportation	James J. Howard	57	1965	New Jersey
Rules	Claude D. Pepper	83	1963	Florida
Science and Technology	Don Fuqua	51	1963	Florida
Small Business	Parren J. Mitchell	62	1971	Maryland
Standards of Official Conduct	Louis Stokes	59	1969	Ohio
Veterans' Affairs	Gillespie V. Montgomery	63	1967	Mississippi
Ways and Means	Dan Rostenkowski	56	1959	Illinois

As of birthdate in 1984.
Source: Congressional Directory, with additional data from the Clerk of the House.

in the chain that finally led to the downfall of the Nixon Presidency.

Most congressional investigations are not nearly so visible, nor are they very often so historic. Their more usual shape can be seen when, say, the House Committee on Agriculture looks at some problem in the farm price support system, or a subcommittee of the Senate Armed Services Committee is interested in the need to upgrade the housing of military dependents abroad.

Joint Committees

A **joint committee** is one that has members from both houses. Some are select committees, set up to serve some temporary purpose. Most are permanent groups which serve on a regular basis.

Some joint committees are investigative in nature and issue periodic reports to the House and Senate—for example, the Joint Economic Committee. Most of them have housekeeping duties, however—for example, the Joint Committee on the Library of Congress.

Because the standing committees of the two houses often duplicate one another's work, many have long urged that Congress make a much greater use of the joint committee device.

Conference Committees

Before a bill may be sent to the President, it must be passed in *identical form* by each house. Sometimes, the two houses pass differing versions of a measure, and the first house will not agree to the changes the other has made. When this happens a **conference committee**—a temporary, joint body—is created to iron out the differences in the bill. Its job is to produce a bill which both houses will accept.

We shall come back to the strategic role of the conference committee soon, on page 314.

 FOR REVIEW

1. What is a standing committee? How many are there in the House? In the Senate? Why are they called "subject-matter committees"? How are the members of each of them chosen?
2. What major role does the Rules Committee play in the House?
3. What is a select committee? A joint committee? A conference committee?
4. Why is the investigative power so important to Congress?

How a Bill Becomes a Law

As many as 20,000 bills are now introduced in the House and Senate during a term of Congress. Fewer than 10 percent of them ever become law. Where do these measures come from? Why are so few of them passed? What steps are taken in the House and the Senate when Congress makes law?

To answer these questions we shall first trace a bill through the House. Then, because the legislative process is quite similar in the upper chamber, we shall note the major differences to be found in the Senate.

Authorship and Introduction

Most of the bills introduced in either house do *not* originate with members of Congress themselves. Most of the more important measures—and the more routine ones, too—start in the executive agencies. Business, labor, agriculture, and other pressure groups often draft measures. Some, or at least the idea for them, come from private citizens who think "there ought to be a law . . ." And many are born in the standing committees of the House and Senate.

SENATE LEADERSHIP, 1984

Position	Name	Age[a]	Year Entered Senate[b]	State
Leadership				
Majority Leader	Howard Baker, Jr.	59	1967	Tennessee
Majority Whip	Ted Stevens	61	1968	Alaska
Minority Leader	Robert C. Byrd	66	1959 (1953)	West Virginia
Minority Whip	Alan Cranston	70	1969	California
Committee Chairmen				
Agriculture, Nutrition, and Forestry	Jesse A. Helms	63	1973	North Carolina
Appropriations	Mark O. Hatfield	62	1967	Oregon
Armed Services	John G. Tower	59	1961	Texas
Banking, Housing and Urban Affairs	Jake Garn	52	1975	Utah
Budget	Pete V. Domenici	52	1973	New Mexico
Commerce, Science, and Transportation	Bob Packwood	52	1969	Oregon
Energy and Natural Resources	James A. McClure	60	1973 (1967)	Idaho
Environment and Public Works	Robert T. Stafford	71	1971 (1961)	Vermont
Finance	Robert Dole	61	1969 (1961)	Kansas
Foreign Relations	Charles H. Percy	65	1967	Illinois
Governmental Affairs	William V. Roth	63	1971 (1967)	Delaware
Judiciary	Strom Thurmond	82	1954	South Carolina
Labor and Human Resources	Orrin G. Hatch	50	1977	Utah
Rules and Administration	Charles McC. Mathias	62	1969 (1961)	Maryland
Small Business	Lowell Weicker, Jr.	53	1971 (1969)	Connecticut
Veterans' Affairs	Alan K. Simpson	53	1979	Wyoming

[a]As of birthdate in 1984.
[b]Date in parentheses indicates first year of prior service in House of Representatives.
Source: Congressional Directory, with additional data from the Secretary of the Senate.

The Constitution states that all bills for the raising of revenue must originate —be first introduced—in the House.[10] All other kinds of bills may be introduced in either chamber. Once the lower house has passed a revenue measure, the Senate may amend it in the same manner as it may any other bill.

Only a member may introduce a bill in the House—and does so by dropping it into the "hopper."[11]

Types of Bills and Resolutions.

The thousands of measures—*bills* and *resolutions*—Congress considers at each session take several forms:

[10]Article I, Section 7, Clause 1.
[11]The hopper is a large box hanging at the edge of the Clerk's desk. Only a Senator may introduce a measure in the upper house; he or she does so by addressing the chair.

Drawing by Richter. ©The New Yorker Magazine, Inc.

"My folks are in the gallery. If you can work it in, would you mind terribly calling me 'my esteemed colleague'?"

Bills are proposed laws, drafts of laws presented to the House or Senate for enactment. Each bill's enacting clause reads: "Be it enacted by the Senate and House of Representatives of the United States of America in Congress assembled, That . . ." and the content of the measure follows.

Public bills are measures applying to the nation as a whole, as, for example, a tax measure, an amendment to the copyright laws, or an appropriation of funds for the armed forces.

Private bills are those measures which apply to certain persons or places rather than to the nation generally. For example, a few years ago Congress passed an act to pay a man in Wyoming $1229.52. This was the amount he would have made on a government contract had a local post office handled his mail promptly.

Joint Resolutions are little different from bills and when passed have the force of law. The wording of the enacting clause is: "Resolved by the Senate and House of Representatives of the United States of America in Congress assembled, That. . . ." They most often deal with unusual or temporary matters. For example, they may appropriate money for the presidential inauguration ceremonies, or correct an error in a statute already passed. Joint resolutions are also used to propose constitutional amendments (see page 56) and have been used for territorial annexations (page 395).

Concurrent Resolutions deal with matters in which the House and Senate must act jointly but for which a law is not needed. They usually begin in this form: "Resolved by the Senate, the House of Representatives concurring, That . . ." They are used most often by Congress to state a position, an opinion, on some matter—for example, in foreign affairs.

Resolutions deal with matters concerning either house alone and are taken up only by that house. A simple resolution regularly begins: "Resolved by the Senate [or House], That . . ."

A bill or resolution usually deals with a single subject, but sometimes a *rider* dealing with a quite unrelated matter is included. A **rider** is a provision, not likely to pass on its own merit, attached to an important measure certain to pass. Its sponsors hope that it will "ride" through the legislative process on the strength of the other measure. (Presidents sometimes veto a bill because of an objectionable rider.)

Reference to Committee

The Clerk of the House *numbers* each bill as it is introduced. Thus, H.R. 3410 would be the 3410th measure introduced in the House during the congressional term.[12] The Clerk also gives each bill a *short title* (a very brief summary of its principal contents).

Having received its number and short title, the bill is then entered in the House *Journal* and in the *Congressional Record* for the day.[13]

With these actions the bill has received its *first reading*. Each bill that is

---

[12]Bills originating in the Senate receive the prefix "S."—as S. 210. Resolutions are similarly identified in each house in order of their introduction. Thus, H.J. Res. 12 would be the 12th joint resolution introduced in the House during the term and, similarly, S.J. Res. 19. Concurrent resolutions are identified as H. Con. Res. 16 or S. Con. Res. 4 and simple resolutions as H. Res. 198 or S. Res. 166.

[13]The *Journal* contains the minutes, the official record, of the daily proceedings in the House (Senate). The *Journal* for the preceding day is read at the beginning of each daily session, unless the chamber agrees to dispense with that reading (as almost always happens). The *Congressional Record* is a voluminous account of the daily proceedings (speeches, debates, other comments, votes, motions, etc.) in each house. The *Record* is not quite a word-for-word account, however. Members have five days in which to make changes in each temporary edition. They often insert lengthy speeches that were in fact never made on the floor, reconstruct "debates," and take out or revise thoughtless or inaccurate remarks. The *Record* is, nonetheless, extraordinarily valuable, both politically and historically.

Hazel Rollins, who served as Deputy Administrator of DOE's Economic Regulatory Administration during the Carter Administration, gives testimony on the costs of nuclear power plant shutdowns.

finally passed in either house is given three "readings" along the legislative route. In the House *second reading* comes during floor consideration, if the measure gets that far. And *third reading* takes place just before the final vote on the measure.[14]

Each of these readings is usually by title only: "H.R. 3410, A bill to provide . . ." However, the more important or controversial bills are read in full and taken up line by line, section by section, at second reading—that is, during consideration on the floor.

After first reading, the Speaker refers the bill to the standing committee with jurisdiction over its subject matter.

The Committee Stage

The standing committees have been described as "sieves," sifting out most bills and considering and reporting only those they judge to be the more important or worthwhile ones. As Woodrow Wilson once wrote, "Congress in its committee rooms is Congress at work."

Most bills die in committee. They are "pigeonholed,"[15] and most deserve that fate. At times, however, a committee pigeonholes a measure that a majority of the House wishes to consider. When that happens, the bill can be "blasted out" of the committee with a discharge petition.[16] But this is not often successful.

Those bills that a committee, or at least its chairman, does wish to consider

---

[14]All bills introduced are immediately printed and distributed to the members. The three readings, an ancient parliamentary practice, are intended to ensure careful consideration of bills and prevent any of them from slipping by with little or no notice. The practice is not very significant today; in effect, the readings are now way stations along the legislative route. But they were quite important in the day when, quite literally, some members of Congress could not read.

[15]The term comes from the old-fashioned roll-top desks with pigeonholes into which papers were put and promptly forgotten. Most of the so-called "by-request" bills are routinely pigeonholed. These are measures that many members introduce—but only because some person or some pressure group has asked them to.

[16]After a bill has been in committee for at least 30 days (seven days in the Rules Committee) any member may file a *discharge motion*. If that motion (in effect, a petition) is signed by a majority (218) of House members, the committee has seven days in which to report the bill. If it does not, any member who signed the petition may (on the second and fourth Mondays of each month) move that the committee be discharged (relieved of the bill). Debate on the motion to discharge is limited to 20 minutes. If the motion carries, the House turns to floor consideration of the discharged bill at once.

are discussed and considered at times chosen by the chairman. Most committees work through **subcommittees**—"committees within committees." Where more important or controversial measures are involved, committees usually hold public hearings on them. Interested persons, pressure groups and other private organizations, and government officials are invited to testify at those hearings.[17]

At times subcommittees make **junkets** (trips) to areas affected by a measure. Thus, some members of the House Agriculture Committee may journey to the Southwest to look into drought conditions. Or, members of the Senate Energy and Natural Resources Committee may visit the Pacific Northwest to gather information on a public power bill.

These junkets are made at public expense, and members of Congress are sometimes criticized for taking them. But an on-the-spot investigation often proves to be the best way a committee can inform itself.

After examining a bill, the full committee may do one of several things. It may:

(1) Report the bill favorably, with a "do pass" recommendation. It is then the chairman's job to steer the bill through debate on the floor.

(2) Refuse to report the bill—pigeonhole it.

(3) Report the bill in amended form. Many bills are changed in committee, and several bills on the same subject may be combined into a single measure before they are reported out.

(4) Report the bill with an unfavorable recommendation. This does not often happen. But sometimes a committee feels that the full body should have a chance to consider a bill or does not want to take the responsibility for killing it.

(5) Report a "committee bill." In effect, this is an entirely new bill which the committee has substituted for one or more referred to it.

The Rules Committee and the Calendars

Before it goes to the floor for consideration, a bill reported by a standing committee is placed on one of several calendars. A **calendar** is a schedule of the order in which bills will be taken up on the floor. There are five of these calendars in the House:

(1) *The Calendar of the Committee of the Whole House on the State of the Union*, commonly known as the *Union Calendar*—for all bills having to do with revenues, appropriations, or government property.

(2) *The House Calendar*—for all other public bills.

(3) *The Calendar of the Committee of the Whole House*, commonly called the *Private Calendar*—for all private bills.

(4) *The Consent Calendar*—for all bills from the Union or House Calendar which are taken up out of order by unanimous consent of the House of Representatives. These are most often minor bills to which there is no opposition.

(5) *The Discharge Calendar*—for petitions to discharge bills from committee.

In theory, bills are taken from each of these calendars on a regularly scheduled basis, under the rules of the House. Bills from the Consent Calendar are to be considered on the first and third Mondays of each month. Measures relating to the District of Columbia are to be taken up on the second and fourth Mon-

---

[17]If necessary, a committee may *subpoena* witnesses. A **subpoena** is an order compelling one to appear. Failure to obey a subpoena may lead the House (or Senate) to pass a resolution citing the offender for contempt of Congress—a federal crime punishable in court.

RECOGNIZING BIAS

ON THE LEVEL?

Congressional Candidate A: During my last term, more new jobs were created than when the other party was in power. Re-elect me and together we will work for an even stronger economy!

Congressional Candidate B: During my opponent's term in office, unemployment rose to a very high level. We cannot afford any more of that. Elect me and together we will work for a strong economy!

Which candidate should you believe? How can you tell if candidates and other people are presenting information fairly or if they are slanting it to favor their own positions? The ability to detect *bias* is important because it keeps us from being misled and making poor decisions. **Bias** is an attitude for or against something or someone. When we say that a presentation is biased, we usually mean that it misrepresents information to favor or discredit a particular position.

Biases develop from previous experience, beliefs, and self-interest (personal goals). Everyone has biases, and most of us act in a biased manner some of the time. Our biases often influence how we see and interpret things.

Biased information can take several forms. It can be inaccurate, incomplete, or distorted by propaganda devices; see Chapter 10. Card-stacking, for example, is a propaganda device that is common in politics. It occurs when the people and groups taking different sides of an issue stack or slant the facts to favor their position. They do this by emphasizing some facts (the ones that support their position) and ignoring others. They tell the truth—but not the whole story—thus distorting the information we receive.

Bias often occurs in the presentation of numbers· or statistics. Usually the numbers are accurate, but they are chosen and used in ways that attempt to convince people to support a particular candidate or policy. Both Republicans and Democrats, for example, oppose high rates of unemployment and claim that their policies are the best way to create more jobs. In periods of high unemployment, the party in power is likely to claim that its policies are working because unemployment has dropped, say from 9.8 to 9.2 percent. The opposing party, in contrast, is likely to claim that new policies are needed because a 9.2 percnt unemployment rate is too high. The parties agree on the numbers, but they interpret and use them differently.

In the example at the beginning, both candidates were correct about jobs and unemployment, but neither was telling the whole story. Each candidate's presentation is biased because it is incomplete, presenting only the information that supports the candidate's position and self-interest. How can there be more jobs *and* higher unemployment rates? (As the total population increases, it takes more jobs to maintain the same rate of employment. So, if the number of jobs increases, but not as much as the total population, the unemployment rate also will increase.)

days, and private bills every Friday. On "Calendar Wednesdays" the various committee chairmen may call up any bills that have cleared their committees.

None of these arrangements is followed too closely, however. What often happens, instead, is quite complicated. First, remember, the Rules Committee plays a critical role here. It must grant a rule before most bills can in fact reach the floor. That is, before a measure can be taken from a calendar the Rules Committee must approve that step, set a time for its appearance on the floor.

By failing or refusing to grant a rule for a bill, the Rules Committee can quite effectively kill it. Or, when it does grant a rule, that rule may be a **special rule**—one setting conditions under which the measure will be considered. A special rule regularly sets a time limit on floor debate. It may even provide that amendments may not be offered to certain or even any of the bill's provisions.

Then, too, certain bills are "privileged." They may be called up at almost any time—ahead of any other less privileged business before the House. The most highly privileged measures include general revenue (important tax) and major appropriations (spending) bills, conference committees reports, *and* special rules from the Rules Committee.

On certain days (usually the first and third Mondays and Tuesdays), the House may suspend its rules. To do so, a motion to that effect must be approved by a two-thirds vote of the members present. When that happens, as it sometimes does, the House moves so far away from its established procedures that a measure can go through all of the steps necessary to enactment in a single day.

All of this—the calenders, the role of the Rules Committee, and the other complex procedures have developed over time, and for several reasons. In major part, they have because of (1) the large size of the House and (2) the sheer number and variety of bills its members introduced. And they have, too, because no one member could possibly know the contents, let alone the merits, of every bill upon which he or she may have to vote.

Consideration on the Floor

When a bill does finally reach the floor it receives its *second reading.*

Many of the bills the House passes are minor ones, to which there is little or no opposition. Most of them are called from the Consent Calendar, get their second reading by title only, and are quickly disposed of.

Nearly all of the more important measures are dealt with in a much different manner, however. They are considered in *Committee of the Whole,* an old parliamentary device for speeding business on the floor.

The **Committee of the Whole** is the House sitting not as itself but as one large committee of itself. Its rules are much less strict and floor action moves along at a faster pace. A **quorum** (majority of the full membership, 218) must be present in order for the House to do business; but only 100 members need be present in Committee of the Whole.

When the House resolves itself into Committee of the Whole, the Speaker steps down, for the House is not legally in session. Another member presides.

General debate is held, and then the bill receives its second reading, section-by-section. As each section is read, amendments may be offered. Under the "five-minute rule," supporters and opponents of each amendment have just that long to make their case. Votes are taken on each section and its amendment as the reading proceeds.

When the bill has been gone through —and many run to dozens of pages—the Committee of the Whole has completed its work. It then "rises"—dissolves it-self. The House is now back in session, the Speaker resumes the chair and the committee's work is formally adopted.

Debate. Its large size has long since forced the House to impose severe limits on floor debate. A rule first adopt-ed in 1841 forbids any member to hold the floor for more than one hour, unless he or she has unanimous consent to speak for a longer time. Since 1880 the Speaker has had the power to force any member who strays from the subject at hand to give up the floor—in short, to stop talking and sit down.

The majority and minority floor leaders generally decide in advance how they will split the time to be spent on a bill. But, at any time, any member may "move the previous question." That is, any member may demand a vote on the issue before the House. If that motion passes, only 40 minutes of further de-bate is allowed before a vote is taken. This device is the only motion that can be used in the House to **close** (end) debate, but it is a very effective one.

Voting. A bill may be (often is) the subject of several different votes on the floor. If amendments are offered to it, as they frequently are, each of them must be voted up or down. Then, too a num-ber of procedural motions may be presented—for example, one to **table** the bill (lay it aside), another for the previ-ous question, and so on. (These several other votes can be a better guide to a bill's friends and foes than is the final vote itself. Sometimes, a member votes for a bill which is now certain to pass—even though he/she supported amend-ments to it which, if they had been adopted would in fact have scuttled it.

The House uses four different meth-ods for the taking of floor votes:

(*1*) **Voice votes** are the most com-mon. The Speaker calls for the "ayes" and then the "noes," the members an-swer in chorus, and the Speaker then announces the result.

(*2*) If any member thinks the Speaker has erred in judging a voice vote, he or she may demand a **standing vote** (also known as **a division of the House**). All in favor, and then all opposed, stand and are counted by the Clerk.

(*3*) A **teller vote** may be demanded by one-fifth of a quorum (44 members in the House or 20 in Committee of the Whole). When this procedure is used, the Speaker names two tellers, one from each party; the members pass between them and are counted, for and against. (Teller votes are rare today; the practice has been replaced by electronic voting; see below.)

(*4*) A **roll-call vote,** also known as a **record vote,** may be demanded by one-fifth of the members present.[18]

In 1973 the house installed a compu-terized voting system for all quorum calls and record votes—to replace the roll-call by the Clerk. Members now vote at any of 48 stations on the floor, by inserting a personalized plastic card in a box and then pushing one of three buttons—"Yea," "Nay," or "Present."[19]

A large master board, high above the Speaker's chair, shows instantly how each member has voted. Smaller summary boards on the balcony ledges on either side of the chamber show the running vote totals and the time remaining for members to cast votes. The leadership tables on either side of the center aisle have consoles so that the majority and minority floor leaders may

[18]The Constitution (Article I, Section 7, Clause 2) requires a record vote on the question of overriding a presidential veto. No record votes are taken in Commit-tee of the Whole.

[19]The "Present" button is most often used for a **quorum call**—a check to make sure that a quorum of the members is in fact present. Otherwise, it is used when a member does not wish to vote on a question but still wants to be recorded as present. A "present" vote is not allowed on some questions—for example, overrid-ing a veto.

Floor proceedings in the House (but not the Senate) have been regularly televised since 1979. Occasionally, segments of the televised coverage are broadcast on national network news programs.

follow voting patterns and the behavior of each member.

The House rules allow the members 15 minutes in which to answer quorum calls or cast record votes. Voting ends when the Speaker pushes a button to lock the electronic system. That action also produces a permanent record of the vote. (Under the former roll-call process, it took the Clerk anywhere from 25 to 45 minutes to call each member's name and record his or her vote. (Before 1973, roll-calls took up about *three months* of House floor time each session.)

The computer also keeps track of every measure in both the House and Senate, reporting its legislative history and current status through an information retrieval system.

Voting procedures are much the same in the Senate. That is, the upper house uses voice, standing, and roll-call votes. But the Senate does not take teller votes. Nor does it use an electronic voting process. Only six or seven minutes are needed for the taking of a roll-call vote in the upper chamber.

Final Steps in the House

Once a bill has been approved at second reading, it is **engrossed**—that is, printed in its final form. Then it is read a third time, by title, and a final vote is taken. If it is approved at *third reading*, as nearly all bills which reach that stage are, it is signed by the Speaker. A page then carries it to the Senate and places it on the Vice President's (Senate President's) desk.

The Bill in the Senate

The steps in the lawmaking process are quite similar in both houses. So, we need not trace a bill through the Senate in the detail with which we reviewed that process in the House. Rather, we shall look at the major contrasts to be found in the upper house.

Bills are introduced by Senators, who are formally recognized for that purpose. A measure is then given a number and short title, read twice, and then referred to committee—where bills are dealt with much as they are in the House.

All in all, the Senate's proceedings are less formal and its rules less strict than those of the much larger House. Thus, for example, the Senate has only one calendar for all bills reported out by its committees. Bills are called to the floor at the discretion of the majority floor leader.[20]

Debate

The major differences in House and Senate procedures are found in floor debates. They are strictly limited in the House but almost unfettered in the Senate. Indeed, most Senators are intensely

---

[20]The Senate does have another, nonlegislative calendar, the **Executive Calendar**—for treaties and appointments made by the President and awaiting Senate approval (or, rarely, rejection). The majority leader controls that schedule, too.

HOW BILLS BECOME LAWS

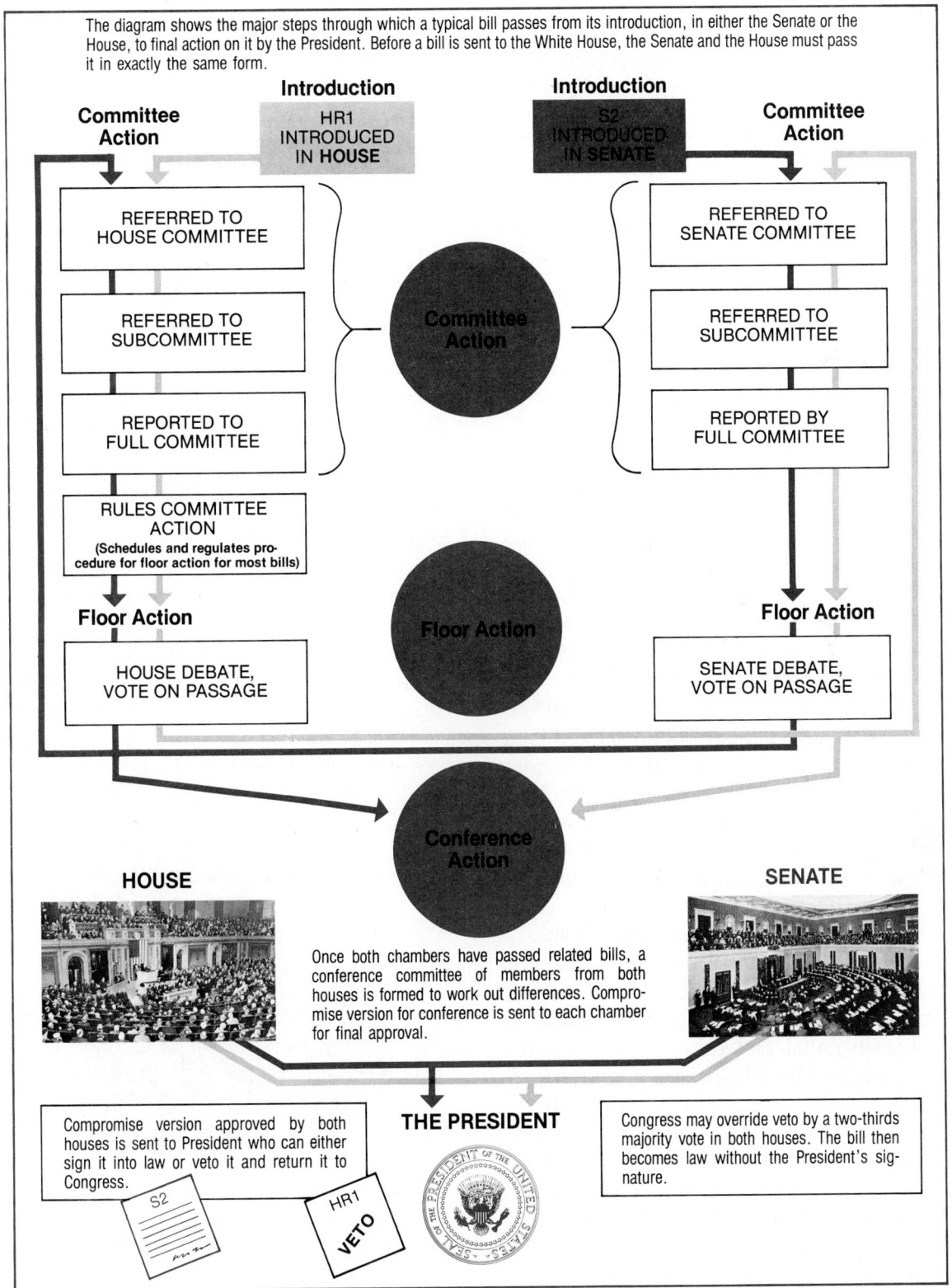

The diagram shows the major steps through which a typical bill passes from its introduction, in either the Senate or the House, to final action on it by the President. Before a bill is sent to the White House, the Senate and the House must pass it in exactly the same form.

Introduction
HR1 INTRODUCED IN **HOUSE**

Introduction
S2 INTRODUCED IN **SENATE**

Committee Action

REFERRED TO HOUSE COMMITTEE

REFERRED TO SUBCOMMITTEE

REPORTED TO FULL COMMITTEE

RULES COMMITTEE ACTION
(Schedules and regulates procedure for floor action for most bills)

Committee Action

REFERRED TO SENATE COMMITTEE

REFERRED TO SUBCOMMITTEE

REPORTED BY FULL COMMITTEE

Committee Action

Floor Action
HOUSE DEBATE, VOTE ON PASSAGE

Floor Action
SENATE DEBATE, VOTE ON PASSAGE

Floor Action

Conference Action

HOUSE

SENATE

Once both chambers have passed related bills, a conference committee of members from both houses is formed to work out differences. Compromise version for conference is sent to each chamber for final approval.

Compromise version approved by both houses is sent to President who can either sign it into law or veto it and return it to Congress.

THE PRESIDENT

Congress may override veto by a two-thirds majority vote in both houses. The bill then becomes law without the President's signature.

S2 / HR1 VETO

Heather Hutchins

proud of belonging to what has often been called "the greatest deliberative body in the world."

As a general matter, Senators may speak on the floor for as long as they please. There is no rule that they speak only to the measure under consideration. And, unlike the House, the Senate's rules do not allow the moving of the previous question.

The Senate's consideration of most major bills is brought to a close by **unanimous consent** agreements. That is, discussion ends and a final vote is taken at a fixed time previously agreed to by the majority and minority leaders. But if any Senator objects—prevents unanimous consent—the device fails.[21]

The Senate's dedication to freedom of debate is, well-nigh unique among modern legislative bodies. It is intended to encourage the fullest possible discussion of matters on the floor, of course. But the great latitude it allows can be—and has been and is—abused by the *filibuster.*

The Filibuster.   Essentially, a **filibuster** is an attempt to "talk a bill to death." It is a stalling tactic. It is a process in which a minority of Senators seeks to delay or prevent Senate action on a measure. The filibusterers try to so monopolize the floor and the time of the Senate that that body must either drop the bill before it or change it in some manner acceptable to the minority.

Talk is the filibusterers' major weapon—talking, holding the floor, on and on. But many time-killing motions, quorum calls, and other parliamentary maneuvers are also used.

---

[21]The Senate does have a "two-speech rule." Under it, no Senator may speak more than twice on a given question on the same legislative day. By **recessing** (temporarily interrupting) rather than adjourning (ending) a day's session the Senate can prolong a "legislative day" indefinitely. Thus, the two-speech rule does have some limiting effect on the amount of time the Senate spends on some matters on its agenda.

The history of the Senate is liberally dotted with filibusters—many of them prolonged and dramatic. Most of them have been team efforts, in which a small group of Senators speak in relay, passing the possession of the floor back and forth among themselves, indefinitely.

Among the many better known filibusterers, Senator Huey Long (D., Louisiana) spoke for more than 15 hours in 1935. He stalled along by reading from the Washington telephone directory and a mail-order catalogue and gave his colleagues his recipes for "pot-likker," corn bread, and turnip greens. In 1947, Glen Taylor (D., Idaho) used more than eight hours of floor time, talking of his children, Wall Street, baptism, and fishing.

The current filibuster record was set 25 years ago. Senator Strom Thurmond (R., South Carolina) held the floor for 24 hours and 18 minutes in an unsuccessful, one-man effort against what later became the Civil Rights Act of 1957.

No later efforts have come close to matching that one. But the practice remains often used and often effective in the Senate. Over the past century and

Drawing by Richter. ©New Yorker Magazine, Inc.

"And as the ant said to the grasshopper . . ."

more, well over 200 measures have been killed by filibusters. And the *threat* of a filibuster has resulted in the Senate's failure to consider a number of bills, and the amending of many more.

The Senate often tries to beat off a filibuster with lengthy (even day-and-night) sessions, to wear down the participants. At times, some little-observed rules are quite strictly enforced—for example, the requirement that Senators stand, not sit, lean on their desks, or walk about as they speak; or that they not use "unparliamentory language." But these tactics seldom work.

The Cloture Rule. The Senate's real check on the filibuster is its *Cloture Rule*—Rule XXII in the Standing Rules of the Senate. It was first adopted in 1917, after one of the most notable of all of the many filibusters in Senate history.[22]

Rule XXII provides for **cloture** (limiting debate). But the rule is not in regular and continuing force. It can be brought into play only by a special procedure. As it now stands: A vote to invoke the rule must be taken two days after a petition calling for that action has been submitted by at least 16 members of the Senate. If at least 60 Senators—three-fifths of the full Senate—then vote for the mo-

tion, the rule becomes effective. Each member is then allowed no more than one hour of debate on the pending bill. Then the measure *must* be brought to a final vote.

Invoking the rule is no easy matter. Thus far, from 1917 to 1983, 187 attempts have been made. Only 60 of them succeeded.

The record shows that the Senate is now more willing to invoke cloture than was the case only a few years ago, however. Nearly three-fourths of all of the attempts to close debate—138 of them—have come since 1970. Nearly all of the successful ones (52) have come in that same period.

☑ FOR REVIEW

1. Who may introduce a bill in the House? The Senate?
2. Identify the different types of measures that are introduced in either house.
3. What happens at first reading in the House?
4. Who refers bills to committee in the House? The Senate?
5. What is the function of the various calendars in the House?
6. What is the Committee of the Whole?
7. By what four methods does the House take floor votes? What three are used in the Senate?
8. Contrast the regulation of floor debate in the House and Senate. What is a filibuster? The Cloture Rule?

---

[22]That filibuster lasted for some three weeks, and took place less than two months before the United States entered World War I (April 6, 1917). In February, German submarines had renewed their attacks on shipping in the North Atlantic. Immediately, President Wilson asked Congress for legislation to permit the arming of American merchant vessels. The bill, widely supported in the country, was quickly passed by the House, by a vote of 403–12. The measure died in the Senate, however. It had strong support there, but 12 Senators filibustered it until the end of the congressional term on March 4th. The public was outraged. President Wilson declared: "A little group of willful men, representing no opinion but their own, has rendered the great Government of the United States helpless and contemptible." The Cloture Rule was passed by the Senate at its next session, later that same year.

The Final Stages

Any measure enacted by Congress *must* have been passed by both houses in *identical* form. Most often, a bill

Shown in session is the Senate Foreign Relations Committee. Third from the the front is the Committee's Chairman, Senator Charles Percy (R., Illinois).

passed by one house and then approved by the other is not amended in the second chamber. When the House and Senate do pass different versions of the same bill, the first house usually "concurs" in the other's amendments—and, so, congressional action is completed.

The Conference Committee

There are times, however, when the House or the Senate will not accept the other's version of a bill. When this happens, the measure is turned over to a conference committee—a temporary joint committee of the two houses. It seeks to "iron out" the differences and come up with a compromise bill.

The conferees ("managers") are named by the respective presiding officers. Mostly, they are leading members of the standing committee that first handled the measure in each house.

Both the House and Senate rules restrict a conference committee to the consideration of those points in a bill on which the two houses disagree. They also say that the committee cannot in-

clude any entirely new material in its compromise version. But, in practice, the "conferees' product very often contains provisions that were not even considered in either house.

Once the conferees agree, their report—the compromise bill—is submitted to both houses. It must be accepted or rejected without amendment —and only rarely does either house turn down a conference committee's work. (That a bill hammered out by a conference committee is seldom rejected by either house is not too surprising, for two major reasons: (1) the potent membership of the typical conference committee, and (2) the fact that its report usually comes in the midst of the rush to adjournment at the end of a congressional session.)

In short, the conference committee stage is a most strategic step in the legislative process. It is a point at which a number of major legislative decisions are made. Indeed, the late Senator George Norris (R., Nebraska) once quite aptly described conference committees as "the third house of Congress."

The President's Action

The Constitution requires that

Every bill which shall have passed the House of Representatives and the Senate [and] every order, resolution, or vote, to which the concurrence of the Senate and House of Representatives may be necessary (except on a question of adjournment) shall be submitted to the President. . . .[23]

and the Constitution presents the President with four options at this point:

First, the President may sign the bill, and it then becomes law.

Second, the President may veto the

---

[23]Article I, Section 7, Clauses 2 and 3. We shall return to the President's veto power in Chapter 15, on pages 399–400.

bill. The measure must then be returned to the house in which it began, together with the President's objections (a veto message). Although it seldom does, Congress may then pass the bill over the President's veto, by a two-thirds vote in each house.

Third, the President may allow the bill to become law without signing it—by not acting upon it (neither signing nor vetoing it) within 10 days (not counting Sundays) of receiving it.

The *fourth* option is a variation of the third. If Congress adjourns its session within 10 days of submitting a bill to the President, and the Chief Executive does not act upon it, the measure dies—the "pocket veto" has been applied to it.

☑ FOR REVIEW

1. When is a conference committee formed? What is its job?
2. Why is a conference committee's report seldom rejected by either house?
3. What four options does the President have upon receiving a measure passed by Congress?

the small society   by Brickman

© King Features Syndicate

S U M M A R Y

Opening day in the House of Representatives each term is filled with ceremony. A Speaker must be chosen, the members sworn, non-member officers selected, rules adopted, and committee and other organization posts filled. The Senate's first day is a much more routine one, for it is a continuous body.

Once organized, the two houses await the President's State of the Union Message. In this annual address the Chief Executive reports on the condition of the nation and generally makes several legislative recommendations and other policy pronouncements.

The Speaker is the presiding officer of the House of Representatives and its most powerful member. The Vice President (or, in that officer's absence, the President *pro tem*) presides over the Senate.

In both houses, each party has an organizational structure dominated by the majority (or minority) floor leader, chosen by the party's caucus.

Congress does much of its work in committees. The standing committees are the regular, permanent committees of both chambers, and they are dominated by their respective chairmen (who are chosen under the seniority rule). The select committees are temporary, special committees in each house. Joint committees (made up of members of both houses) are usually permanent bodies. Conference committees are temporary joint committees formed to "iron out" differences in measures passed by the two chambers.

Bills may be introduced in the House only by Representatives and in the Senate only by the members of that body—but they usually come from some other source such as the executive branch or a pressure group. Following introduction, bills go to the appropriate standing committees, where most of them die. Bills reported out of committee in the House go on one of five calendars and must clear the Rules Committee in order to reach the floor. There is but one calendar in the Senate, and bills are called up by the majority floor leader.

Bills are debated in the House at the second of three readings. The House, but not the Senate, considers most important bills in Committee of the Whole. Debate is severely limited in the House, but not in the Senate. A filibuster, the practice of talking a bill to death, may be stopped in the Senate by the difficult process of invoking cloture.

The House takes voice votes, standing votes, teller votes, and roll-call (record) votes.

The Senate does not use teller votes. The House, but not the Senate, now uses an electronic voting system for its roll-calls.

A measure enacted by Congress must have passed both houses in the same form, and a conference committee is sometimes necessary to that end. From Congress, a bill goes to the President, who may sign it, veto it, allow it to become law without signature, or (at the close of a session) pocket veto it. Congress may override a presidential veto by a two-thirds vote in each house.

CHAPTER REVIEW

Key Terms/Concepts

Bill (304)
Calendar (306)
Caucus (293)
Clerk of the House (293)
Cloture (313)
Committee (298)
Committee of the Whole (308)
Concur (314)
Concurrent resolution (304)
Conference Committee (314)
Congressional Record (304)
Convene (292)
Discharge petition (305)
Division of the house (309)
Filibuster (312)
First, second, third reading (304, 305)
House (Senate) *Journal* (304)
House Rules Committee (300)

Joint committee (302)
Joint resolution (304)
Junket (306)
Majority floor leader (297)
Minority floor leader (297)
Oversight function (300)
Party whip (297)
Pigeonhole (305)
Pocket veto (315)
President *pro tem* (296)
President of the Senate (296)
Presiding officer (294)
Private bill (304)
Public bill (304)
Recess (312)
Record vote (309)
Resolution (304)
Rider (304)
Roll-call vote (309)
Select committee (300)

Seniority rule (298)
Speaker of the House (294)
Special rule (308)
Standing committee (299)
Standing vote (309)
State of the Union Message (294)

Subcommittee (306)
Teller vote (309)
Unanimous consent procedure (312)
Veto (314)
Vice President (296)
Voice vote (309)

Keynote Questions

1. Who is the presiding officer of the House? The Senate? How is each of them selected?
2. Who chooses the floor leaders in each house? The whips? What are their functions?
3. How are committee chairmen chosen? Why are they so powerful? What is the seniority rule?
4. Identify the several types of committees involved in the legislative process. Describe the special role of the House Rules Committee.
5. Identify the different types of measures that may be introduced in either house.
6. Outline the legislative process in both houses and cite the major differ-

ences between Senate and House procedures.

7. What is a filibuster? The Cloture Rule?

8. What is the function of a conference committee?

9. What three options does the President usually have when Congress sends a measure to the White House? What is the pocket veto?

For Thought and Discussion

1. The daily sessions of the House are now carried by many cable TV systems around the country. If these broadcasts are available in your area, you can learn much about the House, the legislative process, and much more by watching them, of course. Do you think that the sessions of the House and/or the Senate should be televised? Why, or why not?

2. The *Congressional Record* reports the way in which each member responds to every roll-call vote in either house. Why might a Representative or a Senator not wish to vote on certain roll calls?

3. Many have long urged that the Senate do away with the filibuster and that both houses give up the seniority rule. How do you feel about each of these practices? What other reforms in congressional organization or procedure do you think should be made?

4. Senator Bob Packwood (R., Oregon) was first elected to the Senate in 1968. He won his seat in a close contest with the then-senior Senator from his State, Wayne Morse, who had been in the Senate for 24 years. In his bid to unseat Morse, Packwood was a strong critic of the seniority rule. He has since changed his mind, however. Now he says: "The longer I'm in the Senate, the better I like the rule." What is he really saying in that comment?

5. Explain this comment: "Ideally, a member of Congress should be both responsive and responsible." Are either or both of these characteristics desirable? Are they necessary? Is one of them more important (or more desirable) than the other?

6. Why do you think the Framers of the Constitution provided that: (a) "All bills for raising revenue shall originate in the House of Representatives . . ." (Article I, Section 7, Clause 1), and (b) "No money shall be drawn from the treasury, but in consequence of appropriations made by law" (Article I, Section 9, Clause 7)?

Suggested Activities

1. Stage a debate or class forum on one of the following questions: (2) *Resolved,* That the seniority rule be abolished in both houses of Congress; (b) *Resolved,* That filibusters be prohibited in the Senate; (c) *Resolved,* That the members of each house of Congress be required to vote for or against major pieces of legislation in accord with the positions taken by their respective party caucuses.

2. Select some major (or at least interesting) bill now in either house in Congress. Trace its origins and follow its progress through the legislative mill. Newspaper files, Congressional Quarterly's *Weekly Report,* the *Congressional Record,* and information and other materials from your Representative and/or Senators would be most helpful in this project.

3. Prepare a report on one or more of these topics: (a) The Speaker of the House; (b) The House Rules Committee; (c) The Seniority Rule; (d) Filibusters in the Senate; (e) Congressional reform; (f) Conference committees; (g) The Library of Congress.

13

The Powers of Congress

CHAPTER OBJECTIVES

To help you to
Learn ▪ Know ▪ Understand

The scope of the powers of Congress, in a governmental system both limited and federal in character.

The concepts of expressed and implied powers.

The several expressed powers of Congress.

The Necessary and Proper Clause and the broad field of implied powers.

The nonlegislative powers exercised by Congress.

All legislative powers herein granted shall be vested in a Congress of the United States. . . .

Article I, Section 1, Constitution of the United States

As the opening words of Article I of the Constitution state, the basic function of the Congress is to legislate, to make law. As we've pointed out several times, that function is of pivotal importance to democratic government. It is the function of translating the public will into public policy in the form of law.

In this chapter we look at the two basic categories of power held and exercised by Congress: First, its *legislative powers*—those constitutional powers which form the base upon which Congress can and does make law. And, secondly, its *nonlegislative powers*—those constitutional powers with which the two houses can and do carry out other functions closely connected to its role as the lawmaking branch of the National Government.

Scope of Congressional Powers. At this point it would be well to remember two fundamentally important facts—for each of them has a large impact upon each and all of the powers held by Congress. First, that government in the United States is *limited* government. And, secondly, that the American system of government is a *federal* system.

In 1868, the House *impeached* (brought charges against) President Andrew Johnson for removing several public officials from office. The Senate (shown above) served as *judge* (sat as a court to try) in the case; it found Johnson not guilty. *Facing page:* "The Mace," symbol of authority in the House of Representatives.

The Constitution places a great many restrictions and prohibitions upon Congress—as it does upon the National Government as a whole. Large areas of power are denied to Congress. They are denied in so many words by the Constitution, because of its silence on many matters, and because of the federal system itself.

In short, Congress has *only* those powers delegated to it by the Constitution. The power to do many things is not granted to it. Thus, Congress cannot create a national public school system, require that all eligible citizens vote on election day, nor insist that all persons attend church. It cannot pass a marriage and divorce law for the nation, set a minimum age for drivers' licenses, nor prohibit trial by jury. It cannot do these and a great many other things because it has not been given the power to do them.

Remember too, that Congress *does* have the power to do a great many things. The Constitution delegates specific powers to Congress in three different ways. It does so: (1) Expressly, in so many words (the *expressed powers*). (2) By implication, that is by reasonable deduction from the expressed powers (the *implied powers*). And (3) from the fact that it creates a *national* government for the United States (the *inherent powers*).

Strict Versus Liberal Construction

The Framers of the Constitution intended to create a stronger National Government. As we know, the ratification of their plan was stoutly opposed. The Federalist-Anti-Federalist conflict continued into the early years of the Republic.

Through those early years, that conflict centered on the extent of the powers granted to Congress. How broad, in fact, were they?

The **strict-constructionists**, led by Thomas Jefferson, continued to argue the Anti-Federalist position from the ratification period. They believed that Congress should be able to exercise *only* those powers spelled out in the Constitution. They wanted the States to keep as much power as possible. In short, they agreed with Jefferson that "that government is best which governs least."

The **liberal-constructionists**, led by Alexander Hamilton, had led the fight to adopt the Constitution. Now, they favored a liberal or broad interpretation of the Constitution. Most of all, they wanted a broad construction of the powers given to Congress.

The liberal-constructionists won, as we shall see (page 335). Their victory set a pattern which has been generally followed to the present day.

Several factors, working together with a liberal construction of the Constitution, have been responsible for a marked growth in national power. Wars, economic crises, and other national emergencies have been prominent causes. The spectacular advances we have made—especially in transportation and communication—have also had a real impact. And so have the demands of the people themselves for more and still more services from government.

Congress has been led by these and other factors to view its powers in broader and broader terms. Most Presidents have regarded and exercised their powers in similar fashion. The Supreme Court, in deciding cases involving the extent of the powers of the National Government, has generally taken a like position. And the American people have generally agreed with a liberal rather than a strict interpretation of the Constitution. This consensus has prevailed

even though our political history has been marked—and still is—by controversies over the proper limits of national power.

✔ FOR REVIEW

1. What two very important facts about the American system of government have a large impact upon the scope of the powers of Congress?
2. What was the position of the strict-constructionists in the early years under the Constitution? Of the liberal-constructionists? Which group's view prevailed?
3. What major factors have been largely responsible for the vast growth in the powers of the National Government since 1789?

The Expressed Powers

Most, but not all, of the expressed powers of Congress are found in Article I, Section 8 of the Constitution. There, in 18 separate clauses, some 27 different powers are explicitly given to Congress.[1]

These grants of power are quite brief. What they do—and do not—allow Congress to do often cannot be discovered merely by reading the few words involved. Rather, their content is to be found in the ways in which Congress has in fact exercised its different powers since 1789. And one must look, too, to

[1] Several of the expressed powers of Congress are set out elsewhere in the Constitution. Thus, Article IV, Section 3 grants it the power to admit new States to the Union (Clause 1) and to manage and dispose of federal territory and other property (Clause 2). The 16th Amendment gives Congress the power to levy an income tax. And, importantly, the 13th, 14th, 15th, 19th, 24th, and 26th Amendments each vest in Congress the "power to enforce" their provisions "by appropriate legislation."

COMING DOWN PARK ROW, N.Y. CITY

The motor vehicle not only transformed American life, but has also prompted dramatic changes in the ways in which interstate commerce is regulated by Congress.

scores of Supreme Court cases arising out of many of the actions taken by Congress.

As a case in point, take the Commerce Clause. Article I, Section 8, Clause 3 gives to Congress the power

> To regulate commerce with foreign nations, and among the several States, and with the Indian tribes.

Its wording is both brief and broad. Congress and the Court have had to answer dozens upon hundreds of questions about its scope and content.

Here are a *few* examples: What does "commerce" include? Does it include persons entering or leaving the country or crossing State lines? Radio and television broadcasts? Air transportation? Business practices? Labor-management relationships? Does the Commerce Clause give Congress the power to do such things as fix a minimum wage, set maximum hours of work, and spell out other labor conditions? Does it allow Congress to prohibit the shipment of certain goods? To regulate banks and other financial institutions? Prohibit discrimination? Provide for the con-

struction of highways, airports, and multi-purpose dams? What commerce is *foreign* and what is *interstate?* And what commerce is neither, and thus is *intrastate* and not subject to congressional regulation?

In answering these and hundreds of other questions on this *one* brief provision, Congress and the Court have spelled out, and are still spelling out, the meaning of the Commerce Clause. And so it is with nearly all of the many other provisions of the Constitution which grant power to Congress.

Before we turn to the several powers of Congress, remember this: Each of these powers has its historic significance. Most of them have a very substantial and continuing present-day importance. It should be fairly clear that such powers as those to tax, to borrow, to declare war, and to regulate foreign and interstate commerce are of that order.

A few of them are of little real moment, however. For example, Congress has the power to grant letters of marque and reprisal, but it has not used that power in well over a hundred years.[2]

The Power to Tax

Article I, Section 8, Clause 1 gives Congress the power

> To lay and collect taxes, duties, imposts, and excises, to pay the debts and provide for the common defense and general welfare of the United States. . . .

Recall, the Articles had not given Congress the power to tax. Without it,

the government under the Articles was impotent; and the lack of that power was a leading cause for the coming of the Constitution.

The Federal Government will take in some $650 billion in fiscal year 1984—and that huge sum will almost certainly be greater in fiscal 1985. Most of that money—well over 90 percent of it—will come as a direct result of the various taxes levied by Congress.

The basic purpose of the power to tax is both obvious and well-known: to raise the money needed to finance the operations of government. Dictionaries tell us that a "tax" is "a charge laid by government upon persons or property to meet the public needs." But notice that this usual dictionary definition is not altogether complete.

Taxes are most often imposed in order to raise money—that is, "to meet the public needs." But they are often imposed for other purposes, too. The *protective tariff* is perhaps the oldest example of the point. It does bring in some revenue, but its real goal is to "protect" domestic industry against foreign competition. Or, as another illustration, note that taxes are sometimes levied to protect the public health and safety. The Federal Government's regulation of the use of narcotics is a case in point. Most of that regulation is based on licensing. Only those who have a proper federal license may legally manufacture, sell, or otherwise deal in those drugs—and licensing is a form of taxation.

The power to tax is not unlimited. As with all of the other powers of the National Government, it must be used in accord with all of the other provisions of the Constitution. Thus, Congress cannot lay a tax on church services or the publication of a newspaper. Such taxes would be clear violations of the 1st Amendment.

---

[2]Article I, Section 8, Clause 11. *Letters of marque and reprisal* are relics of the past. They are (were) commissions (written grants of power) authorizing private persons to fit out vessels to capture and destroy the enemy in time of war. In short, a form of legalized piracy. (The States cannot issue them, Article I, Section 10, Clause 1.) They are forbidden in international law by the Declaration of Paris, 1856, and the United States honors the rule in practice.

TAX COLLECTIONS

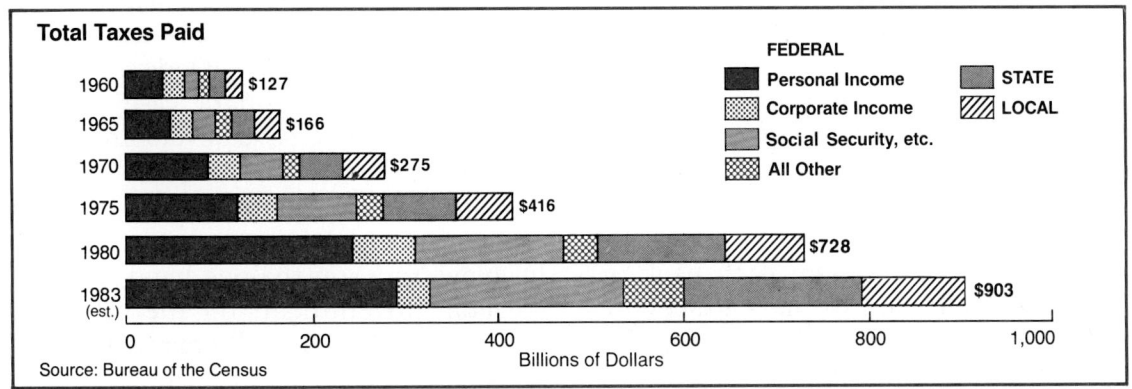

Total Taxes Paid

FEDERAL
- Personal Income
- Corporate Income
- Social Security, etc.
- All Other

STATE
LOCAL

Year	Total
1960	$127
1965	$166
1970	$275
1975	$416
1980	$728
1983 (est.)	$903

0   200   400   600   800   1,000
Billions of Dollars

Source: Bureau of the Census

The Average Taxpayer's Burden

Based on a man (with wife and 2 children) who had income of $25,000 in 1983 (estimates).

Federal Income Tax	$2,445
Social Security Tax	$1,675
Other Federal Taxes	$2,203
State Income Tax	$ 550
Local Property Tax on Home (includes School Tax)	$ 935
State and Local Sales Taxes	$ 360

TOTAL BASE TAXES $8,168

Source: The Tax Foundation Inc.

In addition some or all of these approximate taxes will be paid

On cigarettes at 21¢ a pack, a pack a day	$76.85
On gasoline at 12¢ a gallon, 11 gallons a week	$68.64
A substantial tax on all spirits (including wine and beer)	

Plus varying rates per dollar on toll telephone calls, air-travel, fishing equipment, and other items.

. . . So more than 33 cents of each dollar is taken by Federal, State and Local taxes

More exactly, the Constitution places four explicit limitations on the taxing power. *First*, Congress may tax only for *public purposes*, not for private benefit. Remember that Article I, Section 8, Clause 1 says that taxes may be levied only "to pay the debts, and provide for the common defense and general welfare of the United States."

Secondly, Congress may not lay any tax upon exports. Article I, Section 9, Clause 5 declares

No tax or duty shall be laid on articles exported from any State.

Thus, customs duties (tariffs, which are taxes) may be placed only on imports.

Thirdly, direct taxes must be apportioned among the States, according to their populations. Article I, Section 9, Clause 4 declares

No capitation, or other direct tax, shall be laid, unless in proportion to the census or enumeration herein before directed to be taken.

A **direct tax** is one which must be paid by the person upon whom it is imposed —for example, a tax on the ownership of land or buildings, or a *capitation* (head or poll) tax. An income tax is a direct tax. But, notice, it may be laid without regard to population because of the 16th Amendment:

The Congress shall have power to lay and collect taxes on incomes, from whatever source derived, without apportionment among the several States, and without regard to any census or enumeration.

Finally, Article I, Section 8, Clause 1 provides that

. . . all duties, imposts, and excises shall be uniform throughout the United States.

That is, all *indirect taxes* must be levied at the same rate in all parts of the country.

Whether any given tax is direct or indirect really rests with Congress and the Supreme Court. As a general rule an **indirect tax** is one which is actually paid by one person but is in fact passed on to another. That is, it is indirectly paid by that second person. Take, for example, the federal excise tax on each pack of cigarettes. It is paid to the Treasury by the tobacco company that makes the cigarettes. But the company then passes the tax on up the retail chain until it is in fact paid by the person who finally buys the cigarettes.

The Commerce Power

The commerce power is as vital to the existence and the welfare of the nation as the taxing power. As we've seen, it, too, played a large role in the formation of the Union. The weak Congress of the Articles had no power to regulate interstate trade and only very little authority over foreign commerce. The Critical Period of the 1780s was marked by intense commercial rivalries and bickerings among the States. High trade barriers and spiteful State laws created chaos and confusion in much of the country.

To overcome these conditions, the Framers wrote the Commerce Clause, Article I, Section 8, Clause 3. It gives Congress the power:

> To regulate commerce with foreign nations, and among the several states, and with the Indian tribes.

The Commerce Clause has been more responsible for building a strong Union of States out of a weak confederation than has any other provision in the Constitution. It has allowed the growth in the United States of the greatest open market area in the world. Together with the taxing power, it has contributed most to the vast growth in the power and authority of the National Government.

The very first case to reach the Supreme Court involving the Commerce Clause was *Gibbons* v. *Ogden*, decided in 1824. That landmark case set the stage for the extensive development the provision has since undergone.

The case arose out of a clash over the regulation of steam vessels by the State of New York, on the one hand, and the Federal Government, on the other. In 1807 Robert Fulton's steamboat, the *Clermont*, had made its first successful run up the Hudson River, from New York City to Albany. The State legislature then gave Fulton an exclusive, long-term grant to navigate the waters of the State by steamboat. From that monopoly, Aaron Ogden secured a permit for steam navigation between New York City and the New Jersey shore.

Thomas Gibbons, operating with a coasting license from the Federal Government, began to carry passengers on a competing line. Ogden sued him, and the New York courts held that Gibbons could not sail by steam in New York waters.

Gibbons appealed that ruling to the Supreme Court. He claimed that the New York grant conflicted with the congressional power to regulate commerce. The Court agreed. It rejected Ogden's argument that "commerce" should be defined narrowly, as simply "traffic" or the mere buying and selling of goods. Instead, siding with Congress, it read the Commerce Clause in very broad terms. Wrote Chief Justice John Marshall:

> Commerce undoubtedly is traffic, but it is something more—it is intercourse. It describes the commercial intercourse between nations, and parts of nations, in all its branches, and is regulated by prescribing rules for carrying on that intercourse.

This broad view of the scope of the commerce power has led to the reach of federal authority into many areas far beyond any thoughts of the Framers of the Constitution. We cited a number of those areas a moment ago, on page 321.

As another of the many examples of the point, note this: It is on the basis of the commerce power that the Civil Rights Act of 1964 prohibits discrimination in access to or service in hotels, motels, theaters, restaurants, and other public accommodations on grounds of race, color, religion, or national origin.[3]

It is on the basis of the expressed power to regulate commerce, and to tax, that Congress and the courts have built nearly all of the field of implied powers. Put another way: Most of what the Federal Government does, day to day and year to year, it does as the result of legislation passed by Congress in the exercise of these two powers.

The commerce power is not an unlimited one, of course. It, too, must be used in accord with all other provisions in the Constitution. Thus, Congress could not say that only those companies that employ only native-born citizens may carry on business in more than one State. Such an arbitrary and unreasonable regulation would violate the 5th Amendment's Due Process Clause.

More exactly, the Constitution places four explicit limitations on the use of the commerce power. *First*, as we have seen, Article I, Section 9, Clause 3 forbids Congress the power to lay any tax on exports. *Secondly*, Article I, Section 9, Clause 6 prevents Congress from favoring the ports of one State over those of any other in the regulation of trade.

All ports of entry in the United States must be treated with an even hand. *Thirdly*, the same provision forbids Congress to require that "vessels bound to, or from, one State, be obliged to enter, clear, or pay duties in another."

The *fourth* limitation is the curious "slave trade compromise" found in Article I, Section 9, Clause 1. It is, of course, obsolete—and has been for more than 170 years now (see page 42).

✓ FOR REVIEW

1. Where in the Constitution are most of the expressed powers of Congress?
2. What is the major purpose of the power to tax? Are taxes ever imposed for any other purpose?
3. What four specific limits does the Constitution place upon the taxing power?
4. What is a *direct tax?* An *indirect tax?*
5. The Constitution gives to Congress the expressed power to regulate what trade?
6. Why is *Gibbons* v. *Ogden* so important?
7. What four specific limits does the Constitution place upon the commerce power?

The Currency Power

The Constitution gives to Congress the power "to coin money [and] regulate the value thereof."[4] The States are forbidden to do so.[5]

---

[3]The Supreme Court upheld this use of the commerce power in *Heart of Atlanta Motel, Inc.* v. *United States*, 1964. In doing so, the unanimous Court noted that there was "overwhelming evidence of the disruptive effect of racial discrimination . . . on commercial intercourse." See page 156.

[4]Article I, Section 8, Clause 5.

[5]Article I, Section 10, Clause 1 forbids the States the power to coin money, issue bills of credit (paper money), or make anything but gold and silver legal tender. (**Legal tender** is any kind of money a creditor must accept by law in payment of a monetary debt.)

Until the Revolution, the English money system, built on the shilling and pound, was in general use in the colonies. With independence, that stable currency system collapsed, however. The Second Continental Congress and then the Congress under the Articles issued paper money. But without sound backing, and no taxing power behind it, it was practically worthless. Each of the 13 States also issued its own currency. In several of them, this amounted to little more than the State's printing its name on paper and calling it money.

DISTINGUISHING FACTS

IS THAT A FACT?

Many situations in politics, as in other places in everyday life, call for distinguishing *facts* from other statements. Whenever we are faced with a choice, it helps to identify the facts before we make a decision. Whatever the decision—whether a defendant is guilty or innocent, which candidate to support, which brand of stereo equipment to buy—we are less likely to be misled if we first identify and then rely on the available facts.

How can you tell whether or not statements such as these are facts?

1. Atlanta, Georgia is west of Pittsburgh, Pennsylvania.
2. If more people voted in congressional elections, members of Congress would do a better job of regulating interstate commerce.
3. Pressure groups should be more strictly regulated.
4. Save Money—Buy Generic Brands!

Facts are statements that have been verified, found to be accurate. To **verify** a statement means to establish its accuracy. A statement is accurate when there is information that supports (agrees with) it and no information that refutes (contradicts, disagrees with) it.

The information used to verify a statement is called **evidence.** Only two of the statements above (#1 and #4) are verifiable; so, of the four, only they can be facts. Are they? How can you verify them?

Some statements cannot be verified. That is, they cannot be shown to be accurate. While evidence can be provided to support them, evidence refuting them also can be found. You can agree or disagree with such statements, but you cannot either confirm or disprove them. Therefore, they are not facts.

Statement #2 cannot be verified because you cannot tell with confidence what would happen if more people participated in congressional elections. The evidence needed for verification is not available. Statements like this one that predict the future are often called hunches or speculation.

See how well you can distinguish facts from other statements in newspaper and magazine articles which deal with, say, a bill now before Congress. Or, in an upcoming election, examine the campaign advertisements to see if you can separate fact from opinion in the statements of the competing candidates.

Nearly all the Framers agreed on the need for a single, national system of "hard" money. So the Constitution gave the currency power to Congress, all but removing the States from the field. From 1789 on, among the most important of all of the many tasks performed by the Government has been this very one: To provide the nation with a uniform, and stable, monetary system.

From the beginning, the United States has issued coins—in gold (until 1933), silver, and other metals. Congress chartered the First Bank of the United States in 1791 and gave it the power to issue bank notes. But those notes (paper money) were not made legal tender: no one had to accept them as payment of a debt. Congress did not make paper currency legal tender until 1863.[6]

At first, the new national notes ("greenbacks") could not be redeemed for gold or silver coin at the Treasury. Their worth fell to less than half of their face value on the open market. Then, in 1870, the Supreme Court held their issuance to be unconstitutional. It said in *Hepburn* v. *Griswold*, "to coin" meant to stamp metal and, hence, the Constitution did not authorize paper money.

The Court soon changed its mind, however—in the *Legal Tender Cases* in 1871 and again in *Juliard* v. *Greenman* in 1884. In both cases it held the issuing of paper money as legal tender a proper use of the currency power.

The Borrowing Power

In Article I, Section 8, Clause 2 Congress has the power "to borrow money on the credit of the United States."

The power permits the Government to face both short- and long-term problems with the funding needed to meet them. Thus, the borrowing power was much used in World War II, as it had been during the economic crisis of the 1930s. It has been heavily used to help finance the extraordinary costs of war and defense over the years since then, as well.

There is no constitutional ceiling on the amount that may be borrowed. Congress has placed a statutory ceiling on the public debt, but it changes the ceiling whenever fiscal realities seem to call for it. At the start of fiscal year 1984, the nation's public debt was $1,377 trillion.

The Government most often borrows by selling bonds. They are much like the *promissory notes* ("IOU's") given by individuals when they borrow—a promise to pay a certain sum at a certain time.

The Government's bonds are issued as both short-term and long-term obligations—for lengths of time as short as 30 days to as much as 10 years or more. Interest rates are competitive with those paid in the private market.

The fact that the Constitution gives Congress the power to borrow makes borrowing a national function. Thus, the interest the Government pays cannot be taxed by the States—which makes its bonds quite attractive to investors, of course. The borrowing power also implies the power to create the Federal Reserve System and to regulate the nation's banking and other financial institutions.

Bankruptcy

Congress has power "to establish . . . uniform laws on the subject of bankruptcies, throughout the United States."[7] A **bankrupt** person is one

---

[6]Although they could not issue paper money themselves, the States chartered (licensed) private banks and their notes did circulate as money. As these private bank notes interfered with the new national currency, Congress levied a 10 percent tax on their issue in 1865; and they soon disappeared. The Supreme Court upheld the 1865 law as a proper exercise of the taxing power in *Veazie Bank* v. *Fenno*, 1869.

[7]Article I, Section 8, Clause 4.

whom a court has found to be insolvent, not able to pay his or her debts in full. **Bankruptcy** is the legal proceeding in which the bankrupt's assets are then distributed among those to whom a debt is owed. That proceeding frees the bankrupt from legal responsibility for debts acquired before bankruptcy.[8]

Both the States and the National Government have the power to regulate bankruptcy. It is, then, a concurrent power. Except for three short periods, Congress left the matter in the hands of the States for more than 100 years. In 1898, however, it passed a general bankruptcy law, and today that law is so broad that it all but excludes the States from the field.

Naturalization

The Constitution gives to Congress alone the power "to establish a uniform rule of naturalization.[8] **Naturalization** is the legal process by which a citizen of one country becomes a citizen of another country.

As it was originally written, the Constitution contained several references to "citizens of the United States" and "citizens of the States." It contained no definition of either national or State citizenship, however.

The coming of the Civil War, and then the adoption of the 13th Amendment (abolishing slavery) in 1865, brought the need for such a definition into sharp focus.[9] That need was met in the 14th Amendment, in 1868.

The first sentence of Section 1 of the 14th Amendment lays down the basic statement of American citizenship. It reads:

All persons born or naturalized in the United States, and subject to the jurisdiction thereof, are citizens of the United States, and of the States wherein they reside.

Thus, the 14th Amendment declares that a person may become an American citizen in one of two ways: by birth or by naturalization.

Citizenship by Birth. Nearly all of us—more than 220 million Americans today—are citizens of the United States because we were born in this country. But some—more than three million today—are also citizens by birth even though they were born abroad. Citizenship by birth is determined by either of two basic rules: (1) ***jus soli***—the law of the soil, *where* born, and (2) ***jus sanguinus***—the law of the blood, to *whom* born.

Jus Soli. The 14th Amendment confers citizenship according to the *location* of a person's birth: "All persons born . . . in the United States. . . ." By law, Congress has defined the United States to include for purposes of citizenship Puerto Rico, Guam, the Virgin Islands and the Northern Mariana Islands. And it includes, as well, all American embassies abroad and all American public vessels anywhere in the world.[10]

Jus Sanguinus. A child born abroad can become a citizen at birth under certain circumstances. At base, that child must be born to parents at

---

[8]Article I, Section 8, Clause 4.

[9]In the historic *Dred Scott Case* (*Scott* v. *Sanford,* 1857), the Supreme Court had ruled that neither the States nor the National Government had the power to confer national citizenship on Negroes, slave or free.

---

[10]Some few persons are born physically in the United States but are not "subject to its jurisdiction" and so do not become American citizens at birth. The very small number involved here includes mostly the children born to foreign diplomats stationed in this country. Until 1924, Indians born to tribal members living on reservations were not considered to be citizens; rather, they were wards, persons under the legal guardianship of the Government. In that year, however, Congress granted citizenship to all Indians in this country not already possessing it.

Under the international law doctrine of *extraterritoriality,* United States embassies abroad are, in effect, parts of the United States. A public vessel is any ship or aircraft operated by an agency of the Government.

least one of whom is a citizen who has at some time lived in the United States.

Although the 14th Amendment does not provide for *jus sanguinus*, Congress has included it as a part of American citizenship law since 1790. Its constitutionality has never been challenged; but if it were, it would now almost certainly be upheld—if for no reason other than its longstanding history.

Citizenship by Naturalization. As we have noted, naturalization is the legal process by which a person acquires a new citizenship at some time after birth. That process may be either an individual or a collective one.

Individual Naturalization. The process is most often an individual one, conducted by a court. At present, some 160,000 persons are naturalized each year.

As a general rule, any person who has come to the United States as an **immigrant**—that is, an alien who has been legally admitted as a permanent resident—is eligible to become a naturalized citizen.

The Immigration and Naturalization Service, in the Department of Justice, makes the necessary investigation of each applicant. An INS examiner then reports to the judge of the court in which the petition for naturalization has been filed. If the judge is satisfied, the person involved takes an oath (or an affirmation) of citizenship. The new citizen pledges that he or she will "support and defend the Constitution and laws of the United States against all enemies foreign and domestic."

Collective Naturalization. At various times, an entire group of persons has been naturalized *en masse,* at single stroke. This has usually happened when new territory has been acquired, and residents of the areas were collectively naturalized by terms of treaties, by acts, or by joint resolutions of Congress.

NATURALIZATION PROCESS

● **DECLARATION OF INTENTION** (Optional)
Filed with clerk of court; petitioner must be at least 18 years of age; states intention to renounce allegiance to former country.

● **PETITION**
Filed with clerk of court after 5 years of residence (3 if married to an American citizen); renounces allegiance to former country and declares not opposed to organized government nor a polygamist.

● **PETITION ATTESTED**
2 American citizens (witnesses) verify petitioner's 5 years of continuous residence, good moral character, and belief in principles of Constitution in sworn statement to clerk of court.

● **EXAMINATION**
By judge, or appointee who reports findings and makes recommendations to judge.

● **CITIZENSHIP GRANTED**
Not less than 30 days after filing of petition; judge administers oath of allegiance and signs certificate of citizenship.

Expatriation. Although it rarely happens, an American citizen may renounce (voluntarily give up) his or her citizenship. (**Expatriation** is the legal term for the process by which a loss of citizenship occurs.)

The Supreme Court has several times held that the Constitution prohibits automatic expatriation. That is, Congress cannot provide for the involuntary loss of a person's citizenship for something he or she has done—for example, voting in a foreign election or serving in the armed forces of another country. In the leading case, *Afroyim* v. *Rusk,* 1967, the Court declared that every citizen has "a constitutional right to remain a citizen unless he voluntarily relinquishes that right."

However, a naturalized citizen can be stripped of citizenship (*denaturalized,* expatriated involuntarily) if it can be shown that he or she became a citizen by fraud or deception.

The Postal Power

Congress has the sole power "to establish post offices and post roads."[11] Here, Congress is given the power to provide for the carrying of the mails. That power covers the authority to protect the mails and to insure their quick and efficient distribution. It carries with it, too, the power to prevent the use of the mails for fraud or for the carrying of outlawed materials.

The United States Postal Service traces its history to the early colonial period. Benjamin Franklin is generally credited as the "father" of the present-day postal system. It now operates on the basis of the Postal Reorganization Act of 1970; see page 410.

There are now more than 30,000 post offices, and more than 660,000 postal workers, across the country. They do more than $18 billion in business and handle well over 100 billion pieces of mail each year.

Congress has established a number of crimes based on the postal power. Thus, it is a federal crime for any person to obstruct the mails, or to use the mails to commit any fraud, or to use them as a part of any other criminal act.

The States cannot interfere with the mails unreasonably. Nor can they require a license for vehicles owned by the Postal Service or tax the gas they use. And they cannot tax the post offices or any other property of the Postal Service.

Articles which are not allowed by a State's laws—for example, firecrackers or switch-blade knives—cannot be sent into that State through the mails. A great many other items—including alcoholic beverages, lottery tickets, and obscene materials—are also barred from the mails.

Electronic equipment enables a mail sorter to process a great volume of mail in a relatively short time.

Copyrights and Patents

Article I, Section 8, Clause 8 in the Constitution gives to Congress the power

> To promote science and useful arts, by securing, for limited times, to authors and inventors, the exclusive right to their respective writings and discoveries.

A **copyright** is the exclusive right of an author to reproduce, publish, and sell his or her literary, musical, artistic, or other creative work. That right may be assigned (transferred by contract) to another—as to a publishing firm.

Copyrights are registered by the

---

[11]Article I, Section 8, Clause 7. **Post roads** are all postal routes, including railroads, airways, and waters within the United States, during the time that mail is being carried thereon.

Copyright Office in the Library of Congress. Under present law they are good for the life of the author plus 50 years. They cover a wide range of creative efforts—books, magazines, newspapers, musical compositions (and lyrics), dramatic works, paintings, sculptures, cartoons, maps, photographs, motion pictures, sound recordings, and much else.

The Copyright Office does not enforce the protections of a copyright. If a copyright is infringed, the owner of the right may sue for damages in the federal courts.

A **patent** grants one the sole right to manufacture, use, or sell "any new and useful art, machine, manufacture, or composition of matter, or any new and useful improvement thereof." A patent is good for a varying number of years—today, 17 years on a patent of invention. The term of a patent may be extended only by a special act of Congress. The patent laws are administered by the Patent and Trademark Office, in the Department of Commerce.

Weights and Measures

In Article I, Section 8, Clause 5 the Constitution gives to Congress the exclusive power "to fix the standards of weights and measures" for all of the United States. The power is a reflection of the need for accurate, uniform gauges of time, distance, area, weight, volume, and the like in practically every segment of the nation's daily life.

In 1838 Congress set the English system (of pound, ounce, mile, foot, gallon, quart, and so on) as the legal standards of weights and measures in the United States. In 1866 it also agreed to the use of the metric system (gram, meter, kilometer, liter, and so on). The original standards by which all other measures in the United States are tested and corrected are kept by the Bureau of Standards, in the Commerce Department.

By 1884, some 700 patents for velocipedes were granted by the U.S. Patent Office. A drawing submitted for one of them included a design for a unicycle in 1869.

In 1975 Congress created the United States Metric Board. Its major job is to promote greater use of and a change over to the metric system in this country.

Power Over Territories and Other Areas

Congress has power to acquire, manage, and dispose of various federal areas.[12] Of course, that power relates to the District of Columbia and to the several federal territories, including Puerto Rico, Guam, and the Virgin Islands. It covers, as well, hundreds of military and naval installations, arsenals, dockyards, post offices, prison facilities, park and forest preserves, and other federal holdings.

The Federal Government may acquire property by purchase or gift, of course. It may do so, too, through the exercise of the power of **eminent domain** —the inherent power to take private

---

[12]Article I, Section 8, Clause 17; Article IV, Section 3, Clause 2.

One of the most famous vessels in the U.S. Navy, the U.S.S. *Constitution* ("Old Ironsides") is berthed at Boston's Naval Shipyard, on federal property. Its site is now a National Historic Park, and attracts some 200,000 visitors each year. Launched in 1797, it is the oldest warship still afloat in any of the world's navies.

property for public use.[13] Territory may also be acquired from a foreign state based on the power to admit new States, the war powers, and the President's treaty-making power.[14] Under international law, any sovereign state may acquire unclaimed territory by discovery.

☑ FOR REVIEW

1. What is the currency power? Is it a concurrent power? What is legal tender?
2. The Government most often borrows by what means? Is there a legal limit on the amount of the public debt?
3. What is bankruptcy? The postal power?
4. What is a copyright? A patent?
5. What two basic standards of weights and measures has Congress recognized by law?
6. What does the congressional power over territories and other areas include? How may the United States acquire territory?

Judicial Powers

As an important part of the principle of checks and balances, Congress has several judicial powers. Thus, it has the expressed power to create all of the federal courts below the Supreme Court and to provide for the organization and composition of the federal judiciary.[15] We shall look at the federal courts in Chapter 18.

Congress has the power to define federal crimes and provide for their punishment.[16] It also has the power to impeach and remove any civil officer of the United States.[17]

Powers Over Foreign Relations

The National Government has greater powers in the field of foreign affairs than it has in any other. Congress shares power in this field with the President, who is primarily responsible for the conduct of our relations with other states.

---

[13]The 5th Amendment restricts the Government's use of the power with these words: "nor shall private property be taken for public use, without just compensation." Each of the State constitutions has a similar provision. Private property may be taken by eminent domain only: (1) for a public use, (2) with proper notice to the owner, and (3) for a fair price. What really is a public use, proper notice, or a fair price often becomes a court matter.

[14]Article IV, Section 3, Clause 1; Article I, Section 8, Clauses 11–16; Article II, Section 2, Clauses 1 and 2.

[15]Article I, Section 8, Clause 9; Article III, Section 1.

[16]The Constitution mentions only four types of federal crimes: counterfeiting, piracies and felonies committed on the high seas, and offenses against the law of nations (in Article 1, Section 8, Clauses 6 and 10), and treason (in Article III, Section 3). But Congress has the implied power to define many other offenses and provide for their punishment; see pages 67, 334.

[17]The impeachment power is one of the nonlegislative powers to which we shall turn shortly; see page 337.

Because the States in the Union are not sovereign, they have no standing in international law. The Constitution does not allow them to take part in foreign relations.[18]

Congressional authority in the field of foreign relations comes from two sources. *First,* from several of its expressed powers—most of all from the war powers and the commerce power. *Secondly,* Congress has power to act in the field because the United States is a sovereign nation. As the nation's lawmaking body, it has the inherent power to act on matters which affect the security of the nation.

We shall study this whole matter at much greater length in Chapter 17.

The War Powers

Eight of the expressed powers given Congress by Article I, Section 8 deal with war and national defense.[19]

Here, too, Congress shares power with the Chief Executive. The Constitution makes the President the Commander in Chief of the nation's armed forces,[20] and the President dominates the field. The congressional war powers, however, are both extensive and substantial.

Congress—and only Congress—may declare war. It has the power to raise and support armies, to provide and maintain a navy, and to make rules governing the land and naval forces.[21] It also has the power to provide for "calling forth the militia," and for the organizing, arming, and disciplining of it. Also, Congress has the power to make rules concerning captures on land and water.

With the War Powers Resolution of 1973, Congress may restrict the use of American forces in combat in areas where a state of war does not exist; see page 398.

FOR REVIEW

1. What judicial powers does Congress have?
2. With whom does Congress share authority in the field of foreign relations? What specific powers does it have in that field?
3. With whom does Congress share authority in the field of war and national defense? What specific powers does it have in that field?

Midshipmen learn the rudiments of sailing at the United States Naval Academy at Annapolis, Maryland.

[18]Article I, Section 10, Clauses 1 and 3; see pages 69–70.

[19]The war powers of Congress are set out in Clauses 11 through 16.

[20]Article II, Section 2, Clause 1; see pages 396–398.

[21]Congress cannot appropriate funds for "armies" for longer than a two-year period (Clause 12). The Constitution does not place that restriction on funding for the Navy (nor, under a 1948 Attorney General's opinion, on funding for the Air Force). It is intended to make certain that the Army will always remain under civilian authority.

THE POWERS VESTED IN CONGRESS BY ARTICLE I, SECTION 8 OF THE CONSTITUTION

Expressed Powers

I. Peace Powers
  1. To lay taxes.
     a. Direct (not used since the War Between the States, except income tax).
     b. Indirect.
        customs = tariffs.
        excises = internal revenue.
  2. To borrow money.
  3. To regulate foreign and interstate commerce.
  4. To establish naturalization and bankruptcy laws.
  5. To coin money and regulate its value; to regulate weights and measures.
  6. To punish counterfeiters of federal money and securities.
  7. To establish post offices and post roads.
  8. To grant patents and copyrights.
  9. To create courts inferior to the Supreme Court.
  10. To define and punish piracies and felonies on the high seas; to define and punish offenses against the law of nations.
  17. To exercise exclusive jurisdiction over the District of Columbia; to exercise exclusive jurisdiction over forts, dockyards, national parks, federal buildings, and the like.

II. War Powers
  11. To declare war; to grant letters of marque and reprisal; to make rules concerning captures on land and water.
  12. To raise and support armies.
  13. To provide and maintain a navy.
  14. To make laws governing land and naval forces.
  15. To provide for calling forth the militia to execute federal laws, suppress insurrections, and repel invasions.
  16. To provide for organizing, arming, and disciplining the militia, and for its governing when in the service of the Union.

Implied Powers

  18. To make all laws necessary and proper for carrying into execution the foregoing powers. For example—To define and provide punishment for federal crimes.
      To establish the Federal Reserve System.
      To improve rivers, canals, harbors, other waterways.
      To fix minimum wages, maximum hours of work.

The Implied Powers

The Necessary and Proper Clause

Up to this point we have looked at the expressed powers of Congress, most of which are to be found in Article I, Section 8, Clauses 1 through 17. The last clause there, Clause 18, is the dramatically important Necessary and Proper Clause. It gives to Congress the power

To make all laws which shall be necessary and proper for carrying into execution the foregoing powers, and all other powers vested by this Constitution in the Government of the United States, or in any department or officer thereof.

Much of the vitality and adaptability of the Constitution can be traced directly to this provision—and, even more so, to the manner in which both Congress and the Supreme Court have interpreted and used it over the years. For good reason, the Necessary and Proper Clause is often called the "Elastic Clause."

Liberal Versus Strict Construction

The Constitution had barely come into force when the meaning of Clause 18 was called into question. In 1790 Alexander Hamilton, as Secretary of the Treasury, urged Congress to set up a national bank. That proposal touched off one of the most important disputes in all of our political history.

The opponents of Hamilton's plan said that nowhere in the Constitution was Congress given the power to set up such a bank. These "strict-constructionists," led by Thomas Jefferson, argued that the new Government had no powers beyond those expressly granted to it by the Constitution.

Hamilton and other "liberal-constructionists" looked to the Necessary and Proper Clause. They said it gave Congress the power to do anything that might be reasonably "implied" from any of the expressly delegated powers. As for setting up the bank, they argued that it was necessary and proper in order to carry out the taxing, borrowing, commerce, and currency powers.

The Jeffersonians answered this claim of "implied powers" by insisting that such reasoning would give the new Government almost unlimited authority and would just about destroy the reserved powers of the States.[22]

---

[22]In 1801 a bill was introduced in Congress to incorporate a company to mine copper. As Vice President, Jefferson ridiculed that measure with this comment: "Congress is authorized to defend the nation. Ships are necessary for defense; copper is necessary for ships; mines necessary for copper; a company necessary to work the mines; and who can doubt this reasoning who has ever played at 'This Is the House that Jack Built'?" While Jefferson himself was President (1801–1809), he and his party were many times forced to reverse their earlier stand. Thus, for example, it was only on the basis of the implied powers doctrine that the Louisiana Purchase in 1803 and the embargo on foreign trade in 1807 could be justified.

Reason and practical necessity carried the day for Hamilton and his side. Congress established the Bank of the United States in 1791. Its charter (the act creating it) was to expire in 1811. Over those 20 years, the constitutionality of both the Bank and the concept of implied powers went unchallenged in the courts.

McCulloch* v. *Maryland, 1819. In 1816 Congress created the Second Bank of the United States. Its chartering came after another hard-fought battle over the extent of the powers of Congress.

Having lost the fight in Congress, several States tried to cripple the Bank in operation. In 1818 Maryland placed a tax upon all notes issued by any bank doing business in the State but not chartered by the State legislature. The tax was aimed directly at the Second Bank's branch in Baltimore. James McCulloch, the bank's cashier, purposely issued notes on which no tax had been paid. The State sought and won a judgment against him in its own courts. Acting for McCulloch, the United States then appealed to the Supreme Court.

Maryland took the strict-construction position before the High Court. It argued that the creation of the Bank had been unconstitutional. In reply, the United States took a two-fold position: (1) a defense of the concept of implied powers, and (2) the contention that no State could lawfully place a tax on any agency of the Federal Government.

Chief Justice John Marshall handed down one of the Supreme Court's most important and far-reaching decisions in the case. Here, for the first time, the Court was squarely faced with the 30-year-old question of the constitutionality of the implied powers doctrine.

The Court unanimously reversed the Maryland courts. It found the creation of the Second Bank to be necessary and proper in order to carry out the taxing, borrowing, and currency powers. Far more important, it thereby upheld the doctrine of implied powers.

The Court's decision in *McCulloch* v. *Maryland* is so significant that we quote these three key sentences from it:

> We admit, as all must admit, that the powers of the government are limited, and that its limits are not to be transcended. But we think the sound construction of the Constitution must allow to the national legislature that discretion, with respect to the means by which the powers it confers are to be carried into execution, which will enable that body to perform the high duties assigned to it, in the manner most beneficial to the people. Let the end be legitimate, let it be within the scope of the Constitution, and all means which are appropriate, which are not prohibited, but consist with the letter and spirit of the Constitution, are constitutional.

This broad interpretation of the powers granted to Congress has become firmly fixed in our constitutional system. Indeed, it is impossible to see how the nation could have developed as it has under the Constitution without it.[23]

The Doctrine in Practice. Both the way Congress has looked at and used its powers and the supporting decisions of the Supreme Court have made Article I, Section 8, Clause 18 truly the Elastic Clause. Today the words "necessary and proper" really read "convenient and useful." This is most especially true when applied to the power to regulate interstate commerce and the power to tax.

Yet, there is a real limit to how far the doctrine of implied powers may be pushed. Neither the Congress nor any other element of the Federal Government has a blanket authority to do anything that may seem desirable or that may be for the "general welfare" or in the "public interest." The basis for *any* implied power must *always* be found among the expressed powers. Or, put it this way: The implied powers are those which may be *reasonably* drawn from one or more of the expressed powers.

☑ **F O R   R E V I E W**

1. What does the Necessary and Proper Clause provide? The Elastic Clause?
2. What is the doctrine of implied powers?
3. Why is *McCulloch* v. *Maryland* so profoundly important?
4. How far the doctrine of implied powers may be carried is subject to what fundamental limitation?

The Nonlegislative Powers of Congress

Congress makes laws. But the Constitution gives to it a number of *nonlegislative* powers and duties, as well.

Electoral

On rare occasion, the House of Representatives may be called upon to elect a President. If no candidate receives a majority of the electoral votes for President, the House, voting by States, must then choose one. It must choose by majority vote and from among the three top contenders in the electoral college. The Senate must choose a Vice President when no candidate for that office wins a majority in the electoral college.[24]

The House has had to choose a Presi-

---

[23]The Court also invalidated the Maryland tax. Because, said the Court, "the power to tax involves the power to destroy," no State may tax the United States or any of its agencies or functions; see page 602.

[24]12th Amendment; see pages 367–368.

The 25th Amendment brought Gerald Ford to the Vice Presidency, December 6, 1973. Chief Justice Warren Burger administered the oath of office, as President Richard Nixon, Mrs. Ford, and others looked on.

dent only twice: Thomas Jefferson in 1801 and John Quincy Adams in 1825. The Senate chose Richard M. Johnson as Vice President in 1837.

Remember, too, that the 25th Amendment provides for the filling of a vacancy in the Vice Presidency. When and if one occurs, the President nominates a successor, subject to a majority vote in both houses of Congress. That process has been used twice in recent years. Gerald Ford was confirmed as Vice President in 1973 and then Nelson Rockefeller in 1974.

Constitutional Amendment

As we have seen, Congress may propose amendments to the Constitution, by a two-thirds vote in each house. It may also call a national convention to propose an amendment if so requested by two-thirds of the State legislatures.[25]

Impeachment

The Constitution provides that the President, Vice President, and all civil officers of the United States may "be removed from office on impeachment for, and conviction of, treason, bribery, or other high crimes and misdemeanors.[26] The House has the sole power to **impeach** (bring charges) and the Senate the sole power to **judge** (sit as a court, try) in impeachment cases.[27]

The House may impeach by a majority vote. A two-thirds vote of the Senators present is needed for conviction. The Chief Justice must preside over the Senate when (if) a President is tried. The penalty for conviction is removal from office. The Senate may add a prohibition against the person ever holding a federal office again. Also, a person who has been impeached and convicted can also be

---

[25]Article V; see pages 55–59.

[26]Article II, Section 4. Military officers are not "civil officers" and may be removed by court-martial. Nor are members of Congress. When the House impeached Senator William Blount of Tennessee in 1798, the Senate refused to try the case on the grounds that it had the power to expel one of its own members if it chose to do so. Blount was expelled. The precedent thus set has been followed ever since; see page 284.

[27]Article I, Section 2, Clause 5, and Section 3, Clause 6.

In July of 1974, the House Judiciary Committee voted that impeachment charges be brought against President Nixon. Shortly afterward, Nixon resigned.

indicted, tried, convicted, and punished according to law in the regular courts.[28]

To date, there have been but 12 impeachments and only four convictions. Some officers have resigned under the threat of impeachment. The most notable, of course, was Richard Nixon who resigned the Presidency in 1974. When the House impeached President Andrew Johnson in 1868, the Senate failed by a single vote to convict him.[29]

Executive

The Constitution gives two "executive powers" to the Senate. One of them has to do with appointments and the other with treaties made by the President.[30]

All major appointments made by the President must be confirmed by the Senate by majority vote. Each nomination by the President is referred to the appropriate standing committee of the Senate. When that committee's recommendation is brought to the floor, it may be (but seldom is) considered in executive (secret) session.

The appointment of a Cabinet officer or of some other top member of the President's "official family" is very seldom turned down by the Senate.[31] But the unwritten rule of "senatorial courtesy" comes into play with the appointment of federal officers who serve at the State level—for example, District Court judges, United States attorneys, and federal marshals. The Senate will turn down such an appointment if it is opposed by a Senator of the President's party from that State. What this means is that some Senators practically dictate certain presidential appointments. We shall return to this whole matter in Chapter 15.

Treaties are made by the President "by and with the advice and consent of the Senate, . . . provided two-thirds of

[28]Article I, Section 3, Clauses 6 and 7.
[29]The four persons removed were federal judges. One other judge resigned after the House had impeached him and just before the Senate began his trial, and the case was dropped. Four other judges were acquitted by the Senate. On these judicial impeachments, see page 496. Aside from Senator Blount and President Johnson, W. W. Belknap, who was President Grant's Secretary of War, was impeached in 1876. He was acquitted by the Senate, however, on grounds that that body no longer had jurisdiction because he had resigned from office.
[30]Article II, Section 2, Clause 2.

[31]All told, only nine of the more than 500 Cabinet appointments made since 1789 have been rejected by the Senate; see page 385.

In investigating the nuclear accident at Three Mile Island, Pennsylvania, Congress heard testimony from many sources, including the panel shown here.

the Senators present concur."[32] For a time after the adoption of the Constitution, the advice of the Senate was asked when a treaty was being prepared. Now the President most often consults the members of the Senate Foreign Relations Committee and other influential Senators of both parties.

The Senate may accept or reject a treaty as it stands. It may, however, offer amendments, reservations, or understandings to it. Because the House has a hold on the public purse strings, influential members of that body are often consulted in the treaty-making process, too. See page 395.

Investigations

Congress, through its committees, has the power to investigate matters for three purposes: *First*, to gather informa-

[32]Article II, Section 2, Clause 2. It is often said that the Senate "ratifies" a treaty. It does not. The Senate may give (or withhold) its "advice and consent" to a treaty made by the President. Once the Senate has consented to (approved) a treaty, the President then ratifies it by exchanging the "instruments of ratification" with the other party or parties to the agreement.

tion that may be of use to Congress in the making of law. *Second*, to review the present-day effectiveness of laws it has passed. And, *third*, to find out whether programs are in fact being administered as Congress intended they should be. See pages 300–302.

☑ FOR REVIEW

1. If the electoral college cannot select a President, who then makes that choice? A Vice President?

2. How is a vacancy in the Vice Presidency now filled?

3. What roles does Congress play in the constitutional amendment process?

4. Where is the power to impeach located? The power to try those who are impeached?

5. What two "executive powers" are held by the Senate?

6. For what three purposes does Congress have the power to investigate?

Scenes from the Rotunda Frieze in the Capitol Building (left to right): Reading of the Declaration of Independence and the surrender of Cornwallis at Yorktown, 1781.

S U M M A R Y

The scope of the many and important powers of Congress is fundamentally affected by the principles of limited government and of federalism. Its powers are those delegated to it by the Constitution: (1) those *expressly* granted to it by the Constitution, (2) those reasonably *implied* by the expressed powers, and (3) those *inherently* possessed because the Constitution creates a national government for the sovereign United States.

Most of the expressed powers of Congress are set out in Article I, Section 8, Clauses 1–18. Several are also found elsewhere in the Constitution.

Early in our history the question of strict or liberal interpretation of the powers given to Congress became a hard-fought issue. It was very largely settled by the Supreme Court in the landmark case of *McCulloch* v. *Maryland*, 1819. The Court gave a sweepingly broad interpretation to the Necessary and Proper Clause. In short, it upheld the doctrine of implied powers.

Congress performs several nonlegislative functions—in the electoral, constituent, impeachment, executive, and investigative fields.

C H A P T E R   R E V I E W

Key Terms/Concepts

Bankruptcy (327)
Borrowing power (327)
Commerce power (324)
Copyright (331)
Currency power (325)
Elastic Clause (334)
Electoral power (336)
Eminent domain (331)
Executive powers (338)
Expatriation (329)
Expressed powers (320)
Gibbons v. *Ogden* (324)
Impeachment (337)
Implied powers (334)
Investigative power (339)
Jus sanguinus (328)
Jus soli (328)
Legislative power (318)
Liberal construction (335)
McCulloch v. *Maryland* (335)
Naturalization (328)
Necessary and Proper Clause (334)
Nonlegislative powers (336)
Patent (331)
Strict construction (335)
War powers (333)
Weights and measures (331)

Keynote Questions

1. In what three distinct ways does the Constitution delegate powers to Congress?
2. What have been the major causes for the growth in the powers of the National Government over time?
3. What is the basic purpose of the power to tax? Are taxes ever imposed for any other purpose? What four specific limits does the Constitution place upon the exercise of the taxing power? For what does the 16th Amendment provide?
4. Congress has the expressed power to regulate what trade? What four specific limits does the Constitution place upon the commerce power?
5. What is the basic shape of the currency power? What is legal tender?
6. What is the basic shape of the borrowing power? Is there a legal limit on the size of the public debt?
7. What is bankruptcy? The postal power? A copyright? A patent?
8. How can American citizenship be acquired? What is the rule of *jus soli*? *Jus sanguinus*?
9. What two systems of weights and measures may be legally used in the United States?
10. What power does Congress have over territories and other areas?
11. What judicial powers does Congress have?
12. What specific powers does Congress have in the fields of foreign affairs and defense? With whom does it share authority to act in those fields?

For Thought and Discussion

1. Great Britain has no written constitution, and Parliament may pass any law it believes to be necessary. Why has Congress only the expressed, implied, and inherent powers?
2. In the Court's opinion in *McCulloch v. Maryland* Chief Justice Marshall wrote that "the power to tax involves the power to destroy." What did he mean by that observation?
3. In what ways might the general wellbeing of the American people be affected if each of the States had its own monetary system? Its own system of weights and measures? Its own postal system?
4. How do each of the several nonlegislative powers of Congress illustrate the principle of checks and balances?

Suggested Activities

1. Select one of the expressed powers of Congress and prepare a report to the class covering: (1) the reasons why it was granted to Congress, (2) its historic development, and (3) its present-day scope and use.
2. Identify 10 of the major pieces of legislation thus far enacted or still being considered in the present session of Congress. In a report, identify those measures based upon one or more of the expressed powers and those which are applications of the doctrine of implied powers. Do any of them exemplify the doctrine of inherent powers?
3. Stage a debate or class forum on one of the following: (a) *Resolved,* That Congress be allowed to exercise only those powers expressly delegated to it by the Constitution; (b) *Resolved,* That the federal monopoly over the postal system be ended; (c) *Resolved,* That the metric system be made the sole standard of weights and measures in the United States; (d) *Resolved,* That Congress reassert its authority to grant letters of marque and reprisal.
4. Prepare a bulletin board or other display to show the meaning, scope, and importance of one of the powers of Congress.

UNIT FIVE

The Executive Branch: The Presidency and the Bureaucracy

In Unit Five, we turn to the vast, complex, sprawling and critically important executive branch of the National Government. Governments may operate without either legislatures or courts; but no government, whatever its form, can exist without some type of executive authority. Recall that a major weakness of the Articles of Confederation was the lack of such authority. Obviously a government with neither legislature nor courts could not be a democratic one, but it would still be a government. Laws could be made by executive order, and public and private disputes could be settled in the same fashion.

Thus our governmental system, like all others, demands an executive authority. And, it demands a strong one. Alexander Hamilton put the case for a strong executive in 1788 in *The Federalist* No. 70:

> Energy in the Executive is a leading character in the definition of good government. It is essential to the protection of the community against foreign attacks; . . to the steady administration of the laws; to the protection of property . . . ; to the security of liberty. . . . A feeble Executive implies a feeble execution of the government. . . . [and] in practice, a bad government.

The first two chapters of Unit Five, Chapters 14 and 15, deal with the presidency. Chapter 16 addresses the bureaucracy—that is, the vast number of offices and agencies, and their staffs, that make the government work, and the public dollars with which they do so. And Chapter 17 closes the unit with a discussion of foreign affairs and the formation and administration of American foreign policy.

The Oval Office of the President

14

The Presidency

He is the vital center of action in the system, whether he accepts it as such or not, and the office is the measure of the man—of his wisdom as well as of his force.

Woodrow Wilson

On April 30, 1789, George Washington placed his left hand on the Bible, raised his right hand, and swore that he would "preserve, protect, and defend the Constitution of the United States." As he did so, at New York which was then the temporary capital, he became the first President of the United States. Over the long course of 190 years, each of his successors has repeated that ceremony and spoken the words of the constitutional oath. Most of them have done so in Washington, D.C., as Thomas Jefferson did for the first time in 1801. And, most of them have done so on the steps of the Capitol, as James Madison did for the first time in 1817.

Ronald Wilson Reagan repeated the solemn words of the Constitution at noon in the nation's capital on January 20, 1981—and so became the 40th President of the United States.

As the nation's Chief Executive, Mr. Reagan holds the most important and the most powerful office known to history. His powers are vast, his responsibilities are well-nigh immeasurable, and his functions are many.

In an earlier and a simpler day, Admiral George Dewey said that "the office of President is not such a very difficult one to fill, his duties being mainly to execute the laws of Congress." That view of the Presidency was

As did George Washington in 1789 (bottom/left), Ronald Reagan recited the constitutional oath of office as he became the nation's 40th President in 1981.

wrong-headed at the time. Let us see why that view—still held by some—is so much further from the truth today.

The President's Many Roles

At any given time, only one person is President of the United States, of course. But, whomever that person may be, he—and perhaps someday she[1]—must fill a number of different roles, and all of them at the same time.

The President is, to begin with, *Chief of State*, the ceremonial head of the government of the United States. He is, then, the symbol of all of the people of the nation—in President William Howard Taft's words, "the personal embodiment and representative of their dignity and majesty."

In many countries, the chief of state reigns but does not rule—among them,

the Queens of England and of Denmark, the Emperor of Japan, the Kings of Norway and of Sweden, and the Presidents of Italy and of West Germany. It is most certainly *not* true of the President of the United States. He both reigns *and* rules.

The President is the nation's *Chief Executive*, vested by the Constitution with "*the* executive power of the United States." The President is also the *Chief Administrator* of the Federal Government—heading one of the largest governmental machines the world has known. Today, the President directs an administration with some 2.8 million civilian employees and which spends more than $800 billion a year.

The President is also the nation's *Chief Diplomat*, the chief architect of American foreign policy and the nation's chief spokesman to the rest of the world. "I make foreign policy," President Harry Truman once said—and he did. What the President says, and does, are

---

[1]To this point all of the Presidents have been men, but there is nothing in the Constitution to prevent the selection of a woman to that office.

Left: President Reagan signs the Social Security Reform Act into law.
Right: In 1945, President Truman met with Britain's leader, Clement Atlee, and the Soviet Union's Josef Stalin at Potsdam to discuss plans for the postwar world.

carefully followed, not only in this country but everywhere abroad.

The Constitution makes the President the *Commander in Chief* of the nation's armed forces. Two million men and women in uniform, and all of the incalculable power in the nation's military arsenal, are thus made subject to the President's direct and immediate control.

Importantly, the President is also the nation's *Chief Legislator*, the chief architect of its public policies. It is the President who sets the overall shape of the congressional agenda—initiating, suggesting, requesting, supporting, insisting, and demanding that Congress enact most of the major legislation that it does.

These six presidential roles all come directly from the Constitution. But they do not complete the list. The President must fill still other vital roles.

The President is *Chief of Party*, the acknowledged leader of the political party in control of the executive branch. A great deal of the real power and influence wielded by the Chief Executive depends upon the manner in which this critical role is played.

The office also automatically makes of its occupant the nation's *Chief Citizen*. The President is expected to be "the representative of *all* of the people," the one to work for and represent the *public* interest against the many different and competing private interests. "The Presidency," said Franklin Roosevelt, "is not merely an administrative office. That is the least of it. It is preeminently a place of moral leadership."

Each of these roles is inseparable from, and closely interrelated with each of the others. The manner in which the President plays any one of them can have a very decided effect upon the ability to play another or several or all of them.

As but two illustrations, take the experiences of Presidents Lyndon Johnson and Richard Nixon. Each was a strong and a relatively effective President during his first years in office. But the agonizing and increasingly unpopular war in Vietnam persuaded Mr. Johnson not to run for reelection in 1968. In effect, the manner in which he acted as Commander in Chief seriously eroded his stature and effectiveness in the White House. And the many-sided and sordid Watergate affair—and the manner in which he filled the roles of party leader and chief citizen—so destroyed his Presidency that Mr. Nixon was forced to leave office in disgrace in 1974.

Surely, enough has been said to this

point to confirm our description of the Presidency as "the most important and the most powerful office known to history." Enough has been said, too, to dismiss Admiral Dewey as, at best, a naive commentator.

Qualifications, Term, Compensation

Formal Qualifications

Whatever else a President must be, the Constitution sets out three qualifications for the office.[2] It says that the President must:

(1) Be "a natural-born citizen." Under the doctrine of *jus sanguinus* (page 329), it is apparently quite possible for a person born abroad to become President. Some dispute that view; and the real shape of this requirement cannot be known unless and until someone born a citizen, but born abroad, does in fact become President.[3]

(2) Be at least 35 years of age. At 43, John F. Kennedy was the youngest person ever to be elected to the office. Theodore Roosevelt reached it by succession at age 42. Only five other Presidents entered office at less then 50 years of age: James K. Polk, Franklin Pierce, Ulysses Grant, James Garfield, and Grover Cleveland. Ronald Reagan, who was 69 when he was elected in 1980, is the oldest man ever elected and ever to hold the office. (Before Mr. Reagan, William Henry Harrison was the oldest ever elected, at age 68; and Dwight D. Eisenhower, who left the White House at 70, was the oldest ever to hold the office.)

---

[2]Article II, Section 1, Clause 5.

[3]Martin Van Buren, who was born December 5, 1782, was the first President actually born in the United States. His seven predecessors and his immediate successor were each born before the Revolution. But notice that the Constitution anticipated that situation ("or a citizen of the United States at the time of the adoption of this Constitution").

An anti-FDR button from the presidential campaign of 1940.

(3) Have lived in the United States for at least 14 years.[4]

These formal qualifications are clearly important; but they are really not very difficult to meet. We shall look at the much more telling informal qualifications shortly.

Term

The Framers of the Constitution considered a number of different limits on the length of the presidential term. Most of their debate centered around a four-year term, with the President to be eligible for reelection, versus a single six- or seven-year term. They finally settled upon a four-year term.[5] They agreed, as Alexander Hamilton put it in *The Federalist*, that that was a long enough period for a President to gain experience, demonstrate abilities, and establish stable policies.

Until 1951, the Constitution placed no limit upon the number of terms a President might serve. Several Presidents, beginning with George Washington, refused to seek more than two terms, however. Soon, the "no-third-term tradition" became an unwritten rule in presidential politics.

After Franklin D. Roosevelt broke the tradition by winning a third term in 1940, and then a fourth in 1944, the unwritten custom became a part of the written Constitution. The 22nd Amend-

---

[4]The 14-year requirement means any 14 years in a person's life, not just those immediately before election.

[5]Article II, Section 1, Clause 1.

ment, adopted in 1951, reads in part:

> No person shall be elected to the office of the President more than twice, and no person who has held the office of President, or acted as President, for more than two years of a term to which some other person was elected President shall be elected to the office of the President more than once.

As a general rule, then, each President may now serve a maximum of two full terms—eight years—in office. *But* a President, who has *succeeded* to the office *beyond the midpoint* in a term to which another was originally elected, may serve for more than eight years. At the very outside, however, a President may not serve more than 10 years.

Several Presidents—most recently Jimmy Carter—have urged a single, six-year term for the office. Significantly, they have each come to this view *after* having won the office.

Compensation

The President's salary is fixed by Congress, and it can neither be increased nor decreased during a term.[6]

The salary was first set at $25,000 a year in 1789. Congress put the figure at its present level—$200,000—in 1969. Since 1949 the President has also received a $50,000-a-year expense account. It is taxable as income and, in effect, is really a part of the President's pay.

The Constitution forbids the President "any other emolument from the United States, or any of them."[7] But this

does not prevent the President from being provided with the White House, a magnificent 132-room mansion set on an 18.3-acre (7.8-hectare) estate in the heart of the nation's Capital; a sizable suite of offices and a large staff; a yacht a fleet of automobiles, three lavishly fitted Boeing 707 jets, and several other planes and helicopters; Camp David, the resort hideaway in the Catoctin Mountains in Maryland; the finest medical, dental, and other health care available; generous travel and entertainment funds; and a many other perquisites

Many of these services and facilities cannot be measured in dollar terms, of course. However, to have all of the material benefits the Chief Executive receives, it has been estimated that a private citizen would have to have an after-taxes income of more than $15 million a year. That amount of "take-home pay" would require a gross income of about $30 million a year.

Since 1958 each former President has received a lifetime pension, now $80,100 a year; and each presidential widow is entitled to a pension of $20,000 a year.

✔ **FOR REVIEW**

1. What several roles does (must) the President play?
2. Why can none of them be played separately?
3. What are the formal qualifications for the Presidency?
4. For what term is a President elected?
5. To how many terms may a President be elected? What is the maximum length of time any person may serve as President?
6. Who fixes the President's pay? How much is it today?

[6]Article II, Section 1, Clause 7. At Philadelphia, Benjamin Franklin argued that, as money *and* power might corrupt a man, the President ought to receive nothing beyond his expenses; his suggestion was not put to a vote at the Convention, however. The present salary was set in the first measure passed by Congress in 1969; it was signed by President Johnson on January 17—three days before the new presidential term, President Nixon's first, began.

[7]Article II, Section 1, Clause 7.

PRESIDENTS OF THE UNITED STATES

Name	Party	State[a]	Born	Died	En-tered Office	Age on Taking Office	Vice Presidents
George Washington	Federalist	Virginia	1732	1799	1789	57	John Adams
John Adams	Federalist	Massachusetts	1735	1826	1797	61	Thomas Jefferson
Thomas Jefferson	Dem.-Rep.[b]	Virginia	1743	1826	1801	57	Aaron Burr
							George Clinton
James Madison	Dem.-Rep.	Virginia	1751	1836	1809	57	George Clinton
							Elbridge Gerry
James Monroe	Dem.-Rep.	Virginia	1758	1831	1817	58	Daniel D. Tompkins
John Q. Adams	Dem.-Rep.	Massachusetts	1767	1848	1825	57	John C. Calhoun
Andrew Jackson	Democrat	Tenn. (S.C.)	1767	1845	1829	61	John C. Calhoun
							Martin Van Buren
Martin Van Buren	Democrat	New York	1782	1862	1837	54	Richard M. Johnson
William H. Harrison	Whig	Ohio (Va.)	1773	1841	1841	68	John Tyler
John Tyler	Democrat	Virginia	1790	1862	1841	51	. . . .
James K. Polk	Democrat	Tenn. (N.C.)	1795	1849	1845	49	George M. Dallas
Zachary Taylor	Whig	La. (Va.)	1784	1850	1849	64	Millard Fillmore
Millard Fillmore	Whig	New York	1800	1874	1850	50	. . . .
Franklin Pierce	Democrat	New Hampshire	1804	1869	1853	48	William R. King
James Buchanan	Democrat	Pennsylvania	1791	1868	1857	65	John C. Breckinridge
Abraham Lincoln	Republican	Illinois (Ky.)	1809	1865	1861	52	Hannibal Hamlin
							Andrew Johnson
Andrew Johnson	Democrat[c]	Tenn. (N.C.)	1808	1875	1865	56	. . . .
Ulysses S. Grant	Republican	Illinois (Ohio)	1822	1885	1869	46	Schuyler Colfax
							Henry Wilson
Rutherford B. Hayes	Republican	Ohio	1822	1893	1877	54	William A. Wheeler
James A. Garfield	Republican	Ohio	1831	1881	1881	49	Chester A. Arthur
Chester A. Arthur	Republican	N.Y. (Vt.)	1830	1886	1881	50	. . . .
Grover Cleveland	Democrat	N.Y. (N.J.)	1837	1908	1885	47	Thomas A. Hendricks
Benjamin Harrison	Republican	Indiana (Ohio)	1833	1901	1889	55	Levi P. Morton
Grover Cleveland	Democrat	N.Y. (N.J.)	1837	1908	1893	55	Adlai E. Stevenson
William McKinley	Republican	Ohio	1843	1901	1897	54	Garret A. Hobart
							Theodore Roosevelt
Theodore Roosevelt	Republican	New York	1858	1919	1901	42	. . . .
							Charles W. Fairbanks
William H. Taft	Republican	Ohio	1857	1930	1909	51	James S. Sherman
Woodrow Wilson	Democrat	N.J. (Va.)	1856	1924	1913	56	Thomas R. Marshall
Warren G. Harding	Republican	Ohio	1865	1923	1921	55	Calvin Coolidge
Calvin Coolidge	Republican	Mass. (Vt.)	1872	1933	1923	51	. . . .
							Charles G. Dawes
Herbert Hoover	Republican	Calif. (Iowa)	1874	1964	1929	54	Charles Curtis
Franklin D. Roosevelt	Democrat	New York	1882	1945	1933	51	John N. Garner
							Henry A. Wallace
							Harry S. Truman
Harry S. Truman	Democrat	Missouri	1884	1972	1945	60	. . . .
							Alben W. Barkley
Dwight D. Eisenhower	Republican	N.Y.-Pa. (Tex.)	1890	1969	1953	62	Richard M. Nixon
John F. Kennedy	Democrat	Massachusetts	1917	1963	1961	43	Lyndon B. Johnson
Lyndon B. Johnson	Democrat	Texas	1908	1973	1963	55	. . . .
							Hubert H. Humphrey
Richard M. Nixon	Republican	N.Y. (Calif.)	1913		1969	55	Spiro T. Agnew[d]
							Gerald R. Ford[e]
Gerald R. Ford	Republican	Michigan (Neb.)	1913		1974	61	Nelson A. Rockefeller[f]
James E. Carter	Democrat	Georgia	1924		1977	52	Walter F. Mondale
Ronald W. Reagan	Republican	Calif. (Ill.)	1911		1981	69	George H. W. Bush

[a]State of residence when elected; if born in another State that State in parentheses. [b]Democratic-Republican. [c] Johnson, a War Democrat, was elected Vice President (as Lincoln's running mate) on the coalition Union Party ticket. [d]Resigned October 10, 1973.[e]Nominated by Nixon, confirmed by Congress December 6, 1973. [f]Nominated by Ford, confirmed by Congress December 19, 1974.

Presidential Succession

Section 1 of the 25th Amendment states that:

> In case of the removal of the President from office or of his death or resignation, the Vice President shall become President.

In strictest terms, then, before the 25th Amendment was added in 1967, the Constitution did *not* say that in such situations the Vice President should become President. Rather, it declared that the *powers and duties* of the office (not the office itself) were to "devolve on the Vice President."[8]

The practice, however, begun by John Tyler in 1841, had been that should the office become vacant the Vice President succeeds to it. The only real effect of this addition to the Constitution was to make what had been one of its many informal amendments a part of the written document itself.

Congress fixes the order of succession following the Vice President.[9] The present law on the matter is the Presidential Succession Act of 1947. By its terms, the Speaker of the House and then the President *pro tem* of the Senate are next in line. They are followed, in turn, by the Secretary of State and each of the other 12 heads of the Cabinet departments, in order of precedence.[10]

President Warren Harding died in office in 1923, of an undisclosed illness. He was succeeded by Calvin Coolidge.

Presidential Disability

Before the 25th Amendment, there were serious gaps in the succession arrangement. Neither the Constitution nor Congress had made any provision for deciding *when* a President was so disabled that presidential duties could not be carried out. Nor was there anything to indicate *by whom* such a decision was to be made.

For nearly 180 years, then, the nation played with fate. President Eisenhower suffered three serious, but temporary, illnesses while he was in office—a heart attack in 1955, ileitis in 1956, and a mild stroke in 1957. Two other Presidents were disabled for much longer periods of time. James Garfield lingered for 80 days before he died from an assassin's bullet in 1881. In all of that time, the only official act he was able to take was to sign an extradition warrant. Woodrow Wilson suffered a paralytic stroke in 1919. He was so ill that he could not meet with his Cabinet for seven months after the attack.

Sections 3 and 4 of the 25th Amendment fill the disability gap, and in detail. The Vice President is to become Acting President if (1) the President informs Congress, in writing, "that he is unable to discharge the powers and duties of his office," or (2) the Vice President and a majority of the members of the Cabinet inform Congress, in writing, that the President is so incapacitated.[11]

---

[8]Article II, Section 1, Clause 6. On removal of the President by impeachment, see Article I, Section 2, Clause 5; Article I, Section 3, Clauses 6 and 7; Article II, Section 4; and page 337.

[9]Article II, Section 1, Clause 6.

[10]This is, in the order in which their offices were created by Congress; see page 385. A Cabinet member is to serve only until a Speaker or President *pro tem* is available and qualified. But notice that Section 2 of the 25th Amendment provides for the filling of any vacancy in the Vice Presidency. That provision almost certainly guarantees that the line of presidential succession will never pass below the Vice Presidency.

---

[11]The 25th Amendment gives this authority to the Vice President and the Cabinet or to "such other body as Congress may by law provide." To 1983, no "such other body" has been established.

In either case, the President may resume the powers and duties of the office by informing Congress that no inability exists. However, the Vice President and a majority of the Cabinet may challenge the President on this score. If they do, Congress has 21 days in which to decide the matter.

Fortunately, these provisions have not been put to the test.

☑ FOR REVIEW

1. If the Presidency becomes vacant, why does the Vice President succeed to the office?
2. Who follows the Vice President in the line of presidential succession? Why?
3. Who serves as Acting President if the President becomes disabled? Has this ever happened?
4. Who decides the question of presidential disability?

The Vice Presidency

"I am Vice President. In this I am nothing, but I may be everything." So said John Adams, the nation's first Vice President. Those words could have been repeated, very appropriately, by each of the 42 Vice Presidents who have followed him in that office.

The Constitution pays little attention to the office. It assigns the Vice President only two formal duties: (1) to preside over the Senate,[12] and (2) to help decide the question of presidential disability.[13] Beyond them, the Constitution makes the Vice President a "Presi-

Vice President George Bush addresses a multi-agency task force structured to curtail traffic in illegal drugs.

dent-in-waiting"—to become "everything" should the President die, resign, or be removed from office.

Through much of our history the Vice Presidency has been slighted—treated as an office of little real consequence and, often, as the butt of jokes.

Several—in fact, nearly all—Vice Presidents themselves have had a hand in this. John Adams described his post as "the most insignificant office that ever the invention of man contrived or his imagination conceived." And Thomas Jefferson who followed him, found the office "honorable and easy" and "tranquil and unoffending."

Theodore Roosevelt, who had come to the White House from the Vice Presidency, was annoyed by the tinkling of the prisms of a chandelier in the presidential study. He ordered it removed, saying: "Take it to the office of the Vice President. He doesn't have anything to do. It will keep him awake." The handsome fixture has been in the Vice President's office, just off the Senate floor, ever since.

John Nance Garner, who served for two terms as Franklin Roosevelt's Vice

---

[12]Article I, Section 3, Clause 4, see page 296.

[13]25th Amendment, Sections 3 and 4. The 12th Amendment declares that the Vice President must meet the same qualifications for office as those set out for the Presidency.

President once said; "The Vice Presidency isn't worth a warm pitcher of spit." And Alben Barkley, who served during Harry Truman's second term, often told the story of a woman who had two sons. One of them, he said, went away to sea and the other one became Vice President, "and neither of them was ever heard from again."

Despite these—and a great many other—slightings, the office is important, of course.

Its occupant is, literally, "only a heartbeat away from the Presidency." Remember, eight Presidents have died in office—and one, Richard M. Nixon, was forced to resign in 1974.

Much of the blame for the low state of the Vice Presidency belongs to the two major parties and the process they use to nominate their candidates for the office. Traditionally, each convention names the hand-picked choice of its just-nominated presidential candidate. And, invariably, the presidential candidate picks someone who will "balance the ticket"—that is, a running mate who can improve the electoral chances of the presidential nominee. In short, fate and the Vice Presidency do not have a very high priority in the vice-presidential candidate selection process.

Gerald R. Ford became the 38th President of the United States following the resignation of Richard M. Nixon in 1974.

The Vice Presidency has been vacant 18 times thus far—nine times by succession to the Presidency, twice by resignation, and seven times by death.[14] Yet, not until the 25th Amendment did the Constitution deal with the matter. Section 2 states that:

> Whenever there is a vacancy in the office of the Vice President, the President shall nominate a Vice President who shall take office upon confirmation by a majority vote of both houses of Congress.

VICE PRESIDENTS WHO SUCCEEDED TO THE PRESIDENCY

John Tyler—upon the death (pneumonia) of William Henry Harrison, April 4, 1841.

Millard Fillmore—upon the death (gastroenteritis) of Zachary Taylor, July 9, 1850.

Andrew Johnson—upon the death (assassination) of Abraham Lincoln, April 13, 1865.

Chester A. Arthur—upon the death (assassination) of James A. Garfield, September 19, 1881.

Theodore Roosevelt—upon the death (assassination) of William McKinley, September 14, 1901.

Calvin Coolidge—upon the death (undisclosed illness) of Warren G. Harding, August 2, 1923.

Harry S. Truman—upon the death (cerebral hemorrhage) of Franklin D. Roosevelt, April 12, 1945.

Lyndon B. Johnson—upon the death (assassination) of John F. Kennedy, November 22, 1963.

Gerald R. Ford—upon the resignation of Richard M. Nixon, August 9, 1974.

[14]John C. Calhoun resigned to become a Senator from South Carolina in 1832. Spiro T. Agnew resigned in 1973, after a conviction for income tax evasion and in the face of charges of corruption dating from his service as a county executive and then governor of Maryland. The seven who died in office: George Clinton (1812), Elbridge Gerry (1814), William R. King (1853), Henry Wilson (1875), Thomas H. Hendricks (1885), Garret A. Hobart (1899), and James S. Sherman (1912).

The provision was first implemented in 1973—when President Nixon selected and Congress confirmed Gerald Ford to succeed Spiro Agnew as Vice President. And it came into play again in 1974 when President Ford named and Congress approved Nelson Rockefeller as Mr. Ford's successor.

The more recent Presidents—from Eisenhower to Reagan—have made greater use of their Vice Presidents. Today, Vice President Bush takes part in Cabinet meetings and is a member of the important National Security Council. Mr. Bush also carries out a number of social, political, diplomatic, and administrative chores for the President.

Many have long urged that the Vice President be given a larger role in the executive branch. But, so far, no President has "upgraded" the Vice President to the role of a true "Assistant President." The major reason: Of all of the President's official family, only the Vice President is not subject to the ultimate discipline of removal from office by the President.

FOR REVIEW

1. What duties does the Constitution give to the Vice President?
2. On what basis do the major parties regularly pick their vice presidential candidates?
3. How many Vice Presidents have succeeded to the Presidency? Who were they, and when and why did they succeed?
4. How is a vacancy in the Vice Presidency filled? Has this ever happened?
5. Why has no President yet made the Vice President a true "Assistant President"?

Presidential Nomination and Election

In strictly formal terms, the President is chosen according to the provisions of the Constitution.[15] In practice, however, the President is elected through an altogether extraordinary process—which has developed over now 49 presidential elections. It is a composite of constitutional provisions, a few State and federal laws, and—in largest measure—a number of practices born of and applied by the nation's political parties.

No other election—here or abroad—can match its color, drama, or suspense. None can match the tremendous popular interest it attracts nor the huge amounts of time, effort, and money it consumes.

Original Constitutional Provisions

The Framers of the Constitution gave more time to the method for choosing the President than to any other matter. It was, said James Wilson of Pennsylvania, "the most difficult of all on which we have had to decide." It was a difficult one largely because most of the Framers were against selecting the President by either of the obvious ways: by Congress or by a direct vote of the people.

Early in the Convention, most of the delegates favored selection by Congress. But nearly all of them later came to the view that it would, as Hamilton said, put the President "too much under the legislative thumb."

Only a few of the Framers favored choosing the President by popular vote. Nearly all agreed that that would lead "to tumult and disorder." Most of them felt that the people, scattered over

[15]The Constitution deals with the process of presidential selection in these several places: Article II, Section 1, Clauses 2 and 4, and the 12th, 20th, and 23rd Amendments.

so wide an area, could not possibly know enough about the available candidates to make wise, informed choices. George Mason of Virginia spoke for most of his colleagues when he said on the floor of the Convention:

> The extent of the country renders it impossible that the people can have the requisite capacity to judge of the respective contentions of the candidates.

The Framers finally agreed on a plan first put forward by Hamilton. Under it, the President was to be chosen by a body of electors. They agreed that:

(1) Each State would have as many presidential electors as it has Senators and Representatives in Congress;

(2) These electors would be chosen in each State in a manner the State legislature directed;

(3) The electors, meeting in their own States, would each cast two votes—each for a different person;

(4) The electoral votes from the several States would be opened and counted before a joint session of Congress;

(5) The person receiving the largest number of electoral votes, provided that total was a majority of all of the electors, would become President;

(6) The person with the second highest number of electoral votes would become Vice President;

(7) If a tie occurred, or if no one received the votes of a majority of the electors, the President would then be chosen by the House of Representatives, voting by States;

(8) If a tie occurred for the second spot, the Vice President would then be chosen by the Senate.

The Framers thought and spoke of the electors as "the most enlightened and respectable citizens" from each State. They were to be "free agents" who would "deliberate freely" in choosing the persons best qualified to fill the nation's two highest offices.

Impact of the Rise of Parties

The original version of the electoral college system worked as the Framers intended only for as long as George Washington was willing to seek and hold the Presidency. He was twice, and unanimously, elected President. That is, in 1789 and again in 1792, each elector cast one of his two ballots for the great Virginian.

Flaws began to appear in the system in 1796, however. By then, political parties had begun to form. John Adams, the Federalist candidate, was elected to the Presidency. Thomas Jefferson, an archrival and Democratic-Republican, who lost to Adams by just three votes in the electoral balloting, became his Vice President.

The system broke down in the election of 1800. By then there were two well-defined parties—the Federalists, led by Adams and Hamilton, and the Democratic-Republicans, headed by Jefferson. Each of these parties nominated presidential and vice presidential candidates. They also nominated elector-candidates in the several States. Those elector-candidates were picked with the clear understanding that, if elected, they would then vote for their party's presidential vice presidential nominees.

Each of the 73 Democratic-Republicans who won posts as electors voted for their party's nominees: Jefferson and Aaron Burr. In doing so, they produced a tie for the Presidency. Remember that the Constitution gave each elector *two* votes, each to be cast for a *different* person but each to be cast for someone *as President*. Popular opinion clearly favored Jefferson for the Presidency, and the party had intended Burr for the Vice Presidency. But, still, the House of Representatives had to take 36 separate ballots before it finally chose Jefferson.

The spectacular election of 1800 marked the introduction of three new elements into that process: (1) party nominations for the Presidency and Vice Presidency; (2) the nomination of candidates for presidential electors pledged to vote for their party's presidential ticket; and (3) the automatic casting of the electoral votes in line with those pledges.

The 12th Amendment. The 12th Amendment was added to the Constitution to make certain there would never be another fiasco of 1800. The amendment is a lengthy one, but it made only one major change in the electoral college system. It *separated* the presidential and vice presidential elections: "The Electors . . . shall name in their ballots the person voted for as President, and in distinct ballots the person voted for as Vice President."[16]

---

[16]Not only does the amendment mean there cannot be a repetition of the circumstances that led to the tie of 1800; it also certainly guarantees that the President and Vice President will always come from the same party.

THE PATH TO THE PRESIDENCY

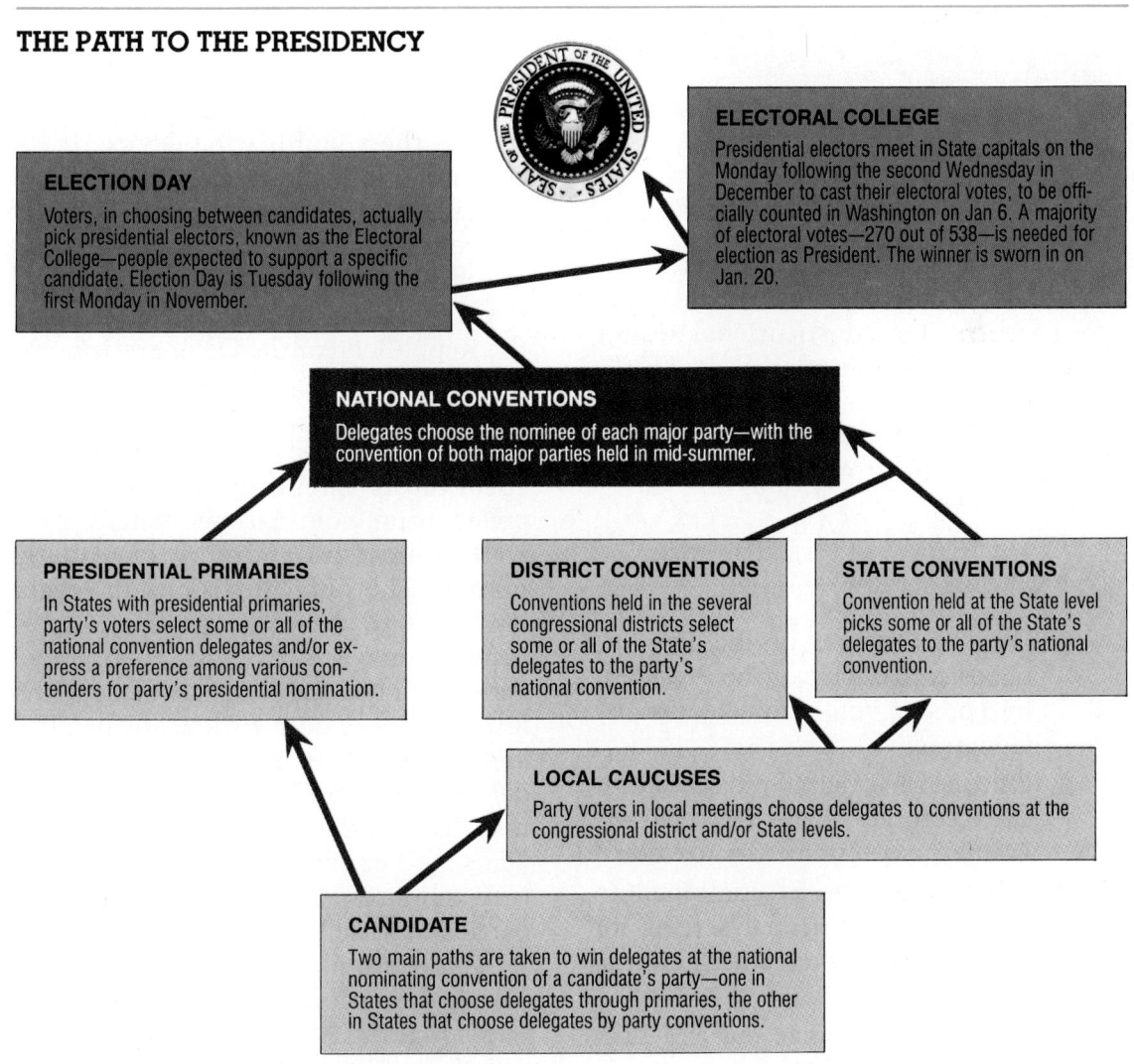

ELECTION DAY

Voters, in choosing between candidates, actually pick presidential electors, known as the Electoral College—people expected to support a specific candidate. Election Day is Tuesday following the first Monday in November.

ELECTORAL COLLEGE

Presidential electors meet in State capitals on the Monday following the second Wednesday in December to cast their electoral votes, to be officially counted in Washington on Jan 6. A majority of electoral votes—270 out of 538—is needed for election as President. The winner is sworn in on Jan. 20.

NATIONAL CONVENTIONS

Delegates choose the nominee of each major party—with the convention of both major parties held in mid-summer.

PRESIDENTIAL PRIMARIES

In States with presidential primaries, party's voters select some or all of the national convention delegates and/or express a preference among various contenders for party's presidential nomination.

DISTRICT CONVENTIONS

Conventions held in the several congressional districts select some or all of the State's delegates to the party's national convention.

STATE CONVENTIONS

Convention held at the State level picks some or all of the State's delegates to the party's national convention.

LOCAL CAUCUSES

Party voters in local meetings choose delegates to conventions at the congressional district and/or State levels.

CANDIDATE

Two main paths are taken to win delegates at the national nominating convention of a candidate's party—one in States that choose delegates through primaries, the other in States that choose delegates by party conventions.

Note: This outline indicates general procedures; many states vary them.

GOP presidential nominees—1856 to 1908

With the appearance of parties, the elections of 1800, and then the 12th Amendment, the constitutional setting was laid for the development of the presidential selection system as we know it today. What we now have is, indeed, a far cry from what was agreed upon in 1787.

☑ FOR REVIEW

1. Why were most of the Framers opposed to choosing the President by popular vote? To selection by Congress?

2. Outline the original provisions for the electoral college. How did the Framers expect electors to vote?

3. What three events combined to lay the constitutional setting for the present-day electoral college system?

4. What major change did the 12th Amendment make?

National Conventions

The Constitution makes no provision for the nomination of candidates for the Presidency. As the Framers set up the system, the electors would, out of their own knowledge, select the "wisest and best man" as President. But, as we have seen, the rise of parties altered that system, drastically—and with the change came the need for nominations.

The first method the parties developed to nominate presidential candidates was the congressional caucus. As we saw on page 219, that method was regularly used in the elections of 1800 to 1824. But, as we know, its closed character led to its downfall in the mid-1820s. For the election of 1832, both major parties turned to the national convention as their nominating device. It has continued to serve them ever since.

Extent of Control by Law. By the convention process, the final selection of the President is, for all practical purposes, narrowed to one of two persons: the Republican or the Democratic nominee. Yet, there is almost no legal control of that vital process.

We have already noted that the Constitution is silent on the subject of presidential nominations. There is, as well, almost no statutory law on the matter. The only provisions in federal law have to do with the financing of conventions; see page 238. Also, only a very small body of State law deals with a few aspects of convention organization and procedure—such as the choosing of delegates and the manner in which they may cast their votes; see pages 358–361. Thus, the convention is largely a creature and a responsibility of the political parties themselves.

Convention Arrangements. In both parties the national committee is charged with making the plans and arrangements for the national convention. As much as a year before it is held, the committee meets (usually in Washington D.C.) to set the time and place for the convention. July has been the favored month; but each party has met in convention as early as mid-June and also as late as the latter part of August.

Where the convention is held is a matter of prime importance. There must be an adequate convention hall, sufficient hotel accommodations, plentiful entertainment outlets, and convenient transportation facilities. Political considerations are also brought to bear. A city in a doubtful state (one likely to go either way in the election)—is usually picked—in the hope of swaying the election outcome, of course. Aspirants for the party's nomination often lobby for the selection of a city in a section of the country in which they have a strong base of popular support.

Many of the nation's larger cities bid for the "honor"—and the financial return to local business—of hosting a national convention. For 1984, the GOP chose Dallas, with their meeting slated for August. The Democrats picked San Francisco and July.

Both major parties have met in Chicago more often than in any other city—a fact which points to that city's central location and other physical attractions. Its selection points up, as well, the significance of Illinois as a doubtful or "pivotal" State.

The Democrats held each of their first six conventions—from 1832 through 1852—in Baltimore. Since 1856 —when the Republicans held their first convention, in Philadelphia, and the Democrats moved to Cincinnati—the two parties have met in the cities shown in the accompanying table.

The Apportionment of Delegates. With the date and the location set, the national committee sends out its "call." That formal announcement names the time and place and also tells the party's

A tumultuous moment at the Democratic National Convention in 1980, held at Madison Square Garden in New York.

City	Republicans	Democrats
Atlantic City		1964
Baltimore	1864	1860, 1872 1912
Chicago	1860, 1868, 1880 1884, 1888, 1904, 1908, 1912, 1916, 1920, 1932, 1944, 1952, 1960	1864, 1884, 1892, 1896, 1932, 1940, 1944, 1952, 1956, 1968
Cincinnati	1876	1856, 1880
Cleveland	1924, 1936	
Dallas	1984	
Detroit	1980	
Denver		1908
Houston		1928
Kansas City, Mo.	1928, 1976	1900
Los Angeles		1960
Miami Beach	1968, 1972	1972
Minneapolis	1892	
New York		1868, 1924, 1976, 1980
Philadelphia	1856, 1872, 1900, 1940, 1948	1936, 1948
St. Louis	1896	1876, 1888, 1904, 1916
San Francisco	1956, 1964	1920, 1984

organization in each State how many delegates it may send to the convention.[17]

As a rule, both parties give each State organization a number of convention votes based upon that State's electoral votes. Over the past several conventions, however, both parties have awarded bonus delegates to those States which have supported the party's candidates in recent elections.

For 1984, the Republican's apportionment formula produced a convention of 2235 delegates, and the Democrat's more complicated plan 3933.[18] Given those numbers, it should be fairly clear that neither party's convention can be called "a deliberative body."

Selection of Delegates. There are really two campaigns for the Presidency in both of the major parties every four years. One of them is the contest between the Republican and the Democratic nominees, of course. The other, earlier and quite different one takes place *within* each of the parties: the struggle for convention delegates.

State laws and/or party rules fix the procedures by which the delegates are chosen in each State. That fact is a reflection of federalism, of course—and it has produced a crazy-quilt pattern of presidential primaries, conventions, and caucuses among the States.[19]

Presidential Primaries

Well over half of all the delegates to both national conventions now come from States where presidential primaries are held. Several of those primaries are major media events every fourth year—and, with their extensive television and other press coverage, they dominate much of the pre-convention scene. Each of the serious contenders for either party's nomination has to try to make the best possible showing in at least most of them.

As we noted on page 225, a presidential primary is one or both of two things. Depending upon the State, it is a process in which those who vote in a party's primary (1) elect some or all of a State party organization's delegates to the national convention, *and/or* (2) choose (express a preference) among various contenders for that party's presidential nomination.

The presidential primary first appeared in the early 1900's, as a part of the reform movement aimed at the boss-dominated convention system. Wiscon-

---

[17]In strictest fact, the call sets the number of convention *votes* each State organization will have. In several States the Democrats select more delegates than their quota of convention votes; some of the delegates from those States cast a fraction of a vote at the convention. Republicans do not permit fractional voting.

[18]In addition to the delegates assigned to their State organizations, each party allots delegates to the District of Columbia, Guam, Puerto Rico, and the Virgin Islands. The Democratic convention also includes delegates representing American Samoa, Democrats Abroad (Europe), and Latin American Democrats.

For 1984, the Democrats added a varying number of "superdelegates" to each State's delegation—to give convention seats (and votes) to the top party officers in each State and also to Democrats provided for 561 of these "superdelegates": 370 party leaders and State and local officeholders (governors, mayors, legislators, and so on), chosen by their respective State party organizations, and 191 members of Congress (164 Representatives and 27 Senators), picked by the House and Senate Democratic caucuses.

[19]To a very large extent, the GOP leaves the matter of selecting national convention delegates to its State party organizations and to State law.

The Democrats have added several such rules in recent years, however. In effect, they have nationalized much of the delegate selection process. Their rules are a direct result of the divisive Democratic convention in Chicago in 1968 and of their loss of the presidential election later that year. Most of them are aimed at prompting broader involvement in the choosing of delegates (especially by the young, blacks, other minority groups, and women) and at making other aspects of convention organization and procedure more democratic. Those rules have been adopted by the Democratic National Committee, and they are enforced by it.

As an example of all of this, from 1980 on the DNC's rules require each State party organization to choose an equal number of men and women as convention delegates. (The RNC "requests" their State parties to do so.) Its rules also provide that *only* Democrats may take part in the party's delegate selection process. Thus Democratic delegates cannot be chosen in an open primary (page 221) or by any other method in which Republicans, independents, or others may take part. (The GOP has no such rule.)

sin passed the first presidential primary law in 1905, providing for the popular election of national convention delegates. Several States soon followed that lead, and Oregon added the preference feature in 1910.

By 1916 nearly half of the States had adopted presidential primary laws. But many later dropped the device. By 1968 it was found in only 16 States and the District of Columbia.

Efforts to reform the national convention process—and especially in the Democratic Party—reversed that trend in the 1970's, however. Some form of the presidential primary was in place for 1984 in 27 States[20]—and also in the District of Columbia and Puerto Rico.

Again, a presidential primary is either or both of two things: a delegate selection process and/or a preference election. But once that much has been said, the device becomes very hard to describe—except on a State-by-State basis. The difficulty here comes largely from two sources. One is the fact that the details of the process vary from State to State, and sometimes very considerably. The other is the ongoing effects of reform efforts in both parties. In recent years, they—and especially the Democratic Party at the national level—have written and rewritten rules to prompt more grassroots participation in the delegate selection process. Those new rules have prompted many and frequent changes in State election laws.

Even a matter that seems so simple as the date for the primary shows the crazy-quilt pattern of State laws here. By tradition, New Hampshire holds the first of the presidential primaries every four years; and it guards its first-in-the-nation distinction very jealously. For 1984, its primary fell on February 28th. All of the others were then scattered over the next three months. The last ones took place on June 5th.

Until fairly recently, most of these primaries were both delegate-selection *and* preference exercises. Several of them were also "winner-take-all" contests. That is, the presidential aspirant who won the preference vote automatically won the support of all of the delegates chosen at the primary.

Winner-take-all primaries have all but disappeared, however—at least at the State-wide level.[21] For both 1976 and 1980—but not for 1984— the Democrats imposed a "proportional representation" rule. It required that, no matter how Democratic delegates were chosen, they (and their convention votes) had to be apportioned among the contenders for the party's presidential nomination in line with the support each of them had within the party in that particular State. States with winner-take-all contests had to change their laws to accommodate the Democrats rule. Most of them did so by doing away with the winner-take-all feature.

This rule had yet another major impact on the shape of these primaries. It led several States to give up the popular selection of delegates—among them both Oregon and Wisconsin, the two States that pioneered the presidential primary idea.

---

[20]In Alabama, California, Connecticut, Florida, Georgia, Idaho, Illinois, Indiana, Maryland, Massachusetts, Montana, Nebraska, New Hampshire, New Jersey, New Mexico, New York, North Carolina, Ohio, Oregon, Pennsylvania, Rhode Island, South Dakota, Tennessee, Texas, Vermont, West Virginia, Wisconsin. In some of those States the law permits but does not require a major party to hold one of these primaries. Thus, in 1984, the Republicans held presidential primaries in Texas and Wisconsin, but the Democrats did not. Also, these primaries sometimes occur in States without a presidential primary law—under party rules, instead.

[21]For 1984, the Democrats adopted a new rule which does allow for winner-take-all primaries—but only if they are held at the congressional district level. That is, the Democrats now permit winner-take-all primaries in those States where the presidential primary is held, separately, in each of the State's congressional districts.

More than half of the presidential primary States now hold *only* a preference primary (often called a "beauty contest"). The delegates themselves are chosen later, at party conventions and/or by party committees.[22]

Most of the States with preference contests now hold what are sometimes known as "all-candidate" primaries." They require that the names of all the generally recognized contenders for a party's presidential nomination be listed on that party's preference ballot.[23]

Evaluation of the Presidential Primary.
No one who surveys the presidential primary system, as we have, needs to be told that it is very complicated-nor that it is filled with a number of confusing variations.

Nevertheless, these primaries play a vital role in the presidential nominating process. Overall, they are important for two major reasons: *First,* they tend to democratize the delegate-selection process. *Second,* they usually force would-be nominees to test their candidacies in actual political combat.

Hard-fought contests seldom occur in the party in power. This tends to be true either because the President (1) is himself seeking reelection or (2) has groomed a successor. In either case the President is almost always able to get his way.

Both 1976 and 1980 were exceptions to that rule—but not altogether. In 1976 Ronald Reagan made a stiff run at President Ford in the Republican Party. And

Senator Edward Kennedy gave President Carter a real fight in the Democratic Party in 1980. But one useful way of looking at both of those events is to begin with the fact that the incumbent President *did* win his party's nomination.

The primaries are often "knock-down, drag-out" battles in the other party, however. Without the unifying force of the President as party leader, the several leaders and factions in the party vie with one another, vigorously, for the presidential nomination. Here one of the major functions of the presidential primaries can usually be seen—the screening out of the lesser contenders to the point where only one or a few are really available for the nomination.

The recent "explosion" in the number of presidential primaries has had any number of consequences. Not the least of them center on the candidates and their problems of time, effort, money, scheduling, and fatigue—to say nothing of the public's fatigue. Adlai Stevenson once said, in a day when there were less than half as many primaries: "The hardest thing about any political campaign is how to win without proving that you are unworthy of winning."

Many critics think that each of the major parties should hold a single, *nationwide* presidential primary. Some of them would have both parties nominate their presidential candidates in those contests. They would do away with the conventions—except, perhaps, to pick vice presidential nominees or to write platforms. Indeed, President Wilson favored a constitutional amendment to that end back in 1913.

Other critics see a national primary as the best way for the parties either (1) to select all of their convention delegates or (2) to allow their voters to express their candidate preferences, that would then bind (instruct) the delegates from their States.

[22]In most of these States the delegates must be picked in line with the results of the preference primary—*e.g.*, in 1980, so many delegates for Carter, so many for Kennedy; so many for Reagan, so many for Bush, and so on.

[23]Until fairly recently, each of the contenders could decide whether to enter a State's preference primary, or not. They ran only in those States where they expected to win or at least do reasonably well. The "all-candidate" primary takes the enter-or-not decision out of the hands of the contenders; it allows the voters to choose among the various contenders for a party's presidential nomination.

The pre-convention fight for the presidential nomination is almost always a "knock-down, drag-out" affair in the party out of power. Eight major contenders sought the Democrats' nod in 1984.

Still other critics favor a different plan. They would have a series of *regional* primaries—held at two-or three-week intervals in groups of States across the country.

Hope for any of these plans is dim at best. Each of them would require joint action by Congress, the States, and both major parties. Beyond that hurdle, recall this point from Chapter 9: The nominating process is an *intra*-party process; however it is conducted, it can have a very *divisive* effect on a party; and the primary *magnifies* that ever-present possibility. In short, neither major party has ever been much interested in abandoning its national convention. Both of them see the convention as a device to promote compromise and, out of it, party unity.

Caucuses and Conventions. In those States that do not hold presidential primaries, delegates are chosen in a system of caucuses and conventions.[24] Here, too the details of the process are different from State to State. At base, however, it works pretty much as we described it in Chapter 9 (page 219).

The party's voters meet in local caucuses, generally at the precinct level. There they choose delegates to a local or district convention where delegates to the State convention are picked. At the State level, and sometimes in the district conventions, delegates to the national convention are chosen.

The caucus-convention process is the oldest method for picking national convention delegates. But, notice, less than half of all of the delegates to either party's convention now come from those States that still use it. The Iowa caucuses generally get the most attention every fourth year—largely because they are now the first to be held in every presidential election season.

☑ FOR REVIEW

1. To what extent does federal law deal with the national conventions? State law?

2. What body handles arrangements for a party's convention?

3. What is the general shape of each party's delegate apportionment formula?

4. A presidential primary is either or both of what two things?

5. By what other process are convention delegates now chosen?

6. Why are hard-fought presidential primaries fairly common in the party out of power? Rather rare in the President's party?

7. Why has neither of the two major parties shown any interest in abandoning its national convention in favor of a national primary?

---

[24]More of the crazy-quilt point: Remember that in several of the presidential primary States some and often all of the national delegates are actually picked in party conventions.

The Convention Setting

Each party's national convention meets in a huge auditorium lavishly hung with flags, bunting, and various party symbols. Portraits of great figures from the party's past adorn the hall. The front of it is dominated by a large platform and the speaker's rostrum from which the proceedings are managed. The floor itself is jammed with row upon row of hundreds of chairs. Standards and placards mark the seating reserved for each State delegation. Microphones and telephones are spotted at strategic points. There are extensive facilities for the army of press, radio, and television reporters, commentators, camera operators, technicians, and all their equipment. The galleries seat thousands who come from all over the country to see the "greatest political show on earth." They come to see a spectacle H. L. Mencken once described this way:

> [T]here is something about a national convention that makes it as fascinating as a revival or a hanging. It is vulgar, it is ugly, it is stupid, it is tedious, it's hard upon both the cerebral centers and the *gluteus maximus,* and yet it is somehow charming. One sits through long sessions wishing heartily that all the delegates were dead and in hell—and then suddenly there comes a show so gaudy and hilarious, so melodramatic and obscene, so unimaginably exhilarating and preposterous that one lives a gorgeous year in an hour.

In the middle of all of this—and the turbulence and confusion that is a part of nearly all that happens—the convention meets to do two major things. First, to adopt the party's platform and, most importantly, to nominate its presidential and vice presidential candidates.

The Opening Session

Each party's convention generally runs four, sometimes five, days, and the order of business is much the same in both.

The opening session is called to order by the chairperson of the party's national committee. The *Star Spangled Banner* is played, the official call is read, prayer is offered, and the temporary roll of delegates is called. Welcoming speeches are made by the national chairperson and a number of other party dignitaries.

The national chairperson then announces a slate of temporary officers for the convention, one of whom is the temporary presiding officer—all named by the national committee. The delegates promptly elect them.

The temporary chairperson then takes the rostrum to give the first major speech. Both it, and the *keynote address* that follows it, run to a predictable pattern: the party is praised, the opposition is attacked, a plea for party harmony is made, and a smashing victory at the polls is forecast.

Following the keynoter's oratorical efforts, the delegates routinely elect the convention's standing committees. There are four major committees at every convention: rules and order of business, permanent organization, credentials, and platform and resolutions. Each State delegation now has two members (a man and a woman) on each of them. After these committees are selected, the first session generally ends.

The Second and Third Sessions

The next two or three, and sometimes four, sessions of the convention are given over to more speeches by leading party figures and to the receipt of committee reports. In the more recent conventions, both parties have slated these sessions to for the late afternoon and/or early evening—hoping for prime time on network television, of course.

Typically, the committee on rules and order of business reports first. It regularly recommends the adoption of the rules of the last convention with, perhaps, a few changes. Its report, which also presents an agenda for the rest of the convention, is generally accepted with little or no dissent. But at times there have been vigorous rules fights.

The credentials committee prepares the permanent roll of delegates entitled to seats and votes in the convention. Occasionally, there are contests over the seating of particular delegates and even whole delegations. When this happens, it generally involves a State in which the party is faction-ridden and where the delegates are chosen by the caucus-convention process.

The committee on permanent organization nominates the permanent convention officers. When elected, they direct the remaining sessions of the convention. Selecting the permanent chairperson is often a test of the strength of the rivals for the presidential nomination. Upon election, the permanent chairperson delivers another of

Scenes from the national conventions held in 1980. *Left:* Floor activity at the Democratic National Convention. *Top/center:* A delegate from the Lone Star State. *Bottom/center:* Media personnel at work. *Right:* Republican delegates applaud a speaker.

PERSONALITY PROFILE

DELEGATE
TO A NATIONAL CONVENTION

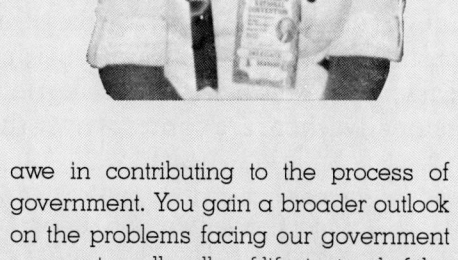

Betty J. DeVito first became interested in politics at age 13 when she was excused from school to see presidential candidate, Harry Truman, speak from the caboose of a train in Sharon, PA. She got her own start in politics by "licking envelopes" in campaigns. Since then, the busy wife and mother of seven (who is also a State auditor) has had many adventures in politics. Among many other things, she's been a presidential elector, a guest at the White House, and a delegate to the 1976 and 1980 Democratic conventions.

On her experiences as a national convention delegate, she says:

> It's a totally exhausting physical experience. You're up at 6:30 every morning and work until late at night. It can also be quite expensive. You have to miss work, and the cost of attending a National Convention can exceed $1000.
>
> Despite the drawbacks, it's exciting, vigorous and renews your political spirit. You have the opportunity to converse and exchange ideas with groups that share mutual concerns. You also get an overwhelming sense of participation and

awe in contributing to the process of government. You gain a broader outlook on the problems facing our government concerning all walks of life, instead of the narrow restraints of your own locale.

And on why she spends endless hours on her many political activities:

> Contributing to the political process on all levels and aspects of campaigns gives you a great sense of self-satisfaction in that you are "doing something" about government. I take pride in the fact that others may complain whereas I try to contribute.

1. Do you know someone who is as politically active as Betty DiVito?
2. What motivates (prompts) people like Mrs. DiVito to become so actively involved in the political process?

those lengthy speeches in which the party is praised, the opposition party is attacked, unity is prayed for, and a smashing victory is foreseen.

The report of the committee on platform and resolutions—in the form of a proposed platform—usually reaches the floor by the third session.

Much of the party's platform emerges from a draft drawn up by party leaders or, for the party in power, by the Presi-

dent and his advisors. A struggle may—and often does—develop within the committee, and at times the fight spills over to the convention floor.

Platform-writing is a fine art. The document is supposed to be a basic statement of the party's principles and its stands on major policy matters. But it is also a campaign statement—intended to win as many votes as possible, while alienating none. So, both parties tend to produce somewhat generalized, less than specific comments on many of the hard questions of the day.

Still, they do contain many hard and fast policy positions—and, at the same time, they reflect the compromise nature of both our politics and each of the two major parties.

The Final Sessions. By its fourth, sometimes the fifth, session, the convention at last comes to the nomination of the party's presidential candidate.

The names of any number of contenders may be offered to the delegates. For each of them there is a nominating speech and then several seconding speeches. They are lavish hymns of praise, extolling the virtues of "The man who. . . ." Although the "who" is well known before the nominator begins to speak, tradition has it that that person's name is little more than hinted at until the very end of the speech. Its final announcement sets off a lengthy, wild, noisy demonstration on the floor. These "spontaneous" demonstrations—supposed to show widespread support for the aspirant, whether real or not—are carefully planned, of course.[25]

After all of the nominating speeches, and their seconds, have been made, the balloting begins. The secretary calls the States alphabetically and each chairperson announces the vote of his or her delegation. Each complete roll call is known as a "ballot." In both parties a majority vote is needed to select the presidential candidate. Balloting goes on until someone has the magic number.

Most often, the first ballot produces a choice. In the 21 conventions each party has held in the period 1900–1980, the Republicans have made a first-ballot

nomination 17 times and the Democrats 16 times.[26]

Once the presidential nomination has been decided, the choice of a running mate comes as an anti-climax. The vice presidential nominee is almost invariably the choice of the just-nominated presidential candidate; see page 352.

With the candidates named, the convention comes to the last major item on its agenda: the presidential candidate's acceptance speech. And, as that speech ends, the delegates—all of them super-patriots of the party—nearly tear the convention hall apart.

Whom Does the Party Nominate? If an incumbent President wants another term, the answer is almost always easy—the President is almost certain to get the nomination, and usually with no real opposition from within the party. Indeed, each time in this century that the incumbent has sought the nomination he has received it. The President's advantages are immense: the majesty and publicity of the office and close control of the party machinery.[26a]

But when the President is not in the field, from two or three to a dozen or so more-or-less serious contenders surface in the preconvention period. At least two or three of them usually survive to contest the prize at the convention.

[25]Some of the candidates offered to a convention have no real chance of becoming the party's presidential nominee, but are put forward for some other reason. Thus, a "favorite son" may be offered because a State delegation wants to honor one of its own.

[26]From 1832 until 1936 the Democrats required a two-thirds vote for nomination. The Republicans have required a simple majority for nomination from their first convention in 1856. A convention can (and a few in both parties have) become deadlocked—that is, find itself unable to make a choice between the top two, or sometimes three, contenders for the nomination. In that event, a "darkhorse" (someone who did not appear to be a likely choice before the convention) may finally be nominated. The most spectacular deadlock occurred at the Democratic convention in New York in 1924; 123 separate ballots were taken over the course of nine days before John W. Davis became the party's candidate.
[26a]In fact, only four sitting Presidents have ever been denied nomination: John Tyler, by the Whigs in 1844; Millard Fillmore, by the Whigs in 1852; Franklin Pierce, by the Democrats in 1856; and Chester Arthur, by the Republicans in 1884.

Who among them will win the nomination? The record argues this answer: the one who is, in the jargon of politics, the most **available**—the one who is the most nominatable and electable. The nominating process tries to come up with candidates who can *win*.

Most presidential candidates have come to their nominations with substantial and well-known records in public office. *But* those records have not been studded with controversies which could have antagonized important elements within the party or among the voting public. And, generally, they have served in *elective* office, where they have shown a considerable vote-getting ability. Seldom does one step from the business world or from the military directly into the role of candidate, as did Wendell Willkie in 1940 or Dwight Eisenhower in 1952.

Historically, the governorships of the larger States have produced the largest number of presidential candidacies. Eleven of the 20 men nominated by the two major parties between 1900 and 1956 were either then serving or had once served as a governor.

For a time, the Senate became the prime source, however. In the four elections from 1960 through 1972, each of the major party nominees had been a Senator; and none had ever been a governor.

But the old pattern seems to have been restored. Jimmy Carter, the former governor of Georgia, was nominated by the Democrats in 1976 and 1980; and Ronald Reagan, former governor of California, was the GOP choice in 1980.

Despite the few exceptions, most notably Democrats Alfred E. Smith in 1928 and John F. Kennedy in 1960, most of the leading contenders for major party presidential nominations have been Protestants. Most have also come from the larger and doubtful States. Thus, candidates from such "pivotal" States as New York, Ohio, Illinois, or California are more available than those from smaller States. From this standpoint, the nominations of Senator Barry Goldwater of Arizona by the Republicans in 1964 and Senator George McGovern of South Dakota by the Democrats in 1972 were more than just a little exceptional. So, too, was the Democratic nomination of Jimmy Carter from Georgia in 1976.

Neither party has, at least to this point, seriously considered a woman as its candidate for the Presidency or the Vice Presidency. Nor has either party seriously contemplated a black for either role.

The candidates usually have a pleasing and healthy appearance, seem to be happily married, and have a happy (and exploitable) family. Adlai Stevenson, the Democratic nominee in 1952 and 1956, and Ronald Reagan, the GOP candidate in 1980, are the only major party nominees ever to have been divorced.

A well-developed speaking ability has always been a major factor of availa-

Democratic nominees Jimmy Carter and Walter Mondale are joined by their wives as they accept the cheers of the delegates.

bility. And, of course, being able to project well over television has become an absolute must over the past 20 years or so.

Presidential candidate Ronald Reagan delivers his acceptance speech to the cheers of the Republican National Convention in 1980.

☑ **FOR REVIEW**

1. Around what four committees is much of a national convention's work organized?
2. What is the general tone of the typical party platform? Why?
3. What is *the* major purpose of a national convention?
4. Why are incumbent Presidents almost certain to win their party's nomination to another term if they want it?
5. What does the term "availability" mean in presidential politics?

The Presidential Campaign

For a short period after the conventions, the opposing candidates rest and plan their campaigns. Then the presidential campaign—the grinding effort to win votes—begins in earnest. Every means to put the candidates and their ideas before the voters, and in the best light, is used. Radio and television speeches, "whistle-stop" tours, press conferences, press releases, public rallies, party dinners, newspaper, radio, and television advertisements, campaign stickers and buttons, placards and pamphlets, billboards and matchcovers —all bombard the voters in behalf of each party's nominees. The candidates pose for hundreds of photographs, shake thousands of hands, and strive to convince the electorate that a victory for the other side would mean hard times for the country. Whether the campaign really changes an important number of votes or not—and the point is debatable —the massive efforts continue right up to election eve.

The Electoral College Today

The presidential campaign ends with election day, when millions of voters go to the polls.

Here we come to one of the least well understood parts of the American political process. As the people vote in the presidential election, they do *not* choose among the contenders for the Presidency. Instead, they vote to elect presidential electors.

Remember, the Constitution provides for the election of the President by the electoral college—in which each State has as many electors as it has members of Congress. The Framers expected that the electors would use their own judgment in selecting a President. But for more than 180 years now, the parties have nominated slates of elector candidates in each State. The electors, once chosen, are automatons—"rubber stamps." Despite the Framers' intent, they are expected to vote, automatically, for their party's candidates for President and Vice President.

In short, the electors go through the *form* set out in the Constitution, in order to meet the *letter* of the Constitution—but their behavior is a far cry from its original *intent*. The electors are chosen by popular vote in every State,[27] and on the same day everywhere in the country—the Tuesday after the first Monday in November every fourth year. In 1980 the presidential election fell on November 4th; in 1984 it will be held on November 6th.

They are chosen at-large—from the entire State—in every State now except Maine.[28] That is, the electors are chosen on a "winner-take-all" basis. The presidential candidate (technically, the slate of elector-candidates) receiving the largest popular vote in a State wins *all* of that State's electoral votes. (Today, the names of the individual elector-candidates appear on the ballot in less than a fourth of the States. In most, only the names of the presidential and vice presidential candidates are listed—they stand as "shorthand" for the elector slates)

The electors meet at their State capitol on the date set by Congress—now the Monday following the second Wednesday in December.[29] There they each cast their electoral votes—one for President and one for Vice President. Their ballots, signed and sealed, are sent by registered mail to the President of the Senate in Washington.[30]

Which party has won a majority of the electoral votes—and who then will be the next President of the United States—is usually known by midnight of election day, more than a month before the electors cast their ballots. But the *formal* election of the President and Vice President *finally* takes place on January 6th.

On that date, the President of the Senate opens the electoral votes from each State and counts them before a joint session of Congress. The candidate who receives a majority of the electors' votes for President is declared elected—as, too, is the one with a majority of the votes for Vice President.

If no one has a majority for President (at least 270 of the 538 electoral votes), the election is thrown into the House of Representatives. This happened, as we saw, in 1800, and again in 1824. The House chooses a President from among the top three candidates in the electoral college. Each State delegation has one vote, and it takes a majority of 26 to elect. If the House fails to choose a President by January 20, the 20th Amendment provides that the newly elected Vice President shall act as President until it does.[31]

[27]The Constitution (Article II, Section 1, Clause 2) says that the electors are to be chosen in each State "in such manner as the legislature thereof may direct." In several States the legislatures themselves chose the electors in the first several elections. By 1832, however, every State except South Carolina had provided for popular election. The electors were picked by the legislature in South Carolina through the elections of 1960. Since then, all presidential electors have been chosen by popular vote in every State, with but two exceptions. The State legislature chose the electors in Florida in 1868 and in Colorado in 1876.

[28]Beginning with the 1972 election, Maine now uses the "district plan." Two of that State's four electors are chosen from the State at-large and the other two from each of the State's congressional districts. The district plan was used by several States in the first several presidential elections, but every State (except South Carolina) had provided for the choice of the electors from the State at-large by 1832. Since then, the district plan has been used only by Michigan in 1892 and by Maine in 1972, 1976, and 1980.

[29]Article II, Section 1, Clause 4 provides that the date Congress sets "shall be the same throughout the United States." The 12th Amendment provides that the electors "shall meet in their respective States."

[30]Two copies are also sent to the Archivist of the United States, two to the State's secretary of State, and one to the local federal district court.

[31]The 20th Amendment further provides that "the Congress may by law provide for the case wherein neither a President-elect nor a Vice President-elect shall have qualified" by inauguration day. Congress has done so in the Succession Act of 1947; see page 350. In such an event, the Speaker of the House would "act as President . . . until a President or Vice President shall have qualified."

In the "Stolen Election" of 1876, the Republican candidate, Rutherford B. Hayes, won the Presidency. He received 185 electoral votes, to the 184 won by his opponent, Samuel J. Tilden, the Democrat. (The basic facts involved in the electoral vote count are set out in note 33, on page 371.) Here, the results of the Electoral Commission's review of the 20 disputed electoral votes are handed to the President *pro tem* of the Senate—in a joint session of Congress (meeting in the House Chamber), at 4:00 A.M. on March 2, 1877.

1. Who was the Senate's President *pro tem* who, with the Speaker of the House, presided at that joint session of Congress?
2. Why was he sitting in the place that would normally have been occupied by the Vice President?
3. Who was then the Speaker of the House?

If no person receives a majority for Vice President, the Senate decides between the top two candidates. It takes a majority of the whole Senate to elect. The Senate has had to choose a Vice President only once. It elected Richard M. Johnson in 1837.

Defects in the Electoral College System

Criticisms of the electoral college system have been heard almost from the beginning—and so, too, have proposals for its reform. There are three major weaknesses in the present arrangement.

The First Major Defect. There is the ever-present threat that the electoral vote will contradict the popular vote, that the winner of the popular vote will *not* win the Presidency.

This continuing threat is largely the result of two factors:

The most important of them is the "winner-take-all" feature—the fact that in each State the winning candidate customarily receives *all* of that State's electoral vote. The other major party candidate's popular votes count for nothing in terms of the final outcome. In 1976, for example, Jimmy Carter carried the State of Ohio by a paper-thin margin—by only 9,333 votes, less than three-tenths of one percent. Despite the fact that more

ELECTORAL VOTE OF EACH STATE — 1980

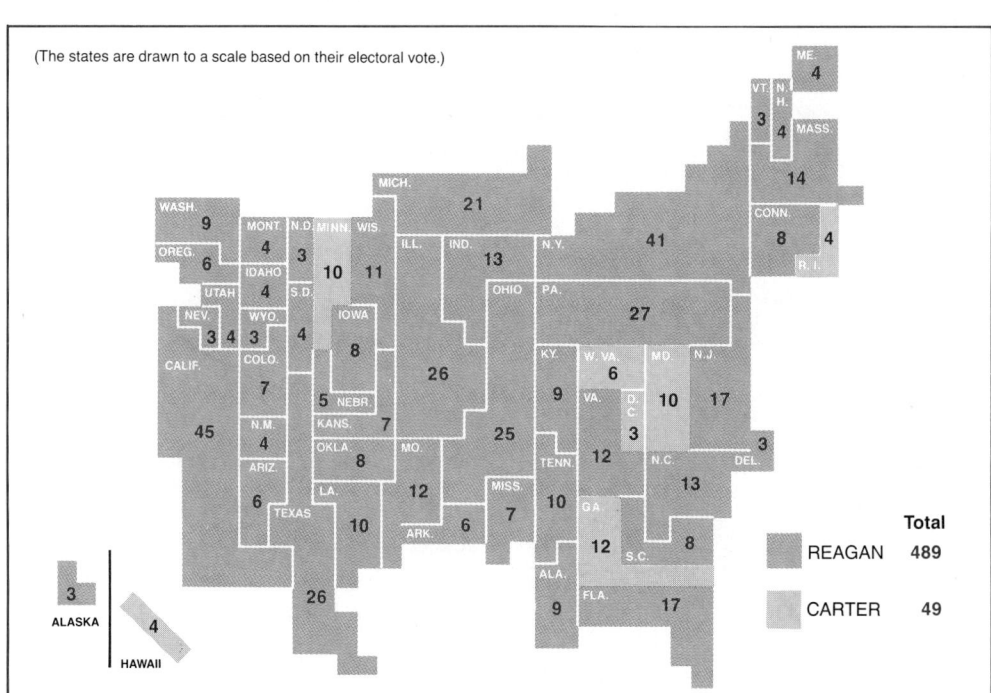

(The states are drawn to a scale based on their electoral vote.)

Total
REAGAN   489
CARTER   49

than two million people in Ohio voted for Gerald Ford, Carter won all 25 of the State's electoral votes.

The other major culprit here is the way in which the electoral votes are distributed among the States. Remember that each State has two electors because of its Senate seats, regardless of its population. Because of them, the distribution of electoral votes cannot begin to match the facts of population (and voter) distribution.

Take the extreme case to illustrate this situation: California, the largest State, now has 47 electoral votes—or one for each 503,586 persons, based on its 1980 population of 23,668,562. Alaska has three electoral votes—or one for each 133,494 persons, with its 1980 population of 400,481.

The popular vote winner has, in fact, failed to win the Presidency three times —in 1824, 1876, and 1888.

In 1824, Andrew Jackson won the largest share (a plurality, but not a majority) of the popular votes—151,174, or 40.3 percent of the total. Jackson's nearest rival, John Quincy Adams, received 113,122 votes, or 30.9 percent. Ninety-nine of the 261 electors then voted for Jackson—again a plurality, but far short of the constitutionally required majority. The election thus went to the House of Representatives and, early in 1825, it elected Adams to the Presidency.[32]

---

[32]Both Adams and Jackson were Democratic-Republicans; remember that the election of 1824 occurred during the one-party Era of Good Feeling; see page 175. Popular votes were cast in only 18 of the 24 States in 1824; the electors were chosen by the legislatures in Delaware, Georgia, Louisiana, New York, South Carolina, and Vermont. The popular vote figures given here are only approximately correct; vote counts were neither well-kept nor -recorded in 1824. These figures, as most of the popular vote results cited in this book, are drawn from the authoritative *Guide to U.S. Elections,* Congressional Quarterly, Inc., 1975.

In the election of 1876, Rutherford B. Hayes, the Republican candidate, received 4,034,311 popular votes and his Democratic opponent, Samuel J. Tilden, won 4,288,548. Tilden, with a popular plurality of 254,237, received 184 electoral votes. Hayes won 185 electoral votes and so became President.[33]

In 1888 President Grover Cleveland won 5,534,488 popular votes—90,596 more than his Republican opponent, Benjamin Harrison. But Harrison received 233 electoral votes to Cleveland's 168—and so became the 23rd President.

The system has not "misfired" since 1888, but it *could* have happened on *several* occasions. Take the close election of 1976. Jimmy Carter defeated his Republican opponent, Gerald Ford, by 1,678,069 popular votes—and won only a bare majority of the popular vote.[34]

If only a handful of voters in a few States had voted for Ford, instead of Carter, Ford would have had a majority of the electoral votes, and so kept the Presidency. Several States can be used to play this game, but the simplest one involves Ohio and Hawaii. If only 4667 of the 2,009,959 Carter votes in Ohio (25 electoral votes) and only 3687 of the

147,375 Carter votes in Hawaii (4 electoral votes) had gone to Ford instead, Ford would have received 270 electoral votes. Thus, Ford would have had a bare majority of the electoral votes and so won the election.

	Popular Vote	%	Electoral Vote	%
Carter	40,825,839	50.03	297	55.2
Ford	39,147,770	47.97	240	44.6
Others	1,629,737	2.00	1	0.2

Several other presidential elections can be used to illustrate the point, as well. In 1960, John F. Kennedy won a popular plurality of 114,673 votes over the Republican candidate, Richard M. Nixon—less than two-tenths of one percent of all of the votes cast:

	Popular Vote	%	Electoral Vote	%
Kennedy	34,221,334	49.7	303	56.4
Nixon	34,106,671	49.6	219	40.8
Byrd	—	—	15	2.8
Others	500,945	0.7	—	—

If only a comparatively few voters in a few States had voted for Nixon rather than Kennedy—for example, 4430 in Illinois (27 electoral votes in 1960), and 23,122 in Texas (24 electoral votes), Nixon would have won. And, like Carter in 1976, Kennedy would still have been the popular vote winner.

In short, the "winner-take-all" factor produces an electoral vote result which is, at best, only a very distorted reflection of the popular vote. Even the lopsided results in the 1980 race demonstrate the point:

[33]The election of 1876 is often called "the Stolen Election." Two conflicting sets of electoral votes were received from Florida (4 votes), Louisiana (8 votes), and South Carolina (7 votes), and the validity of one vote from Oregon was disputed. Congress set up an Electoral Commission—with five Senators, five Representatives, and five Supreme Court Justices—to decide the matter. The Commissioners—eight Republicans and seven Democrats—voted on strict party lines, awarding all of the disputed votes, and so the Presidency, to Hayes.

[34]To this point, 13 Presidents have been elected although they did not win a majority of the popular vote: John Quincy Adams won in the House in 1824, and Rutherford B. Hayes in 1876 and Benjamin Harrison in 1888. Each won the electoral vote count while losing the popular vote contest, as we have noted. The other 10 all were elected with a plurality, but not a majority, of the popular vote. These "minority Presidents": James K. Polk (1844), Zachary Taylor (1848), James Buchanan (1856), Abraham Lincoln (1860), James A. Garfield (1880), Grover Cleveland (1884 and 1892), Woodrow Wilson (1912 and 1916), Harry Truman (1948), John F. Kennedy (1960), Richard Nixon (1968).

	Popular Vote	%	Electoral Vote	%
Reagan	43,899,248	50.8	489	90.9
Carter	35,481,435	41.0	49	9.1
Anderson	5,719,437	6.6	—	—
Others	1,395,558	1.6	—	—

The Second Major Defect.   There is nothing in the Constitution, nor in any federal statute, *requiring* the electors to vote for the candidate favored by the popular vote in their States. (Several States do have such laws but they are of highly doubtful constitutionality, and none has ever been enforced.)

The electors are expected to vote for the candidate who carries their State and, as loyal partisans, they almost always do. Thus far, electors have "broken their pledges"—voted for someone other than their party's presidential nominee —on only eight occasions: in 1796, 1820, 1948, 1956, 1960, 1968, 1972, and 1976. In the most recent case, one Republican elector from Washington voted for Ronald Reagan instead of Gerald Ford, who had turned back Reagan's bid for the GOP nomination in 1976.

In no case has the vote of a "faithless elector" had a bearing on the outcome of a presidential election—but the potential is certainly there.

The Third Major Defect.   In any presidential election it is possible that the contest will be decided in the House of Representatives. This has happened only twice, as we know—and not since 1824. But in several other elections a strong third party bid has threatened to win enough electoral votes to make it impossible for either major party candidate to win in the electoral college— especially in 1912, 1924, 1948, and most recently in 1968. Look at 1968:

	Popular Vote	%	Electoral Vote	%
Nixon	31,785,148	43.4	301	55.9
Humphrey	31,274,503	42.7	191	35.5
Wallace	9,901,151	13.5	46	8.6
Others	242,568		—	—

George Wallace, the American Independent Party's candidate, won five States and received 46 electoral votes, as the map on page 211 shows. If Democrat Hubert Humphrey had carried Alaska, Delaware, Missouri, Nevada, and Wisconsin—States where Richard Nixon's margin was thin and in which Wallace also had a substantial vote— Nixon's electoral vote would have been 268 and Humphrey's 224. Neither would have had a majority. The House would then have had to choose among Humphrey, Nixon, and Wallace.[35]

[35]In 1968 Wallace received more popular votes than any other third-party presidential candidate, before or since; but Theodore Roosevelt in 1912 and Robert M. LaFollette in 1924 each received a *larger share* of the popular vote, 27.4 percent and 16.6 percent, respectively; see page 181.

From *Herblock's State of the Union* (Simon & Schuster, 1972).

"Don't be chicken—try it once more"

Three serious objections can be raised to election by the House: (1) The voting in such cases is by States, not by individual members. A small State—such as Alaska or Nevada—would have as much weight as even the most populous States, California and New York. (2) If the Representatives from a State were so divided that no candidate were favored by a majority of them, the State would lose its vote. (3) The Constitution requires a majority of the States for election in the House—today 26, of course. If a strong third party candidate were involved, it could prove to be almost impossible for the House to make a decision by inauguration day.[36]

☑ **F O R R E V I E W**

1. How many electors does each State have? How are they chosen? How are they expected to vote?

2. What is the total number of electors? At least how many electoral votes are needed to win the Presidency? The Vice Presidency?

3. If no candidate has at least that many votes, how is the President then chosen? The Vice President?

4. What are the three major weaknesses in the electoral college system? What is its winner-take-all feature?

5. Has the electoral college ever chosen a President who lost the popular vote contest? If so, when?

[36]In such a case, Section 3 of the 20th Amendment states that "the Vice President-elect shall act as President until a President shall have qualified"; and if no Vice President-elect is available, the Presidential Succession Act (page 350) would come into play. Notice that it is even mathematically possible for the minority party in the House to have control of a majority of the individual State delegations. That party could then elect its candidate—even though he or she may have run second (or even third) in both the popular and the electoral vote contests.

Proposed Reforms

The defects in the electoral college system have long been recognized, of course. Constitutional amendments to change the process have been introduced in every term of Congress since 1789. Most of the reforms which have been offered can be grouped under three headings:

(1) THE DISTRICT PLAN. Under this plan, the electors would be chosen in each State as are members of Congress. That is, two electors would be chosen from the State at-large and the others would be elected from each of the State's congressional districts.[37]

[37]Maine now uses the district plan, as we noted on page 368. Any other State could do so; but it would take a constitutional amendment to make its use mandatory in all States.

On a specified day, all the electors of each of the States assemble at their State capitols. Here, John W. McCormack of Massachusetts, formerly a Speaker of the House of Representatives, casts an electoral vote for George McGovern in 1972. His vote was one of 14 cast by Massachusetts electors.

The district plan would do away with the "winner-take-all" problem in the present system, of course. Its supporters —including former Presidents Johnson and Nixon—argue that it would make the electoral vote a more accurate reflection of the popular returns.

The strongest argument against the district plan is that it would *not* eliminate the possibility that the loser of the popular vote could still win the electoral vote. In fact, if the plan had been in effect in 1960, Richard Nixon would have received 278 electoral votes and he, not John Kennedy, would have won the Presidency.

Further, the results under the district plan would depend very much upon how the congressional districts were drawn in each State.

(2) THE PROPORTIONAL PLAN. Under this arrangement, each presidential candidate would receive the same share of a State's electoral vote as he or she received of that State's popular vote. If, for example, a candidate won 40 percent of the votes cast in a State with 20 electoral votes, he or she would receive eight electoral votes from that State.

Clearly, this plan would cure the "winner-take-all" problem. And, it would also do away with the "faithless elector" possibility. Also, it would most certainly produce an electoral vote more nearly in line with the popular vote—at least for *each State.*

It would not, however, necessarily produce the same result *nationally.* Because each of the smaller States is overweighted by its two Senate-based electors, the proportional plan would still make it possible for the loser of the popular vote to win the Presidency in the electoral vote. In fact, this would have happened in 1896 if the plan had been in effect for that election. William Jennings Bryan would have defeated William McKinley even though McKin-

ley had a comfortable popular vote margin of 596,985 (5.1 percent).[38]

Many who are against the proportional plan worry about its consequences for the two-party system—and, therefore, for the whole fabric of the American political system. The adoption of the plan would almost certainly mean a substantial increase in both the number and the vigor of minor parties. Minor party candidates would regularly receive at least some share of the electoral vote. The chance that one or more of them might be able to force a presidential election into the House would be much greater, too.[39]

(3) DIRECT POPULAR ELECTION. The proposal most often made—and most supported—is the most obvious one. It is: do away with the electoral college system altogether and provide for the direct popular election of the President.

The arguments for direct election seem overpowering. The strongest one is that it would support the democratic ideal: each vote would count, and equally, in the national result. The winner would always be the majority or plurality choice. The dangers and confusions of the present system would be ended— replaced by a simple and easily understood process. Opinion polls have long shown that there is overwhelming public support for direct election.

---

[38] And in the closest of all of the presidential elections, Winfield S. Hancock would have defeated James A. Garfield in 1880—even though Garfield had a popular plurality (of only 1898 votes, 0.0213 percent). But, on the other hand, there would have been no "Stolen Election" in 1876, and Cleveland would have defeated Harrison in 1888; see page 371.

[39] Most of the plan's backers agree that an increase in minor party clout would mean that the popular vote winner would often fail to gain a clear majority of the electoral vote. In 1976, for example, Jimmy Carter would have received 261.148 electoral votes to Gerald Ford's 258.860. (The typical proportional plan would carry the arithmetic to three decimal points.) Hence, they would reduce the majority requirement to that of a plurality of at least 40 percent. If no candidate won at least 40 percent of the electoral votes, a second election, with only the two front runners, would be held.

From *The Herblock Gallery* (Simon & Schuster, 1968)

"You go first, sonny, then point me toward him"

Several "practical" obstacles stand in the way of this proposal, however; and, because of them, there seems little real chance of its adoption any time soon.[40]

The constitutional amendment process itself is a major stumbling block. Remember two things here. *First*, there are three built-in minority vetoes in the amendment process. Two of them are in Congress, where one-third plus one of the members of *either* house can block the proposal of an amendment. And one-fourth plus one of the State legislatures (or conventions) can defeat an amendment once it is proposed.

Second, the smaller States are greatly overrepresented in the electoral college. They would lose that advantage in a direct election plan. It is likely that enough Representatives, or Senators, or small States, would oppose a direct election amendment, and so kill it.

In addition to those who take the small State view here, many others oppose the reform. Some argue that it would weaken federalism—because the

States, as *States*, would lose their role in the choice of a President.

Others believe that direct election would put too great a load on the election process. They say that because *every* vote cast in *each* State would count in the *national* result, the candidates would have to campaign strenuously in *every* State. The consequences that that would have in terms of campaign time, effort, and finance would be huge—and, probably unmanageable.[41]

Some insist that direct election would be an added spur to ballot-box stuffing and other forms of vote fraud. And, they add, it would be sure to mean lengthy, bitter, highly explosive post-election challenges. They fear that those disputes could tear the nation apart.

In many States, a State-wide election often hangs on the behavior of some minority in the electorate. The result often depends on how those voters cast their ballots or, even more important, on how heavily they do or do not turn out to vote. Thus, for example, the black vote in Chicago is often decisive in the presidential election in Illinois. But in a direct election these groups would not hold the balance of power, the clout, they now have—and so many of them are against direct election.

All in all, given these objections, there seems little real chance for the adoption of the direct election proposal within the foreseeable future. Little real

---

[40] The House of Representatives did approve a direct election amendment by the necessary two-thirds vote in 1969; that measure was killed by a Senate filibuster in 1970, however. President Carter championed a similar proposal, but it was rejected by a Senate floor vote in 1979.

[41] Under the present winner-take-all system, the candidates give most of their attention to (1) the doubtful States (rather than those States which are fairly safe or those in which there is little real chance of winning) and, especially (2) the larger States, because of their large blocs of electoral votes. In fact, it is possible for a candidate to win the Presidency by carrying only the 12 largest States—because they now have a total of 279 electoral votes, nine more than the 270 needed to win. Those 12 States (and their electoral votes): California (47), New York (36), Texas (29), Pennsylvania (25), Illinois (24), Ohio (23), Florida (21), Michigan (20), New Jersey (16), North Carolina (13), Massachusetts (13), and Indiana (12). (Georgia and Virginia also have 12 electoral votes apiece.)

The electoral votes for the President and Vice President are opened and counted in the presence of members of both houses Congress. Here, on January 6, 1981, Ronald Reagan was officially declared to have been elected President, and George Bush Vice President.

possibility, that is, *unless* the electoral college system malfunctions in another presidential election. Should that happen, a direct election amendment would very likely be adopted in short order.

The National Bonus Plan. Another, and very different, plan for reform has recently surfaced. It is the "national bonus plan." At first glance, it seems quite complicated—indeed, odd, even "off the wall;" in fact, it is not.

The national bonus plan would keep much of the present electoral college system, and especially its winner-take-all feature. It would weigh that system very heavily in favor of the winner of the popular vote, however.

Under the plan, a national pool of 102 electoral votes would be awarded, automatically, to the winner of the popular vote contest. That is, that bloc of electoral votes would be added to the electoral votes that that candidate won in the election. If all of those votes added up to a majority of the electoral college (at least 321, then) that candidate would be declared the winner of the Presidency. In the highly unlikely event that they did not, a runoff election between the two front-runners in the pop-

ular vote race would then be held.

The proponents of this plan see the electors themselves as unnecessary to it, and so would do away with them. They say that their plan meets all of the major objections to the present electoral college system and all of those raised against the other proposals for its reform, too. And, they claim their plan would almost certainly guarantee that the winner of the popular vote would also be the winner of the electoral vote.

☑ FOR REVIEW

1. How would the district plan revise the electoral college system? What major arguments are made for and against it?

2. How would the proportional plan change the system? The major arguments for and against it?

3. The direct election plan? The arguments for and against it?

4. Which of these proposals for change is most widely favored? Is it likely to be adopted in the foreseeable future?

5. What is the national bonus plan?

Election night excite-
ment and jubilation at
the President-elect's
head-quarters in
Dixon, Illinois, one of
the towns in which
Ronald Reagan lived
as a youth.

S U M M A R Y

The Presidency is the most important and the most powerful office known to history. The President's many roles include those of chief of state, chief executive, chief administrator, chief diplomat, commander in chief, chief legislator, party chief, and chief citizen. The problems of the Presidency are as many and difficult as its powers are vast.

The Constitution states that the President must be a natural-born citizen, at least 35 years of age, and must have lived in the United States for at least 14 years. The Chief Executive is chosen to a four-year term and is limited to serving two full terms or not more than ten years. The President receives a salary of $200,000 a year and many other compensations, as well.

A vacancy in the Presidency is filled by the Vice President who succeeds to the office. The line of succession passes to the Speaker of the House, the President *pro tem* of the Senate, and the now 13 Cabinet Department heads. The question of presidential disability is treated by the 25th Amendment.

The Vice President, long regarded as a "fifth wheel," occupies a most significant office, particularly because of possible succession. Recent Presidents have "upgraded" the office, but none has made its occu-

pant a true "Assistant President." The 25th Amendment provides for filling a vacancy in the Vice Presidency.

In strictly formal terms, the President is elected in accord with the Constitution's provisions for the electoral college system. In fact, the President is chosen through a largely extralegal process which is chiefly the product of party practices. Presidential candidates are nominated by the parties in huge, boisterous, and complex national conventions. Technically, the President is elected by presidential electors chosen by the voters in each State; but the electors have become rubber stamps for their parties, reflecting the popular vote result in their States.

The electoral college system suffers several shortcomings. The most serious are that: it can produce a President who has won a majority of the electoral votes even though losing the popular vote contest; the electors can break their pledges; and, a presidential contest can be decided in the House of Representatives. Most of the reforms have called for presidential selection by a district or proportional electoral vote system or by direct election. Most recently, the national bonus plan has appeared. None of the reforms, including direct election, seems likely to be approved in the near future.

CHAPTER REVIEW

Key Terms/Concepts

All-candidate primary (360)
Availability (366)
Caucus-convention (361)
Chief Administrator (345)
Chief Citizen (346)
Chief Diplomat (345)
Chief Executive (345)
Chief Legislator (346)
Chief of Party (346)
Chief of State (345)
Commander in Chief (346)
Delegate (358)
Delegate apportionment (358)
Direct popular election (374)
District plan (373)
Electoral college (367)
Electoral votes (368)
Inauguration (344)
National bonus plan (376)
National convention (356)
National
presidential primary (358)
No-third-term-tradition (347)
Permanent chairperson (363)
Platform (364)
Preference primary (358)
Presidency (345)
Presidential disability (350)
Presidential electors (367)
Presidential primary (358)
Presidential roles (345)
Presidential succession (350)
Proportional plan (374)
Proportional representation rule (359)
Regional presidential primaries (361)
Temporary chairperson (362)
Vice Presidency (351)
Winner-take-all system (359)

Keynote Questions

1. What several roles does the President play?
2. What are the formal qualifications for the Presidency?
3. For what term is the President elected? What limit(s) does the 22nd Amendment put on presidential tenure?
4. For what does the 25th Amendment provide with regard to: (a) presidential succession? (b) a vice-presidential vacancy? (c) presidential disability?
5. Who follows the Vice President in the line of presidential succession?
6. What duties does the Constitution give to the Vice President?
7. Cite several reasons for the historically low state of the Vice Presidency.
8. Outline the Constitution's original provisions for the selection of the President and Vice President.
9. What major change did the 12th Amendment make in those provisions?
10. How did political parties soon change the constitutionally prescribed process?
11. By what device do the two major parties nominate their presidential candidates? What is a presidential primary? By what other processes are convention delegates chosen?
12. What does the term "availability" mean in presidential politics?
13. What two factors are responsible for the possibility that a candidate who loses the popular vote can nonetheless win the Presidency in the electoral college?
14. What is a "faithless elector"?
15. Outline the major proposals for electoral college reform. Which of them is the most widely favored? Is it likely to be adopted in the foreseeable future? Why, or why not?

For Thought and Discussion

1. Beyond the formal constitutional qualifications for the office and the political factors of availability, what characteristics do you think a President ought to have?

2. When James Earl Carter became President he insisted on being called "Jimmy" Carter. One commentator has suggested that that "was one of Mr. Carter's early important mistakes". Do you agree/disagree with this comment? Why?

3. The inauguration of a new President can be described in several different ways. Among other things, it is a public pageant, a television spectacular, and a celebration of a political victory. It is also described as an important demonstration of this nation's continuing commitment to its basic principles of popular sovereignty and limited government. Why?

4. A noted French political writer once described the major parties' national conventions as "a colossal travesty of popular institutions." Do you agree with that view? On what grounds can you *defend* the continued use of the convention as the major party device for presidential nominations?

5. Maine now uses the district plan to select its presidential electors. Why would you favor (or oppose) the adoption of this procedure in your State?

6. The authors of the national bonus plan gave it that title in part to emphasize the fact that there is a "federal bonus" in the present electoral college arrangement. What is that "federal bonus"? Do you think that an amendment embodying the national bonus plan should be adopted? Why, or why not?

6. If you were to defend the electoral college system, why would terms as federalism, decisive result, legitimacy, and national unity be important?

Suggested Activities

1. Put together a wall or bulletin board display to illustrate (perhaps with newspaper and magazine clippings and photographs) the different roles the President plays (pages 345–346). In that display, try to show the interrelated nature of each and all of those "different hats the President wears."

2. Invite someone who has been a delegate to a national convention in either major party or a presidential elector to speak to the class on his/her experiences and role in the nomination or election of a President. (The local party organizations can almost certainly help you locate such persons.)

3. Stage a debate or class forum on one of the following topics: (a) *Resolved*, That the 22nd Amendment be repealed; (b) *Resolved*, That the Vice Presidency be abolished; (c) *Resolved*, That the major parties be required to nominate their presidential candidates in a nationwide primary; (d) *Resolved*, That the 26th Amendment be repealed; (e) *Resolved*, That the electoral college be abolished and that the President be elected by direct popular vote.

4. Prepare a report to the class on one of the following topics: (a) The Stolen Election of 1876; (b) The presidential election of 1980; (c) The "youth vote" in 1976 and 1980; (d) the effects of the new federal campaign finance laws on the 1976 and 1980 elections; (e) The 1980 presidential campaign in this State; (f) The presidential election of 1984; (g) the proposal and adoption of the 22nd Amendment; (h) the proposal and adoption of the 25th Amendment; (i) The resignation of President Richard Nixon; (j) the role of Vice President Bush in the Reagan Administration.

15

The Presidency in Action

CHAPTER OBJECTIVES

To help you to
Learn ▪ Know ▪ Understand

The nature and the extent of "the executive power" of the President.

The Executive Office of the President, the several agencies within it, and their functions.

The Cabinet and its role in the executive branch.

The several factors which have worked to strengthen the role and powers of the Presidency.

The President's several executive, diplomatic, military, legislative, and judicial powers.

When I ran for the Presidency . . . I knew this country faced serious challenges, but I could not realize—nor could any man who does not bear the burdens of this office—how heavy and constant would be those burdens.

John F. Kennedy

Article II of the Constitution begins:

> The executive power shall be vested in a President of the United States. . . .

With those few words the Framers established the Presidency. And with them they laid the basis for the vast power and influence the nation's chief executive has today.

The Constitution does set out several other, and somewhat more specific, grants of presidential power. The President is given the power to command the armed forces, to make treaties, to approve or veto acts of Congress, to send and receive diplomatic representatives, to grant pardons and reprieves, and "to take care that the laws be faithfully executed."[1]

But, notice, the Constitution deals with the powers of the Presidency in only very sketchy fashion. Article II has been called "the most loosely drawn chapter" in the nation's fundamental

---

[1]Most of the specific grants of presidential power are found in Article II, Sections 2 and 3. A few are elsewhere in the Constitution, however—such as the veto power, in Article I, Section 7, Clause 2.

President Kennedy committed the United States to a program to make the nation first in space exploration. Here, he visits a NASA space center in Houston, Texas, in 1962. *Facing page:* President Truman opens the 1951 baseball season.

law.[2] It does not define "the executive power," and the other grants of presidential authority are put in equally broad terms.

Much has been added to the constitutional outline of the Presidency over the past 190 years and more. Thus, the ways in which the stronger Presidents have used their powers has done much to shape both the office and the scope of its powers. The most notable of those Presidents have been Washington, Jefferson, Jackson, Lincoln, Wilson, the two Roosevelts, Truman, and the second Johnson. A large number of acts of Congress and many court decisions have also helped to define and extend the powers of the Presidency. Very importantly, too, the way in which the public has viewed the presidential office has been a large factor in its development.

In this chapter we survey the whole field of presidential powers. First, however, we must take a look at the ways in which the Presidency is organized for the use of those powers.

The Executive Office of the President

Every officer, employee, and agency of the huge executive branch of the Federal Government is legally subordinate to the Chief Executive. All of them exist to aid the President in the exercise of the executive power.

The President's chief right arm, however, is the Executive Office of the Presi-

---

[2]Edward S. Corwin, *The President: Office and Powers.* New York: New York University Press, 4th ed., 1957, page 3. "To those who think that a constitution ought to settle everything beforehand it [Article II] should be a nightmare; by the same token, to those who think that constitution makers ought to leave considerable leeway for the future play of political forces, it should be a vision realized." *Ibid.,* pp. 3–4. This is *the* classic study of the Constitution's treatment of the Presidency.

dent. It is an umbrella agency with several separate offices, staffed by most of the President's closest advisers and assistants.

The Executive Office was created by Congress in 1939, and it has been reorganized in every administration since then —including President Reagan's.

The White House Office

The White House Office is the "nerve center" of the entire executive branch. It houses the President's key personal and political staff, including a score of senior advisers and other top aides and several hundred professional and clerical people. Most of them have offices in the two wings on either side of the White House.

The "Big Three" in the White House Office today are Counsellor Edwin Meese, Chief of Staff James Baker, and Deputy Chief of Staff Michael Deaver. They are President Reagan's closest advisers and, together, they direct the operations of the whole presidential staff. A number of other top officials, Assistants and Special Assistants to the President, also aid him in such vital areas as foreign policy, defense, the economy, political affairs, congressional relations, and contacts with the news media and with the public at large.

The White House staff also includes such other major aides as the Counsel to the President, the Press Secretary, the President's Physician, and the Director of Staff for the First Lady.

Altogether, the White House staff now numbers about 400 men and women who, in a very real sense, work for the President.

The National Security Council

Most of the President's major steps in foreign affairs are taken in close consultation with the NSC. It meets at the President's call, often on short notice, to advise him in all matters—domestic, foreign, and military—that bear on the nation's security.

The President chairs the Council. Its other members are the Vice President and the Secretaries of State and Defense. The Director of the CIA and the Chairman of the Joint Chiefs of Staff also attend all of its meetings.

The NSC has a small, highly competent staff of foreign and military policy experts. They work under the direction of the President's Assistant for National Security Affairs—another of his most influential advisers. The NSC also directs the operations of the super-secret Central Intelligence Agency (the CIA); see page 454.

The Office of Policy Development

Domestic affairs—matters of home-front policy—demand the President's constant attention, too, of course. The

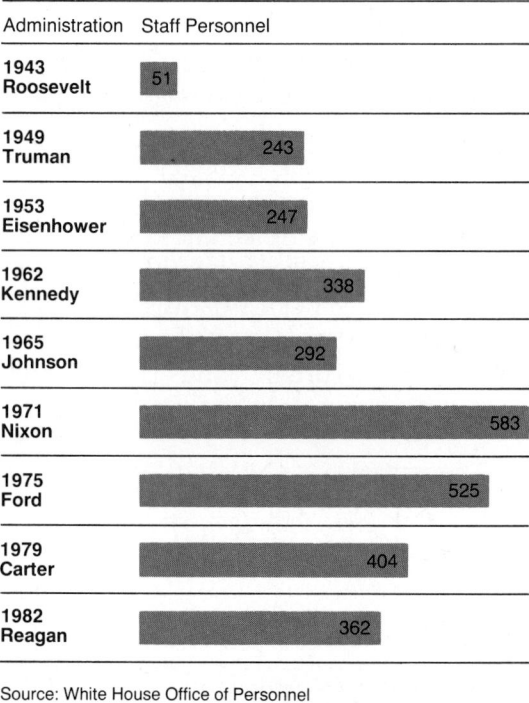

GROWTH OF THE WHITE HOUSE STAFF 1943-1982

Administration	Staff Personnel
1943 Roosevelt	51
1949 Truman	243
1953 Eisenhower	247
1962 Kennedy	338
1965 Johnson	292
1971 Nixon	583
1975 Ford	525
1979 Carter	404
1982 Reagan	362

Source: White House Office of Personnel

On a day-to-day basis the President interacts with many different groups. *Left:* President Reagan confers with members of his staff. *Right:* He handles a barrage of questions from reporters at a televised press conference.

Office of Policy Development gives him the staff help he must have in order to stay on top of that whole many-sided field. It is headed by another leading White House figure, the Assistant to the President for Policy Development.

The Office of Management and Budget

The OMB is the largest, and after the White House Office, the most influential unit in the Executive Office. It directs the preparation of the federal budget which the President must submit to Congress in January each year.

The budget-making function is far more than a routine bookkeeping chore. It is, in a very real sense, the preparation of an annual statement of the public policies of the United States—put into dollar terms.

The federal budget is, at base, a financial document. It is a very detailed estimate of receipts and expenditures—an anticipation of federal income and outgo—during the next fiscal year.[3] And,

more than that, it is also a *plan*—a carefully drawn, closely detailed work plan for the conduct of public policy.

The budget-making process begins more than a year before the start of the fiscal year for which it is intended. In its first stages, each federal agency prepares detailed estimates of its spending for that 12-month period. Those spending proposals are then reviewed by the OMB —generally in a series of budget hearings, at which agency officials must defend their dollar requests. Following that agency-by-agency review, the revised (and usually lowered) spending estimates of all of them are fitted into the President's overall program. They become a part of the budget document the Chief Executive presents to Congress— early in each of its yearly sessions, as we shall see on page 399.

The OMB is more than simply the President's budget-*making* arm. It also oversees the *execution* of the budget. That is, it monitors the spending of the funds once they have been appropriated by Congress. The President's close control over both the preparation and the execution of the budget is a major tool with which the Chief Executive is

---

[3]A *fiscal year* is the 12-month period used by a government for its record-keeping, budgeting, revenue-collecting, and other financial management purposes. The Federal Government's fiscal year now runs from October 1 through the following September 30.

able to manage the huge and sprawling executive branch.

Beyond its budget chores, the OMB is a sort of presidential "handy-man" agency. It makes continuing studies of the organization and management of the executive branch and keeps the President up to date on the work of all of its agencies. It checks and clears agency stands on all legislative matters (to be certain that they agree with the President's own positions). It helps the President with executive orders and veto messages, and does much else to live up to the word "management" in its title.

The Council of Economic Advisers

Three of the country's leading economists, chosen by the President with the consent of the Senate, make up the Council of Economic Advisers. They are the Chief Executive's major source of information and advice on the state of the nation's economy.

The Council, with the aid of a small professional staff, keeps a close watch on the economy and keeps the President informed of economic developments and problems. It also helps the President prepare his annual Economic Report to Congress.

Other Units in the Executive Office

There are a number of other agencies within the Executive Office. Each of them also houses key presidential assistants—men and women who give the President the information, advice, and other help needed to carry out the executive function.

The Council on Environmental Quality aids the President in all environmental policy matters and in the writing of the annual "state of the environment" report to Congress. Its three members are named by the President, with the Senate's consent. They work closely with the Environmental Protec-

tion Agency and various agencies in the Department of the Interior, Agriculture, and Energy.

The Office of United States Trade Representative advises the Chief executive in all matters of foreign trade. The Trade Representative, appointed by the President and Senate, carries the rank of ambassador and represents the President in foreign trade negotiations.

The Office of Science and Technology Policy is the President's major adviser in all scientific, engineering, and other technological matters with a bearing on national policies and programs. Its Director, who is chosen by the President and Senate, is drawn from the nation's scientific community.

The Office of Administration is the general house-keeping agency for all of the other units in the Executive Office. It provides them with all of the many support services they must have in order to do their jobs. The list of those things is almost endless: clerical help, data processing, library services, transportation, and much else.

The Cabinet

The Cabinet is an informal advisory body brought together by the President to serve his needs. The Constitution makes no mention of it,[4] nor did Congress create it. It is, instead, the product of custom and usage, developed over the years since George Washington's first term of office.

At its first session in 1789, Congress established four executive posts: Secretary of State, Secretary of the Treasury,

---

[4]The closest approach to it is in Article II, Section 2, Clause 1, where the President is given the power to "require the opinion, in writing, of the principal officer in each of the executive departments, upon any subject relating to the duties of their respective offices." The Cabinet was first mentioned in an act of Congress in 1907, well over a century after its birth.

THE PRESIDENT'S CABINET

Cabinet Post*	Year Created
Secretary of State	1789
Secretary of the Treasury	1789
Secretary of Defense[a]	1947
Attorney General[b]	1789
Secretary of the Interior	1849
Secretary of Agriculture	1889
Secretary of Commerce[c]	1903
Secretary of Labor[c]	1913
Secretary of Health and Human Services[d]	1953
Secretary of Housing and Urban Development	1965
Secretary of Transportation	1967
Secretary of Energy	1977
Secretary of Education	1979

*The Cabinet posts are listed in order of precedence—i.e., the order in which each was established. This ranking is followed for formal and ceremonial purposes (protocol) and also is the order in which the Cabinet officers rank in the line of presidential succession; see page 350.

[a]Congress created the National Military Establishment, as an executive department headed by the Secretary of Defense, in 1947. It was renamed the Department of Defense in 1949. Since 1947 it has included the former Cabinet-level Department of War (1789) and Department of the Navy (1798), and the Department of the Air Force (1947). The Secretaries of Army, Navy and Air Force do not hold Cabinet rank.

[b]Although the post of Attorney General was created in 1789, the Department of Justice was not established until 1870.

[c]The Secretary of Commerce was originally the Secretary of Commerce and Labor. The Department of Commerce and Labor, created in 1903, was replaced by the separate Departments of Commerce and of Labor in 1913.

[d]The Secretary of Health and Human Services was originally the Secretary of Health, Education, and Welfare. The Department of Health, Education, and Welfare was created in 1953. HEW's education functions were transferred to a separate Department of Education in 1979 and HEW was renamed at that time.

The Postmaster General, who headed the Cabinet-level Post Office Department, was a member of the Cabinet from Andrew Jackson's first year in the Presidency (1829) until Congress replaced the Department with an independent agency, the United States Postal Service, in 1971.

The first Cabinet (left to right): Henry Knox, Thomas Jefferson, Edmund Randolph (in background), Alexander Hamilton, and President George Washington.

Secretary of War, and Attorney General. By his second term, President Washington was regularly seeking the views and advice of the four outstanding men he had named to those offices—Thomas Jefferson in the Department of State, Alexander Hamilton at the Treasury, Henry Knox in the War Department, and Edmund Randolph, the Attorney General. And so the Cabinet was born.

By tradition, the heads of the executive departments form the Cabinet. A number of the President's topmost aides often attend its meetings, too. And every recent Vice President, from Alben Barkley to George Bush, has been a regular participant, as well.

Selection of Cabinet Members. The President appoints the head of each of the 13 executive departments. This is another way of saying that the President names the members of the Cabinet, of course. Each of these appointments is subject to confirmation by the Senate. Of the more than 500 appointments made to 1984, only nine have been turned down by the Senate.[5]

[5]The last rejection was in 1959, when the Senate turned down President Eisenhower's selection of Lewis Strauss as Secretary of Commerce.

President Reagan meets with his Cabinet.

Many factors influence these presidential choices. Party considerations are always important. Republican Presidents do not often pick Democrats, and vice versa. One or more of a new President's appointees usually comes from among those who had a large hand in the recent presidential campaign.

Professional qualifications and practical experience are also taken into account, of course—particularly in selecting the Secretaries of State and Treasury and the Attorney General. Geography plays a part, too. In broad terms, each President tries to give some sectional balance to the Cabinet. Thus, the Secretary of the Interior almost always comes from the West—where most of the department's work is carried out.

A number of special interest groups are especially interested in certain departments and have an influence on some of the choices. Thus, the Secretary of Agriculture is almost always a farmer or at least has a background closely related to agriculture. The Secretary of the Treasury comes from the financial community and the Secretary of Commerce from the ranks of business. The Secretary of Labor must be acceptable to labor, and the Secretary of Housing and Urban Development almost always has a "big-city" background.

Considerations of sex and race,[6] an appointee's stand on the "hot" issues of the day, management abilities and experience, and other personal characteristics—these and a host of other factors

---

[6]To January 1, 1984, only eight women and four blacks have served in the Cabinet. Franklin Roosevelt appointed the first woman, Frances T. Perkins; she was Secretary of Labor from 1933 to 1945. Olveta Culp Hobby, the first Secretary of Health, Education, and Welfare, served in the Eisenhower Cabinet from 1953 to 1955. Lyndon Johnson named the first black to the Cabinet, Robert C. Weaver as the first Secretary of Housing and Urban Development in 1966. Gerald Ford was the first President to select both a woman (Carla Hills, Secretary of HUD) and a black (William T. Coleman, Secretary of Transportation); both were named in 1975. Among Jimmy Carter's first selections were two women Juanita M. Kreps as Secretary of Commerce and Patricia R. Harris, the first black woman to hold a Cabinet post, as Secretary of HUD (and, in 1979, as Secretary of Health and Human Services); he also picked Shirley Hufstedler to head the new Department of Education in 1979. Ronald Reagan's first Cabinet appointments (1981) included one black, Samuel R. Pierce, Secretary of HUD, and no women; he did appoint two women in 1983, however: Elizabeth H. Dole, Secretary of Transportation, and Margaret M. Heckler, Secretary of Health and Human Services.

are a part of the decision mix in selecting Cabinet members. Indeed, those factors, and the group pressures also at work here, are so many and so different that they really cannot be catalogued.

The Cabinet's Role. The members of the Cabinet have *two* major jobs. *Individually*, each of them is the administrative head of one of the executive departments. *Together*, they are advisers to the President.

How, and how much, the President *uses* the Cabinet—how important it really is, then—is something for each President to decide. A number of them have given great weight to it, and to its advise; others have given it only a secondary role. Cabinet meetings have a large place in the Reagan administration. John Kennedy, on the other hand, thought that those sessions were "a waste of time."

William Howard Taft put the role of the Cabinet in its proper light years ago:

> The Constitution . . . contains no suggestion of a meeting of all of the department heads in consultation over general governmental matters. The Cabinet is a mere creation of the President's will. It exists only by custom. If the President desired to dispense with it, he could do so.[7]

The Reagan Cabinet usually meets twice a week. Reports are made and discussed, and advice is offered to the Chief Executive. That advice need not be taken, of course. Abraham Lincoln once laid a proposition he favored before his Cabinet. Each member opposed it, whereupon Lincoln declared: "Seven nays, one aye: the ayes have it."

Several Presidents have leaned upon other, unofficial advisory groups—and sometimes more heavily than upon the Cabinet. Andrew Jackson began the

---

[7] *Our Chief Magistrate and His Powers.* New York: Columbia University Press, 1916, pages 29–30.

practice. Several of his close friends often met with him in the kitchen at the White House—and came to be known as "the Kitchen Cabinet." Franklin Roosevelt's "Brain Trust" of the 1930s and Harry Truman's "Cronies" in the late 1940s were in the same mold.

At times, one or a few individuals have become close advisers, working with the President on a highly confidential and personal basis. These "President's Men" have had different titles with each administration. Some of them have held no public office; but they have each had a large hand in the shaping of White House decisions.

✓ FOR REVIEW

1. To whom does the Constitution give *the* executive power?
2. From what sources have the President's powers been filled out?
3. What is the Executive Office of the President? Name its agencies.
4. What is the federal budget? Why is the budget power a major administrative tool for a President?
5. What is the Cabinet? How was it created? Who are its members? What is its role?

The Powers of the Presidency

Again, the Constitution gives "the executive power" to the President of the United States. But, as we have seen, the specific powers of the Presidency are set out in only very sparse fashion.

The Growth of Presidential Power

Much of the story of the development of the American system of government can be told in terms of the growth of the Presidency and of presidential power. A large part of our political history, that is, has revolved about a continuing struggle over the meaning of the constitutional phrase "executive power." That struggle has pitted those who have argued for a weaker Presidency, subordinate to Congress, on the one hand, against those who have pressed for a stronger, independent and coequal Chief Executive, on the other.

The debate over the nature and extent of "the executive power" has gone on now for more than 190 years. Over that period, and for many reasons, the champions of a stronger Presidency have prevailed.

One of the leading reasons they have is the *unity* of the Presidency. The office and its powers are held by *one* person. The President is the *single*, commanding head of the executive branch. On the other hand, the Congress—though its powers are many and substantial—consists of *two* houses. And *both* of them must agree on a matter before the Congress can do anything. Moreover, remember, one of those two houses is made up of 100 separately-elected members and the other 435 of them.

Several other factors have worked to strengthen the role and the powers of the Presidency, and so to enhance the scope of "the executive power." One highly important one we have referred to a number of times—the influence the Presidents themselves, especially the stronger one, have had upon the office.

Yet another has been pressures from the increasingly complex nature of the nation's social and economic life. As the United States has become more and still more highly industrialized and technologically centered, the people have demanded that the Federal Government play a larger and still larger role—in transportation, communications, labor-management relations, education, welfare, housing, civil rights, health, environmental protection, and a host of other fields. And it has been to the Presidency that the people have most often looked for leadership in these matters.

Congress itself has had a major part in the strengthening of the Presidency. This has been especially true as it has passed the thousands of pieces of legislation necessary to the growth of the scope of the activities of the Federal Government. Congress has neither the time nor the technical knowledge to do much more than set up the basic outlines of public policy in many new fields. It has been literally forced to delegate substantial authority to the President.

Yet another of these factors has been the frequent need for extraordinary and decisive action in times of national emergency, and—most notably—in time of war. The ability of the President—the *single*, commanding Chief Executive —to act in such situations has done much to strengthen "the executive power."

If one were to draw a graph of the growth of presidential power, that graph would not show a steadily rising line. It would show, instead, several periods of gradual increase, a few years of decline, and, at some points, spectacular jumps. The sharpest upward leaps would come in these Presidencies: Abraham Lincoln's, during the Civil War, Woodrow Wilson's, in World War I, and Franklin Roosevelt's, through the Great Depression and then World War II.

A number of other factors have fed the growth of "the executive power." Among them have been the President's roles as chief legislator, party leader, and chief citizen, to which we referred on page 346. Another, the huge amount of staff support a President has, as we noted on page 382. Yet another is the unique position from which the President can catch and hold the public's attention, and so gather support for policies and actions. Each of the most recent

Presidents, from Franklin Roosevelt through Lyndon Johnson to Ronald Reagan, has very purposely used the press, radio, and television to that end.

Presidential Views of Presidential Power. What the Presidency is at any given time depends, in no small part, upon the manner in which the President views the office and uses its powers.

Historically, two general and contrasting views of the Presidency have been held by the several Presidents. The stronger, and the more effective of them, have taken a broad view of their powers. Theodore Roosevelt defined their position in what he called the "stewardship theory":

> My view was that . . . every executive officer in high position, was a steward of the people bound actively and affirmatively to do all he could for the people, and not to content himself with the negative merit of keeping his talents undamaged in a napkin. I declined to adopt the view that what was imperatively necessary for the Nation could not be done by the President unless he could find some specific authorization to do it. My belief was that it was not only his right but his duty to do anything that the needs of the Nation demanded unless such action was forbidden by the Constitution or by the laws . . . I did not usurp power, but I did greatly broaden the use of executive power. In other words, I acted for the public welfare, I acted for the common well-being of all our people, whenever and in whatever manner was necessary, unless prevented by direct constitutional or legislative prohibition.[8]

Ironically, the strongest presidential statement of the opposing view was made by Roosevelt's handpicked successor in the office, William Howard Taft.

Looking back upon his Presidency, Taft has this to say about Roosevelt's view:

> My judgment is that the view of Mr. Roosevelt, ascribing an undefined residuum of power to the President, is an unsafe doctrine. . . . The true view of the executive function is, as I conceive it, that the President can exercise no power which cannot be fairly and reasonably traced to some specific grant of power or justly implied and included within such express grant. . . . Such specific grant must be either in the Federal Constitution or in an act of Congress passed in pursuance thereof. There is no undefined residuum of power which he can exercise because it seems to be in the public interest.[9]

In the last chapter we pointed out that the Presidency and its powers may be viewed from the standpoint of the different roles the President plays. The

---

[9]*Our Chief Magistrate and His Powers*, pages 139–40., 144.

Teddy Roosevelt believed that a President should act boldly. During his "Rough Rider" days, he established an image of boldness, energy, and optimism.

---

[8]*Theodore Roosevelt: An Autobiography.* New York: Macmillan, 1913, page 389.

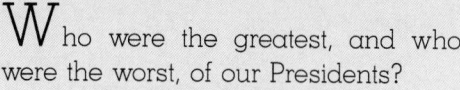

Mt. Rushmore

A CASE IN POINT

RANKING THE PRESIDENTS

Who were the greatest, and who were the worst, of our Presidents?

A number of surveys of the Presidency —by historians, political scientists, and other authorities—show this:

Four men deserve to be ranked as truly great Presidents: Abraham Lincoln, Franklin Roosevelt, George Washington, and Thomas Jefferson, in that order.

Six other Presidents rank in the "near great" category: Theodore Roosevelt, Woodrow Wilson, Andrew Jackson, Harry Truman, John Adams, and James K. Polk.

Nearly all of these experts on the Presidency agree that two men clearly deserve to be called "failures" in the White House: Ulysses Grant and Warren Harding. And most of them also say that James Buchanan, Franklin Pierce, Andrew Johnson, and Richard Nixon also stand very close to the bottom of the list.

Each of the other Presidents is most often placed somewhere in the "above average" to "below average" range.

Among the most recent Presidents: Lyndon Johnson, Dwight Eisenhower, and John Kennedy are regularly ranked toward the top of the "above average" category. Gerald Ford and Jimmy Carter usually place in the lower middle of the scale. (Clearly, Ronald Reagan's standing cannot be measured until some time after he leaves office. And most students of the Presidency agree that neither William Henry Harrison nor James A. Garfield were in office long enough to be properly assessed.)

1. On what basis would you judge a President's greatness? Which Presidents would you rank high? Low? Why?
2. Why do many people's evaluations of a President change over time?
3. Why might the evaluations made by historians and political scholars differ from those made by the general public?

President must be, at one and the same time, each and all of these vital things: Chief of State, Chief Executive, Chief Administrator, Chief Diplomat, Commander in Chief, Chief Legislator, Chief of Party, and Chief Citizen.

Another and useful way to describe presidential powers is to group them under five broad headings: the President's executive, diplomatic, military, legislative, and judicial powers.

Executive Powers

As the nation's Chief Executive, the President has to execute—to enforce, put into effect, carry out—the provisions of federal law. The power to do so rests upon two brief constitutional provisions. The first of them is the oath of office the President must take:

> I do solemnly swear (or affirm) that I will faithfully execute the office of President of the United States, and will, to the best of my ability, preserve, protect, and defend the Constitution of the United States.[10]

The other is the Constitution's command that "he shall take care that the laws be faithfully executed."[11]

The President's power to execute the law covers *all* federal laws, of course. Their number, and the different subject matters they cover, nearly boggle the mind. The armed forces, social security, civil rights, housing, taxes, environmental pollution, collective bargaining, farm price supports, public health immigration—these 10 only begin the list; there are scores of others.

Just as do Congress and the courts, the President, and the President's subordinates, have much to say about the meaning of the law. That is, in executing and enforcing law, the executive branch also *interprets* it. The Constitution requires the President to execute *all* federal laws, no matter what the Chief Executive's own views of any of them may be. But the President may (and does) use some discretion as to how vigorously and in what particular way any given law will be applied in practice.

To look at the point more closely: Many of the laws that Congress passes are written in fairly broad terms. In them, Congress sets out the basic policies and standards to be followed. The details necessary to the actual, day-to-day administration of the law are usually left to be worked out in the executive branch.

To take an example, the immigration laws require that all immigrants seeking permanent admission to this country must be able to "read and understand some dialect or language." But what does this literacy requirement mean in actual practice? How well must an alien be able to read and write? What words in some language must he or she know, and how many of them? What kind of

test is to be given to meet this requirement? The law does not say. Rather, the answers to these and any number of other such questions come from within the executive branch—here from the Immigration and Naturalization Service in the Department of Justice.

Direction of Administration. From what has just been said, it should be clear that the President deserves the title Chief Administrator as well as Chief Executive. The day-to-day job of administering and applying most federal law is carried out through the many bureaus, offices, boards, commissions, councils, and other agencies that make up the huge executive branch. All of the some 2.8 million men and women who staff these agencies work are subordinate to the President. They are all subject to the President's control and direction.

The Ordinance Power. The President has the power to issue *executive orders* which have the effect of law. The power to do so, the **ordinance power,** arises from two sources: the Constitution and acts of Congress.

Several helicopters are available for use by the President as well as three Boeing 707 jets.

---

[10] Article II, Section 1, Clause 8.
[11] Article II, Section 3, this provision gives to the President what is often called the "take care power."

The Constitution does not mention the ordinance power, but it is clearly intended. In conferring certain powers on the President the Constitution anticipates their use. In order to exercise those powers, the President must have the power to issue the necessary orders —directives, rules, regulations—and to implement them. The President must also have, the power to authorize subordinates to issue such orders, too.[12]

As the number, the scope, and the complexity of problems in government have grown, Congress has had to delegate more and still more discretion to the President, and to presidential subordinates, to spell out the policies and programs it has passed. Members of Congress are not, and cannot be expected to be, experts in all of the fields in which they must deal—nor do they have all-seeing crystal balls.

When it does delegate authority to the executive branch, Congress cannot give away its constitutional power to legislate, to make basic public policy. Rather, it sets out the broad standards within which the President and other executive officers and agencies must work. There are many, many, examples. One we have just noted involves the literacy of immigrants. For another, Congress has provided for the payment of subsidies to support the prices of certain farm products. It has named 12 commodities to be supported, and it has given the Secretary of Agriculture the power to add other commodities to that list. The additions are made by executive order.

Power of Appointment. A President cannot hope to succeed without loyal subordinates who support the administration's policies. No matter how able a President, no matter how wise those policies, no administration can work effectively without such loyalty and support.

The Constitution provides that the President

> by and with the advice and consent of the Senate, shall appoint ambassadors, other public ministers, and consuls, judges of the Supreme Court, and all other officers of the United States whose appointments are not otherwise herein provided for; but the Congress may by law vest the appointment of such inferior officers, as they think proper, in the President alone, in the courts of law, or in the heads of departments.[13]

Acting alone, the President names only a handful of the some 2.8 million federal civilian employees—and many of those are members of the staff of the White House Office.

With Senate consent, the President names most of the top-ranking officers of the Federal Government—ambassadors and other diplomats, Cabinet members and their top aides, the heads of such independent agencies as the Environmental Protection Agency, all federal judges, attorneys and marshals, and all officers in the armed forces.

When the President makes one of these apointments, the "nomination" is sent to the Senate—where the support of a majority of the Senators present and voting is needed for confirmation.

The unwritten rule of *senatorial courtesy* plays an important part in this process. It applies to the choice of those federal officers who serve within a State —for example, a federal district judge or a federal marshal. The rule holds that the Senate will approve only those feder-

---

[12]All executive orders are published in the *Federal Register*, which appears five times a week. At least annually, all orders currently in force are published in the *Code of Federal Regulations*.

[13]Article II, Section 2, Clause 2. Those whose appointments are "otherwise provided for" are the Vice President, Senators, Representatives, and presidential electors.

al appointees acceptable to the Senator or Senators of the President's party from the State involved. The practical effect of this custom, which is closely followed in the Senate, is to place a meaningful part of the appointment power in the hands of particular Senators.

Well over half of all the federal civilian workforce is selected on the basis of competitive civil service examinations. Today, the Office of Personnel Management examines applicants for some two million positions; see page 436.

Removal Power. The power to remove is the other side of the appointment coin—and it is as critically important to presidential success. Except for the cumbersome and little-used impeachment process,[14] however, the Constitution is silent on the matter. It does not say how or by whom appointed officers may be dismissed—for incompetence, for opposition to presidential policies, or for any other cause.

The question was hotly debated in the first session of Congress in 1789. Several members argued that for those offices for which Senate approval was needed for appointment, Senate consent should also be required for removal. They insisted that this restriction on presidential authority was essential to congressional supervision (oversight) of the executive branch. Others said that the President could not "take care that the laws be faithfully executed" without a free hand to dismiss those who were incompetent or otherwise undesirable in the Chief Executive's administration.

The latter view prevailed. The 1st Congress gave to the President the power to remove any officer whom he appointed, except federal judges. Over the years since then, Congress has sometimes tried to restrict the President's

---

[14]Article II, Section 4; see pages 337–338.

Sandra Day O'Connor, appointed to the Supreme Court by President Reagan, responds to a question during Senate confirmation hearings.

freedom to dismiss—but with little success.

One notable instance of this came in 1867. Locked with Andrew Johnson in the fight over Reconstruction, Congress passed the Tenure of Office Act. The law's plain purpose was to prevent President Johnson from removing several top officers in his administration—especially the Secretary of War, Edwin M. Stanton. The law provided that any person holding an office by presidential appointment with Senate consent should remain in that office until a successor had been confirmed by the Senate. The President vetoed the bill, charging that it was an unconstitutional invasion of executive authority. The veto, which was overridden, sparked the move for Johnson's impeachment. The law was ignored in practice and never challenged in the courts. It was finally repealed in 1887.

The question of the President's removal power did not reach the Supreme Court until *Myers* v. *United States*, 1926. In 1876 Congress had passed a law requiring Senate consent before the President could dismiss any first-, second-, or third-class postmaster.

In 1920 President Woodrow Wilson removed Frank Myers as the postmaster at Portland, Oregon, and did so without consulting the Senate. Myers then sued for the salary for the rest of his four-year term. He based his claim on the point that he had been removed in violation of the 1876 law. The Court found the law unconstitutional, however. Its opinion was written by Chief Justice William Howard Taft, himself a former President. It held that the power of removal was an essential part of the executive power, clearly necessary to the faithful execution of the laws.

The Supreme Court did place some limit on the President's removal power in 1935, in *Humphrey's Executor* v. *United States.* President Herbert Hoover had appointed William Humphrey to a seven-year term on the Federal Trade Commission in 1931. When President Franklin D. Roosevelt entered office in 1933, he found Humphrey in sharp disagreement with many of his policies. He asked Humphrey to resign, saying that his administration would be better served with someone else on the FTC. Humphrey refused, and Roosevelt then removed him. Humphrey challenged the legality of the action but died before a case could be brought. His heirs then filed a suit for back salary.

The Supreme Court upheld their claim. It based its decision on the act creating the FTC. That law provides that a member of the Commission may be removed only for "inefficiency, neglect of duty, or malfeasance in office." The President had given none of these reasons. He had dismissed Humphrey because of political disagreements.

The Court further held that Congress does have the power to set the conditions under which a member of the FTC

and other such agencies might be removed by the President. It did so because those agencies, the independent regulatory commissions, are not purely executive agencies; they are, instead, **quasi-legislative** and **quasi-judicial** in character.[15]

As a general rule, however, the President may remove those whom the President appoints.

FOR REVIEW

1. Around what two competing views of "the executive power" can much of our political history be written?
2. What are at least three main reasons for the historical growth of presidential power.
3. What two contrasting views of the Presidency have been taken by those who have held the office?
4. How does the executive branch have a good deal to say about the meaning of the law?
5. Why is the President the Chief Administrator as well as the Chief Executive?
6. What is the ordinance power? From what two sources does it arise?
7. Why is the President's appointing power so critically related to the President's success in office?
8. What officers does the President appoint? What is the Senate's role in the appointment process? What is senatorial courtesy?
9. What is the general rule of the President's removal power?

[15]That is, their duties are partly legislative and partly judicial; they *make rules* and *decide controversies.* The prefix *quasi-* is from the Latin, meaning "in a certain sense, resembling, seemingly." See pages 428–429. **Malfeasance** is wrongful conduct, especially by a public officeholder.

Diplomatic Powers

The Constitution makes the President the nation's Chief Diplomat. It does so by giving the President the power to make treaties (with the consent of two-thirds of the Senate) and to appoint ambassadors to other nations and other diplomatic officers (subject to Senate confirmation). It also gives Presidents the power to receive foreign diplomatic representatives (that is, to *recognize* foreign governments).[16]

The Treaty Power. A treaty is a formal agreement between two or more sovereign states. The President, usually acting through the Secretary of State, negotiates these international agreements. The Senate must give its approval, by a two-thirds vote of the members present, before a treaty made by the President can become effective.[17]

The Framers considered the Senate—with, originally, only 26 members—a suitable council to advise the President in foreign affairs. Secrecy was thought to be necessary and was seen as an impossibility in a body as large as the House.

Turn the two-thirds rule around and it becomes a one-third-plus-one veto rule. That is, only one more than a third of the Senators present and voting may

President Carter signs the two Panama Canal treaties—transferring control of the Canal to Panama, in a process begun in 1979 and to be completed by the year 2000.

defeat a treaty—no matter how important it might be to the nation's interests.

In 1919 the Senate rejected the Versailles Treaty, the general peace agreement to end World War I. The treaty included provisions for the League of Nations. Forty-nine Senators voted for the pact and 35 against—but the vote was seven short of the necessary two-thirds. More than once a President has been forced to bow to the views of a few Senators in order to get a treaty passed—even when this meant making concessions opposed by the majority.

At times, a President has had to turn to roundabout methods. When a Senate minority defeated a treaty to annex Texas, President Tyler was able to bring about annexation in 1845 by a joint resolution—a move which needed only a majority vote in each house. And in 1898 President McKinley used the same tactic to annex Hawaii, again after a treaty had failed in the Senate.

[16]Article II, Section 2, Clause 2; Section 3; see also Chapter 17.

[17]In spite of what many believe, the Senate does *not* "ratify" treaties. The Constitution requires Senate "advice and consent" to a treaty made by the President. *After* Senate approval, the President ratifies a treaty by the exchange of formal notifications with the other parties. Treaties have the same legal standing as do acts passed by Congress. Congress may repeal *(abrogate)* a treaty by passing a law contrary to its provisions, and an existing law may be repealed by the terms of a treaty. When a treaty and a statute conflict, the courts consider the latest enacted to be the law, *The Head Money Cases,* 1884. The terms of a treaty cannot conflict with the higher law of the Constitution, *Missouri v. Holland,* 1920; but the Supreme Court has never found a treaty provision to be unconstitutional. Money cannot be appropriated by a treaty. But in practice, whenever the Senate has approved a treaty which calls for an expenditure, the House has agreed to a bill providing the money.

Executive Agreements. More and more, international agreements, especially the more routine ones, are made as **executive agreements.** These are pacts between the President and the head of a foreign state, or their subordinates. They do not require Senate consent.

Most executive agreements either flow out of legislation already passed by Congress or implement treaties the Senate has agreed to. But the President can make these agreements without any congressional action.[18]

Dozens of executive agreements are made each year, most of them of a fairly routine sort. But at times they are used for extraordinary purposes—for example, in the "Destroyer-Bases Deal" of 1940 in which the United States gave the hard-pressed British 50 "overage" destroyers during World War II. In return, the United States received 99-year leases to several island bases extending from Newfoundland to the Caribbean.

Power of Recognition. When the President receives the diplomatic representatives sent to the United States by another sovereign state, the President exercises the power of **recognition.** That is, the President, acting for the United States, acknowledges the legal existence of that country and its government. By doing so, the President indicates that the United States accepts that country as an equal in the family of nations and is prepared to have relations with it.[19]

Recognition does not mean that one government approves of the character and conduct of another. The United States recognizes several governments about which we have serious misgivings, most notably those of the USSR and China. The facts of life in world politics make relations with these governments necessary, of course.

Recognition is often used as a weapon in foreign relations, too. Prompt recognition of a new state or government may do much to guarantee its life. In the same way, the withholding of recognition may have a serious effect on its continued existence.

President Theodore Roosevelt's quick recognition of the Republic of Panama in 1903 is one of the classic examples of American use of the power as a diplomatic weapon. He recognized the new state less than three days after the Panamanians had begun a revolt against Colombia. His quick action guaranteed their success. In a very similar way, President Truman's recognition of Israel, within 24 hours of its creation in 1948, helped that new state to survive among its hostile Arab neighbors.

The President may show United States displeasure with the conduct of another country by asking for the recall of that nation's ambassador or other diplomatic representatives in this country. (The official recalled is declared to be *persona non grata.*) The same point can be made by the recalling of an American diplomat from a post in another country. The withdrawal of recognition is the sharpest diplomatic rebuke one government may give to another and has often been a step to war.

Military Powers

The Constitution makes the President the Commander in Chief of the nation's armed forces.[20] Congress also has several important war powers. They

---

[18]The Supreme Court has held executive agreements to be as binding as treaties and a part of the supreme law of the land, *United States* v. *Belmont,* 1937; *Pink* v. *United States,* 1942.

[19]Sovereign states generally recognize one another through the exchange of diplomatic representatives. Recognition may be carried out in any of several other ways, however. For example, it may be accomplished by proposing to negotiate a treaty, since under international law only sovereign states can make such agreements.

[20]Article II, Section 2, Clause 1; see also Chapter 17.

include, especially, the power to declare war, to provide for the raising and maintaining of the armed forces, to make the rules by which they are governed, and to appropriate money for the nation's defense.[21]

Even though Congress shares the war powers, the President's position in military affairs is as dominant as it is in the field of foreign affairs. In fact, it does not stretch the matter too far to say that the President's powers as Commander in Chief are almost without limit.

Take this illustration of the point: In 1907 Theodore Roosevelt sent the Great White Fleet around the world. He did so partly as a training exercise for the Navy, but even more to impress other nations with America's naval strength. Several members of Congress objected to the cost and threatened to hold back the necessary appropriation. To which TR replied: "Very well, the existing appropriation will carry the Navy halfway around the world and if Congress chooses to leave it on the other side, all right."

Presidents almost always delegate much of their command authority to military subordinates. But he is not required to do so. George Washington actually took command of federal troops himself and led them into Pennsylvania in the Whiskey Rebellion of 1794. Abraham Lincoln often visited the Army of the Potomac and instructed his generals in the field during the Civil War.

Most Presidents have not become so directly involved in military operations, however. Still, the President always has the final authority over and responsibility for any and all military matters. The most critical decisions are made by the Commander in Chief—for example:

—President Truman's decision to use

Acting under his authority as Commander in Chief, President Reagan ordered the use of the Marines as part of an international peace-keeping force in war-torn Beirut in 1982.

the atomic bomb against Japan to end World War II; and to send American troops to defend South Korea in 1950.

—President Johnson's decision to commit massive air and then ground forces in Viet Nam in 1965.

—President Nixon's decisions to bomb targets in Cambodia (in secret) in 1969, to send American troops into that country in 1970, to resume bombing North Viet Nam and mine its seaports in 1972, and to bomb Cambodian targets again in 1973.

---

[21]Article I, Section 8, Clauses 11–17, see also pages 66, 333.

—President Reagan's decision to use the Marines as part of an international peace-keeping force in war-torn Beirut in 1982.

Several Presidents have used the armed forces abroad, in combat, without a declaration of war by Congress. In fact, most of them have—and on no fewer than 150 separate occasions in our history.

John Adams was the first to do so, in 1798. At his command, the Navy fought and won a number of battles with French warships harassing American merchantmen in the Atlantic and the Caribbean. Thomas Jefferson and then James Madison followed that precedent, in the war against the Barbary Coast pirates of North Africa in the early years of the 1800s. There were many other and similar foreign adventures on through the last century and into the present one.

The long military conflicts in Korea and then in Viet Nam were the largest of those "undeclared wars," of course.

President Reagan has twice used the armed forces in combat abroad: to repel attacks on the Marines in Lebanon, and in the quick and successful invasion of Grenada in late 1983.

In today's world there can be no doubt that the President must be able to respond rapidly and effectively to threats to this nation's security. But many have long warned of the dangers inherent in the President's power to involve the nation in "undeclared wars." They have insisted that the Constitution never intended the President to have the power to do so.

The nation's frustrations and growing anguish over the war in Viet Nam finally moved Congress to pass the War Powers Resolution of 1973. It is designed to place close limits on the President's war-making powers. President Nixon vetoed the measure, calling it "both unconstitutional and dangerous to the best interest of our nation." But Congress overrode the veto. The Resolution's central provisions require that:

—Within 48 hours after committing American forces to combat abroad, the President must report to Congress, detailing the circumstances and the scope of his actions.

—The use of American forces in combat must end within 60 days, unless Congress authorizes a longer commitment. But the deadline may be extended 30 days if the President certifies the extension necessary to the safe withdrawal of the forces involved.

—American forces engaged in combat abroad without a declaration of war or other specific congressional authorization must be withdrawn immediately should Congress pass a concurrent resolution to that effect.

The constitutionality of the War Powers Resolution remains in dispute. A determination of the question must await a situation in which Congress demands that its provisions be obeyed but the President refuses to do so.

The President's military powers—his powers as Commander in Chief—are far greater during a war than they are in more normal times. In fact, his wartime authority goes far beyond the traditional military field. Thus, in World War II, for example, Congress gave the President the power to do such things as ration food and gasoline, control wages and prices, and seize and operate private industries vital to the nation's war effort.

The President may also use the armed forces to keep the domestic peace, as we saw in Chapter 4;[22] and he also has the power to call any of the State's militia (or all of them) into federal service when necessary.[23]

---

[22]See page 73 and Article IV, Section 4.
[23]Article I, Section 8, Clause 15; Article II, Section 2, Clause 1.

Presents often find it necessary to explain, as well as promote, their programs and policies. Here, President Reagan meets with governors of several States at the White House.

✓ FOR REVIEW

1. By whom are treaties made? Ratified? What part does the Senate have in the treaty process?

2. What are executive agreements?

3. What is the power of recognition? How does the President ordinarily exercise it?

4. What is the President's major military power? How broad is that power? What is the War Powers Resolution?

Legislative Powers

As part of its system of checks and balances, the Constitution gives certain legislative powers to the President. With them—and the power that comes from being Chief of Party—the President can have a considerable influence over the actions of Congress. The President is in effect, then, the nation's Chief Legislator.

Power to Recommend Legislation. The Constitution requires that the President:

> shall, from time to time, give to the Congress information of the state of the Union, and recommend to their consideration such measures as he shall judge necessary and expedient.[24]

Soon after the beginning of each congressional session, the President gives the State of the Union Message to Congress. This is quickly followed by the proposed budget and the annual Economic Report. At times, the President also submits special messages on certain subjects. In all of them the legislators are called upon to enact those laws the President feels are needed.

The Veto Power. The Constitution says that "every bill" and "every order, resolution, or vote to which the concurrence of the Senate and House of Representatives may be necessary (except on a question of adjournment) shall be presented to the President" for his action.[25]

As we noted in Chapter 12, the Constitution presents the President with four options when the Congress sends a measure to the White House:

First, the President may sign the bill —thus making it law.

Second, the President may veto[26] the bill—and then must return it to the house in which it originated, together with a written statement of objections. Though it does not often do so, Congress may override a presidential veto by a two-thirds vote in each house.

---

[24]Article II, Section 3; see also page 294.

[25]Article I, Section 7, Clauses 2 and 3. Notice, however, that practice has it that joint resolutions proposing constitutional amendments and concurrent resolutions, which do not have the force of law, are not sent to the President.

[26]*Veto*, from the Latin, literally, "I forbid."

Third, the President may allow the bill to become law without signature—by not acting upon it, neither signing nor vetoing it, for 10 days (not counting Sundays). This rarely happens.

The *fourth* option, the "pocket veto," can be used only at the end of a congressional session. If Congress adjourns within 10 days of sending a bill to the President and the Chief Executive does not act upon it, the measure dies. The "pocket veto" has been applied.

The veto power allows the President, who is the only representative of *all* of the people, to act as a check on Congress. Often, just the *threat* of a veto is enough to defeat a bill or to bring about some changes in it before it is passed by Congress.

The historical record of presidential vetoes—and the fact that they are rarely overridden—can be seen in the table on this page.

Bills must be vetoed in their entirety. The President has no "item veto," as do most State governors. With that power, needless or wasteful projects might be eliminated from an appropriations measure, or an objectionable provision from a bill the President might otherwise wish to become law. On the other hand, the power could be used as a weapon to punish or pressure the President's opponents in Congress. Every president since Woodrow Wilson has favored a constitutional amendment to add the item veto to the President's legislative arsenal.

Other Legislative Powers. Only the President may call special sessions of Congress, as we noted on page 276. The President also has the power to adjourn (*prorogue*) Congress when the two houses cannot agree upon an adjournment date (which has never happened).

Judicial Powers

The Constitution states that the

PRESIDENTIAL VETOES

President		Vetoes	Vetoes Overridden
Washington	1789–97	2	–
Madison	1809–17	7	–
Monroe	1817–25	1	–
Jackson	1829–37	12	–
Van Buren	1837–41	1	–
Tyler	1841–45	10	1
Polk	1845–49	3	–
Pierce	1853–57	9	5
Buchanan	1857–61	7	–
Lincoln	1861–65	6	–
Johnson	1865–69	29	15
Grant	1869–77	93	4
Hayes	1877–81	13	1
Arthur	1881–85	12	1
Cleveland	1885–89	414	2
Harrison	1889–93	44	1
Cleveland	1893–97	170	5
McKinley	1897–01	42	–
Roosevelt	1901–09	82	1
Taft	1909–13	39	1
Wilson	1913–21	44	6
Harding	1921–23	6	–
Coolidge	1923–29	50	4
Hoover	1929–33	37	3
Roosevelt	1933–45	635	9
Truman	1945–53	250	12
Eisenhower	1953–61	181	2
Kennedy	1961–63	21	–
Johnson	1963–69	30	–
Nixon	1969–74	42	5
Ford	1974–77	66	12
Carter	1977–81	29	2
Reagan	1981–82	14	2
		2401	94

Source: Congressional Research Service, Library of Congress. Presidents not listed vetoed no measures.

President: shall have the power to grant reprieves and pardons for offenses against the United States, except in cases of impeachment.[27]

A **reprieve** is the postponement of the carrying out of a sentence. A **pardon**

[27]Article II, Section 2, Clause 1.

President Gerald Ford signs an amnesty resolution which restored citizenship to Robert E. Lee. The ceremony took place 110 years after the Virginia general surrendered his Confederate forces at Appomattox Court House, in 1865.

is legal (though not moral) forgiveness of a crime.

The President's power to grant reprieves and pardons is absolute, except in cases of impeachment where they may never be granted. These powers of *clemency* (of mercy, leniency) may be used only in cases of federal offenses, however. The President has no authority to pardon a person for any violation of a State's laws.

Presidential pardons are usually granted to persons accused of federal crimes *after* they have been convicted in court. The President may pardon a federal offender *before* that person is tried however, and even before there has been a formal charge.

Pardons in advance of a trial or charge have been rare. The most noteworthy pardon, by far, was granted in 1974. In that year, President Gerald Ford gave "a full, free and absolute pardon unto Richard Nixon for all offenses against the United States which he . . . has committed or may have committed or taken part in during the period from January 20, 1969, through August, 9, 1974."

To be effective, a pardon must be accepted by the person to whom it is granted. When one is granted before charge or conviction—as in Mr. Nixon's case—its acceptance is regularly seen as an admission of guilt by the person to whom it is given.

The pardoning power includes the power to grant *conditional* pardons, if the conditions are reasonable. It also includes the power of **commutation**—that is, the power to commute (reduce) the length of a sentence and/or the fine to be paid.

It also includes the power of **amnesty**—in effect, a general pardon offered to a group of law violators. Thus, in 1889 President Benjamin Harrison issued a proclamation of amnesty forgiving all Mormons who had broken the antipolygamy laws in the federal territories.

 FOR REVIEW

1. Why does the Constitution give certain legislative powers to the President? What are they?

2. Outline the veto power. By what vote may Congress override a presidential veto? Why is the threat of a veto at times an important presidential tool?

3. Does the President have the item veto?

4. Under what circumstances may a President pardon someone? What must rank as the most noteworthy of all presidential pardons?

5. What is a reprieve? A commutation? An amnesty?

S U M M A R Y

Every officer, employee, and agency of the executive branch is subordinate to the President and aids the President in carrying out the executive function. The President's chief right arm is the Executive Office of the President—a group of agencies staffed by key advisers and assistants. The Cabinet, made up of the heads of the 13 executive departments, is also a major source of advice to the President.

The President's powers arise from the Constitution, acts of Congress, and usage. The nature of the President's powers has been most tellingly shaped by the manner in which the stronger Presidents have used their powers. They include:

(1) *Executive powers:* to execute and en-

force the law, to direct administration, to issue executive orders, and to appoint and remove major officers.

(2) *Diplomatic powers:* to make treaties, to make executive agreements, to send and receive diplomatic representatives, and otherwise conduct foreign relations.

(3) *Military powers:* to act as Commander in Chief and to keep domestic peace.

(4) *Legislative powers:* to recommend legislation, to approve or veto acts of Congress, to call special sessions of Congress, and to adjourn Congress when the two houses cannot agree on an adjournment date.

(5) *Judicial powers:* to exercise executive clemency (pardons, reprieves, amnesties, commutations).

C H A P T E R   R E V I E W

Key Terms/Concepts
Amnesty (401)
Appointment/removal powers (392)
Budget (383)
Budget-making power (383)
Cabinet (384)
Chief Administrator (390)
Chief Diplomat (395)
Chief Executive (388)
Chief Legislator (399)
Commander in Chief (396)
Commute (401)
Diplomatic powers (395)
Executive agreements (396)
Executive clemency (401)
Executive Office of the President (381)
Executive ordinances (391)
Executive powers (390)
Judicial powers (400)
Legislative powers (399)
Message power (399)
Military powers (396)
Ordinance power (391)
Pardon (400)
Pocket veto (400)
Recognition (396)
Reprieve (400)
Senatorial courtesy (392)
Take-care power (390)
"the executive power" (381)
Treaty-making power (395)
Unity of the Presidency (388)
Veto power (399)
War Powers Resolution (398)
White House Office (382)

Keynote Questions
1. What basic power does the Constitution assign to the President?
2. Why is the fact that the Constitution deals with the Presidency in very broad and even outline-like terms so important a matter?
3. What is the main function of the Executive Office of the President? Why is it called an "umbrella agency"?

4. What is the Cabinet? Who are its members? What role does it play?

5. What is meant by the phrase "the unity of the Presidency"? Why is it a leading reason for the growth and present-day scope of presidential power? Cite at least three other factors that have led to the expansion of presidential power.

6. The Constitution gives the President the power to execute what laws? Why does that mean that the President and his subordinates in the executive branch have much to say about the actual content of these laws?

7. From what two sources does the President draw the power to exercise the ordinance power?

8. Why is the power of appointment so critically important to the President's ability to exercise any and all of his other powers? What role does the Senate play in the appointment process? What is the general shape of the President's removal power?

9. By whom are treaties made? Ratified? What is the Senate's role in the treaty-making process? What are executive agreements?

10. What is the power of recognition? How is it most often exercised?

11. What is the President's major military power? How broad is it? What is the War Powers Resolution?

12. Why does the Constitution give certain legislative and judicial powers to the President? What are those powers?

For Thought and Discussion

1. While he was President, Harry Truman kept a small sign on his desk; it read: "The buck stops here." Can you explain its meaning? Why do you suppose that Jimmy Carter had that same sign on his desk while he was President?

2. Each of the President's powers is limited in one or more important ways—by constitutional provision, by congressional action, by court decision, by custom, and/or by political realities. What illustrations can you give to support that statement?

3. Who were Edward M. House, Harry Hopkins, Sherman Adams, Bill Moyers, H. R. Halderman and John Ehrlichman, and Hamilton Jordan? What role did each of them play in the White House?

4. At various times it has been suggested that we should have two Presidents, one for foreign affairs and one for domestic affairs. What do you think of this idea?

5. Who are the present members of the Reagan Cabinet? What is the background of each of them? Why do you think each was appointed to the Cabinet?

Suggested Activities

1. Prepare a bulletin board or other display to illustrate the several powers of the President and/or the Cabinet and its role.

2. Stage a debate or class forum on one of the following topics: (a) *Resolved,* That the Constitution be amended to give the President the item veto; (b) *Resolved,* That the Constitution be amended to forbid the President to use the armed forces in combat without a declaration of war by Congress; (c) *Resolved,* That all Cabinet officers and other major presidential appointees be chosen to serve fixed terms of office; (d) *Resolved,* That the Constitution be amended to repeal the Senate's power to confirm or reject major presidential appointments.

3. Draw organizational charts comparing the Executive Office of the President with the structure of the governor's office in your State.

16

Running the Federal Government: Bureaucracy/Dollars

To help you to
Learn ▪ Know ▪ Understand

The need for and growth of the federal bureaucracy.

The overall shape of the organization of the executive branch and the staff/line functions in the federal government.

The organization/functions of the executive departments and of the independent agencies.

The continuing need for reorganization in the executive branch.

The development and present shape of the federal civil service.

The Federal Government's finances.

The true test of good government is its aptitude and tendency to produce a good administration.

Alexander Hamilton

As we have said several times, and in several different ways, the basic function of government in the United States is to translate the public will into public policy. In short, what the people want is what government is supposed to do.

In its broadest sense, public policy may be defined as what government does. Government does *many* different things, of course—and, so, public policy is in fact made up of many different policies on many different matters. Clearly, those policies must first (1) be made and then (2) administered, put into effect. And, of course, they must be paid for.

To this point, we have been very largely concerned with the *making* of public policy in the United States. We have looked at the constitutional setting in which that happens, at the roles of public opinion, pressure groups, parties, and voters, and at Congress and the Presidency. Now we turn to its administration—to "policy in action."[1]

---

[1]We shall look at the institutions and process by which public policy is made, and financed, at the State and local levels of government in Chapters 19–24.

The vast amounts of data gathered by the Census Bureau are indispensable to both the making and administration of public policy. *Above:* Taking the census in 1870. *Facing page:* The Bureau of Census Computer Center in Washington, D.C.

In Chapter 1 we said that there is nothing about democracy that guarantees that those who make public policy decisions will always find the "right" or the "best" answers to public problems. In fact, the democratic process is not even designed to find those kinds of answers. It looks, instead, for *satisfactory* solutions,. But, notice, even if Congress and the President make the wisest of policies, their decisions still must be carried out. Without an **administration** —without administrators and administrative agencies—the best of public policies amount to just so many words.

In other words, a **bureaucracy**—a large and complex administrative structure in the executive branch—is an absolute necessity in the Federal Government today. A number of factors have produced the need for it. Certainly, the many and extensive powers of the Presidency is a leading one. No single person, alone and unaided, could possibly do the huge job that the Constitution assigns to the Chief Executive. The size of the nation's population, the sweep of its geography, and ongoing scientific, technological, and industrial developments —are also major contributors to that need. So, too, are government's concerns for economic growth, for social welfare and social justice, and for the nation's security at home and abroad, and for all of the other things that make up the policies of the Federal Government.

As we go on here, come back to this thought, often: A large and extensive executive branch—often called "the administration" or "the bureaucracy"—is a common feature of modern governments, both here and abroad. One of the central problems for democracy is to keep that structure responsive to the law and to the elected representatives of the people. The growth in the number, reach, and power of administrative agencies makes effective control of them absolutely necessary. They cannot be allowed to obstruct rather than promote the policies, the interests, and the wishes of "government by the people."

The Federal Bureaucracy

As we know, the Constitution makes the President the *Chief Administrator* of the Federal Government. Article II, Section 3 states that "he shall take care that the laws be faithfully executed."

The Constitution makes only the barest mention of the administrative machinery through which the President is to exercise that power, however. Article II does suggest the existence of several executive departments—by giving to the President the power to "require the opinion, in writing, of the principal officers in each of the executive departments."[2] And it suggests the existence of two departments in particular, for military and for foreign affairs—by making the President the "commander in chief of the army and navy," and by giving him the power to make treaties and to appoint "ambassadors, other public ministers, and consuls."[3]

As the chart on page 407 shows, the executive branch is now made up of three major groups of administrative agencies: (1) the Executive Office of the President, (2) the 13 Cabinet Depart-

ments, and (3) a large number of independent agencies.[4]

We talked about the Executive Office, and its several agencies, in Chapter 15. We shall look at the other two groups in a moment. But, first, a word on two matters: What is often called the "name game" and the difference between *staff* and *line* agencies and functions.

The Name Game. The titles given to the many units that make up the executive branch vary a great deal. The name *department* is reserved for agencies of Cabinet rank. Beyond that, however, there is not very much in the way of standardized use of titles—and that can be confusing.

The term *agency* is often used to refer to any governmental body. It is sometimes used to identify a major unit headed by a single administrator of near-Cabinet status—such as, the Environmental Protection Agency and the United States Arms Control and Disarmament Agency. But so, too, is the title *administration*—for example, the National Aeronautics and Space Administration and the Veterans Administration.

The name *commission* is usually given to those agencies charged with the regulation of business activities—as the Interstate Commerce Commission and the Securities and Exchange Commission. The same title, however, is also given to some investigative, reporting, advisory, and other bodies including the Civil Rights Commission and the Federal Election Commission.

Either *corporation* or *authority* is the title most often given to agencies headed by a board and a manager and that con-

---

[2]In Section 2, Clause 1. There is also a reference to "heads of departments" in Clause 2, and to "any department or officer" of the government in Article I, Section 8, Clause 18, the Necessary and Proper Clause.

[3]In Section 2, Clauses 1 and 2.

[4]The chart is adapted from the current edition of the *United States Government Manual*, a yearly publication of the Office of the Federal Register in the General Services Administration. The *Manual* contains a brief description of the creation, authority, and functions of each of the agencies operating in each of the three branches of the Federal Government.

THE GOVERNMENT OF THE UNITED STATES

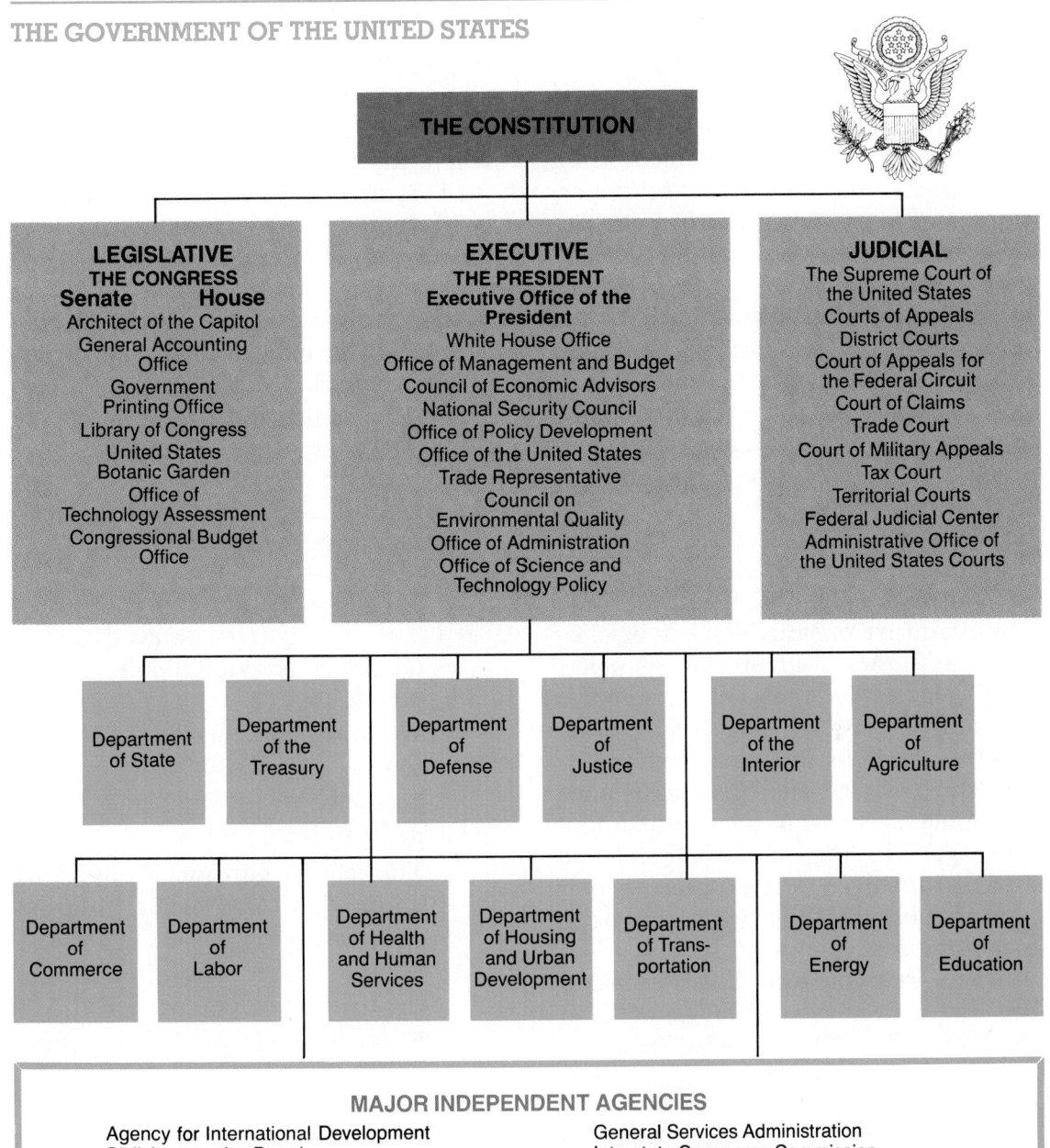

THE CONSTITUTION

LEGISLATIVE
THE CONGRESS
Senate   House
Architect of the Capitol
General Accounting
Office
Government
Printing Office
Library of Congress
United States
Botanic Garden
Office of
Technology Assessment
Congressional Budget
Office

EXECUTIVE
THE PRESIDENT
Executive Office of the President
White House Office
Office of Management and Budget
Council of Economic Advisors
National Security Council
Office of Policy Development
Office of the United States
Trade Representative
Council on
Environmental Quality
Office of Administration
Office of Science and
Technology Policy

JUDICIAL
The Supreme Court of
the United States
Courts of Appeals
District Courts
Court of Appeals for
the Federal Circuit
Court of Claims
Trade Court
Court of Military Appeals
Tax Court
Territorial Courts
Federal Judicial Center
Administrative Office of
the United States Courts

Department of State

Department of the Treasury

Department of Defense

Department of Justice

Department of the Interior

Department of Agriculture

Department of Commerce

Department of Labor

Department of Health and Human Services

Department of Housing and Urban Development

Department of Transportation

Department of Energy

Department of Education

MAJOR INDEPENDENT AGENCIES

Agency for International Development
Civil Aeronautics Board
Commission on Civil Rights
Consumer Product Safety Commission
Environmental Protection Agency
Equal Employment Opportunity Commission
Export-Import Bank of the U.S.
Farm Credit Administration
Federal Communications Commission
Federal Deposit Insurance Corporation
Federal Election Commission
Federal Home Loan Bank Board
Federal Maritime Commission
Federal Mediation and Conciliation Service
Federal Reserve System
Federal Trade Commission

General Services Administration
Interstate Commerce Commission
National Aeronautics and Space Administration
National Labor Relations Board
National Transportation Safety Board
Nuclear Regulatory Commission
Office of Personnel Management
Pension Benefit Guaranty Corporation
Securities and Exchange Commission
Selective Service System
Small Business Administration
Tennessee Valley Authority
U.S. Arms Control and Disarmament Agency
U.S. International Trade Commission
U.S. Postal Service
Veterans Administration

Note: There are, altogether, more than 200 independent agencies in the Executive Branch.

duct business-like activities—as the Federal Deposit Insurance Corporation and the Tennessee Valley Authority.

Within each major agency we find the same confusion. *Bureau* is the name often given to the major elements in a department, but *service, administration, office, branch,* and *division* are titles often used for the same purpose.

Many federal agencies are very often referred to by their initials rather than their full titles. EPA, IRS, VA, FBI, CIA, FCC, and TVA are but a few of dozens of familiar examples of the practice. A few are also known by nicknames. The Federal National Mortgage Association is often called "Fannie Mae"; and the National Railroad Passenger Corporation is much better known as Amtrak.

Staff and Line.   The units of any administrative organization can be classified as either *staff* or *line* agencies. **Staff** agencies and their personnel serve in a support capacity. They aid the chief executive and other administrators by furnishing advice and other assistance in the management of the organization. **Line** agencies, on the other hand, are directly involved with, actually perform, the basic task for which the organization exists.

Take, as two quick illustrations of this distinction, the several agencies in the Executive Office of the President and, in contrast, the Environmental Protection Agency.

The agencies which make up the Executive Office—the White House Office, the National Security Council, the Office of Management and Budget, and so on—each exist as staff support to the President. Their primary mission is to assist the President in the exercise of the executive power and in the overall management of the executive branch. They are *not* operating agencies. That is, they do not operate (administer) public programs.

The Environmental Protection Agency has a quite different mission. It is responsible for the day-to-day enforcement of the several federal anti-pollution laws. It operates "on the line," where the action is.

This difference between staff and line can help us to understand the complexities of the federal bureaucracy. But, remember: it can be oversimplified or pushed too far. For example, most line agencies do have staff units of their own—to aid them in their line operations. Thus, the Office of Legislation in the EPA assists the agency's Administrator in the critical matter of relations with Congress, its appropriate committees, and its individual members.

FOR REVIEW

1. Of what is public policy composed?
2. What is a bureaucracy?
3. Why is a bureaucracy an absolute necessity in the Federal Government today?
4. The federal bureaucracy is made up of what three major groups of agencies?
5. What terms are most often used in the titles of federal agencies?
6. What are staff agencies and functions? Line agencies and functions?

The Executive Departments

Much of the work of the Federal Government is done by the 13 executive departments. They are the traditional units of federal administration, and each of them is built around a broad field of activity.

The 1st Congress set up three of these departments, in 1789: State,

PERSONALITY PROFILE

DAVID STOCKMAN

In the time it takes to read this page, the Federal Government will spend more money than the average American earns in a lifetime. Much of the awesome task of preparing the spending plan (the federal budget) the President must present to Congress each year rests with the Office of Management and Budget (OMB). As President Reagan's Director of the OMB, David Stockman is one of the most influential and, at times, one of the least popular people in Washington. As a leader in the battle to cut federal spending, Stockman often finds himself at odds with members of Congress, many potent pressure groups, and even many of his colleagues in the Administration.

Stockman came to admire individual enterprise and hard work growing up on a farm near St. Joseph, Michigan. At Lakeside High School, he played football and basketball and served on the student council. His first political involvement came at 17 when he campaigned for Barry Goldwater for President. After attending Michigan State and Harvard Universities, Stockman became a staff member of the House Republican Conference (see page 297) and then served two terms in the House of Representatives (1977–1981). As a conservative Congressman from Michigan, the young bachelor worked for reduction of the role of government in American life. When Ronald Reagan was rehearsing for the 1980 television debates, Stockman helped him by playing the roles of both John Anderson and Jimmy Carter. His performance and keen intellect made a deep impression on the future President.

Since he became Director of the OMB at age 34, Stockman has often worked 16- and 18-hour days. With the goal of bolstering the nation's economy and achieving a balanced federal budget, the self-taught economist has drafted plans to cut or reduce many of the Federal Government's domestic programs. Despite many setbacks and much opposition in Congress, the current federal budget reflects many of Stockman's efforts to curb federal spending.

1. What more can you discover about David Alan Stockman?

2. Have his policy views and his influence in the Reagan Administration had any impact on you, personally?

David Stockman, Director of the OMB.

Treasury, and War. As the size and the workload of the Federal Government grew, new departments were added. Some of the later ones took over various duties originally assigned to older departments, and they gradually assumed new functions, as well. And a few departments have been created and later abolished by Congress.

The head of each department is known as the Secretary—except for the Attorney General, who directs the work of the Justice Department, of course. Each of them is named by the President subject to Senate confirmation.

Together, the department secretaries serve as the members of the President's Cabinet—a matter we talked about in the last chapter. Their duties as the chief officers of their own agencies generally take most of their time, however. Each of them is the primary link between presidential policy and his/her own department. But, just as importantly, each tries to promote and protect that department with the President, congressional committees, the rest of the bureaucracy, and the public.

The secretary is aided in that many-sided role by an under secretary or deputy secretary and several assistant secretaries. They, too, are named by the President and Senate. Staff help for the secretary comes from assistants and aides (with a wide range of titles) in such areas as personnel, planning, legal advice, budgeting, and public relations.

Each department is made up of a number of sub-units, both staff and line. As we noted a moment ago, these agencies are known as bureaus, offices, services, divisions, and so on. And each of them is divided into smaller units.

The internal structure of most of the departments is also arranged on a geographic basis. That is, many of its activities are conducted through regional offices which direct the work of agency

employees in the field. For example, the Treasury Department's Internal Revenue Service is head-quartered in Washington. But most of its tax collection and enforcement work is carried out through seven regional offices, 58 district offices, and some 200 local offices.

The organizational chart of the Department of Labor, on the next page, presents a fairly typical picture of the structure of the executive departments.

Over the next 13 pages we summarize the work/functions of the principal agencies of 11 of the 13 executive departments. The Departments of State and Defense are treated in Chapter 17.

THE EXECUTIVE DEPARTMENTS TODAY

Department	Created
State	1789
Treasury	1789
Defense[a]	1949
Justice[b]	1870
Interior	1849
Agriculture	1889
Commerce[c]	1903
Labor[c]	1913
Health and Human Services[d]	1953
Housing and Urban Development	1965
Transportation	1967
Energy	1977
Education[d]	1979

[a]Congress created National Military Establishment, as an executive department headed by Secretary of Defense, in 1947; renamed Department of Defense in 1949. Since 1947 has included former Cabinet-level Departments of War (1789) and Navy (1798) and Department of the Air Force (1947).
[b]Post of Attorney General established by Congress in 1789.
[c]Department of Commerce and Labor, established in 1903, replaced by separate Departments of Commerce and of Labor in 1913.
[d]Education functions transferred from Department of Health, Education, and Welfare to new Department of Education in 1979; HEW renamed in 1979.

Another executive department, the Post Office Department, was abolished by Congress in 1971. Originally established in 1789, it was made an executive department in 1872. Congress transformed it into a government corporation, the United States Postal Service, in 1971.

DEPARTMENT OF LABOR

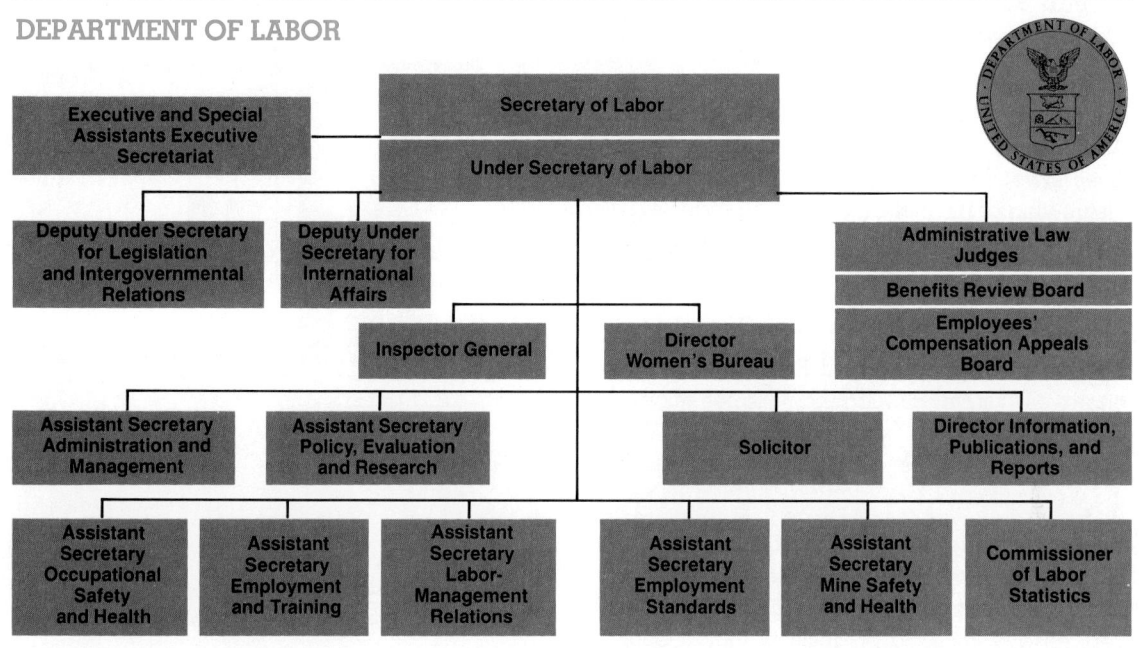

	Secretary of Labor	

Executive and Special Assistants Executive Secretariat

Under Secretary of Labor

Deputy Under Secretary for Legislation and Intergovernmental Relations

Deputy Under Secretary for International Affairs

Administrative Law Judges

Benefits Review Board

Employees' Compensation Appeals Board

Inspector General

Director Women's Bureau

Assistant Secretary Administration and Management

Assistant Secretary Policy, Evaluation and Research

Solicitor

Director Information, Publications, and Reports

Assistant Secretary Occupational Safety and Health

Assistant Secretary Employment and Training

Assistant Secretary Labor-Management Relations

Assistant Secretary Employment Standards

Assistant Secretary Mine Safety and Health

Commissioner of Labor Statistics

THE EXECUTIVE DEPARTMENTS:
Principal Agencies and Functions[a]

DEPARTMENT OF THE TREASURY
Established: 1789
Head: Secretary of the Treasury
Employees, 1984: 127,000[b]

Internal Revenue Service. Administers, enforces most federal tax laws; collects nearly all federal taxes (including, especially, personal and corporate income, social security, excise, estate, and gift taxes).

United States Customs Service. Administers, enforces customs laws; collects duties on imports; combats smuggling, other illegal practices in international trade.

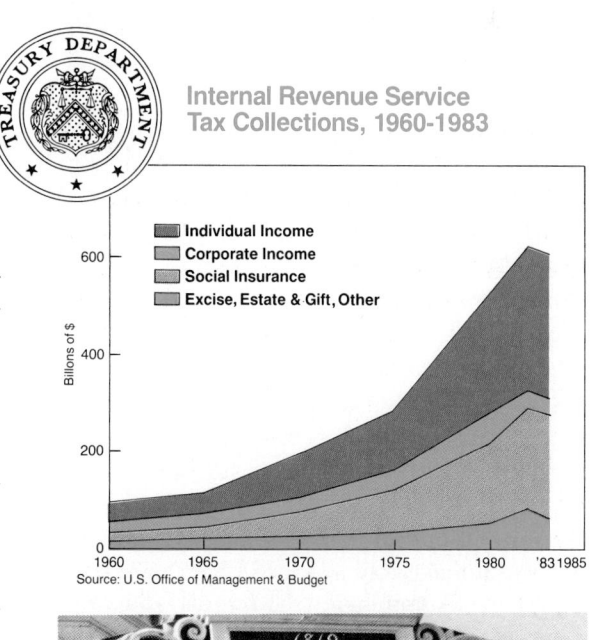

Internal Revenue Service
Tax Collections, 1960-1983

Billions of $

- Individual Income
- Corporate Income
- Social Insurance
- Excise, Estate & Gift, Other

Source: U.S. Office of Management & Budget

---

[a]The several agencies listed on these pages are the major units within Cabinet-level departments treated here. There are a number of other agencies within each of those Departments; see the current edition of *The United States Government Manual.*

[b]This figure, and the corresponding figure for each of the other departments, supplied by the Office of Personnel Management.

CUSTOM HOUSE.

Bureau of the Public Debt. Supervises most federal borrowing operations; manages the public debt.

Bureau of Alcohol, Tobacco and Firearms. Administers, enforces federal firearms, explosives laws, and those covering production, use, distribution of alcohol and tobacco products.

Bureau of Government Financial Operations. Government's central bookkeeper and principal financial reporting agency.

Bureau of Engraving and Printing. Designs, engraves, prints all currency (paper money), Treasury bonds and notes, postage stamps, food coupons and similar financial items issued by the Government.

Bureau of the Mint. Manufactures all U.S. coins; holds Government's stocks of gold, silver; operates United States Mints (Philadelphia, Denver), Assay Office (San Francisco), Gold Depository (Fort Knox, Kentucky), Silver Depository (West Point, N.Y.).

Office of the Comptroller of the Currency. Headed by the Comptroller of the Currency; administers federal banking laws and generally supervises the operations of 4500 national banks; directs staff of 2100 bank examiners to assure the soundness of the operations and financial condition of all national banks.

United States Secret Service. Protects the President and Vice President, the members of their immediate families, former Presidents and their wives or widows, presidential and vice-presidential candidates, and visiting heads of foreign states; enforces laws against counterfeiting.

DEPARTMENT OF JUSTICE
    Established: 1870
    Head: Attorney General
    Employees, 1984: 57,800

Solicitor General. Represents the United States in the Supreme Court; decides which lower court decisions Government should ask Supreme Court to review and position Government should take in cases heard by High Court.

Antitrust Division. Handles court cases involving violations of antitrust laws, other federal statutes covering illegal business practices.

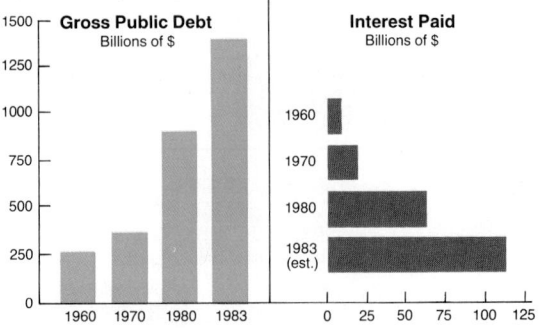

Public Debt of Federal Government, 1960-1983

Source: U.S. Office of Management & Budget

The Small Society

FROM ONE SENATOR TO ANOTHER—

TELL ME, CHARLIE. EXACTLY HOW MUCH IS A HUNDRED BILLION DOLLARS IN REAL MONEY?

Cartoon by Brickman   Washington Star Syndicate, Inc.

The *Fugio* cent of 1787, the first coin to be struck by authority of the United States.

Confiscated marijuana is unloaded at a dock in New York City.

Land and Natural Resources Division. Handles most civil (non-criminal) cases involving the public lands and other real property owned by the United States; represents the Government's interests in civil cases involving Indians and Indian affairs; handles both civil and criminal cases arising out of federal environmental protection laws.

Tax Division. Handles both civil and criminal cases arising out of the tax laws; most often, acts as in-court attorney for the Internal Revenue Service.

Civil Rights Division. Handles both civil and criminal cases involving acts of discrimination prohibited by the various federal civil rights laws.

Civil Division. Handles most of the civil cases to which the United States is a party (all of those civil cases not handled by one of the other Divisions).

Criminal Division. Handles most court cases involving federal crimes (all criminal cases not handled by one of the other Divisions).

Federal Bureau of Investigation. Investigates most cases involving violations of federal criminal laws; pursues, arrests most persons suspected of or charged with federal crimes.

Drug Enforcement Administration. Administers, enforces federal laws relating to controlled substances (principally narcotics and dangerous drugs).

DEPARTMENT OF THE INTERIOR
Established: 1849
Head: Secretary of the Interior
Employees, 1984: 80,000

Bureau of Land Management. Controls, manages some 340 million acres of public lands (most of the land owned by the United States, located chiefly in the Far West and Alaska); manages timber, oil, gas, minerals, rangeland, recreation, and other resources of those lands; leases (and sometimes sells) public lands for various purposes; leases Outer Continental Shelf lands for oil, gas, and other resource exploration and development.

Bureau of Prisons. Operates the federal penal system (including five penitentiaries and several other correctional insitutions).

Immigration and Naturalization Service. Administers, enforces the immigration laws (involving aliens who seek to enter or remain in the United States) and the naturalization laws (relating to aliens who seek to become American citizens).

Bureau of Reclamation. Builds, operates water projects to reclaim arid and semiarid lands in the Western States; most BLM projects are multipur-

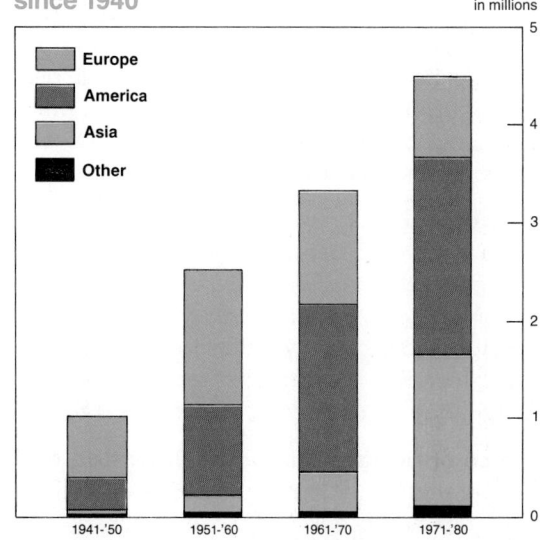

Immigrants by Continent since 1940

in millions

- Europe
- America
- Asia
- Other

Source: U.S. Immigration & Naturalization Service

Camping in California's Tahoe National Forest

pose. That is, in addition to water conservation, storage, and irrigation, they serve such other purposes as hydroelectric power generation, flood control, municipal and industrial water supply, navigation, and outdoor recreation.

National Park Service. Administers the more than 330 units of the National Park System (including national parks, national monuments of natural and scientific value, scenic rivers, lakeshores and seashores, recreation areas, and historic sites); plays host to more than 300 million tourist visits each year.

United States Fish and Wildlife Service. Responsible for protecting and increasing the nation's fish and wildlife resources; maintains more than 400 wildlife refuges, 77 fish hatcheries, and a number of laboratories, and a nationwide network of wildlife law enforcement agents.

Geological Survey. Conducts surveys and other research to describe (map) the geography and geology of the United States and locate the nation's oil, gas, mineral, water, power, and other natural resources; its very detailed topographic and geologic maps and other reports now cover more than half of the land area of the U.S.

Office of Surface Mining Reclamation and Enforcement. Administers, enforces federal laws to protect people and the environment from the harmful effects of coal mining; regulates strip mining activities; works to reclaim abandoned mines and mined lands; aids the States in the development and enforcement of their own similar regulatory programs.

Bureau of Mines. Conducts research, issues factual reports on mining techniques, mine health and safety, environmental pollution, the recycling of solid wastes, and nearly all other phases of mining activity in this country.

Bureau of Indian Affairs. Administers educational, public health, and other social assistance programs for the nation's Indian population, especially the approximately 600,000 Indians who now live on or near some 260 reservations.

Office of Territorial and International Affairs. Works to promote the economic, social, and political development of the territories of the Virgin Islands, Guam, American Samoa, and the Trust Territory of the Pacific Islands.

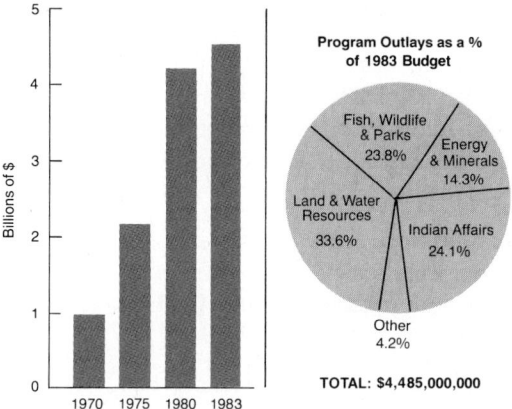

Interior Budget Outlays, selected years

Program Outlays as a % of 1983 Budget

Fish, Wildlife & Parks 23.8%
Energy & Minerals 14.3%
Land & Water Resources 33.6%
Indian Affairs 24.1%
Other 4.2%

TOTAL: $4,485,000,000

Source: U.S. Office of Management & Budget

A Geological Survey cartographer at work.

Logs destined for a Navajo-owned lumber mill.

DEPARTMENT OF AGRICULTURE

Established: 1889
Head: Secretary of Agriculture
Employees, 1984: 119,100

Farmers Home Administration. Makes several different types of low-interest, long-term loans to farmers and farm groups who are unable to get credit at reasonable terms from other (private) lenders; most FHA loans are made for the purchase, enlargement, improvement, or operation of family-sized farms.

Rural Electrification Administration. Makes low-interest, long-term loans to farm cooperatives and other rural-based nonprofit groups to provide electric power and/or telephone service to people in rural areas.

Agricultural Cooperative Service. Helps farmers to form and run cooperatives, especially to market their crops and to purchase farm supplies.

Agricultural Marketing Service. Aids farmers to market their products; issues daily reports on crop conditions, demands, prices, and other local and national agricultural market data, through press, radio, and television; enforce several laws that prohibit fraud and other deceptive market practices.

Animal and Plant Health Inspection Service. Conducts inspections to prevent, control, or eradicate animal and plant pests and diseases; may impose quarantines to prevent shipments in both interstate and foreign commerce; licenses, regulates the manufacture and sale of chemical and nonchemical products used in the prevention or the treatment animal and plant pests and diseases.

Food and Nutrition Service. Administers the food stamp program (which provides coupons to low-income persons and families to increase their food purchasing power); provides grants and/or foodstuffs for several other food assistance programs (most notably, the National School Lunch Program).

Food Safety and Inspection Service. Inspects food and meat processing plants and grades their products under federal laws that require that those products are safe, of good quality, and properly labelled.

Grain is harvested in Indiana.

Agriculture Budget Outlays, selected years

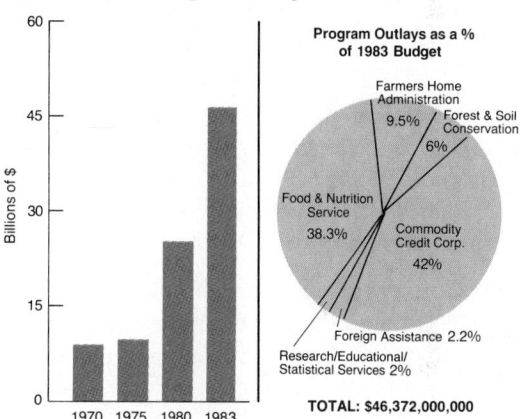

Program Outlays as a % of 1983 Budget

- Farmers Home Administration 9.5%
- Forest & Soil Conservation 6%
- Commodity Credit Corp. 42%
- Foreign Assistance 2.2%
- Research/Educational/Statistical Services 2%
- Food & Nutrition Service 38.3%

TOTAL: $46,372,000,000

Source: U.S. Office of Management & Budget

Food stamps are issued by the U.S.D.A.

Agricultural Stabilization and Conservation Service. Administers several price support, commodity loan, and subsidy payment programs to "stabilize" (*i.e.*, maintain, bolster) farm incomes and market prices for certain crops.

Commodity Credit Corporation. Holds (stores) crops purchased or accepted as payments of loans under the various programs administered by the ASCR; reduces surplus crop holdings (mostly by donations to federal, State, and private welfare agencies and programs).

Federal Crop Insurance Corporation. Offers (sells) insurance to producers of certain crops to protect them against unavoidable losses from such causes as weather, insects, and diseases.

Agricultural Research Service. Conducts a wide range of both basic and applied research programs, covering all phases of agriculture; makes grants to support research and other activities at State agricultural experiment stations and land-grant universities; provides financial support for the Cooperative Extension Service (which operates through land-grant universities and county extension agents, to promote "beyond-the-classroom" education and other farm-related activities, especially in rural areas); administers grants and other financial aid for higher education in food and agricultural sciences and veterinary medicine.

Forest Service. Manages the National Forest System (155 national forests and 19 national grasslands, totalling 191 million acres in 44 States and Puerto Rico); provides grant support for research in all phases of forestry.

Soil Conservation Service. Directs and/or provides financial and other assistance for a broad range of soil conservation, watershed protection, and related programs; promotes the creation of and gives technical help to local soil conservation districts (which now number nearly 3000 and cover more than 90 percent of the nation's farms and farmlands).

DEPARTMENT OF COMMERCE

Established: 1903
Head: Secretary of Commerce
Employees, 1984: 35,900

Bureau of the Census. Takes a census of the nation's population every 10 years (as required by the Constitution, particularly for the apportionment of seats in the House of Representatives); collects, analyzes, and publishes a wide variety of other statistical data about the people and the economy of the nation.

National Bureau of Standards. Develops and maintains the uniform standards of all weights and measures which, by law, may be used in the United States; performs a wide range of advanced scientific and other experimental and

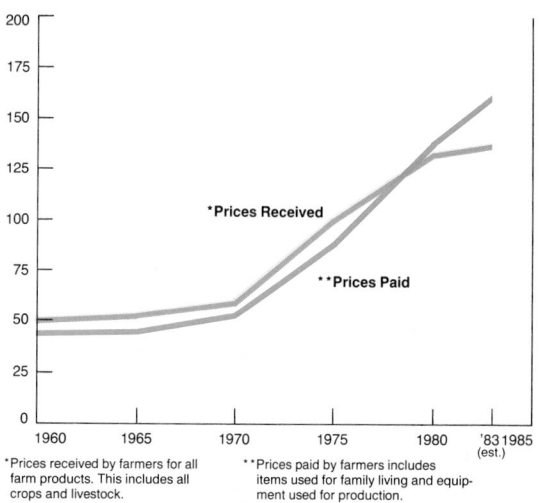

Farm Prices and Costs
Index: 1977 = 100

*Prices Received

**Prices Paid

*Prices received by farmers for all farm products. This includes all crops and livestock.

**Prices paid by farmers includes items used for family living and equipment used for production.

Source: U.S. Dept. of Agriculture

Alfalfa, a soil-enriching plant, is harvested.

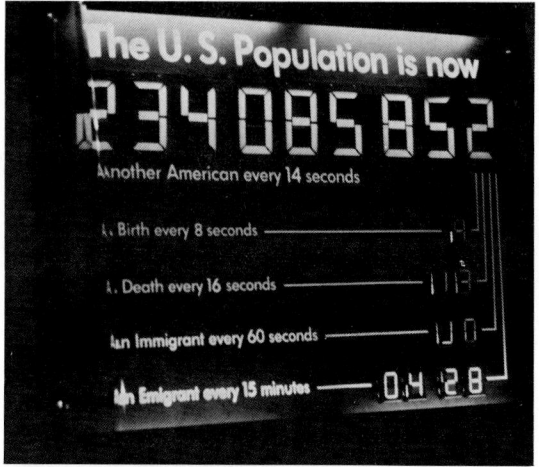

A Census Clock reading on September 6, 1983.

testing functions; furnishes scientific and technological services to both government and private industry.

Patent and Trademark Office. Issues more than 60,000 patents each year (patents of invention, good for 17 years; patents of design, good for 14 years; and plant patents, good for 17 years); registers some 30,000 trademarks each year (good for 20 years, and renewable).

National Oceanic and Atmospheric Administration. Operates the National Weather Service, which forecasts and reports weather conditions throughout the country; makes satellite observations of weather and other features of the earth's environment; conducts oceanic, atmospheric, seismological, and other environmental research; publishes its findings in nautical and aeronautical maps, charts, and other reports; administers the Sea Grant program (which provides grants for marine research and education).

Maritime Administration. Administers several programs to promote the development and operation of the nation's merchant marine; subsidizes shipbuilding and certain ship operating costs (especially to counter foreign competition); conducts research and development programs to improve the merchant marine; trains officers for the merchant marine (at the U.S. Merchant Marine Academy, at Kings Point, N.Y.).

Minority Business Development Agency. Promotes and coordinates federal and other public and private efforts to help organize and strengthen businesses owned and operated by members of minority groups; furnishes management and technical assistance to minority firms.

Bureau of Economic Analysis. Collects, analyzes, and publishes data to provide a reliable and detailed picture of the structure, condition, and prospects of the nation's economy; makes continuing reports on the gross national product (the GNP, the total national output of goods and services, measured in dollar terms).

International Trade Administration. Promotes American interests in foreign trade; maintains a network of Foreign Commercial Service offices to report on business conditions and trade and investment opportunities abroad; conducts trade fairs and operates trade centers in other countries.

A weather map is updated.

A biologist checks for clam infection.

The Gross National Product (GNP) 1960-1983

Billions of $

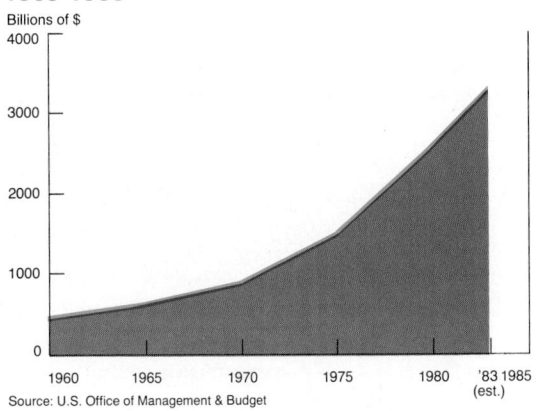

Source: U.S. Office of Management & Budget

DEPARTMENT OF LABOR
Established: 1913
Head: Secretary of Labor
Employees, 1984: 19,400

Employment and Training Administration.
An umbrella agency. Through the *United States Employment Service,* aids the States to operate a system of local employment offices; through the *Unemployment Insurance Service,* supervises the States' administration of their unemployment compensation programs (largely financed by a federal tax on employers); through the *Office of Employment and Training Programs,* makes grants for and administers several job-training, work experience, and public service employment programs; through the *Bureau of Apprenticeship and Training,* works to improve the standards of apprenticeship and training for various skilled jobs.

Employment Standards Administration. An umbrella agency. Through the *Wage and Hour Division,* enforces federal minimum wage and maximum hours laws; through the *Office of Federal Contract Compliance Programs,* enforces laws prohibiting discrimination in employment on all federal or federally-supported construction projects; through the *Office of Workers' Compensation Programs,* administers laws providing injury and accident benefits for federal employees.

Labor-Management Services Administration. Administers laws guaranteeing the reemployment rights of veterans; enforces federal laws regulating the operations of private pension and welfare plans; acts as an advisory agency to help in the collective bargaining process.

Occupational Safety and Health Administration. Enforces federal laws setting minimum

Quitting time for a construction crew.

Federal Minimum Hourly Wage Rates 1950-1983

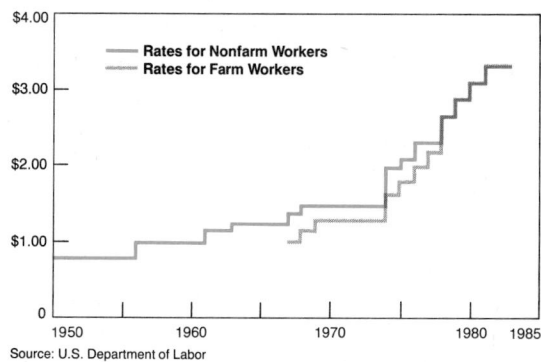

Source: U.S. Department of Labor

safety and health standards in most work situations.

Mine Safety and Health Administration.
Enforces federal laws setting minimum safety and health standards for mining operations.

Bureau of Labor Statistics. Collects, analyzes, and publishes data on employment, unemployment, hours of work, wages, and prices.

Trends in the Labor Force: 1960-1983

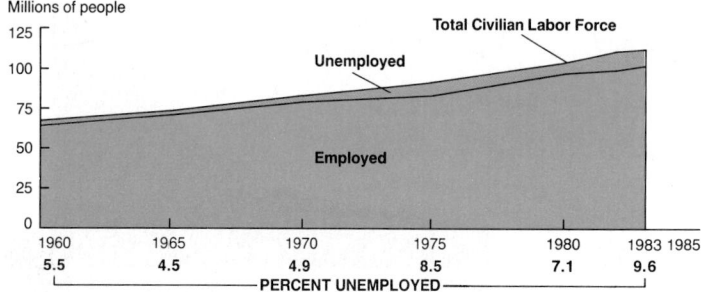

Source: U.S. Bureau of Labor Statistics

Consumer Price Index: 1960-1983

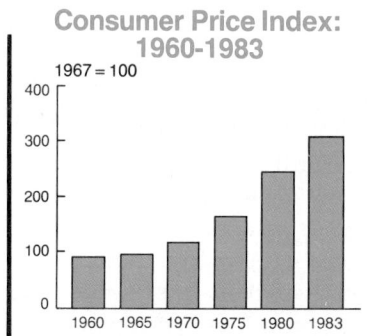

DEPARTMENT OF HEALTH AND HUMAN SERVICES

Established: 1953
Head: Secretary of Health and
   Human Services
Employees, 1984: 149,400

Office of Human Development Services. An umbrella agency. Through the *Administration on Aging,* makes grants, gives other support to State and local programs to provide social services to older persons; through the *Administration for Native Americans,* makes grants, gives other support to social and economic development programs for American Indians, Alaskan Natives, and Native Hawaiians; through the *Administration on Developmental Disabilities,* makes grants, gives other support to rehabilitation and similar programs for handicapped persons.

Public Health Service. An umbrella agency. Through the Centers for Disease Control (based at Atlanta), conducts research and treatment programs for the prevention and control of communicable and other diseases; through the *Food and Drug Administration,* conducts research and administers federal laws which prohibit the manufacture, shipment, or sale of impure and unsafe foods, drugs, commetics, medical devices, and similar items; through the *Health Resources and Services Administration,* makes grants to strengthen State, local, and private nonprofit hospital and other health care facilities and programs; provides medical and other health care services to certain groups (*e.g.,* Coast Guard personnel and their dependents, federal

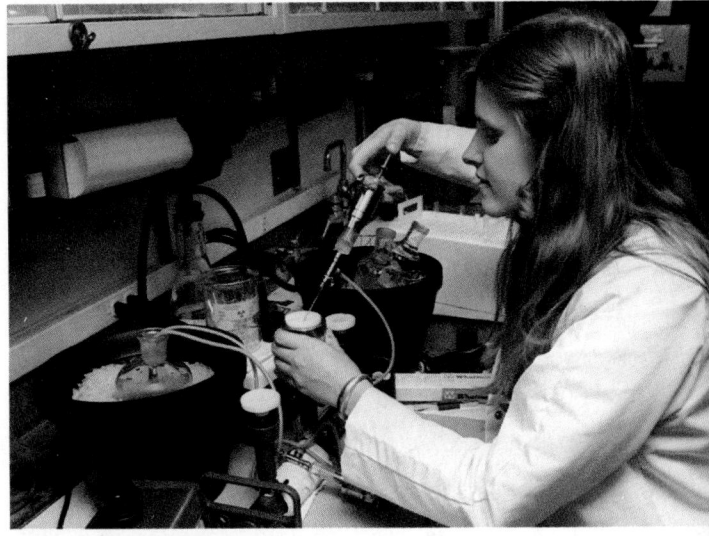

An FDA scientist at work

prisoners, American Indians); through the *National Institutes of Health,* makes grants to support medical research and operates several research institutes (*e.g.,* National Cancer Institute, National Institute of Allergy and Infectious Diseases, and National Institute of Environmental Health Services).

Social Security Administration. Administers several major elements of the social security programs, especially: (1) the Old-Age, Survivors, and Disability Insurance (OASDI) program— under which compulsory payroll taxes paid by employers, employees and the self-employed finance payments (pensions, other benefits) to persons covered under the program when they retire or become permanently disabled, and to their dependents or survivors; (2) the Supplemen-

Highlights of Social Security

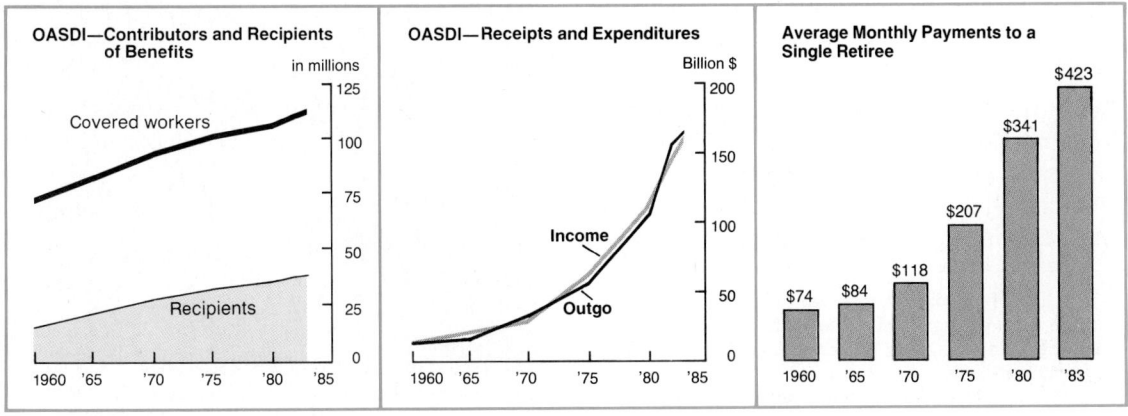

Source: U.S. Department of Health & Human Services, Social Security Administration

tal Security Income (SSI) program—which gives direct federal assistance (payments) to needy aged, blind, and disabled persons; and (3) the Aid to Families with Dependent Children (AFDC) program—under which federal grants help the States to give financial assistance to children who lack adequate parental support.

Health Care Financing Administration. Administers two other major elements of the social security program: (1) *Medicare*—a health insur-

ance program for most elderly persons (those over 65 who receive OASDI benefits), to help pay at least most of their hospital, medical, and other health care bills (financed by a combination of compulsory payroll taxes and optional monthly fees); and (2) *Medicaid*—a federal grant program, to help the States help to pay the hospital, medical, and other health care bills of the poor (principally, families who receive AFDC payments and the needy aged, blind, and disabled who receive SSI payments).

National Health Expenditures

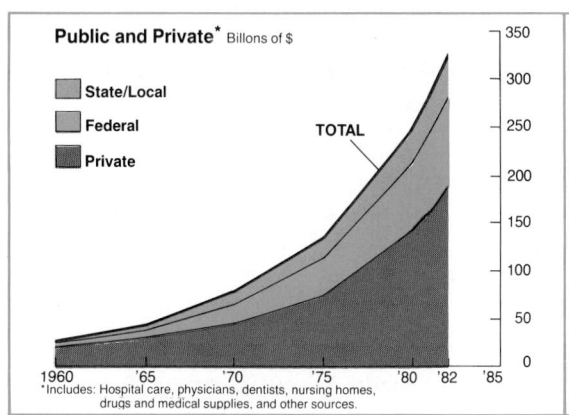

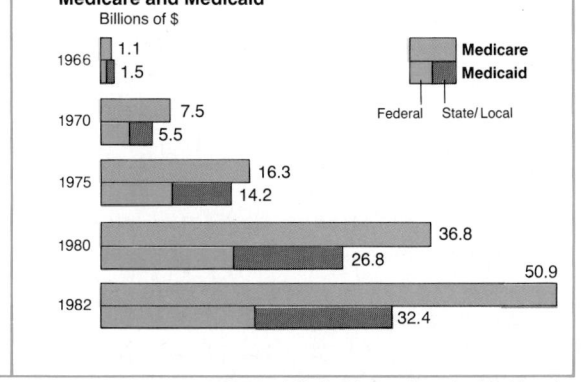

Source: U.S. Bureau of Labor Statistics

Source: U.S. Health Care Financing Administration

DEPARTMENT OF HOUSING AND URBAN DEVELOPMENT[c]

> Established: 1965
> Head: Secretary of Housing and
>   Urban Development
> Employees, 1984: 14,000

Assistant Secretary for Community Planning and Development. Administers several grant programs to aid State and local government efforts to improve housing conditions in urban areas (*e.g.,* water, sewer, slum clearance projects).

Assistant Secretary for Housing (Federal Housing Commissioner). Administers several programs, including: (1) mortgage insurance programs—in which the Government guarantees loans made by private lenders (mortgages)

---

[c]HUD and two other departments (Energy and Education) are not organized in quite the same way as the other Cabinet Departments. Most of their functions and programs are administered directly by a number of Assistant Secretaries (rather than by several bureaus, services, or similar line agencies).

One in four homes built in the past 40 years have been built with FHA-backed loans.

for the purchase of private housing (mostly single-family residences and such multifamily units as apartment houses and condominiums); (2) loan programs—to help both public and private borrowers finance housing projects for the elderly and the handicapped (*e.g.*, nursing homes); (3) the Rent Supplement Program—in which HUD pays a portion of the monthly rents of low-income families; and (4) public housing programs—in which loans, subsidies, and other aid are given to local agencies to build, operate

public housing projects (mostly for low-income families).

Assistant Secretary for Neighborhoods, Voluntary Associations, and Consumer Protection. Administers grants, gives other aid to neighborhood-oriented development projects in low-income urban areas; enforces federal laws setting construction, safety standards for mobile homes; enforces federal laws regulating the interstate sale of land.

Housing Highlights

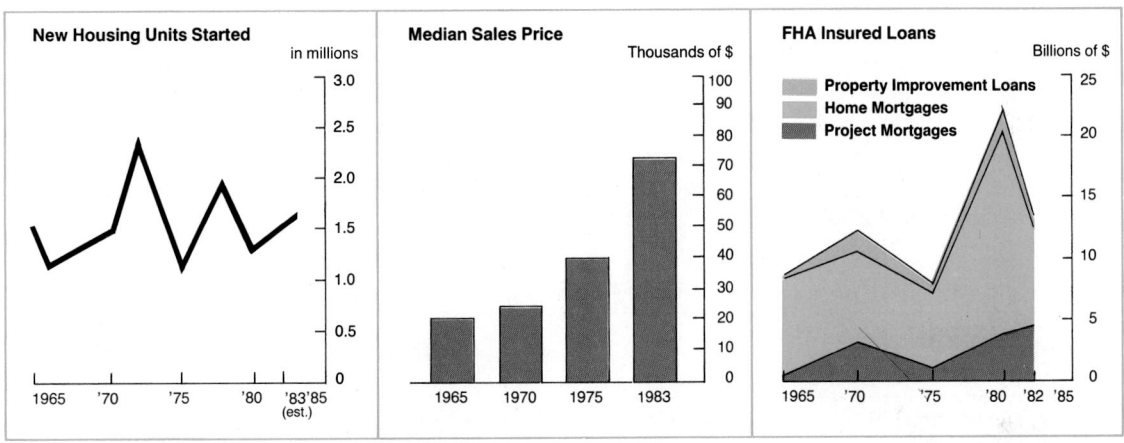

Sources: Bureau of the Census: Department of Commerce

DEPARTMENT OF TRANSPORTATION

Established: 1967
Head: Secretary of Transportation
Employees, 1984: 63,400

United States Coast Guard. Enforces federal maritime laws (laws relating to the high seas and the navigable waters of the United States—*e.g.*, smuggling, ship safety, port security, and spillage, pollution, and other marine enviromental protection statutes); maintains ships and other vessels, aircraft, and communications facilities, especially for search and rescue operations; operates an extensive network of aids to navigation (*e.g.*, lighthouses, buoys, icebreakers, radio and other electronic devices); operates the U.S. Coast Guard Academy (at New London, Ct.).

Federal Aviation Administration. Enforces federal laws regulating air commerce (including, for example, aircraft safety, pilot licensing, and air traffic); operates an extensive network of aids to air navigation (*e.g.*, air traffic control towers and centers, radio and other electronic communi-

The National Airport at Washington, D.C.

cations facilities); makes grants for the construction, improvement of public airports; conducts a wide range of aviation-related research projects.

Federal Highway Administration. Administers several grant programs to aid State, local construction, maintenance of highways and other roads (including the 42,500-mile interstate freeway system); makes grants for such other purposes as highway safety (*e.g.,* traffic signs and signals, projects to eliminate traffic hazards) and beautification; enforces federal highway safety laws (*e.g.,* laws regulating the movement of such dangerous cargoes as explosives, hazardous wastes); builds, maintains roads in such federal areas as nation parks, national forests, Indian reservations; conducts research on a wide range of highway-related matters.

National Highway Traffic Safety Administration. Enforces federal motor vehicle safety laws; makes grants to support State, local motor vehicle safety and accident prevention programs (including driver training); conducts research on matters relating to motor vehicle safety.

Federal Railroad Administration. Enforces federal rail safety laws; gives financial and other aid to certain railroads (especially those in financial difficulty); conducts research on most phases of rail transportation; operates the 482-mile Alaska Railroad.

Urban Mass Transportation Administration. Administers several grant and loan programs to help State, local governments develop and operate bus, rail, and other mass transit systems in urban areas; conducts research covering most phases of urban mass transportation.

Saint Lawrence Seaway Development Corporation. Operates that part of the Seaway within the United States (the American side of the stretch between Montreal and Lake Erie); sets and collects tolls and otherwise works in close cooperation with the St. Lawrence Seaway Authority of Canada.

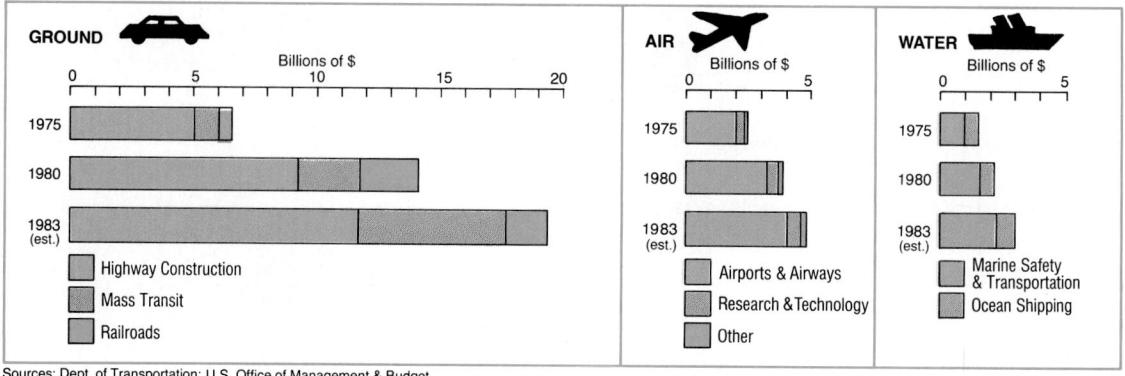

Federal Outlays for Transportation: 1975-1983

Sources: Dept. of Transportation; U.S. Office of Management & Budget

DEPARTMENT OF ENERGY
Established: 1977
Head: Secretary of Energy
Employees, 1984: 17,400

Assistant Secretary, Fossil Energy. Directs research and development programs involving fossil fuels—coal, petroleum, and gas (*e.g.,* study and demonstration projects relating to mining, drilling, and other methods of fuel extraction).

Assistant Secretary, Nuclear Energy. Directs R & D programs involving fission energy (*e.g.,* projects relating to the disposal of commercial nuclear reactor wastes).

A solar energy research lab in New Mexico

Assistant Secretary, Defense Programs. Directs nuclear weapons research, development, testing, and production programs.

Assistant Secretary, Environmental Protection, Safety, and Emergency Preparedness. Monitors departmental programs to insure compliance with environmental safety and health regulations; manages the Strategic Petroleum Reserve and other petroleum storage projects.

Assistant Secretary, Conservation and Renewable Energy. Directs R & D programs designed to promote more efficient uses (conservation) of energy and to increase the production and use of solar, wind, tidal, and other energy from renewable sources; makes grants to support State, local efforts in those areas (*e.g.,* local projects to weatherize housing).

Energy Information Administration. Collects, analyzes, publishes a broad range of data relating to energy (*e.g.,* information on energy resources, production, and consumption).

Economic Regulatory Administration. Enforces laws regulating aspects of energy production, sale, and use (*e.g.,* laws regulating drilling on leased federal lands, placing controls on fossil fuel exports, requiring increased industrial use of coal in place of oil and natural gas).

Bonneville Power Administration. Markets electric power generated by the vast network of federal multipurpose dams (constructed, operated by the Army's Corps of Engineers and Interior's Bureau of Reclamation) in the Pacific Northwest. (Smaller-scale operations are also conducted in four other regions.

Highlights of the Energy Situation

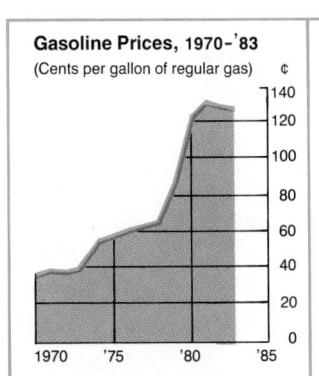
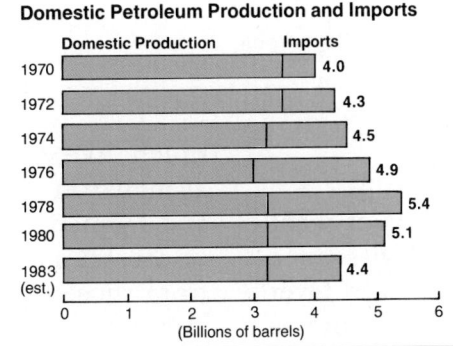
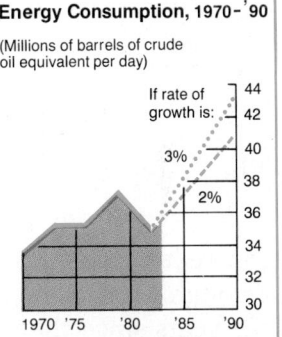

Source: U.S. Department of Energy

DEPARTMENT OF EDUCATION
Established: 1979
Head: Secretary of Education
Employees, 1984: 5,500

Assistant Secretary for Elementary and Secondary Education. Administers grant programs to support a variety of State and local school efforts in pre-school, elementary, and secondary education.

Assistant Secretary for Educational Research and Improvement. Directs research and administers grant programs to support State, local school efforts in a wide range of instructional service and resource areas (*e.g.,* basic skills, alcohol and drug abuse, and health education; library, laboratory resources).

A high school chemistry class

Assistant Secretary for Special Education and Rehabilitative Services. Makes grants for research and to support teacher training and other State, local programs for the education of handicapped children, and for rehabilitation programs for those children.

Assistant Secretary for Postsecondary Education. Administers several grant programs to support and expand instructional and other edu-

cational services and facilities in colleges, universities, and similar institutions; administers several different types of student grant and loan programs.

Assistant Secretary for Vocational and Adult Education. Administers several grant and other programs to support and expand State, local efforts in the fields of vocational training and adult education.

Education in the U.S. (Public and private)

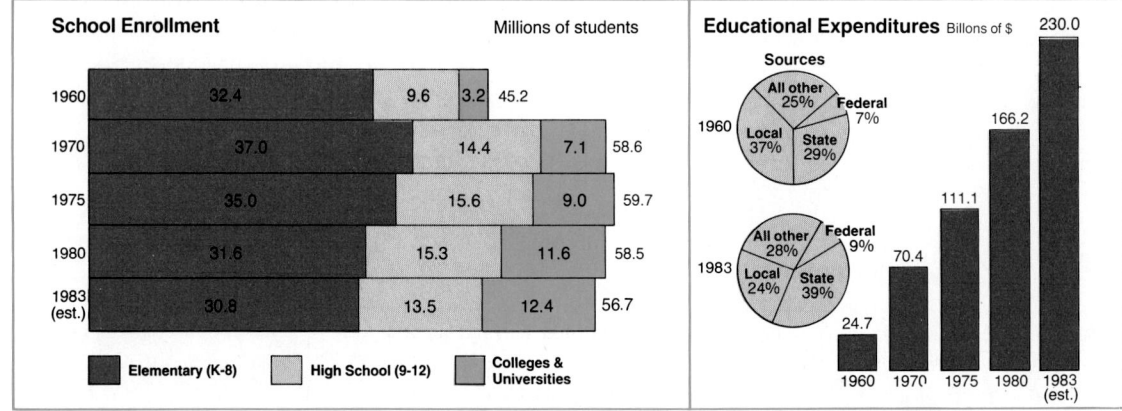

Source: U.S. National Center for Educational Statistics

The Independent Agencies

Until the 1880s, nearly all of what the Federal Government did was done through the Cabinet Departments. Over the years since then, however, Congress has created a large number of additional agencies—the *independent agencies*—located outside any of the departments. Many have come, and some have gone. Today, they number close to 200. Their functions range from the fields of transportation and communications through labor-management relations and finance to veterans affairs, nuclear energy, and natural resources. Most of the more important of them are shown in the chart on page 407.

Several of these independent agencies administer programs that cannot be very easily distinguished from the major responsibilities of the Cabinet departments. Much of the work of the Veterans Administration, for example, is very

much like that done by a number of agencies in the Department of Health and Human Services; and the concerns of the VA are not too very far removed from those of the Defense Department, either.

Neither the size of its budget nor the number of its employees provides a very good dividing line between many of these agencies and the executive departments, either. Thus, the VA's budget now runs to more than $25 billion a year—more than that of any of the departments except Defense, Labor, and Health and Human Services. And it now has some 240,000 employees—a total exceeded only by Defense.

The reasons for the separate existences of these agencies are nearly as many as the agencies themselves. A few of the major reasons stand out, however. Some of them have been set up outside of the regular departmental structure because they do not fit well there.

INTERPRETING CHARTS

HOW DOES THAT GO?

Charts are drawn outlines, printed diagrams of some particular thing. Like tables and graphs, they are visual displays of information. They try to show their information in a way that can be more easily understood than it can when that same information is presented in written form.

Charts can be used for several different purposes. Thus, on page 8 we used two of them to compare and contrast the presidential and the parliamentary forms of government. On page 311 we used another one to outline the legislative process in Congress. And on page 329 we have a chart that sets out the basic facts about how citizen-

ship is acquired through naturalization.

Below, we present yet another one. It is an organizational chart, showing the structure of the Federal Trade Commission. As you study it (and similar ones, like the chart on page 407), notice that organizational charts tend to resemble pyramids—broader at the base and narrower at the top. Why?

We have just mentioned charts that have been used for four purposes: to compare and contrast concepts, to outline a process, to clarify a complex matter, and to describe an organization. For what other purposes can charts be used? What examples of those other uses can you find?

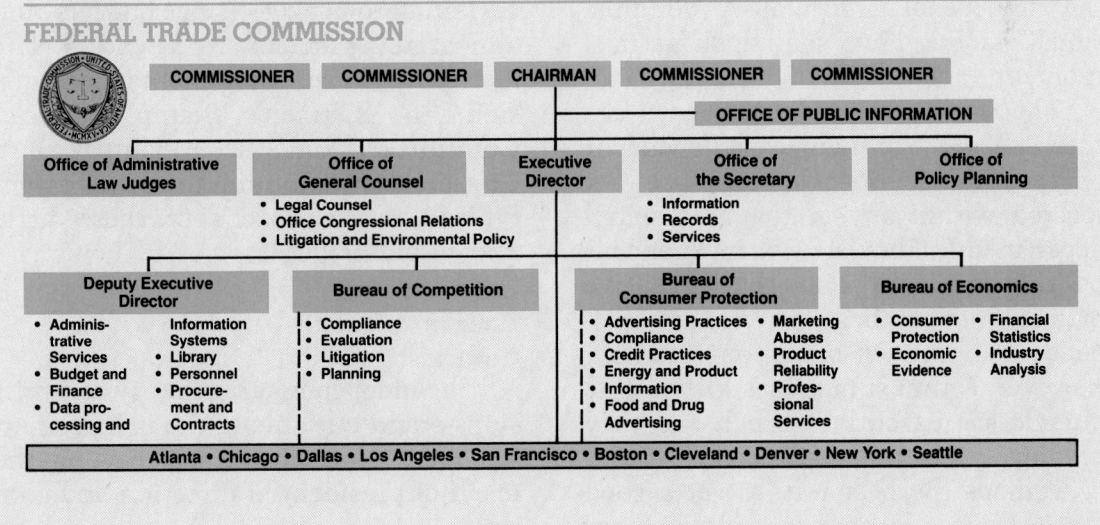

FEDERAL TRADE COMMISSION

| COMMISSIONER | COMMISSIONER | CHAIRMAN | COMMISSIONER | COMMISSIONER |

OFFICE OF PUBLIC INFORMATION

| Office of Administrative Law Judges | Office of General Counsel | Executive Director | Office of the Secretary | Office of Policy Planning |

Office of General Counsel:
• Legal Counsel
• Office Congressional Relations
• Litigation and Environmental Policy

Office of the Secretary:
• Information
• Records
• Services

Deputy Executive Director
• Administrative Services
• Budget and Finance
• Data processing and
• Information Systems
• Library
• Personnel
• Procurement and Contracts

Bureau of Competition
• Compliance
• Evaluation
• Litigation
• Planning

Bureau of Consumer Protection
• Advertising Practices
• Compliance
• Credit Practices
• Energy and Product
• Information
• Food and Drug Advertising
• Marketing Abuses
• Product Reliability
• Professional Services

Bureau of Economics
• Consumer Protection
• Economic Evidence
• Financial Statistics
• Industry Analysis

Atlanta • Chicago • Dallas • Los Angeles • San Francisco • Boston • Cleveland • Denver • New York • Seattle

The General Services Administration is a leading example. The GSA is the Federal Government's major house-keeping agency. Its main chores include the management of buildings, furnishing of supplies and equipment, storage of rec-

ords, and providing similar help to most other federal agencies. The Office of Personnel Management is another; the OPM is the hiring agency for nearly all other federal agencies, as we shall see in a moment.

Congress has given some of these agencies an independent status to protect them from the play of partisan politics and from pressure groups. Take the OPM, again; it is one of the several agencies that can be cited as an example of this point. But the point can be turned on its head, too. Some agencies are located outside the Cabinet departments because that's where certain pressure groups wanted them. Thus, several veterans organizations were responsible for the separate identity of the VA, and they have fought hard for years to keep it that way.

Then, too, some federal agencies have been born as independents largely by accident. In short, no thought was given to the problems of administrative hodge-podge when they were created.

Finally, some agencies are independent because of the peculiar and sensitive nature of their functions. This is especially true of what are often called the "independent regulatory commissions"—a breed we shall look at in a moment.

The label "independent agency" is a catch-all. Most of them are independent only in the sense that they are not located within any of the 13 Cabinet departments. They are *not* independent of the President and the executive branch. Some of these agencies are independent in a much more concrete way, however. For most purposes, they *do* lie outside the executive branch and they *are* largely free of presidential control.

Perhaps the best way to get a good grasp on these agencies is to divide them into three main groups: (1) the independent executive agencies, (2) the independent regulatory commissions, and (3) the government corporations.

The Independent Executive Agencies

This group includes most of the independent agencies. Some of them are large, with thousands of employees, multi-million or even billion-dollar budgets, and hugely important public tasks to perform. The VA, NASA, and the EPA are three leading examples of the larger ones. They are organized much like the Cabinet departments—headed by a single administrator, with sub-units operating on a regional basis, and so on. The most important difference between them and the 13 executive departments is simply this: They do not have Cabinet status.

Some of the agencies in this group are not administrative and policy giants. They do important work, however, and sometimes attract public notice. The Civil Rights Commission, the Farm Credit Administration, the Federal Election Commission, and the Small Business Administration all fall into this category.

Most of them live far from the limelight, however. They have few employees, small to pocket-change budgets, and almost never attract any attention. The American Battle Monuments Commission, the Citizen's Stamp Advisory Committee, and the Migratory Bird Conservation Commission are rather typical of the dozens of these little known public bodies.

The Independent Regulatory Commissions

The independent regulatory commissions stand out among the independent agencies. They are largely beyond the reach of presidential direction and control.

There are 12 of these agencies today, each created to regulate (police) important aspects of the nation's economy. Their vital statistics are set out in the chart on page 427.

Their large measure of independence from the White House comes mainly from the way in which Congress has

THE INDEPENDENT REGULATORY COMMISSIONS

AGENCY, DATE ESTABLISHED	MEMBERS NUMBER / TERM		MAJOR FUNCTIONS
Interstate Commerce Commission (ICC), 1887	11	7 years	Licenses, fixes rates, regulates other aspects of commercial transportation by railroad, highway, domestic waterway.
Board of Governors, Federal Reserve System (the Fed), 1913	7	14 years	Supervises banking system, practices; regulates money supply, use of credit in economy.
Federal Trade Commission (FTC), 1914	5	7 years	Enforces antitrust, other laws prohibiting unfair competition, price-fixing, false advertising, other unfair business pracitces.
Securities and Exchange Commission (SEC), 1934	5	5 years	Regulates securities, other financial markets, investment companies, brokers; enforces laws prohibiting fraud, other dishonest investment practices.
Federal Communications Commission (FCC), 1934	7	7 years	Licenses, regulates all radio and TV stations, operators, all satellite communications systems; regulates interstate telephone, telegraph rates, services.
National Labor Relations Board (NLRB), 1935	5	5 years	Administers federal labor-management relation laws; holds collective bargaining elections; prevents, remedies unfair labor practices.
Federal Maritime Commission (FMC), 1936	5	5 years	Regulates waterborne foreign, domestic offshore commerce, of the United States; supervises rates, services.
Civil Aeronautics Board (CAB), 1938[a]	5	6 years	Supervises rates, licenses air carriers in domestic, foreign commerce; regulates some other aspects of air transportation.
Consumer Product Safety Commission (CPSC), 1972	5	5 years	Sets, enforces safety standards for consumer products; directs recall of unsafe products; conducts safety research, information programs.
Nuclear Regulatory Commission (NRC), 1974	5	5 years	Licenses, regulates all civilian nuclear facilities, all civilian uses of nuclear materials.[b]
Commodities Futures Trading Commission (CFTC), 1974	5	5 years	Regulates commodity exchanges, brokers, futures trading in agricultural, metal, other commodites.
Federal Energy Regulatory Commission (FERC), 1977[c]	5	4 years	Regulates, fixes rates for transportation, sale of natural gas, transportation of oil by pipelines, interstate transmission, sale of electricity.[c]

[a]Under terms of Airline Deregulation Act of 1978, CAB is to be abolished by January 1, 1985.

[b]These functions performed by Atomic Energy Commission from 1946 to 1974 (when AEC was abolished); other AEC functions now performed by agencies in Energy Department.

[c]These functions performed by Federal Power Commission (created in 1930) unitl FPC was abolished in 1977. FERC within Energy Department, but only for administrative purposes; otherwise independent (except Energy Secretary may set reasonable deadlines for FERC action in any matter before it). Under terms of National Energy Act of 1978, FERC's authority to regulate natural gas prices to end no later than 1985.

structured them. Each is headed by a board or commission made up of from five to 11 members named by the President with Senate consent. However, those officials are chosen for terms of such length (five to 14 years) that it is quite unlikely that a President can gain control over any of these agencies through the appointment process—at least not a single presidential term.

Several other features of the make-up of these boards and commissions puts them beyond the reach of effective presidential control, too. No more than a bare majority of the members of each board or commission can belong to the same political party—so, several of those officers must belong to the party out of power. Also, the appointed terms of all of them are staggered. Finally, most of these officers can be removed from office by the President *only* for those causes Congress has specified.[5]

As with the other independent agencies, the regulatory commissions are executive bodies. That is, Congress has given them the power to administer the programs for which they are created. *But,* unlike those other agencies, these commissions are also **quasi-legislative** and **quasi-judicial** bodies.[6] That is, Congress has also given them certain legislative-like and judicial-like powers.

These agencies exercise their quasi-legislative powers when they make rules and regulations. Those rules and regulations have the force of law. They implement (spell out the details of) the laws Congress has directed these regulatory bodies to enforce. For example, ever since it passed the Act to Regulate Commerce (now known as the Interstate

Commerce Act) of 1887, Congress has said the railroads must offer "reasonable service" to the public and to charge "just and reasonable" rates for that service. The Interstate Commerce Commission implements those requirements—sets out how they are to be met by the railroads—by issuing detailed rules and regulations.

The regulatory commissions exercise their quasi-judicial powers when they decide disputes in those fields in which Congress has given them their policing authority. For example, if a railroad asks the ICC for permission to raise its rates for carrying goods between two points, that request will very likely be opposed by the companies that ship those goods. The ICC holds a hearing to determine the merits of the matter. It then makes a decision, much as a court would do. Appeals may be taken to the United States Courts of Appeals, as we shall see in Chapter 18.

In a sense, Congress has created these agencies to act for it, to act in its place. Congress *could* do the many things it has directed these regulatory commissions to do. But these are complex and time-consuming matters, and they demand constant and expert attention. If Congress did all of these things, it would then have no time for its other and important legislative work.

As we've just seen, these regulatory bodies have all three of the basic governmental powers—executive, legislative, and judicial. They are, then, exceptions to the principle of separation of powers. Several authorities, and most recent Presidents, have urged that at least their administrative functions be given to regular Cabinet department agencies.

Even larger questions have been asked about these agencies, and prompted proposals to abolish or redesign them. The most troubling ones are these: Have some of them been captured by the

---

[5]Recall, we discussed this point in Chapter 15, at page 394. The members of five of these bodies (the SEC, FCC, CPSC, NRC, and CFTFC) are exceptions here, however. Congress has provided that any of them may be removed at the President's discretion.

[6]The prefix *quasi* is from the Latin, meaning "in a certain sense, resembling, seemingly."

special interests they are expected to regulate? Are all the rules made by these agencies really needed? Do some of them have the effect of stifling legitimate competition in the free enterprise system? Do some of them add unreasonably to the costs of doing business and so the prices consumers must pay?[7]

Back to our central point here: the location of these agencies in the federal bureaucracy. Notice that they really should not be grouped with the other independent agencies as they are in the chart on page 407. Instead, they should be located somewhere between the executive and the legislative branches. And, at the same time, they should be placed somewhere between the executive and the judicial branches, too.

The Government Corporations

Several of the independent agencies are government corporations. Like most of the others, they are within the executive branch and subject to the President's direction and control. Unlike the others, however, they have been set up by Congress to carry out certain commercial or business-like activities.

Congress established the first government corporation nearly 200 years ago, when it chartered the First Bank of the United States in 1791; see page 335. The device was little used until the First

The ICC regulates commercial transportation by domestic waterway, as well as by highway and by rail.

World War and then the Depression of the 1930s, however. In both of those periods Congress set up dozens of corporations to carry out "crash" programs. Most of those agencies have long since disappeared. But several are still with us—among them, for example, the Federal Deposit Insurance Corporation (FDIC), which insures bank deposits, and the Export-Import Bank, which makes loans to help the export and sale of American goods abroad.

There are at least 60 of these government corporations today. They have been formed to carry out a wide range of business-like operations. For example: the generation and distribution of electric power (the Tennessee Valley Authority), intercity passenger trains (the National Railroad Passenger Corporation—Amtrak), mail service (the United States Postal Service), and the insurance of savings accounts (the FDIC and the Federal Savings and Loan Insurance Corporation).

---

[7]Because Congress sets the basic shape of the policies of these regulatory bodies, it is mainly responsible for any answers to these questions. It has responded to some of them in the past few years. In particular, it has given transportation businesses much greater freedom in many of their activities. For example, in the Airline Deregulation Act of 1978 it reshaped the basic policies of the CAB. That law all but did away with that agency's authority over the rates airlines may charge and the domestic air routes they may fly. It declares that the promotion of competition in the air transport industry is now the CAB's chief purpose. Congress has also done much the same thing with the ICC's authority over freight rates and other practices of railroads (in the Railroad Reorganization and Regulatory Reform Act of 1976) and truckers (in the Motor Carrier Act of 1980). The Reagan Administration is pushing for still more deregulation; one of its major targets is the FCC.

The typical government corporation is set up much like a private business. It is run by a board of directors, with a general manager to direct its operations in line with the policies set by that board. Most of them produce income which is plowed back into the "business."

There are several striking differences between government and private corporations, however. Among the major ones: Congress decides the purposes for which the public agencies exist and the function they may perform. Their officers are *public* officers; in fact, all who work for those corporations are *public* employees. Their top officers—board members and manager—are most often chosen by the President with Senate confirmation. The public agencies are financed (capitalized) by public monies appropriated by Congress, not by the funds of private investors; and the Government owns the stock.

The major advantage most often claimed for the use of the corporation is its flexibility. That is, it is said that the public agency—freed from the controls of the regular departmental organization —can carry on its business-like activities with the incentive, efficiency, and ability to experiment that is often found in private concerns. Whether that claim is valid or not is at least open to question. At the very least, it raises this sticky point: How can a public corporation's need for flexibility in its operations be squared with democratic government's requirement that all public agencies be held responsible and accountable to the people?

The degree of independence and flexibility government corporations really have varies quite a bit. In fact, some of them are not independent at all. They are attached to some executive department, and so are subject to the control of the secretary of that department.

Some of these corporations do have considerable independence, however. The Tennessee Valley Authority (TVA) is a case in point. It operates under a statute in which Congress has given it considerable discretion over its policies and programs. Although its budget is subject to review by the OMB and the President, and then by Congress, it has a large say in the uses of the income its several operations produce. It even has its own civil service system.[8]

☑ FOR REVIEW

1. What agencies are the traditional units of federal administration?

2. Why has Congress created many independent agencies in the executive branch? Of what three general types are they? In what sense is each type "independent"?

3. Why has Congress created a number of independent regulatory commissions? In what ways are they most strikingly different from other independent agencies?

4. What major advantage is claimed for the creation of some agencies as government corporations?

---

[8]Measured by any standard, TVA is one of the major illustrations of government in business. It was set up by Congress, after years of controversy, in the Tennessee Valley Authority Act of 1933. That law provided for the "orderly and proper physical, economic, and social development" of the Tennessee River Valley. It called for the coordinated development and use of the natural resources of a huge area that today includes large parts of seven States: Tennessee, Kentucky, Virginia. North Carolina, Georgia, Alabama, and Mississippi.

TVA is headed by a Board of Directors; its three members are appointed by the President and Senate for nine-year terms. Its operations are supervised by a General Manager, chosen by and answering to the Board. Those operations include electric power development, flood control and navigation work, reforestation, soil conservation, fertilizer production, agricultural research, recreational facilities, and the promotion of industrial growth in the Tennessee River Valley. TVA's power program is self-supporting. Much of the support for its other activities comes from Congress. Still, it generates considerable revenues from sales of electricity and fertilizer and from its power to issue bonds.

Reorganization of the Executive Branch

We have just looked at the overall structure of the huge executive branch of the Federal Government. As we have seen, there are many good reasons for the shape of that bureaucracy. But, at the same time, some of it can be best described as confusingly complex—or as a sprawling hodgepodge, a disjointed jumble, even a hopeless mess.

Why? One very important reason is that the government of the United States is dynamic, not static; it is always changing—often growing here and sometimes shrinking there. The march of time, fresh circumstances, the adoption of new policies and programs, the expansion, de-emphasis, or even abandonment of older ones all call for changes. They bring about the creation, reshuffling, and/or elimination of agencies. Wars, economic recessions, and other crises have a very hefty impact on the shape of government organization. So, too, do changes in party control of the White House and Congress. In short, the tale of the structure of the executive branch can be told in good part as a *continuing* story of organization and *re*organization.

Congress has created nearly all of the agencies under the President. But, over the years, Congress has been slow to react to the continuing need for change.

Because of this, every President, beginning with President Taft in 1911, has asked Congress for the authority to reorganize the executive branch. Since the Depression years of the 1930s, Congress has answered with several statutes. The earlier ones usually set up a commission to study the problems involved and to make recommendations for their solution. Among those bodies three were especially important: the President's Committee on Administrative Management, which made its report in 1937, and the two Commissions on Organization of the Executive Branch (the first and second Hoover Commissions), which reported in 1949 and in 1955.

The work of these groups did lead to several changes and improvements. The

As the size of the federal bureaucracy has grown over the years, so has the volume of records and forms generated by government regulations.

© 1981, *Chicago Sun-Times*

NEVER UNDERESTIMATE THE ABILITY OF A BUREAUCRAT...

...TO START A NEW BUREAU.

1937 (Brownlow) Committee's report led to the creation of the highly important Executive Office of the President. The first Hoover Commission brought about a number of important steps, among them the creation of the Department of Health, Education, and Welfare. HEW brought dozens of agencies together under one more or less manageable roof. The first Hoover Commission's report also led to the Reorganization Act of 1949 and several later and similar laws.

The Reorganization Acts. Since 1949 Congress has several times given the President a substantial authority to reshape executive branch agencies.

The latest of these Reorganization Acts was passed in 1977 and then extended for another year in 1980. When the extension ran out in 1981, however, Congress did not renew it. Nor has it done so since (to 1984, at least).

Under the 1977 law, the President could submit reorganization plans to Congress. If neither house turned down a plan within 60 days it became effective. In effect, Congress provided an arrangement in which it could make law by doing nothing.

Over the time the 1977 and earlier laws were in force, there was always the chance of a "legislative veto," of course. But of the 103 reorganization plans sent to Congress by six Chief Executives, 94 were accepted.

Several major federal agencies were created by this process—among them: the Office of Management and Budget and the Environmental Protection Agency (both by President Nixon in 1970) and the Office of Personnel Management (by President Carter in 1978). A number of lesser but important reorganizations were put in place under the reorganization laws, too.

Beyond the "legislative veto," there were only three significant restrictions on the President's reorganization authority under the 1977 law: (1) No plan could create, merge, or abolish an entire Cabinet department or any independent regulatory commission. (2) No plan could abolish any government function that Congress had by law required the executive branch to perform. And (3) no more than three reorganization plans could be before Congress at any one time.

The Civil Service

The Federal Government is the largest single employer in the United States. Some 2.8 million people now work in the federal bureaucracy.[9] Of that huge number, only about 2500 are appointed by the President. The Chief Executive names the top-ranking men and women (and their immediate aides and assistants) who serve in the Executive Office, in the 13 Cabinet departments, in the many independent agencies, and in American embassies and other diplomatic posts. Most of the other jobs in the Federal Government are now filled through the competitive civil service system.

Development of the Civil Service

The Constitution says very little about the staffing of the federal bureaucracy. In fact, its only direct reference is in Article II, Section 2, Clause 2. There the Constitution says that the President

shall nominate, and by and with the consent of the Senate, shall appoint ambassadors, other public ministers, and

[9]Another 2 million men and women serve in the armed forces; see chapter 17. Altogether, there are now about 15 million civilian public employees in this country. Some 3.5 million work for the States, and another 8.6 million for local governments (including 4.2 million persons employed by school districts). About 2.5 million of all of those who work for State and local governments are employed on a part-time basis.

consuls, judges of the Supreme Court, and all other officers of the United States whose appointments are not herein otherwise provided for, and which shall be established by law; but the Congress may by law vest the appointment of such inferior officers, as they think proper, in the President alone, in the courts of law, or in the heads of departments.

The Beginnings. When he became President in 1789, George Washington knew that the success of the new government under the Constitution would depend in large part on those whom he appointed to office. Those to be chosen, he said, would be "such persons alone . . . as shall be the best qualified." Still, most of the appointments he made went to members of his own party, the Federalists. So did those of his successor, John Adams.

When Thomas Jefferson took over the White House in 1801, he found that most federal posts were held by men who were both politically and personally opposed to him. He agreed in principle with Washington's standard of "fitness for office," but he quickly combined it with "political acceptability." Several hundred Federalists were fired, and they were replaced by good Democratic-Republicans. Overall, not very many positions were involved, however. When the national capital was moved to the new city of Washington in 1800, there were fewer than a thousand federal employees.

The Spoils System. By the late 1820s, the number of federal employees had risen above 10,000. When Andrew Jackson became President in 1829 he dismissed more than 200 presidential appointees and nearly 2000 other federal officeholders. They were replaced by tried and true Jacksonian Democrats.

Ever since, Jackson has been called the father of the **spoils system**—the

Cartoonist Thomas Nast (1840–1902) comments on the corruption that prevailed in the administration of public affairs in the 1870s.

practice of giving offices and other favors of government to political supporters and friends.[10] This is not altogether fair. Jefferson had laid its foundations at the federal level in 1801, and it was in wide use at the State and local levels long before Jackson's Presidency.

Jackson saw his appointing policy as "democratic." In his first message to Congress he explained and defended it on four grounds: (1) Since the duties of public office are, at base, simple, any normally intelligent person can fill such office. (2) There should be a "rotation in office" so that a large number of people can have the privilege of serving in government. (3) Long service in office by any person can lead to both tyranny and inefficiency. And (4) the people are entitled to have the party they have placed in power in control of all of the

---

[10]The phrase comes from a statement made on the floor of the Senate in 1832. Senator William Learned Marcy of New York, defending Jackson's appointment of an ambassador, declared: "To the victor belongs the spoils of the enemy."

offices of government, top to bottom.

Whatever Jackson's view, many saw the spoils system as a way to build and hold power. For the next half-century every change of administration brought a new round of rewards and punishments. As the Government's activities, agencies, and payrolls grew, so did the spoils. Huge profits were made on public contracts at the people's expense, and much of the nation's natural wealth was plundered. Inefficiency and even corruption became the order of the day.

The Movement to Reform. Able people, in and out of government, pressed for reforms. Congress did make some move in that direction in 1851 and again in 1853. Department heads were required to fill several thousand clerkships by examinations. But all of that came to nothing. Party loyalists passed those tests; others did not, and could not. Congress tried again in 1871, when it set up the first Civil Service Commission and coupled it with the requirement of *competitive* examinations. That move soon faltered, too—in good part because Congress would not give the new agency enough money to cover its operations.

The cry for change went on. By 1880 civil service reform had become a major political cause and a leading issue in the presidential and congressional elections that year.

A tragedy at last brought fundamental changes in the hiring and other staffing practices of the Federal Government. President James Garfield was assassinated by a deranged and disappointed office-seeker in 1881. The nation was outraged. Congress, pushed hard by Garfield's successor, Chester Arthur, passed the Pendleton Act—the Civil Service Act of 1883.

The Pendleton Act. The 1883 law laid the foundations of the present federal civil service. Its main goal was to take the civil service out of politics—to make merit the major basis for hiring, promotion, and other personnel actions in the federal workforce.

An independent agency, the United States Civil Service Commission, was formed to administer the law. That bipartisan body lasted for 95 years—until it was replaced, as we shall see in a moment, by two new agencies in 1979.

The law named two categories of employment in the executive branch: one, the *classified,* and the other the *unclassified* service. The President was given the key power to decide into which of these categories most federal agencies (and so their personnel) were to be placed. All hiring for the classified service was to be based on merit—and that was to be decided through "practical" examinations given by the Civil Service Commission.

To further its central purpose, the law stated that classified employees

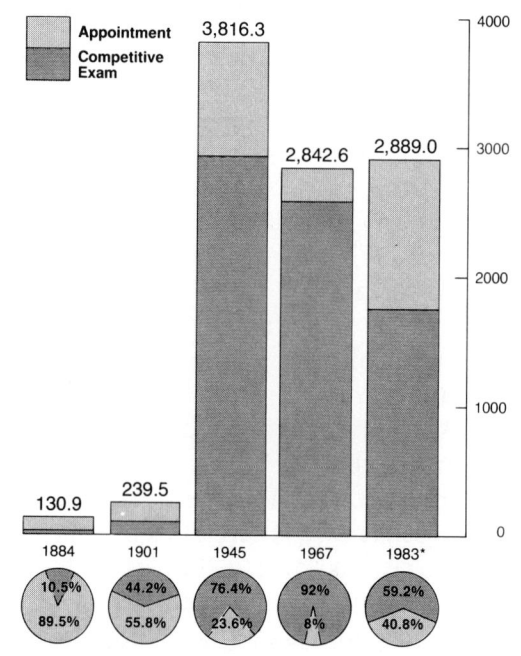

GROWTH OF THE CIVIL SERVICE
in thousands

*Postal employees no longer included in competitive service.
Source: U.S. Office of Personnel Management

could take no part in partisan politics. Its emphasis on merit was undercut to some extent by two other provisions, however. One was the requirement that all classified hiring be geared to geography. The federal workforce was to be made up of men and women from every State, and the number from each of them had to bear a close relationship to that State's share of the total population. The other was the matter of veterans preference. All veterans, and especially disabled veterans and veterans' widows, were given a preferred ranking in all federal hiring.

The Pendleton Act itself put only about 10 percent of the Federal Government's then 130,000 employees into the classified service. The merit system grew by fits and starts, and fairly slowly, over the next 20 years. It began to grow rapidly when Theodore Roosevelt became President, however. When TR left office in 1909, the classified umbrella covered two-thirds of the federal workforce—which by then had climbed to 365,000. Roosevelt's successors, and Congress, have generally followed his lead over the years since then. Today about 90 percent of all of the men and women who work for executive branch agencies are in the classified service.[11]

Civil Service Today

The first goal of civil service reform—doing away with the spoils system—was largely reached in the early part of this century. Gradually, a newer goal emerged: recruiting and keeping the best available people in the federal workforce.

---

[11]That is, 90 percent not counting the Postal Service and a few other federal agencies. The Postal Service, with about 600,000 persons, is the largest agency not covered by the civil service system. It is the only federal agency in which employment policies are set by collective bargaining and labor union contracts. The other major agencies not counted in fixing that 90 percent figure are the FBI, CIA, and TVA; each of those agencies has its own merit system.

On the whole, efforts to reach that goal have been generally successful. Sometimes they have stumbled over themselves, however. That is, they have most often stressed job *security* and too often neglected the equally important matters of job *performance* and *quality*. To put it another way, as critics often have: not enough attention has been paid to "merit" in the merit system.

President Carter put it this way in 1978:

The Pendleton Act, . . . the Civil Service Commission and the merit system . . . have served our nation well in fostering the development of a federal workforce which is basically honest, competent, and dedicated. . . .

But the system has serious defects. It has become a bureaucratic maze which neglects merit, tolerates poor performance, and mires every personnel action in red tape, delay, and confusion.

Most civil service employees perform with spirit and integrity. Nevertheless, the public suspects that there are too many government workers, that they are underworked, overpaid, and insulated from the consequences of incompetence.

Such sweeping criticisms are unfair; but we must recognize that the only way to restore public confidence in the vast majority who work well is to deal effectively with the few who do not.

Reorganization. Large changes in the civil service system were brought about both by the President through a major reorganization plan and by the Congress when it passed the Civil Service Reform Act of 1978.

The Civil Service Commission was replaced by two new independent agencies:

The *Office of Personnel Management* is now the Government's central personnel agency. It is headed by a single director appointed by the President and

Senate. OPM examines and recruits most new federal employees, carries on extensive training programs for career civil servants, sets position classifications, and manages the salary and other job benefits for some 2.1 million of the people who work for Uncle Sam.

The *Merit System Protection Board* handles the rest of the work once done by the Civil Service Commission. It is a bipartisan three-member panel picked by the President and Senate. It is *the* agency which polices and protects the merit principle in the federal bureaucracy.[12]

The Office of Personnel Management can best be described as the clearinghouse in the federal recruiting, examining, and hiring process. It advertises for new employees, gives oral and written examinations, and keeps lists (**registers**) of those persons who pass its tests.

OPM has registers for hundreds of different types of jobs. In fact, the Federal Government hires people for more than 2000 separate occupational specialties. Included are clerks, typists, secretaries, telephone operators, janitors, doctors, nurses, lab technicians, chemists, botanists, psychologists, teachers, computer programmers, carpenters, plumbers, lawyers, truck drivers, pilots, and many, many more.

When there is a job opening in some agency, OPM usually sends it the names of the top three persons on its register for that type of position.[13] The agency then hires one of those three (and the other two names go back on the register). Or, if it turns down all three, it asks OPM for another set, and the "rule of three" is used again.

All new federal employees must swear (or affirm) that they will support and defend the Constitution and laws of the United States. They must also sign a pledge not to strike against the Government or any of its agencies. Such strikes are outlawed by the Labor-Management Relations (Taft-Hartley) Act of 1947. Within that framework, they may join any of several labor unions and other groups that promote the interests of government employees.

The merit system was put in place to protect federal workers from political pressures. At the same time, several laws and many OPM regulations place close restrictions on the partisan political activities of civil servants.

Federal employees *may* do a number of things in politics. They can vote, join

Assembled (written) civil service tests are usually made up of short-answer (true-false, multiple-choice, and similar) questions.

---

[12]Another independent agency, the *Federal Labor Relations Authority*, now handles labor-management relationships in federal employment. It, too, is a bipartisan, three-member body appointed by the President and Senate. The Director of the OPM is the Government's chief representative in its dealings with public employee unions.

[13]The place each applicant for a federal job has on a register is fixed by three factors: (1) time of application, (2) OPM test scores, and (3) veterans preference points, if any. Nearly half of all federal jobs are now held by veterans, wives of disabled veterans, and unremarried widows of veterans. Some jobs, such as guards and messengers, are reserved especially for veterans.

a party and other political organizations, make voluntary campaign contributions, wear campaign buttons (off duty), and put bumper stickers on their own cars. They can voice their opinions on all political matters, attend and take part in (but not organize or lead) partisan rallies, take part in non-partisan activities, run for and serve in nonpartisan local offices, and do many other such things. But they *cannot* take an active part in party politics or campaigns. That is, they cannot do such things as run for a partisan office, serve as an officer in a party organization or as a delegate to a party convention, or raise funds for a party or any of its candidates.

Many federal employees, and many others, are against these restrictions. They see them as both unnecessary and unjustifiable limits on their political and civil rights.[14] Supporters of them say that they prevent two main evils: the use of federal workers in presidential and congressional campaigns and the possibility that job security might come to depend on party loyalty.

Congress sets the pay and other job conditions for everyone who works for the Federal Government.[15] At the lower and middle levels, civil service pay compares quite well with salaries paid in the private sector. Government can never hope to compete dollar-for-dollar with private industry at the upper levels, however. How to attract—and keep— the better people for its higher positions is a major headache in the civil service system. On the whole, the fringe benefits in federal employment—vacations, sick leave, retirement, and so on—are at least on a par with those to be found in most jobs outside of government.

[14]The Supreme Court has upheld them, however— as reasonable restrictions on 1st Amendment rights. The leading case is *Civil Service Commission* v. *National Association of Letter Carriers, AFL-CIO*, 1973.

[15]Except postal workers; see page 435, note 11.

FOR REVIEW

1. Why has every recent President asked Congress for the authority to reorganize the executive branch?
2. Outline the provisions of the Reorganization Act of 1977.
3. What standard did George Washington set for federal employment? What was the spoils system? How did Andrew Jackson defend his version of it? What conditions did it produce?
4. What event prompted the passage of the Pendleton Act? Out line its major features.
5. Over time, the primary goal of civil service efforts has shifted from what original aim to what major concern today?
6. What role does OPM have in the civil service system? The Merit System Protection Board?
7. What are OPM's registers? The "rule of three"?
8. Can federal workers strike? They may not take part in what kinds of political activity?

Those who work in government agencies are sometimes swamped by paperwork.

Federal Finance

For fiscal year 1984, the Federal Government expects to collect, from all sources, some $660 billion. And it will spend much more—at least $850 billion —in that same period.[15]

Here, we take a brief look at many of the details of those huge numbers—at where all that money comes from and where it goes. As we do so, keep this very important point in mind: All of the dollar signs and all of the amounts we are dealing with here are a direct result of public policy decisions.

How much is collected? By what means, and from whom? How much is spent, and for what? These and a host of similar questions can be answered in dollar terms, of course. But these dollar-answers are also public-policy-answers. They tell us a great deal about both the content and the general direction of the nation's public policies. In short, in public finance public dollars = public policy decisions.

Sources of Revenue. Most of the Federal Government's revenue (the money it takes in each year) comes from taxes. However, a sizable chunk of it also comes from several nontax sources, as we shall see.

Current Federal Taxes. Recall, we considered Congress' power to tax in Chapter 13 (pages 322–324). Now, we look at the several taxes it has imposed.

THE FEDERAL GOVERNMENT'S INCOME, by Major Source
(For selected fiscal years, in billions of dollars)

	1970	1975	1980	1983	1984 est.
Individual income taxes	$90.4	$122.4	$244.1	$288.9	$295.6
Corporation income taxes	32.8	40.6	64.6	37.0	51.8
Social insurance taxes and contributions	45.3	84.5	157.8	209.0	242.9
Excise taxes	15.7	16.6	24.3	35.3	40.4
Estate and gift taxes	3.6	4.6	6.4	6.1	5.9
Customs duties	2.4	3.7	7.2	8.6	9.1
Miscellaneous receipts	3.4	6.7	12.7	15.6	14.0
Total receipts	$193.7	$279.1	$517.1	$600.6	$659.7

Source: Office of Management and Budget

Income Taxes. The 16th Amendment gave Congress the power to levy taxes on income; see pages 42, 323. Income taxes first became the major source of federal revenue during World War I, and (except for a few years during the Depression of the 1930s) they have remained so ever since.

Incomes of both individuals and corporations are taxed. The rates have always been **progressive**—that is, the higher the income the higher the tax rate applied to it.

The *individual income tax* regularly produces the larger amount. It is levied on a person's taxable income—one's total income in the previous year minus certain exemptions and deductions.

Each taxpayer has a personal exemption of $1000 plus another $1000 exemption for each of his/her dependents; an additional $1000 exemption is also allowed for each person over age 65 or blind. Deductions are allowed for several things—mainly for medical and hospital care costs, most State and local taxes, interest payments, and charitable contributions.

---

[15]As we noted on page 383, the Federal Government's fiscal year runs from October 1 through the following September 30 of each calendar year.

By April 15 all persons with taxable income in the preceding year must file tax returns (declarations of that income) with the Internal Revenue Service. The rates applied to taxable income received in 1983 (and reported on 1984 returns) began at 11 percent in the lowest brackets ($2300 to $3400 for single persons, $3400 to $5500 for married couples) and ranged on up to a maximum of 50 percent in the top brackets (above $55,300 for single persons, $109,400 for married couples).[16]

The *corporation income tax* is applied to all of a corporation's **net income**—all of its earnings above its costs of doing business. (Nonprofit organizations—such as churches, labor unions, charitable foundations, and cooperatives—are not subject to the tax.) This levy has been called the most complicated of federal taxes, largely because of the many deductions allowed in figuring a corporation's net (taxable) income.

The tax rates now run from 15 percent on the first $25,000 of taxable earnings on up to a top rate of 46 percent on that income above $100,000.

Social Insurance Taxes. Three major social welfare programs are supported by "payroll taxes." (1) The Old-Age, Survivors, and Disability Insurance (OASDI) program—the basic social security program, established by the Social Security Act of 1935; (2) Medicare—health care for the elderly, added to the social security program in 1965; and (3) the unemployment insurance program—to pay unemployment compensation benefits to jobless workers, also established by the Social Security Act of 1935.

The payroll taxes for both OASDI and Medicare are collected from most employees and their employers, and from self-employed persons. Employees now (1984) pay a 6.7 percent tax on their salaries or wages (up to a ceiling of $37,800 of yearly pay—a maximum tax, then, of $2532.60 for the year). Their employers now pay a tax of 7 percent on those salaries or wages. The self-employed pay 11.3 percent on the first $37,800 of yearly income (a maximum of $4271.40).

The unemployment insurance program is a joint federal-State operation, to make payments to workers who lose their jobs for reasons beyond their own control. It is financed by a 3.4 percent federal tax on the payrolls of nearly all businesses. The States administer the program, paying jobless benefits according to federal guidelines.

Excise Taxes. Taxes laid on the production, transportation, sale, or consumption of goods or services are **excises.** Federal excise taxes are imposed on a great many items today, including: gasoline, oil, tires, the "windfall profits" of oil companies, cigarettes, pipe and chewing tobacco, liquor, wine, beer, firearms, telephone service, and airline tickets. (Many of them are called "hidden taxes"—because they are collected from producers who then figure them into the prices they charge to their retail customers.)

Estate and Gift Taxes. The federal estate tax, levied since 1916, is a tax on the property of deceased persons. Congress added the gift tax in 1924, to plug a loophole in the estate tax (the giving of money or other property before death to avoid that tax).

The estate tax is applied to one's net estate—its full value minus certain exemptions and deductions. For 1984, the first $325,000 of an estate

FEDERAL BUDGET TRENDS

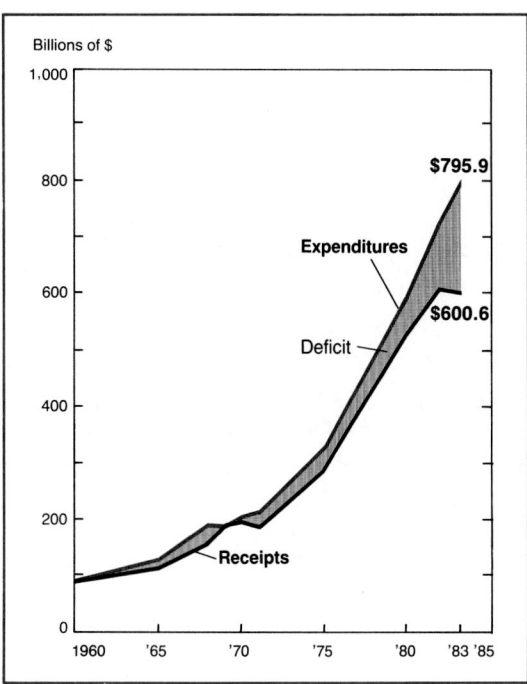

Source: U.S. Dept. of the Treasury

---

[16]The rates and other details of the various taxes dealt with here are accurate as of January 1, 1984. At President Reagan's urging, Congress made many changes in the tax laws in 1981 and 1982—including a 25 percent personal income tax cut over three years.

FEDERAL SPENDING, FISCAL YEARS 1981–1983
(By agency, in billions of dollars)

	Fiscal 1981	Fiscal 1982	Fiscal 1983
Legislative Branch	$1.2	$1.4	$1.4
Judicial Branch	.6	.7	.8
Executive Office of the President	.1	.1	.1
Funds appropriated to the President (Mostly for foreign economic/military aid)	7.0	6.1	5.4
Department of Agriculture	26.0	36.2	46.4
Department of Commerce	2.2	2.0	1.9
Department of Defense—Military	156.0	182.9	205.0
Department of Defense—Civil	3.1	3.0	2.9
Department of Education	15.1	14.1	14.6
Department of Energy	11.8	7.6	8.3
Department of Health and Human Services	227.0	251.3	274.1
Department of Housing and Urban Development	14.0	14.5	15.3
Department of the Interior	4.3	3.9	4.5
Department of Justice	2.7	2.6	2.8
Department of Labor	30.1	30.7	38.2
Department of State	1.9	2.2	2.3
Department of Transportation	22.6	19.9	20.6
Department of the Treasury	92.6	110.5	116.8
Interest on the Public Debt	(95.6)	(117.4)	(128.8)
Other	(11.3)	(11.6)	(13.0)
Offsetting receipts	(−14.3)	(−18.5)	(−25.8)
Environmental Protection Agency	5.2	5.0	4.3
National Aeronautics and Space Administration	5.4	6.0	6.7
Veterans Administration	22.9	23.9	24.8
Other independent agencies	35.5	33.1	34.3
Deductions (undistributed offsetting receipts)			
Contributions to federal employee retirement	−6.4	−7.0	−8.1
Interest received by various trust funds	−13.8	−16.0	−17.0
Rents, royalties on Outer Continental Shelf	−10.1	−6.3	−10.5
Total Outlays	**$657.2**	**$728.4**	**$795.9**
Deficit (Outlays greater than Receipts)	**−58.0**	**−110.7**	**−195.4**

Source: Bureau of Government Financial Operations, Deparment of the Treasury

THE PUBLIC DEBT
(At end of selected fiscal years, in billions of dollars)

1916 (pre-World War I)	$ 1.3	1950 (pre-Korean War)	$ 256.1
1919 (post-World War I)	25.5	1954 (post-Korean War)	271.3
1930 (start of Depression)	16.2	1964 (pre-Vietnam War)	308.1
1940 (decade of depression)	43.0	1974 (post-Vietnam War)	474.2
1941 (pre-World War II)	48.9	1982 (preceding fiscal year)	1,142.0
1946 (post-World War II)	269.4	1983 (latest fiscal year)	1,377.2

Source: Bureau of the Public Debt, Department of the Treasury

is exempt (so, in fact most estates are not taxed). Deductions are allowed for such things as State death taxes (see page 606) and bequests to religious and charitable groups. Anything a husband or wife leaves to the other is taxed, if at all, only when the surviving spouse dies.

Any person may make up to $10,000 in tax-free gifts to any other person in any one year. Gifts husbands/wives make to one another are not taxed, regardless of value.

The estate and gift taxes are separate federal taxes, but both are taxes on the transfer of property (before or after death)—and so they are now levied at the same rates. For 1984, those rates range from a minimum of 18 percent on up to a maximum of 55 percent on a net estate or a gift worth more than $2.5 million.

Customs Duties. Customs duties (tariffs) are taxes on goods brought into the United States. Congress decides which imports will be taxed (dutied) and at what rates. Most imports (some 30,000 different items) are dutied; but some are not—for example, Bibles, coffee, and up to $300 of an American tourist's purchases. Many duties are set purposefully high (the "protective tariff"), to protect industries and jobs in this country.

Miscellaneous Receipts. Huge sums come every year from a multitude of nontax sources, including interest payments on many types of loans, court fines, sales/leases of public lands, sales of surplus property, canal tolls, fees for passports, copyrights, trademarks, and patents, seignorage (the profit on minting coins), and many others.

S U M M A R Y

As Chief Administrator, the President heads the federal bureaucracy—the large and complex administration structure within the executive branch of the Federal Government. The realities of the modern world make bureaucracy a standard feature of government, both here and abroad.

The Constitution says little about the federal bureaucracy. Nearly all of it has been created by Congress. It is now made up of three major groups of administrative agencies: (1) the Executive Office of the President (which we treated in Chapter 15), (2) the 13 Cabinet departments, and (3) the many independent agencies.

The several units of an administrative organization can be classed as either (1) staff agencies—those which serve in a support capacity, or (2) line agencies—those which carry out the tasks for which the organization exists. Except at the departmental level, there is little uniformity in the use of such organizational titles as bureau, service, office, and so on in the federal bureaucracy.

The now 13 Cabinet departments are the traditional units of federal administration; each of them is built around a major field of governmental activity.

The many independent agencies are a part of the executive branch but outside of any of the Cabinet departments. They are independent of the regular departmental structure for a number of reasons, carry out a wide range of functions, and are of three main types. Most of them are (1) independent executive agencies; the others are either (2) independent regulatory commissions or (3) government corporations.

The Federal Government now employs some 2.8 million people. As the nation's first Chief Administrator, George Washington insisted upon "fitness for office" as the chief qualification for federal employment. Beginning with Andrew Jackson's Presidency (1829), the spoils system became the rule in the executive branch, however. The present-day federal civil service system was begun with the passage of the Pendleton Act in 1883. That system, based upon merit, is now managed by two independent agencies: the Office of Personnel Management and the Merit Systems Protection Board.

C H A P T E R   R E V I E W

Key Terms/Concepts

Administration (405)
Agency (406)
Bureaucracy (405)
Cabinet department (406)
Chief Administrator (406)
Civil service (432)
Classified employee (435)

Executive Office of the President (416)
Government corporation (429)
Independent agency (424)
Independent executive agency (425)
Independent regulatory commission (425)

Line agency, function (408)
Merit system (434)
Merit System Protection Board (436)
Office of Personnel Management (435)
Pendleton Act (434)
Quasi-judicial (428)

Quasi-legislative (428)
Registers (436)
Reorganization Acts (432)
Spoils system (433)
Staff agency, function (408)
United States Civil Service Commission (434)

Keynote Questions

1. What is a bureaucracy? Why is a bureaucracy a very necessary part of the Federal Government today?
2. The federal bureaucracy is now composed of what three major groups of agencies?
3. What is the essential difference between a staff agency and a line agency?
4. Why has Congress created so many independent agencies in the executive branch? In what sense is each of them "independent"? How do the several independent regulatory commissions differ from each of the other independent agencies?
5. Why is reorganization both a continuing necessity and a continuing problem in the executive branch?
6. What was the original goal of civil service reform at the federal level? Over time, that goal was replaced by what newer aim?
7. What role does the Office of Personnel Management play in the civil

service system? The Merit System Protection Board?
8. What is the meaning of the expression "public dollars—public policy decisions"?
9. Approximately how much money does the Federal Government expect to collect in fiscal year 1984? To spend in the period? What is the approximate size of the federal debt today?
10. Which of the various federal taxes produces the largest amount of revenue each year? What major social welfare programs are supported by payroll taxes?
11. What are excise taxes? Customs duties? Estate and gift taxes? Identify five significant nontax sources of federal revenue.

For Thought and Discussion

1. On what grounds can you challenge the comment by Alexander Hamilton quoted at the beginning of this chapter?

2. On page 405 we said that the dynamic character of the Federal Government is a leading reason for the complexities and confusions in the organization of the executive branch. What other reasons can you suggest?

3. In 1807 Thomas Jefferson said: "When a man accepts a public trust, he should consider himself as public property." On what grounds might you *disagree* with Jefferson in this?

4. On page 432 we noted the fact that some 2500 federal jobs are filled by appointment by the President today. When he became President in 1981 why might Ronald Reagan have recalled William Howard Taft's complaint that every time he made an appointment he created "nine enemies and one ingrate"?

5. Why do you think that civil service merit systems have been generally much slower to develop at the State and local levels than in the Federal Government?

6. When it passed the Civil Service Reform Act of 1978 Congress made no changes in the policy of veterans preference in civil service. Why? Should it have done so?

7. How might the Federal Government make a civil service career more attractive to young people today?

Suggested Activities

1. Ask a representative of some federal agency in your locale to describe that agency and its organization and functions for the class.

2. From newspaper or other sources describing the early organization of the Reagan administration, discover what "the plum book" is, and then prepare a report on it.

3. Prepare a chart of the organization of the Federal Government that places the independent regulatory commissions in their proper relationship to the President and to Congress and to the courts.

4. From such sources as local newspaper advertisements and post office bulletin boards, discover what federal jobs are currently available in your area. Learn the details of the federal hiring process from the many films and publications of OPM. In addition to such local sources as libraries and media resource centers, you might contact the Office of Public Affairs, OPM, 1900 E Street NW, Washington, DC. 20415 (or see the list of OPM's regional offices in the *Government Manual*).

5. Stage a debate or class forum on one of the following topics: (a) *Resolved*, That the independent regulatory commissions be abolished and their functions assigned to the regular Cabinet departments; (b) *Resolved*, That the legal restrictions on the political activities of federal employees be abolished; (c) *Resolved*, That the geographic quota requirements in federal hiring be abolished; (d) *Resolved*, That all federal employees be given the right to strike.

"First of all, You need to set up a Department of paperwork . . ."

CHAPTER 17

Foreign Affairs and National Security: Providing for the Common Defense

CHAPTER OBJECTIVES

To help you to
Learn ▪ Know ▪ Understand

The one, historic, continuing, and overriding goal of America's foreign and defense policies.

The important and inseparable linkage of the nation's foreign relations and its defense.

The institutions and process of foreign and defense policy-making.

The major features of American foreign policy, both historically and presently.

We have no choice as to whether or not we shall play a great part in the world. That has been determined for us by fate. The only question is whether we will play that part well or badly.

Theodore Roosevelt

It would be impossible to overstate the importance of our foreign relations and the manner in which they are conducted. Here we turn to foreign affairs and national defense—to the highly important ways in which the might and influence of the United States are used in world affairs.

Today—as, indeed, through all of our history—our foreign and defense policies are directed to one overriding end. They are designed to safeguard the security of the United States. So, in a very real sense, our subject here can be accurately described as the national security policy of the United States.

Through much of our history American politics turned very largely on questions of domestic policy. For more than 150 years we were chiefly concerned with what was happening at home. Our relationships with other countries were very largely shaped by a policy of

In 1916, many Americans endorsed a policy of noninvolvement in World War I, then being waged in Europe (see facing page). But, Germany's submarine campaign against U.S. shipping led, finally, President Wilson to ask Congress to declare war on Germany in 1917.

isolationism—by a purposeful refusal to become generally involved in the affairs of the rest of the world.

The years since World War II, however, have been marked by a profound change in the place of the United States in world affairs. And that historic shift—from isolationism to internationalism—has brought major changes in our foreign and defense policies. World War II taught us that we cannot live in isolation in today's world. We have learned that, in many ways, and whether we like it or not, we live in "one world."

That we do live in "one world" can be seen most clearly in terms of national security. The well-being of the American people and in fact the very survival of the United States are closely affected by much that happens elsewhere on the globe. If nothing else, the ultra-rapid travel and instantaneous communica-

tions of today's world make that point quite clear.

Wars and other political upheavals anywhere in the world have a decided impact on the interests of the United States—and on the daily lives of each and of all Americans. Four times in this century we have become involved in wars thousands of miles from our shores. Our security has been threatened by events abroad, too—by an outbreak in the Middle East, by unrest in Poland, by an incident in Berlin, by strife in Southern Africa, by a revolution in Latin America, and by many others.

Economic conditions elsewhere are felt quite directly in this country, too. Japanese automobiles, European steel, Arab oil, Brazilian coffee, Australian wheat, and the many other things we import make that a daily fact of life.

In these and several other ways, then,

we live in "one world." In some ways, however, we do not. The communist world, and especially the Soviet Union, and the free world, led by the United States, confront one another on many issues and in many places. Most of the newer nations of Africa and Asia make up yet another grouping, a "non-aligned" or neutralist bloc of growing power in world politics. In this other—divided—world of today, we have come to see that only through policies designed to promote and protect the security and well-being of all nations can the security and well-being of the United States ever be assured.

Foreign Policy

Every nation's foreign policy is actually many different policies on many different topics. It is made up of all of the stands that that nation takes in its relationships with other countries—diplomatic, military, commercial, and all others. Or, to put it another way, a nation's foreign policy is made up of all of its many foreign policies.

Thus, American foreign policy deals with such matters as treaties and alliances, international trade, the defense budget, foreign economic and military aid, the United Nations, nuclear weapons testing, and disarmament negotiations. It also includes the American position on oil imports, grain exports, immigration, space exploration, fishing rights in the Atlantic and Pacific Oceans, cultural exchange programs, and a great many other matters, as well.

Some of our foreign policies remain fixed (largely unchanged) over time. For example, an insistence on freedom of the seas has been a basic part of American policy from the beginning of our history. Other policies are more flexible, subject to change as circumstances change. Thus, little more than a generation ago, opposition to the German and Japanese dictatorships was a major part of our foreign policy. But, today, West Germany and Japan are among our closest and staunchest allies.

Sometimes the United States is able to take the lead in international relations. We are able to launch new policies that win support and heighten American power and prestige abroad. Take, as an example, the decision to rebuild the war-torn countries of Europe and restore their shattered economies after World War II (the Marshall Plan). It was a bold and effective step at that critical point in history, and it was a major signal of American intentions in the postwar world.

Very often, American policy must be defensive in nature. It must be adjusted to meet the actions of some other country. Thus, "containment"—resisting the spread of Soviet influence in the world—became a basic part of our foreign policy more than 30 years ago.

Making Foreign Policy

The President is both the nation's chief diplomat and the commander in chief of its armed forces. As we have seen, Congress does have significant powers in the fields of foreign and military affairs, too—especially with its power of the purse, its power to declare war, and in the Senate's role in the treaty-making and the appointment processes.[1] But, it is the President who dominates those policy fields. Both constitutionally and by tradition, he bears the major responsibility for both the making and conduct of foreign policy.[2]

[1]See, especially, Chapter 13, pages 332–333.
[2]See Chapter 15, pages 395–398. Recall, the Constitution forbids to the States any role in foreign relations, Article I, Section 10, Clause 1 and 3.

The President depends upon a number of officials and agencies to meet his immense responsibilities as chief diplomat and commander in chief. Recall that we considered the National Security Council, in the Executive Office of the President, in Chapter 15 (page 382). Here we turn to the other elements of what is often called "the foreign policy bureaucracy"—first with the Departments of State and Defense, and then with several others.

The Department of State

The State Department, headed by the Secretary of State, is the President's right arm in both forming and carrying out American foreign policy. The Secretary is appointed by the President, subject to Senate confirmation.

The Secretary of State ranks first among the members of the President's Cabinet. This is in part because of the importance of the office, but also because the Department of State was the first of the now 13 executive departments set up by Congress in 1789; see page 385.

The duties of the Secretary relate almost solely to foreign affairs—to the making and conduct of policy and to managing the work of the Department, its many overseas posts, and its more than 24,000 employees.[3]

Some Presidents have relied very heavily upon the Secretary of State; others have chosen to keep foreign policy more tightly in their own hands. But, in either case, the Secretary has been an important and influential officer in every administration.

The Department is organized along both geographic and functional lines.

Israel's Prime Minister Yitzhak Shamir (at left) listens as Secretary of State George Schultz makes a point to the Israeli Defense Minister, Moshe Arens.

Some of its agencies deal with matters involving certain countries or regions of the world—such as the Bureau of African Affairs and the Bureau of Near Eastern and South Asian Affairs. Others have broader responsibilities—such as the Bureau of Economic and Business Affairs and the Bureau for Refugee Programs. Most of these Bureaus are headed by an Assistant Secretary and include several "offices"—for example, the Office of Soviet Union Affairs in the Bureau of European Affairs, and the Passport Office and the Visa Office in the Bureau of Consular Affairs. This arrangement makes it possible for the Department to keep abreast of the many different and often fast-breaking events of world politics.

The Foreign Service. More than 3400 men and women now represent the United States abroad as members of the Foreign Service.

---

[3]The Secretary does have some domestic responsibilities. Thus, when Richard Nixon resigned the Presidency on August 9, 1974, his formal, legal announcement of that fact had to be submitted to the Secretary of State (at the time, Henry Kissinger).

Under *international law*[4] every nation has the **right of legation**—the right to send and receive diplomatic representatives. The practice is ancient; its roots can be traced back to the Egyptian civilization of 6000 years ago.

The Second Continental Congress named this nation's first foreign service officer in 1778—when it chose Benjamin Franklin to be our minister to France.

Ambassadors. Today the United States is represented by an ambassador stationed at the capital of each of the states the United States *recognizes*.[5] By 1984, there were American embassies in more than 140 countries around the world.

Ambassadors are appointed by the President, with Senate consent, and they serve at the President's pleasure. Some of their posts are much-desired political plums; and there are many new appointments wherever there is a shift in the party in power in Washington. Too often, amateurs have been picked—usually because of their record of service in the President's party. Fortunately, most of our ambassadors are now career Foreign Service officers.

President Truman named the first woman as an ambassador, to Denmark, in 1949. President Johnson appointed the first black (also a woman), as our ambassador to Luxembourg in 1965. Now, several women, blacks, and other minority persons hold high rank in the Foreign Service.

Each American ambassador is the personal representative of the President of the United States, and he or she reports to the President through the Secretary of State. Each of them must keep the President fully informed of events in the host country, negotiate diplomatic agreements, protect the rights of American citizens abroad, and do whatever else the best interests of the United States may require.

To carry out these duties effectively, an ambassador must have the closest possible contacts with the leaders of the country to which he or she is sent—and with its people, too. A well-grounded knowledge of the language, history, customs, and culture of that country is an almost indispensable qualification for the job.

Every ambassador is assisted by one or more *diplomatic secretaries;* and every embassy's top staff also includes a *counsellor,* a high-ranking Foreign Service officer who advises the ambassador on matters of international law and diplomatic practice. Trade, agricultural, and communications experts, military attaches, clerks, interpreters, and a number of other people are stationed at each American embassy, too.[6]

Diplomatic Immunity. In international law, every sovereign state is supreme within its own boundaries, and all persons or things found within its territory are subject to its jurisdiction.

As a major exception to that rule, ambassadors are regularly given **diplomatic immunity.** That is, they are not subject to the laws of the state to which they are accredited. They cannot be arrested, sued, or taxed. Their official resi-

---

[4]**International law** consists of those rules and principles that guide sovereign states in their dealings with one another and their treatment of foreign nationals (private persons and groups). Its sources include treaties, decisions of international courts, reason, and custom, with treaties the most important source today.

[5]See page 396. An ambassador's official title is *Ambassador Extraordinary and Plenipotentiary.* When there is an opening in the office, or the ambassador is absent, the post is generally filled by a lesser-ranking Foreign Service officer. That officer, temporarily in charge of embassy affairs, is known as the *charge d'affaires.*

[6]The United States also has some 130 consular offices abroad. There, Foreign Service officers promote American interests in a multitude of ways—*e.g.,* encouraging trade, gathering intelligence data, advising persons who seek to enter this country, and aiding American citizens who are abroad and in need of legal advice or other help.

PERSONALITY PROFILES

THE COONS: CAREER DIPLOMATS

The Coons share a meal
at the U.S. Embassy in Dacca, Bangladesh.

In the spring of 1981, President Reagan appointed Carleton S. Coon, Jr. as the U. S. Ambassador to Nepal. Shortly afterward, Jane Abell Coon, Carleton's wife, was appointed U. S. Ambassador to Bangladesh, approximately 500 miles southeast of Nepal. Both career diplomats welcomed the assignments and have managed to spend one week together each month in alternating countries. The Coons are only the second husband-wife team of U. S. ambassadors. The previous husband-wife team was Mr. and Mrs. Ellsworth Bunker; in the 1970s, he served as Ambassador-at-Large and envoy to South Vietnam while she served as Ambassador to Nepal.

Both the Coons are in their 50s and have spent most of their careers working for the State Department. Each earns more than $60,000 a year at their post. Carleton was born in Paris, studied at Harvard, and joined the foreign service following World War II. He has held many diplomatic posts abroad and at the State Department in Washington. Prior to his appointment as Ambassador, he served as Director of North African Affairs. Jean Abell Coon was raised in New Hampshire and attended the College of Wooster in Ohio where she studied history and political science. After joining the Foreign Service, she spent time as a political officer in Pakistan and India. Prior to her most recent appointment, she was Deputy Assistant Secretary of State for Near Eastern and South Asian Affairs.

While in the past many ambassadorships were given as political "plums" or favors, today the trend is toward appointment of people like the Coons who have had extensive experience in the Foreign Service.

Those who wish to enter the Foreign Service must first pass a very difficult and highly competitive examination. The State Department has a pamphlet entitled "Foreign Service Careers." It describes the diplomatic corps and its work and contains a sample of the written exam given to all Foreign Service Officer candidates. For a copy, write to: The Recruitment Division, Department of State, Box 9317, Rosslyn Station, Arlington, Virginia 22209-0317.

1. What qualities do you think a person should have to be an ambassador?
2. Would you like to be an ambassador or member of the Foreign Service? Why, or why not?

dences (embassies) cannot be entered or searched without their consent; and their official communications, papers, and other properties are protected in the same way. This same immunity is normally given to all other embassy personnel and to their families, as well.

The granting of diplomatic immunity is intended to help each nation conduct its foreign relations. The practice assumes that diplomats will not abuse their position, of course. If a host government finds a diplomat's conduct unacceptable, that official may be declared *persona non grata* and be expelled from the country. The mistreatment of diplomats can lead to a serious break in the relationships of the countries involved.

Diplomatic immunity is a generally accepted and widely honored practice. But sometimes there are exceptions. The seizure of the American embassy in Iran in late 1979, and then the holding of 52 Americans as hostages for more than a year, is an outrageous illustration of that fact.

Special Diplomats. Those persons whom the President names to certain other top diplomatic posts also carry the rank of ambassador. Two such posts are the United States Representative to the UN and the American member of the North Atlantic Treaty (NATO) Council. There are also times when the President gives the *personal* rank of ambassador to those who take on special assignments abroad—such as representing the United States at an international conference on arms limitations.

Passports. **Passports** are certificates issued by a government to its citizens who travel or live abroad. They entitle their holders to the privileges accorded to them by international custom and treaties. Few states will admit persons who do not hold valid passports. Legally, no American citizen may leave the United States without a passport—

except for trips to Canada, Mexico, and a few other nearby places.

The State Department's passport Office issues some 3.5 million passports to American citizens each year. (Passports are not the same as *visas*. A **visa** is a permit to enter another state, and must be obtained from the country one wishes to enter. Most visas to enter this country are issued at American consulates abroad.)

FOR REVIEW

1. Why can the foreign and defense policies of the United States be properly called this country's national security policy?
2. In what ways do we live in "one world"? In what ways do we not?
3. Who is the nation's chief diplomat? The commander in chief of its armed forces?
4. What is the Secretary of State's first responsibility?
5. Why is the State Department organized along both geographic and functional lines?
6. What is the Foreign Service? The principal duties of an ambassador? What does the term *diplomatic immunity* mean?

The Department of Defense

The Defense Department also plays a leading role in the foreign policy process. The Secretary of Defense is always among the President's closest advisers in all matters touching on national security.[7]

Civil Control of the Military. The

---

[7]Congress created the Defense Department in order to unify the nation's armed forces–that is, to bring the then-separate Army (including the Air Force) and the Navy under the control of a single Cabinet department.

authors of the Constitution understood, absolutely, the importance of the nation's defense. They emphasized that fact in the Preamble, and they underscored it in the body of the Constitution by speaking of defense more often than any other governmental function.

The Framers also saw the dangers inherent in military power. They knew that its very existence can pose a threat to free government. For that reason, the Constitution is studded with provisions to keep the military always subject to the control of the nation's civilian authorities.

The Constitution makes the elected President the commander in chief of the armed forces. To the same end, it gives several very significant military powers to Congress—that is, to the elected representatives of the people. And it reinforces the principle of civilian control by giving to Congress the tremendously important power of the purse. As it exercises that power, Congress decides such basic matters of military policy as the size of the armed forces and decides how much money there will be available for military pay, for training, for equipment, and for all other military purposes.[8]

We have obeyed the principle of civilian control throughout our history. It has been a major factor in the making of defense policy, and in setting up and staffing the agencies to carry out that policy. The point is clearly illustrated by the fact that the Secretary of Defense cannot have served on active duty in any of the armed forces for at least 10 years before being named to that post.

The Secretary of Defense. The Secretary, who serves at the President's pleasure, has two major responsibilities: (1) as the President's chief aide and adviser in making and carrying out defense policy and (2) as the operating head of the Defense Department, with its more than two million men and women in uniform and its more than one million civilian employees.

The Secretary's huge domain is often called "the Pentagon"—because of its massive five-sided headquarters building on the Virginia side of the Potomac River, just across from the Capitol. Year in and year out, its operations take a large slice of the federal budget. Military spending reached a record high of more than $239 billion in fiscal year 1983; and President Reagan has called for military expenditures of more than $258 billion in 1984 and $305 billion in 1985.

Chief Civilian Aides. The Secretary's chief assistant, the Deputy Secretary, directs the day-to-day operations of the Department. There are a number of other civilians at the top levels of the Pentagon. The most important of them: the two Under Secretaries—one for Policy and the other for Research and Engineering; the several Assistant Secretaries of Defense—often referred to as ASD's; and the Secretaries of the Army, the Navy, and the Air Force. All of them are named by the President with Senate consent.

Chief Military Aides. The five members of the Joint Chiefs of Staff

---

[8]Recall, too, that the Constitution makes defense a *national* function and just about excludes the States from that field. Article I, Section 10, Clause 3 provides: "No State shall, without the consent of Congress . . . keep troops or ships of war, . . . or engage in war, unless actually invaded, or in such imminent danger as will not admit of delay." Each State does have a *militia* which it may use to keep the peace within its own borders. Each State's militia is legally separate from that of every other, but all are, collectively, "the militia of the United States." Congress has the power (Article I, Section 8, Clauses 15, 16) to "provide for calling forth the militia to execute the laws of the Union, suppress insurrections, and repel invasions," and to provide for organizing, arming, and disciplining it. Since 1795, the President has had the power to call the militia into federal service. Today the governor of each State is the commander of that State's units of the Army and the Air National Guard, except when the President has ordered any or all of those units into federal service; see page 545.

serve as the principal military advisers to the Secretary—and to the President and the National Security Council, as well. They are the highest ranking uniformed officers in the armed services: the Chairman of the Joint Chiefs, the Army Chief of Staff, the Chief of Naval Operations, the Commandant of the Marine Corps, and the Air Force Chief of Staff. Each of them is also named by the President, subject to Senate approval.

The *Armed Forces Policy Council* is the Department's major planning and decision-making body. Its meetings are chaired by the Secretary. Its other members are the Deputy Secretary, the two Under Secretaries, the Secretaries of the Army, the Navy, and the Air Force, and the members of the Joint Chiefs of Staff.

The Military Departments. The three military departments—the Departments of the Army, the Navy, and the Air Force—are sub-Cabinet departments in the Department of Defense.[9] Each of them is headed by a civilian Secretary, answering to the Secretary of Defense and so to the President.

The Department of the Army. The Army is the largest of the armed services. It is also the oldest of them. The American Continental Army, now the United States Army, was established by the Second Continental Congress on June 14, 1775—more than a year before the Declaration of Independence.

The Army is essentially a ground-based force, responsible for military operations on land. Its primary mission is two-fold. It must be ready (1) to defeat

Equipped for all forms of combat, paratroopers of the 82nd Airborne Division can go into action on short notice.

any attack upon the United States itself and (2) to take swift and forceful action to protect American interests in any other part of the world. It must organize, train, and equip its active duty forces (the Regular Army) and its reserve units (the Army National Guard and the Army Reserve) for those purposes. All of its forces are under the direct command of the Army's Chief of Staff.

The Regular Army is the nation's standing army, the heart of its land forces. It now has a strength of about 710,000 men and 65,000 women—officers and enlisted personnel, professional soldiers and volunteers. The women on active duty today serve in nearly all of the Army's units; they are excluded only from direct combat roles.

The Army's combat units are made up of soldiers trained and equipped to fight enemy forces. The infantry takes, holds, and defends land areas. The artillery supports the infantry, smashes enemy concentrations with its heavier guns, and gives antiaircraft cover. The armored cavalry also supports the infantry, using armored vehicles, and helicopters to spearhead assaults and oppose

---

[9]The United States Marine Corps is a separate branch of the armed forces but, for organizational purposes, it is located within the Department of the Navy.

The United States Coast Guard is also, and at all times, a branch of the armed forces. Since 1967, the Coast Guard has been located in the Department of Transportation; see page 421. In time of war, or at any other time at the President's direction, it becomes a part of the United States Navy.

enemy counteroffensives.

The other units of the Army provide the many services and supplies for the soldiers in these combat organizations. They could not fight without the help of those other troops—the soldiers of the engineer, quartermaster, signal, ordnance, transportation, chemical, military police, finance, and medical corps.

The Department of the Navy. The United States Navy was first formed as the Continental Navy—a fledgling naval force formed by the Second Continental Congress on October 13, 1775. From that day to this, its major responsibility has been sea warfare and defense.

The Chief of Naval Operations is the Navy's highest ranking officer and is responsible for its preparations and readiness for war and for its use in combat. The CNO has direct command of all of its seagoing forces and of all of its shore units and land-based facilities. Some 540,000 officers and enlisted personnel including nearly 33,000 women serve in the Navy today.

The United States Marine Crops was established by the Second Continental Congress on November 10, 1775. Today it operates as a separate armed service—within the Navy Department but not under the control of the Chief of Naval Operations. Its Commandant answers directly to the Secretary of the Navy for the efficiency, readiness, and performance of the Corps.

The Marines are essentially a combat-ready land force for the Navy. They have two major combat missions: (1) to seize or defend land bases from which the ships of the fleet and the Navy and Marine air arms can operate and (2) to carry out other land operations essential to a naval campaign. Today some 180,000 men and nearly 7000 women serve in the USMC.

MILITARY EXPENDITURES

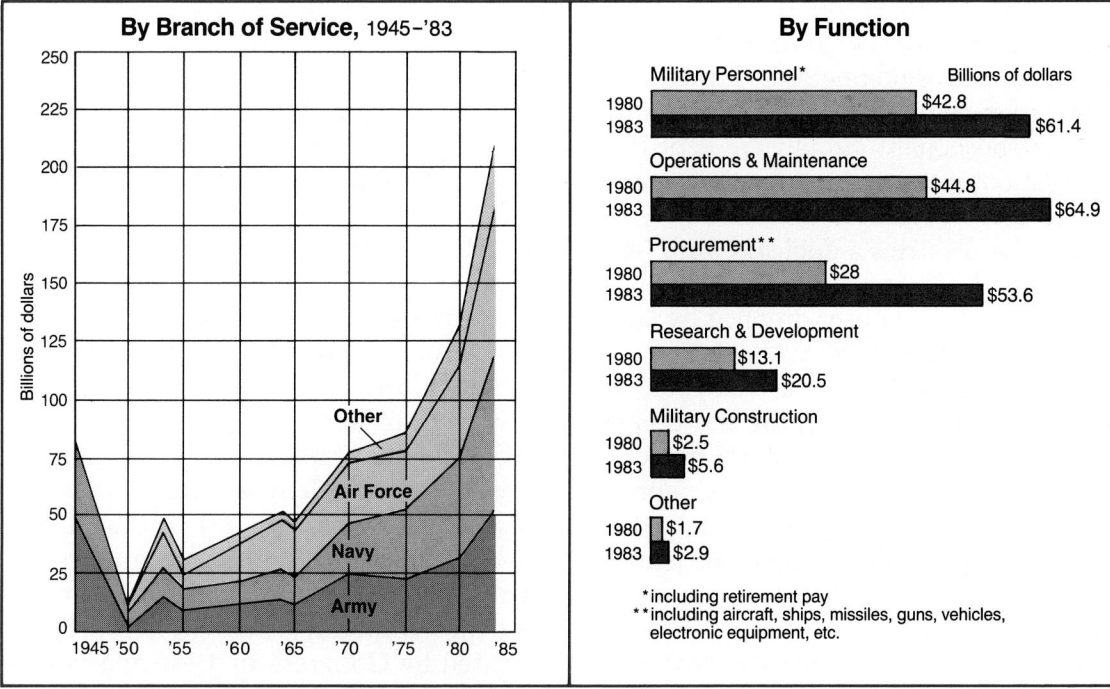

Source: U.S. Dept. of the Treasury

The Department of the Air Force.
The Air Force is the youngest of the military services. Congress established the United States Air Force, and made it a separate branch of the armed forces, in the National Security Act of 1947. However, its history dates back to 1907—when the Army assigned an officer and two enlisted men to a new unit, the Aeronautical Division of the Army's Signal Corps.

Today the USAF is the nation's first line of defense. It has primary responsibility for military air and aerospace operations. In time of war, its major duties are to defend the United States, attack and defeat enemy air, ground, and sea forces, strike military and other war-related targets in enemy territory, and provide transport and combat support for American land and naval operations.

The Air Force now has about 565,000 officers and enlisted personnel, including nearly 60,000 women. All of them are under the direct command of the Chief of Staff of the Air Force.

The striking power of the Air Force is truly awesome. Huge, eight-engined B-52s are the backbone of its strategic—long-range-bomber fleet. Several hundred of those giant aircraft are kept in a state of constant combat readiness, at a number of bases here and abroad. Just *one* of them carries a nuclear bomb load with a greater destructive power than that of all of the bombs dropped by both sides during all of World War II.

Today's B-52's are improved versions of planes that first flew in the 1950s. Plans now are to replace them with supersonic, missile-firing B-1s, sometime in the late 1980s.

All of the USAFs tactical (short-range) aircraft—jet fighters and interceptors and attack bombers—are now armed with air-to-air missiles. Most of them now carry air-to-ground missiles, as well. The Air Force also flies weather, reconnaissance, and hospital planes, transports, trainers, and several other types of aircraft. Like the other services, the Air Force is also armed with different surface-launched missile weapons—and, especially, the long-range intercontinental (ICBM) and intermediate-range (IBM) ballistic missiles. Many of its newest missiles can seek out and destroy fast-flying targets even hundreds of miles away.

Other Foreign/Defense Policy Agencies

We have already said that several federal agencies outside the Departments of State and Defense are involved in the field of foreign affairs. A few quick illustrations of the point:

The Immigration and Naturalization Service, in the Department of Justice, deals with those who come here from abroad. The Customs Service, in the Treasury Department, is concerned with goods imported from other nations and combats international smuggling operations. The Public Health Service, in the Department of Health and Human Services, works with a number of UN agencies and foreign governments to conquer disease and other health problems in many parts of the world. The Coast Guard, in the Department of Transportation, keeps an iceberg patrol in the North Atalantic to protect the shipping of all nations.

A listing of that sort could go on for several pages. In fact, nearly *all* federal agencies are in some way or another involved in the fields of foreign and defense policy. But here we turn to the several independent agencies with the most direct involvements in that field.

The Central Intelligence Agency.
The CIA is a very important part of the foreign policy establishment. It was created by Congress in 1947 and works under the direction of the National Security Council. The "agency," as it is

often called, is headed by the Director of Central Intelligence appointed by the President with Senate consent.

Clearly, the President and his chief advisers must have vast amounts of accurate and timely information upon which to base foreign policy and national security decisions. The CIA fills that need. On paper, it has three major tasks: (1) to coordinate the information-gathering activities of all of the State, Defense, and other federal agencies involved in the areas of foreign affairs and national defense, (2) to analyze and evaluate all of the data collected by those agencies, and (3) at all times to keep them informed of all of that material.

The CIA is far more than a coordinating and reporting body, however. It also conducts its own worldwide intelligence operations. In fact, it is a major "cloak-and-dagger" agency. Much of the information it gathers comes from such more or less open (overt) sources as foreign newspapers and other publications, radio broadcasts, travellers, satellite photos, and the like. But a large share comes from its own **clandestine** (secret, covert) activities. Those operations cover the full range of espionage.

The nature of the CIA's work, its methods, the results it achieves, and the its reports are regularly shrouded in deepest secrecy. Even Congress has generally shied away from more than a surface check on its activities; only a few key members are closely informed about them. Indeed, the agency's operating funds—which now run to several billions of dollars a year—are hidden in the federal budget each year.

The International Communications Agency. The International Communications Agency is, at base, a propaganda unit. Its mission is to promote the image of the United States and to sell its policies and its way of life abroad. The agency describes its work as building "two-way bridges of understanding between the people of the United States and the other peoples of the world."

The ICA works to sell America in a number of ways—in radio and television broadcasts, by distribution of books, magazines, and other publications, with films and tapes, by sponsoring educational and culture exchange programs, and through a number of other channels. It now operates more than 200 libraries, film centers, and other posts in more than 120 foreign countries.

It is best-known for the Voice of America. The VOA's round-the-clock radio programs are beamed in English and some 40 other languages to audiences throughout the world.

The National Aeronautics and Space Administration. From the days of the ancient Greeks, more than 2400 years ago, people have dreamed of the exploration and conquest of outer space. The modern space age is little more than 25 years old, however. It began on October 4, 1957, when the Soviet Union put its first satellite, Sputnik I, in space. The first American satellite, Explorer I, was

Space shuttle *Columbia* thunders away from its launch pad on its third mission in space in April of 1982.

fired into orbit a few months later, on January 31, 1958. From that point on, a great number of space vehicles—manned and unmanned, with one U.S. and one Russian satellite carrying a woman—have been thrust into the heavens by both of the superpowers.

NASA is an independent agency formed by Congress in 1958 to handle this nation's space programs. The military importances of those programs can hardly be exaggerated; but Congress has ordered the space agency to bend its efforts "to peaceful purposes for the benefit of all humankind," as well. NASA's work has opened new frontiers in several fields–in astronomy, physics, and the environmental sciences, in communications, medicine, and weather forecasting, and in many more.

The United States Arms Control and Disarmament Agency.   For more than a generation now, the world has lived under the shadow of nuclear war—with the danger of a holocaust, begun by design or by accident, that could destroy all forms of life in this planet. That awesome terrifying fact has given new and compelling urgency to the ancient hope for the day when, in the words of Isaiah:

> They shall beat their swords into plowshares, and their spears into pruning-hooks; nation shall not lift up sword against nation, neither shall they make war any more.

The USACDA is responsible for American participation in arms limitations and disarmament negotiations with the Soviet Union and other countries. Its Director also serves as the principal adviser to the President, the National Security Council, and the Secretaries of State and Defense in all matters dealing with those policy areas.

Much of the agency's work to date has centered on nuclear test ban and

"Lurie's Opinion," by Ranan Lurie. King Features Syndicate.

"Boy are we lucky it was only a limited nuclear war!"

arms limits negotiations, which have been held, on and off, since 1958.

The Selective Service System. Through most of our history, as today, the armed forces have depended on voluntary enlistments to fill their ranks. But from 1940 to 1973, military conscription (compulsory service) was a major source of military manpower. At present, the draft, which is administered by the Selective Service System, exists only on a standby basis.

Conscription has a long history in this country. Several of the colonies and later nine States required all able-bodied males to serve in their militia. Proposals for a national draft, made by the first Secretary of War, Henry Knox, and endorsed by George Washington, were rejected by Congress in the 1790s.

Both the North and the South did have a limited conscription program during the Civil War. It was not until 1917 that a national draft was first used in this country, even in wartime.

The nation's first peacetime draft came with the Selective Service and Training Act of 1940, as World War II raged in Europe. More than 10 million of the 16.3 million Americans who were in uniform in World War II entered the service under that law.

The World War II draft was ended in 1947. The crises of the postwar period, however, quickly moved Congress to revive it, in the Selective Service Act of 1948. The present law is the Military Selective Service Act of 1971. From 1948 to 1973, nearly 5 million young men were drafted for the armed forces—most notably during the Korean War and, later, the war in Southeast Asia.

Mounting criticisms of compulsory military service, fed by opposition to Vietnam policy, led many Americans to call for an end to the draft in the late 1960s. Fewer than 30,000 men were drafted in 1972, and selective service was suspended in 1973. But the draft, and its administrative arm, the Selective Service System, are still on the books. Compulsory military service can be reactivated if Congress finds it necessary.

The draft law places a military obligation on all males in the United States between ages 18½ and 26. Over the years in which the draft in fact operated, it was largely conducted through local selective service boards—hundreds of them, across the country. All young men had to register for service at age 18. The local boards then "selected" those who were to enter the armed forces.

The registration requirement is now back in place. President Carter reactivated it in 1980, and President Reagan has kept it in force. All young men—but not women—must sign up soon after they reach their 18th birthday.[10]

---

[10]The President's power to order the induction of men into the armed forces expired on June 30, 1973. If the draft is ever to be reactivated, Congress must first renew that presidential authority. Recall that the Supreme Court first upheld the constitutionality of the draft in the *Selective Draft Law Cases* in 1918 and also ruled that its all-male features are constitutional in *Rotsker* v. *Goldberg* in 1981; see pages 129, 154.

 FOR REVIEW

1. Why does the Constitution provide for civilian control of the nation's military forces? How does it do so?
2. What is the primary role of the Secretary of Defense?
3. Describe the basic features of the structure of the Department of Defense.
4. Why is it incorrect to view the making and execution of national security policy only in terms of the President and the State and Defense Departments?
5. What is the primary function of each of these agencies: the CIA? ICA? NASA? USACDA?
6. What is the status of the Selective Service System today?

American Foreign Policy: Past and Present

The basic purpose of America's foreign policy has always been to protect the security of the United States—and so it is today. It would be quite impossible to present all of the history of our foreign relations in these pages, of course. But we can review its major themes and highlights here. And we should, because history is *not* "bunk," as Henry Ford once said it is. It is, instead, the stuff out of which today is made.

Isolationism

From its beginnings, and for 150 years, American foreign policy was very largely built upon a policy of *isolationism*. Through all of that time, the United States refused to become generally and permanently involved in the affairs of the rest of the world.

Isolationism was born in the earliest years of our history. In his Farewell Address in 1796, George Washington declared "our true policy" to be "to steer clear of permanent alliances with any portion of the foreign world." Our "detached and distant situation," he said, made it desirable for us to have "as little political connection as possible" with other nations. In 1801 Thomas Jefferson added his own warning against "entangling alliances."

At the time, and for years to come, isolationism seemed a wise policy to most Americans. The United States was a new and a relatively weak nation. We had a great many problems of our own, a huge continent to explore and settle, and two oceans to separate us from the rest of the world. That policy did not demand a complete separation, however. From the first, the United States developed ties abroad—by exchanging diplomatic representatives with other nations, making treaties with many of them, building an extensive foreign commerce, and in other ways. In fact, isolationism was, over time, more a statement of our desire for noninvolvement *outside* the Western Hemisphere than within it.

The Monroe Doctrine

James Monroe gave the policy of isolationism a wider shape in 1823. In an historic message to Congress he proclaimed what has ever since been known as the *Monroe Doctrine.*

A wave of revolutions had swept Latin America, destroying the old Spanish and Portuguese empires there. The prospect that other European powers would now help them to take back their lost possessions was seen as a threat to our own security and a challenge to our economic interests.

In his message, President Monroe restated America's intentions to stay out of the affairs of Europe. And, at the same time, he warned the nations of Europe—including Russia, then in control of Alaska—to stay out of the affairs of the New World. He declared that the United States would look upon

> any attempt on their part to extend their system to any portion of this hemisphere as dangerous to our peace and safety.

The Monroe Doctrine is not a law. Rather, it is a self-defense policy, a policy of "America for the Americans." It opposes any non-American encroachment on the independence of any country in the Western Hemisphere. It has been consistently supported by Congress and by every President for more than a century and a half.

At first, most Latin Americans paid little attention to the Doctrine. Later, as the United States became more powerful, many Latin Americans came to view the Doctrine as a selfish policy. They felt that we were more concerned with our own security and commercial fortune than with their independence. Happily, matters have taken a somewhat brighter turn in recent decades, as we shall see.

Continental Expansion

At the close of the Revolutionary War, the United States was a confederation of 13 States stretching for some 1300 miles along the Atlantic seaboard. By the Treaty of Paris, which officially ended that war in 1783, the new nation also held title to all of the territory from the Great Lakes on the north to Spanish Florida in the south and westward to the Mississippi.

We began to fill out the continent almost at once. Taking advantage of France's conflict with England in the early 1800s, President Jefferson negotiated the Louisiana Purchase in 1803. At a single stroke, the nation's size was

By W.A. Rogers in *New York Herald*, 1902.

"That's a live wire, gentlemen!"

doubled—with territory reaching from the mouth of the Mississippi up to what is now Montana. With the Florida Purchase in 1819 we completed our expansion to the south.

Neither isolationism nor the Monroe Doctrine stood in the way of further expansion to the west. Texas was annexed in 1845. We obtained the Oregon Country (and British Columbia became a part of Canada) by treaty with Great Britain in 1846. Mexico ceded California and the land between after its defeat in the Mexican War of 1846–1848. The southwestern limits of the United States were rounded out by the Gadsden Purchase in 1853. By treaty, we bought from Mexico a strip of territory, in what is now the southern parts of Arizona and New Mexico, as the best rail route to the Pacific. In 1867 we bought Alaska from Russia and so became a colonial power.

In that same year, 1867, the Monroe Doctrine got its first real test. While we were beset by the Civil War, France, under Napoleon III, had invaded Mexico and installed Prince Maximilian of Austria as its puppet emperor. We backed the Mexicans in forcing the French to withdraw, and the Maximilian regime fell.

The United States, a World Power

The United States emerged as a first-class power in world politics with the Spanish-American War in 1898. Spain's mistreatment of its few remaining possessions in the Caribbean had fanned wide resentment in this country. The war was triggered by the mysterious sinking of an American battleship, the *U.S.S. Maine*, in Havana Harbor on February 15, 1898. The fighting lasted only four months. With Spain's decisive defeat, we gained the Philippines and Guam in the Pacific and Puerto Rico in the Caribbean. Cuba became independent, under American protection. We also annexed Hawaii in 1898.

By 1900, the United States had become a colonial power with interests extending across the continent, to Alaska and the Arctic, to the tip of Latin America, and across the Pacific to the Philippines.

The Good Neighbor Policy

Our relations with Latin America have ebbed and flowed. The Monroe Doctrine has always served two purposes. It has (1) guaranteed the independence of Latin American countries, and (2) protected our position (our "backyard") in the New World.

The threat of European intervention, which gave rise to the Doctrine, declined in the last half of the 19th century. It was replaced by problems within the hemisphere. Political instability, revolutions, unpaid foreign debts, and injuries to citizens and property of the United States and other countries plagued Central and South America.

Under what came to be known as the "Roosevelt Corollary" to the Monroe Doctrine, the United States began to police Latin America in the early 1900s. Several times, the Marines were used to put down domestic disorders in Nicaragua, Haiti, Cuba, and elsewhere. Political and financial conditions were stabilized, boundry disputes were settled, foreign lives and property were protected, and order was more or less generally maintained.

In 1903 Panama revolted and became independent of Colombia, with American blessings. In the same year, we gained the right to build a canal across the Isthmus, and the Panama Canal was opened in 1914. In 1917 we bought the Virgin Islands from Denmark to help guard the Canal. All of these and other steps taken by the United States were resented by many in Latin America. They complained of "the Colossus of the North," of "Yankee imperialism," and of "dollar diplomacy" (and many still do).

Our Latin American policies took an important turn in the 1930s. Theodore Roosevelt's Corollary was replaced by Franklin Roosevelt's *Good Neighbor Policy*, a conscious attempt to win friends to the south. New life was breathed into the Pan American Union, first formed in 1890 and now known as the Organization of American States (the OAS). Over the past several years, we and most of our Latin American neighbors have worked to promote "hemispheric solidarity" and "Inter-American cooperation."

The central proviso of the Monroe Doctrine—the warning against foreign encroachments—is now set out in the Inter-American Treaty of Reciprocal Assistance (the Rio Pact) of 1947; and it is enforced by both the United States and the OAS. Still, the United States is, without question, *the* dominant power in the Western Hemisphere—and the Monroe Doctrine is still a vital part of American foreign policy. Today, our most serious problems in the region revolve about the existence of a communist government in Cuba, its close ties with the Soviet Union, and its efforts to promote revolution in Central and South America.

The Open Door in China

Historically, American foreign policy interests have centered on Europe and on Latin America. Our involvements in the Far East do reach back to the middle of the 1800s, however. Forty-five years before the United States acquired territory in the far Pacific, the Navy's Commodore Matthew Perry had opened Japan to American trade. The next several decades were marked by intense rivalries among a number of European powers to win territorial holdings and trade advantages in the Far East, most of all in China.

By the latter years of the century, America's thriving trade in the Orient was seriously threatened. The British, French, Germans, and Japanese were each ready to take slices of the Chinese coast as their own exclusive trading preserves. In 1899 Secretary of State John Hay announced this country's insistence on an *Open Door Policy*—a policy of equal trade access for all nations and a demand that China's independence and soverignty over its own territory be preserved.

The other major powers came to accept the American position, however reluctantly. Our relations with Japan worsened from that point on to the climax at Pearl Harbor in 1941. Over the same period, we built increasingly strong ties with China on through World War II; but they came to an end when the communists won control of the Chinese mainland in 1949. For nearly 30 years the United States and the People's Republic of China refused to recognize one another.

The People's Republic took on a new role in world affairs when it replaced Nationalist China in the UN in 1971.

President Nixon's historic visit to Peking in 1972 signalled the beginnings of a new era in American-Chinese affairs. Preliminary diplomatic contacts came with the exchange of "liaison officers" in 1973.

At last, the realities of world politics have led the two powers to a full-fledged relationship. The United States and the People's Republic formally recognized one another in 1979.

World War I, and the Return to Isolationism

Germany's submarine campaign against American shipping in the North Atlantic forced the United States out of its isolationist cocoon in 1917. We entered World War I "to make the world safe for democracy."

With the defeat of Germany and the Central Powers, however, we pulled back from the involvements brought on by the war. The United States refused to join the League of Nations, conceived by President Woodrow Wilson. Europe's problems, and those of the rest of the world, so many Americans thought, were no concern of ours.

The rise of Mussolini in Italy, of Hitler in Germany, and of the militarists in Japan cast dark clouds on the world of the 1920s and the 1930s. But for more than 20 years after World War I an isolationist United States wrapped itself with its two oceans.

World War II

Our historic commitment to isolationism was finally ended by World War II. That massive conflict, which began in Europe in 1939, spread to engulf much of the world and lasted for nearly six years. By the time it ended in 1945, it had cost the lives of at least 45 million people. The war's other costs, in human suffering and in physical destruction, were at least as appalling.

The United States became directly involved in the war when the Japanese attacked Pearl Harbor on December 7, 1941. From that point on, together with the British, the Russians, the Chinese, and our other Allies, we waged an all-out effort to defeat the Axis Powers (Germany, Italy, and Japan).

World War II ended, with the Allies victorious everywhere, in mid-1945. In Europe, Germany—devastated by the attacks of American and British forces from the west and by Russian troops from the east—surrendered unconditionally in May. The war in the Pacific came to a sudden end in August. Japan capitulated soon after the United States dropped two atomic bombs, which destroyed the Japanese cities of Hiroshima and Nagasaki.

An Allied beachhead established on the coast of German-held France in June of 1944. Less than a year later, Germany was forced to surrender unconditionally.

FOR REVIEW

1. What was the policy of isolationism? Why did it dominate our foreign policy for 150 years?

2. What was (is) the Monroe Doctrine? Was it a departure from isolationism?

3. Trace the territorial development of the United States from the original 13 States to the acquisition of the lands that now make up the 50 States.

4. At what point did the United States take its place as a first-class power in world politics?

5. What has been the historic shape of this country's relations with Latin America?

6. What was the Open Door Policy? What is the shape of our relations with China now?

7. Did World War I finally persuade this country to give up isolationism? Explain.

American Foreign Policy Today

World War II led to a fundamental change in the shape of American foreign policy—an historic shift from isolationism to internationalism. In just a few years, the United States rose from a position as *one* of several major powers in the world to its present place as *the* leading power among the free nations of the world. From its isolationist past, this country emerged from World War II as a permanent and global participant in international affairs.

Our foreign policy has been following that new direction for some 40 years now. Even so, the overall objective of that policy remains what it has always been: the protection of the security of the United States.

Peace through Collective Security

The United States, and most of the rest of a war-weary world, looked to the principle of **collective security** to keep international peace and order after World War II. That is, we hoped to forge a worldwide system of security—a world community, in which all or at least most nations would agree to act together against any nation that threatened or broke the peace.

We were determined not to repeat the error of 1919–1920, when the United States refused to join the League of Nations. To that end, we took the lead in creating the United Nations in 1945. Its Charter declared that the UN was formed to promote international cooperation and so "to save succeeding generations from the scourge of war . . . and to maintain international peace and security." See pages 471–475.

It soon became clear that the future of the world would not be shaped in the UN, however. Rather, it would depend upon the nature of the relations between the world's two superpowers, the United States and the Soviet Union. Those relations, which were never very close, quickly deteriorated, and much of American foreign policy on into the 1980s has been built around that fact.

Still, the principle of collective security remains a cornerstone of our foreign policy. We have consistently supported the United Nations and several other efforts to further international cooperation. And, because the UN has not fulfilled the dreams upon which it was founded, we have taken another path to collective security: We have built a system of defensive alliances (regional collective security treaties) with many of the other free nations of the world; see pages 468–471.

Deterrence

The policy of *deterrence* is another major plank of current American foreign policy. It was begun under President Truman, as the antagonisms between the United States and the Soviet Union grew after World War II; and it has been maintained by every President ever since. At base, **deterrence** is the policy of making ourselves and our allies so militarily strong that its strength will deter (prevent, forestall) any attack upon us.

President Reagan has put that policy in these words:

> We are not a warlike people. Quite the opposite. We always seek to live in peace. We resort to force infrequently. . . . But neither are we naive or foolish. We know only too well that war comes not when the forces of freedom are strong, but when they are weak. It is then that tyrants are tempted.

The President has urged Congress to raise the level of defense spending over each of the next several years, as we noted on page 451. In doing so, he has made much the same point, arguing that this spending is needed in order "to buy peace for the rest of this century." In a very real sense, the policy of deterrence comes down to this: This country's military might is most effective if, in fact, it does not have to be used.

Resisting Soviet Aggression

Much of the content of American foreign policy today is fixed, as it has been for more than a generation now, by one crucial factor: the state of our relations with the Soviet Union. Ever since the end of World War II those relations have been at least tense. More often than not, they have been hostile.

We had planned to work with the Russians, particularly through the UN, to build international cooperation and keep the peace in the postwar world. Those plans were quickly dashed, however, by the aggressive, expansionist policies of the Soviet Union.

At the Yalta Conference, in early 1945, Soviet Premier Josef Stalin had agreed (with President Franklin Roosevelt and British Prime Minister Winston Churchill) that "democratic govern-

"HERMAN," by Unger. © 1980 Universal Press Syndicate.

"Let's hope we never have to use it!"

The first hydrogen bomb was exploded in a test conducted in the South Pacific in 1952. Nuclear devices developed since then are even more destructive.

ments" would be established by "free elections" in the liberated countries of Eastern Europe. Instead, the Russians imposed communist governments on those countries. Very quickly, they erected an empire of Soviet-dominated satellites along their western frontier. What Mr. Churchill promptly described as an "iron curtain" had dropped across Europe, dividing it between East and West. What soon became known as the Cold War had begun.

As they took over Eastern Europe, the Russians tried to move in several other directions, as well. They attempted to take over the oil fields of Iran, to the south. At the same time, they supported communist guerillas in a civil war in Greece. And, following the historic Russian dream of a "window to the sea," they demanded military and naval bases in Turkey.

The Truman Doctrine and Containment. The United States began to counter the Soviet Union's aggressive thrusts in the early months of 1947. The *Truman Doctrine* marked the first step in that now long-standing process. Both Greece and Turkey were in danger. Without immediate American help they were certain to fall under Soviet control. At President Harry Truman's urgent request, Congress approved a massive program of economic and military aid, and both countries were saved. In his message to Congress, the President declared that it was now

> the policy of the United States to support free peoples who are resisting subjugation by armed minorities and outside pressures.

The Truman Doctrine soon became part of a broader American plan for dealing with the Soviet Union. Since mid-1947 we have generally followed the policy of **containment.** The policy is based on the belief that, if Soviet expan-

sion can be stopped, then Soviet communism will collapse under the weight of its own internal problems. The United States has taken many different actions in line with that strategy—a number of political economic, and military moves intended to contain (halt, check) the spread of communist power.

The policy of containment dominated our relations with the Soviet Union during the Cold War—from the late 1940s on through the 1950s and the 1960s. First put in place under President Truman, it was followed by Presidents Dwight Eisenhower, John Kennedy, and Lyndon Johnson. Each of them applied the policy many times—and with mixed results, sometimes successfully and sometimes not.

The United States and the Soviet Union confronted one another often, and in many places, during the Cold War years. Two of those confrontations were of major, near-war proportions: in Berlin in 1948–1949 and in Cuba in 1962. And, during that same time, the United States fought two wars against communist forces in Asia.

The Berlin Blockade. At the end of World War II, the city of Berlin, surrounded by Russian-occupied East Germany, was divided into four sectors. One sector (East Berlin) was controlled by the Soviet Union; the other three (comprising West Berlin) were occupied by the United States, Britain, and France.

In 1948 the Soviets tried to force their three former allies to withdraw. They clamped a land blockade around the city, stopping the shipment of food and other supplies to the western sectors. The United States mounted a massive airlift that kept the city alive until the blockade was finally lifted, a year-and-a-half after it had been imposed.

The Cuban Missile Crisis. The United States and the Soviet Union

Athenians celebrate the one-millionth ton of aid received by 1949 from the United States, aid sent to prevent a Soviet take-over of Greece during the Cold War years.

came very close to a nuclear shoot-out during the Cuban missile crisis in 1962.

Cuba had slipped into the Soviet orbit not long after Fidel Castro gained power there in 1959. Cuban-American relations quickly broke down, and the United States cut diplomatic ties with the Castro regime in early 1961. Cuba was pushed deeper into the Soviet camp when a band of CIA-trained Cuban exiles attempted to invade the island, at the Bay of Pigs in April of 1961.

By mid-1962 huge quantities of Soviet arms and thousands of Russian "technicians" had been sent to Cuba. Both Cuba and the Soviet Union insisted that the military buildup was purely defensive, to protect Cuba from an American invasion. Suddenly, in October, the buildup became unmistakably offensive in character. Despite Moscow's repeated assurances to the contrary, aerial photographs showed several Soviet missiles placed in Cuba, ones capable of nuclear strikes against this country and much of Latin America.

Immediately, President Kennedy declared that the United States would "not tolerate deliberate deception and offensive threats by any nation, large or small." He ordered a naval blockade of Cuba, to prevent the delivery of any more missiles. He warned both Cuba and the Soviet Union that the United States would attack Cuba unless the existing Soviet missiles were removed.

After several tension-filled days, the Soviets backed down. Rather than risk all, so far from home, they dismantled their missile installations and the weapons were returned to the USSR.

The Korean War. During the years of the Cold War, the United States fought two hot wars against communist aggression in Asia. The first was fought in Korea, and the other in Vietnam.

The Korean War began on June 25, 1950. South Korea (the UN-sponsored Republic of Korea) was attacked by communist North Korea (the People's Democratic Republic of Korea). Immediately, the UN's Security Council called upon all UN members to help South Korea repel the invasion. President Truman ordered U.S. forces into action at once.

The war lasted for more than three years. It pitted the United Nations Command, largely made up of American and South Korean forces, against Soviet-trained and -equipped North Korean and Communist Chinese troops.[11] A cease-fire agreement was signed in July of 1951; but sporadic fighting continued for another two years, until an armistice was finally signed on July 27, 1953. Final peace terms have never been agreed to, however. American and South Korean forces still stand guard against any further aggression from the north.

The long and bitter Korean conflict

[11]The UN Command also included combat and/or support units from 15 other UN members: Australia, Belgium, Canada, Colombia, Ethiopia, France, Great Britain, Greece, Luxembourg, the Netherlands, New Zealand, the Philippines, Thailand, Turkey, and South Africa.

did not end in a clear-cut UN victory in the sense that the enemy was beaten to its knees. The war cost the United States 157,530 casualties, including 33,629 combat dead, and more than $20 billion. South Korea's military and civilian casualties ran into the hundreds of thousands, and much of Korea, north and south, was laid to waste.

Still, much was accomplished. The invasion was turned back and the Republic of Korea was saved. Perhaps more importantly, for the first time in history, armed forces fought under an international flag against aggression. In the hope of preventing World War III, the tide of communist aggression had to be stopped somewhere, and soon.

The War in Vietnam.   Beginning in the early 1950s the United States became more and more involved in Vietnam. The involvement grew largely out of the collapse of French colonial rule in Southeast Asia in 1954. It developed, finally, into the most controversial and unpopular war in this nation's history.

A Vietnamese nationalist movement, seeking independence from France and made up mostly of communist forces led by Ho Chi Minh, fought and defeated the French in lengthy political and military struggle that had begun soon after World War II. Under truce agreements signed at Geneva in 1954, France withdrew from Southeast Asia entirely. What had been French Indochina was divided into two zones: a communist-dominated North Vietnam, with its capital in Hanoi, and an anti-communist South Vietnam, based in Saigon.

Almost at once, communist guerillas (the Viet Cong), supported by the Ho Chi Minh government in Hanoi, began a civil war in South Vietnam. The Eisenhower administration responded with first economic and then military aid to Saigon. This aid was increased by President Kennedy. By the end of 1963, more than 16,000 American military advisers were on duty in Vietnam—building and training the South Vietnamese army, and often leading it in combat. But, even with stepped-up American support, the Viet Cong—and ever growing numbers of North Vietnamese troops, supplied with (mostly) Russian and (some) Chinese weapons—continued to make substantial gains.

It was President Johnson who, in early 1965 committed the United States to full-scale war in Vietnam. Military operations were quickly stepped up and "Americanized," as the United States took over the major burdens of the fight against both the Viet Cong and North Vietnam. By 1968, more than 540,000 Americans were involved in a fierce ground and air conflict. By that time, however, the war had become a seemingly endless struggle—and increasingly unpopular in this country.

In 1969, President Nixon began what he called the "Vietnamization" of the war. Over the next four years, American troops were pulled out of combat and responsibility for the fighting was turned over to the South Vietnamese. Finally, a cease-fire agreement was signed in early 1973. The United States, said President Nixon, had won "peace with honor" in South Vietnam, and the last American units were withdrawn from that country. (In spite of the cease-fire, the war between North and South Vietnam started up again almost at once. By 1975, South Vitenam had been overrun and the two Vietnams became the Socialist Republic of Vietnam.)

The ill-fated war in Vietnam cost the United States a staggering $200 billion and, irreplaceably, more than 56,000 American lives. The issue of our taking part in that conflict divided the American people for more than a decade, and more deeply than had any other issue

U.S. Army infantrymen guard a bridge in Vietnam as villagers flee a battle zone.

since the Civil War. It caused many to lose faith in the workings of the American political system—and, for that reason alone, its costs will be with us for many years to come.

Detente, and the Return to Containment. As the United States withdrew from Vietnam, the Nixon administration set out upon a policy of *detente*[12] with the two major communist powers—that is, a purposeful attempt to improve our relations with the Soviet Union and, separately, with the People's Republic of China.

Secretary of State Henry Kissinger was the chief architect of this new direction in American foreign policy—a moving away from containment toward a thawing of the tensions of the Cold War. It was built upon a number of factors. A major concern was over the rapidly rising costs, and dangers, of the nuclear arms race between this country and the Soviet Union. Another was a belief that improved relations would lead to a big increase in international trade; another was a desire to exploit worsening relations between the USSR and China.

President Nixon flew to Peking in 1972, to begin a new era in American-Chinese relations. His visit paved the way to further contacts and led finally to formal diplomatic ties between the United States and the People's Republic; see pages 460, 461.

Less than three months later, the President also journeyed to Moscow. There, he and the Soviet Premier Leonid Brezhnev signed the first Strategic Arms Limitations Talks agreement—SALT I, a five-year pact in which the two superpowers agreed to a measure of control over their nuclear weapons.

Our relations with mainland China have improved fairly steadily, on into the 1980s. Efforts at detente with the Soviet Union, proved far less successful, however. Moscow continued to apply its expansionist pressures on a global scale and provided increasing economic and military support to revolutionary movements in the Middle East, Africa, Asia, and Latin America. The spread of Soviet influence was checked in some places—in Egypt, for example, where Soviet troops and civilian technicians were expelled in 1972. But the Soviets made substantial gains elsewhere—and often with the use of Cuban troops, as in Angola in 1975 and Ethiopia in 1977.

The short-lived period of detente was ended altogether by the Russians' inva-

---

[12]The term is French, meaning a relaxation of tensions, and has long been used in international politics to describe an easing of strained relations between two or more countries.

sion of Afghanistan in 1979. From that point, an American foreign policy—under President Carter and now President Reagan—has placed renewed emphasis on containing Soviet power.

 FOR REVIEW

1. What decisive impact did World War II have on the overall shape of American foreign policy?

2. When and why did collective security become a basic plank in our foreign policy? What role did we hope the United Nations would play in the postwar world?

3. What is the policy of deterrence? Of containment?

4. Identify, describe: The Cold War. The Berlin Blockade. The Cuban Missile Crisis. The Korean War. The War in Vietnam. Detente.

Foreign Aid

The providing of economic and military aid to other countries has been a basic feature of American foreign policy for more than 40 years now. It began with the Lend-Lease program of the early 1940s, in which we gave nearly $50 billion in food, munitions, and other supplies to our allies in World War II. Since then, we have given more than $315 billion to more than 100 countries.

Foreign aid became a part of the containment policy with our aid to Greece and Turkey in 1947. Under the Marshall Plan (named for its author, Secretary of State George C. Marshall), the United States poured some $17 billion into 16 nations in Western Europe between 1948 and 1952. That massive American help prompted Western Europe's remarkable postwar economic recovery.

Our aid policy has taken several directions over time. Immediately after World War II, most of it was economic in form; in the 1950s and 1960s much of it was military. More recently, most of it has become once again economic. Until the mid-1950s, Europe received the lion's share of our help; since then, the largest amounts have gone to nations in Asia and Latin America.

On balance, most of our aid has been sent to those countries regarded as the most critical to the realization of our foreign policy objectives. Over the past 25 years, South Vietnam, Israel, and Taiwan have been the major recipients of military aid; and India has received the most in economic assistance.

Most of the foreign aid we provide must be used to buy American goods and services—and, so, most of the billions we spend for that purpose amount to a substantial subsidy to both business and labor in this country. Most of our economic aid programs are administered by the independent Agency for International Development (AID), in close cooperation with the Departments of State and Agriculture. Military aid is channeled through the Defense Department.

Security Through Alliances

Present-day American foreign policy is also based upon the concept of security through defensive alliances. Over the past 40 years the United States has concluded mutual defense treaties with more than 50 countries. Through those pacts, we have set up a network of **regional security alliances.** In each of them, the United States and the other countries involved have agreed to take collective action to meet aggression.

The *North Atlantic Treaty,* signed in 1949, established NATO—the 16-member North Atlantic Treaty Organization. The chief object of the NATO alliance is the collective defense of Western Europe—particularly against Soviet aggression. Each of its members has agreed that "an armed attack against

AMERICAN FOREIGN AID (U.S. Overseas Loans & Grants) in billions of dollars

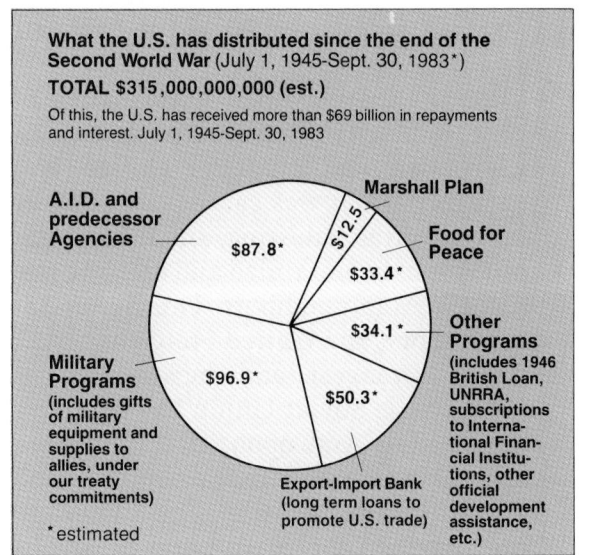

What the U.S. has distributed since the end of the Second World War (July 1, 1945-Sept. 30, 1983*)
TOTAL $315,000,000,000 (est.)
Of this, the U.S. has received more than $69 billion in repayments and interest. July 1, 1945-Sept. 30, 1983

Marshall Plan $12.5
Food for Peace $33.4*
A.I.D. and predecessor Agencies $87.8*
Other Programs (includes 1946 British Loan, UNRRA, subscriptions to International Financial Institutions, other official development assistance, etc.) $34.1*
Export-Import Bank (long term loans to promote U.S. trade) $50.3*
Military Programs (includes gifts of military equipment and supplies to allies, under our treaty commitments) $96.9*

*estimated

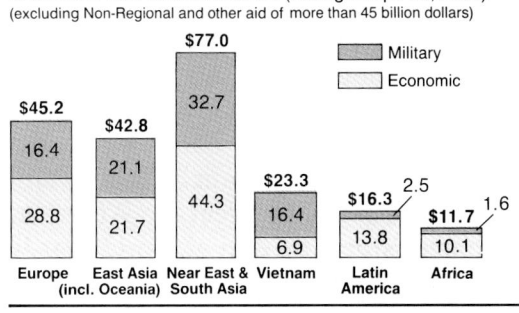

Where the U.S. distributed Aid (through Sept. 30, 1982)
(excluding Non-Regional and other aid of more than 45 billion dollars)

■ Military
□ Economic

	Europe	East Asia (incl. Oceania)	Near East & South Asia	Vietnam	Latin America	Africa
Total	$45.2	$42.8	$77.0	$23.3	$16.3	$11.7
Military	16.4	21.1	32.7	16.4	2.5	1.6
Economic	28.8	21.7	44.3	6.9	13.8	10.1

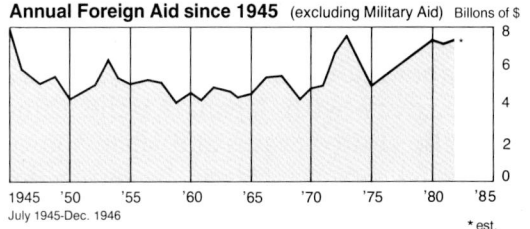

Annual Foreign Aid since 1945 (excluding Military Aid) Billons of $

1945 '50 '55 '60 '65 '70 '75 '80 '85
July 1945-Dec. 1946
* est.

Sources: Department of State, International Development Cooperation Agency; Office of Management and Budget

one or more of them in Europe or in North America shall be considered an attack against them all."

NATO was orginally composed of the United States and 11 other countries: Canada, Great Britain, France, Italy, Portugal, the Netherlands, Belgium, Luxembourg, Denmark, Norway, and Iceland. Greece and Turkey joined the alliance in 1952. West Germany did so in 1955, and Spain bacame NATO's newest member in 1982.

The NATO alliance has been the cornerstone of American foreign policy in Europe ever since its beginning. The North Atlantic Treaty Council is, made up of the foreign ministers of the 16 NATO countries. Through it, we and our allies in Western Europe have worked out political-military responses to actions of the Soviet Union.[13]

The *Rio Pact*, the Inter-American Treaty of Reciprocal Assistance, was signed in 1947. In it, the United States and now 24 Latin American countries have agreed "that an armed attack by any state against an American state shall be considered as an attack against all the American states." The treaty also pledges those countries to the peaceful settlement of all disputes between or among them.

In effect, the Rio Pact is a restatement of the Monroe Doctrine. Remember, when we made that point earlier, we also noted the fact that the United States continues to dominate the politics of the Western Hemisphere. When President Kennedy moved against the Soviet missile buildup in Cuba in 1962, he acted under the terms of the treaty. The OAS supported our actions.[14]

Economic problems and the growing political unrest in much of Latin America today point up the importance of the Rio Pact in American foreign policy. So, too, do Cuban-Soviet efforts to exploit

[13]In answer to NATO, the Soviets formed the Warsaw Treaty Organization (the Warsaw Pact) in 1955. It is a mutual defense alliance among Albania, Bulgaria, Czechoslovakia, East Germany, Hungary, Romania, and the USSR, with its headquarters in Moscow.

[14]Technically, Cuba (one of the original signers of the Rio Pact) is still a member of the OAS; but that body formally excluded Cuba from all OAS activities in 1962. That ban remains in effect today.

those conditions—most recently in Central America and the Caribbean.

The *ANZUS Pact* of 1951 unites Australia, New Zealand, and the United States in another of these defensive alliances. It reflects how important the Pacific region is to this nation's security and also the fact that much of the Pacific Ocean has been, in effect, an American lake ever since the end of World War II.

The *Japanese Pact* also dates from 1951. After six years of American military occupation, we and our World War II allies (but not the Soviet Union) signed a peact treaty with Japan. At the same time the United States and Japan signed a mutual defense treaty. In return for American protection, we are permitted to maintain land, sea, and air force in and about Japan. We have added to our own security by making a close political friend of a former enemy.

The *Philippines Pact* was also signed in 1951. As we know, the United States acquired the Philippines as a result of the Spanish-American War in 1898 and gave the islands independence in 1946. The 1951 pact is a continuing American guarantee of that independence.

The *Korean Pact* of 1953 pledges this country to come to the aid of South Korea should it be attacked again. American military forces have been stationed there since the end of the Korean War.

The United States and the Middle East. Our network of regional alliances covers several areas of the globe, each critical to American security. It does not cover all of them, however—and, most importantly today, not the Middle East.

The Middle East is both oil-rich and conflict-ridden. Its vast oil resources and its deeply-rooted frictions make it the one region of the world in which there is the greatest danger that the United States and the Soviet Union could become involved (either directly or indirectly) in a shooting war. Our foreign policy interests in the region are often torn in two quite opposite directions—by our support of Israel, and by our need for Arab oil.

Israel, the "historic homeland" of the Jewish people, was established as an independent state by the United Nations in 1948. It was carved out of what had been Arab Palestine, and it has been continuously embroiled and often at war with its Arab neighbors. During its 35-year history, the United States has been Israel's strongest and most steadfast ally; and the Soviet Union has regularly supported its Arab opposition. The more militant Arab nations, and the Palestine Liberation Organization (the PLO), are committed to the destruction of Israel.

In spite of our support of Israel, we have gone to considerable lengths to promote friendly relations with most of the Arab states—and especially because of our dependence on Arab oil. Today we import about 30 percent of all of the oil we consume in this country, and the bulk of it comes from the Middle East.

With the active involvement of President Carter, Israel and Egypt negotiated

The Camp David peace agreement is signed by Egypt's President Sadat, President Carter, and Israel's Prime Minister Begin.

THE UNITED STATES AND ITS COLLECTIVE DEFENSE ARRANGEMENTS

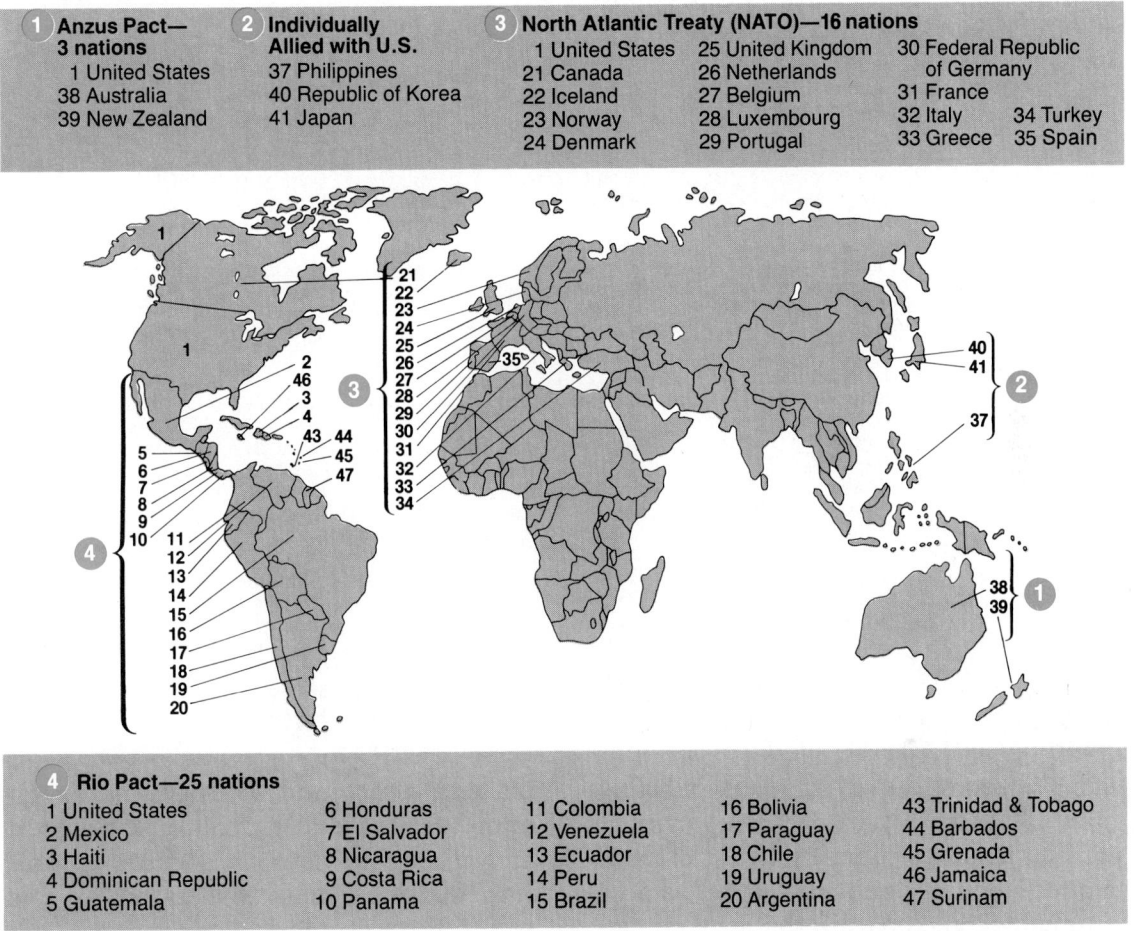

1 Anzus Pact— 3 nations
1 United States
38 Australia
39 New Zealand

2 Individually Allied with U.S.
37 Philippines
40 Republic of Korea
41 Japan

3 North Atlantic Treaty (NATO)—16 nations

1 United States	25 United Kingdom	30 Federal Republic of Germany
21 Canada	26 Netherlands	31 France
22 Iceland	27 Belgium	32 Italy 34 Turkey
23 Norway	28 Luxembourg	33 Greece 35 Spain
24 Denmark	29 Portugal	

4 Rio Pact—25 nations

1 United States	6 Honduras	11 Colombia	16 Bolivia	43 Trinidad & Tobago
2 Mexico	7 El Salvador	12 Venezuela	17 Paraguay	44 Barbados
3 Haiti	8 Nicaragua	13 Ecuador	18 Chile	45 Grenada
4 Dominican Republic	9 Costa Rica	14 Peru	19 Uruguay	46 Jamaica
5 Guatemala	10 Panama	15 Brazil	20 Argentina	47 Surinam

a peace treaty, which became effective in 1979. That agreement (the Camp David Accord) ended more than 30 years of hostilities between those two countries. But none of the other Arab states has joined the ongoing American-Israli-Egyptian effort to build peace in the Middle East—and so our precarious diplomatic balancing act there continues.

The United Nations

A major change in the pattern of American foreign policy took place dur-ing and right after World War II. That change—the shift from isolationism to a full-scale involvement in international affairs—is very clearly shown by our participation in the United Nations.

The United Nations was formed at the UN Conference on International Organization, which met in San Francisco from April 25 to June 26, 1945. There, the representatives of 51 nations—the victorious allies of World War II—drafted the United Nations Charter, which serves as its constitution.

The United States became the first nation to ratify the UN Charter. The

U.N. MEMBERSHIP, 1945 AND NOW

51 Charter Members (in alphabetical order)	
Argentina	Iraq
Australia	Lebanon
Belgium	Liberia
Bolivia	Luxembourg
Brazil	Mexico
Byelorussian S.S.R.	Netherlands
Canada	New Zealand
Chile	Nicaragua
China	Norway
Colombia	Panama
Costa Rica	Paraguay
Cuba	Peru
Czechoslovakia	Philippines
Denmark	Poland
Dominican Republic	Saudi Arabia
Ecuador	South Africa
Egypt	Syria
El Salvador	Turkey
Ethiopia	Ukrainian S.S.R.
France	Union of Soviet
Greece	Socialist Republics
Guatemala	United Kingdom
Haiti	United States
Honduras	Uruguay
India	Venezuela
Iran	Yugoslavia

Admitted since 1945			
Afghanistan	Equatorial	Malawi	Seychelles
Albania	Guinea	Malaysia	Sierra Leone
Algeria	Fiji	Maldives	Singapore
Angola	Finland	Mali	Solomon Islands
Antigua	Gabon	Malta	Somalia
and Barbuda	Gambia	Mauritania	Spain
Austria	Ghana	Mauritius	Sri Lanka
Bahamas	Grenada	Mongolia	Sudan
Bahrain	Guinea	Morocco	Suriname
Bangladesh	Guinea-Bissau	Mozambique	Swaziland
Barbados	Guyana	Nepal	Sweden
Belizes	Hungary	Niger	Tanzania
Benin	Iceland	Nigeria	Thailand
Bhutan	Indonesia	Oman	Togo
Botswana	Ireland	Pakistan	Trinidad and
Bulgaria	Israel	Papua-	Tobago
Burma	Italy	New Guinea	Tunisia
Burundi	Ivory Coast	Portugal	Uganda
Cameroon	Jamaica	Qatar	United Arab
Cape Verde	Japan	Romania	Emirates
Central African	Jordan	Rwanda	Upper Volta
Republic	Kampuchea	St. Lucia	Vanuata
Chad	(Cambodia)	St. Vincent	Vietnam
Comoros Islands	Kenya	and the	West Germany
Congo	Kuwait	Grenadines	Yemen Arab Rep.
Cyprus	Laos	Samoa	Yemen Dem. Rep.
Dominica	Lesotho	Sao Tome	Zaire
Djibouti	Libya	and Principe	Zambia
East Germany	Madagascar	Senegal	Zimbabwe

Senate approved it by an overwhelming vote, 89–2, on July 24, 1945. It was then ratified in quick order by Great Britain, France, China, and the other states which had taken part in the San Francisco Conference. The Charter went into force on October 24, 1945; and the UN held its first formal meeting in London on January 10, 1946.

The UN Charter

The Charter is a lengthy document. It consists of a preamble and 111 articles that set forth the purposes, structure, and powers of the United Nations.

The Charter opens with an eloquent preamble which states that the UN was created "to save succeeding generations from the sourge of war." The body of the document begins in Article I with a statement of the organization's purposes. They are: the maintenance of international peace and security, the development of friendly relations between and among all nations, and the promotion of justice and cooperation in the solution of international problems.

Membership. Today the UN has 157 members. Under the Charter, membership is open to those "peace-loving states" which accept the obligations of the Charter and are, in the UN's judgment, able and willing to carry them out. New members may be admitted by a two-thirds vote of the General Assembly, upon recommendation by the Security Council.

Basic Organization. The Charter sets forth the complicated structure of the UN, built around six "principal organs": the General Assembly, the Security Council, the Economic and Social Council, the Trusteeship Council, the International Court of Justice, and the Secretariat.

The General Assembly

The General Assembly has been called "the town meeting of the world." It is composed of representatives of each of the UN's now 157 member nations, each having one vote.

The Assembly meets once a year, normally in September. Most of its sessions are held at the UN's permanent headquarters, in New York. Special sessions may be called by the Secretary General, either at the request of the Security Council or a majority of the members of the UN.

The Assembly may take up and debate any matter within the scope of the Charter,[15] and it may make whatever recommendation it chooses to the Security Council, the other UN organs, and any or all of the member-states. The recommendations it makes to UN members are not legally binding upon them; but they do carry weight because they have been approved by a significant number of the governments of the world. On important questions, such as those on finances, decisions must be made by a two-thirds vote. On lesser matters, a simple majority vote is enough.

The Assembly elects the 10 nonpermanent members of the Security Council, the 54 members of the Economic and Social Council, and the elective members of the Trusteeship Council. With the Security Council, it also selects the Secretary General and the 15 judges of the International Court of Justice. It also shares with the Security Council the power to admit, suspend, or expel members of the UN. It alone may propose amendments to the Charter.

The Assembly controls the UN's finances. It sets the biennial budget and the share of it that each member must pay. The UN's regular budget for 1983–1984 is slightly less than $2 billion. The United States pays about one-fourth of that total. The minimum payment for any member, paid by many of the smaller states, is now 1/100 of one percent of the budget—less than $100,000 per year.

The Security Council

The Security Council is made up of 15 members. Five of them—the United States, Britain, France, the Soviet Union, and China—are permanent members of the Council. The 10 nonpermanent members are chosen by the General Assembly for two-year terms; they cannot be immediately reelected. The Council meets in continuous session at the UN's headquarters.[16]

The Security Council bears the UN's major responsibility for maintaining international peace, and it may take up any matter involving a threat to or a breach of that peace. It may adopt measures which range from calling upon the parties to settle their differences peacefully to placing economic and/or military sanctions upon an offending nation. The only time the Security Council has undertaken a military operation against an aggressor came in answer to North Korea's invasion of South Korea in 1950. It has provided for a number of UN peace-keeping forces in trouble spots however—notably in the Middle East.

On *procedural* questions—routine matters—decisions of the Security Council can be made by the affirmative vote of any nine members. On the more important matters—*substantive* questions—nine affirmative votes are

---

[15]Except those matters currently under consideration by the Security Council. This restriction is to prevent the confusion that could come from a simultaneous consideration of some matter by the UN's two major organs.

[16]The number of nonpermanent members on the Security Council was increased from 6 to 10 by a 1965 amendment to the Charter. In 1971 the People's Republic of China replaced the Nationalist Chinese regime on Taiwan as a permanent member of the Security Council (and acquired China's membership in the UN in all other respects, as well.)

THE UNITED NATIONS

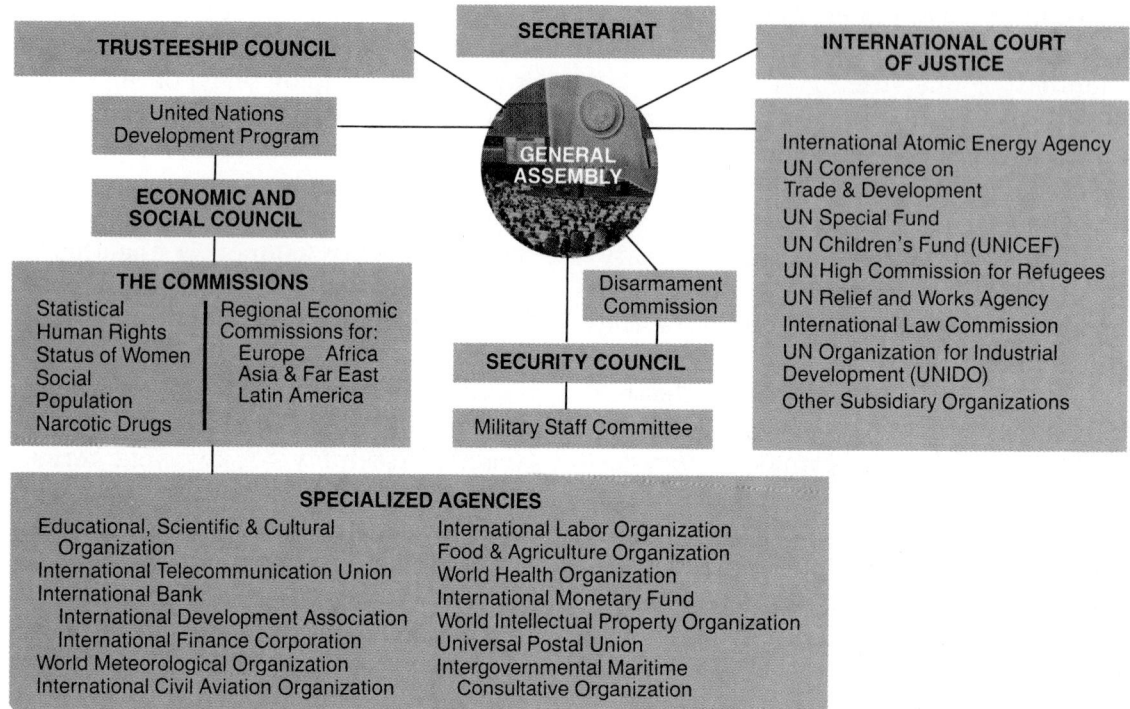

also needed, *but* they *must* include the vote of each of the permanent members. Thus, each of the five permanent members has a veto power which it can use to prevent Security Council action on any important matter.

Because of the veto power, the Security Council is effective only when and if the Big Five (the permanent members) cooperate. The Soviet Union has often used its veto to block UN actions; to date, it has cast more than 115 vetoes. The other permanent members have used it much less often. The United States did not cast its first veto until 1970 and has since done so only some 35 times (to 1984).[17]

The United Nation's Security Council works to maintain international peace and deals with incidents which threaten that peace.

---

[17]When, on June 25, 1950, the Security Council called upon all UN members to aid South Korea to repel the North Korean invasion, the Soviet delegate was boycotting sessions of the Security Council and so was not present to veto that action. The Soviets have not repeated their boycott tactic in more than 30 years now.

The Economic and Social Council

The Economic and Social Council is made up of 54 members elected by the General Assembly to three-year terms. It is responsible to the Assembly for carrying out economic, cultural, educational, health, and related activities. It also coordinates the work of the UN's Specialized Agencies—see facing page.

The Trusteeship Council

The UN Charter requires each member to promote the interests and well-being of the peoples of all "non-self-governing territories" as a "sacred trust." It sets guidelines for the government of all dependent areas and makes rules for the administration of all UN trust territories.[18] The Council receives periodic reports from all of the member-states with non-self-governing possessions and seeks to encourage self-government for all dependent peoples.

The International Court of Justice

The International Court of Justice is the UN's judicial arm. All members of the UN are automatically parties to the ICJ Statute; and under certain conditions the services of the Court are also available to non-member states. A UN member may agree to accept the Court's jurisdiction over cases in which it may become involved either unconditionally or with certain reservations, so long as they do not conflict with the ICJ Statute.

The ICJ is made up of 15 judges selected for nine-year terms by the General Assembly and the Security Council. It sits in permanent session at The Hague, in the Netherlands. It handles cases brought to it voluntarily by both members and non-members of the UN. The ICJ also advises the other UN organs on legal questions arising out of

their activities. If any party to a dispute fails to obey a judgment of the Court, the other party may take that matter to the Security Council.

The Secretariat

The Secretariat is the civil service branch of the UN. It is headed by the Secretary-General, who is chosen to a five-year term by the General Assembly upon the recommendation of the Security Council. The staff of the Secretariat now members some 18,000 men and women, drawn from UN member-states.

José Perez de Cuellar, a Peruvian diplomat, is now the Secretary General. He became the UN's top administrative officer in 1982. In addition to his housekeeping chores, the Charter gives him a very important power. He may bring before the Security Council any matter which he believes poses a threat to international peace and security.

☑ **FOR REVIEW**

1. Why has the United States provided massive amounts of foreign aid since the end of World War II?

2. Why have we built a network of regional security alliances covering much of the globe? What is the nature of each of those alliances?

3. Our foreign policy interests in the Middle East are torn by what two often conflicting considerations?

4. When, where, and by whom was the UN Charter drafted? What, according to the Charter, are the UN's basic purposes?

5. The UN began with how many members? How many are there today?

6. What are the UN's six principal organs? Their major functions? What organ has the veto power?

---

[18]There were at one time 11 of those territories. Today there is but one: the Trust Territory of the Pacific Islands, administered by the United States.

S U M M A R Y

America's foreign and defense policies have one major purpose. They are designed to protect the security of the United States.

American foreign policy consists of all of the official statements and actions of the Government of the United States that have a bearing on foreign relations. In effect, then, our foreign policy is made up of all of our many foreign policies. Although Congress has a number of important powers in the field, the President is the country's chief diplomat. The Secretary of State is the President's principal aide in both making and carrying out foreign policy. The State Department, headed by the Secretary, is set up on both a functional and a geographic basis. It includes the Foreign Service, made up of our diplomatic agents abroad.

The Constitution makes defense a national function and places control of the nation's military establishment in civilian hands. Congress has several important war powers and the President is the commander in chief of the armed forces. The Secretary of Defense is the President's chief aide in all defense matters. The Defense Department, headed by the Secretary includes the sub-Cabinet Departments of the Army, the Navy, and the Air Force.

Several other federal agencies also work in the fields of foreign affairs and defense—in particular, the Central Intelligence Agency, the International Communications Agency, the National Aeronautics and Space Administration, the United States Arms Control and Disarmament Agency, and the Selective Service System.

World War II brought about a major change in American foreign policy—from an historic pattern of isolationism to a full-scale involvement in world politics. That dramatic shift is reflected in these basic features of present-day American foreign policy: collective security, deterrence, containment, foreign aid, and regional security alliances.

C H A P T E R   R E V I E W

Key Terms/Concepts

Central Intelligence Agency (454)
Chief Diplomat (446)
Civil control of the military (450)
Clandestine (455)
Cold War (464)
Collective security (462)
Containment (464)

Department of Defense (450)
Detente (467)
Deterrence (463)
Diplomatic immunity (448)
Draft (456)
Foreign aid (468)
Foreign policy (446)
Good Neighbor Policy (459)
Isolationism (445)

Monroe Doctrine (458)
National security (457)
"One world" (445)
Open Door Policy (460)
Passport (450)
Regional security alliances (468)
Right of legation (448)
Selective service (456)

Truman Doctrine (464)
United Nations (471)
Veto (474)
Visa (450)

1. What is, and always has been, the basic aim of this nation's foreign and defense policies?
2. To whom does the Constitution assign powers in the field of foreign affairs? National defense?
3. Who is the nation's chief diplomat? The commander in chief?
4. What is the primary role of the Secretary of State? Of Defense?
5. Why does the Constitution provide for civilian control of the nation's military forces?
6. What is the function of the CIA? The ICA? NASA? The USACDA?
7. What is the status of the draft today?
8. Why was isolationism the dominant feature of American foreign policy for 150 years? Was the Monroe Doctrine a departure from that policy?
9. World War II brought what fundamental change to the basic shape of American foreign policy?
10. Identify the major features of present-day American foreign policy.
11. The UN Charter declares that the international organization exists to serve what three major purposes?
12. What are the six principal organs of the UN? Their major functions? What is the veto power?

1. It is often said that the only truly effective checks on the Government's powers in foreign affairs are political, not legal in character. Explain the meaning and gauge the accuracy of that observation.
2. Constitutionally, the President and Congress share power in the fields of foreign affairs and defense. What factors have led to the fact of presidential supremacy in both?
3. What did President Eisenhower mean when he said: "Americans, indeed all free men, remember that in the final choice a soldier's pack is not so heavy a burden as a prisoner's chains"?
4. Some say that the history of the United States demonstrates that we are not in fact "a peace-loving people." How do you respond to that view?
5. The United States (as well as the Soviet Union) insisted upon the veto power in the Security Council when the UN Charter was drafted. Why? The United States has never favored the abolition of the veto. Why?

1. List as many illustrations as you can of the ways in which the content and the conduct of U.S. foreign and defense policies are reflected in the everyday life of your community.
2. Select one of the 58 men, from Thomas Jefferson to George Shultz, who have served as Secretary of State. Write a brief biography of that personality and a summary of our foreign relations during the period in which he served as Secretary.
3. Invite a veteran and/or a present member of the armed forces to speak on the subject of military service.
4. Stage a debate or class forum on one of the following questions: (a) *Resolved*, That Congress provide for a system of universal military training and service; (b) *Resolved*, That the United States withdraw from the United Nations; (c) *Resolved*, That the Constitution be amended to provide that the United States cannot make war in any circumstances until such action is approved by a vote of the people.
5. Prepare a report on some current or recent problem or event in foreign relations—for example, our policy toward China, the OPEC nations, or the PLO; Soviet-Cuban involvements in Central America; the American-Soviet arms race; or the current status of the NATO alliance.

UNIT SIX

The Federal Judiciary

In the American system of separation of powers, it is the prime function of the legislative branch to make the law, of the executive branch to enforce and administer the law, and of the judicial branch to interpret and apply the law. As the great Chief Justice John Marshall declared in *Marbury* v. *Madison*, "It is emphatically the province and the duty of the judicial department to say what the law is." By "the judicial department" he meant the federal courts.

As with the Congress and the Presidency, the federal "judicial department"—and particularly the Supreme Court of the United States—has played a major part in the building of the American constitutional system. Throughout our history, it has been true—and it is true today—that, as Chief Justice Charles Evans Hughes put it, "The Constitution means what the judges say it means."

The democratic ideal insists that there are areas of activity prohibited to government and into which government may not intrude. In America, it is upon the courts that major reliance is placed for the preservation of this concept of limited government.

One of the distinctive features of the American legal system is its two-fold organization. There are two separate and distinct judicial structures, one for the Federal Government, and the other for the 50 States—actually 50 separate structures. Unit Six in this book deals with the federal courts. (The State courts are dealt with in the next unit, in Chapter 22.)

In the single chapter of Unit Six we deal with the structure, jurisdiction, and operations of the national court system. We also consider the judges and other court officers. Finally, we look at the several responsibilities of the Department of Justice.

The Old Supreme Court Chamber, used from 1810 to 1860, has many of the original furnishings.

18

The Federal Court System

To help you to
Learn ▪ Know ▪ Understand

The basic role of the judiciary in the governmental process.

The structure of the federal judiciary, the jurisdiction of the several different federal courts, and the role of the Supreme Court as the nation's highest court.

Judicial review and its extraordinary significance in the American governmental system.

The process by which federal judges are selected.

It is emphatically the province and the duty of the judicial department to say what the law is.

Chief Justice John Marshall
Marbury v. Madison (1803)

We have spoken of the Supreme Court and the other courts in the federal judiciary often to this point. We shall now take a systematic look at the judicial branch of the National Government.

Most of the authors of the Constitution pointed to the lack of a national judiciary as a major weakness in the government set up by the Articles of Confederation. They believed that an independent judiciary—a system of *national* courts—was needed if the new government they had put together at Philadelphia was to work.

Over the time the Articles were in force (from 1781 to 1789), the laws of the United States were interpreted and applied among the States as each of them chose (or chose not) to do. Disputes between States, and between residents of different States, were decided—if at all—by the courts of one of the States involved.[1] Often, decisions by the courts of one State were neither accepted nor enforced in the others.

Alexander Hamilton spoke to the point in *The Federalist* No. 78. He described "the want of a national judiciary" as a "circumstance which crowns

---

[1]The Articles of Confederation did provide (in Article IX) a complicated procedure for the settlement of disputes between States, but it was not often used.

The nation's highest court met in several places in Washington before it moved to the United States Supreme Court Building in 1935 (see photo, page 478).

the defects of the Confederation." And, he added:

> Laws are dead letters without courts to expound and define their true meaning and operation.

To meet the need, the Framers wrote Article III, which creates the national judiciary in a single sentence:

> The judicial power of the United States shall be vested in one Supreme Court, and in such inferior courts as the Congress may from time to time ordain and establish.

And Congress is given the expressed power "to constitute tribunals inferior to the Supreme Court," in Article I, Section 8, Clause 9.

A Dual Court System

In this chapter we are especially concerned with the national court system—that is with the Supreme Court, created by the Constitution, and with the other federal courts, set up by act of Congress. But keep this point in mind: There are in fact *two* separate court systems in the United States.[2] On the one hand there is the national judiciary, with its more than 100 courts across the country. On the other, each of the 50 States has its own system of courts. Their number runs well into the thousands. We shall turn to the State courts in Chapter 22.

Types of Federal Courts

Beneath the Supreme Court, Congress has created two distinct types of federal courts: (1) constitutional courts and (2) special courts.

The **constitutional courts** are the fed-

---

[2]Notice that federalism does not require two separate court systems. In fact, in most other federal governments the principal courts are those of the states (or provinces) which make up the federation. The only significant federal court is a national supreme court which serves as a court of last resort.

eral courts that Congress has formed under Article III, to exercise "the judicial power of the United States." They are sometimes called the "regular courts." Together with the Supreme Court, they now include: the Courts of Appeals, the District Courts, and the Court of International Trade.

The **special courts** do not exercise the broad "judicial power of the United States." Rather, they have been created by Congress to hear cases arising out of certain of the expressed powers given to Congress in Article I. They hear a much narrower range of cases than those which may come before the constitutional courts.

These special courts are sometimes called the "legislative courts." Today, they include the Court of Military Appeals, the Claims Court, the Tax Court, the various territorial courts, and the courts of the District of Columbia.

✔ **F O R   R E V I E W**

1. Why did the Framers provide for a national judiciary?
2. Which Article in the Constitution deals mostly with the judiciary? What does it provide?
3. Why is there a dual system of courts in the United States?
4. What is the chief difference between the constitutional and the special courts?

The Constitutional Courts

Jurisdiction

The term **jurisdiction** may be defined as the authority of a court to hear (to *try* and to *decide*) a case. The term means, literally, the power "to say the law."

Under Article III the federal courts have jurisdiction over a case either be-

cause of (1) the subject matter or (2) the parties involved in the case.

Subject Matter. In terms of subject matter, the federal courts may hear a case if it deals with:

(1) the interpretation and application of a provision in the Constitution or in any federal statute or treaty; or
(2) a question of admiralty or maritime law.[3]

Any case which falls into either of these categories can be brought in the proper federal court.

Parties. A case comes within the jurisdiction of the federal courts if any of the parties (one of the *litigants*) in the case is:

(1) the United States or one of its officers or agencies;
(2) an ambassador, consul, or other official representative of a foreign government;
(3) a State suing another State, or a citizen of another State, or a foreign government or one of its subjects;[4]
(4) a citizen of one State suing a citizen of another State;
(5) an American citizen suing a foreign government or one of its subjects;
(6) a citizen of one State suing a citizen of that same State where both claim land under grants from different States.

Any case in the above categories can be brought in the proper federal court.

---

[3]**Admiralty law** relates to matters which arise on the high seas or the navigable waters of the United States—*e.g.*, crimes committed aboard ships, collisions, and the like. **Maritime law** relates to matters arising on land but directly related to the water—*e.g.*, a contract to deliver ship's supplies at dockside. The Framers gave the federal courts exclusive jurisdiction in all admiralty and maritime cases to make certain of national supremacy in the regulation of all waterborne commerce.

[4]Note that the 11th Amendment says that a State may not be sued in the federal courts by a citizen of another State or of a foreign state. A State may be sued without its consent in the federal courts only by the United States, another State, or a foreign state.

All of those cases which are not heard by the federal courts are within the jurisdiction of the States' courts. (As we shall see in Chapter 22, the State courts hear by far the larger number of court cases in this country.)

Still more must be said on the federal courts' power "to say the law."

Exclusive and Concurrent Jurisdiction. In several of the categories of cases which we have just listed, the federal courts have **exclusive jurisdiction.** That is, those cases can be heard *only* in the federal courts. For example, a a trial for a federal crime cannot be heard in a State court; it must be held in a federal District Court.

Many cases may be tried in *either* a federal *or* a State court, however. That is, the federal and State courts have **concurrent jurisdiction** over them. Cases involving citizens of different States are fairly common examples of the type. They are known in the law as cases in *diverse citizenship.*[5]

Congress has provided that the federal District Courts may hear cases in diverse citizenship only if the amount of money in each case is over $10,000. In these cases the *plaintiff*[6] may bring the suit in the proper State or federal court, as he or she chooses. If the case is brought before the State court, the *defendant*[7] may have it moved to the federal District Court.

Original and Appellate Jurisdiction. A court in which a case is heard first-hand is said to have **original jurisdiction** over it. A court which hears a case on appeal from a lower court has **appellate jurisdiction.**

In the federal court system, the Dis-

---

[5]The major reason cases in diverse citizenship may be heard in federal courts is to provide a neutral forum to settle the disputes involved.

[6]A **plaintiff** is one who brings a suit in law against another.

[7]A **defendant** is a party who must make answer, defend against a complaint, in a legal action.

Drawing by Joseph Mirachi; © 1977 The New Yorker Magazine, Inc.

"Quasi-innocent, Your Honor."

trict Courts have only original jurisdiction and the Courts of Appeals have only appellate jurisdiction. The Supreme Court has both.

The District Courts

The United States District Courts are the federal trial courts. They now handle over 200,000 cases a year—some 90 percent of all of the federal case load.

The District Courts were set up by Congress in the Judiciary Act of 1789. There are now 91 of them. The 50 States are divided into 89 judicial districts, with one court in each district. There is also a District Court in the District of Columbia and another in Puerto Rico.

Each State forms at least one federal judicial district. The larger, more populous States are divided into two or more districts—because of the greater amount of judicial business arising in them, of course.

At least one judge is assigned to each district, but many have several. Thus, New York is divided into four judicial districts; and one, the United States Judicial District for Southern New York, now has 27 judges. All told, 507 judges now preside over the 91 federal District Courts.

Cases tried in the District Courts are

most often heard by a single judge; but certain cases may be heard by a three-judge panel.[8]

Jurisdiction.   The District Courts have original jurisdiction over most of the cases heard in the federal courts. Clearly, then, they handle many different kinds of cases. They hear criminal cases ranging from bank robbery, kidnapping, and mail fraud to counterfeiting, tax evasion, and treason. They try civil cases arising under the bankruptcy, postal, tax, labor relations, public lands, civil rights, and other laws of the United States.[9] The District Courts are the only federal courts that regularly use *grand juries* (to indict) and *petit juries* (to try) defendants.

Cases decided in the District Courts do not often go further in the judicial process. But they may be appealed to the Court of Appeals in that judicial circuit, as we shall see. In a few instances, they may be taken directly to the Supreme Court, as we shall also see shortly.

The Courts of Appeals

The Courts of Appeals were formed in 1891. They were intended to relieve the Supreme Court of much of the burden of hearing appeals from the District Courts.[10] There were so many appeals

that the High Court was then three years behind its docket.

There are now 12 Courts of Appeals. The United States is divided into 11 judicial circuits. There is a Court of Appeals for each of those circuits and also one in the District of Columbia.

Altogether, 132 circuit judges sit on these appellate courts. In addition, a Justice of the Supreme Court is assigned to each of them. Take the United States Court of Appeals for the Seventh Circuit, for example. The Seventh Circuit covers three States: Illinois, Indiana, and Wisconsin. The court has nine circuit judges, and Supreme Court John Paul Stevens is also assigned to the circuit. The court sits in Chicago. As another: the Fifth Circuit encompasses three States: Louisiana, Mississippi, and Texas. Its Court of Appeals has 13 judges, plus Associate Justice Byron R. White. It holds its sessions in a number of different cities within the circuit.

Each of the Courts of Appeals usually sits in panels of three judges. Once in a while, to hear an important case, a court will sit *en banc*—that is, with all of the circuit judges participating.

Jurisdiction.   The Courts of Appeals have only appellate jurisdiction. Most often, their cases come from the District Courts within their circuits. They hear cases appealed from the United States Tax Court and from the territorial courts, as well. They also hear appeals from the decisions of several federal regulatory agencies—from such quasi-judicial agencies as the Interstate Commerce Commission, the Civil Aeronautics Board, and the Federal Trade Commission, as we noted earlier on page 428.

The Courts of Appeals now handle about 25,000 cases a year. Their decisions are final—except in those (very few) cases the Supreme Court agrees to hear on appeal.

---

[8]Congress has directed that three-judge panels hear certain cases. Chiefly, these are cases that involve congressional districting or State legislative apportionment questions, those arising under the Civil Rights Act of 1964 or the Voting Rights Acts of 1965, 1970, 1975, and 1982, and certain anti-trust actions.

[9]In the federal courts, a **criminal case** is one in which a defendant has been charged with and is tried for committing a federal crime (*i.e.,* some action that Congress has declared by law to be a crime, a wrong against the public). A federal **civil case** involves some non-criminal matter—such as a dispute over the terms of a contract or a claim of patent infringement.

[10]These tribunals were originally known as the Circuit Courts of Appeals. Before 1891, Supreme Court Justices "rode circuit" to hear appeals from the District Courts. Congress renamed them in 1948, but they still are often called the Circuit Courts.

There is yet another federal court with a quite similar title but a quite different role—the Court of Appeals for the Federal Circuit. It was created by Congress in 1982; see 493.

FEDERAL JUDICIAL CIRCUITS AND DISTRICTS

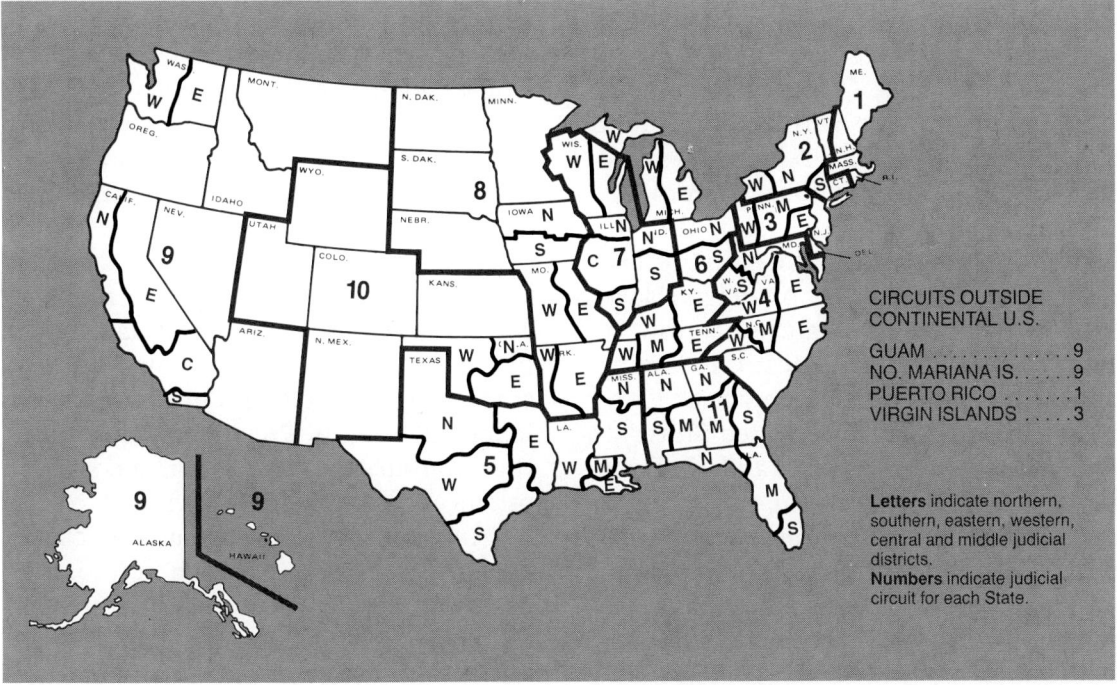

CIRCUITS OUTSIDE
CONTINENTAL U.S.

GUAM 9
NO. MARIANA IS. 9
PUERTO RICO 1
VIRGIN ISLANDS 3

Letters indicate northern, southern, eastern, western, central and middle judicial districts.
Numbers indicate judicial circuit for each State.

 FOR REVIEW

1. On what two general bases do the federal courts have jurisdiction over cases?

2. Distinguish between *exclusive jurisdiction* and *concurrent jurisdiction; original jurisdiction* and *appellate jurisdiction.*

3. There are how many federal District Courts today? How many District Court judges?

4. What is a United States Judicial District? How many are there?

5. Over what cases do the District Courts have jurisdiction?

6. Why were the Courts of Appeals created? How many are there today? How many circuit judges?

7. What is a Judicial Circuit? How many are there?

8. From where do cases reach the Courts of Appeals?

The Supreme Court

The Supreme Court of the United States is the only court specifically created in the Constitution.[11] It is made up of the Chief Justice of the United States, whose office is also established by the Constitution,[12] and eight Associate Justices.[13]

---

[11]Article III, Section 1.
[12]Article I, Section 3, Clause 6.
[13]Congress sets the number of Associate Justices and thus the size of the Supreme Court. The Judiciary Act of 1789 created a Court of six Justices, including the Chief Justice. Its size was reduced to five members in 1801, but increased to seven in 1807, to nine in 1837, and to 10 in 1863. It was reduced to seven in 1866 and raised to its present size in 1869.

It would be just about impossible to overstate the significance of the role of the Supreme Court in both the development and the present-day operations of the American system of government. The Framers of the Constitution placed it on an equal plane with the President and Congress. It was designed as the apex of the nation's judicial system. As the highest court in the land, the Supreme Court stands as the court of last resort in *all* questions of federal law. That is, it is the final authority in *any* case involving *any* question arising under the Constitution, an act of Congress, or a treaty of the United States.

The Supreme Court and Judicial Review. As we've noted, most courts in this country, federal and State, may exercise the highly important power of *judicial review.* That is, they have the extraordinary power to decide the constitutionality of an act of government, whether executive, legislative, or judicial (see page 54). The *ultimate* exercise of that power rests with the Supreme Court of the United States. That single fact makes the Supreme Court the final authority on the Constitution's meaning.

The Constitution does not *in so many words* provide for the power of judicial review. But there is little room for doubt that the Framers intended that the federal courts—and in particular, the Supreme Court—would have the power, and exercise it.

The Court first asserted that it had the power in the classic case of *Marbury* v. *Madison* in 1803.[14] The case arose after the stormy elections of 1800. Thomas Jefferson and his Anti-Federalists had won the Presidency and

control of both houses of Congress.

The outgoing Federalists, stung by their defeat, then tried to pack the judiciary with loyal party members. Several new federal judgeships were created by Congress in the early weeks of 1801. President John Adams quickly filled those posts with good Federalists.

William Marbury had been appointed a justice of the peace for the District of Columbia. The Senate had confirmed his appointment and, late the night of March 3, 1801, the President had signed his and a number of other new judges' commissions of office. On the next day Jefferson became President—and found that Marbury's commission, and several others, had not been delivered.

Angered by the Federalists' court-packing, Jefferson at once told James Madison, the new Secretary of State, not to deliver those commissions to the "midnight justices." Marbury then sued Madison in the Supreme Court, seeking a *writ of mandamus*[15] to compel delivery.

Marbury based his suit on a provision of the Judiciary Act of 1789, in which Congress had given the Supreme Court the right to hear such suits in its *original* jurisdiction (not on appeal from a lower court).

In a unanimous opinion written by Chief Justice John Marshall, the Court refused Marbury's request.[16] It did so because it found the pertinent section of the Judiciary Act in conflict with the

---

[14]It is often said that the Court first *exercised* the power in this case; but, in fact, the Court did so at least as early as *Hylton* v. *United States* in 1796. In that case it *upheld* the constitutionality of a tax Congress had levied on carriages.

[15]A court order compelling an officer of government to perform an act which that officer has a clear legal duty to perform.

[16]Marshall was appointed Chief Justice by President John Adams, and he took office on January 31, 1801. He served in the post for 34 years, until his death on July 6, 1835. He also served as Adams' Secretary of State, from May 13, 1800 to March 4, 1801. Thus he served as Secretary of State *and* as Chief Justice for more than a month at the end of the Adams administration. What is more, he was the Secretary of State who had failed to deliver Marbury's commission in timely fashion.

PERSONALITY PROFILE

SANDRA DAY O'CONNOR

In January 1980, Donna Gallus, a St. Cloud, Minnesota high school student, wrote to Supreme Court Justice Potter Stewart. She wrote her letter as part of a class assignment. In it, among other things, she asked the 65-year-old jurist about his plans for leaving the

post he had held for more than 20 years. And, when he announced his retirement the next year, Stewart said that that letter had triggered his thoughts about stepping down.

Little could Donna know that her

letter would set off a chain of events that would lead to the appointment of the first woman to the nation's High Court. In July, 1981, President Reagan named Sandra Day O'Connor to succeed Justice Stewart. She was confirmed, unanimously, by the Senate in September and so became the 102nd Justice to be appointed to the Supreme Court.

Mrs. O'Connor brought years of experience to the Court. Born in 1930, she was raised on a ranch near Duncan, Arizona. She graduated from Stanford University Law School at the age of 22, with highest honors. After several years in private practice in Arizona, she became an assistant attorney general there in 1965. In 1969, the staunch Republican was elected to the State senate, where she became the first woman to serve as majority leader. In 1974, she was elected to the Superior Court for Maricopa County, and in 1979 Governor Bruce Babbitt, a Democrat, appointed her to the State Court of Appeals.

1. Why do you suppose that a woman was not appointed to the Supreme Court until 1981?
2. What more can you discover about Justice O'Connor's background? Her appointment? The positions she has taken in cases before the Court?

Constitution and, therefore, void. More exactly, it found the statute in conflict with Article III, Section 2, Clause 2 which reads in part:

In all cases affecting ambassadors,

other public ministers and consuls, and those in which a State shall be a party, the Supreme Court shall have original jurisdiction. In all other cases before mentioned, the Supreme Court shall have appellate jurisdiction . . .

Marshall's powerful opinion was based upon these three propositions: (1) The Constitution is, by its own terms, *the* supreme law of the land. (2) All legislative enactments, and all other actions of government, are subordinate to and cannot be allowed to conflict with the supreme law. And (3) judges are sworn to enforce the provisions of the Constitution and therefore must refuse to enforce any governmental action they find to be in conflict with it.

The dramatic and often far-reaching effects of the Supreme Court's exercise

INTERPRETING PICTURES

WHAT DO YOU SEE?

Much of our information comes from pictures, especially photographs and film (including television). Before photography, film, and television people had to depend on listening and reading for the information they desired. Today, watching or viewing is a common means of obtaining information. In an average week, how much time do you spend watching movies and television? (The national average is about six hours per day.)

Although the claim that "one picture is worth a thousand words" is probably exaggerated, pictures are useful sources of information. But, they can be misleading. If you had several photographs taken of yourself on the same day, each one would be different from the others. They might differ in terms of the angle, the amount of light, the distance (close up or a longer shot), and your facial expression. As a result, each photo would present a different impression of you. Film also can be misleading when it emphasizes some things and leaves out others. Here are some suggestions for developing the skill of careful, critical viewing.

First, describe the content of the picture. What do you see? What else do you notice? For example, what objects, people, and actions are shown? How are they related?

Second, try to interpret the picture by identifying its main idea or purpose. What message does the picture send? What impression does it create? What clues or details in the picture contribute to that impression?

Third, try to determine how accurately the picture represents the subject. In what ways, if any, does it distort things? For example, what does it emphasize? What does it leave out? One way to tell is by comparing the picture in question with other pictures or sources of information. An unflattering picture of a presidential candidate, for example, might be used by an opponent to influence voters.

Look at the Supreme Court Justices on the next page and answer the following questions.

1. What do you see? What else do you notice?
2. What impression does the photo create? How does it do that?
3. How fairly does this photo seem to portray the Justices?
4. What do you see, with a second look, that you missed the first time?

JUSTICES OF THE SUPREME COURT

Name	State From Which Appointed	President By Whom Appointed	Year of Birth	Year Appointed
Chief Justice:				
Warren E. Burger	Minnesota	Nixon	1907	1969
Associate Justices:				
William J. Brennan, Jr.	New Jersey	Eisenhower	1906	1956
Byron R. White	Colorado	Kennedy	1918	1962
Thurgood Marshall	Maryland	Johnson	1908	1967
Harry A. Blackmun	Minnesota	Nixon	1908	1970
Lewis F. Powell, Jr.	Virginia	Nixon	1907	1972
William H. Rehnquist	Arizona	Nixon	1924	1972
John Paul Stevens	Illinois	Ford	1916	1975
Sandra Day O'Connor	Arizona	Reagan	1930	1981

of the power of judicial review tends to overshadow much of its other work. Each year it hears dozens of cases in which questions of constitutionality are *not* raised but in which federal law still is interpreted and applied. Thus, many of the more important statutes Congress has passed have been brought to the Supreme Court time and again for decision. So, too, have many of the lesser ones. In interpreting those laws and applying them to specific situations, the Court has had a real impact upon their meaning and effect.

Remember, too, that the Court has a very large role as the "umpire" in the federal system, as we noted on page 71.

Jurisdiction. The Supreme Court has both original and appellate jurisdiction. Most of all, however, it is an appellate tribunal. Most of the cases it hears come to it on appeal from the lower federal courts and from the State supreme courts.

Article III, Section 2 spells out two classes of cases which may be heard by

From left to right, the nine Justices of the Supreme Court today: Justices Blackmun, Marshall, and Brennan, Chief Justice Burger, and Justices O'Connor, White, Powell, Rehnquist, and Stevens.

the High Court in its *original* jurisdiction: (1) those to which a State is a party; and (2) those affecting ambassadors, other public ministers, and consuls.

Congress cannot enlarge upon this constitutional grant of original jurisdiction.

Recall, this is what the Court held in *Marbury* v. *Madison.* If Congress could do so, it would in effect be amending the Constitution. But Congress can implement the constitutional provision, and it has. It has provided that the Court shall have original *and* exclusive jurisdiction over: (1) all controversies between two or more States; and (2) all cases *against* ambassadors or other public ministers (but not consuls). But the Court *may* take original jurisdiction over any other case covered by the broad wording in Article III, Section 2.

How Cases Reach the Court. Some 3500 to 4000 cases are now appealed to the Supreme Court each year. Of these, only a few hundred are accepted for decision. In most cases, then, the petitions for review are denied —usually because at least most of the Justices agree with the decision of the lower court or believe that the case involves no significant point of law.

More than half of the cases which are decided by the Court are disposed of in brief orders. For example, an order may *remand* (return) a case to a lower court for reconsideration in the light of some other recent and related cases decided by the High Court. All told, the Court

CHIEF JUSTICES OF THE UNITED STATES

Name	State From Which Appointed	President By Whom Appointed	Years Of Service	Life Span	Age When Appointed
John Jay	New York	Washington	1789–1795	1745–1829	44
John Rutledge[a,b]	South Carolina	Washington	1795	1739–1800	55
Oliver Ellsworth	Connecticut	Washington	1796–1800	1745–1807	51
John Marshall	Virginia	John Adams	1801–1835	1755–1835	46
Roger B. Taney	Maryland	Jackson	1836–1864	1777–1864	59
Salmon P. Chase	Ohio	Lincoln	1864–1873	1808–1873	56
Morrison R. Waite	Ohio	Grant	1874–1888	1816–1888	58
Melville W. Fuller	Illinois	Cleveland	1888–1910	1833–1910	55
Edward D. White[b]	Louisiana	Taft	1910–1921	1845–1921	65
William Howard Taft	Connecticut	Harding	1921–1930	1857–1930	64
Charles Evans Hughes[b]	New York	Hoover	1930–1941	1862–1948	68
Harlan F. Stone[b]	New York	F. D. Roosevelt	1941–1946	1872–1946	69
Fred M. Vinson	Kentucky	Truman	1946–1953	1890–1953	56
Earl Warren	California	Eisenhower	1953–1969	1891–1974	62
Warren E. Burger	District of Columbia	Nixon	1969–	1907–	61

[a]Rutledge was appointed Chief Justice by President George Washington on July 1, 1795, while the Congress was not in session. He presided over the August 1795 term of the Supreme Court; but the Senate refused to confirm his appointment, rejecting it on December 15, 1795. Rutledge subsequently went insane.

[b]Four men served as Associate Justice before being appointed as Chief Justice: John Rutledge, from 1789 to 1791; White, 1894 to 1910; Hughes, 1910 to 1916; and Stone, 1925 to 1941. Rutledge was appointed an Associate Justice when the Supreme Court was first organized in 1789; but he resigned a year and a half later, having attended no sessions of the Court. Hughes resigned as an Associate Justice in 1916 to seek the Presidency. White and Stone each were serving as Associate Justice when elevated to Chief Justice.

decides, after hearing arguments and with full opinions, only 120 or so cases each year.

Generally, cases come to the Supreme Court either by *certiorari* or on *appeal*. Most cases reach the Court by **writ of certiorari** (from the Latin, "to be made more certain"). This is an order by the Court directing a lower court to send up the record in a given case because one of the parties says there was some error in the lower court's handling of that case. An **appeal** is a petition by one of the parties to a case asking the Court to review the lower court's decision in the case. A few cases do reach the Court in a third way, by **certificate.** The process is used when a lower court is not clear about the procedure or the rule of law that should apply in a case. The lower court asks the Supreme Court to certify the answer to a specific question in the matter.

The Supreme Court at Work. The Supreme Court sits for a term of about nine months each year—from the first Monday in October until some time the following June or July. As a rule, the Justices hear arguments in the cases before them for two weeks, then recess for two weeks. While arguments are being heard, the Court opens at 10 A.M., Monday through Thursday.

Monday is usually "decision day." The decisions ready for release are announced at the beginning of that day's session.[17] As the decisions are announced, the Justices read the opinions which accompany them. The Court then listens to the arguments in the next cases on its docket.

The lawyers for each side in a case are normally allowed one hour to present their oral arguments. The Justices

Grin and Bear It by George Lichy © Courtesy of Field Newspaper Syndicate
"I think we should find him guilty and let the Supreme Court worry about it!"

often interrupt them with questions. The lawyers also prepare written **briefs,** detailed and systematic arguments which often run to hundreds of pages. As a rule, the Justices depend a great deal upon those briefs in reaching their decisions and writing their opinions.

On Friday of most weeks of a term the Justices meet in conference. There, they discuss the cases they have heard and try to decide their disposition. These conferences are held in the closest secrecy, and no formal report of them is ever made. More than fifty years ago, Chief Justice Harlan Fiske Stone wrote one of the very few first-hand accounts which exist:

At Conference each case is presented for discussion by the Chief Justice, usually a brief statement of the facts, the question of law involved, and with such suggestions for their disposition as he may think appropriate. No cases have been assigned to any particular judge in advance of the Conference. Each Justice is prepared to discuss the case at length and to give his views as to the proper solution of the questions presented. In Mr. Justice Holmes' pungent phrase, each must be able to "recite" on the case. Each Judge is requested by the Chief Justice, in the order of seniority, to give his views and the conclusions which he has reached. The discussion is of the freest character and at its end, after full opportunity for each member of the Court to be heard and for the asking and answering of questions, the vote is taken and recorded in the reverse order of the discussion, the youngest, in point of service, voting first.

On the same evening, after the conclusion of the Conference, each member of the Court receives at his home a memorandum from the Chief Justice advising him of the assignment of cases for opinions. Opinions are written for the most part in recess, and as they are written, they are printed and circulated among the Justices, who make suggestions for their correction and revision. At the next succeeding Conference these suggestions are brought before the full Conference and accepted or rejected as the case may be. On the following Monday [usually] the opinion is announced by the writer as the opinion of the Court.[18]

Six justices make up a quorum for the decision of a case, and at least four must agree before a case can be decided. If all nine Justices take part (as they mostly do), a case may be decided by a 9–0, 8–1, 7–2, 6–3, or 5–4 vote. Many cases are decided unanimously, but several find the Court "split" (divided).

Some criticize the Court for its many "split decisions." But, notice, the "easy" cases don't very often get that far in the judicial process.

As Chief Justice Stone indicated, a **majority opinion** regularly accompanies the deciding of a case. A Justice who does not agree with the majority often writes a **dissenting opinion.** Indeed, two, three, or even four dissents may be presented. A Justice who agrees with the Court's decision, but not with the rea-

soning by which it was reached, often prepares a **concurring opinion.** One or more of these opinions are often presented.

The written opinions are really not necessary to the decision of a case. In fact, decisions are sometimes handed down without opinion.

But the opinions are valuable. The majority opinions stand as precedents to be followed in similar cases as they arise in the lower courts or reach the Supreme Court. The concurring opinions may bring the Supreme Court to modify its present stand in future cases. Chief Justice Hughes once described dissenting opinions as "an appeal to the brooding spirit of the law, to the intelligence of a future day." Once in a while, the Supreme Court does reverse itself; the minority opinion of today could become the Court's majority position in some future case.

☑ FOR REVIEW

1. Which is the only federal court specifically created in the Constitution? The only judicial office?
2. How is the size of the Supreme Court set? What is it now?
3. What is the power of judicial review? Why is its use by the Supreme Court so vitally important?
4. Why is *Marbury* v. *Madison* so important?
5. Over what cases does the Supreme Court have original jurisdiction? Exclusive jurisdiction?
6. From what courts are cases appealed to the Supreme Court? About how many cases are decided, after arguments and with full opinions, each year?
7. What is a majority opinion? A concurring opinion? A dissenting opinion?

[18]"Fifty Years of Work of the United States Supreme Court," Report of the American Bar Association, 1928.

The Other Constitutional Courts

There are two other consitutional courts today.

The Court of International Trade.
The Trade Court was originally created as the Board of United States General Appraisers in 1890. That body became the Court of Customs in 1926, and it was renamed by Congress in 1980.

The Trade Court now has nine judges, one of whom is its chief judge. It hears civil cases arising out of the tariff and other trade-related laws. Its judges sit in panels of three and often hold trials at such major ports of entry as New Orleans, San Francisco, Boston, and New York.

Appeals from decisions of the Trade Court are taken to the Court of Appeals for the Federal Circuit.

The Court of Appeals for the Federal Circuit. Congress created the Court of Appeals for the Federal Circuit in 1982. It established the new tribunal especially to centralize—and so speed up—the handling of appeals in certain kinds of civil cases. To that end, this Court, unlike the 12 other federal Courts of Appeals (page 484), has a nationwide jurisdiction.

It hears appeals from several places. Many of its cases come from the Trade Court, and others from the Claims Court (one of the special courts we shall look at in a moment). It also hears appeals in certain cases decided by any of the 91 District Courts around the country—those involving patents, trademarks, or copyrights. Then, too, it takes cases that arise out of the administrative rulings made by the International Trade Commission (page 407), the Patent and Trademark Office (in the Department of Commerce, page 417), and the Merit Systems Protection Board (page 436).

The Court of Appeals for the Federal Circuit has 12 judges—and appeals from their decisions may be carried to the Supreme Court.

Law clerks at work in the Supreme Court Library.

The Special Courts

The special courts are often called the *legislative courts*. They are the federal courts Congress has set up to exercise jurisdiction only in certain cases—cases dealing with particular subjects that fall within the expressed powers of Congress. That is, these courts have *not* been set up under Article III, and they do *not exercise* "the judicial power of the United States."

The United States Claims Court

The United States cannot be sued, by anyone, in any court, for any reason, without its consent. It may be taken to court only in those cases in which Congress has declared that the Government is open to suit.[19]

---

[19]The government is shielded from suit by the doctrine of *sovereign immunity*. It comes down from an ancient principle of English public law summed up by the phrase: "The King can do no wrong." The rule is not intended to protect public officials from charges of corruption or any other wrong-doing. Congress has long since agreed to a long list of legitimate court actions against the Government.

One of several U.S. Customs Service small boat inspection stations. Criminal violations of the customs laws (smuggling and the like) are tried in federal District Courts; civil disputes are heard in the Court of International Trade.

Originally, any person with a claim against the United States could secure **redress** (satisfaction of the claim, payment) only by an act of Congress. In 1855, however, Congress set up a special court, the Court of Claims, to hear these pleas. It did so acting under its expressed power to pay the debts of the United States.[20] Congress restructured the Court of Claims—as the United States Claims Court—in 1982.

The Court now has 16 judges. They hold trials—hear claims for damages against the Government—throughout the country.[21] Those claims they uphold cannot in fact be paid until Congress appropriates the money (which it does almost as a matter of course).

Appeals from the Court's decisions may be carried to the Court of Appeals for the Federal Circuit.

The Territorial Courts

Acting under its power to "make all needful rules and regulations respecting the territory . . . belonging to the United States,"[22] Congress has created courts for the nation's territories. Today these territorial courts sit in the Virgin Islands, Guam, and the Northern Mariana Islands (in the Pacific Trust Territory). They work in much the same way as the local courts in the 50 States. (There is a regular federal District Court in Puerto Rico.)

The Courts of the District of Columbia

Acting under its power "to exercise exclusive legislation in all cases whatso-

[20]Article I, Section 8, Clause 1.
[21]Under the Federal Tort Claims Act of 1946 the District Courts also have jurisdiction over many claims cases; but only where the amount sought is not more than $10,000. The same statute also gives executive agencies the authority to settle claims under $1000.

[22]Article IV, Section 3, Clause 2; see page 331.

THE NATIONAL JUDICIARY

Court	Created	Number of Courts	Number of Judges	Term of Judges	Judges Appointed By[a]	Salary of Judges
District Court	1789	91	507	Life	President	$73,100
Court of Appeals	1891	12	132	Life	President	$77,300
Supreme Court	1789	1	9	Life	President	$96,700[b]
Trade Court	1926	1	9	Life	President	$73,100
Court of Appeals for the Federal Circuit	1982	1	12	Life	President	$77,300
Claims Court	1982	1	16	15 years	President	$73,100
Court of Military Appeals	1950	1	3	15 years	President	$77,300
Tax Court	1969	1	19	12 years	President	$73,100

[a]With Senate confirmation.
[b]Chief Justice receives $100,700.

ever, over such District . . . as may . . . become the seat of the Government of the United States,"[23] Congress has set up a judicial system for the nation's capital. Both the federal District Court and the Court of Appeals for the District of Columbia hear many local cases as well as those they try as constitutional courts. Congress has also established two *local* courts, much like the courts in the States: a Superior Court, which is the general trial court, and a Court of Appeals.

The Court of Military Appeals

Acting under its power "to make rules for the government and regulation of the land and naval forces,"[24] Congress created the Court of Military Appeals in 1950. It has a chief judge and two associate judges, appointed by the President and Senate for 15-year terms.

[23]Article I, Section 8, Clause 17.
[24]Article I, Section 8, Clause 14. This provision, and the 5th Amendment, allow Congress to regulate the conduct of members of the armed forces under a separate (non-civilian) code of military law.

The Court is sometimes called the "GI Supreme Court." It is the court of last resort in dealing with offenses against military law.

The United States Tax Court

Acting under its power to tax, Congress established the Tax Court in 1969.[25] It has 19 judges, one of whom

[25]Article I, Section 8, Clause 1.

Drawing by Richter, © 1968 The New Yorker Magazine, Inc.
"These steps are killing me. I say we settle out of court."

serves as chief judge. Each of these judges is named by the President and Senate for a 12-year term.

The Tax Court hears civil—not criminal—cases involving disputes over the application of the tax laws. Most of its cases, then, are generated by the Internal Revenue Service and other Treasury agencies.

☑ FOR REVIEW

1. Which of the constitutional courts were first created as special courts?

2. Over what types of cases does the Court of International Trade have jurisdiction? The Court of Appeals for the Federal Circuit?

3. Which are the special courts in the national judiciary?

4. Over what types of cases do the territorial courts have jurisdiction? The courts of the District of Columbia? The Court of Military Appeals? The Tax Court?

The Judges

Appointment

The President appoints all federal judges, subject to confirmation by the Senate. The Constitution declares that the President "shall nominate, and, by and with the advice and consent of the Senate, shall appoint . . . judges of the Supreme Court."[26] And Congress has provided the same procedure for the selection of all other federal judges. Hence the President is free to name to the federal bench anyone the Senate will confirm.

Most federal judges are drawn from the ranks of leading attorneys, legal scholars and law school professors, former members of Congress, and from the State courts. Judicial selections are shaped by the same sorts of considerations as other exercises of the Chief Executive's appointing power—which we reviewed on pages 392–393. The President and his closest political and legal aides—especially, the Attorney General—take leading parts, of course. But major roles are also played by influential Senators—most of all those from the nominee's home State; by the legal profession—especially the American Bar Association's Committee on the Federal Judiciary; and by other persons in the President's political party.

Term

Article III, Section 1 reads, in part:

> The judges, both of the Supreme and inferior courts, shall hold their offices during good behavior . . .

This means, then, that all judges of the constitutional courts are appointed for life—until they resign, retire, or die in office. They may be removed only through the impeachment process. Only nine federal judges have ever been impeached; none, in almost 50 years. Of the nine impeached by the House, only four were found guilty by the Senate.[27]

Giving life tenure to judges is intended and works to insure the independence of the judiciary.

---

[26]Article II, Section 2, Clause 2.

[27]Judge John Pickering of the District Court in New Hampshire, for irregular judicial procedures, loose morals, and drunkenness, in 1803; Judge West H. Humphreys of the District Court in Tennessee, for disloyalty, in 1862; Judge Robert W. Archibald of the old Commerce Court, for improper relations with litigants in his court, in 1913; and Judge Halstead L. Ritter of the District Court in Florida, for bringing his court into "scandal and disrepute," in 1936.

The judges of the territorial courts and those of the District of Columbia are appointed for terms varying from four to eight years. The judges of the Claims Court and the Court of Military Appeals serve 15-year terms and those of the Tax Court 12 years.

Compensation

Article III, Section 1 also states that federal judges:

> . . . shall, at stated times, receive for their services a compensation which shall not be diminished during their continuance in office.

Congress sets the salaries for all federal judges. For the salaries they receive today, see the table on page 495.

Congress has provided a fairly generous retirement arrangement for the judges of the constitutional courts. They may retire at age 70 and, if they have served for at least 10 years, they receive their full salary for the rest of their lives. Or, they may retire at full salary at age 65, after at least 15 years of service on the federal bench. The Chief Justice may call any retired judge back into service in the lower federal courts at any time, however.

Court Officers

Today, federal judges are little involved in the day-to-day administrative operations of the courts over which they preside. Their primary mission is to hear and decide cases. Other judicial personnel provide the support services necessary to permit them to perform that basic task.

Each federal court appoints a **clerk** who has custody of the seal of the court and keeps a record of the court's proceedings. The clerk is helped by deputy clerks, stenographers, bailiffs, and others as needed.

Each of the 91 federal District Courts

One of the judges of the District of Columbia's federal District Court, Norma Johnson hears a great variety of cases arising from violations of federal law, both civil and criminal.

now appoints at least one **United States Magistrate,** court officers who handle a number of legal matters once dealt with by the judges themselves. Magistrates issue warrants of arrest, and often hear evidence to decide whether or not a person who has been arrested on a federal charge should be held for action by the grand jury. They also set bail in federal criminal cases, and even have the power to try those who are charged with certain minor offenses.

The President appoints, subject to Senate confirmation, a **United States Attorney** for each federal judicial district. Attorneys and their assistants are responsible for the prosecution of all persons charged with the commission of federal crimes in the district. They also represent the United States in all civil actions to which it is a party in the district.

The President and Senate also appoint a **United States Marshal** to serve each District Court. Each federal marshal and the marshal's deputies carry out duties much like those handled by a county sheriff and the sheriff's deputies. They make arrests in federal criminal cases, keep accused persons in custody, secure jurors, serve legal papers, keep order in the courtroom, and execute court orders and decisions.

United States Attorneys and Marshals are each appointed for four-year terms. They are officers of the court, but they serve under the direction of the Attorney General and are officials of the Department of Justice.

✓ FOR REVIEW

1. Who appoints all federal judges? For what terms?
2. How may federal judges be removed from office?
3. What restriction does the Constitution place on Congress' power to set judicial salaries?
4. What are the major functions of the clerks of the federal courts?
5. What are the major duties of United States Magistrates? Attorneys? Marshals?

The Administration of Justice

No matter is, or can be, of greater importance to a democratic government than justice. To establish it, declares the Preamble to the Constitution, is one of the high purposes for which that great charter was written. To provide it, said Thomas Jefferson, is "the most sacred of the duties of government."

But what, precisely, is "justice"? The question is a far from simple one—for justice is a concept, an idea. It has no physical existence; it cannot be seen or touched or weighed or measured. Rather, like "truth" and "liberty" and "good" and all other concepts, it is an invention of the human mind. And, precisely, because it is a product of human thought, it means what human beings make it mean.

As the concept has been developed over time in American thought and practice, it has come to mean this: That the law, in both its content and its administration, must be reasonable, fair, and impartial.

As we have suggested before, those standards of justice have not always been met in practice in this country. We have not in fact attained our professed goal of "equal justice for all." But we have also made this crucial point: Our history can be told very largely in terms of our efforts to reach that goal—and very largely, too in terms of our ever-improving attempts to do so.

Clearly, the courts play a very special role in those efforts. In fact, courts are often described as "tribunals for the administration of justice according to law." As you know, we have just examined the federal court system—the judicial machinery by which the Federal Government seeks to do justice. And, later, we shall consider the much larger network of State and local courts, as well, in Chapter 22.

But, recall, justice is a matter of vital concern to *all* of government in this country—not just to the courts alone. The concept is supposed to guide the behavior of all legislative and executive agencies, too.

The reality—the practical day-to-day fact—of a government's committment to the concept of justice can be measured by a close look at its policies and its actions. In short, how does all that it says and all that it does square with that concept?

The Department of Justice

Of all of the many agencies in the executive branch of the Federal Government, one in particular is an especially telling indicator of that government's committment to the concept: the Department of Justice.

We identified the Department's major agencies and summarized their principal functions in Chapter 16; and a review of that material (on pages 412–413) will demonstrate its central role here. So, too, do these words, chiselled into the marble outside the office of the Attorney General of the United States: "The United States wins its point whenever justice is done one of its citizens in the courts."

The Department, headed by the Attorney General, was created by Congress in 1870. The post of Attorney General was established much earlier, however —by the very first session of Congress, in 1789; and, the nation's first Attorney General, Edmund Randolph, was a member of Washington's original Cabinet. Most of Randolph's now 73 successors have followed him in the role of intimate advisor to the Presidents they have served.

Until 1870, the Attorney General's only official duties were to provide legal advice to the President and his aides and to represent the United States in court. Over the years since then, those duties have multiplied considerably.

Today, the Department describes itself as "the largest law firm in the nation."[28]

Through its thousands of lawyers, investigators, agents, and other employees—some 55,000 in all—the Justice Department: furnishes legal advice to the President and to the heads of the other executive departments; enforces most of the federal criminal laws; investigates violations of those statutes and arrests those who commit federal offenses; supervises the work of the United States Attorneys and Marshalls throughout the country; represents the United States in court; operates the federal prison system; and enforces the nation's immigration, naturalization, and narcotic laws.

---

[28]Altogether, some 20,000 attorneys work for the Federal Government. They hold positions throughout the executive branch. The Treasury Department (especially the IRS) and the several independent regulatory commissions have large legal staffs; however, well over half of all federal attorneys are employed by the Justice Department.

S U M M A R Y

Among its several weaknesses the Articles of Confederation did not provide for a national judiciary. The Framers corrected this in Article III of the Constitution. There, the Supreme Court is established, Congress is given the power to create lower federal courts, and the jurisdiction of the national judiciary is set out. The federal system gives rise to a dual system of courts in this country: national and State.

Congress has created two types of federal courts: (1) the constitutional (or regular) courts—today, the District Courts, the Courts of Appeals, the Supreme Court, and the Court of International Trade; and (2) the special (or legislative) courts—the territorial courts, those of the District of Columbia, the Claims Court, the Court of Military Appeals, and the United States Tax Court.

The constitutional courts have the broad judicial power of the United States. They have jurisdiction over a case either because of its subject matter or the parties involved. Some cases are within their exclusive jurisdiction; those heard on appeal are within their appellate jurisdiction.

The 91 District Courts hear most federal cases. The 12 Courts of Appeals hear cases appealed from the District Courts and the independent regulatory commissions.

The Supreme Court is the highest court in the land. The importance of its exercise of the power of judicial review cannot be overstated. The High Court generally chooses the cases it will hear on appeal from the lower federal courts and the highest State courts. It has original jurisdiction over cases against ambassadors and other public ministers and cases involving disputes between two or more States.

The Trade Court hears cases arising out of the tariff and other laws relating to international trade. Appeals from its decisions are taken to the Court of Appeals for the Federal Circuit which also hears appeals from the Claims Court, certain decisions in the District Courts, and administrative rulings made by some executive agencies.

The special courts are not created under Article III. They do not have the judicial power of the United States; rather, they handle cases arising out of the exercise of particular congressional powers.

The President appoints all federal judges, subject to Senate confirmation. The judges of the constitutional courts serve for life (during good behavior); those of the special courts are appointed for various terms. Each of the federal courts is aided by a judicial staff. Magistrates serve the District Courts, as do United States Attorneys and Marshals.

C H A P T E R   R E V I E W

Key Terms/Concepts
Appeal (491)
Appellate
 jurisdiction
 (483)
Briefs (491)

Concurrent juris-
 diction (483)
Concurring
 opinion (492)
Constitutional
 courts (481)

Dissenting
 opinion (492)
Dual court system
 (481)
Exclusive juris-
 diction (483)

Judicial review
 (486)
Jurisdiction (482)
Legislative courts
 (482)
Magistrate (497)

Majority opinion
(492)

National judiciary
(480)

Original juris-
diction (483)

Regular courts
(482)

Special courts
(482)

Writ of *certiorari*
(491)

Writ of *man-
damus* (486)

Keynote Questions

1. To whom does the Constitution give "the judicial power of the United States"?
2. What is the chief distinction between the constitutional courts and the special courts in the federal judiciary?
3. Whether or not a particular case lies within the jurisdiction of the federal courts hinges on one or another of what two factors?
4. Most of the cases heard in the federal courts begin (and end) where?
5. What is the major role of the Courts of Appeals in the federal court system?
6. What is the power of judicial review? Why is the Supreme Court's possession and exercise of that power a matter of such extraordinary importance?
7. Why does *Marbury* v. *Madison* rank as one of the very most important of all of the cases ever decided by the Supreme Court?
8. What particular types of cases does the Court of International Trade hear? The Court of Appeals for the Federal Circuit?
9. What particular types of cases are heard by the Court of Military Appeals? The Tax Court?
10. How are all federal judges chosen? For what terms?

For Thought and Discussion

1. What qualifications do you think a President should set in appointing federal judges? Would you favor or oppose the popular election of federal judges? Why?

2. Frequently, federal judges must interpret provisions in statutes or in the Constitution and apply them to cases before their courts. When they do so, do they "make law"? Explain.
3. Do you agree or disagree with this observation: The principles of popular sovereignty and of majority rule, on the one hand, and that of judicial review on the other, are contradictory and cannot logically exist together in a governmental system. Why?
4. Why did Woodrow Wilson describe the High Court as "a constitutional convention in continuous session"?

Suggested Activities

1. Write an essay on this comment by Chief Justice Charles Evans Hughes:

   Democracy will survive only as long as the quick whims of the majority are held in check by the courts in favor of a dominant and lasting sense of justice. If democratic institutions are long to survive, it will not be simply by maintaining majority rule and by the swift adaptation to the demands of the moment, but by the dominance of a sense of justice which will not long survive if judicial processes do not conserve it.

   Compare this comment with Judge Learned Hand's, quoted on page 90.
2. If possible, attend a session of the nearest United States District Court. Report your observations to the class.
3. Invite a local judge or attorney to speak to the class on the nature of the law, the legal profession, and our court system.

UNIT SEVEN

State and Local Governments

One of the most distinctive characteristics of the American governmental system is the division of powers between the National Government and the States. The Articles of Confederation had set up a loose union of 13 States in which those States held virtually all the power. At the Constitutional Convention in 1787, many delegates feared that a strong National Government would mean the end of the States' powers. Charles Pinckney of South Carolina asked if Edmund Randolph's proposal for a "national government . . . consisting of a supreme Legislative, Executive, and Judiciary" did not mean that he "intended to abolish the State Governments altogether," as James Madison tells us in his *Notes.*

In fact, the federal system set up by the Constitution gives the States vast powers. It reserves to them, or to the people, all of those "powers not delegated to the United States by the Constitution nor prohibited by it to the States."

Most of the contacts that most citizens have with government in this country are with the States and their local governments, not the National Government. Operating under written constitutions, the States make and enforce laws, build and maintain schools, roads, and other facilities, and provide for public health and safety. The States also create local governments—counties, towns, townships, boroughs, cities, and other districts.

In Unit Seven we turn to the States and their thousands of units of local government. We shall look, first, at the 50 State constitutions and at the legislative, executive, and judicial branches of State government. Then we shall consider the many different kinds of local government which exist across the country and, finally, the various ways in which we pay for all of those governments and all that they do.

An interior view of the dome of California's Capitol Building, in Sacramento.

CHAPTER 19 — State Constitutions

CHAPTER OBJECTIVES

To help you to
Learn ▪ Know ▪ Understand

The nature of State constitutions and their place in the American federal system.

The nature of the first State constitutions and that of their present-day descendants.

The processes of constitutional change and development among the States.

The various methods of formal constitutional change and, specifically, those available in your State.

The general and urgent need for constitutional revision among the States today.

CONSTITUTION

OR

FORM OF GOVERNMENT

OF THE

STATE OF LOUISIANA

BY AUTHORITY

NEW-ORLEANS:

PRINTED BY JO BAR BAIRD, PRINTER TO THE CONVENTION

1812.

Constitutions govern governments.

Thomas R. Dye

Each of the 50 States has a *written* constitution—and that fact, in itself, is very important.

From the very beginning, government in this country has been based upon written constitutions. In fact, the United States has sometimes been described as "a land of constitutions."

Our experience with such documents dates from as early as 1606, when King James granted a charter to the Virginia Company. That act led to the settlement at Jamestown in the following year and, with it, the beginning of the first government in British North America. Later, each of the other colonies was established, and governed, on the basis of a written charter.

Since 1776, the States have written and approved nearly 150 constitutions. Each of the present-day State constitutions is a link in a chain of written documents that now stretches over nearly 400 years of American history.

Constitutions govern governments—and each of the State constitutions does just that. It is its State's fundamental law. It sets out the way in which the government of that State is organized and it distributes power among its various branches. It authorizes the exercise of power by government and, at the same time, it places limits on the exercise of governmental power.

In this chapter we take a close look at State constitutions. As we do, remember their place in the scheme of Ameri-

504

James Madison addresses the chair at the Virginia Constitutional Convention of 1829-30. Other prominent delegates included James Monroe, John Marshall, and John Randolph. *Facing page:* The title-page of a pamphlet containing Louisiana's first constitution.

can federalism. A State constitution is that State's supreme law. It is superior to any and all other forms of State (and local) law within that State. *But*, recall, each State's constitution is subordinate to the Constitution of the United States, and may not conflict with any form of federal law.[1]

The First State Constitutions

When the 13 colonies became independent, each of them faced the problem of establishing a new government. On May 15, 1776, the Second Continental Congress advised each of the new States to adopt

> . . . such governments as shall, in the opinion of the representatives of the

people, best conduce to the happiness and safety of their constituents in particular, and America in general.

Despite their several shortcomings, most of the colonial charters served as models for the first State constitutions. Indeed, in Connecticut and Rhode Island, the old charters seemed so well suited to the needs of the day that they were carried over as constitutions almost without change.

The earliest State constitutions were adopted in a number of ways. The people played no direct part in that process, anywhere. In Connecticut and in Rhode Island the legislature made the small changes it thought necessary in the charters, and no further action was taken in either State.

Six of the Revolutionary legislatures drew up new documents and proclaimed them in force in 1776. In none of those States—Maryland, New Jersey, North

[1]Reread Article VI, Section 2, the Supremacy Clause in the national Constitution, and pages 70–71.

Carolina, Pennsylvania, South Carolina, and Virginia—was the new constitution offered to the people for judgment.

In Delaware and New Hampshire in 1776 and in Georgia and New York in 1777 new constitutions were prepared by conventions called by the legislature. In each case, the new document had to be approved by the legislature and then became effective; but in none was popular approval required.

In 1780 a popularly elected convention prepared a new constitution for Massachusetts; it was ratified by a vote of the people. Thus, Massachusetts set the pattern of popular participation in the constitution-making process.[2]

All of the present State constitutions were drafted by assemblies representing the people, and most of them became effective only after a popular vote.[3]

Contents

The first State documents differed in many ways. But, as we saw in chapter 2, they each came out of the same revolutionary ferment—and so they shared many basic features.

Each of them proclaimed the twin principles of *popular sovereignty* and *limited government*. That is, in each of them the people were recognized as the sole source of authority, for the government, and the powers given to the new government were very closely limited. Seven began with a lengthy bill of rights. All of them made it clear that the sover-

eign people held "certain unalienable rights" that government must respect.

The doctrines of *separation of powers* and of *checks and balances* were also built into each of the new charters. In practice, however, the memory of the hated royal governors was yet fresh, and most of the authority each State government had was given to the legislature.

Everywhere, except in Georgia (until 1789) and Pennsylvania (until 1790), the legislature was *bicameral* (two-chambered).[4] At first, only Massachusetts and South Carolina allowed the governor to veto acts of the legislature. The governor was generally limited to a one-year term, and he was chosen by the legislature in each of the States except Massachusetts and New York.

For their time, the early State constitutions were democratic documents. Each of them had, however, several provisions (and some important omissions) that, by today's standards, were quite undemocratic. Thus, none of them provided for full religious freedom, each set rigid qualifications for voting and for office-holding, with property owners given a highly favored standing.

☑ FOR REVIEW

1. What is a State's constitution?
2. What is the relationship between each State's constitution and the national Constitution? Other forms of federal law? Other forms of State law?
3. What pattern of constitution-making was first set by Massachusetts? When?
4. Describe the general shape of the first State constitutions.

---

[2]As we noted on page 33, with independence Massachusetts relied upon the colonial charter in force (1691) before as, in effect, its first State constitution.

New Hampshire adopted its second and present constitution in 1784. It followed the Massachusetts pattern of popular convention and popular ratification in doing so. The Massachusetts constitution of 1780 and New Hampshire's constitution of 1784 are the oldest written constitutions in force anywhere in the world today.

[3]Only the present constitution of Delaware (1897), Mississippi (1890), South Carolina (1895), and Vermont (1793) came into force without popular ratification.

[4]Vermont, which became the 14th State in 1791, had a unicameral legislature until 1836. Only Nebraska (since 1937) has a one-house legislative body today.

State Constitutions Today

The present-day State constitutions are, of course, the direct descendants of those earlier documents. They are somewhat like and, at the same time, very different from their predecessors. This is not too surprising. On the one hand, only 17 of them were written in this century. But, on the other, most of them have been amended several dozens of times, as we shall see.

Each of them sets up a framework of government much like that to be found in the other States. All of them rest upon nearly uniform principles.

THE STATE CONSTITUTIONS

State	Present Document Became Effective In[a]	State Entered Union In[b]	Number of Previous Documents	State	Present Document Became Effective In[a]	State Entered Union In[b]	Number of Previous Documents
Alabama	1901	1819	5	Montana	1973	1889	1
Alaska	1959	1959	0	Nebraska	1875	1867	1
Arizona	1912	1912	0	Nevada	1864	1864	0
Arkansas	1874	1836	4	New Hampshire	1784	1788	1
California	1879[c]	1850	1	New Jersey	1948	1787	2
Colorado	1876	1876	0	New Mexico	1912	1912	0
Connecticut	1965	1788	3	New York	1895	1788	3
Delaware	1897	1787	3	North Carolina	1971	1789	2
Florida	1969	1845	5	North Dakota	1889	1889	0
Georgia	1983	1788	9	Ohio	1851	1803	1
Hawaii	1959	1959	0[d]	Oklahoma	1907	1907	0
Idaho	1890	1890	0	Oregon	1859	1859	0
Illinois	1971	1818	3	Pennsylvania	1874	1787	3
Indiana	1851	1816	1	Rhode Island	1843	1790	1
Iowa	1857	1846	1	South Carolina	1896	1788	6
Kansas	1861	1861	0	South Dakota	1889	1889	0
Kentucky	1891	1792	3	Tennessee	1870	1796	2
Louisiana	1975	1812	10	Texas	1876	1845	4
Maine	1820	1820	0	Utah	1896	1896	0
Maryland	1867	1788	3	Vermont	1793	1791	2
Massachusetts	1780	1788	0	Virginia	1971	1788	5
Michigan	1964	1837	3	Washington	1889	1889	0
Minnesota	1858	1858	0	West Virginia	1872	1863	1
Mississippi	1890	1817	3	Wisconsin	1848	1848	0
Missouri	1945	1821	3	Wyoming	1890	1890	0

[a]Twenty-four of the present-day State constitutions were actually ratified in a year prior to the year in which they became effective: Alaska (1956), Arizona (1911), Florida (1968), Georgia (1982), Hawaii (1950), Idaho (1889), Illinois (1970), Kansas (1859), Louisiana (1974), Maine (1819), Michigan (1963), Minnesota (1857), Montana (1972), New Jersey (1947), New Mexico (1911), New York (1894), North Carolina (1970), Oregon (1857), Pennsylvania (1873), Rhode Island (1842), South Carolina (1895), Utah (1895), Virginia (1970), Wyoming (1889).

[b]For each of the original 13 States, the year in which the State ratified the national Constitution.

[c]California's constitution became effective July 4, 1879, for purposes of the election of officers, the beginning of their terms of office, and the meeting of the legislature; it became effective for all other purposes January 1, 1880.

[d]Prior to 1898, Hawaii (as a kingdom and then a republic) had five written constitutions.

A close look at your State's constitution will show that it can be fairly well described in terms of the following categories.[5]

Basic Principles

Every State's fundamental law is built upon the principles of popular sovereignty and limited government. That is, each of them recognizes that government exists only with the consent of the people and that it must operate within certain, often closely defined, bounds.

In every State, the powers of government are divided among executive, legislative, and judicial branches. Each of the 50 documents proclaims the concepts of separation of powers and checks and balances. Each of them provides, too, either in so many words or by implication, for the power of judicial review.

Protections of Civil Rights

Each document has a bill of rights—a listing of the rights which individuals hold against the State and its officers and agencies. Most set out guarantees much like those found in the first 10 amendments to the National Constitution. Several have a number of others, as well—for example, the right to self-government, to be safe from imprisonment for debt, to migrate from the State, and to organize labor unions and bargain collectively.

Structure of Government

Any constitution is, in major part, a statement of governmental organization. Every State document deals with the structure of government at both the State and the local levels. Most cover the subject of governmental organization at considerable length and often in quite specific detail.

Governmental Powers and Processes

All State constitutions deal with the powers and processes of government at some length. The powers vested in the governor and other elements of the executive branch, the legislature, the courts, and units of local government generally take up large amounts of space.

The powers to tax, spend, borrow, and provide for education are very prominent. So, too, are such processes as elections, legislation, and intergovernmental (State-local) relations, and (in several States) the initiative, referendum, and recall.

Constitutional Change

Constitutions are the product of human effort. None is perfect. Sooner or later, changes become necessary, or at least desirable. Each of the State constitutions recognizes that fact. It sets out the means by which it may be formally changed—that is, revised or amended.

As constitutions are *fundamental* laws, they cannot be changed as ordinary law is changed. Rather, they require more complex procedures, somewhat more difficult to bring about.

Miscellaneous Provisions

Every State constitution has several provisions of a miscellaneous or "other" character. Thus, most begin with a **preamble** which has no legal force but does set out the purposes of those who drafted and adopted the document.

Most also have a **schedule** for putting a new document into effect and avoiding conflicts with its predecessor. All of them contain a number of "dead letter" provisions—those with no current force and effect but which still remain a part of the constitution.

---

[5]If a copy cannot be found in the school or other local library, one can usually be obtained from the secretary of state's office in the State capital.

Constitutional Change

A constitution is an expression of the time in which it was made. Times change, circumstances and attitudes change. Inevitably, a constitution—or at least some parts of it—become outdated. So, an essential part of any constitution is its provisions for change.

Formal and Informal Amendment

Like the national Constitution, the State documents have been altered over the years by both the *formal* and the *informal* amendment process.

But—and this is a very important *but*—the informal process has not been nearly so important at the State as at the national level. State constitutions are much less flexible (more rigid and detailed) than the national document. The structures, powers, and procedures of State government are treated at great length, so there is much less room for the play of informal change. And the State courts have generally been quite strict in their role as constitution-interpreters. States have had to depend largely on formal amendments for constitutional change and development.

As we turn to the methods of formal change, the meanings of two distinct sets of terms—"proposal-ratification" and "amendment-revision"—must be kept in mind. First, the process of formal change involves two basic steps: *proposal* and then *ratification*. Proposals for change may be made by a constitutional convention, by the legislature, or by the voters themselves. Ratification is by popular vote, except in Delaware.

As to the second set of terms, *amendment* generally describes a limited change, dealing with only one or a few provisions in a constitution. The term *revision* is regularly used to describe changes of a broader scope—for example, an entire new document.

Constitutional Conventions

The convention is the usual device by which new constitutions have been written and older ones revised. To this point, at least 230 of them have been held among the States.[6]

In every State the legislature has the power to call a convention, and that call is generally subject to voter approval.[7] In 14 States the question of calling a convention must be submitted to the voters at regular intervals.[8] The people commonly vote three times during the process of constitution-making by convention: (1) to authorize the calling of the convention, (2) to elect delegates, and (3) to ratify or reject the document framed by the convention.

Proposal of Amendments

Most changes in State constitutions come as amendments (additions or modifications or deletions of particular provisions) rather than by revision (large-scale changes in much of the document or an entirely new one).

Convention Proposal The convention is most often used for the broader purpose of revision, but it can be and sometimes is used in several States to

---

[6]In several States another body, a *constitutional revision commission*, may be used to propose extensive changes in the existing document or frame a new one. Only the Florida constitution expressly provides for one; there it must assemble every twentieth year and may itself submit unlimited changes to the voters. In other States, a revision commission is generally set up by and reports to the legislature, which may modify and send some or all of its proposals on to the voters.

[7]In seven States (Alaska, Georgia, Louisiana, Maine, South Carolina, South Dakota, and Virginia) the legislature may call a convention without first submitting the question to the voters. In Florida, Montana, and South Dakota a convention may be called by the initiative process.

In California, Georgia, and Oregon the legislature itself (by a two-thirds vote in each house) may propose a new constitution to the people. In those States, then, the legislature has the power (1) to call a constitutional convention and (2) to act as such a body itself.

[8]Every 20 years in Connecticut, Illinois, Maryland, Missouri, Montana, New York, Ohio, and Oklahoma, 16 years in Michigan, 10 years in Alaska, Iowa, New Hampshire, and Rhode Island, and 9 years in Hawaii.

propose amendments. But conventions are both costly and time-consuming—and so they are not widely used for amendment purposes.

Legislative Proposal.   Most amendments added to State constitutions are proposed by the legislature. The process varies from State to State.

AMENDMENT BY LEGISLATIVE PROPOSAL

Legislative Vote Required	Popular Vote for Ratification	States
Majority vote, each house	Majority on amendment	Arizona, Arkansas, Missouri, New Mexico[a], North Dakota, Oklahoma, Oregon[b], Rhode Island, South Dakota
Majority vote, each house	Majority at election	Minnesota
Two-thirds vote, each house	Majority on amendment	Alaska, California[b], Colorado, Georgia[b], Idaho, Kansas, Louisiana, Maine, Michigan, Mississippi, Montana, South Carolina[e], Texas, Utah, Washington, West Virginia
Two-thirds vote, each house	Majority at election	Wyoming, Hawaii[c]
Three-fourths vote, each house	Majority on amendment	Connecticut[c]
Three-fifths vote, each house	Majority on amendment	Alabama, Florida, Kentucky, Maryland, Nebraska[d], New Jersey[c], North Carolina, Ohio
Three-fifths vote, each house	Majority at election or three-fifths on amendment	Illinois
Three-fifths vote, each house	Two-thirds on amendment	New Hampshire
Majority vote, each house at two successive sessions	Majority on amendment	Connecticut[c], Hawaii[c], Indiana, Iowa, Nevada, New Jersey[c], New York, Pennsylvania[f], Virginia, Wisconsin
Majority vote in joint session, at two successive sessions	Majority on amendment	Massachusetts
Two-thirds vote, each house, two successive sessions	(No popular vote required)	Delaware
Majority vote, each house at one session; two-thirds vote each house at next session	Majority of votes cast for governor	Tennessee
Two-thirds vote of senate, majority vote of house at one session; majority vote of each house at next session	Majority on amendment	Vermont

[a]Amendments relating to voting qualifications or to the guarantee of equal treatment of Spanish-speaking students in public schools may be proposed only by a three-fourths vote of each house, and must be approved by three-fourths of all voting in the election, including at least two-thirds of those voting in each county.
[b]By a two-thirds vote in each house, legislature may propose a revision of all or a part of the constitution.
[c]Either method may be used in these States (Connecticut, Hawaii, New Jersey).
[d]Majority for ratification must equal at least 35 percent of total vote cast in election.
[e]Subsequent majority vote of each house required to complete ratification.
[f]An "emergency amendment" may be proposed by two-thirds vote of each house at a single session; such an amendment must be ratified by a majority of voters who vote in election.

The process is comparatively simple in some States, quite difficult in others. As a general rule, and as one might expect, the easier the process the more often are amendments proposed (and adopted). The California constitution, which dates from 1879, has now been amended some 450 times (to 1984). But the Massachusetts document of 1780, in force for twice as long, has been changed only some 115 times.[9]

Only a few States limit the number of amendments that may be submitted to the voters at any one election. For example, no more than four may be offered in Kentucky and five in Kansas.

Proposal by Initiative. The voters themselves can propose (initiate) constitutional amendments in 17 States. They may do so by the **initiative**—a process in which a certain number of qualified voters must sign petitions in favor of the proposal. The proposal then goes directly to the ballot—for approval or rejection by the people.

The process varies among these 17 States. As you can see in the table on page 512, Illinois and Massachusetts place large restrictions on its use.

Ratification of Amendments

In every State except Delaware an amendment must be approved by vote of the people in order to become a part of the constitution.[10] As with the matter of proposal, the ratification process varies

---

[9]The number of amendments which have been proposed (and added) to each State's constitution is the result of several other factors, too. Two factors figure most prominently: the *content* of the document (whether well-drawn or not, flexible or rigid and detailed, and so on) and its *age*, of course.

[10]In Delaware if an amendment is approved by a two-thirds vote in each house of the legislature at two successive sessions, it then becomes effective. In South Carolina, *final* ratification, after a favorable vote by the people, depends upon a majority vote in both houses of the legislature. Both the Alabama and South Carolina constitutions provide that amendments of only local (as opposed to Statewide) application need be approved only by the voters in the affected locale.

DADE COUNTY QUESTION — VOTE FOR ONE

Shall the ordinance

(a) prohibiting smoking in enclosed public places, places of employment, educational facilities and health facilities, but

(b) permitting smoking in bars, retail tobacco stores, hotel and motel rooms, at certain private social gatherings, designated smoking sections in lobbies or waiting areas physically separated by walls or partitions, designated smoking sections in student or faculty lounges in educational facilities, designated smoking areas in employee lounges, enclosed rooms designated as smoking rooms, outdoor areas, private hospital rooms, semiprivate hospital rooms where both patients request that smoking be permitted, designated smoking areas in employee cafeterias, places where boxing or wrestling matches will occur, pool halls, and designated smoking areas in restaurants and cafeterias, and

(c) requiring the posting of signs reading that smoking is prohibited by law in all areas where smoking is prohibited, be enacted?

| FOR THE ORDINANCE | 48 ➤ |
| AGAINST THE ORDINANCE | 49 ➤ |

A proposal for a county ordinance, which reached the ballot by the initiative process in a county in Florida, was defeated in 1982.

among the States—as, again, the tables on pages 510 and 512 show.

Generally, the approval of a majority of those voting on an amendment adds it to the State constitution. A greater margin, however, is needed in some States.

And, on many occasions, constitutional amendments have been defeated in those States even though they received more *yes* than *no* votes. Most often, that has happened because, as we suggested on page 202, many voters fail to vote on ballot measures.

☑ FOR REVIEW

1. What are the major features of the 50 State constitutions today?
2. Why must constitutions provide for formal change?
3. Why has the process of informal amendment been less significant at the State than at the national level?
4. What is the device usually used for the writing of a new constitution or the revision of one?
5. How are amendments to State constitutions usually proposed? Ratified? What is the initiative?

AMENDMENT BY INITIATIVE PROPOSAL

State	Number of Petition Signatures Required[a]	Distribution of Signatures	Popular Vote for Ratification
Arizona	15% of votes cast for governor	—	Majority on amendment
Arkansas	10% of votes cast for governor	Must be at least 5% in each of 15 counties	Majority on amendment
California	8% of votes cast for governor	—	Majority on amendment
Colorado	8% of votes cast for secretary of state	—	Majority on amendment
Florida	8% of votes cast for presidential electors	Must be 8% in each of one-half of congressional districts	Majority on amendment
Illinois[b]	8% of votes cast for governor	—	Majority at election, or three-fifths on amendment
Massachusetts[c]	3% of votes cast for governor	Not more than one-fourth from any one county	Majority on amendment[d]
Michigan	10% of votes cast for governor	—	Majority on amendment
Missouri	8% of votes cast for governor	Must be 8% in each of two-thirds of congressional districts	Majority on amendment
Montana	10% of votes cast for governor	Must be 10% in each of two-fifths of legislative districts	Majority on amendment
Nebraska	10% of votes cast for governor	Must be at least 5% in each of two-fifths of counties	Majority on amendment[e]
Nevada	10% of highest vote cast	Must be 10% in each of three-fourths of counties	Majority on amendment in two consecutive general elections
North Dakota	4% of the population	—	Majority on amendment
Ohio	10% of votes cast for governor	Must be at least 5% in each of one-half of counties	Majority on amendment
Oklahoma	15% of highest vote cast	—	Majority on amendment
Oregon	8% of votes cast for governor	—	Majority on amendment
South Dakota	10% of votes cast for governor	—	Majority on amendment

[a]Based on number of votes cast in most recent general election, except in North Dakota.
[b]Initiative process may be applied only to Article IV, The Legislature.
[c]Initiated measure must first be approved by at least one-fourth of legislature, sitting in joint session, at two successive legislative sessions before submission to voters for ratification.
[d]Majority must equal at least 30% of all votes cast in election.
[e]Majority must equal at least 35% of all votes cast in election.

FEDERALISM / STATE CONSTITUTIONS / SCHOOL FINANCE

In every State except Hawaii, the public schools are financed mainly by local property taxes. Several recent State court decisions foreshadow a major change in that pattern, however.

California's Supreme Court triggered the matter in a case it first decided in 1971 and then again, with the same result, in 1976. In *Serrano* v. *Priest,* it held that State's reliance on local property taxes as the principal means of local school finance to be unconstitutional—as a violation of the equal rights guarantees in the California constitution.

It found that there are often very large variations between and among school districts—especially in terms of the amount and the assessed values of taxable properties in each of them. The net effect of these variations, it said, was flagrant inequalities—differences which made the quality of a child's education "dependent upon the wealth of his parents and neighbors."

Similar rulings have now been made in several other States. And, as a direct result, most of the States have revamped their programs of aid to local schools and upped their financial support of them.

The U.S. Supreme Court has come to a somewhat different conclusion in this matter, however—in a case from Texas, *San Antonio Independent School District* v. *Rodriguez,* 1973. There, it held that the right to an education is *not* one of the "fundamental rights" covered by the 14th Amendment's Equal Protection Clause; see page 150.

In effect, the Court ruled that, whatever a State's own constitution may mean on this point, the 14th Amendment does not forbid a State to rely on the local property tax as the principal source of the financing of its public schools.

1. Which of these contrasting views of "equal rights" do you think is the proper one? Why?
2. How have the courts of your State ruled in this matter?

General Observations

The Need for Reform

Almost without exception, State constitutions are in urgent need of reform. The typical document is sorely outdated. It is cluttered with unnecessarily detailed provisions, overly burdensome restrictions, and obsolete sections. It carries much repetitious, even contradictory, material and much clumsy, often confusing, language. Not least among its sins are those of omission—it fails to deal with many of the pressing problems that the States and their local governments face in the latter part of the 20th century.

Unfortunately, this indictment may be read against even the newest, the most recently rewritten, documents—

QUESTION 1

PROPOSED AMENDMENT TO THE CONSTITUTION

Do you approve of the adoption of an amendment to the constitution summarized below, *which was approved by the General Court in joint sessions of the House of Representatives and the Senate on July 2, 1980 by a vote of 171-4, and on June 21, 1982 by a vote of 144-44?*   **YES** ▶   **NO** ▶

SUMMARY

The proposed constitutional amendment would remove the present constitutional prohibition against the use of public funds to aid or maintain private primary or secondary schools.

It would permit the Commonwealth, cities and towns to make public funds available to pupils attending private primary and secondary schools in the form of either aid, materials or services subject, however, to three specific limitations. First, the private school could not be one that discriminates on the basis of race or color in its admission requirements. Second, the grant of aid must be consistent with the First Amendment to the United States Constitution which guarantees the free exercise of religion and prohibits the establishment of religion. Third, individual pupils would have to request the aid, materials or services. In addition to these three specific limitations, the amendment would authorize the legislature to enact other laws imposing conditions or restrictions on the grant of public aid, materials or services.

The proposal would also change the state constitution to allow public money to be spent to aid infirmaries, hospitals, charitable or religious undertakings if they are either publicly owned or under the control of public officials. The state constitution now prohibits such spending unless these institutions are both publicly owned and under the control of public officials.

In 1982, voters in Massachusetts voted down a legislative proposal to amend the State constitution—one that, under certain conditions, would have permitted State funds to be used to aid private schools.

for they carry over much, with little or no change, from their predecessors.

The need for reform can be pointed up in several ways. And the odds are very good that, wherever you live, a close look at your State's constitution is one of them. As another, look at the 50 documents as a whole in terms of two points: length and age.

The Problem of Length. The first State constitutions were quite short. They were meant to be statements of basic principle and organization. Purposely, they left to the legislature and to time and practice the task of filling in the details as they became necessary.

The longest of the original documents was the Massachusetts constitution of 1780, with some 12,000 words. The shortest was New Jersey's constitution of 1776; it ran to only some 2500 words.

Through the years State charters have become longer, and longer, and longer still. Today, most are between 15,000 and 30,000 words. The shortest are those of Vermont (1793), with fewer than 7000 words, and Connecticut (1965), not quite 8000 words long. On the other hand, the Alabama document of 1901 now contains nearly 130,000 words—

more than those to be found in most novels today.

Why are the documents so long? The reasons are easy to find. The leading one: popular distrust of government, a long-established fact of American political life. It has often led to quite detailed provisions, specifically aimed at preventing the misuse of governmental power. Also, many restrictions on that power, which might be set out in ordinary law, have been purposefully placed in the fundamental law, where they cannot be easily ignored nor readily (and quietly) changed.

Special interest groups—veterans organizations, private utilities, the liquor industry, and many others—long ago learned that public policies of benefit to them are much safer in the constitution than they are in a mere statute. These groups, which usually have a good deal of political clout, have managed to carve out their special preserves in the constitutions of most States.

Then, too, court decisions can be and often have been overridden by constitutional amendments. This is exactly what has happened in the whole matter of capital punishment (page 148), for example.

There has been a marked failure in nearly every State to separate **fundamental law** (that which is of basic and lasting import and ought to be in the constitution) from **statutory law** (that which should be the subject of laws passed by the legislature).

To pick from dozens of examples: Who can seriously argue the fundamental character of the New York constitution's provision authorizing an exchange of 10 acres of State land for 30 acres owned by the village of Saranac Lake, in order to give the village a place for a dump? Or the California ban on taxing fruit and nut trees planted within the past four years? Or, too, the Oregon constitutional guarantee of the right to sell liquor by the glass?

Two other factors have had much to do with the ever-lengthening shape of State constitutions: (1) The functions carried out by the States (and their local governments) have grown greatly in the past few decades, and (2) the "people" (in fact, organized groups) have not been stingy in the use of the initiative in those States where it is available.

The Problem of Age. If you look again at the table on page 507, you can see that most of the State constitutions are rather old. Though most of them have been amended dozens of times, those changes have, as often as not, added to the clutter of the documents.

The Oregon constitution offers a *typical* example. It was written by delegates —most of them farmers—to a territorial convention in 1857, and it became effective in 1859. It has now been amended more than 170 times, runs to some 30,000 words, and contains *two* Articles VII and *ten* Articles XI!

Like most of the other State constitutions, it is overloaded with statutory material and in serious need of reform. For example, one of its Articles XI gives nearly 2000 closely detailed words to the subject of veterans' farm and home loans. Another of them spends some 500 words to give the State and its local governments the right to issue bonds "for the purpose of planning, acquisition, construction, alteration or improvement of facilities for the collection, treatment, dilution, and disposal of all forms of waste in or upon the air, water, and lands of this State."

And, it includes a number of outdated provisions. One of them, for example, forbids the legislature to tax, spend any money, or contract any debt for the construction of a capitol building before the year 1865. Still another requires that all voters in school district elections be at least 21 years of age.

In all, 19 States still have the constitutions with which they entered the Union. Twenty-two States have documents at least 100 years old, and 15 others were written 50 to 100 years ago.

Several States have adopted new (revised) constitutions in recent years— Michigan in 1963, Connecticut in 1965, Florida in 1968, Illinois, North Carolina, and Virginia in 1970, Montana in 1972, Louisiana in 1974, and, most recently, Georgia in 1982. Even counting them, the average age of the 50 State constitutions is nearly 90. (And most of the more recent documents are subject to the same criticisms we have aimed at State constitutions over the past few pages.)

✔ **FOR REVIEW**

1. Why are most State constitutions in urgent need of reform?
2. Why has the typical State constitution become a longer and still longer document?
3. Which is the oldest of the present-day documents? The most recently revised? When was your State's present constitution adopted?

S U M M A R Y

Each State has a written constitution, the State's fundamental law. It sets out the structure of that State's government and divides its powers among its several branches. It both authorizes the exercise of power by the State (and its local) government and restricts the use of governmental power. It is the supreme form of State law; however, it may not conflict with any provision in the national Constitution nor with any other form of federal law.

With independence, 11 of the original States adopted new constitutions; in Connecticut and Rhode Island the colonial charters were adapted to that purpose. Generally, the people had little part in the constitution-making process until 1780. In that year, the Massachusetts constitution was written by a popularly elected convention and then ratified by a vote of the people. Since then, popular participation has been the rule in State constitution-making.

Despite their many variations, the first State constitutions were born out of the common revolutionary atmosphere and were quite similar documents. Each of them stated the principles of popular sovereignty, limited government, separation of powers, and checks and balances. In each State, the legislature was relatively strong, the governor weak, and the suffrage confined to the propertied class.

The present-day constitutions, direct descendants of those early documents, also vary in many particulars. But all have major sections making quite similar provision for certain basic principles, civil rights guarantees, the structure of State and local government, the powers and process of government, and methods of constitutional change.

The details of the process of formal constitutional change differ among the States. The proposed revision or replacement of a constitution is generally the function of a convention. Amendments may be proposed by the legislature in every State, and in 17 of them by initiative petition. Ratification must be by popular vote in all but Delaware.

Nearly every one of the State constitutions is in urgent need of reform. Most are sorely outdated, too lengthy and detailed, and overloaded with statutory material.

C H A P T E R   R E V I E W

Key Terms/Concepts

Amendment-revision (509)
Bill of Rights (508)
Checks and balances (506)
Colonial charters (505)
Constitution (504)
Constitutional convention (509)

Formal amendment (509)
Fundamental law (515)
Informal amendment (509)
Initiative (511)
Judicial review (508)

Limited government (508)
Popular sovereignty (508)
Preamble (508)
Proposal-ratification (510)
Separation of powers (506)

Statutory law (515)
Supremacy Clause (505)
Written constitution (504)

Keynote Questions

1. What is a State's constitution? Why may it be said that that document "governs governments"?
2. What is the relationship of each State's constitution to the national Constitution? Other forms of federal law? Other forms of State law?
3. Describe your State's constitution in terms of the six categories set out on page 508.
4. Why are the provisions for formal change so important a part of each of the 50 State constitutions?
5. By what method(s) may your State's constitution be amended?
6. Why have most of the State constitutions become increasingly longer documents over time?

For Thought and Discussion

1. If each of the State constitutions were abolished would government then be more or less democratic?
2. How well does your State's constitution meet this standard, set by Alexander Hamilton in *The Federalist*, No. 57:

   The aim of every political constitution is, or ought to be, first to obtain men who possess most wisdom to discern, and most virtue to pursue, the common good of the society; and in the next place, to take the most effectual precautions for keeping them virtuous whilst they continue to hold their public trust.

3. How do you rate the process by which your State's constitution may be amended: as too easy or too difficult? Why? How many times has it been amended? What amendments (if any) were added at the most recent election? Rejected?
4. What provisions (if any) in your State's constitution would you class as statutory rather than fundamental? Why do you think those provi-

sions were placed in the document? What provisions (if any) are outdated or obsolete? Repetitious or contradictory? Why do those provisions remain in the document?

Suggested Activities

1. Outline your State's constitution. (The outline of the national Constitution on pages 628–629 might be used as a model.) Then answer these questions: (1) How long is the document? (2) How can it be amended? (3) How many times has it been amended? (4) Does it deal largely with basic principles and the basic framework of government, or contain much material that might be better handled in ordinary legislation? (5) What specific changes (if any) would you recommend be made in it?
2. Write a brief description of the background, drafting, ratification, and development of your State's present constitution.
3. Invite a State legislator, judge, or some other public figure to discuss your State's constitution, its contents, and the changes he/she recommends be made in it.

"Now, you try to get a fire started while I draft a constitution."

From the *Rotarian*, June 1972. By permission of the publisher.

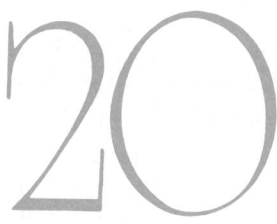

The State Legislatures

CHAPTER OBJECTIVES

To help you to:
Learn ▪ Know ▪ Understand

Why the legislature is "the powerhouse of State government."

Why all but one of the 50 State legislatures are bicameral.

The structure, organization, and powers of the State legislatures.

The legislative process at the State level.

The process of direct legislation: the initiative and referendum.

Representative government is in essence self-government through the medium of elected representatives of the people.

Chief Justice Earl Warren
Reynolds v. *Sims,* 1964

The size of the legislature, the details of its organization, the frequency and the length of its sessions, and even its official name vary among the States. The chief reason for its existence is everywhere the same, however: The legislature is the lawmaking branch of State government. It is charged with the high duty of translating the public will into the public policy of the State.

The legislature has been described as "the powerhouse of State government." With its vast lawmaking powers, it creates the energy needed to operate the governmental machinery of the State and its local units.

What is generally called "the Legislature" is officially known by that title in 27 of the States. In 19 others it is "the General Assembly."[1] In North Dakota and Oregon it is called "the Legislative Assembly," and in Massachusetts and New Hampshire "the General Court."

Forty-nine of the 50 State legislatures are two-chambered. In each of them the upper house is called "the Senate."[2]

---

[1] Arkansas, Colorado, Connecticut, Delaware, Georgia, Illinois, Indiana, Iowa, Kentucky, Maryland, Missouri, North Carolina, Ohio, Pennsylvania, Rhode Island, South Carolina, Tennessee, Vermont, Virginia.

[2] Nebraska applies that name to its single chamber.

Nebraska's unicameral legislature has 49 members elected on a nonpartisan ballot for four-year terms. *Facing page:* As do members of the United States Congress, State legislators do much of their work in committee meetings.

The lower house in most is "the House of Representatives." But in California, Nevada, and New York it is "the Assembly," and in Maryland, Virginia, and West Virginia "the House of Delegates."

Bicameralism

Except for Nebraska, all of the State legislatures are bicameral today.[3] Bicameralism has been the dominant pattern for two major reasons : (1) The influence of both English and colonial experience, and (2) the tendency among the newer States to follow the lead of the original States and the National Government.

The first colonial legislatures were typically unicameral; the elected representatives commonly sat with the governor and his council in the making of colonial laws. As the popularly chosen legislators gained in political power in most of the colonies, the governor's council took on the role of a second, upper chamber. Thus, well before the Revolution, most of the colonies had bicameral bodies structured much like the British Parliament. After independence, those States which had not already done so soon established two-chambered legislatures.

Unicameralism vs. Bicameralism

Unicameralism is often recommended as one of the major steps that could raise the quality of State legislatures, their procedures, and their product.

Those who support bicameralism have long made the argument that one house can act as a check on the other in a two-chambered body, and so prevent unwise legislation. But the critics of

---

[3]Nebraska's voters approved the creation of a *unicameral* legislature in 1934 and that body held its first session in 1937. Georgia until 1789, Pennsylvania until 1790, and Vermont until 1836 also had unicameral legislatures.

bicameralism point to many examples to show that, in fact, the theory has not worked altogether well in practice. Indeed, very often, the real check on "hasty and ill-considered legislation" comes from places outside the legislature—from the governor's veto, from coverage in and comment by the news media, and from public opinion.

The fact that bicameralism has worked well in Congress is often used to support it at the State level. The bicameral Congress is a reflection of the *federal* character of the Union, however. The States are not federal; they are, instead, *unitary* in form. Also, remember, a bicameral Congress came out of the Connecticut Compromise—a practical solution to a very serious political dispute at the Philadelphia Convention in 1787.

Until fairly recently, many supported bicameralism because they favored a "little federal plan" for their own State's legislature. That is—despite the nonfederal character of the States—a body with one house based upon area and the other on population. Otherwise, they claimed, the more populous cities would so control the lawmaking process that small-town and rural interests would be almost unrepresented. As we shall see in a moment, the Supreme Court destroyed their position in 1964, however,—when it ruled that the 14th Amendment's Equal Protection Clause requires that *both* houses of a State's legislature *must* be apportioned on the basis of population.

Critics of bicameralism argue that in the complicated structure and procedures of a two-house system, special interests have more opportunities to block popular legislation. As an example of this, they point to conference committees—which are not needed in a unicameral legislature; see pages 302–314.

The advocates of unicameralism also point out that with two chambers involved in the lawmaking process it is almost impossible to fix the responsibility for some legislative action, or inaction. With but one house to watch, the people can more readily discover and understand what the legislature is doing. And, they add, the legislature itself can much more easily watch the activities of the lobbyists for special interest groups in a one-house system.

The Nebraska experience has not proved a cure-all. But it does appear to have worked quite well for more than 45 years now. Legislative costs have been cut, greater efficiency has been achieved, and lobbyist influence has been reduced. A generally higher caliber of legislator has been chosen. And, the typical legislator has been more responsive to his/her constituents than was the case under the old two-house system.

All in all, the weight of the argument favors unicameralism. But proposals to adopt it elsewhere have made almost no headway since the Nebraska reform. Both tradition and inertia stand on the side of bicameralism—and so, too, do a lack of knowledge and interest on the part of the general public.[4]

FOR REVIEW

1. What is the basic function of each State's legislature?
2. By what official name is the legislature, and each of its houses, known in your State?
3. For what two major reasons are all but one of the State legislatures bicameral today?
4. What major arguments are usually made for bicameralism? For unicameralism?

[4]Notice, however, that nearly all *local* legislative bodies (city, county, and special district) are composed of only one chamber; see Chapter 23.

Size and Apportionment

There is no exact figure for the ideal size of a legislative body. Two basic considerations are important, however. First, a legislature (and each of its houses) should not be so *large* as to hamper the orderly conduct of the people's business. Secondly, it should not be so *small* that the many views and interests within the State cannot be adequately represented.

The *upper house* in most States has from 30 to 50 members. There are only 20 seats in the Senate in both Alaska and Nevada. Minnesota's upper house is the largest with 67 members.

The *lower house* usually ranges between 100 and 150 members. However, there are only 40 seats in Alaska's and Nevada's lower chamber. In Pennsylvania, on the other hand, there are 203 seats in the house and in New Hampshire an almost incredible 400.

Apportionment

Each State's constitution makes some provision for the **apportionment** of legislative seats in the State. That is, it states how those seats will be allocated, distributed among districts, in the State.

On what basis should the legislature be apportioned? Should the seats be distributed among districts of about equal populations? Or should they be apportioned on the basis of area, with district lines drawn according to area and/or economic factors? Or should, say, one house be based upon population and the other upon area?

Clearly, these are vital questions. The answers very largely identify the groups and regions within a State that control is legislative machinery—and, so, shape its public policies.

Most State constitutions have always provided for population as the only or at least the major basis for the distri-

Copyright © *St. Louis Dispatch*. Reproduced by courtesy of Bill Mauldin.

"RUSTY SCALES"

bution of legislative seats. As we shall see, population is now the only standard that may be used—no matter what a State's constitution may say.

Reapportionment. Most State constitutions direct the legislature to make periodic adjustments in the distribution of its seats to account for increases, decreases, and shifts of population in the State. Usually, the constitution orders the legislature to reapportion itself every 10 years, in line with the most recent federal census.[5]

The "Reapportionment Revolution." Although the pattern has now changed, most State legislatures were long controlled by the rural, less populated sections of the State.

This general pattern of rural over-representation and urban under-representation lasted long after the United States became a nation of mostly city-dwellers. Two practices accounted for

---

[5]In some States reapportionment is no longer a legislative function—a direct result of the "reapportionment revolution." In Ohio, for example, it is now done by a commission composed of the governor, secretary of state, auditor, and a representative from each of the major parties. A few States now provide that if the legislature fails to reapportion itself, or does so inadequately, it will be done otherwise—in Maine, for example, by the Supreme Judicial Court.

this imbalance: (1) The fact that many legislatures failed to reapportion themselves and (2) the frequent use of area as well as (or instead of) population as a basis for reapportionment.

Baker v. Carr, 1962.   The long-standing fact of rural domination has now come to an end in nearly all States.

In *Baker* v. *Carr,* 1962, the Supreme Court held, for the first time, that federal courts could properly hear cases in which it is claimed that the way in which a State legislature is apportioned violates the 14th Amendment's Equal Protection Clause.[6]

In *Baker* the Court decided only a *jurisdictional* question. It did not face this critically important, and controversial, question: On what factor(s) can a reapportionment be based? But the handwriting was large on the constitutional wall, and cases presenting the question were not long in coming.

Reynolds v. Sims, 1964.   In a now lengthy series of cases, the Court has consistently applied the "one-man, one-vote" rule. That is, it has consistently held that population is the *only* constitutionally acceptable basis for the apportionment of seats in a legislative body. Said the Court in the leading case, *Reynolds* v. *Sims,* from Alabama in 1964:

> Legislators represent people, not trees or acres. Legislators are elected by voters, not farms or cities or economic interests . . . The Equal Protection Clause requires that the seats in both houses of a bicameral State legislature must be apportioned on a population basis.

Since 1964, the Court has regularly rejected all other bases of apportionment.

The significance of the "reapportionment revolution" that was begun with *Baker* v. *Carr* in 1962 cannot be overstated. Within only a couple of years, some redistribution of legislative seats took place in each one of the 50 States. In a few States only minor adjustments were needed to meet the one-man, one-vote standard; but in many the redistricting was extensive. In most, changes came only after hard-fought court, legislative, and ballot battles.

Today there is very little malapportionment at the State legislative level. A majority of the seats in most State legislatures are now held by lawmakers from metropolitan areas—from the cities and their suburbs. Only in the few largely rural States—where the economy is mostly agricultural—has the "reapportionment revolution" had little effect.

To grasp the vital importance, and the practical meaning, of all of this, look at it in these terms. The *location* of political power, *where* that clout is based, has recently shifted in most of the States. Most of the real muscle in State politics was moved from the once-dominant rural interests to the cities and suburbs. And, remember this: the State legislatures draw congressional districts—and so have a large impact on the election of the members of the national House of Representatives.

✓ **FOR REVIEW**─────────

1. How many members serve in each house of your State legislature?
2. What did the Supreme Court hold in *Baker* v. *Carr,* 1962? Why was that decision so important?
3. What did the Supreme Court hold in *Reynolds* v. *Sims,* 1964? Why was that decision so important?

─────────

[6]Before *Baker,* both federal and State courts regularly refused to hear cases involving the composition of legislative bodies. Such cases were held to involve "political questions," to be decided by legislatures or voters, not by the courts.

Qualifications, Election, Terms, Compensation

Qualifications

Every State's constitution sets out formal qualifications for membership in the legislature. They do vary but, on the whole, they are easy to meet.

In most States, representatives must be at least 21; but in several the minimum age for service in either house is now 18. Most States set a higher minimum age for senators, usually 25.

Regularly, a legislator must be a citizen of the United States, a legal resident of his or her State, and also live in the district he or she represents.

The realities of politics place still other—*informal* and more meaningful—qualifications on those who seek seats in the legislature. These factors of *political availability* vary somewhat from State to State, and even from district to district within a State. They have to do with a candidate's vote-getting abilities and are based on such characteristics as occupation, name familiarity, party identification, race, national origin, and the like. The "right" combination of these factors will help a candidate to win nomination and then election to the legislature; and one or more "wrong" ones can spell defeat.

Election

Legislators are chosen by popular vote in every State. Nearly everywhere, candidates for seats in the legislature are nominated in party primaries and opposing candidates face one another in a partisan general election. Legislative nominees are picked by party conventions in only a few States. In only one State, Nebraska, the candidates are nominated in nonpartisan primaries; and there the opposing candidates are not identified by party in the general election, either.

In most States the lawmakers are elected in November of the even-numbered years. This is not the case in four of them, however. In Mississippi, New Jersey, and Virginia legislative elections are held in November, and in Louisiana in December, of the *odd*-numbered years. This is done in the hope of separating consideration of State and local issues from national politics.

Terms

From the table on page 524 you can see that legislators serve either two- or four-year terms. Senators are usually elected for longer terms than are their colleagues in the lower chamber. They serve for four years in 37 States and Nebraska and for two years in the other 12. Representatives are picked for two-year terms in all but four—Alabama, Louisiana, Maryland, and Mississippi.

The rate of turnover in legislative seats—the number of new members in each session—is fairly high among the States. Typically, there are more new faces in the lower house than in the senate each term. This is mostly the re-

Posters of office seekers line the way to a polling place in Potomac, Maryland.

THE STATE LEGISLATURES

State	Year Held	Regular Sessions Limitations on Length*	Regular Sessions Month Convenes	Upper House No. of Members	Upper House Term of Members	Lower House No. of Members	Lower House Term of Members	Salary of Members[d]
Alabama	annual	30 L days	Feb	35	4	105	4	$10 per day
Alaska	annual	None	Jan	20	4	40	2	$46,800 ann.
Arizona	annual	None	Jan	30	2	60	2	$15,000 ann.
Arkansas	odd[g]	60 C days	Jan	35	4	100	2	$7500 ann.
California	[f]	None	Dec	40	4	80	2	$28,110 ann.
Colorado	annual[b]	None	Jan	35	4	65	2	$14,000 ann.
Connecticut	annual[b]	5 months[e]	Jan	36	2	151	2	$10,500 ann.
Delaware	annual	June 30	Jan	21	4	41	2	$12,198 ann.
Florida	annual	60 C days	Apr	40	4	120	2	$12,000 ann.
Georgia	annual	40 L days	Jan	56	2	180	2	$7200 ann.
Hawaii	annual	60 L days	Jan	25	4	51	2	$13,650 ann.
Idaho	annual	None	Jan	35	2	70	2	$4200 ann.
Illinois	annual	None	Jan	59	4	177	2	$28,000 ann.
Indiana	annual	61 L days / 30 L days	Jan	50	4	100	2	$9600 ann.
Iowa	annual	None	Jan	50	4	100	2	$13,700 ann.
Kansas	annual	None / 90 C days	Jan / Jan	40	4	125	2	$47 per day
Kentucky	even	60 L days	Jan	38	4	100	2	$100 per day
Louisiana	annual	60 L days	Apr	39	4	105	4	$16,800 ann.
Maine	annual[b]	100 L	Dec	33	2	151	2	$10,000 bien.
Maryland	annual	90 C days	Jan	47	4	141	4	$21,000 ann.
Massachusetts	annual	None	Jan	40	2	160	2	$30,000 ann.
Michigan	annual	None	Jan	38	4	110	2	$33,200 ann.
Minnesota	odd[g]	120 L days	Jan	67	4	134	2	$18,500 ann.
Mississippi	annual	90 C days[e]	Jan	52	4	122	4	$8100 ann.
Missouri	annual	6 months[e]	Jan	34	4	163	2	$15,000 ann.
Montana	odd	90 L days	Jan	50	4	100	2	$4502 session
Nebraska	annual	90 L days / 60 L days	Jan / Jan	49	4	—	—	$4800 ann.
Nevada	odd	60 C days	Jan	20	4	40	2	$104 per day
New Hampshire	odd	90 C days[a]	Jan	24	2	400	2	$200 session
New Jersey	annual	None	Jan	40	4	80	2	$25,000 ann.
New Mexico	annual[b]	60 C days / 30 C days[b]	Jan	42	4	70	2	$75 per day
New York	annual	None	Jan	60	2	150	2	$32,960 ann.
North Carolina	odd[g]	None	Jan	50	2	120	2	$6936 ann.
North Dakota	odd	80 L days	Jan	50	4	100	2	$90 per day
Ohio	annual	None	Jan	33	4	99	2	$22,500 ann.
Oklahoma	annual	90 L days	Jan	48	4	101	2	$20,000 ann.
Oregon	odd	None	Jan	30	4	60	2	$16,800 bien.
Pennsylvania	annual	None	Jan	50	4	203	2	$35,000 ann.
Rhode Island	annual	60 L days[a]	Jan	50	2	100	2	$5 per day
South Carolina	annual	5 months[e]	Jan	46	4	124	2	$10,000 ann.
South Dakota	annual	40 L days / 30 L days	Jan / Jan	35	2	70	2	$3200 session / $2800 session
Tennessee	odd[g]	90 L days[a]	Jan	33	4	99	2	$8308 ann.
Texas	odd	140 C days	Jan	31	4	150	2	$7200 ann.
Utah	annual[b]	60 C days / 20 C days[b]	Jan / Jan	29	4	75	2	$25 per day
Vermont	odd[g]	None	Jan	30	2	150	2	$275 per wk.
Virginia	annual	30 C days / 60 C days	Jan	40	4	100	2	$8000 ann.
Washington	annual	105 C days / 60 C days	Jan	49	4	98	2	$13,750 ann.
West Virginia	annual	60 C days	Jan	34	4	100	2	$5136 ann.
Wisconsin	annual	None	Jan	33	4	99	2	$22,632 ann.
Wyoming	annual[b]	40 L days / 20 L days[b]	Jan / Feb	30	4	64	2	$30 per day

Note: See footnotes on facing page.

sult of the larger size of the house and the (usually) longer senate term, of course. It also reflects the fact that members of the lower house often seek "promotion" to the upper chamber.

In any given year more than one-fourth of all of the 7,489 State legislators in the country are serving their first term in office. The major reasons for this high turnover seem to be two: low pay and partisan politics. The fact that legislators generally remain in office longer in those States where the pay is higher and where one party regularly wins most of the elections suggests just how important these reasons are.

Compensation

How much legislators are paid is a very important matter—and not only to legislators themselves. Some people feel that it is payment enough for one to have the honor, to enjoy the supposed prestige, of sitting in the State's law-making body. And some apparently think that legislators are not worth paying at all. Most people seem to be quite unaware of the matter, however.

The cold, hard facts are these: It costs money for legislators to live, and it costs them money to take time away from their normal occupations to serve the State. Far too often, capable men and women refuse to run for the legislature —and very often because of the financial sacrifices they would have to make.

From the table at the left, you can see the salaries paid in each State. Most

of them also provide some sort of additional allowances. Oregon is a fairly typical example. The basic salary is now $700 a month ($16,800 for the *biennium*, a two-year period). In addition, each member receives an expense allowance —$44 for each day of the legislative session (which usually lasts for about 180 days) and for each day he or she attends interim committee meetings (between sessions). Each member also has a $300 per month expense allowance for each month in which the legislature is not in session. The total compensation per member, both salary and allowances, comes to about $16,000 a year.

Legislative pay is set by the constitution in a few States; in most, however, the legislature itself decides the matter. (Lawmakers often hesitate to vote for higher salaries for themselves—usually because of their worries about voter reactions. They often attain the same end by raising the expense allowances.)

Legislative Sessions

As the table on the left shows, 37 States now (1984) hold their regular legislative sessions on an annual basis, and the California legislature meets in a continuous two-year session. The other 12 States hold regular sessions only every other year.

Most of the States have turned to holding annual sessions only in the past decade or so—as it has become more apparent that the workload cannot be handled on an every-other-year basis.

PARTY CONTROL OF GOVERNORSHIPS AND STATE LEGISLATURES

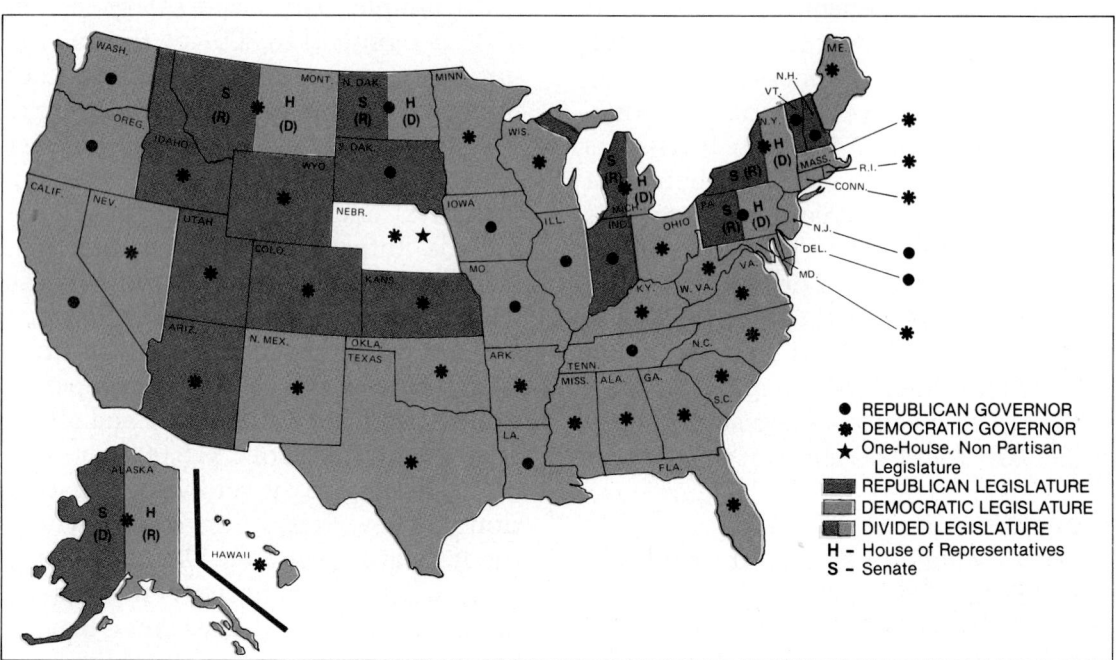

In six of the annual session States—Colorado, Connecticut, Maine, New Mexico, Utah, and Wyoming—the second (that is, every other) session is a budget session. That meeting is limited entirely or mainly to budget and related fiscal matters.

As a general rule, regular sessions, whether annual or biennial, are becoming longer and longer. As the table shows, some State constitutions put a time limit on sessions; but those are gradually disappearing.

Special Sessions

A special session of the legislature may be called by the governor in every State, and by the legislature itself in just over half of them.

As the term suggests, special sessions are held to allow the lawmaking body to take up urgent matters between its regularly scheduled meetings. These sessions are fairly common today, especially where regular sessions still meet only every other year.

Another kind of special session, a "veto session," now meets in seven of the States—in Connecticut, Hawaii, Louisiana, Missouri, Washington, Utah, and Virginia. They meet soon after the end of each regular session—to give legislators an opportunity to reconsider those bills the governor vetoed in the period immediately following the adjournment of that regular session.

Powers of the Legislature

In the American federal system, governmental power is divided between the nation and the States. The National Government has only those powers *delegated* to it by the Constitution, and the States have those powers *reserved* to them by that document. As you recall, the 10th Amendment lays out the basic division of powers between the nation and the States:

> The powers not delegated to the United States by the Constitution, nor prohibited by it to the States, are reserved to the States, respectively, or to the people.

Nearly all of the reserved powers each of the States has are in fact held by its legislature.

None of the 50 State constitutions sets out a complete list of all of the powers held by the legislature. Nor could it—for in the complex arrangements of federalism, and of separation of powers, all of those powers which are not given to some other agency of government in the United States belong to the State legislatures.

To put this rather complicated point another way:

In each State the legislature has all of those powers that (1) the State constitution does not grant exclusively to the executive or judicial branches of the State's government or its local units, and (2) neither the State nor the United States Constitution denies to the legislature.

Legislative Powers

Each State's legislature can pass any law that does not conflict with any federal law or with any part of that State's constitution. It is, therefore, not possible to put together a complete listing of any State legislature's powers. Even so, most of the State constitutions do list several of the legislature's more important powers. The ones most often mentioned include the powers to tax, spend, borrow, establish courts, define crimes and provide for their punishment, regulate commercial activities, and maintain public schools.

The powers of every legislature include the extremely important *police power*—the State's power to protect and promote the public health, safety, morals, and welfare, as we noted on pages 125–127. Although this broad power cannot be more exactly defined, it is the basis for thousands of State laws. Among them are laws that require vaccinations and authorize quarantines, restrict automobile exhaust emissions, forbid certain forms of gambling, regulate the sale and use of alcoholic beverages, prohibit the ownership of dangerous weapons, fix highway speed limits, impose safety requirements in industrial plants, limit campaign contributions and spending, forbid the sale of soft drinks in nonreturnable bottles or cans, compel school attendance, set the minimum legal age for marriage, provide for food inspections, and bar immoral or indecent entertainments. In a word, the powers of the State legislatures are huge, indeed.

Nonlegislative Powers

Each of the State legislatures has certain non-legislative powers—powers in addition to those it exercises in the making of law.

Executive Powers. Some of its powers are *executive* in nature. For example, the governor's power to appoint certain State officials is often subject to approval by the legislature, or at least its upper house. In some States the legislature itself appoints one or more executive officeholders. Thus, the secretary of state, elected by the voters in most of the States, is chosen by the legislature in Maine, New Hampshire, and Tennessee.

Judicial Powers. Each of the State legislatures also has certain judicial powers. The chief illustration is the power of impeachment, of course. In every State except Oregon the legislature can remove any executive officer or judge through that process.

Each legislature also has judicial powers with regard to its own members. Thus, disputes about the election or the qualifications of a member-elect are generally decided by the house involved in the matter. Then, too, because legislators themselves are not subject to impeachment, each chamber has the power to discipline—and, in extreme cases, even expel—any of its members.

Constituent Powers. As we saw in Chapter 19, each State legislature plays a significant role in both the constitution-making and the constitutional amendment processes. When the legislature calls a constitutional convention or proposes an amendment to the State constitution it does not make law; rather, it exercises a nonlegislative power—the *constituent* power.

☑ **F O R   R E V I E W**

1. Why are the informal qualifications for membership in the legislature more meaningful than the formal ones?

2. By what process are all State legislators chosen?

3. For what terms are the members of each house chosen in your State? How much are they paid?

4. How often are regular sessions held in your State? Why do most State legislatures now meet yearly?

5. What powers do each of the State legislatures have? What is the police power?

Organization of the Legislature

In general terms, each of the State legislatures is organized in much the same manner as Congress.

Maryland's senate in session. Its presiding officer is elected from that chamber's membership.

The Presiding Officers

Those who preside over the sessions of the nation's 99 State legislative chambers are almost always powerful political figures—in the legislature itself and elsewhere in State politics, as well.

The lower house in each of the 49 bicameral legislatures elects its own presiding officer—known everywhere as the *speaker*.

The senate chooses its own presiding officer in only 21 States. In the other 29 the lieutenant governor serves as the *president of the Senate*.[8] Where the lieutenant governor does preside the senate selects a *president pro tempore* to serve when he or she is absent.[9]

Except for the lieutenant governors, each of these presiding officers is chosen by a vote of the full membership in his or her legislative chamber. In fact, they are usually picked by the majority party's caucus in that body just before the legislature meets.

Their chief duties center around the

---

[8] The office of lieutenant governor exists in 43 States today; see pages 541, 548. In 14 of them the lieutenant governor does not double as the president of the senate, however. The Tennessee senate elects its presiding officer (known, uniquely, as the "speaker") and that officer is also, by statute, that State's lieutenant governor.

[9] The term *pro tempore* means "temporary." In practice this officer's title is generally shortened to *president pro tem*.

conduct of the legislature's floor business—and are a major source of their power. They refer bills to committee, recognize members who seek the floor, and interpret and apply the rules of their body to its proceedings.

Unlike the Speaker of the House in Congress, the speaker in nearly every State appoints the chairperson and all other members of each house committee. The senate's president or president *pro tem* has the same power in only just over half of the States. The presiding officers regularly use the power to name committees as they do their other powers—to reward their friends, punish their enemies, and otherwise work their influence on the legislature.

The Committee System

The number of measures introduced at each session of a legislature varies widely among the States—from 500 or so in some of the smaller States to several thousand in many of the larger ones. This flood makes the committee system as necessary at the State level as it is in Congress. As in Congress, much of the actual work of the legislature is done in its committee rooms.

Committees make their most important contributions to the lawmaking process (1) as they sort out those bills which should reach the floor and (2) when they inform the full chamber on those measures they have handled.

The standing committees in each house are generally set up by subject matter, as: committees on highways, local government, elections, the judiciary, education, and so on. It is to them that all bills are sent and it is in them that most bills are given the closest attention they receive. A bill may be amended or even very largely rewritten in committee, or—as often happens—ignored altogether. The question of whether a bill will ever reach the floor is

usually decided by the committee to which it has been sent.[10]

There are, on the average, 15 to 20 standing committees in each house of the typical legislature. In recent sessions the number in the lower house has run from as few as five in Massachussetts to as many as 59 in North Carolina. And in the senate, standing committees have ranged in number from five in Massachusetts to 38 in North Dakota.

The number of members per committee also varies greatly. Ten to 12 is a fairly common size, but in some States some committees have as many as 40 or more members. A legislator may serve on three or four committees at the same time. In short, in too many States too little attention is given to the relationship between the number and the size of committees on the one hand, and how well the legislature can and does function, on the other.

Joint committees—permanent groups made up of members of both houses—can produce substantial savings of legislative time and effort. They have been used extensively in a few States for several years—notably in Massachusetts, Maine, and Connecticut. In fact, the legislatures in Maine and Connecticut use *only* joint committees. There are now one or more joint committees in nearly half of the State legislatures.

The use of *interim committees*—which function *between* legislative sessions—is also growing. These groups study particular problems and then report their findings and recommendations to the next session.

---

[10]The "pigeon-holing" of bills is as well known in the States as it is in Congress; see page 305. In fact, in most States one of the standing committees in each house is regularly the "graveyard committee"—a body to which bills are sent to be buried. The judiciary committee, to which bills may be referred "on grounds of doubtful contitutionality," often fills this role. A vivid illustration of a graveyard committee existed for several years in the lower house in landlocked Oklahoma: the Committee on Deep Sea Navigation.

The Legislative Process

The basic function of the legislature is, of course, to make law. You can follow the major steps in the legislative process in a typical State in the diagram on the next page. Because that diagram is fairly descriptive, and the lawmaking machinery in each State is much like that in Congress (pages 302–314), we shall comment only briefly here.

Sources of Bills

Legally, only a member may introduce a bill in either house in any of the State legislatures. So, in the strictest sense, legislators themselves are *the* source for all of the measures introduced. In broader terms, however, the lawmakers are the real source, the authors, of only a relative handful of bills.

A large number of bills come from *public* sources—officers and agencies of State and of local government. The governor's office is always a major source. Every governor has a legislative program of some sort—and, often, an extensive and ambitious one. Much of what the lawmakers do is shaped by proposals from the governor's office.

Many bills are born in other public places, too. Take, for example, a measure to raise the maximum interest rate the State can pay on the money it borrows. It would very likely be prepared in the State treasurer's office. A change in the compulsory school attendance law might come from the superintendent of public instruction; and so on.

Bills also come from a wide range of *private* sources, too. In fact, the largest single source for proposed legislation in the States appears to be pressure groups. Remember, those groups, and their lobbyists, have one overriding purpose: To influence public policy to benefit their own interests. Of course, some bills do originate with private individuals—lawyers, business people, farmers, and other citizens who, for one reason or another, think that "there ought'a be a law . . ."

Voting

In most States votes on the floor may be taken in a number of ways. And they are taken for a number of purposes, too.

The most important vote on a measure usually comes at the point at which the bill is finally approved or rejected by the chamber—in most States at third reading. Votes are taken at several other steps in the legislative process, however —for example, on amendments, on motions to limit or close debate, on motions to re-refer (send a measure back to committee), and so on.[11]

Viva Voce. Most of the votes taken on the floor are voice votes (*viva voce*). The presiding officer puts the question and then judges the outcome from the shouts of "aye" versus the shouts of "no." The major advantage of voice votes is the speed with which they

A Georgia legislator listens to constituents as they argue their point of view and ask him to vote in support of ERA.

---

[11]One of these other votes may in fact be the critical vote that decides the fate of a measure. The real test of a bill may come with the vote on a key amendment to it. Once that vote is taken, the question of final passage (or defeat) may be just a formality.

THE COURSE OF A BILL

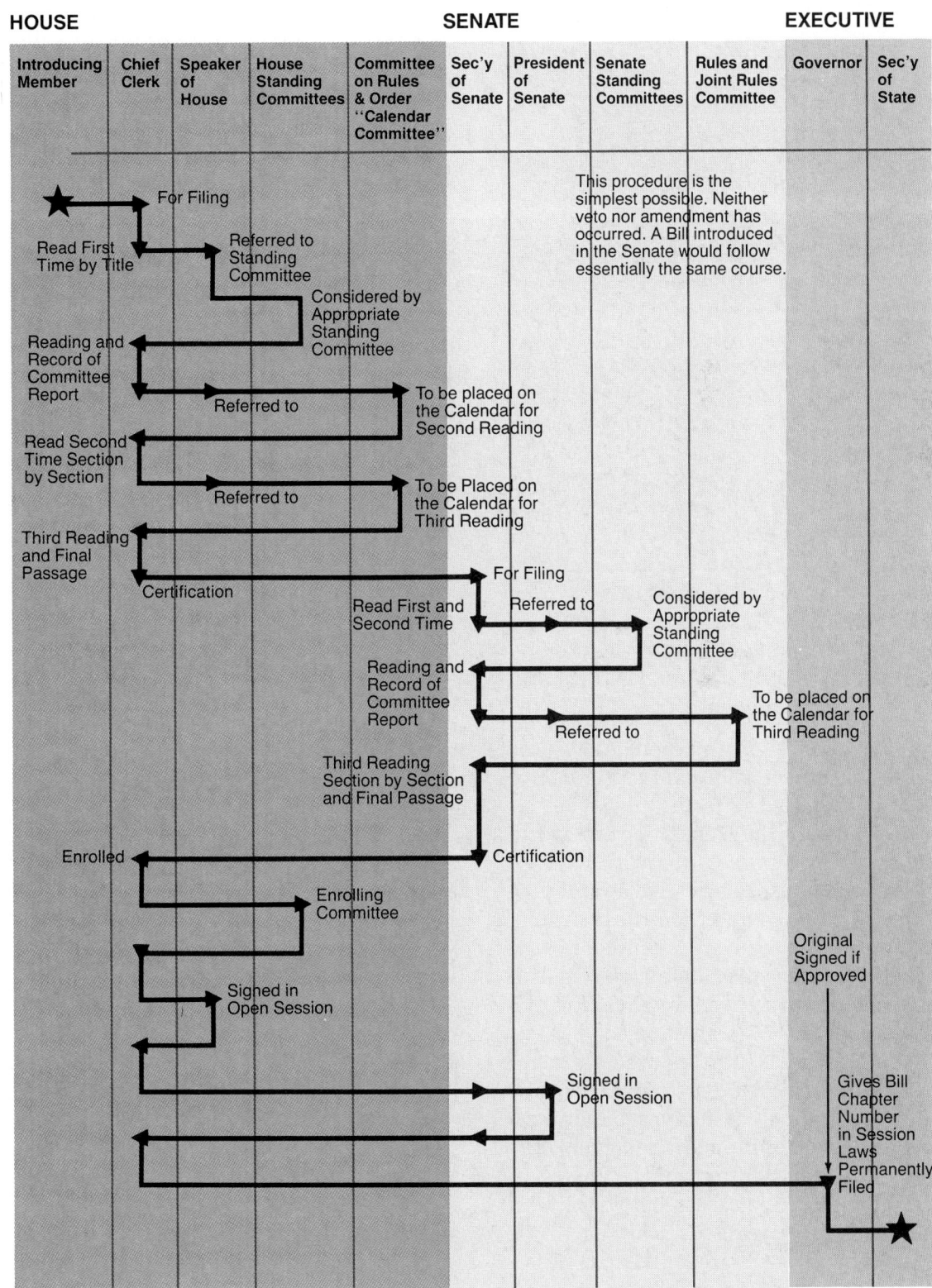

HOUSE

| Introducing Member | Chief Clerk | Speaker of House | House Standing Committees | Committee on Rules & Order "Calendar Committee" |

SENATE

| Sec'y of Senate | President of Senate | Senate Standing Committees | Rules and Joint Rules Committee |

EXECUTIVE

| Governor | Sec'y of State |

For Filing

Read First Time by Title

Referred to Standing Committee

Considered by Appropriate Standing Committee

Reading and Record of Committee Report

Referred to

To be placed on the Calendar for Second Reading

Read Second Time Section by Section

Referred to

To be Placed on the Calendar for Third Reading

Third Reading and Final Passage

Certification

For Filing

This procedure is the simplest possible. Neither veto nor amendment has occurred. A Bill introduced in the Senate would follow essentially the same course.

Read First and Second Time

Referred to

Considered by Appropriate Standing Committee

Reading and Record of Committee Report

Referred to

To be placed on the Calendar for Third Reading

Third Reading Section by Section and Final Passage

Certification

Enrolled

Enrolling Committee

Signed in Open Session

Original Signed if Approved

Signed in Open Session

Gives Bill Chapter Number in Session Laws

Permanently Filed

The electronic vote register board in the lower house of Wisconsin's State legislature.

can be taken. The method allows the presiding officer some very useful latitude in judging the result, however.

Division of the House. Some votes are taken by a process known as a *division of the house*, also called a "standing vote." Those for and then those against a motion rise and are counted by the presiding officer. A standing vote is usually taken when the chair's reading of a voice vote has been challenged.

Teller Vote. In this process members' votes are cast and counted as they file past "tellers." Usually two members (the tellers, one for and one against the question) stand in front of the chamber —telling their votes as they do so. It gives a more accurate tally than either the voice or division methods.

Record Vote. Commonly called a "roll-call vote," a record vote is one in which each member's vote is recorded— put in the permanent record. Roll calls are time-consuming, and they are often used as a delaying tactic.

The time a legislature spends in the voting process can be substantial over the course of a session. As a result, many States now use electronic devices ("scoreboards") to speed matters along.

The Governor's Veto

Once the legislature has approved a measure, it must go to the governor— who, in every State except North Carolina, has the veto power.

We shall look at the veto and the governor's other legislative powers in the next chapter. For now, these quick points. Unlike the President, the governors of 43 States have the "item veto"— the power to veto parts of a bill without rejecting the whole measure.[11] Bear in mind, too, the fact that the governor, like the President, can use the *threat* of a veto as a lever to influence the actions of the legislature.

☑ FOR REVIEW

1. Who presides over the lower house in your State? The upper house?
2. Why must and does the legislature rely so heavily upon its committees?
3. What are joint committees? Interim committees?
4. What appears to be the largest single source for bills in the several State legislatures?
5. By what four methods are floor votes taken in a legislature?

[11]In all States except Indiana, Maine, Nevada, New Hampshire, Rhode Island, Vermont and, of course, North Carolina.

6. Does the governor of your State have the item-veto power? Why is the governor's ability to threaten to use the veto an important part of the legislative process?

Improving the State Legislatures

The State legislatures are human creations; and, like their creators, none of them is perfect. Quite happily, we are now seeing some real improvements among them, however. Among the more important ones: the move to annual sessions, significant pay increases, the growing use of electronic data processing, and greatly expanded staff and research support for legislators.

Much remains to be done. Several authorities—and especially the Council of State Governments and the National Conference of State Legislatures—have long urged certain steps to upgrade the 50 State lawmaking bodies. They recommend that:

(1) Restrictions on the length of regular sessions be removed. The legislature should be able to meet as often and for as long as needed.

(2) Adequate salaries and allowances, enough to permit competent persons to serve as legislators, be provided.

(3) Legislative terms of office be lengthened, and staggered to provide for continuity in membership.

(4) The lieutenant governor be eliminated as a legislative figure.

(5) More effective regulation of lobbyists and of legislators' conflicts of interest be enacted.

(6) Legislators and committees be given adequate professional research, secretarial, and other staff aides and facilities.

(7) Legislative rules be revised as needed to speed up procedures, but with due regard for deliberation and for minority viewpoints.

(8) Committees be reduced in number where possible, and be organized in terms of subject matter, equalization of workload, and cooperation between the two houses.

(9) Committees operate "in the sunshine"—that is, hold open meetings; public hearings should be held on all major bills, and permanent and public records of all committee actions should be kept.

(10) The legislature control the auditing function, to make sure that public funds are spent in the manner and proposes for which the legislature appropriated them; see page 550.

Direct Legislation

Beginning with South Dakota in 1898, several States allow voters to take a direct part in the lawmaking process—through the *initiative* and the *referendum.*

The Initiative

On page 511 we noted that the voters may propose (initiate, by petition) constitutional amendments in 17 States. In 21 States they may initiate ordinary statutes, as well.[12]

Among these 21 States the initiative takes two quite different forms: the more common *direct initiative* and the little-used *indirect initiative.*[13]

---

[12]Alaska, Arkansas, Arizona, California, Colorado, Idaho, Maine, Massachusetts, Michigan, Missouri, Montana, Nebraska, Nevada, North Dakota, Ohio, Oklahoma, Oregon, South Dakota, Utah, Washington, Wyoming.

[13]Maine and Massachusetts provide only for the indirect form. Michigan, Nevada, Ohio, South Dakota, Utah, and Washington have both.

In both forms a certain number of qualified voters must sign initiative petitions to propose a law. The key difference between them lies in what happens to the proposed measure once enough valid signatures have been collected.

Where the **direct initiative** is used, the measure goes directly to the ballot, usually at the next general election. If the voters approve it, it becomes law; if not, it dies, of course.

In the **indirect initiative,** the proposal goes *first* to the legislature. That body may pass it, making it a law. If it

---

A CASE IN POINT

STATE DRINKING LAWS

Since the mid-1970s, many State legislatures have reversed earlier decisions to lower the legal drinking age. In recent years, Connecticut, Iowa, Maine, Maryland, Massachusetts, Michigan, Minnesota, and Montana have raised the minimum drinking age from 18 to 19, 20, or 21. Similar legislation is pending in other States. Citizens groups such as MADD (Mothers Against Drunk Drivers) have been influential in bringing about this change. The following is a conversation between two 18-year-old seniors from a State whose legislators are currently debating this issue.

Shawn: I hope the legislature votes to raise the drinking age to 21. There are too many teenagers being killed in traffic accidents. I think it would also cut down on the amount of vandalism we have in the school. Too many people our age are selling alcohol to younger kids.

David: I disagree. What right do our State legislators have to define maturity? If, by law, I'm mature enough to vote, get married, or get drafted, I don't see why I can't drink. Besides, the State can't enforce morals. Look what happened during Prohibition. Anyhow, if our State raised the legal age, kids will just go across the State border to get liquor.

Shawn: I know raising the age won't solve the whole problem, but it will help. States that have raised the age report a big decrease in traffic fatalities. Eventually, there should be federal laws setting the same drinking age everywhere.

David: Laws are too simplistic an approach. I think that parents and the schools should educate students to deal responsibly with alcohol. Besides, the laws punish all 18-year-olds when only a few abuse alcohol. Sometimes I think the older people who vote for such laws just resent the freedom that teenagers have.

1. What is the legal drinking age in your State?
2. What is your opinion on what the legal drinking age should be?

does not, the measure *then* goes to the voters.

The number of voters who must sign petitions to initiate a statute varies. In North Dakota, for example, that number must be at least two percent of the population of the State. In Arkansas, Michigan, and Washington it is eight percent of the votes cast for governor in the last election.

As fairly typical examples of the process, Oregon's voters dealt with three initiative measures in the 1980 general election. They approved one of them—a ban on the building of any new nuclear power plant in the State until a safe nuclear waste storage facility is built there. One of the measures they defeated would have placed a very tight lid on local property taxes. The other would have banned the use of leg-hold traps (used to catch coyotes, which attack cattle, sheep, and other ranch animals).

The Referendum

The referendum involves the submission (referral) of legislative acts to the voters. Three different forms of the referendum are now used among the States—the *mandatory*, the *optional*, and the *popular*.

The **mandatory referendum** is involved whenever the legislature *must* refer a measure to the voters. Thus, in every State except Delaware the legislature must submit proposed amendments to the constitution to the electorate. In several States some other measures must also go to the voters for final action—for example, bond and other borrowing measures.

An **optional referendum** measure is one which the legislature refers to the voters voluntarily. Such measures are rare. When one appears on a State's ballot it usually involves a "hot potato" question—one the lawmakers would rather not decide themselves.

High school students urge the defeat of a referendum in Massachusetts; they fear it will result in reduced funding for public education.

The **popular referendum** is the form most often connected with the idea of "direct legislation." It is now found in 24 States—the 21 States with the statutory initiative (page 533), and three others: Maryland and New Mexico, and Kentucky (where it may be used *only* for measures relating to property taxes.)

Under this form, the people may demand that a measure passed by the legislature be referred to them for final action. In short, they may insist on the right to veto an act of the legislature.[14]

Their demand must be made by petitions, signed by a certain number of qualified voters. That number varies—for example, five percent of the votes cast for governor at the last election in California and Nebraska, and six percent of all qualified voters in Ohio.

To illustrate the popular referendum process, we turn to Oregon again. In 1979 the legislature raised the State's gasoline tax from 7¢ to 9¢ a gallon. Opponents of the tax increase, having

---

[14]In most States, a measure passed by the legislature does not become effective at the time it is enacted. Rather, it becomes law at some later time, as fixed by the State constitution—usually 60 or 90 days after the legislature has adjourned. This delay permits time to circulate petitions against a measure before it goes into effect. Thus, if the petition campaign is successful, the measure does not become effective unless and until it is finally approved by the voters.

lost their fight in the legislature, mounted a referendum campaign—and soon gathered more than enough signatures. The new tax law was referred to the voters at the general election in November of 1980—and it was voted down.

The voters now face some 300 initiative and referendum measures among the States in each two-year span. Most of them appear on the general election ballots every other November.

 FOR REVIEW

1. Summarize the 10 recommendations for the improvement of State legislatures.
2. What is the initiative? Compare the two basic forms of this device.
3. What is the referendum? Compare the three forms of this device.
4. Does your State have the referendum? If so, in what form(s)?

S U M M A R Y

The legislature is the lawmaking branch of State government. It is a *bicameral* (two-chambered) body in all but one of the States; only Nebraska has a *unicameral* (single-chambered) legislature today.

The size of the legislature, and of each house, varies considerably among the 50 States. In each of them, however, the seats in both houses are now apportioned on the basis of population equality. The long-standing pattern of rural over-representation in most States was swept away by the "reapportionment revolution" of the 1960s and early 1970s. That dramatic change was set off by the Supreme Court in *Baker* v. *Carr*, 1962. In a series of cases, beginning with *Reynolds* v. *Sims*, 1964, the Court has again and again applied the "one-man, one-vote" rule. It has consistently held that the Equal Protection Clause requires that legislative districts in each State contain substantially equal numbers of persons.

Each State's constitution sets out formal qualifications for membership in the legislature. The informal qualifications, those imposed by practical politics, are far more important, however. Legislators are elected by popular vote in every State. Senators are chosen for four-year terms in 38 States and for two-years terms in the other 12. Representatives serve two-year terms in 45 States and four-year terms in only four. Legislative pay is relatively low in most States and, because of this, many qualified men and women refuse to run for legislative office.

The steadily increasing volume of legislative business has led most of the States to provide for annual legislative sessions. Only 12 States now schedule regular sessions on a biennial basis. Special sessions may be called by the governor in every State and by the legislature itself in just over half of them.

In each State the legislature possesses all of those governmental powers that (1) the State constitution does not give exclusively to the executive or judicial branches of the State's government or to its local units and (2) neither the State nor the National Consitution denies to the legislature. Its very extensive powers include the broad police power and a number of nonlegislative powers.

The organization and the lawmaking procedures of the typical State legislature are much like those of Congress. The presiding officers are powerful figures within the legislature and elsewhere in the politics of the State. As in Congress, a major share of the legislature's work is done in committees. Bills originate with public and private sources. The governor holds the veto power in every State except North Carolina; that power includes the item veto in 43 States.

Through devices of direct legislation—the initiative and the referendum—the voters in several States may take a direct part in the lawmaking process.

CHAPTER REVIEW

Key Terms/Concepts
Apportionment (521)
Bicameral (519)
Constituent power (528)
Direct legislation (533)
Division of the house (532)
Initiative (533)
Interim committee (529)
Item veto (532)
Joint committee (529)
Legislative powers (527)
Nonlegislative powers (527)
One-man, one-vote rule (522)
Police power (527)
Reapportionment (521)
Record vote (532)
Referendum (535)
Roll call (532)
Session (525)
Special session (526)
Standing committee (529)
Teller vote (532)
Unicameral (519)
Veto (532)
Veto session (526)
Voice vote (530)

Keynote Questions

1. What is the basic function of State legislatures?
2. Why are all but one of the State legislatures bicameral?
3. What major arguments are usually made for bicameralism? For unicameralism?
4. Why is the basis of apportionment of a State's legislature so important a matter?
5. What is the only standard for legislative apportionment today?
6. By what process are all State legislators chosen?
7. Why do most of the State legislatures now meet in regular session each year?
8. Why is it impossible to list all of the powers held by the State legislatures today?
9. Who usually presides over the lower house in a State legislature? The upper house? In your State?
10. Why does a State legislature rely so heavily upon its committees?
11. What is the initiative? The referendum? What several forms of these devices are there?

For Thought and Discussion

1. In his classic study, *The American Commonwealth*, Lord Bryce said in 1888: "The legislature is so much the strongest force in the several States that they may almost call it the Government and ignore all other authorities." How accurate do you think that judgement is today?
2. Should the elected term of the members of either or both houses of your State's legislature be longer? Shorter? Should the size of either or both houses be increased? Reduced?
3. On page 525 we noted that low pay and partisan politics appear to be the major reasons for the high rate of turnover in legislative seats in most States. Are there other reasons?

Suggested Activities

1. If possible, arrange for the class to visit the legislature when it is in session. (One or more of your legislators will almost certainly help make the necessary arrangements.)
2. Prepare a diagram of the legislative process in your State's legislature. (See page 531 for a useful model.)
3. Stage a debate or class forum on one of the following questions: (a) *Resolved*, That the legislature of this State be restructured as a unicameral body; (b) *Resolved*, That this State (adopt/repeal) the direct initiative and/or the popular referendum.

21 The Governor and State Administration

To help you to
Learn ▪ Know ▪ Understand

The origins and development of the office of governor.

The shape of the office today, in terms of formal and informal qualifications, selection, tenure, compensation, and succession.

The many different, interacting roles governors must play.

The scope and content of gubernatorial powers and the fragmented nature of executive power in State government.

The other executive offices and their principal functions.

Energy in the Executive is a leading character in the definition of good government.

Alexander Hamilton

The governor is the principal executive officer in each of the 50 States. He—or she[1]—is always a central figure in State politics and is often a well-known national personality, as well.

The governor today holds an office that is the direct descendant of the earliest public office in American politics—the colonial governorship, first established in Virginia in 1607.

Much of the colonial resentment that finally exploded into revolution was directed at the royal governors. That attitude was carried over into the first State constitutions. The new State governors were given, for the most part, very little real authority. Most of the powers the State governments did have were given to the legislature. In every State except Massachusetts and New York, the governor was chosen by the legislature, and in most of them only for

---

[1]Only one of the 50 governors today (1984) is a woman: Governor Martha Layne Collins of Kentucky, elected in 1983. Only five other women have ever been elected to a governorship: Nellie T. Ross (Wyoming, 1925–1927; Miriam A. Ferguson (Texas, 1925–27, 1933–35); Lurleen Wallace (Alabama, 1967–1968); Ella T. Grasso (Connecticut, 1975–1980); and Dixy Lee Ray (Washington, 1977–1981). Unlike Governors Grasso, Ray, and Collins, the three earlier women followed their husbands in the office of governor.

Governor John D. Rockefeller IV (D., West Virginia) was first elected in 1976 and re-elected in 1980. He cannot seek another term in 1984 and plans to run for a seat in the United States Senate, instead.

PARTY CONTROL OF GOVERNORSHIPS

Following Elections of	Republicans	Democrats
1946	25	23
1948	18	30
1950	25	23
1952	30	18
1954	21	27
1956	20	28
1958	14	34
1960	16	34
1962	16	34
1964	17	33
1966	25	25
1968	31	19
1970	21	29
1972	19	31
1974[a]	13	36
1976	12	37
1978	18	32
1980	23	27
1982	16	34
1984	?	?

[a]James B. Longley, an independent, was elected to a four-year term as governor of Maine in 1974.

Succession

Every State constitution provides for a successor should the governorship become vacant. In 43 States the lieutenant governor is first in the line of succession; see page 548. In four others—Maine, New Hampshire, New Jersey, and West Virginia—the president of the senate succeeds. In the other three—Arizona, Oregon, and Wyoming—the office passes to the secretary of state.

Governors are mortal; occasionally one of them dies in office. Many are also politically ambitious; every so often, one of them resigns in mid-term—to become a U.S. Senator, for example. When a vacancy does occur, it usually sets off a game of political musical chairs in the State.[6]

Removal. The governor may be removed from office by the impeachment process in all but one State, Oregon. But only four governors have been thrown out of office since Reconstruction days —and none in over 50 years.[7]

The governor may be *recalled* by the voters in 15 States.[8] Only one ever has been, however. Governor Lynn J. Frazier was removed by the voters of North

[6]Over time, most newly elected Presidents have appointed one or more governors (of their own party) to high federal posts. (Ronald Reagan did not follow this historical pattern, however.) With a vacancy in the governorship, the political plans and timetables of ambition of several public figures are affected.

[7]William Salzer of New York in 1913; James E. Ferguson of Texas in 1917; J.C. Walton of Oklahoma in 1923; and Henry S. Johnston of Oklahoma in 1929. "Pa" Ferguson was later pardoned by the Texas legislature and announced at once his candidacy for the governorship. But the State Supreme Court held the legislature's pardon unconstitutional in 1920. His wife, Miriam T. ("Ma") Ferguson, then ran for and won the office in 1924 (and again in 1932), as we noted on page 538.

[8]Alaska, Arizona, California, Colorado, Georgia, Idaho, Kansas, Louisiana, Michigan, Montana, Nevada, North Dakota, Oregon, Washington, Wisconsin. The **recall** is a procedure by which voters may remove an elected official from office before the completion of his or her regular term. The process generally works this way: If a certain number of qualified voters (usually 25 percent of the number who voted in the last general election) sign recall petitions, a special election must be held at which the voters decide whether to remove (recall) the officeholder or not.

STATE GOVERNORS

State	Term in Years	Annual Salary
Alabama	4	$50,000 and residence
Alaska	4	$81,648 and residence
Arizona	4	$56,000
Arkansas	2	$35,000 and residence
California	4	$49,100 and residence
Colorado	4	$60,000 and residence
Connecticut	4	$65,000 and residence
Delaware	4	$35,000 and residence
Florida	4	$69,550 and residence
Georgia	4	$71,214 and residence
Hawaii	4	$59,400 and residence
Idaho	4	$50,000 and residence
Illinois	4	$58,000 and residence
Indiana	4	$47,996 and residence
Iowa	4	$60,000 and residence
Kansas	4	$52,425 and residence
Kentucky	4	$50,000 and residence
Louisiana	4	$73,440 and residence
Maine	4	$35,000 and residence
Maryland	4	$75,000 and residence
Massachusetts	4	$60,000
Michigan	4	$70,000 and residence
Minnesota	4	$66,500 and residence
Mississippi	4	$63,000 and residence
Missouri	4	$55,000 and residence
Montana	4	$47,962 and residence
Nebraska	4	$40,000 and residence
Nevada	4	$65,000 and residence
New Hampshire	2	$58,803 and residence
New Jersey	4	$85,000 and residence
New Mexico	4	$60,000 and residence
New York	4	$100,000 and residence
North Carolina	4	$60,768 and residence
North Dakota	4	$60,862 and residence
Ohio	4	$65,000 and residence
Oklahoma	4	$70,000 and residence
Oregon	4	$55,423 and residence
Pennsylvania	4	$85,000 and residence
Rhode Island	2	$49,500
South Carolina	4	$60,000 and residence
South Dakota	4	$50,975 and residence
Tennessee	4	$68,226 and residence
Texas	4	$90,700 and residence
Utah	4	$52,000 and residence
Vermont	2	$50,000
Virginia	4	$75,000 and residence
Washington	4	$63,000 and residence
West Virginia	4	$60,000 and residence
Wisconsin	4	$75,337 and residence
Wyoming	4	$70,000 and residence

Sources: State constitutions and statutes and information furnished by appropriate State officials.

Dakota in 1921—but he was elected to the United States Senate the very next year.

Compensation

A glance at the table on this page will show that gubernatorial salaries now average just about $61,000 a year among the States. There is a fairly wide spread among them, however—from the few where the pay is quite low on up to as much as $100,000 in New York. Most States also provide the governor with an official residence (generally called "the governor's mansion") and a more or less generous expense account.

To the governors' salary and other material compensation must be added the intangibles of honor and prestige that go along with the office. Indeed, it is this factor, along with a sense of public duty, that often brings many of our better citizens to seek the office. About a fourth of the members of the United States Senate are former governors, and a number of Senators later served as governors. Former Chief Justice Earl Warren went to the High Court from the governor's chair in California. Several Presidents were governors of their States before entering the White House—including, since 1900: Theodore Roosevelt, Woodrow Wilson, Calvin Coolidge, Franklin Rossevelt, Jimmy Carter, and now, Ronald Reagan.

✓ FOR REVIEW

1. Outline the general pattern of the development of the office of governor from independence to the present.
2. Distinguish the formal and the informal qualifications one must meet in order to become governor.
3. How is the governor chosen in every State?

4. For what term is the governor elected in your State? Is that tenure limited? Salary?

5. How may the governor be removed from office in your State?

6. Who succeeds to the office in case of a vacancy?

The Governor at Work

The Many Roles

The powers and duties of the governor of each State may be grouped under three major headings, and one lesser one: (1) executive, (2) legislative, (3) judicial, and (4) miscellaneous and ceremonial. A useful understanding of the nature of the office can be had by examining each of these categories.

But, first, notice that the governor, like the President, plays many roles—wears many different hats. He, or she, is at the same time, an executive, an administrator, a legislator, a party leader, an opinion leader, and a ceremonial figure. What the office in fact amounts to depends very largely on how the governor plays each, and all, of those roles. And how he or she does so depends, in turn, upon the strength of the governor's personality, political muscle, and overall abilities.

Some, often most, of the governor's formal powers are hedged with constitutional and other legal restrictions. But the powers the office does have, together with its prestige, make it quite possible for a capable, persuasive, dynamic incumbent to be a "strong" governor, accomplishing much for the State and the public good.

One noted authority on State politics insists that the powers of any and all of the governors rest very largely on their talents of persuasion:

Their power depends on their ability to persuade administrators over whom they have little authority, legislators who are jealous of their own powers, party leaders who are selected by local constituents, federal officials over whom governors have little authority, and a public that thinks governors have more authority than they really have. Thus, the role of governors is, above all, that of a persuader—of their own administrators, State legislators, federal officials, party leaders, the press, and the public.[9]

Executive Powers

The Presidency and the governorship can be likened in several ways, but the comparison can be pushed too far. Remember that the Constitution of the United States makes the President *the* executive in the National Government. State constitutions, on the other hand, regularly describe the governor as the *chief* executive in State government.

This difference between *the* and *chief* is a critical one. Most of the State constitutions divide the executive power among several "executive officers." This has the effect of making the governor only "first among equals." As we shall see, these other executive officers are almost always popularly elected. And, because they are, they are very largely beyond the governor's control.

In most States, then, the executive authority is fragmented. It is held by several separate, and independently chosen, officers. Only a part of it is in fact held by the governor. Yet, whatever the realities of power may be, it is the governor to whom the people look for leadership in State affairs—and hold responsible for their conduct and condition.

The basic legal responsibility of the

---

[9]Thomas R. Dye, *Politics in States and Communities.* (Englewood Cliffs, N.J.: Prentice-Hall, 4th ed., 1981), p. 162.

governor is regularly found in a constitutional provision directing the chief executive to "take care that the laws be faithfully executed." And, though the executive authority may be divided, the governor is given a number of specific powers with which to do that job.

Appointment and Removal. The governor can best carry out the duty to execute—enforce and administer—the law with subordinates of his or her own choosing. Hence, the powers of appointment and removal are, or should be, among the most important in the chief executive's arsenal.

A leading test of any administrator is the ability to select loyal and able assistants. Two major factors work against the governor's effectiveness here, however. First, of course, is the existence of those other elected executives; the people choose them and the governor cannot remove them.

Secondly, the State's constitution and statutes place restrictions on the governor's power to hire and fire. In most States the constitution requires that most of the governor's major appointees be confirmed by the State senate. And the legislature often sets qualifications and other conditions that must be met by those appointed to the offices it has created by statute. In a vigorous two-party State, for example, the law often requires that not more than a certain number of the members of each board or commission be from the same political party. This means, of course, that the governor must appoint some members of the opposing party to posts in his/her administration.

There are many other limits of this sort. As but one more example: The law often requires that those persons the governor appoints to any of the State's professional licensing boards must themselves be licensed to practice in the particular field that that board regulates.

Thus, only licensed realtors can be appointed to the real estate board; only licensed MDs can serve on the board of medical examiners; and so on.

Still, the governor must fill many important posts. To help make it possible for that to be done more effectively, recent reorganization efforts have stressed this recommendation: Place governmental functions in the hands of a small number of agencies—each headed by a single administrator, chosen by and answering directly to the governor.

Supervision of Administration. The governor is the State's chief administrator—again, not *the* and not the *only* but the *chief* administrator.

Alone, the governor cannot possibly "take care that the laws be faithfully executed." Unaided, he or she cannot enforce all of the State's laws, perform all of its many functions, provide all of its many services. That work is done, day-to-day, by the thousands of men and women who staff the agencies that make up the State's executive branch, of course. The governor must supervise that work—must manage and oversee the administration.

That is, the governor must do so—so far as he or she *can.* Many of the State's agencies are subject to the governor's direct control. But, remember, many are not. They are headed by other elected officials. For instance: an elected attorney general regularly heads the department of justice and an elected secretary of state administers the election laws.

At base, the governor's ability to supervise State administration depends, *first,* upon the extent to which the constitution and statutes make that possible. And, *second,* upon the governor's ability to operate by such means as party leadership, appeals to the public, and the like—or, as Dye told us on page 543, on the governor's talents of persuasion.

The Budget.   We shall take a close

look at the budget-making process in Chapter 24. But we must look into that subject for a moment here.

As we suggested earlier, a budget is much more than a balance sheet, much more than a dull recitation of dollars from here and dollars for that. It is a *political* document, a highly important policy statement. Its numbers reflect the struggle over "who gets what"—and who doesn't.

Public agencies, no less than private businesses, can do little without money. Clearly, those who hold the purse-strings have a large measure of control over the activities (and even the very lives) of public agencies.

In most States the governor now has the power to make the State's budget. That is, the governor prepares the annual (or biennial) budget that goes to the legislature. The legislature may make changes in the governor's financial plan, of course. It may appropriate this or that amount, or nothing, for this agency and that program, as it chooses. *But*—and this is the vital point—the governor's budget recommendations carry a great deal of weight.

In short, the governor's budget-making power can be—and often is—a powerful tool with which he or she can control State administration. Although unable to appoint or remove the head of a certain agency, for example, the governor can use the budget-making power to affect that agency's programs—and so have a real impact on the attitudes and behavior of that official.

Military Powers. Every State constitution makes the governor the commander-in-chief of the State militia —effectively, of the State's units of the National Guard.

The National Guard is the *organized* part of the State militia. In a national emergency it may be "called up"—

ordered into federal service by the President.[10]

When the State's Guard units are not in federal service—which is most of the time—they are commanded by the governor. The governor's chief military aide, the adjutant general, serves as the highest ranking officer of the State's National Guard.

At certain times, governors find it necessary to call out the Guard—to deal with such emergencies as prison riots, to aid in relief and evacuation and prevent looting during and after a flood or some other natural disaster, to help State police reduce holiday traffic accidents, and so on.

Legislative Powers

The State's principal *executive* officer has three quite important formal *legislative* powers: (1) to send messages to the legislature, (2) to call the legislature into special session, and (3) to veto measures passed by the legislature. These powers, together with the governor's own political clout, often make the governor, in fact, the State's chief legislator.

The Message Power. The message power is really the power to recommend legislation—and a strong governor can do much with it.

As we noted earlier, much of what the legislature does centers on the governor's program for legislative action. That program is given to the lawmakers in a yearly State of the State address and in the budget, and in several special messages, too. The most effective governors regularly push their programs by

---

[10]All of the States' National Guard units were federalized in 1940 and served as part of the nation's armed forces in World War II. Many units also saw extensive combat duty in both Korea and Vietnam. National Guard units are not often called into federal service in domestic crisis situations, however; see pages 73, 398.

using the formal message power together with a number of informal tactics—appeals to the people, close contacts with key legislators, a shrewd use of the appointing power, and so on.

Special Sessions.   The governor in every State has the power to call the legislature into special session.[11]

Special sessions have become fairly common among the States, as both the volume and the complexity of State business have grown. This is most true in those States which still schedule regular biennial sessions—and even more so where the biennial session is limited as to length.

The basic purpose of the governor's power here is to permit the State to meet extraordinary situations, of course. But the power can also be an important part of the governor's legislative arsenal, too. On occasion, a governor has persuaded reluctant legislators to pass a bill by threatening to call them back in a special session if they adjourn the regular session without having done so.

The Veto Power.   Except for North Carolina, the governor in every State has the power to veto measures passed by the legislature. This power, as well as the *threat* to use it, is often the most potent power the governor has in influencing the work of the legislature.

In most States the governor has only a few days in which to sign or veto a measure—most often five.[12] If no action is taken within the period set—and the

legislature remains in session—the measure then becomes law.[13]

The Pocket Veto.   Unlike the President, the governor does not have the **pocket veto** in most States. That is, those bills the governor neither signs nor vetoes *after* the legislature adjourns become law without his/her signature.

The governor does have the pocket veto in 15 States, however.[14] Take Oklahoma, for example. There the governor has five days (not counting Sunday) to act on a measure while the legislature remains in session. But if the session ends during that five-day period the governor then has another 15 days in which to act. If the bill is neither signed nor vetoed within that 15-day period, it dies—the pocket veto has been applied.

The Item Veto.   In 43 States[15] the governor's veto power includes the **item veto.** That is, the governor may veto one or more provisions (items) in a bill without rejecting the entire measure. The power is most often—but not always—restricted to money items.

The item veto is regularly used to check extravagant legislative appropriations. But, notice, the fact that the governor has this power sometimes means that legislators will vote for certain spending proposals and "pass the buck" for balancing the State's budget on to the governor. Often, the governor finds the item veto a useful weapon with which to persuade or punish lawmakers who oppose the governor's program.

The Legislature's Power to Override.   The governor does not have an abso-

---

[11]See page 526. In most States, the lawmakers may deal with any matters they choose; and this fact sometimes makes a governor slow to call a special session.

[12]Three days in Iowa, Minnesota, New Mexico, North Dakota, Wyoming; six days in Alabama, Georgia, Maryland, Rhode Island, Wisconsin; seven days in Florida, Indiana, Virginia; 10 days in Colorado, Delaware, Hawaii, Kansas, Kentucky, Louisiana, Maine, Massachusetts, New Jersey, New York, Ohio, Pennsylvania, Tennessee, Texas; 12 days in California; 14 days in Michigan; 15 days in Alaska, Missouri, 60 days in Illinois; and five days in the other 17 States. In most States Sundays are excluded from the count.

[13]The period *after* adjournment is somewhat longer in several States—*e.g.*, 20 days in Arkansas and Texas; 30 days in Georgia and Iowa; 45 days in Alaska and New Jersey. On "veto sessions" in some States, see page 526.

[14]Alabama, Delaware, Hawaii, Iowa, Massachusetts, Michigan, Minnesota, New Hampshire, New Jersey, New Mexico, New York, Oklahoma, Vermont, Virginia, Wisconsin.

[15]All except Indiana, Maine, Nevada, New Hampshire, Rhode Island, Vermont, and North Carolina.

lute veto power in any State—except where the pocket veto is involved. That is, the governor's veto is subject to a vote to override it in the legislature.

The size of the vote needed to override varies among the States, but two-thirds of the full membership in each house is most common.

In actual practice, not many bills are vetoed. Less than five percent of all measures passed by the State legislatures are rejected. But when the power is used it is quite effective. Fewer than ten percent of all vetoed bills are then passed over the governor's veto.

Judicial Powers

In every State the governor has several powers of a judicial nature. Most of them are usually referred to as the powers of **executive clemency**—powers of mercy which may be shown toward those convicted of crime. They include:

The power to **pardon**—that is, to release a person from the legal consequences of a crime. In most States, a pardon may be either full or conditional and cannot be granted until *after* conviction. In most, too, a pardon cannot be granted in cases involving either treason or impeachment.

The power to **commute**—that is, to reduce the sentence imposed by a court. Thus, a death sentence may be commuted to life imprisonment, or the commutation may be to "time served"—which means that the prisoner is then released.

The power to **reprieve**—that is, to postpone the execution of a sentence. Reprieves are usually granted for a few hours or a few days—to allow more time for an appeal or because some new piece of evidence in a case has been found.

The power to **remit**—that is, to eliminate or reduce a fine imposed upon conviction.

The power to **parole**—that is, to release a prisoner short of the completion

of the term of a sentence. Paroles are usually conditional and supervised. They are also a regular—and often controversial—part of the criminal corrections process.

The governor may have some or all of these powers, but they are often shared with one or more boards—as with a board of pardons and/or a parole board. Receiving an extradition warrant from another State also places the governor in a judicial role; see page 79.

Miscellaneous Duties

The governor of every State has many other time-consuming duties. A list a few of them gives an idea of their scope. The governor receives official visitors and welcomes other distinguished persons to the State, dedicates new buildings and parks, opens the State fair and attends countless local celebrations, addresses many organizations and public gatherings, and crowns beauty contest, spelling bee, and soap-box derby winners. He or she is an *ex officio* (by virtue of office) member

A flood-ravaged town in north-central Oklahoma, where high flood waters routed some 600 families from their homes. Surveying the damage is Lieutenant Governor Spencer Bernard.

of several boards and commissions and must attend their meetings, of course. Then, too, the governor is often called upon to help settle labor disputes, to travel elsewhere in the country and sometimes abroad, to endorse worthy causes—indeed, the list is almost endless.

✓ FOR REVIEW

1. What is meant by the observation that "the governor wears many different hats"?

2. In what major way is the executive power fragmented in most States?

3. What is the governor's basic legal responsibility in every State?

4. Why are the governor's powers of appointment and removal important? The budget-making power?

5. What are the governor's legislative powers? Judicial powers?

Other Executive Officers

As we've noted several times, in nearly every State the governor must share the control of his or her administration with other elected officials.

Only three States—Maine, New Jersey, and Tennessee—make the governor the only popularly elected executive officer. And, among the three, only New Jersey now allows the governor to appoint all of the other principal officers in the executive branch of the State's government.[16]

The other executive officers most often found among the States include the lieutenant governor, secretary of state, treasurer, auditor, attorney general, and superintendent of public instruction. No useful treatment of the executive function can overlook them.

The Lieutenant Governor

The office of lieutenant governor now exists in 43 States and is filled by the voters in 42 of them.[17]

The formal duties of the lieutenant governor are much like those of the Vice President—that is, there is little to do. He or she succeeds to the governorship if there is a vacancy, and presides over the senate in most (but a declining number) of States; see page 528.

The office is often regarded as a stepping-stone to the governorship—sometimes by succession, of course, but often in terms of future elections. Seven States seem to get along quite well without the office. Many feel that it should

[16]In Maine the secretary of state, treasurer, and attorney general are elected by the legislature. In Tennessee the secretary of state and treasurer are also chosen by the legislature and the attorney general is selected by the State supreme court.

[17]In Tennessee the presiding officer of the senate (the speaker) is also, by statute the lieutenant governor. The office does not exist in seven States: Arizona, Maine, New Hampshire, New Jersey, Oregon, West Virginia, Wyoming.

THE "TYPICAL" GOVERNOR

As we noted at the beginning of this chapter, the governor is everywhere a central figure in State politics and is often a well-known national personality, as well.

Governors (and gubernatorial candidates) come in a wide range of shapes and sizes. That is, they do with one large exception: They are very seldom female. Of the more than 2000 persons who have served as State governors over the past two centuries, only six have been women—and only one woman holds that office today; see page 538. (Thirty-six of the 50 governorships were up for election in 1982. Among the 72 major party gubernatorial candidates, only two were female—one in Iowa and the other in Vermont; both of them lost.)

The "typical" State governor today can be described in these terms: He is a native of the State, in his middle 40s, married, a college graduate, a veteran of the armed forces, and an attorney by profession.

The governor most often began his political life in the State legislature or as a prosecuting attorney. Some moved from the legislature directly to the governor's office. More often, however, the State's chief executive was the lieutenant governor or held some other State-wide elective office immediately before becoming governor.

1. Write a short biography of the governor of your State. How does he fit the profile of the "typical" governor?
2. Why is the governor's office a much sought after post in every State?
3. Why do so few women seek the office of governor today? Why have so few ever held the office? Does any woman have a reasonable chance of becoming the governor of your State any time soon?

be abolished everywhere. In 1981, David O'Neal, then the lieutenant governor of Illinois, made that proposal in a forthright way. He resigned—because, he said, "the office gave him" nothing to do."

The Secretary of State

The office of secretary of state exists everywhere but in Alaska, Hawaii, and Utah. The post is filled by the voters in 36 States, by the governor in eight,[18] and

by the legislature in the other three States—Maine, New Hampshire, and Tennessee.

The secretary of state is the State's chief clerk and records-keeper. He or she has charge of a great variety of public documents, records the official acts of the governor and the legislature, usually administers the election laws, and is "the keeper of the Great Seal of the State." As with most of these other elected executives, little discretion is given to the secretary of state; most duties of the office are closely detailed by law.

[18]Delaware, Maryland, New Jersey, New York, Oklahoma, Pennsylvania, Texas, Virginia. In Alaska, Hawaii, and Utah the usual duties of the office are assigned to the lieutenant governor.

The Treasurer

The voters in 38 States elect a treasurer. The governor appoints the treasurer in Michigan, New Jersey, New York, and Virginia; and the legislature does so in Maine, Maryland, New Hampshire, and Tennessee.[19]

The treasurer is the custodian of State funds, often the State's chief tax collector, and regularly the State's paymaster. The treasurer's major job is to make payments out of the State treasury. Most of those payments go to meet the many agency payrolls and to pay bills from those who have supplied goods or services to the State. Here, the treasurer must work closely with the auditor, as we shall see in a moment.

The State often has surplus monies, dollars not currently at work—funds not yet appropriated by the legislature, contributions to the public employees retirement system, and the like. In most States the treasurer manages these surplus monies—placing them in banks and in such other places as the short-term notes of the Federal Government, bonds issued by local governments, and even the private stock and bond market. The interest on those investments usually brings a nice little profit to the State's treasury. In short, the treasurer is the State's banker.

The Auditor or Comptroller

Every State's constitution forbids the spending of any State money unless the legislature has authorized that spending—that is, money cannot be spent unless the legislature has first passed a law appropriating the funds for it.

The Pre-Audit and the Post-Audit. *Before* a particular spending is made, some public official must carry out the *pre-audit* function. That is, that officer must issue a **warrant** (a check), certifying that that outlay is legal and that the money for it is in the State treasury.

Some public official must also carry out the *post-audit* function. That is, that officer must review and verify the accounts of all officers and agencies handling public funds, *after* expenditures are made. That officer must make periodic checks to see that the spending was in fact made in accord with the law.

Most experts in public finance agree that these two safeguarding functions should be carried out by two quite separate officers. They recommend that someone, named by and responsible to the governor, do all of the pre-audit work. And they urge that someone else, named by and responsible to the legislature, conduct all post-audits. In other words, they recommend that the governor's agent—a **comptroller**—keep public officers and agencies on the straight and narrow path as they spend the public's money. And they urge that the legislature's agent (an **auditor**) police the books and weed out misdeeds and other unauthorized practices.

Only 12 States presently give the pre-audit job to a gubernatorial appointee and the post-audit task to a legislative appointee.[20] In most of the other States some elected official—the auditor or the comptroller—is involved in one or both of these functions.

Only 19 States now give the all-important post-audit task to an officer chosen by and answerable to the legislature.[21] Putting the post-audit

---

[19]Elsewhere, the duties of the treasurer are handled by the Commissioner of Revenue in Alaska, the Director of Fiscal Services in the Department of Administrative Services in Georgia, the Director of the Department of Budget and Finance in Hawaii, and the Director of the Department of Administration in Montana. Each of these officials is appointed by the governor.

[20]Alaska, Arizona, Colorado, Connecticut, Florida, Kansas, Louisiana, Maine, Michigan, Minnesota, Montana, New Hampshire.

[21]The 12 States listed in note 20 and Georgia, Idaho, Illinois, South Dakota, Tennessee, Texas, Wyoming.

function in the hands of an officer in the executive branch runs the same sort of risks as those involved in asking the fox to guard the chicken coop.

The Attorney General

The attorney general is the State's lawyer. The voters fill the post in 43 States. The governor names the AG in five States: Alaska, Hawaii, New Hampshire, New Jersey, and Wyoming. Maine's legislature chooses the AG and Tennessee's supreme court does so.

The AG acts as the legal adviser to the governor and other State officers and agencies, and often to the legislature. He or she represents the State in court and oversees the work of local prosecutors.

Much of the power and importance of the office centers on the attorney general's **opinions.** These are formal written interpretations of constitutional and statutory law. They are issued in answer to questions raised by the governor, other executive officers, legislators, and local officials—regarding the lawfulness of their actions or proposed actions. In most States these opinions have the force of law unless and until they are successfully challenged in the courts.

The Superintendent of Public Instruction

Known by a variety of titles, the chief school administrator is the overall supervisor of the public school system in every State. Most often this officer is known as the superintendent of public instruction or the commissioner of education. He or she usually shares authority with a State board of education.

The voters still choose the chief school officer in 17 States, in most cases on a nonpartisan basis.[22] The post is

Jon Kennedy in the *Arkansas Journal*

"One of us has got to go"

filled by the governor in but 9 States,[23] and by the board in the other 24.[24]

Other Officers and Agencies

The offices we have just reviewed are the major ones to be found in all or most of the 50 States. There are, of course, many others. They vary in number, name, and function from State to State. Some were created by constitutional provision, others by statute. Some are elected by the voters, others are appointed by the governor or, in some cases, by someone else.[25]

---

[22]Arizona, California, Florida, Georgia, Idaho, Indiana, Kentucky, Louisiana, Montana, North Carolina, North Dakota, Oklahoma, Oregon, South Carolina, Washington, Wisconsin, Wyoming.

[23]Connecticut, Iowa, Maine, Mississippi, New Jersey, Pennsylvania, South Dakota, Tennessee, Virginia.

[24]The members of the board are themselves chosen by the voters in 14 States today: Alabama, Colorado, Hawaii, Idaho, Kansas, Louisiana, Massachusetts, Michigan, Nebraska, Nevada, New Mexico, Ohio, Texas, Utah. Generally they are picked by the governor elsewhere in the country (but there is no State board of education in Wisconsin.).

[25]These officers (and various boards and commissions) are so numerous and vary so much from State to State that it would be pointless to try to treat them here. Nearly every State puts out a *Blue Book* or other directory which at least lists—and often describes the organization and functions of—all State agencies.

Each year, governors of each of the States are invited to take part in the National Governors' Conference, held in Washington, D.C., in 1983. At such conferences, common problems are discussed and interstate cooperation is promoted.

In many States several public functions are handled by boards or commissions—rather than by an agency headed by a single administrator. Thus, the management of correctional, mental, or educational institutions is often in the hands of a several-member board —for example, the State Board of Prisons and Parole or the State Board of Education. Laws relating to agriculture, public health, or highways are the responsibility of a State Board of Agriculture, a State Board of Health, or a State Highway Commission. Public utilities and other corporations are regulated by a Public Service Commission. And there are also a number of licensing and examining bodies in every State—as the Board of Medical Examiners, the Board of Barber Examiners, the Department of Motor Vehicles, and so on.

Administrative Reorganization

As one function after another was added to the work of State government, boards and commissions were established to handle them. Often these new agencies were set up to meet a need of the moment but with little concern for their place in an orderly structured executive branch. Usually, they were made independent of one another, and often even of the governor. The certain result was confusion and, at times, chaos.

Overlapping and duplication of effort, waste and inefficiency, a lack of coordination—sometimes mixed with graft and often touched with favoritism —came to characterize most State administrations. Yet today some States are plagued by the jerry-built way in which the executive branch developed.

Every State has made at least some progress in executive branch reorganization in the past few decades; and those reform efforts have been stepped up in most States in recent years. Among the most effective administrations today are those in Alaska, California, Hawaii, Michigan, Missouri, New Jersey, New York, and North Carolina. But much remains to be done in most States.

Experts in public administration have put together a number of guidelines for State executive branch reorganization. Their recommendations have been conveniently summarized by the Council of State Governments:[26]

---

[26]The Council, founded in 1935, is a research and reporting agency supported by each of the 50 States. It maintains a central headquarters at Lexington, Kentucky, and other offices in New York, Chicago, Atlanta, San Francisco, and Washington, D.C. It publishes a monthly newsletter, State Government News, a quarterly journal, State Government, and a biennial volume of current statistical information and commentary, The Book of the States, as well as many specialized reports.

(1) Consolidate all administrative agencies into a relatively small number of departments (usually 10 to 20), on the basis of function or general purpose. The number of these departments should be small enough to fit within the governor's effective "span of control."

(2) Establish clear lines of authority and responsibility running from the governor at the top of the hierarchy down through the entire organization.

(3) Establish appropriate staff (advisory, planning, budget) agencies immediately responsible to the governor.

(4) To the greatest extent possible, eliminate multi-headed agencies (boards and commissions) for administrative work.

(5) Establish an independent auditor, with authority for post-audit only.

There is a promising move among the States to reorganize along departmental lines—that is, to place all similar and related activities under a single overall agency (a department). In the most thorough-going reorganizations, each department is headed by a single administrator, appointed by and answering to the governor. The departments most commonly found today are: administration, agriculture, corrections, education, environmental protection, finance, health, insurance, justice, labor, military, natural resources, public works, transportation, and welfare.

✓ FOR REVIEW

1. Identify the other major executive officers found in most States, and their functions. Which of them are found in your State? How are these officers chosen in most States? In your State?

2. What are the basic guidelines for State administrative reorganization identified by the Council of State Governments?

SUMMARY

The present-day office of governor is the direct descendant of the colonial governorships and is the oldest of all of the elective offices in American politics. Most of the limited powers of the first State governments were given to the legislature; the early State governors had very little authority. Gradually that original separation of powers was revised, especially as the legislatures tended to abuse their powers. The governorship has been strengthened in greater or lesser degree, everywhere, and especially in the past few decades.

The governor is elected by popular vote in every State. In each of them the State constitution sets out formal qualifications for the office, but in all of them the informal (political) qualifications are more meaningful. Governors are now chosen for two-year terms in four States and for four-year terms in the rest. Half of the States still place some constitutional limit on gubernatorial tenure.

The governor's salary ranges from $35,000 a year in some States up to $100,000 in N.Y. Most governors also receive an expense allowance and live in a home provided by the State. The governor may be removed by impeachment in every State except Oregon and by recall in Oregon and 14 other States. Few have ever been removed from office, and none in more than 50 years. Succession falls first to the lieutenant governor in 43 States, to the president of the senate in four, and to the secretary of state in the other three.

In nearly every State the executive power is fragmented. It is shared by the governor and several other elected executive officers over whom the governor has little or no control. The executive powers are regularly hedged by a number of constitutional and statutory restrictions; they include the powers of appointment and removal, supervision of administration, command of the National Guard, and budget making. The governor's legislative powers are those to send messages to the legislature, to call special sessions of that body, and (except in North Carolina)

to veto measures it enacts (including the item veto in 43 States). The governor's judicial powers are those of executive clemency. The governor must also carry out a number of miscellaneous chores, many of a ceremonial nature. In every State, the governor's real power depends upon his/her personality, political clout, and talents of persuasion.

There are several other major executive offices, usually elective, in every State. The major ones are: lieutenant governor, secretary of state, treasurer, auditor, attorney general, and superintendent of public instruction. Recent years have seen an encouraging amount of executive branch reorganization among the States.

CHAPTER REVIEW

Key Terms/Concepts

Appointment/ removal powers (544)
Attorney general (551)
Auditor (550)
Budget-making power (544)
Chief executive (543)
Commute (547)
Comptroller (550)
Council of State Governments (552)
Executive powers (543)
Impeachment (541)
Item veto (546)
Judicial powers (547)
Legislative powers (545)
Lieutenant governor (548)
Message power (545)
Military powers (545)
Pardon (547)
Parole (547)
Pocket veto (546)
Post-audit (550)
Pre-audit (550)
Recall (541)
Remit (547)
Reprieve (547)
Secretary of state (549)
Special session (546)
Superintendent of public instruction (551)
Succession (541)
Treasurer (550)
Veto power (546)

Keynote Questions

1. Why could James Madison quite correctly describe the State governors as "little more than ciphers" in 1787? How accurate is that description today?
2. How is the governor chosen in every State? Why must a person who wants to be the governor of his/her State meet a series of both formal and informal qualifications for that office?
3. For what term is the governor chosen in your State? Is there a limit on gubernatorial tenure? How may he/she be removed from office?
4. Among the 50 States, who usually succeeds to the governorship if a vacancy occurs? Who succeeds in your State?
5. Why may it be said in each State that "the governor wears many different hats"?
6. In what major way is the executive power fragmented in nearly all of the States today?

7. What is the governor's basic legal duty in each of the States? Why are a governor's powers of appointment and removal so important? Budget-making power?

8. What are a governor's principal legislative powers? Judicial powers?

9. What other major executive offices are to be found in most of the States today? In your State?

For Thought and Discussion

1. At present, only one woman serves as the governor of any of the 50 States. In fact, of the more than 2000 persons who have ever served in that office, only six have been women (see page 538). Why have so few women been elected governor? Do you believe there will be any significant change in this matter in the near future? Why, or why not? Does any woman have a reasonable chance to become the governor of your State in the near future?

2. In recent years nearly half of the States have provided that each party's candidates for governor and lieutenant governor must run "in tandem," as a team (see page 540). Why have so many States adopted this requirement? Should your State adopt/abandon it?

3. Does your State constitution limit the number of terms the governor may serve? If so, what is that limit? Should that limit be repealed? If not, should a limit be added?

4. In New Jersey the governor is the only executive officer elected by the voters, and he/she appoints all of the other principal officers in the executive branch. No other State so completely concentrates executive authority and responsibility in the governorship. Should your State have such an arrangement? Why, or why not?

Suggested Activities

1. Write a short biography of the governor of your State.

2. Prepare a table listing the successive governors of your State, the years in which each served, the manner in which each gained office (by election or succession), the political party to which each belonged, and such other facts as the age at which each took office and the years of birth and death of each of them.

3. From the State constitution and Blue Book, prepare a list of the principal executive offices in the government of your State. Outline each in terms of method of selection, term of office, powers and duties, and similar factors.

4. Invite a present or former State executive officer to describe his/her office and experiences to the class.

Utah's State Capitol, in Salt Lake City

CHAPTER

22

The State Court Systems

Liddy Woods
Heather Fogelberg
Kelley Hatch

I hate exams!

CHAPTER OBJECTIVES

To help you to:
Learn ▪ Know ▪ Understand

The essential purpose and functions of State Courts

The overall organization of the several State court systems (with especial reference to your State's judiciary).

The jurisdiction of the many different State Courts.

The various methods by which judges are selected among the States.

The distinctions between and the duties of the grand jury and the petit jury.

The different kinds of law applied by State courts.

ERIK + Heather

ERIK + Heather

Where law ends, Tyranny begins.

John Locke

Courts are tribunals established by law for the administration of justice according to law. All the courts of a State make up its court system, the State *judiciary.*

Remember, there are two separate and distinct sets of courts in the United States: the federal courts (which we looked at in Chapter 18) and those of each of the 50 States. The federal courts have jurisdiction over certain classes of cases, as we noted on pages 482–483. All other court cases—and the larger number of them—are heard in State courts.

The basic function of the State courts is to decide disputes between private persons and between private persons and government. They protect the rights of individuals guaranteed in both the federal and the State constitutions. They decide the innocence or guilt of persons accused of crime. And they act as checks on the conduct of the executive and legislative branches.

Organization of State Court Systems

Each State constitution creates a court system, and most of them leave the many details of its organization to the legislatures. Over the next few pages we shall look at the structure of the 50 State judiciaries, working our way up the judicial hierarchy.

IN GOD WE TRUST

Law officers were scarce in parts of the West in 1900, when Judge Roy Bean (seated at table) tried a horse thief in Langtry, Texas. *Facing page:* A judge in one of Brooklyn, New York's, municipal courts hears a civil case.

Justices of the Peace

Justices of the peace—JP's—stand on the lowest rung of the State judicial ladder. They preside over what are commonly called *justice courts.*

JP's were once found nearly everywhere in the country. But time has largely passed them by. They, and their justice courts, have been done away in about half of the States, and their number has been greatly reduced in most of the others. Those that are left are usually in small towns and rural areas.

JP's are almost always popularly elected. Most often, they are chosen on a partisan ballot, by the voters of a township or some other district within a county, and for a short term—most often two or four years.

Their jurisdiction[1] usually covers a whole county, but it is generally quite limited. Most JP's can hear only minor *civil cases*[2] and *misdemeanors.*[3]

Mostly, JP's try misdemeanors—cases involving such petty offenses as traffic violations, disturbing the peace, public drunkenness, and the like. They can almost never settle civil disputes involving more than a few hundred dollars. They do issue certain kinds of *war-*

[1]The power of a court to hear (to try and to decide) a case; literally, the power to "say the law"; see page 482.

[2]A **civil case** is a suit brought by one party against another for the enforcement or protection of some private right or for the prevention or redress of a tort (a private wrong). A **criminal case** is one brought by the State against a person accused of committing a crime—a public wrong. The State is at times a party in a civil suit; it is always a party in a criminal trail—as the prosecution. In the strictest sense, the terms "suit" and "trial" may be and are used interchangeably in the law. In general usage, however, "suit" is generally used to refer to civil actions and "trial" to criminal proceedings. A judicial proceeding which is neither a suit nor a trial is usually called a "hearing."

[3]Crimes are of two kinds: felonies and misdemeanors. A **felony** is the greater crime and may be punished by a heavy fine and/or imprisonment or even death. A **misdemeanor** is the lesser offense, punishable by a small fine and/or a short jail term.

rants, hold *preliminary hearings*, and often perform marriages.[4]

In some places, JP's are still paid out of the fines they take in. The more and the heavier the fines they impose, the higher their incomes. This "fee system" can lead to any number of abuses. At the very least, it raises serious questions about the fairness of the trial a defendant can expect and/or the fairness of the verdict a JP hands down.[5]

Magistrates' Courts

Magistrates are the city cousins of JP's. For the most part, **magistrates** handle those minor civil complaints and misdemeanor cases that arise in an urban setting. They preside over what are generally called *magistrates' courts* or, in some places, *police courts*. Those courts are much like the justice courts, with just about the same jurisdiction. Magistrates, like JP's are usually popularly elected, and for rather short terms.

Both the justice courts and the magistrates' courts are sometimes criticized because, very often, their judges are not trained in the law. Some years ago, a California study found that the State's nonlawyer local judges included several ministers, school teachers, real estate agents, druggists, and grocers—including one whose wife held court when he went fishing. Most States, including California, now require that *all* judges be licensed attorneys.

---

[4]A **warrant** is a court order authorizing (making legal) some official action—for example, a search warrant or an arrest warrant. A **preliminary hearing** is generally the first step in a major criminal (felony) prosecution; there the judge decides if the evidence is in fact enough to hold that person (bind that person over) for action by the grand jury or the prosecutor.

[5]Many insist that the fee system means that "JP" really stands for "judgment for the plaintiff." The practice also encourages "fee splitting"—an arrangement in which judges can increase the number of misdemeanors they hear by agreeing to share their fees with those arresting officers who bring such cases to them. The "speed trap" is probably the best known and most common result of a fee-splitting situation.

Municipal Courts

Unhappy experiences with magistrates' courts has led to the creation of *municipal courts* in many cities. The first one was established in Chicago in 1906, and they are now found in most of the nation's larger and many of its middle-sized and smaller cities.

The jurisdiction of **municipal courts** is citywide, and they can often hear civil cases involving several thousands of dollars as well as the usual run of misdemeanors. Many of them are organized into divisions, which hear cases of a given kind—for example, civil, criminal, juvenile, domestic relations, small claims, traffic, and probate divisions.

Take a small claims division—often called the *small claims court*—to illustrate this arrangement. Many people cannot afford the costs of suing for the collection of a small debt. A paper carrier, for example, can hardly afford a lawyer to collect a month's subscription from a customer. An elderly widow may have the same problem with a tenant's back rent; and many merchants are forced to forget an overdue bill or sell it to a collection agency.

Small claims courts have been set up for just such situations. In them, a person can bring a claim for little or no cost. The proceedings are usually quite informal; the judge often handles the matter without attorneys for either side.

☑ FOR REVIEW

1. What is a court? What functions do courts perform?
2. What is a court's jurisdiction?
3. What distinguishes a civil from a criminal case? A felony from a misdemeanor?
4. What courts are commonly at the lowest trial level in a State?

General Trial Courts

Most of the important civil and criminal cases heard in U.S. courts are heard in the State's **general trial courts.**

Each State is divided into a number of judicial districts (or circuits). Each district generally covers one or more counties, and for each of them there is a general trial court. Most legal actions brought under State law are begun in these courts—known variously as district, circuit, county, or superior courts or courts of common pleas.

The judges of these trial courts are popularly elected in two-thirds of the States—usually for four-, six-, or eight-year terms. The governor appoints them in most of the other States, as we shall see. In those districts where the caseload is heavier, each of these courts frequently has several judges.

These general trial courts are courts of "first instance." That is, they exercise original jurisdiction over most of the cases they hear. When cases do come to them on appeal from some lower court, *e.g.*, a municipal court, a trial *de novo* (a new trial, as though the case had not been heard before) is usually held.

The cases heard in these courts are tried before a single judge. Most often, a **petit jury** (the trial jury) hears and decides the facts at issue in a case, and the judge interprets and applies the law in-

volved in it. Criminal cases are presented for trial either by a grand jury or on motion of the prosecuting attorney.

The trial court is seldom limited as to the kinds of cases it may hear. Its decision on the *facts* in a case is usually final; but disputes over questions of *law* may be carried to a higher court.

In the more heavily populated districts of some States, cases involving such matters as the settlement of estates or the affairs of minors are heard in separate trial courts—often called surrogate, probate, or orphans' courts. In most States, and districts, however, these matters are part of the regular caseload of the general trial courts.

Intermediate Appellate Courts

More than half of the States now have one or more **intermediate appellate courts**—courts of appeal which stand between the trial courts and the State's highest court. They serve to ease the burden of the high court.

Like the trial courts, these appellate courts have different names among the States—but, most often, the court of appeals.[6] Their judges are chosen by the governor in a few States—in New York

---

[6] In New York the general trial court is called the Supreme Court; the intermediate appellate court is the Appellate Division of the Supreme Court; the State's highest court is known as the Court of Appeals.

In this small claims court hearing the judge sits at a conference table in his chambers; the plaintiff and defendant face one another across it, while a member of the court's staff records the proceedings.

and New Jersey, for example. Most often, they are picked by the voters, however—usually for terms of six or eight years, but for as long as 12 years in both California and Missouri.

Most of the work of these courts involves the review of cases decided in the trial courts. That is, they exercise mostly **appellate jurisdiction.** Their original jurisdiction, where it exists, is limited to a few specific cases—election disputes, for example. In exercising their appellate jurisdiction, these courts do not hold trials. Rather, they hear oral arguments from attorneys, study the briefs (written arguments) they submit, and review the record of the case in the lower court.

Ordinarily, an appellate court does not concern itself with the *facts* in a case. Rather, its decision turns on whether the *law* was correctly interpreted and applied in the court below. Its decision *may* be reviewed by the State's high court—but, in practice, its disposition of a case is usually final.

The State Supreme Court

The State's **supreme court** is the highest court in its judicial system.[7] Its major function is to review the decisions of the lower courts in those cases which are appealed to it.

The size of the supreme court is fixed by the State constitution. In most States five or seven justices sit on the high bench. But three do in Delaware, and nine in seven other States: Alabama, Iowa, Minnesota, Mississippi, Oklahoma, Texas, and Washington.

The justices, including a chief justice, are appointed by the governor in 23 States.[8] They are selected by the legislature in four States,[9] and by the voters in the other 23.

Only some—a very few—decisions of a State's supreme Court may be reviewed by the United States Supreme Court. An appeal from a State's high court will be heard in the federal Supreme Court *only* if: (1) a "federal question"—some matter of federal law—is involved in the case, *and* (2) the Supreme Court agrees to hear that appeal. (See page 490.)

In short, most State supreme court decisions are final. The oft-heard claim "I'll fight this case all the way to the United States Supreme Court" is, almost always, just so much hot air.[10]

Unified Court Systems

The typical State court system is organized according to the map (geographically) rather than by types of cases. Thus, the general trial courts are most often organized so that each of them hears those cases which arise within its own district, circuit, or county—no matter what the subject matter may be.

In these map-based systems, a judge must hear cases in nearly all areas of the law. A backlog of cases may (often does) build up in some courts while judges sit with little to do in others.

---

[7]The State's highest court is known by that title in 45 States. But in Maine and Massachusetts it is called the Supreme Judicial Court, in Maryland and New York the Court of Appeals, and in West Virginia the Supreme Court of Appeals. Two States actually have *two* high courts. In Oklahoma and in Texas the Supreme Court is the highest court (the court of last resort) in *civil* cases, and a separate Court of Criminal Appeals is the court of last resort in criminal cases.

[8]By the governor alone in Arizona, Delaware, Hawaii, Maine, Massachusetts, New Hampshire, and New Jersey; and by the governor through some version of the Missouri Plan (page 563) in Alaska, California, Colorado, Florida, Idaho, Indiana, Iowa, Kansas, Maryland, Missouri, Nebraska, New York, Oklahoma, Utah, Vermont, and Wyoming.

[9]Connecticut, Rhode Island, South Carolina, and Virginia.

[10]State law regularly gives its lower courts final jurisdiction over many types of minor cases. That is, review cannot be sought in a higher State court; in those cases, the lower court is the State's court of last resort. If any review is to be had, it can be only by the U.S. Supreme Court. Such reviews are extremely rare.

Uneven interpretations and applications of the law may (sometimes do) occur from one part of the State to another.

To overcome these difficulties a number of States have begun to abandon the map in recent years. They have turned, instead, to a **unified court system**—one organized on a functional (case-type) basis.

In a completely unified court system there is technically only one court for the entire State. It is presided over (administered by) a chief judge or judicial council. There are a number of levels within the single court—such as supreme, intermediate appellate, and general trial sections. At each level (within each section), divisions are established to hear cases in certain specialized or heavy-caseload areas of the law—criminal, juvenile, family relations, and other areas that need special attention.

In such an arrangement a judge can be assigned to that section or division to which his/her talents are interests seem best suited. Judges may be moved from one section or division to another, to relieve overcrowded dockets. In short, the unified court system is a modern response to the old common law adage: "Justice delayed is justice denied."

The move to a unified arrangement was pioneered by New Jersey in the late 1940s. Today at least half of the States have taken some steps in that direction.

☑ FOR REVIEW

1. In what type (or level) of courts are most of the more important civil and criminal cases heard? By what title are these courts known in your State?
2. Why do over half of the States now have intermediate appellate courts?
3. What is the primary function of each State's supreme court?
4. Under what circumstances will a decision of a State's highest court be reviewed by the United States Supreme Court?
5. What is a unified court system? Why is it widely recommended?

The Selection of Judges

More than 15,000 judges sit in the nation's State and local courts today. They are most often chosen in one of three ways: by (1) popular election, (2) appointment by the governor, or (3) appointment by the legislature.[11]

In the colonies, judges were regularly appointed by the colonial governor. With independence, selection by the State legislature became the practice. The influence of Jacksonian democracy, which colored much of American political thought in the 19th century, persuaded most States to move to popular election of judges, however.

Selection Today

Most States use only one or another of the major methods of selection—for all or at least most judgeships. But, again, there are many variations.

Popular election is by far the most widely used method by which judges are picked around the country. About three-fourths of all judges sitting in American courts today are chosen by the voters.

In fact, in 13 States popular election is the *only* method by which judges are

[11]Some judges are selected by other means in some States. In Ohio, for example, all judges, except those of the Court of Claims, are elected by the voters; the judges of the Court of Claims are appointed by the Chief Justice of the State Supreme Court. In Alabama, Michigan, Mississippi, Oregon, Texas, and Washington all judges are popularly elected except for municipal court judges; they are chosen in accord with city charter provisions, usually by the city council.

A CASE IN POINT

JUDGING THE JUDGES

Unlike federal court judges, nearly all State judges are either elected or appointed to fixed terms of office.

Still, the rate of judicial turnover is low in every State. Once a judge becomes a judge he or she tends to remain in office over time. Most elected judges seek reelection—most often successfully; and most appointed judges are regularly reappointed.

Most State judges are quite able. But, unfortunately, some few are not. The problem of an unfit judge is sometimes solved by death, resignation, or retirement, or by failure to win reelection or reappointment. But if an unfit judge does stay in office, what then?

Every State (except Oregon) provides for the impeachment process. And two other methods of removal have been available in some States for several decades: (1) the **legislative address** —a process by which the legislature may direct the governor to remove a judge, and (2) the recall—a process we looked at on page 542.

Those methods are cumbersome and are very seldom used, however. (Thus, only one judge has been recalled in the past 40 years—a trial judge in Madison, Wisconsin, in 1977. He was recalled for having made high-

ly sexist remarks during a rape trial in his court.)

Three-fourths of the States have now adopted another method for the judging of judges. Beginning with California in 1960, they have created boards or commissions for that purpose.

California's Commission on Judicial Performance is fairly typical. It has nine members: five sitting judges named by the State supreme court, two lawyers chosen by the State bar, and two citizens appointed by the governor.

The Commission investigates any charge that a judge is unfit for office. If it finds merit in a complaint, it may try to settle matters in confidential discussions with the judge involved. If the facts seem to justify removal, and the judge will not leave office voluntarily, the Commission may take the case to the supreme court.

With that step, the State's high court may take whatever disciplinary action it finds necessary—ranging from public censure to outright removal from office.

1. How are judges chosen in your State? For what terms? How may they be removed from office?
2. Does your State have some kind of judicial qualifications commission?

chosen.[12] And in most of the other States most or at least some judges are also chosen at the polls. About half of all judicial elections are nonpartisan contests today.

Selection by the legislature is the least commonly used of the three major methods. The legislature now chooses all or at least most of the judges in only four States: Connecticut, Rhode Island, South Carolina, and Virginia.

The governor appoints nearly a fourth of all State judges today. In three

---

[12]Arkansas, Illinois, Kentucky, Louisiana, Minnesota, Montana, Nevada, New Mexico, North Carolina, North Dakota, Pennsylvania, West Virginia, Wisconsin.

States—Delaware, Massachusetts, and New Hampshire—all of them are named by the Governor. In several others the governor has the power to appoint all or many of them—but under a "Missouri Plan" arrangement, as we shall see.

How Should Judges Be Selected? Most of us believe that judges should be independent, that they should "stay out of politics." Whatever method of selection is used, then, should be designed with that goal in mind.

Nearly all authorities are agreed that selection by the legislature is the most political of all of the methods of choice—and few favor it. So, the question here really is: Which is better, popular election or appointment by the governor?

Those who agree on popular election generally make the democratic argument, of course. Because judges "say the law," interpret and apply it, they should be chosen by and answer directly to the people. Some also say that the concept of separation of powers is weakened if the executive has the power to name the members of the judicial branch.

Those who favor appointment by the governor argue that the judicial function should be carried out only by those who are well qualified to do so. They insist that executive appointment is the best way to insure that those who preside in courts will have the qualities most needed in that role—absolute honesty and integrity, fairness, and the necessary training and ability in the law.

At best, it is difficult to decide between these two positions. The people have often made excellent choices, and governors have not always made wise and nonpolitical ones. Still, most authorities come down on the side of gubernatorial appointment—largely because those characteristics that make a good judge and those that make a good candidate are not too often found in the same person.

JUDICIAL OFFICES

INDIANA SUPREME COURT:

Shall Justice Alfred J. Pivarnik be retained in office?

YES ☐   NO ☐

INDIANA COURT OF APPEALS:

Second District

Shall Judge V. Sue Shields be retained in office?

YES ☐   NO ☐

Fourth District

Shall Judge Eugene N. Chipman be retained in office?

YES ☐   NO ☐

Shall Judge Stanley B. Miller be retained in office?

YES ☐   NO ☐

A portion of an Indiana ballot lists judges up for approval/rejection by voters in the 1980 general election.

Popular election is both widely used and widely supported; and moves to abandon it have been strongly opposed by party organizations. So, most moves to revise the method of judicial selection have kept at least some element of voter choice.

The Missouri Plan. For some 60 years now, the American Bar Association has sponsored an approach that combines the election and appointment processes. A version of the ABA's plan was first adopted in California in 1934 and then in Missouri in 1940. Because its adoption in Missouri involved much political drama, and so attracted wide attention, the method is often called *The Missouri Plan.*

Missouri's plan is more or less typical. The governor appoints the seven justices of the State's supreme court, the 31 judges of the court of appeals, and all of the judges who sit in certain of the State's trial courts.[13] The governor must make those appointments from a *panel* (list) of three names recommended by a

---

[13]Presently, the judges of the circuit and probate courts in St. Louis City and County, and in the three counties (Jackson, Platte, and Clay) in the Kansas City metropolitan area. All other judges are elected on a partisan ballot; but the plan may be adopted by the voters in any of the State's judicial districts.

judicial nominating commission. It is made up of a sitting judge, several members of the bar, and private citizens.

Each judge named by the governor then serves until the first general election after he or she has been in office for at least a year. The judge's name then appears on the ballot, without opposition. The voters decide if that judge should be kept in office or not.

If the vote is favorable, the judge then serves a regular term—six years for a trial court judge and 12 years for one who sits on a higher court in Missouri. Thereafter, the judge may seek further terms in future retain-reject elections.

Should the voters reject a sitting judge the process begins again—the governor makes a new appointment from the commission's list, and so on.

Some form of the Missouri Plan is now used for selecting at least some judges in nearly half of the States. California and Missouri pioneered the device, and then stood alone for several years. Now, the list of States using the plan is growing.

The Jury System

A jury is a body of persons selected under the law and sworn to state the truth on the evidence laid before it. There are two basic types of juries in the American legal system: (1) the *grand jury* and (2) the *petit jury*.

The major function of the **grand jury** is to determine if the evidence against a person charged with crime is sufficient to justify a trial. It is used only in criminal proceedings. The petit jury is the trial jury, and it is used in both civil and criminal cases.

The Grand Jury

The grand jury has from six to 23 persons, depending on the State. Where larger juries are used, generally at least 12 jurors must agree that an accused person is probably guilty before a formal accusation is made. Similarly, with smaller juries, an extraordinary majority is needed to **indict** (bring the formal charge).

When a grand jury is **impaneled** (selected), the judge instructs the jurors to find a true **bill of indictment** against any and all persons whom the prosecuting attorney brings to their attention and whom they think probably guilty. The judge also instructs them to bring a **presentment** (accusation) against any persons whom they, of their own knowledge, believe have violated the State's criminal laws in that judicial district.

The grand jury meets in secret. To preside over its sessions, either the judge appoints or the jurors select one of their number to serve as the *foreman*. The prosecuting attorney presents witnesses and evidence against persons suspected of crime. The jurors may question those witnesses and summon others to testify against a suspect. No one is allowed in the jury room except the grand jurors themselves, the prosecutor, witnesses, and, in some States, a stenographer. All are sworn to secrecy.

After receiving the evidence and

A procedural matter is discussed with the judge.

hearing witnesses; the grand jury deliberates—with only the jurors themselves present. With the completion of their review they move to the courtroom where their report—including any indictments they may have returned—is read in their presence.

Accusation by Information. The grand jury is cumbersome and time consuming. It adds to the already considerable delay and expense of the criminal process. Hence, most States today depend more heavily upon a much simpler process of accusation—the *information*.

An **information** is a formal charge filed by the prosecutor, without the action of a grand jury. It is now used for most minor offenses. And more than half of the States now use it in most of the more serious cases, as well.

The use of the information is far less costly and time consuming. Then, too, since grand juries most often follow the prosecutor's recommendations, many argue that a grand jury is unnecessary.

The chief objection to giving up the grand jury appears to be the fear that some prosecutors will abuse their powers and harass defendants.

The Petit Jury

The ***petit jury*** is the trial jury. It hears the evidence in a case and decides the disputed facts.

The number of trial jurors may vary. As it developed in England, the jury consisted of "12 men good and true"—and 12 is still the usual number. But a lesser number, often six, now fill jury boxes in several States. Also, women are everywhere qualified for jury duty.

In over a third of the States jury verdicts need not be unanimous in civil and minor criminal cases; rather, some extraordinary majority is needed. In most of the States, however, verdicts must be unanimous in all cases. If a jury cannot agree on a verdict (a "hung jury"), either another trial (with a new jury) is held or the matter is dropped.

Misdemeanor cases and civil proceedings in which only minor sums are involved are often heard without a jury —in a **bench trial,** by the judge alone. In several States the most serious of crimes may be heard without a jury—*if* the accused, fully informed of his or her rights, waives the right to trial by jury.

Selection of Jurors

Jurors are picked in more or less the same way in most States. Periodically, some county official,[14] or special jury commissioners, prepares a list of persons eligible for jury service. The lists are generally quite long. Depending upon the State, the lists are drawn from the poll books or the tax assessor's rolls. When jurors are needed names are picked from these lists at random.

The sheriff serves each person with a court order, a writ of ***venire facias*** (you must come). After eliminating those who, for good reason, cannot serve, the judge prepares a list of those who can— the **panel of veniremen.** Persons under 18 and those over 70 years of age, illiterates, the ill, and criminals are commonly excluded. In many States those in occupations vital to the public interest —physicians, druggists, teachers, firefighters, and the like—are also excused. Those for whom jury service would mean real hardship are often excused too.

As with the grand jury, the States are moving away from the use of the trial jury. The greater time and cost of jury trials are leading reasons. The competence of the average jury and the impulses which may lead it to a particular verdict are often questioned, too.

But much of the criticism is directed

---

[14]Most often the clerk of the court, the sheriff, or the county governing body, and sometimes the presiding judge—and in New England officers of the town.

not so much at the jury system itself as at its *operation*. Several things should be said for the jury system. It has both a long and an honorable place in the development of Anglo-American law. Its high purpose is to promote a fair trial, by providing an impartial body to hear the charges brought in either civil or criminal cases. It tends to bring the common sense of the community to bear upon the law and its application. It gives the citizen a chance to take part in the administration of justice, and it gives the people greater confidence in the judicial system.

☑ F O R   R E V I E W

1. What three major methods are used to select State judges? Which is the most widely used?
2. What is the Missouri Plan? Why is some version of it favored by nearly all students of judicial administration?
3. What is the primary duty of a grand jury? What process is now often used as an alternative to it?
4. What is an indictment? A presentment? An information?
5. What does the petit jury do?

Kinds of Law Applied by State Courts

The law—the code of conduct by which society is governed—is made up of several different forms of law.[15] In

dealing with cases that come before them, State courts apply these various forms:

Constitutional law—the highest form of law, that based upon the provisions of the Constitution of the United States and the State constitution, and judicial interpretations of them.

Statutory law—the law (statutes) enacted by legislative bodies, including the United States Congress, the State legislature, the people (through the initiative or referendum), and city councils and other local legislative bodies.

Administrative law—the rules, orders, regulations which are issued by federal, State, or local executive officers, acting under proper constitutional and/or statutory authority.

Criminal law—that portion of the law which defines public wrongs (offenses against the public order) and provides for their punishment.

Civil law—that portion of the law relating to human conduct, to disputes between private parties, and to disputes between private parties and government, not covered by criminal law.

We have dealt with each of these forms of law at many places to this point, of course. The State courts also apply two other forms of law: *common law* and *equity*.

Common Law.   The **common law** makes up a large part of the law of each of the States, except Louisiana.[16] It is *unwritten, judge-made* law. It has developed, over centuries, from those generally accepted ideas of right and wrong which have gained judicial recognition. It covers nearly all aspects of human conduct. Common law is applied by State courts—*except* when in conflict with written law.

---

[15]In its overall sense, *law* may be defined as the whole body of "rules and principles of conduct which the governing power in a community recognizes as those which it will enforce or sanction, and according to which it will regulate, limit, or protect the conduct of its members." *Bouvier's Law Dictionary*, 3rd revision, vol. II, pp. 1875–76. For us, "community" here refers to the United States, any of the States, and any unit of local government.

[16]Because of the early French influence, Louisiana's legal system is very largely based upon French legal concepts (derived from Roman law). The common law has worked its way into Louisiana law, however.

The common law began in England. It grew out of the decisions made by the king's judges on the basis of local customs. It developed as judges, coming upon situations similar to those found in earlier cases, applied and reapplied the rulings from those earlier cases. Thus, little by little, the law of those cases became *common* throughout the land—and, in time, throughout the English-speaking world.

That is to say, the common law developed as judges followed the *precedent* of earlier decisions—as they applied the rule of **stare decisis,** "let the decision stand."[17]

The common law is *not* a rigidly fixed body of rules controlled in every case by a clear line of precedents which can be easily found and applied. Judges are regularly called upon to interpret and reinterpret the existing rules in the light of changing times and circumstances. Or, the point may be put this way: Most legal disputes in American courts are fought out very largely over the application of precedents. The opposing lawyers try to persuade the court that the precedents support their side of the case—or that the general line of precedents should not, for some reason, be followed. The judge must weigh the precedents—and their applicability—in reaching a decision.

The importance of the common law in the American legal system cannot be overstated. Statutory law does override common law. But many statutes are based on the common law. They are, in effect, common law translated into written law. They are interpreted and applied by the courts according to common law tradition and meaning.

Most of the States' general trial courts sit in courthouses in county seats, as in Carmel, the county seat of Putnam County, New York.

Equity.   **Equity** is a branch of the law which supplements the common law. It developed in England to provide equity—"fairness, justice, and right"— when remedies under the common law fell short of that goal.

Over the years common law became somewhat rigid. Remedies were available only through various *writs* (orders) issued by the courts. If no writ was suited to the relief sought in a case, no action could be taken by the courts.

Those who were thus barred from the courts—for whom there was no adequate remedy at common law—appealed to the king for justice. These appeals became so numerous that they were usually referred to the *chancellor*, a member of the king's council. By the middle of the 14th century, a special court of **chancery,** or equity, was set up. Over time, a system of rules developed, and equity assumed a permanent place in the English legal system.

Perhaps the most important difference between common law and equity today is this: The common law is mostly *remedial* while equity is *preventive.* That is, the common law applies

---

[17]American courts generally follow the rule. A decision, once made, becomes a precedent—a guide to be followed in all later, similar cases, unless compelling reasons call for its abandonment and the setting of a new precedent.

PURPOSEFUL WRITING

PUT THAT IN WRITING

One person *can* make a difference. *You* can influence government decision-making directly by writing letters to government officials. Remember Donna Gallus' letter to Supreme Court Justice Potter Stewart (page 487)?

You also can have an indirect influence by sharing your ideas with others and gaining their support for your position. You can share your ideas in writing with letters to community organizations and interest groups and by writing "letters to the editor." Here are four steps to effective letter writing.

1. *Planning.* Specify your purpose for writing. Then, decide the best audience for your letter. For example, are you interested in obtaining information about proposed legislation? Or, do you want to present your views on some matter? Would it be better to write to your local newspaper or to your representatives in Congress? Next, consider what you will say and how you will say it. Ask yourself these four questions:

a. What is my purpose for writing?

b. To whom should I write?

c. What do I want to say?

d. How can I best organize and present my ideas so that they will be clear to the reader?

2. *Drafting.* When you have an-swered those four questions, write an initial or rough draft of your letter.

3. *Editing.* Very few people write a finished product the first time. More often, it is necessary to review your initial draft and check it for clarity and for spelling, grammar, punctuation, and tone. At this point, make any revisions that seem necessary. *How* you say something, in person or in writing, frequently has as much influence on other people as *what* you say.

4. *Preparing the final copy.* Rewrite or type your letter as neatly as possible, and then sign and mail it.

Thoughtful, sincere letters that clearly state your purpose are likely to be taken seriously and to have an influence. Write a letter stating your position on some public issue that you might send to a community organization or to your representatives in the State legislature or in Congress. Use this checklist to judge how effective your letter is likely to be. Have you:

—addressed the person correctly?

—used a courteous, businesslike tone?

—clearly stated your purpose?

—requested a response (and included your address)?

—kept a copy for yourself?

to (provides a remedy for) matters *after* they have happened; equity seeks to stop wrongs *before* they occur.

To illustrate this, suppose your neighbors plan to add a room to their house. They intend to build, even though you protest. You think that a part of the planned addition will in fact be on your land, and you know that it will destroy your rose garden. You can prevent the construction by getting an **injunction**—a court order prohibiting (enjoining) a specified action by the party named in the order. A court is likely to grant the injunction for two reasons: (1) the immediacy of the threat to your property and (2) the fact that the law can offer no fully satisfactory remedy once your garden has been destroyed. It is true that money damages might be assessed under common law, but no amount of money can give back the pride or the pleasure your plants now give you.

The English colonists brought both equity and the common law to America. At first, the two forms of law were administered by different courts. But, in time, most of the States provided for the administration of both forms by the same courts; and the procedural differences between the two are disappearing.

Advisory Opinions

Ordinarily, a court will not act upon a question unless it is presented in a case actually before it. Even then, it will do so only when the issue is "ripe for decision." Among other things, this means that, as a general rule, courts will not issue advisory opinions.

In 11 of the States, however, the supreme court can render **advisory opinions.** That is, in those States the high court may indicate its views on the constitutionality or legal effects of a law or a proposed change in the law. In each of these States these opinions are available to the governor and, in all except three, to the legislature, as well.[18]

These advisory opinions have a number of advantages. They can be useful guides to the legislature—for example, as a measure which it considers breaks new ground or about which serious con-

stitutional questions have been raised. They can be of similar help to the governor—in deciding whether to sign or veto a bill or whether a law already on the books is in fact enforceable.

As the term suggests, these opinions are *advisory* only. They are not binding on the decision of later cases—except in Colorado. Most legal authorities do not favor giving this power to the State supreme court. Instead, they believe that it should belong to the attorney general; see page 551.

Declaratory Judgments

In nearly all of the States the principal courts may render **declaratory judgments.** These judgments are available *before* an actual case is instituted. The judgments are declarations of the legal rights and obligations of the parties to a controversy before a lawsuit is filed. They may be sought by any person involved in a controversy over his or her rights under any legal instrument, such as a statute, a will, or a contract.

Declaratory judgments are legally binding on the parties involved. They serve to prevent the doing of a wrong, to avoid loss or injury, or to forestall long and costly legal battles.

☑ **F O R R E V I E W**

1. Distinguish these forms of law: Constitutional law, statutory law, administrative law. Civil law, criminal law.
2. What is the common law? How did it originate?
3. What is the rule of *stare decisis?*
4. How did equity originate?
5. What is the chief distinction between common law and equity?
6. What are adivsory opinions? Declaratory judgments?

---

[18]To both the governor and the legislature in Alabama, Colorado, Maine, Massachusetts, Michigan, North Carolina, and Rhode Island; to the governor only in Delaware, Florida, and South Dakota. Neither the Supreme Court nor any other federal court will render advisory opinions.

S U M M A R Y

A court is a tribunal established by law to administer justice according to law. The State courts try most of the cases heard in American courts; only a very small number of cases are heard in the federal courts.

The details of the structure of the 50 separate State court systems are quite complicated, and there are many differences State to State. Justice courts, magistrates' or police courts, and/or municipal courts in all or most of the States hear minor civil and misdemeanor cases.

The general trial courts, known by a variety of names among the States, are the principal courts of first instance. They are the courts in which most of the major civil and criminal cases begin (and generally end) in the United States.

The intermediate appellate courts, now found in over half of the States, stand between the trial courts and the State supreme court. They hear appeals from the lower courts and serve to relieve the highest court much of its appellate burden.

The supreme court stands at the top of the State's judicial system. Except for those cases that might be appealed to the United States Supreme Court, it is generally the court of last resort and the final legal interpreter of the State's constitution and laws.

Most State judges are selected in one of three ways: (1) popular election, (2) appointment by the governor, or (3) appointment by the legislature. About three-fourths of them are chosen by the voters—about as often as not on a partisan ballot. The Missouri Plan is a widely recommended selection process that combines the processes of executive appointment and popular election.

There are two major types of juries in the judicial process: (1) the grand jury, which decides if the evidence against a suspect is sufficient to warrant trial in a criminal case; and (2) the petit (trial) jury, which hears and decides the facts at issue in both civil and criminal cases. In most States an information may be filed by the prosecutor as an alternative to accusation by the grand jury, and the process is frequently used today.

The State courts apply several different kinds of law: constitutional, statutory, and administrative law; civil and criminal law; and common law and equity. Eleven of the State supreme courts may give advisory opinions; and the principal courts in most States may render declaratory judgments.

C H A P T E R   R E V I E W

Key Terms/Concepts

Administrative law (566)
Advisory opinion (569)
Appeal (559)
Appellate jurisdiction (559)
Civil case (557)

Civil law (566)
Common law (566)
Constitutional law (566)
Criminal case (557)
Criminal law (566)

Declaratory judgment (569)
Equity (567)
Felony (557)
General trial court (559)
Grand jury (564)
Hearing (557)
Hung jury (565)

Indict, indictment (564)
Information (565)
Injunction (568)
Intermediate appellate court (559)
Judiciary (556)
Jurisdiction (557)

Jury (564)
Justice court (557)
Justice of the
  peace (557)
Law (566)
Magistrates' court
  (558)
Misdemeanor
  (557)

Missouri Plan
  (563)
Municipal court
  (558)
Original
  jurisdiction
  (559)
Petit jury (565)
Police court (558)

Precedent (567)
Preliminary
  hearing (558)
Presentment (564)
Stare decisis (567)
State supreme
  court (560)
Statutory law
  (566)

Suit (557)
Trial (557)
Trial *de novo*
  (559)
Unified court
  system (560)
Venire facias (565)
Veniremen (565)

Keynote Questions

1. How many separate court systems are there in this country today?
2. What word is regularly used to identify a court's power to hear (*i.e.*, to try and to decide) a case?
3. What distinguishes a civil from a criminal case? A felony from a misdemeaner?
4. What courts are often found at the lowest trial level in a State's court system?
5. Most of the more important civil and criminal cases are first heard in what courts in your State?
6. Why have more than half of the States now established intermediate appellate courts?
7. What is the primary function of each State's supreme court?
8. Under what circumstances will a decision of a State's highest court be reviewed by the United States Supreme Court?
9. How are judges selected in your States? What is the Missouri Plan?
10. What process is often used as an alternative to the grand jury? Why?
11. What is the basic function of a trial (petit) jury?
12. What several different forms of law are applied by State courts?
13. What is the common law? Equity? What is probably the chief distinction between them?
14. What is the rule of *stare decisis*?

For Thought and Discussion

1. What did John Locke mean when he wrote the thought we quoted on page 556: "Where law ends, Tyranny begins"? Who was Locke?
2. How are judges selected in your State? What changes, if any, do you think should be made in that process? Why? Who might be expected to be against such changes? Why?
3. If you had the power to name the judges of the courts of your State, what qualifications would you seek in those you selected? Would those qualifications vary depending upon the court involved?
4. Are *justice* and *law* synonymous terms? Explain your response.

Suggested Activities

1. Go to a session of a local court and write a report describing the proceedings and your impressions of them.
2. Invite a judge, a prosecutor, or a practicing attorney to speak to the class on the courts, their organization, procedures, and functions.
3. Construct a diagram of the courts of your State. Show the jurisdiction of the several courts and by whom and for what term their judges are chosen.
4. Prepare a report to the class on some case currently being tried in a court in your locale. Describe the facts in the dispute and the procedures involved in the trial process.

CHAPTER

23 Governing the Communities

CHAPTER OBJECTIVES

To help you to
Learn ▪ Know ▪ Understand

The role of local government(s) in the United States.

How the nation's 3041 counties vary in terms of geographic size, population, governmental framework, and basic functions.

Towns and townships as units of government and how they differ.

The differences between the legal status of cities and that of other units of local government.

Types of city charters. and the three major forms of city government in this country.

The problems of urban and suburban sprawl, and various responses to them

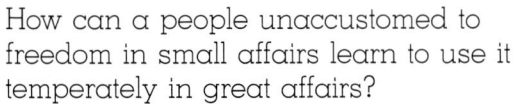

How can a people unaccustomed to freedom in small affairs learn to use it temperately in great affairs?

Alexis De Tocqueville

As we have noted several times, it is the States and especially their local governments which most directly and continuously affect the daily business of living in this country.

As but one measure of their ever-present importance, look at the *sheer number* of local governments in the United States. In a recent tabulation, the 1982 Census of Governments, the Census Bureau reported 82,688 separate units of government across the nation. As the table below shows, 82,637 of these units—nearly all of them—are at the *local* level.

In this chapter we turn to these local units of government so often described as the ones "closest to the people." As we do so, it seems wise to fix their place in the structure of our federal system.

Type of Government	Number of Units
National Government	1
State Governments	50
Local Governments	82,637
Counties	3,041
Municipalities	19,083
Townships	16,748
School Districts	15,032
Special Districts	28,733

The scope and scale of the services provided by small, rural towns (see facing page) are quite different from those provided by such large municipalities as St. Louis, Missouri, a major urban center along the Mississippi River.

The Legal Status of Local Governments

Government in the United States is very often discussed in terms of three basic layers: National, State, and local. The basic components of the federal system, however, are the National Government and the 50 States.

All local governments in the United States are creatures of the States. Each of the 50 States, either through its constitution or its laws, establishes (and may abolish) any or all of these units. To whatever extent any of these governments can provide services, regulate activities, collect taxes, or do anything else, the can *only* because the State has established them and permits them to do so. As they use the powers they have, then, they are really using *State* powers —powers which have been delegated to them by the State.

Another way of putting all of this is to remind you that each of the 50 States has a *unitary* form of government—a point we first made on page 7.

The Counties

The 3,041 counties cover nearly all of the United States. And organized county governments are found in all of the States except Connecticut and Rhode Island. In Louisiana what are known elsewhere as counties are called *parishes*, and in Alaska they are known as *boroughs*. (There are several places across the country where no organized county government exists. About 10 percent of the nation's population lives in those areas today.)

Counties serve almost solely as judicial districts in the New England States. In these States, *towns* carry out most of the functions undertaken by counties elsewhere. The functions of rural local government are shared by counties and *townships* in those States from New York and New Jersey west to the Dakotas, Nebraska, and Kansas. In the South and the West counties are the major units of government in rural areas.

A TYPICAL COUNTY GOVERNMENT

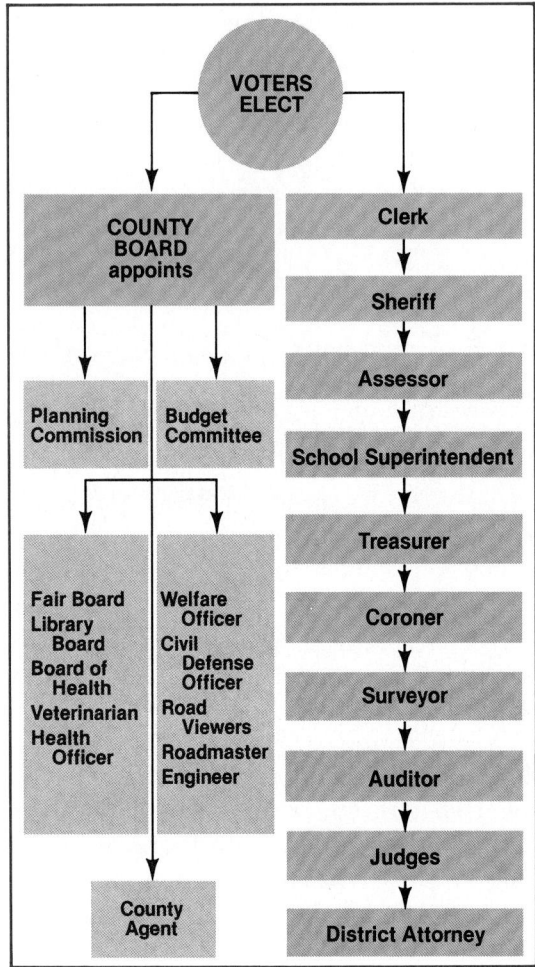

Number, Size, and Population

The number of counties runs from none in Connecticut and Rhode Island and three in Delaware and Hawaii to as many as 254 in Texas. There is no close relationship between the size of a State and the number of counties it has.

In terms of area, San Bernardino County in Southern California is the largest; it covers 52,064 square kilometers (20,102 square miles). Arlington County in Virginia is the smallest, covering only 67.6 square kilometers (26 square miles).

Counties also vary widely in terms of

population. More than 7.4 million persons now live in Los Angeles County in California. At the other end of the scale, only 91 residents were counted in Loving County, in western Texas, in the 1980 census. Most counties serve populations of fewer than 50,000.

County Government— Organized (?) Chaos

County government has long been described as "the dark continent of American politics." Most people know —or, care to know—little about the government of their county.

If county governments have any one principle of organization in common, it is that of confusion. In the typical county, no one official can be called the chief administrator. Rather, authority is divided among a number of elected officials and boards, each largely independent of the others. As a result, it is often impossible to fix the responsibility for laxity, inefficiency, or inaction, or worse, in the conduct of county affairs.

The structures of county government differ, often considerably. But, as you can see from the chart on this page, it typically has four major elements:

(1) <u>A governing body—often called the "county board."</u> This body is known by at least 20 other names among the States—among them, the board of commissioners, board of supervisors, and board of chosen freeholders.

The members of the board, whatever its title, are almost always popularly elected. Their terms of office run from one to eight years, but four-year terms are the most common. They are generally chosen from districts in the county rather than on an at-large basis.[1]

---

[1]In *Avery* v. *Midland County*, 1968, a case from Texas, the U.S. Supreme Court held that the 14th Amendment's Equal Protection Clause "forbids the election of local officials from districts of disparate size." The court there extended the "one-man, one-vote" rule to the local level, and has followed that holding in several later cases; see pages 281, 522.

Generally, county boards may be grouped into two types: *boards of commissioners* and *boards of supervisors.*

The board of commissioners is the smaller and more common type. It is found everywhere in the South and West but is well known elsewhere, too. It most often has three or five, but some have seven or more, members. The members (usually called commissioners) are elected to these bodies, alone. As a rule, they hold no other public office.

The board of supervisors is typically a much larger body—having an average of about 15 members, but sometimes running to as many as 80 or more. The supervisors are elected from each of the several townships in the county—as in New York, Michigan, and Wisconsin. Each of them is generally an officer of his or her township as well as a member of the county-wide governing body.

The powers held by the county governing bodies are prescribed—and often very narrowly defined—in the State constitution and acts of the State legislature. However, restricted they may be, their powers are generally both executive *and* legislative, despite the American tradition of separation of powers.

Their most important legislative powers are those dealing with finance. County boards lay taxes, appropriate funds, and incur limited debts. They also have a number of lesser legislative powers, many in the regulatory field. For example, county boards pass health and zoning ordinances and control amusement places found outside of incorporated communities, especially those where liquor is sold.

Most county boards carry out a number of administrative functions. They supervise the road program and manage county property—such as the courthouse, jails, hospitals, parks, and the like. County boards are often responsible for the administration of welfare programs and the conduct of elections. They also choose certain county officers, deputies, and assistants of many kinds, as well as most other county employees. And they fix the salaries of most of those who work for the county.

Nearly all county boards however, share their executive powers with other elected officials. Because of this, efficiency and economy are often impossible.

(2) <u>A number of separately elected officials with county-wide jurisdiction.</u> These other officers (and their principal duties) are most likely to include:

The **sheriff**—who keeps the jail, furnishes police protection in rural areas, carries out the orders of the local courts, and is often the tax collector.

The **clerk**—who registers and records such documents as deeds, mortgages, birth and marriage certificates, and divorce decrees. The county clerk often administers elections within the county, and acts as secretary to the county board and as clerk of the local courts.[2]

The **assessor**—who appraises (sets the value of) all taxable property in the county.

The **treasurer**—who keeps county funds and makes authorized payments from them.

The **auditor**—who keeps financial records and authorizes payments to meet county obligations.

The **district attorney**—who is the prosecuting attorney, carries out criminal investigations and prosecutes those who break the law.

The **superintendent of schools**—who is responsible for the administration of all or many of the public elementary and secondary schools in the county.

The **coroner**—who investigates vio-

---

[2]In several States a separate officer known as the *recorder* or the *register of deeds* has custody of those documents dealing with property transactions.

LOCAL GOVERNMENTS IN THE UNITED STATES

State	All Local Governments	Counties	LOCAL GOVERNMENTS, BY TYPE			
			Munici-palities	Town-ships*	School Districts	Special Districts
US TOTAL	82,637	3,041	19,083	16,748	15,032	28,733
Alabama	1,019	67	434	—	127	390
Alaska	157	8	142	—	—	6
Arizona	459	14	76	—	231	137
Arkansas	1,430	75	472	—	376	506
California	4,112	57	428	—	1,115	2,511
Colorado	1,568	62	267	—	207	1,031
Connecticut	481	—	33	149	16	282
Delaware	219	3	56	—	19	140
District of Columbia	2	—	1	—	—	1
Florida	972	66	391	—	95	419
Georgia	1,271	158	534	—	188	390
Hawaii	19	3	1	—	—	14
Idaho	1,018	44	198	—	117	658
Illinois	6,464	102	1,280	1,434	1,050	2,597
Indiana	2,873	91	565	1,008	306	902
Iowa	1,874	99	955	—	457	362
Kansas	3,819	105	627	1,380	326	1,380
Kentucky	1,253	119	426	—	180	527
Louisiana	469	62	301	—	66	39
Maine	808	16	22	475	98	196
Maryland	443	23	152	—	—	267
Massachusetts	799	12	39	312	81	354
Michigan	2,646	83	532	1,245	601	184
Minnesota	3,530	87	855	1,795	436	356
Mississippi	860	82	292	—	169	316
Missouri	3,128	114	929	324	559	1,201
Montana	1,045	54	126	—	412	452
Nebraska	3,336	93	535	469	1,080	1,158
Nevada	186	16	17	—	17	135
New Hampshire	507	10	13	221	149	113
New Jersey	1,597	21	323	244	553	455
New Mexico	320	33	96	—	89	101
New York	3,301	57	615	932	773	923
North Carolina	910	100	484	—	—	325
North Dakota	2,798	53	365	1,360	325	694
Ohio	3,353	88	941	1,318	627	378
Oklahoma	2,262	77	582	—	653	949
Oregon	1,460	36	241	—	354	828
Pennsylvania	5,317	66	1,019	1,549	618	2,064
Rhode Island	125	—	8	31	3	82
South Carolina	652	46	265	—	92	248
South Dakota	1,768	64	312	996	195	200
Tennessee	914	94	335	—	13	471
Texas	4,192	254	1,121	—	1,125	1,691
Utah	506	29	224	—	40	212
Vermont	668	14	57	237	274	85
Virginia	408	95	229	—	—	83
Washington	1,735	39	265	—	300	1,130
W. Virginia	637	55	231	—	55	295
Wisconsin	2,596	72	580	1,269	409	265
Wyoming	401	23	91	—	56	230

*Includes "towns" in the six New England States, Minnesota, New York, and Wisconsin.
Source: Census Bureau, *Census of Governments, 1982.*

A county fair in Vermont. Underway is a horse pulling contest, in which horses are urged to pull heavily weighted stone boats that represent heavy wagon loads.

lent deaths and certifies the causes of deaths unattended by a physician.

Many other county officers are often elected. They include: a **surveyor,** who surveys land and sets boundary lines; an **engineer,** who supervises the building of county roads, bridges, drains, and other public improvements; and one or more judges of the local courts.

(3) <u>A number of boards or commissions.</u> These bodies, whose members are also sometimes elected, have authority over a number of county functions. They include a fair board, a library board, a planning commission, a hospital board, a board of road viewers, a board of health, and, sometimes, a civil service commission. And members of the county board often serve *ex officio* on one or more of these other agencies.

(4) <u>An appointed county bureaucracy.</u> Counties now employ more than 1.8 million men and women. They do the day-to-day work of each of the nation's 3,041 counties.

Functions of Counties

Because counties are creatures of the State, they are responsible for the administration of State laws and such county laws as the State's constitution and legislature allow them to make.

Historically, counties have been institutions of *rural* government. And most of them remain rurally oriented today. Though there is some difference from State to State, their major functions reflect that fact. The most common ones are to keep the peace and maintain jails and other correctional facilities; assess property for tax purposes; collect taxes and expend county funds; build and repair roads, bridges, drains and other such public works; and maintain schools. They record deeds, mortgages, marriage licenses, and other documents; issue licenses for such things as hunting, fishing, and marriage; administer elections; care for the poor; and protect the health of the county's people.

Many counties have additional functions as they have become more and still more urbanized. More than two-thirds of all of the people who live in the United States today live within the boundaries of some 300 of the nation's 3,041 counties. Several of the more heavily populated counties now offer many of the public services and facilities generally found in cities.

Reform of County Government

We have already said that the description of the county as the "dark continent of American politics" remains appropriate. And we also pointed out that public apathy is a leading justification for that description. The several weaknesses of county government justify it, too, of course. Three major weaknesses can be readily seen:

(1) Its chaotic and headless structure. It is just about impossible to place responsibility in the jungles of independently elected officers, boards, and commissions that are generally found. Lax, inefficient, and wasteful government, unresponsive government, government by the "courthouse gang," favoritism in awarding public contracts, instances of outright corruption—the list of indictments goes on and on.

(2) The large number of popularly elected offices. Faced by the long ballots that typify county elections, voters are at best hard put to cast the informed votes upon which good government must depend. Further, many elected county officials hold jobs which have nothing to do with the making of basic public policy, but which do demand professional qualifications. Popular election is not the best way to fill those offices with the talented persons who should be in them.

(3) The size and the number of counties in most States. Nearly every one of the counties we now have was laid out in the days of the horse and the stagecoach. Then, it made good sense to draw county lines so that no one lived more than a dozen miles or so from the county seat. But most of them are geographically ill-suited to the realities of today.

The need for thoroughgoing reform of county government has long been recognized. Some steps have been taken in that direction—in some places.

County Home Rule. One of the barriers to real change in the structure of county government lies in the legal status of counties. Their structure and functions are usually closely defined by State constitutions and statutes.

Over half of the States have now lowered that barrier—by providing for county **home rule.** That is, they allow some or all of their counties to decide the details of their own governmental structures—subject to approval by the local voters.

This major step to reform is now available to some 1500 of the nation's counties. Yet, only about 100 of them have adopted home rule charters.[3]

In some States without home rule the legislature has offered counties an optional arrangement—allowing them to choose from different patterns of organization. Each pattern is set out in more or less detail in statutes. In North Dakota, for example, counties may select one of three different plans.

And in a few places striking reforms have come by direct action of the State legislature. There is a very notable example in Tennessee. There, the legislature set up a unique unit of government by combining a county and a major city—the Metropolitan Government of Nashville and Davidson County.

Trend to a Stronger Executive. The most prominent efforts to restructure county government have focused on the most prominent weakness: fragmented executive authority. Three newer patterns of organization have emerged, especially in urban counties:

(1) The **county manager plan**—modeled along the lines of the council-manager form of city government

---

[3]On the encouraging side, the list does include eight of the most populous counties: Los Angeles, San Diego, and Alameda Counties in California; Erie, Nassau, Suffolk, and Westchester Counties in New York; and Dade County in Florida.

now in wide use in middle-sized and smaller cities (see pages 592-593). Under this plan, the elected county board remains the legislative, policy-making, arm of county government. The executive function—the administration of county affairs—is in the hands of a manager, hired by and answering to the board. Ideally, the manager is a trained career administrator who appoints all of the other administrative officers of the county and directs their work.

The county manager plan separates the policy-making and policy-administering functions, placing administrative responsibility in a single and visible officer. It adds professional competence to county management and shortens the ballot. And it has the hearty support of most students of local government.

The plan has not spread among counties as it has at the city level, however. Only some 50 counties use it; but among them are several urban counties —including Sacramento, San Mateo, and Santa Clara Counties in California; Dade County Florida; Anne Arundel and Montgomery Counties in Maryland; Durham County in North Carolina; and McMinn County in Tennessee.

A leading reason why it has not been more widely adopted: Elective county officers are deeply entrenched—both constitutionally and politically—in so many places around the country.

(2) The **chief administrative officer** model—a limited version of the manager plan. Where it is found, a chief administrative officer (often called the CAO) is also chosen by the board and answers to that body. But, unlike a manager, the CAO often has only very limited power, or none, in several important areas—for example, appointments and budgets.

The CAO plan is a sort of compromise between the traditional multiple executive arrangement and the stronger manager system. Los Angeles County was one of the first to provide for a chief executive officer, in 1944. The number of counties with CAO's has grown rapidly in the past decade or so—to more than 500 today.

(3) The **elected chief executive** plan— patterned after the strong mayor-council form of city government (see pages 590–591). The plan features the county board and an elected chief executive—known as the county president, mayor, or supervisor.

It has several advantages. It separates the legislative and executive functions, places administrative responsibility in the chief executive, and cuts the length of the ballot. It is certainly an improvement on the traditional county structure, but it does have the short-comings found in the mayor-council form of city government. In short, its success depends upon the extent of the powers given to the county president *and* that officer's personality and political clout.

Cook County in Illinois (Chicago) has had an elected president since the 1890's. He/she is popularly chosen as a member of the county board, chairs its meetings, and has broad powers of appointment, budget-making, and veto.

COUNTY MANAGER PLAN

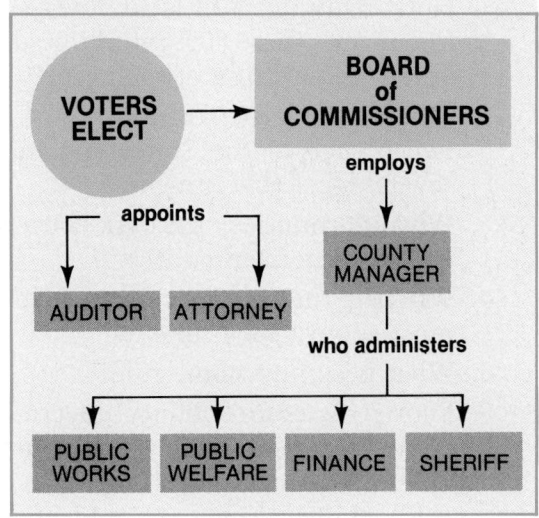

Thirty years ago only three counties had an elected chief executive; today there are some 60 of them.

County Consolidation. As we noted earlier, the boundaries of most counties were horse–drawn. It seems clear that combining two or more adjacent counties would improve them as units of government. Yet, though there have been serious studies and many proposals in several States, little has ever come of that idea. Local pride, politics, and economics stand as major impediments to any such effort.

County-City Consolidation. Consolidation of another sort has met with a bit more success. In several places, a major city and the county around it have been joined into a single unit of government. San Francisco, Denver, and the Metropolitan Government of Nashville and Davidson County are major examples of mergers.

County-City Separation. In a few situations, a quite different path has been taken. Several cities and the counties surrounding them have been separated from each other. Baltimore and St. Louis are two examples of these "independent cities."

✓ FOR REVIEW

1. How many units of local government are there in the United States? How many of each type?
2. What is the basic relationship between each of the States and its several local governments?
3. Why are counties "the dark continent of American politics"?
4. What are the major weaknesses in most county governments?
5. What is county home rule?
6. Efforts to reform county government have been largely aimed at which of its major weaknesses?

Towns and Townships

The *town* or *township* is found as a separate unit of local government in nearly half of the States. Generally, as you can see in the table on page 576, it is found in States stretching from New England through the Middle West. It is little known in the South or the West.[4]

The New England Town

The town is a major unit of local government in New England. Except for just a few cities, each of the six States in the region is divided into towns. Each town generally includes all of the rural *and* urban areas within its boundaries. And, the town is the unit which delivers most of the services which come from cities and counties elsewhere in the country.

The roots of the New England town reach back to colonial beginnings. The Pilgrims landed at Plymouth Rock in 1620 as an organized congregation. They quickly set up a close-knit community in which their church and their government were almost one. Other Puritan congregations followed the Pilgrims' pattern. The desire to be near the church, the real or imagined Indian threat, the severe climate, and the fact that the land was not suited to large farms or plantations all led them to form tight little communities. Their settlements soon came to be known as "towns," as in England.

At least in form, much of town government today is little changed from colonial times. The main feature is the **town meeting**—long praised as the ideal vehicle of direct democracy. It is an

---

[4]The term *town* is used in some States as the legal designation for smaller urban places; it is also sometimes used as another word for township. *Township* is also a federal public lands survey term, used to identify geographic units (often called *congressional townships*) each having exactly 36 square miles (36 *sections*).

assembly open to all of the town's eligible voters. It meets once a year, and sometimes oftener, to levy taxes, make spending and other policy decisions, and elect officers for the coming year.

Between town meetings the **board of selectmen,** chosen at the annual meeting, manage the town's business. Typically, the board is a three-member body and has responsibilities for such things as roads, schools, care of the poor, sanitation, and so on. The other officers regularly selected at the town meeting include the town clerk, a tax assessor, a tax collector, a constable, road commissioners, and school board members.

The ideal of direct democracy is still alive in many smaller New England towns. But it has given way to the pressures of time, population, and the complexities of public problems in many of the larger towns. There, representative government has largely replaced it. The officers of the town are often elected before the yearly gathering. Many towns have gone to a town manager system for day-to-day administration.

Townships

Outside of New England, **townships** are found as units of local government in those States bounded by New York and New Jersey on the east and the Dakotas, Nebraska, and Kansas on the west. In none of them do the townships blanket the State, however. Where they are found, they are mostly county subdivisions.

In New York, New Jersey, and Pennsylvania townships were formed as areas were settled and the people needed the services of local government. As a result, the township maps of those States often resemble crazy-quilts. But from Ohio westward, townships lines are more regular. They mostly follow the lines drawn in federal public land surveys, and many are perfect squares.

About half of these States provide for annual township meetings, like those held in New England towns. Otherwise, most townships have much the same governmental mechanisms. The governing body is a three- or five-member board, generally called the board of trustees or board of supervisors. Often its members are popularly elected to it for two-or four-year terms. But in many places the board's members serve because they hold other elected township offices—such as supervisor, clerk, and treasurer. There is often an assessor, a constable, a justice of the peace, and a body of road commissioners, too.

Unlike in New England, a municipality *within* a township—especially one of

The township hall of Model, North Dakota. In that State, townships serve as units of county government.

any size—usually exists as a separate governmental entity. Thus, township functions tend to be rural—involving such matters as roads, weed control, drainage, and minor law enforcement.

Many believe that townships are no longer useful. More than half of the States get along without them, suggesting that they are not indispensable.

Some of the more densely populated townships appear to have brighter futures than their county cousins, however. This seems true in the suburban areas around some larger cities. In fact, some States, like Pennsylvania, now allow townships to exercise many of the powers and furnish many of the services once reserved to cities.

Special Districts

There are now thousands of **special districts** across the country. These are independent local units which have been set up to carry out a single and occasionally a few related governmental functions at the local level. They are found in almost mind-boggling variety in every one of the States except Alaska.

The school districts are by far the most widely found examples. Counting them, there are more than 43,000 special districts today. The first of these districts were created by New York in 1812, for school purposes. By the 1950s, there were more than 50,000 school districts. But reoganizations have cut that number to some 15,000 today.

Most of the other special districts, which serve a wide range of purposes, have been created since the Depression of the 1930s—and their numbers are still growing. They are found most often —but by no means always—in rural and suburban areas. Many have been created to provide water, sewage, or electrical service; to furnish fire, police, or sanita-

tion protection; and to build and maintain bridges, airports, swimming pools, libraries, or parks; but they exist for a great many other purposes, too.

The reasons for the creation of these units are many. A leading one has been the felt need to provide some service in a wider (or a smaller) area than that covered by a county or a city. Stream pollution may very well be a problem in each of several counties through which a river flows. And (or) there might be a desire to build recreational facilities at several places along the river's course. In many cases, special districts have been formed because other local governments could not, or would not, provide the services desired. For example, police or fire protection might be provided in some out-of-the-way locale by setting up a special district.

An elected board is generally the governing body for a special district. It has the power to lay taxes (usually on the property within the district) or charge fees. Of course, it has the power to spend and to carry out its function(s).

In some communities, rescue teams have been organized and equipped to deal with emergencies unique to their area.

☑ **FOR REVIEW**

1. What is the major unit of local government in New England?
2. Why has the town meeting been praised by political theorists?
3. What is the general condition of township government elsewhere in the country?
4. What are special districts? What is the most common example of this type of governmental unit?

The Cities

To this point we have dealt with those local governments which are, for the most part, rural—in their functions and, very often, in their outlook. Now we turn to *the* principal units of local government in this country: cities.

Urban growth

We are fast becoming a nation of city dwellers. Where once our population was small, largely rural, and agricultural, it is now huge, largely urban, and industrial.

The nation's cities have grown spectacularly—most of all in the past 100 years. When the First Census was taken in 1790, there were only 3,929,214 persons living in the United States. Of these, only 201,655—5.1 percent—lived in the few cities. Philadelphia was then the largest, with 42,000; 33,000 lived in New York and 18,000 in Boston.

Nine years before the First Census, James Watt had patented his double-acting steam engine—and so made large-scale manufacturing possible. Robert Fulton patented his steamboat in 1809 and George Stephenson his locomotive in 1829. These inventions made the transportation of raw materials to factories and, in turn, the wide distribution of manufactured goods readily possible. Almost overnight, home manufacturing gave way to industrial factories and populations began to grow in the new industrial and transportation centers. Cities began to grow rapidly.

The invention of several mechanical farm implements reduced the labor needed on farms. More was grown by fewer people, and the surplus farm population began to move to the cities. By 1860 the nation's population had increased more than seven-fold—and the *urban* population had multiplied *thirty* times. By 1900 nearly two-fifths, and by 1920, more than half of all of our people lived in urban areas.

According to the 1980 census, 166.7 million Americans live in the nation's cities and their surrounding suburbs—73.7 percent, nearly three-fourths of our entire population.

The shift from a predominantly rural to a largely urban society in the United States is a matter of tremendous significance—and it has had dramatic consequences. When large numbers of people live close to one another, the relationships among them are far more complex than those among people who live in less densely settled areas. The rules governing their behavior become more numerous and detailed. Their local governments must furnish them with a wide range of services. The larger the population the more extensive—and expensive—these services become.

The Legal Status of Cities

Depending on local custom and State law, municipalities may be known as "cities," "towns," boroughs," or "villages." The use and meaning of these terms vary among the States. The larger municipalities are everywhere known as cities, and the *usual* practice is to use

A CASE IN POINT

VIDEO-GAME ARCADES

The advent of video games and video-game arcades has aroused concern in many communities across the country. Several cities have passed ordinances to discourage young people from spending time in these places. Some of those ordinances limit attendance at the arcades to certain hours, or require that those under 17 be accompanied by an adult; others attempt to close them down altogether.

Many who favor such ordinances fear that young people are wasting their lunch and other spending money on the machines. And some say that students gamble on the games. In some areas, officials claim that teenagers are breaking into vending machines, parking meters, and other places to get the coins with which to feed the video games.

For their part, many arcade owners argue that the video games provide a "healthy outlet" for young people and also that they help them develop physical and mental skills.

There are now many cases, in several courts, raising a number of questions about the games, the arcades, and their regulation.

To this point, only a very few of those cases have reached the United States Supreme Court—and the High Court has rendered a meaningful judgment in only one of them.

In *Marshfield Family Skateland* v. *Town of Marshfield*, 1983, the Court dismissed a constitutional challenge to an ordinance which bans video arcades in Marshfield, Massachusetts. It rejected, as "trivial," the contention that the playing of games like "Pac-Man" and "Donkey Kong" is a form of expression protected by the 1st and 14th Amendments. The Court's action amounted to a significant setback to the video games industry's efforts to fend off such local restrictions.

The Supreme Court will likely face a number of similar cases over the next few years.

1. Have you been to one of these arcades? What do you think of them? Are they "passing fads," or are they here to stay?

2. What is your view of the various attempts to regulate them? Why have many of those attempts come in the form of licensing ordinances?

THE CITIZEN'S MANY GOVERNMENTS

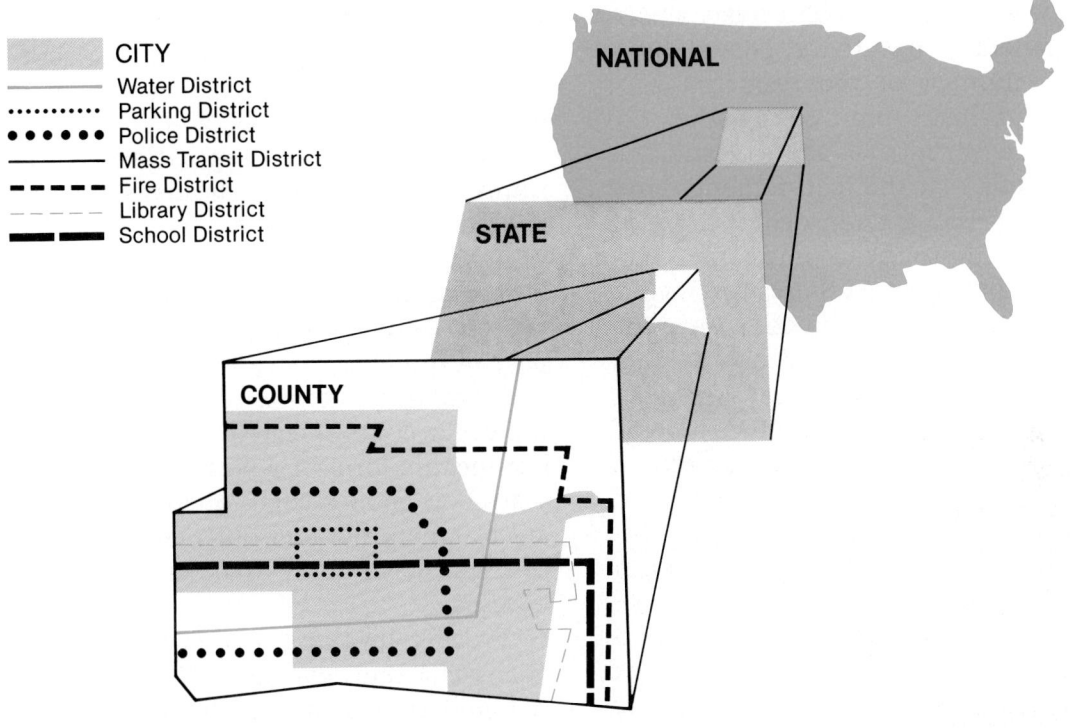

CITY
Water District
Parking District
Police District
Mass Transit District
Fire District
Library District
School District

NATIONAL

STATE

COUNTY

that title only for those communities with a fair-sized population.

Cities Subordinate to the State. Remember that each of the 50 State governments is unitary in form. Consequently, each of them has complete authority and control over *all* of the units of local government within its borders.

The State's authority over cities is reflected in provisions in the State constitution and in laws passed by the legislature. In our early history State constitutions had few provisions relating to cities. The State's authority was largely exercised through the legislature.

As cities grew in size and number, this legislative domination produced many difficult situations. State legislatures, largely dominated by members from the rural areas, were often unfamiliar with the needs and problems of cities. Many of the laws they passed were either very unfair or impractical.

Today, because of this legislative abuse of power, most of the State constitutions contain a large number of provisions relating to municipal government and its problems. Generally, these provisions deal with incorporation, city charters, offices, elections, council meetings and procedures, and financial matters.

Incorporation. Cities are **incorporated**[5]—made into a legal body, by the State. Each State sets out in its constitution or by statute, the conditions and the procedures under which a community may become an incorporated municipality. Generally, a State requires that at least a certain number of persons must live in a given area before incorporation can take place.

In a few States an incorporated community may come into being only by a

---

[5]The term comes from Latin *in* (into) *corpus* (body). To say that cities are incorporated is another, and legal, way of saying that they are creatures of the State.

special act of the legislature. In fact, this is the historic means by which most cities were established. But today a petition generally has to be signed by a certain number of the residents of a locale and then submitted to some public officer. When that officer (usually a judge) finds that the requirements have been met, the area is declared to be incorporated—to be a municipal corporation. But, in most States that declaration cannot become effective until the qualified voters in the area approve that action at a special election.

The fact that cities are incorporated points out a very important difference between city and county government. Cities are called into being largely because of concentrations of population, at the behest of their residents, to provide them with certain public services. Remember that counties, on the other hand, exist largely in order to serve the administrative needs of the State.

The City Charter

The **charter** is the city's basic law, its constitution. Its contents may not be exactly the same from city to city, but commonly the charter names the city, describes its boundaries, and declares it to be a **municipal corporation.** As a municipal corporation, the city is a legal (artificial) person. As such, it has the right to sue and be sued in the courts, to have a corporate seal, to make contracts, and to acquire, own, manage, and dispose of property.

Regularly, the charter also sets out the other powers vested in the city and outlines its form of government. It provides how and for what terms its officers are to be chosen and outlines their duties, and deals with finances and other matters.

Broadly speaking, five distinct types of city charters have been or are presently found among each of the States.

URBAN POPULATION GROWTH

Census	Total Population	Urban Population	Percent Urban
1790	3,929,214	201,655	5.1
1800	5,308,483	322,371	6.1
1810	7,239,881	525,459	7.3
1820	9,638,453	693,255	7.2
1830	12,866,020	1,127,247	8.8
1840	17,069,453	1,845,055	10.8
1850	23,191,876	3,543,716	15.3
1860	31,443,321	6,216,518	19.8
1870	28,558,371	9,902,361	25.7
1880	50,155,783	14,129,735	28.2
1890	62,047,714	22,106,265	35.1
1900	75,994,575	30,159,921	39.7
1910	91,972,266	41,998,932	45.7
1920	105,710,620	54,157,973	51.2
1930	122,775,046	68,954,823	56.2
1940	131,669,275	74,423,702	56.5
1950	150,697,361	96,467,686	64.0
1960	179,323,175	125,268,750	69.9
1970	203,235,298	149,377,944	73.6
1980	226,504,825	166,934,056	73.7

The Special Charter. In colonial days each city received its charter from the governor. With Independence, the State legislatures took on this duty—providing a charter for each city in the State by passing a special act. That practice is still followed in a few States—Delaware, Maine, New Hampshire, and Vermont among them.

The special act arrangement does allow for flexibility. But it also means that each city is subject to continuing and detailed supervision by the legislature. Any real change in its organization, powers, or functions can come only if the legislature acts. In those States which still have this practice, the legislature spends much of its time taking up many bills of purely local concern.

The General Charter. Many State legislatures abused the special charter system. Often those cities where the voters proved loyal to the majority party received better treatment than that given to others. In several States most city charters were hopeless reflections of the ignorance, jealousies, and suspicions of rural legislators.

Reactions to the special charter process grew to the point where, by the mid-1800s, some States went to the other extreme. They adopted a **general charter**—one for *all* cities in the State.

This did away with the practice of singling out one or a few cities for special treatment, good or bad. But it failed to take account of the many differences between and among cities—for example, between a busy industrial center and a small farm community.

No State today provides a single charter for all of its cities. But many cities still operate under a charter dating from the days when the legislature did.

The Classified Charter. The weaknesses of both the special and the gener-

Since the 1960s, vast urban renewal projects have changed San Francisco's skyline. *Inset:* A view of San Francisco's Montgomery Street—now part of the city's busy financial district—as it looked in 1854.

Berthed in Baltimore's new Inner Harbor area is the U.S.S. *Constellation*, the first ship in the United States Navy and a major tourist attraction.

al charter approaches led to the development of the **classified charter** system. Under this arrangement, all of the municipalities in the State are classified by population, and a uniform charter is granted to all of those in the same class.

The classified method minimizes discriminations among cities; and, at the same time, it allows flexibility in meeting the needs of cities of different sizes. Still, it leaves much to be desired. Take, for example, a coastal city where the population is growing and the economy is brisk. Its needs are very different from those of a mining community where the population is static or declining and business is poor.

Where classification is used, the legislature can play games with the population ranges—and in some States it has. There may be only one city in the State with more than 500,000 or only one with a population between 200,000 and 300,000. Where this happens, classification really amounts to the old special charter system in disguise. Several States do have the classified charter arrangement—but most often in combination with the optional approach.

The optional charter. Several States have turned to the **optional charter** system.[6] Under this arrangement, the State offers all cities—or, often those in each population group—a choice from among a number of charters.

The optional charter process is really a compromise between near-domination of cities through special charters and home rule for them.

The Home Rule Charter. Three-fourths of the States now provide for **municipal home rule.** That is, they provide—in the constitution or by statute—that some or all cities may draft, adopt, and amend their own charters.

In most of these States—34 of them—municipal home rule has been established in the constitution.[7] In seven others, however, the grant rests on the basis

---

[6]Cities operating under optional charters are most frequently found today in Illionis, Iowa, Kansas, Massachusetts, Minnesota, New Jersey, and Pennsylvania.

[7]Alaska (1959), Arizona (1912), California (1879), Colorado (1902), Connecticut (1965), Georgia (1950), Hawaii (1959), Illinois (1970), Iowa (1968), Kansas (1960), Louisiana (1946), Maine (1969), Maryland (1915), Massachusetts (1960), Michigan (1908), Minnesota (1896), Missouri (1875), Montana (1972), Nebraska (1912), Nevada (1924), New Mexico (1949), New York (1923), North Dakota (1966), Ohio (1912), Oklahoma (1908), Oregon (1906), Pennsylvania (1922), Rhode Island (1951), South Dakota (1962), Tennessee (1953), Texas (1912), Utah (1932), Washington (1889), West Virginia (1936), Wisconsin (1924), Wyoming (1972).

of legislative enactment alone.[8] The difference here—between *constitutional* and *legislative* home rule—can be a vital one. Legislative home rule is less secure since any later legislature can retract the grant if it chooses to do so.

In some of these States *any* municipality may write and adopt its own charter—in Hawaii, Michigan, Minnesota, Ohio, and Oregon, for example. But in many only *certain* cities may do so—only those with a population of more than 5000 in Missouri, Nebraska, and Texas, for example.

Typically, home rule provisions give to cities "the powers of local self-government" or all powers having to do with "municipal affairs." Home rule is never complete and absolute, however—never creates a "free city." The State always keeps at least some degree of control over its home rule cities—and often a considerable amount of it. There is always difficulty in separating those matters of purely *local* concern from those of general, Statewide import. As routine examples: setting speed limits on city streets which are also State highways, or the regulation of a city sewage system that empties into a river flowing through the State. The questions, and vexations, of city versus State authority in such cases must often be settled in the courts.

A home rule charter may be written and proposed by the city council or by an elected charter commission. To become effective, it must be approved by the city's voters—and in some States by the legislature, as well. Once adopted, amendments may be made by council proposal and voter ratification. In many cities amendments can also be proposed by initiative petition.

---

[8]Delaware, Florida, Indiana, New Hampshire, North Carolina, South Carolina, Vermont.

Changing Municipal Boundaries

As a city grows, the areas around it are likely to grow, too. These areas often cause rather serious problems for the city itself. Shacks may present fire hazards, septic tanks may threaten the city's water, and taverns may make law enforcement difficult.

Methods for the **annexation** (adding) of territory to the city are usually provided by the State constitution or by act of the legislature. Annexation generally must be voted on by the residents of the area that is to be annexed. In some cities, its voters must also act on the question.

Suburbs often resist annexation. So, most States give their cities some *extraterritorial powers*. That is, they can regulate certain matters such as roadhouses, sanitation, and fire hazards in the settled areas around them.

Cities sometimes encourage suburbs to annex by dangling a carrot—for example, an agreement not to raise taxes in the area for a number of years.

Forms of City Government

Which is the more important: the form of government or those who run it?

Certainly good people are essential to good government. They can make at least something of even the worst of forms. But the form is important, too. The better the form of government the more chance there is that capable people will be attracted to public service. And, too, the better the form the greater is the likelihood that the public will be able to get the kind of government it needs.

Every city charter, however adopted, provides for one of three general forms of city government. Although there are variations from this city to that, each has: (1) a *mayor-council*, (2) a *commission*, or (3) a *council-manager* form of government.

The Mayor-Council Form. The **mayor-council** form is the oldest and still the most widely used type. It features an elected mayor as the chief executive and an elected council as its legislative body.

The council is almost always unicameral. In fact, only one city has a two-chambered council today—Everett, Massachusetts. The council regularly has five, seven, or nine members, but there are more in some larger cities. Chicago now has the largest council, with 50 members.

The members of the council are everywhere popularly elected. Terms of office run from one to as many as six years, but four-year terms are the most common. Council members are now most often elected from the city at-large, and that is the trend. But many cities, including several larger ones, choose council members from *wards* (that is, districts) within the city.

A move to nonpartisan city government began in the early 1900s. Today, less than a third of our cities still run their elections on a partisan basis.

The mayor is generally elected by the voters, too—though in some places the office is filled by appointment by the council from among its own members. The mayor presides at council meetings, usually may vote only to break a tie, and may recommend and (usually) veto ordinances. In most cities the veto can be overridden by the council.

Mayor-council governments are often described as either of the *strong-mayor* or the *weak—mayor* type—depending on the powers given to the mayor. This classification is useful for purposes of description. *But,* notice it tends to overlook or blur the importance of *informal power* in city politics.

In the **strong-mayor** type the mayor heads the city's administration, usually has the power to hire and fire employees, and prepares the budget. And, typically, the mayor is otherwise able to exercise strong leadership in the making of city policy and the running of its affairs.

In the **weak-mayor** type the mayor has much less formal power. Executive duties are often shared with such other elected officials as the clerk, treasurer,

STRONG MAYOR–COUNCIL PLAN

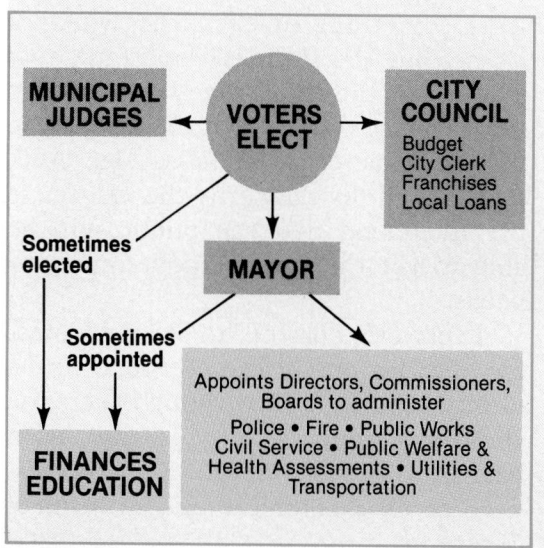

WEAK MAYOR–COUNCIL PLAN

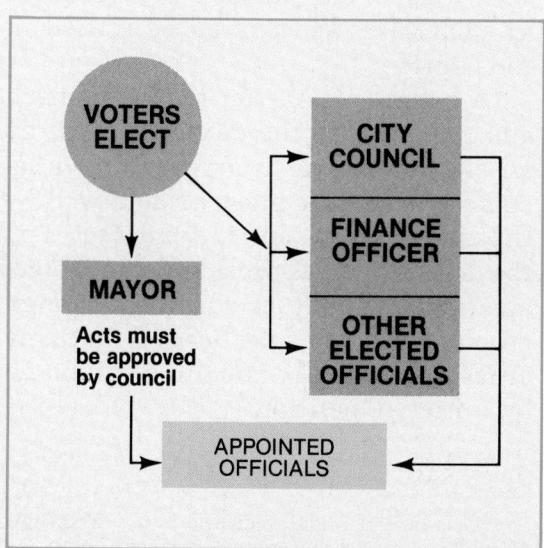

city engineer, and police chief, and with the council. The powers of appointment, removal, and budget are shared with the council or exercised by that body alone, and the mayor seldom has a veto power.

Most mayor-council cities operate under the weak-mayor rather than the strong-mayor plan. But the latter form is generally found in larger cities.

Evaluation. The success of the mayor-council form depends in very large measure on the power, ability, and influence of the mayor. In weak-mayor cities, responsibility for action or inaction is hard to fix.

The strong-mayor plan helps to solve the problems of leadership and responsibility. Still, it has three large weaknesses. First, it depends very heavily on the capacities of the mayor. Second, a major dispute between the mayor and the council can stall the workings of city government. Third, the form is somewhat complicated and so is often little understood by the average citizen.

The Commission Form. Only a handful of the nation's cities now have a *commission form* of government. The larger ones include Portland (Oregon),

St. Paul, Tulsa, Mobile, Lexington (Kentucky), and Jackson (Mississippi).

The **commission form** is rather simple and uncomplicated. Three to nine (usually five) commissioners are popularly elected. *Together*, they form the city council, pass ordinances, and control the purse strings. *Individually*, they head the different departments of city government—police, fire, public works, and so on. Thus, both legislative and executive powers are centered in one body.[9]

In some cities the voters and in others the commissioners themselves choose one of the commissioners to serve as the mayor. Like the other commissioners, the mayor heads one of the city's departments. He or she also runs the council meetings and represents the city on ceremonial occasions. The mayor generally has no more authority than the other commissioners and rarely has the veto power.

The commissioners are usually elected for two- or four-year terms, and almost always from the city at-large and on nonpartisan ballots. Unlike their counterparts in both mayor-council and

[9]The commission form was born in Galveston, Texas in 1901. A tidal wave had swept the island city the year before, killing 7000 persons and laying much of it to waste. The old mayor-council regime was too incompetent (and corrupt) to cope with the emergency. The Texas legislature gave Galveston a new charter, providing for five commissioners to make and enforce the law in the stricken city. Intended to be temporary, the arrangement proved so effective that it soon spread to other Texas cities and then elsewhere in the country. Its popularity has waned, however. In 1960 Galveston's voters approved a new city charter providing for council-manager government.

The mayor of Austin, Texas, Ron Mullen, meets with the city council. As do many cities in that State, Austin has a council-manager form of government.

council-manager cities, they regularly serve as full-time officers.

Evaluation. The simplicity of the commission form, and especially its short ballot, won the support of municipal reformers in the first twenty years or so of this century. However, experience with it pointed up serious defects and the popularity of the form fell off rapidly —from a peak use in some 500 cities in 1920 to little more than 100 today.

Its chief defects: (1) The lack of a single chief executive (or, the presence of several chiefs-among-equals)—which makes it difficult to fix responsibility. This also means that the city generally has no effective political leadership. (2) A built-in tendency toward "empire-building"—or, several separate empires, as each commissioner tries to draw as much of the city's money and power as he or she can to his or her own department. And (3) a lack of coordination at the top-most levels of policymaking and administration. Each commissioner is

The Kingdome, a concrete-domed sports arena built and maintained by the city of Seattle, Washington, has a seating capacity of 64,752.

likely to equate the public good with the peculiar interests and functions of his or her department.

The Council-Manager Form. The **council-manager** plan of government is a modification of the mayor-council form. It features: (1) a strong council, of usually five or seven members, elected at large on a nonpartisan ballot, (2) a weak mayor, chosen by the voters, and (3) a manager, the city's chief administrative officer, named by the council.[10]

The council is the city's policy-making body. The manager carries out the policies the council makes and is directly responsible to that body for the efficient administration of the city. The manager serves at the council's pleasure and may be dismissed at *any* time and for *any* reason the council chooses.

Today most city managers are professionally trained, career administrators— and more and more women are now entering the field. As chief administrator, the manager directs the work of all city employes, has the power to hire and fire, and prepares the budget for council consideration.

Evaluation. The council-manager plan has the backing of nearly every student of municipal affairs, and its use has spread widely. It is now found in nearly 3000 communities, including about half of those with populations of 250,000 or more.

First, it is simple in form. *Second*, it is clear who has the responsibility for policy on the one hand and for its application on the other. And *third*, it relies on experts who can use modern techniques of budgeting, planning, computer-

---

[10]The form was born in Staunton, Virginia, in 1908 when that city hired a general manager to direct the city's work. That step attracted the support of municipal reformers and was soon pushed throughout the country. The first charter to provide for a council-manager form was granted by the South Carolina legislature to Sumter in 1912.

ization, and other administrative tools.

Some critics of the plan hold that it is undemocratic, since the chief executive is not elected. Others say that it does not offer strong political leadership. This, they point out, is needed in larger cities, where the population is often quite diverse and its interests are competitive. Some support for this view can be seen in the fact that only four cities with more than half a million residents now have manager government—Dallas, San Diego, San Antonio, and Phoenix.[11]

Municipal Functions

A city exists primarily to provide services to those who live in it. Those services, which cities provide day in and year out, are so extensive that it is almost impossible to catalog them. Nearly all of our larger, and many smaller, cities issue annual reports on the city's condition. These are often book-length publications.

Consider *some* of the many things that most or all cities do. To list a few, they: provide police and fire protection, and build and maintain streets, sidewalks, bridges, street lighting systems, parks and playgrounds, swimming pools, golf courses, libraries, hospitals, schools, correctional institutions, day-care centers, airports, public markets, parking facilities, auditoriums, and sports arenas. They furnish such public health and sanitation services as sewers and waste water treatment, rubbish and garbage collection and disposal, and disease prevention and eradication programs. They operate water, gas, light, and transportation systems. And they regulate traffic, building practices, noise pollution, and public utilities.

Then, too, many cities build and manage public housing projects, clear slums, provide summer youth camps, build and operate docks and other harbor facilities, and maintain tourist attractions. Several have built their own hydroelectric power dams. Many operate farms in connection with their sewage disposal plants and have set up other recycling programs. The list is endless.

City Planning

Most American cities, like Topsy, just "growed." With few exceptions, they developed haphazardly, without plan, and with no eye to the future. The results of this shortsightedness can be seen almost everywhere.

Industrial plants were placed anywhere their owners chose to build them. Rail lines were run through the heart of the community. Towering buildings shut out the sunlight from the too-narrow streets below. Main roads were laid out too close together and sometimes too far apart. Schools, police and fire stations, and other public buildings were squeezed onto cheap land or put where the political organization could make a profit. Examples are endless.

Fortunately, many cities have set up some sort of planning agency—usually a planning commission, supported by a trained professional staff.[12]

A number of factors have prompted this step. The need to correct past mistakes has often been an absolutely compelling one, of course. *And*, importantly, they have been spurred on by the Federal Government. Most federal grant and loan programs require that cities which seek aid must first have a master plan as a guide to future growth.

[11]Several other major, but smaller, cities also use the manager form, including Cincinnati, Toledo, Oklahoma City, Austin, Fort Worth, Tucson, Oakland, Sacramento, and San Jose.

[12]The first city planning commission was created in Hartford, Connecticut, in 1907. Only a handful of cities with populations of 10,000 or more do not have some kind of planning agency today.

A single-family dwelling has escaped destruction as a new building is constructed around it in Atlantic City, New Jersey.

Washington, D.C., is one of the few cities in the nation that began as, and has remained, a planned city. Its basic plan was drawn before a single building was erected. In 1790 Congress decided to locate the nation's capital along the Potomac River. President Washington gave the task of laying out the new city to an engineer, Major Pierre-Charles L'Enfant.

L'Enfant designed the city on a grand scale, with adequate parks and beautiful circles. Parallel streets, running in an east-west direction, were named according to the alphabet, and those running at right angles were numbered. Twenty-one avenues shortened distances by cutting diagonally through the city, and trees and shrubs were planted at the intersections. Wide streets were provided, and large areas reserved for public buildings.

The original plan has been followed fairly closely through the years. The National Capitol Planning Commission guides the city's development today.

City Zoning. **Zoning** is the practice of dividing a city into a number of districts (zones) and of regulating the uses to which property in each of them may be put. Generally, a zoning ordinance places each parcel of land in the city into one of three zones: residential, commercial, or industrial. Each of these is then divided into sub-zones. For example, each or several of the residential zones may be broken down into several areas. One may be just for single-family residences. Another may allow both one- and two-family dwellings. In still another apartment houses and other multi-family units may be allowed.[13]

Nearly every city of any size in the United States is zoned today; the only major exception is Houston, where zoning was turned down by popular vote.

Zoning ordinances must be *reasonable*. Remember that the 14th Amendment prohibits any State—and its cities, of course—the power to deprive any person of life, liberty, or property without due process of law. Each of the State constitutions has a similar provision.

---

[13]Most zoning ordinances also prescribe limits on the height and area of buildings, determine how much of a lot may be occupied by a structure, and set out several other such restrictions on land use. They often have "set-back" requirements which state that structures must be placed at least a certain distance from the street and from other property lines.

Clearly, zoning *does* deprive a person of the right to use his or her property for certain purposes. Thus, if an area is zoned only for single-family dwellings, one cannot build an apartment house or a service station on his/her property in that zone.[14]

While zoning may at times deprive a person of liberty or property, the key question always is: Does it do so *without due process?* That is, does it do so *unreasonably?*

The question of reasonableness is one for the courts to decide. The Supreme Court first upheld zoning as a proper use of the police power in 1926—in a case involving an ordinance enacted by the city council of Euclid, Ohio.[15]

✓ FOR REVIEW

1. What proportion of our population was urban in 1790? By 1980?
2. What is a city charter? What five distinct types have been or are being used?
3. What are the three major forms of city government?
4. Why did city planning become so generally and vitally necessary?
5. What is meant by *zoning?*

Suburbanites and Metropolitan Areas

Suburbanitis

Most larger cities, and many smaller ones, suffer from what has been called "suburbanitis." Today over a third of our total population—and half of our urban population—live in suburbs.

From 1950 to 1980 the nation's population grew by 53 precent—by more than 75 million persons. Most of that spectacular increase came in the suburban population. It jumped some 42 million—about 85 percent—over those years. Many of the nation's larger cities *lost* population in the 1950s and 1960s, but, at the same time, their fringe areas grew by leaps and bounds. And the move to suburbia continues in the 1980s.

This dramatic shift in population can be explained on several grounds. A plentiful number of quite understandable desires has helped to bring it about—including desires for more room; cheaper land; less smoke, dirt, noise, and congestion; and greater privacy. At the same time, people wished for more neighborliness; less crime; newer and better schools, safer streets and playing conditions; lower taxes; and higher social status. The automobile and the freeway have turned millions of once rooted city dwellers into mobile suburbanites.

Businesses have followed customers to the suburbs, of course—often clustering in modern and convenient shopping centers. Many industries have moved

"The zoning commission would like to point out an irregularity!"

Reprinted through courtesy of the Chicago Tribune-New York News Syndicate, Inc.

---

[14]However, nonconforming uses in existence *before* a zoning ordinance is passed are almost always allowed to continue. And most ordinances give the city council the right to grant exceptions (variances) in cases where property owners might suffer undue hardships.

[15]*Euclid* v. *Amber Realty Co.,* 1926; on the police power, see pages 125–127.

from the central city in search of cheaper land, lower taxes, and a more stable labor supply. Industries have also been looking for an escape from city building codes, health inspectors, and other regulations. And these developments have themselves stimulated growth.

All of this has sharpened a great many problems for core cities. As many of the better-educated, high income families have moved out, they have taken their civic, financial, and social resources with them. They have left behind a central city which, in contrast to its suburbs, has much higher percentages of older persons, low-income families, blacks, and other minorities, more older buildings and substandard housing, more unemployment, and higher crime rates. Inevitably, both the need for and stress on city services have multiplied.

Metropolitan Areas

While the growth and sprawl of suburbia have raised many problems for cities, suburbanites face their share of problems, too. Water supply, sewage disposal, police and fire protection, trans-

The interior of a shopping mall in Queens, New York, one of the many that have become a part of the landscape of suburban America.

portation, and traffic control are only some of them. Duplication of functions by city and city or city and county can be wasteful and dangerous. More than one fire has burned on while neighboring fire departments quibbled over which of them was responsible for fighting it.

Attempts to meet the needs of **metropolitan areas**—that is, of the cities *and* the areas around them—have taken several forms. Over the years, annexation has been the standard means; outlying areas have simply been brought within a city's boundaries. But, as we have noted, many suburbanites resist annexation. Cities, too, have often been slow to take on the burdens involved.

Another approach involves the creation of *special districts*, to which we referred on page 582. The best known and most common of these are school districts, but there are now more than 28,000 sanitary, water, fire protection, and other special districts across the country. Their boundaries may cut across county and city lines, and they

A rapid response to a fire alarm can mean the difference between life and death, as well as that damage to property can be curtailed.

are often called *metropolitan districts.*

These metropolitan districts are generally set up for a single purpose—for example, for park development in the Cleveland Metropolitan Park Development District. There is no reason why a district's authority cannot be expanded to cover other functions, however. The Metropolitan District Commission, created by Massachusetts, controls sewage, water supply, and park development for the City of Boston and several neighboring communities. And the MDC has a number of planning functions in the District as a whole. Boston has only about a third of the District's population; the balance lives within 40 other municipalities.

City-county consolidation and, on the other hand, city-county separation, have also been tried in some places.

Yet another approach is increasing the authority of counties. Among local governments around the country, counties are generally the largest in area and are most likely to include those places demanding new and increased services.

The functions of many urban counties have been increased in recent years,

as we noted on page 578. Dade County (Miami), Florida, has undertaken the nation's most ambitious approach to metropolitan problems. In 1957 its voters approved the first home-rule charter to be designed "to create a metropolitan government." Under it, a county-wide metropolitan government ("Metro") is responsible for area-wide functions. These include fire and police protection; providing an integrated water, sewer, and drainage system; zoning; expressway construction; and the like.

☑ **FOR REVIEW**

1. What factors have been especially responsible for the spectacular growth of the nation's suburban population?

2. What sorts of problems has "suburbanitis" caused for cities? For the suburban areas themselves?

3. What is a metropolitan district? What newer approach has been tried in Dade County? What are the other major approaches attempted elsewhere?

SUMMARY

There are more than 82,000 units of local government in the United States today. Among them are 3,041 counties, more than 16,000 townships, some 44,000 special districts (more than a third of them school districts), and over 19,000 municipalities.

All but two States—Connecticut and Rhode Island have counties. They serve largely as judicial districts in New England, share responsibility for rural government with townships in the northeastern and middle western sections, and are the predominant rural units in the South and West. Only

a few places in the country do not lie within the boundaries of some county.

Counties vary widely in size, population, and number among the States. Legally, they are creatures of the State and administer State law and ordinances the State's constitution and legislature allow them to pass.

With a few exceptions, county government is in urgent need of reform across the country. Its major weaknesses are its headlessness, too many elective offices, and the failure to separate executive and legislative functions. The geographic size and number of counties in most States pose real problems, as well. Reform has made little headway in most States.

Townships are also predominantly rural units, found from the New England States westward to the Dakotas. In New England the *town* is regularly the major vehicle of local government. Elsewhere, townships have been largely outmoded by modern means of transportation and communication and by urbanization.

Special districts are units of local government created to carry out one or occasionally a few specific functions. They are found everywhere except Alaska. School districts are by far the most common example.

The nation's cities have grown spectacularly, especially in the past century. Where our population was once largely agricultural and rural, it is now largely industrial and urban. Three-fourths of all our people live in urban areas today.

Municipalities—known as cities, towns, villages, and boroughs—are creatures of the State. But, importantly, they also exist for the convenience of their residents. The range and variety of their functions and services virtually deny cataloging.

A city's *charter* is its fundamental law and may be *special, general, classified, optional,* or *home rule* in form.

Three major forms of city government are found in the United States: the *mayor-council* form (the most widely used), the *commission form,* and the *council-manager* form.

Most cities have grown haphazardly and with no eye to the future. Most have now recognized the need for effective planning, however. *Zoning* is a principal tool with which orderly growth can be obtained.

"Suburbanitis" has caused many serious problems in and for central cities—and for the suburbs, as well. A number of *metropolitan districts* have been formed and the functions of some urban counties have been increased to meet the problems raised by suburbanization.

C H A P T E R   R E V I E W

Key Terms/Concepts

Annexation (589)
Assessor (575)
Auditor (575)
Boroughs (573)
Board of Commissioners (574)
Board of Supervisors (575)
Chief administrative officer (579)
Cities (583)
City charter (586)
City council (590)
City manager (592)
City planning (593)
Clerk (575)
Commission form (591)
Council-manager form (592)
Counties (573)
County board (574)
County-city consolidation (580)
County-city separation (580)
County consolidation (580)
County manager (578)
Home rule (578, 588)
Incorporation (585)
Mayor-council form (590)
Metropolitan area (596)
Metropolitan districts (596)
Municipal corporation (586)
Municipalities (583)
School districts (582)
Selectmen (581)
Sheriff (575)
Special Districts (582)
Suburbanitis (595)
Suburbs (595)
Towns (580)
Town meeting (580)
Townships (581)
Treasurer (575)
Village (583)
Zoning (594)

Keynote Questions

1. There are approximately how many units of government in the United States today? How many of each type? How many in your State?
2. What is the essential nature of the relationship between each of the States and all of its many units of local government?
3. What is the basic unit of local government in most rural areas of the country? What three major weaknesses are usually associated with it?
4. How do the towns of New England differ from the townships to be found in several other parts of the country?
5. What are special districts? The largest number of them exist for what particular purpose?
6. For what principal reason do cities exist?
7. What is a city charter? Identify the five distinct types of charters to be found among the States.
8. Identify and describe the three major forms of city government to be found in the United States.
9. Why did city planning become so generally necessary in this country? What is zoning?
10. What factors have been especially responsible for the spectacular growth of the nation's suburban population?

For Thought and Discussion

1. Do you think that every city should be allowed to frame its own charter? Every county?
2. What arguments may be made for and against the election of members of a city council (and/or a county governing body) from: (a) wards (districts) and (b) the city (or county) at large?
3. When was your city established? What factors led to its creation? Has its growth been generally orderly and well-planned? If so, why? If not, why not? What are the city's more pressing planning problems today?
4. Why are bicameral city councils now almost wholly unknown among American cities?

Suggested Activities

1. Prepare an organizational chart depicting the major features of the government of your county and/or city.
2. Invite one or more local officials—from the county, city or other local unit—to discuss with the class his or her office and functions.
3. Stage a debate or class forum on one of these topics: (a) *Resolved*, That all counties in this State be abolished; (b) *Resolved*, That this city adopt (or abandon) the council-manager form of government; (c) *Resolved*, That this city's chief of police be hereafter selected by popular vote.
4. Obtain a copy of your city's zoning ordinance(s) and accompanying map(s). Examine and evaluate those documents. Do you recommend any changes in zoning laws? If so, why?

The harbormaster of Noroton, Connecticut, checks applications for small boat mooring spaces.

24 Financing State and Local Governments

CHAPTER OBJECTIVES

To help you to
Learn ▪ Know ▪ Understand

The huge amounts of money involved in State and local government finance today.

The major sources of State and local government income.

The political as well as the financial shape of public budgets and the budget-making process.

The general patterns of State and local government spending.

Finance is not mere arithmetic; finance is great policy.
Woodrow Wilson

Government is an expensive proposition —and it is becoming more so year to year. Just as the costs of government at the national level have risen to astronomical heights in recent decades, so have its costs at the State and local levels. Altogether, the 50 States and their thousands of local governments now take in and spend at a rate of well over $500 billion a year.

State and local spending amounted to less than one billion dollars a year for *all* purposes at the turn of the century. Just 20 years ago, in 1964, that spending came to only some $80 billion a year; today, it is running at a rate of very close to seven times that amount.

This dramatic and continuing rise can be traced to two major casues. One of them is inflation, of course. It affects the price of government in the same way it affects the price of everything else we buy. The other is the fact that, over time, we, the people, have demanded that more and still more services be provided by our many governments.

Government can do little without money. Where does it come from? Where does it go? It is to these *vital* questions we now turn.

State and Local Revenue

The huge amounts of money consumed by State and local government come from both tax and nontax sources. This year (1984) the States will take in over $170 billion in taxes; all of their local units will collect about $110 billion. And the 50 States and their local governments will also receive another $225 billion or so from a number of non-tax sources.

Taxes are charges made by governments, compulsory exactions to raise money for public purposes.

Limitations on State and Local Taxing Powers

The power to tax is one of the major powers reserved to each of the States. In the strictly legal sense, then, it is limited only by those restrictions imposed by the Federal Constitution and by its own fundamental law.[1]

Every local unit acquires its taxing power from its parent State. Thus, its power to tax is limited by State constitutional *and* statutory provisions as well as by the restrictions in the Constitution of the United States.

Federal Limitations. The Federal Constitution places only a few restrictions on State and local taxing powers.

(1) Interstate and Foreign Commerce. As we've already seen, the Constitution forbids the States the power to "lay any imposts or duties on imports or exports" and "any duty of tonnage."[2]

In effect, the States are here prohibited from taxing interstate and foreign commerce. The Supreme Court has often held that, because the Constitution gives to Congress the power to regulate that trade, the States are generally forbidden to do so. But, recall (page 69), a State may *incidentally affect* it. So, States may (and do) tax many kinds of property used in that commerce—for example, land, building, trucks, and much else.

(2) The National Government and

---

[1] The power to tax is also limited by any number of *pratical* considerations, too—i.e., by a variety of quite important economic and political factors in each State.

[2] Article I, Section 10, Clauses 2 and 3.

Its Agencies. The States have been forbidden, ever since the Supreme Court's decision in *McCulloch* v. *Maryland*, 1819, to tax the Federal Government or any of its agencies or functions; see pages 335–336. They are because, as Chief Justice Marshall said: "the power to tax involves the power to destroy."

(3) *The 14th Amendment.* The Due Process and Equal Protection Clauses also place limits on the power to tax at the State and local levels.

Essentially, the Due Process Clause requires that taxes be: (a) imposed and administered *fairly*; (b) *not* so heavy as to actually *confiscate* (seize) property, and (c) imposed only for *public* purposes.

The Equal Protection Clause forbids the making of *unreasonable* classifications for taxing purposes. Notice that most tax laws involve some form of classification. For example, an income tax does, for it is applied only to that class of persons who have income. Likewise, a cigarette tax is collected only from those who buy cigarettes, and a property tax only from those who own property. Of course, the Clause does not prevent these and similar classifications for they are *reasonable* ones. It does forbid tax classifications made on such bases as race, religion, nationality, political party membership, or similarly *unreasonable* factors, however.

State Constitutional Limitations. Each State's own constitution limits the power to tax.

Most State constitutions provide that taxes shall be levied only for public purposes and that they be applied uniformly. Most provide that taxes be collected only within the geographic limits of the units of government which levy them, and that there be no arbitrary or unreasonable classifications made for tax purposes.

Most of them also exempt the properties of churches, private schools, museums, cemeteries, and the like from taxation. Many set maximum tax rates. For example, many fix the State's sales tax at four percent and/or the local property tax at no more than so many *mills*[3] per dollar of assessed valuation. And some prohibit the use of certain kinds of taxes—such as a sales or an income tax.

As local units have no independent powers, the only taxes they may impose are those the State allows them to levy. The States have been notoriously reluctant in the matter. Even those units with home-rule charters are closely restricted in terms of what and how they can tax.

The Principles of Sound Taxation

Any tax, taken by itself, can be shown to be unfair. If all of a government's revenues were to come from one tax—say, a sales, an income, or a property tax—its tax system would be very unfair. Some would bear a much greater burden than others, and some would bear little or none. Yet, each tax should be defensible as *part* of a tax system.

More than 200 years ago, in his classic *The Wealth of Nations*, published in 1776, the English economist Adam Smith laid out four principles of a sound tax system. Most tax experts today cite the same four. Wrote Smith:

> 1.   The subjects of every state ought to contribute towards the support of the government, as nearly as possible, in proportion to their respective abilities; that is, in proportion to the revenue which they respectively enjoy under the protection of the state.
>
> 2.   The tax which each individual is bound to pay ought to be certain and not arbitrary.

---

[3]A *mill* is one-thousandth of a dollar, or one-tenth of a cent. Thus, if the local property tax rate is 50 mills, one who owns property assessed at $10,000 would pay a property tax of $500.

STATE AND LOCAL GOVERNMENT EMPLOYEES AND ANNUAL PAYROLL EXPENDITURES

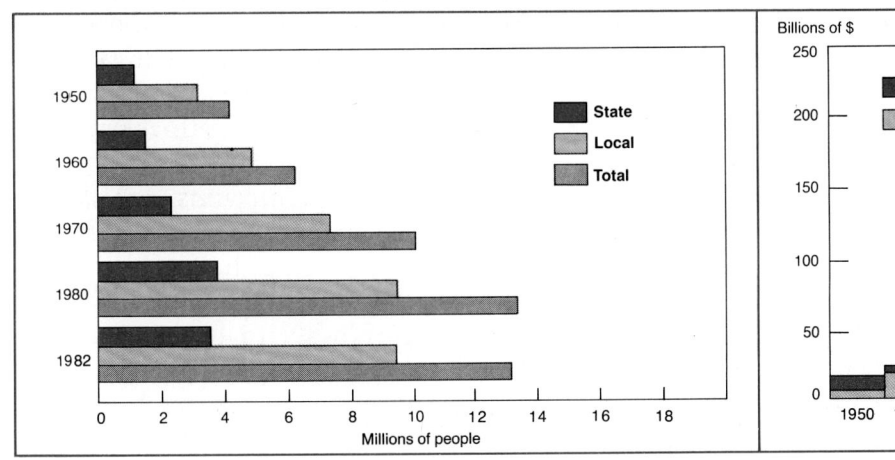
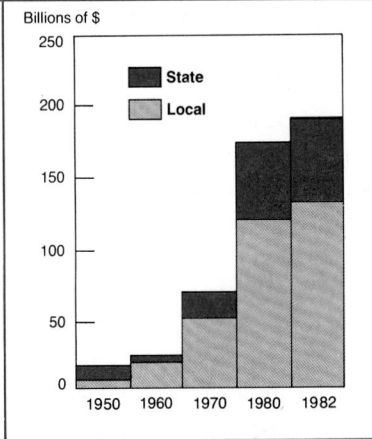

Source: U.S. Bureau of the Census

3. Every tax ought to be levied at the time, or in the manner, in which it is most likely to be convenient for the contributor to pay it.

4. Every tax ought to be so contrived as to take out and to keep out of the pockets of the people as little as possible over and above what it brings into the public treasury. . . .

Shaping a tax system—let alone any single tax—to meet these standards of *equality, certainty, convenience,* and *economy* is just about impossible. Still, that goal should be pursued, always.

☑ FOR REVIEW

1. The 50 States now collect about how much in taxes each year? Their local governments? From nontax sources?

2. What four major restrictions does the Federal Constitution place upon the taxing powers of the States and their local units?

3. What is the other source of legal restriction upon each State's power to tax?

4. Summarize Adam Smith's four principles of a sound tax system.

State and Local Taxes

Beyond the limits we have noted, a State may levy taxes as it chooses. The legislature decides what taxes the State will levy, and at what rates. It also decides what taxes the local units— counties, cities, school districts, and so on—may levy.[4]

The Sales Tax. The sales tax is the single most important source of income among the 50 States today. It now accounts for about half of all of the tax monies collected by the States.

A **sales tax** is a tax placed on the sale of different commodities and is paid by the purchaser. It may be either general or selective in form. A **general sales tax** is one that is placed upon the sale of most commodities. A **selective sales tax** is one placed only on the sale of certain commodities—such as cigarettes, liquor, or gasoline.

Today, 45 States[5] levy a general sales tax. The rate is most often three or four percent; but the rate runs from a low of two percent in Oklahoma on up to seven

---

[4] A State constitution sometimes grants certain taxing powers directly to local governments, but this is not at all common.

[5] All except Alaska, Delaware, Montana, New Hampshire, and Oregon. Each of these States does impose various selective sales taxes, however.

percent in Connecticut. In most States certain items are exempted from the tax—as, all food, or certain food items such as milk or bread, drugs, newspapers, or sales under a certain amount.

In most States the tax is collected by the retailer as each sale is made—that is, it is paid by customers as they buy taxable items. In a few States, however, the tax is not levied on each separate sale but, instead, on a retailer's total sales. Where this is the practice the sales tax is often called a **gross receipts tax.** In either case, it is the customer who pays the tax. The retailer acts as the tax collector and turns the receipts over to the State at regular intervals.

Every State now levies a selective sales tax on gasoline and other motor fuels, alcoholic beverages, insurance policies, and cigarettes. And most also have a selective sales tax on such other things as hotel and motel accommodations, theater and other amusement admissions, restaurant meals, automobiles and parimutuel betting.

There are two major reasons why the sales tax is so widely used. *First*, it is relatively easy to collect. And *second*, it is a fairly dependable revenue producer. But, notice, it is a **regressive tax**—one not geared to ability to pay; it falls most heavily on those with lower incomes.

Several larger and many smaller cities, and some counties, also levy a sales tax—a "piggy-back" tax, added on to and collected with the State tax.

The Income Tax.   The income tax —levied on individuals and/or corporations—yields more than 35 percent of State tax revenues today. Forty-three States now levy an individual income tax; 46 have some form of the corporate income tax.[6]

---

[6]Nevada, Texas, Washington, and Wyoming levy neither type of income tax. Alaska, Florida, and South Dakota impose only the corporate tax. Oil-rich Alaska abolished its tax on personal incomes in 1980.

The *individual income tax* rates are usually **progressive**—that is, the higher the income the higher the tax rate. The rates vary among the States, of course— from one or two percent on lower incomes in most on up to 15 percent or more on the highest incomes in some of them. Various exemptions and deductions are allowed in the figuring of one's taxable income. Over half of the States now tie the details of their own tax return very closely to those of the returns that taxpayers must file with the Federal Government each year.

The *corporate income tax* rates are most often uniform, a certain fixed percentage of income. Only a few States fix the rates on a graduated (progressive) basis.

The progressive income tax is held by many to be the fairest (or least unfair) form of taxation—especially because it may be closely geared to ability to pay. If the rates are too high, however, the tax can discourage incentive. The high federal income tax rates tend to force the States to keep theirs relatively low.

Some cities also levy a small income tax. But local income taxes will never become important revenue producers unless and until both federal and State rates are cut substantially. The chances of that happening are dim, indeed.

The Property Tax.   The property tax is the chief source of income for local governments today. It accounts for approximately 80 percent of all of their tax receipts. Once the principal source

"The Small Society," by Brickman. Washington Star Syndicate, Inc.

INTERPRETING CARTOONS

GETTING THE MESSAGE

Political cartoons are drawn editorials, drawings in which cartoonists express their views on matters of public concern. More often than not, they are satirical—that is, they are meant to criticize, and they try to do so with wit and sarcasm

Cartoons have been a part of the American political scene since colonial days. They can be found in most newspapers, many magazines, and in many other places. Those several other places include this book, of course.

Political cartoons seek to influence public opinion. They attempt to attract our attention to whatever it is they deal with, and affect our views on those topics.

The interpretation of a political cartoon involves a process very much like that involved in analyzing and understanding a picture—and, recall, we looked at that subject on page 488. You should describe its content, identify its main object or purpose, and define the responses it produces.

But, notice, there are some very important differences between cartoons, on the one hand, and pictures (photographs in books and newspapers, images on television screens, and so on), on the other:

1. Cartoons are usually simplified drawings, not accurate and detailed representations of their subjects. Often, details are left out purposely, to emphasize the main point of the cartoonist's message.

2. Cartoons frequently caricaturize.

That is, they often use caricatures (exaggerations, purposeful distortions) to make a point and/or attract attention. Thus, a cartoonist may draw one character in comparatively large form and another much smaller—to suggest that the larger person is the more powerful or notable of the two.

3. Cartoonists often use symbols to identify characters, present information, or produce (favorable or unfavorable) responses. Thus, Uncle Sam = United States; elephant = Republicans; donkey = Democrats; and so on.

4. Signs or labels are frequently used to identify people, objects, or events. They are a cartoonist's short-hand way of making certain that the viewer understands exactly what the cartoonist intends a particular caricature to represent.

When you see a political cartoon, check its caption, then look for caricatures, symbols, and signs and labels. These questions can be a guide for its interpretation: On what matter does the cartoonist comment? What message does the cartoonist want to deliver?

1. Take another look at three of the cartoons in this book—say, those on pages 551, 595, 604. What is the central topic of each of them? What message or point of view does each present?

2. Draw a political cartoon to present your position on some aspect of State and local government finance—for example, the sales tax or the size of public expenditures.

of State income, it now brings in less than two percent of all State revenues.

The property tax may be levied on (1) **real property**—land, buildings, and improvements which go with the property if sold, or (2) **personal property**—either *tangible* or *intangible*. **Tangible** personal property includes all movable wealth which is visible and the value of which can be easily assessed—for example, farm implements, livestock, pianos, television sets, automobiles, and air conditioners. Examples of **intangible personal property** include such things as stocks, bonds, mortgages, promissory notes, and bank accounts. Because intangibles can often be hidden from the tax assessor they are not taxed in many States. In others, they are taxed at a lower rate than tangible personal property.

The process of determining the value of the property to be taxed is known as **assessment**. The task is usually carried out by an elected county, township, or city assessor. Only in a handful of States must he or she be a trained specialist, and in those States the assessor is usually appointed rather than elected. Most tax authorities believe that election is not likely to produce competent assessors. And, there is the possibility that elected assessors will under-assess in order not to antagonize the voters upon whom they depend for their office.

Where personal property is taxed, the assessment is regularly made each year. Real property is usually assessed less often, commonly every second or fourth year. The assessor is expected to visit the property and examine it in order to determine its value. In fact, the assessment is often made simply on the basis of the last year's figures, which were arrived at the same way.

Property is usually assessed at less than its true market value. Most property owners seem better satisfied if the assessment is set at, say, one half of its real value. Thus, a house assessed at $30,000 may actually be worth $60,000. If the tax rate is set at 20 mills (or two percent) the tax will be $600. In reality, of course, this is the same thing as a 10 mill (or a one percent) tax on the $60,000 house.[7]

Three major arguments are commonly made in favor of the property tax: (1) Because property is protected—and its value is often enhanced—by government, it may properly be required to contribute to the support of government. (2) The rate at which the tax is levied may be readily adjusted to meet governmental needs. And (3) it is a dependable source of revenue.

Similarly, there are three major criticisms of the property tax. *First*, the tax is not geared to ability to pay. Although the amount of real property one owns may in our earlier history have been a fair measure of one's wealth, it is not today. *Second*, it is all but impossible, even with the most competent of assessors, to assess all taxable property on a fair and equal basis. And *third*, personal property, especially intangible property, is often, and readily, concealed.

Inheritance or Estate Taxes.   Every State except Nevada levies inheritance or estate taxes—so-called "death taxes." An **inheritance tax** is one levied on the beneficiary's share of an estate, and an **estate tax** is one levied directly on the full estate itself.

Business Taxes.   A wide variety of business taxes, in addition to the corporate income tax, are also an important source of revenue in most States.

---

[7]Several reasons are given for assessing property at a fraction of its market value—none of them valid. Among them: the belief that full assessment means higher taxes; the wish to lessen the share of State or county taxes paid by an assessed area; political considerations, especially the desire of an assessor to be re-elected; and the difficulty of making a fair full-value assessment.

Over half of the States impose **severance taxes.** These are taxes placed on the removal of such natural resources as timber, oil, gas, minerals, and fish from the land or water.

Every State has several different **license taxes**—fees which permit persons to engage in a business, occupation, or activity which is otherwise unlawful. All States require that corporations (artificial persons) be licensed to do business in the State. Certain kinds of businesses —chain stores, amusement parks, bars and taverns, and transportation lines— must also have an additional license to operate. Then, too, persons who wish to engage in certain businesses or occupations must themselves be licensed. Most or all States require the licensing of doctors, lawyers, dentists, morticians, barbers, hairdressers, plumbers, engineers, electricians, and many others. Many local governments impose their own business license taxes, as well.

License taxes other than for business purposes are levied in all States, too— and are an important revenue source. The most important are those for motor vehicles and motor vehicle operators, of course; others include such permits as hunting, fishing, and marriage licenses.

Nearly half of the States have levies known as **documentary and stock transfer taxes.** These are charges made on the recording, registering, and transfer of such documents as mortgages, deeds, and securities. Some States also impose **capital stock taxes,** which are levied on the total assessed value of the shares of stock issued by a business concern.

Poll Taxes. Only New Hampshire now levies a poll tax—a head or capitation tax. In effect, it is a tax on the privilege of living and breathing. Recall that the poll tax was once widely used as a suffrage qualification in the South.

Other Taxes. A number of other taxes are imposed at the State and/or

A home builder applies for a building permit at the Building Inspector's office of Forsyth County, North Carolina.

local levels. More than half the States levy amusement taxes—usually on the tickets of admission to theaters, sports events, circuses, and the like. *Payroll taxes* produce huge sums—in all, some $40 billion among the States today. But money produced by these taxes is held in trust funds for such social welfare programs as unemployment, accident insurance, and retirement programs.

State-Local Tax Sharing. The fact that the States tax so many different sources of revenue often make it impractical for their local governments to do so. So, increasingly, the States now share with their local units portions of certain taxes—either as they are collected or by appropriations made by the legislature.

For example, most States give a portion of the income from gasoline taxes and motor vehicle licenses to cities and counties. Where this is done the State can try to equalize the financial resources of local units—and also attach some strings to the use of the money.

Nontax Receipts

State and local governments now take in some $225 billion a year from a wide range of nontax sources.

Federal Funds. A large portion of that huge amount comes from the federal government each year—much of it in the form of grants-in-aid, as we noted on page 74. The many different federal

A CASE IN POINT

STATE LOTTERIES

Today, 17 States run lotteries to raise revenue. Many other States are now considering them. In those States where lotteries now operate, a person can purchase a lottery ticket for 50 cents or a dollar in the hope of winning many times that amount. Lotteries bring in millions of dollars to State treasuries. The proceeds are sometimes allocated for specific purposes. In Pennsylvania, for example, the income they produce goes to senior citizens programs.

The use of lotteries to raise public funds dates back to colonial times and has met with varying degrees of success. In 1748, Benjamin Franklin helped sponsor a lottery to raise funds to buy cannons for Philadelphia's defense. George Washington reportedly pur-

chased lottery tickets to promote westward expansion. Most of the colonies used lotteries to raise funds to support the American Revolution. The Continental Congress also ran a lottery to help pay the Continental Army. A federal lottery was held to help finance the building of Washington, D.C., in the 1790's.

Due to mismanagement and public opposition on religious or moral grounds, most States had banned lotteries by the 1930s. However, since the 1960s, many States have renewed their interest in them as a viable means of raising needed revenue. Advocates of lotteries claim that they discourage organized crime and provide a "voluntary" means to raise needed funds. Critics argue that it is both morally and fiscally wrong for government to promote gambling.

1. Do you think that the promotion of lotteries serves to "tarnish" the image of State governments? Why, or why not?

2. Does your State have a lottery? Should it? Why, or why not?

A United States lottery ticket of 1776.

grants totalled almost $95 billion in 1981. But, acting on President Reagan's budget recommendations, Congress made substantial cuts in most of the grant programs for 1982 and beyond. The overall total will likely come to less than $85 billion this year.

Government-Operated Businesses. Each of the States and many of their local governments make money from a number of different publically-operated

business enterprises. Toll bridges and toll roads are found in many parts of the country. Several States—most notably Washington—are in the ferry business. North Dakota markets a flour sold under the brand-name "Dakota-Maid" and it is also in the commercial banking business. The city of Milwaukee, Wisconsin, makes and sells a plant fertilizer, "Milorganite." California operates a short railway line in San Francisco.

Eighteen States are in the liquor-dispensing business, selling it through State-operated stores.[8] For several years, Oregon and Washington jointly owned a distillery in Kentucky and sold its product in their own outlets.

Many cities own and operate their water, electric power, and bus transportation systems. Some cities operate farmer's markets and rent out space in their office buildings, warehouses, and housing projects, own and operate dams and wharves, and so on. The receipts from these businesses (often including profits) go toward the support of the governments which own them.

Other nontax sources include such things as court fines, the sale or leasing of public lands, interest earned from investments, and the like. Seventeen States today—Arizona, Colorado, Connecticut, Delaware, Illinois, Maine, Maryland, Massachusetts, Michigan, New Hampshire, New Jersey, New York, Ohio, Pennsylvania, Rhode Island, Vermont, and Washington—conduct lotteries.

Borrowing

Borrowing may be classed as a source of nontax revenue. But, since they must be repaid, loans are hardly in the same class as other nontax receipts.

States and their local governments often must borrow money for unusually large undertakings, such as public buildings or bridges and highways, that cannot be paid for out of current income. That borrowing is most often done by issuing bonds, much as the Federal Government does.

Generally, State and local bonds are fairly easy to market because the inter-est from them is not taxed by any level of government.

Many State and local governments have, in times past, borrowed so heavily that they have had to default on their debts. Thus, most State constitutions now place detailed limits on the power to borrow.

The total of all States' debts now comes to about $150 billion, and all local governments owe not quite twice that much today.

☑ FOR REVIEW

1. What tax produces the largest amount of revenue among the 50 States today?
2. What is the difference between a general and a selective sales tax? What is a gross receipts tax?
3. What two forms of the income tax are levied by most States today?
4. What tax produces the largest amount of revenue for local governments today?
5. Local governments commonly tax what two kinds of property?
6. What are the major arguments usually made for and against the sales tax? The income tax? The property tax? What is a progressive tax? A regressive tax?
7. What other taxes are often laid by a State and/or its local units?
8. From what principal nontax sources do State and local governments draw income?

The State Budget

We have already suggested that a budget is much more than bookkeeping entries and dollar signs. It is a financial plan—a plan for the control and use of public money, public personnel, and public property. It is also a political

[8]Alabama, Idaho, Iowa, Maine, Michigan, Mississippi, Montana, New Hampshire, North Carolina, Ohio, Oregon, Pennsylvania, Utah, Vermont, Virginia, Washington, West Virginia, Wyoming. North Carolina's stores are operated by the counties; Wyoming's liquor monopoly operates only at the wholesale level.

STATE AND LOCAL GOVERNMENT FINANCES

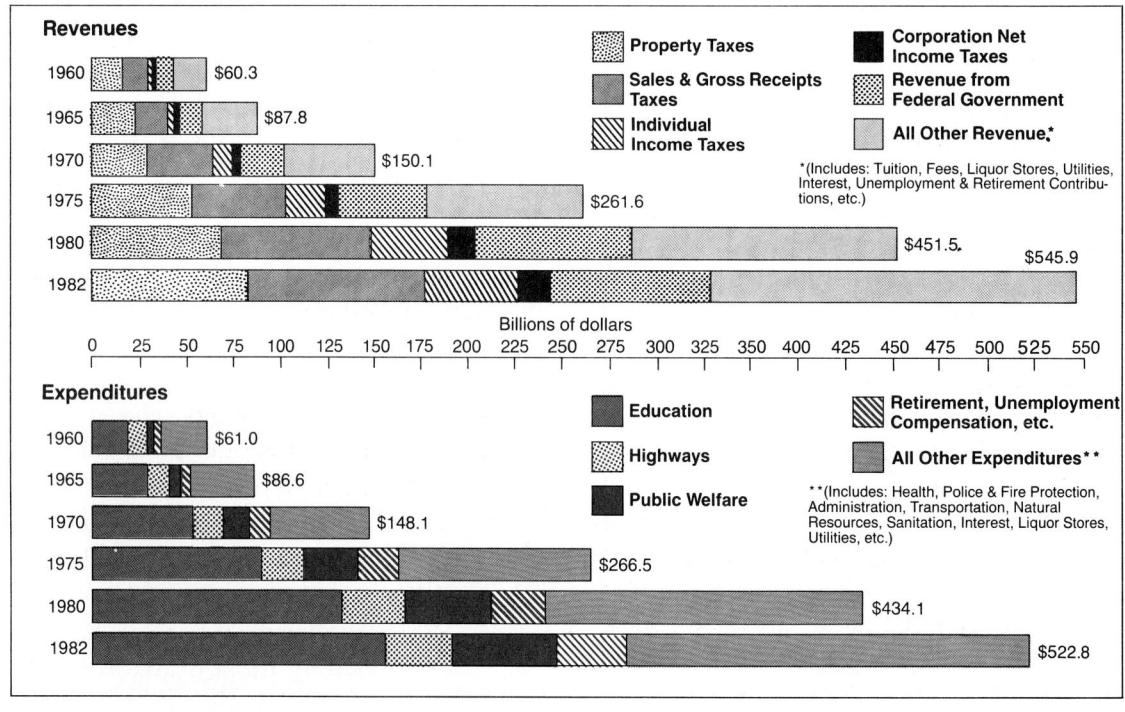

Revenues

1960	$60.3
1965	$87.8
1970	$150.1
1975	$261.6
1980	$451.5.
1982	$545.9

Legend:
- Property Taxes
- Sales & Gross Receipts Taxes
- Individual Income Taxes
- Corporation Net Income Taxes
- Revenue from Federal Government
- All Other Revenue.*

*(Includes: Tuition, Fees, Liquor Stores, Utilities, Interest, Unemployment & Retirement Contributions, etc.)

Billions of dollars
0 25 50 75 100 125 150 175 200 225 250 275 300 325 350 375 400 425 450 475 500 525 550

Expenditures

1960	$61.0
1965	$86.6
1970	$148.1
1975	$266.5
1980	$434.1
1982	$522.8

Legend:
- Education
- Highways
- Public Welfare
- Retirement, Unemployment Compensation, etc.
- All Other Expenditures**

**(Includes: Health, Police & Fire Protection, Administration, Transportation, Natural Resources, Sanitation, Interest, Liquor Stores, Utilities, etc.)

Source: U.S. Bureau of the Census

document—a highly significant statement of public policy. Here, in its budget, the State sets its priorities and decides who gets what and how much, and who doesn't.

Until at least the 1920s, few State budgets could be dignified as a "plan." No officer or agency reviewed the needs of State government and its agencies and measured them against the available resources. No officer or agency cut them where necessary and, then, presented a carefully constructed, cohesive financial program to the legislature.

Instead, State budgets were jerrybuilt, the results of haphazard and uncoordinated steps centering in the legislature. Regularly, the various State agencies appeared before legislative appropriations committees, each seeking its own funding and often in bitter competition with one another. Their chances of success depended far less on either need or merit than upon the political influence they could exert. When the legislature adjourned, no one had any real idea of how much it had appropriated or for what. Extravagance and waste, problems unmet, debt, favoritism, and graft were all parts of the process.

State budgets are very different today. They remain highly charged and vitally important political ducuments, of course; but they are the end-products of what is, by and large, an orderly, planned process.

Forty-seven States have now adopted the **executive budget.** That is, they have given the governor two vital powers: (1) the power to prepare the State budget, and (2) once the legislature has acted upon it, the power to carry out that budget, and authority to administer the different funds the legislature has appropriated. In most states the governor has the help of a director and the professional staff of a budget agency, appointed by and answering to the governor.[9]

The governor's key role in the budget process has been important in strengthening that office among the States, as we noted on page 545. And, recall, the executive budget is a key feature of council-manager government. It has also been put into place in most strong-mayor-council cities.

Steps in the Budget Process

The basic steps in the budget process are much the same at the State and local levels as they are at the Federal level:

(1) Each agency prepares estimates of its needs and expenditures in the upcoming fiscal period.

(2) Those estimates are reviewed by an executive budget agency.

(3) The revised estimates and all supporting information are brought together in a single financial program, the budget, for the governor to present to the legislature.

(4) The budget is considered, part by part, the necessary funds are appropriated, and the necessary revenue measures (if any) are passed by the legislature.

(5) The execution of the budget (the actual spending) approved by the legislature is supervised by the governor.

(6) The execution of the budget is given an independent check (post-audit).

Pattern of Expenditures

On page 600, we talked about the high rate of State and local government spending—now well over $500 billion a year.

Each of the 50 States, and their tens of thousands of local governments, spend for so many different purposes that it would be next to impossible to list them all. Another look at the graphs on page 610 will show that four major functions stand out as the most costly: education, highways, public welfare, and retirement and unemployment compensation. They account for nearly three-fifths of all State and local spending—close to $300 billion in 1984.

Of these four items, education is by far the most expensive entry in most State and local budgets. School spending has climbed ten-fold since 1950, and continues to increase year to year. Highways usually rank next each year, followed by welfare and then by health and hospitals, but not always in that order.

The patterns of spending for other functions are often quite different among the States. The differences depend largely upon the degree to which a given State is urbanized. All the States and their local units now spend more than $100 billion each year for such items as the protection of persons and property, debt payments and interest, developing and conserving natural resources, recreational facilities, correctional institutions, and general government.

☑ **F O R   R E V I E W**

1. What is a budget? Why is it a highly important political document?

2. Why have nearly all of the States given the budget-making power to the governor?

3. Summarize the six basic steps in the budget process.

4. What are the four most costly functions of the States and their local governments today?

---

[9]The preparation of the budget is a shared legislative and executive function in South Carolina and Texas; it is almost completely a legislative one in Mississippi.

S U M M A R Y

Money is just as essential to the existence of government at the State and local levels as it is to the National Government. Just as the cost of government at the national level has increased sharply in the past few decades, so has the cost of State and local government.

Taxes are charges imposed by a legislative body upon persons or property to raise money for public purposes. The canons of sound taxation center around the four concepts of equality, certainty, convenience, and economy.

The Federal Constitution, each State constitution, State laws, and city and county charters place many limits on taxing powers.

The principal State and local tax sources include the property tax, the general and selective sales tax, the individual and corporation income tax, the inheritance or estate tax, and various business and license taxes.

Nontax receipts come chiefly from federal grants and revenue sharing, government-operated businesses, and such other sources as court fines and the sale or leasing of public lands.

Borrowing, which is subject to strict limitations in most States, is only in a sense a nontax source of revenue.

Each State now has a budget system for the planned and more or less effective control of State finances. The budget-making process involves six steps: preparation of estimates, review of estimates, consolidation and presentation of the budget, consideration and adoption of the budget, execution of the budget, and a post-audit.

About three-fourths of all State and local spending today goes for: education, highways, public welfare, and public health and hospitals. Of these, education is by far the most costly.

C H A P T E R   R E V I E W

Key Terms/Concepts

Assessment (606)
Budget process (611)
Corporate income tax (604)
Estate tax (606)
Expenditures (611)
General sales tax (603)
Grants-in-aid (607)
Gross receipts tax (604)
Income tax (604)
Inheritance tax (606)

License tax (607)
Lottery (609)
Individual income tax (604)
Mill (602)
Nontax revenues (607)
Personal property (606)
Progressive tax (604)
Property tax (604)
Real property (606)

Reasonable classification (602)
Regressive tax (604)
Revenues (601)
Revenue sharing (607)
Sales tax (603)
Selective sales tax (603)
Severance tax (607)
Tangible, intangible property (606)

Keynote Questions

1. The dramatic and continuing rise in the cost of State and local government can be traced to what two major causes?
2. The Federal Constitution places what four major restrictions on the taxing powers of the States and their local governments?
3. What four standards are generally accepted as the basic principles for a sound tax system?
4. What tax now accounts for approximately half of all of the tax monies collected by the States today?
5. What two major forms of the income tax are levied by most of the States today?
6. What tax is the chief source of income for local governments today?
7. Identify at least one major argument often made for and another often made against the sales tax. The income tax. The property tax.
8. From which one of their several nontax sources do the States and their local governments now receive the largest amounts of money?
9. What is a government's budget?
10. What are the four most costly items of State and local spending today?

For Thought and Discussion

1. How do you account for the fact that State and local taxes and spending have increased so markedly in the past two decades?
2. What are the major sources of tax revenue for your State? Which one of those taxes produces the most revenue each year? On the basis of the four principles of sound taxation set out on page 602, how do you rate your State's tax structure?
3. Given the fact that both taxes are so regressive, why do most of the States continue to rely so heavily upon the sales tax and local governments upon the property tax?
4. What is the current size of your State's debt? Your city's and county's debts? What were the major purposes of the borrowings that produced those debts? How was the money borrowed, and at what interest? How are those debts being repaid?
5. How much tax-exempt property is there in your city and county? Do you think those exemptions are justified?
6. To what extent is your State, city, and county, engaged in business-like enterprises? Why is each unit involved in each of these enterprises? Should it be?

Suggested Activities

1. Invite State and/or local tax officials to discuss their work with the class.
2. Identify and analyze each of the provisions of your State's constitution which relate to State and local finance.
3. Compare the basic elements of your State's tax system with that of a neighboring State. Identify the similarities and differences between them and comment upon your findings in a report to the class.
4. Obtain copies of the current budgets of your State, city, and county. Compare them, in both form and content, and report your findings to the class. The documents can most likely be obtained from the State budget director's office (see the State Blue Book for exact title and address) and at city hall and the county courthouse.
5. Outline the basic steps in the budget process in your State, city, and county. (See page 611 and the sources of information referred to above.)

STOP THE PRESSES

On these two pages we cite a number of civil rights cases decided by the Supreme Court in 1983. For reasons of time, they could not be included within the main body of the text—in Chapter 5, "Civil Rights: Fundamental Freedoms," and Chapter 6, "Civil Rights: Equal Justice Under Law." The page references here are to the appropriate places in those two chapters, of course.

State Aid to Parochial Schools, pages 99–101. In *Mueller* v. *Allen* the Court upheld a Minnesota law that gives parents a State income tax deduction to help them pay the costs of tuition, textbooks, and transportation for their elementary and secondary school children. Parents are allowed that tax break no matter what schools—public or private—their children attend.

Most public school parents pay little or nothing for tuition or textbooks or transportation; those costs are almost always covered by public (tax) funds. Hence, the law is of particular benefit to parents of private school students—and most of these students attend parochial schools.

By a slim majority, the Court ruled that the Minnoesota law does not violate the excessive entanglement standard. The majority based that ruling very largely on this point: The tax break is available to all parents with children in school and they are free to decide the type of school their children attend.

Freedom of the Press, pages 104–105. The Court struck down another Minnesota law, however, in *Star and Tribune Co.* v. *Minnesota Commissioner of Revenue.* That law had imposed a special tax on the paper and ink used to print the State's larger newspapers (those papers that spent more than $100,000 a year for those items). The court found the law to be a clear violation of the Constitution's guarantee of freedom of the press.

Obscentity, pages 105–106; Advertising, pages 111–112. A federal law which barred the mailing of advertising matter about contraceptives to persons who had not asked for that material were held to be unconstitutional in *Bolger* v. *Young Drug Products Corp.* The Court held that such a ban violates the 1st Amendment's protection of freedom of speech, which includes "commercial speech."

Freedom of Assembly and Petition, pages 116–119. In *United States* v. *Grace* a unanimous Court found unconstitutional a federal law that prohibited a federal law that prohibited parades or other demonstrations on the grounds or within the building of the Supreme Court itself. The case was brought by a woman who had been arrested for picketing the Court in 1980; she and a companion had marched up and down the sidewalk in front of the Supreme Court Building, carrying a sign which bore the words of the 1st Amendment.

Due Process and the Police Power, pages 125–127; Self-Incrimination, pages 144–146. In *South Dakota* v. *Neville* the Court reaffirmed its key ruling in

Schmerber v. *California,* 1966. It held that nothing in the Constitution forbids a State to use a drivers refusal to take a blood test as evidence against him in his trial for drunk driving. South Dakota's law does not provide that a drunk driving suspect *must* take a blood test—and so, said the Court, the use of a refusal to do so does not violate the Constitution's ban of self-incrimination.

Searches and Seizures, pages 131–133.

The court decided two 1983 cases in which police, acting without a warrant, seized evidence in "plain-view"—and in both cases the seizure was upheld.

In *Brown* v. *Texas* a Fort Worth police officer had seized a knotted party balloon from the seat of a car stopped during a routine check for driver's licenses. The officer seized the balloon, which was in plain sight, because he knew that illegal drugs are frequently packaged and carried that way.

In *Illinois* v. *Lafayette* police in Kankakee had arrested a man for disturbing the peace. Later, at the police station, they inspected and inventoried the contents of his backpack—and found ten amphetimine pills.

Federal drug agents may hold a person's luggage, temporarily, without a warrant, in order to have it tested by a dog specially trained to sniff out drugs, *United States* v. *Place.* In fact, said the Court, since the sniff test does not involve opening the luggage, that process is not even a search within the meaning of the Constitution. (However, the Court also held that the agents who detained the luggage held it too long and did not tell the owner why they had it or when and where he might reclaim it. Therefore, the seizure of his property was unreasonable and his conviction for possessing the cocaine it contained was thrown out.)

Cruel and Unusual Punishment, pages 147–148.

In *Solem* v. *Helm* the Court overturned the sentence a South Dakota court had imposed on an habitual criminal—life in prison without the possibility of parole. As it did so, the Court declared, for the first time, that the constitution's ban of cruel and unusual punishment "prohibits not only barbaric punishments, but also sentence that are disproportionate to the crime committed."

The case involved a man who had been convicted of seven relatively minor and nonviolent offenses. He had most recently been found guilty of passing a bad check—a crime for which South Dakota law provides a maximum penalty of five years in prison and a $5000 fine. But, because of his previous record, he had received the much stiffer sentence.

The Court distinguished this case from *Rummel* v. *Estelle,* 1980, by noting that Rummel's life sentence in Texas carried the possibility of parole after ten or twelve years.

Classification by Sex, pages 153–155.

The Court decided two major sex discrimination cases in 1983. Both involve the application of Title VII of the Civil Rights Act of 1964 (page 157). In one, the Court found that a company had illegally discriminated against its male employees, *Newport News Shipbuilding and Dry Dock Co.* v. *Equal Employment Opportunity Commission.* Specifically, it had done so in its medical care plan—which provided greater hospitalization benefits during pregnancy for the company's female employees than those provided for the wives of its male employees.

The other case was *Arizona Governing Committee for Tax Deferred Annuity and Deferred Compensation Plans* v. *Norris.* There, the Court ruled that it is illegal for an employer to offer a retirement plan which provides for smaller monthly benefits to women than it does to men. (Arizona had defended the difference in benefits by arguing that women as a group live longer than do men as a group.)

616

POPULATION OF THE UNITED STATES

Rank 1970	Rank 1980	State	Capital	Population 1970	Population 1980	Percent of Change
21	22	Alabama	Montgomery	3,444,354	3,890,061	+12.9%
50	50	Alaska	Juneau	302,583	400,481	+32.4
33	29	Arizona	Phoenix	1,775,399	2,717,866	+53.1
32	33	Arkansas	Little Rock	1,923,322	2,285,513	+18.8
1	1	California	Sacramento	19,975,069	23,668,562	+18.5
30	28	Colorado	Denver	2,209,596	2,888,834	+30.7
24	24	Connecticut	Hartford	3,032,217	3,107,576	+ 2.5
46	47	Delaware	Dover	548,104	595,225	+ 8.6
–	–	Dist. of Columbia		756,668	637,651	−15.7
9	7	Florida	Tallahassee	6,791,418	9,739,992	+43.3
15	13	Georgia	Atlanta	4,587,930	5,464,265	+19.1
40	39	Hawaii	Honolulu	769,913	965,000	+25.3
42	41	Idaho	Boise	713,015	943,935	+32.4
5	5	Illinois	Springfield	11,110,258	11,418,461	+ 2.8
11	12	Indiana	Indianapolis	5,195,392	5,490,179	+ 5.7
25	27	Iowa	Des Moines	2,825,368	2,913,387	+ 3.1
28	32	Kansas	Topeka	2,249,071	2,363,208	+ 5.1
23	23	Kentucky	Frankfort	3,220,711	3,661,433	+13.7
20	18	Louisiana	Baton Rouge	3,644,637	4,203,972	+15.3
38	38	Maine	Augusta	993,722	1,124,660	+13.2
18	19	Maryland	Annapolis	3,923,897	4,216,446	+ 7.5
10	11	Massachusetts	Boston	5,689,170	5,737,037	+ 0.8
7	8	Michigan	Lansing	8,881,826	9,258,344	+ 4.2
19	21	Minnesota	St. Paul	3,806,103	4,077,148	+ 7.1
29	31	Mississippi	Jackson	2,216,994	2,520,638	+13.7
13	15	Missouri	Jefferson City	4,677,623	4,917,444	+ 5.1
43	44	Montana	Helena	694,409	786,690	+13.3
35	35	Nebraska	Lincoln	1,485,333	1,570,006	+ 5.7
47	43	Nevada	Carson City	488,738	799,184	+63.5
41	42	New Hampshire	Concord	737,681	920,610	+24.8
8	9	New Jersey	Trenton	7,171,112	7,364,158	+ 2.7
37	37	New Mexico	Santa Fe	1,017,055	1,299,968	+27.8
2	2	New York	Albany	18,241,391	17,557,288	− 3.8
12	10	North Carolina	Raleigh	5,084,411	5,874,429	+15.5
45	46	North Dakota	Bismarck	617,792	652,695	+ 5.6
6	6	Ohio	Columbus	10,657,423	10,797,419	+ 1.3
27	26	Oklahoma	Oklahoma City	2,559,463	3,025,266	+18.2
31	30	Oregon	Salem	2,091,533	2,632,663	+25.9
3	4	Pennsylvania	Harrisburg	11,800,766	11,866,728	+ 0.6
39	40	Rhode Island	Providence	949,723	947,154	− 0.3
26	25	South Carolina	Columbia	2,590,713	3,119,208	+20.4
44	45	South Dakota	Pierre	662,257	690,178	+ 4.2
17	17	Tennessee	Nashville	3,926,018	4,590,750	+16.9
4	3	Texas	Austin	11,198,655	14,228,383	+27.1
36	36	Utah	Salt Lake City	1,059,273	1,461,037	+37.9
48	48	Vermont	Montpelier	444,732	511,456	+15.0
14	14	Virginia	Richmond	4,651,448	5,346,279	+14.9
22	20	Washington	Olympia	3,413,244	4,130,163	+21.0
34	34	West Virginia	Charleston	1,744,237	1,949,644	+11.8
16	16	Wisconson	Madison	4,417,821	4,705,335	+ 6.5
49	49	Wyoming	Cheyenne	332,416	470,816	+41.6
		United States		**203,302,031**	**226,504,825**	**+11.4%**

Source: Census Bureau

Number(s) after each definition refer to the page(s) where the term is discussed.

Act Measure approved (passed, enacted) by a legislative body; see *statutory law.* 302, 530

Acquittal Formal determination by a court that one accused of crime is innocent, a finding of "not guilty." 137, 565.

Administrative law Law made up of the rules, orders, regulations issued (under proper constitutional and/or statutory authority) by officers and agencies in the executive branch. 391, 566

Affirmative action Policy that requires that both public and private organizations take positive steps to overcome the effects of past discrimination against blacks, women, and other minority groups, especially in employment and education. 157

Alien One who is not a citizen (or national) of the state in which he/she lives; usually, an alien owes allegiance to a foreign power but may gain citizenship by naturalization. 328

Alienation Individual's sense of separation from (indifference or even hostility to, lack of association with) his/her social environment; in politics, a feeling of powerlessness to affect events; see *political efficacy.* 204

Amendment Formal change (an alteration or addition) made in a bill, motion, or constitution. 55, 509

Anti-Federalists Those persons who opposed the adoption of the Constitution in 1787-1788. 45

Appeal Legal proceeding in which a case is carried from a lower court to a higher court for review. 483, 559

Appellate courts Courts in which appeals of lower court decisions are heard; in the federal court system: the 12 Courts of Appeals, the Court of Appeals for the Federal Circuit, and the Supreme Court. 483, 559

Apportionment Distribution of seats in a legislative body among electoral districts; *e.g.,* the allocation of the 435 seats in the House of Representatives among the 50 States according to their respective populations. 278, 521

Appropriations bills Measures passed by a legislative body granting agencies permission to spend specified amounts of money for specified purposes. 308, 544

Arraignment Court proceeding at which the formal criminal charge against the defendant (the person accused of crime) is read and at which he/she may enter a plea of guilty or innocence. 140, 564

At-large election Election at which members of a public body are chosen by the voters of an entire governmental unit, rather than from separate districts within it; *e.g.,* the election of all members of a city council by voters throughout the city (the city at-large), rather than from several districts (wards) within the city. 280, 590

Authoritarian Form of government in which individual liberty is completely subordinate to the authority of the state, which is itself controlled by one person or a small group; see *dictatorship.* 9

Bail Money the accused may be required to post (deposit with the court) as a guarantee that he/she will appear in court at the proper time. 147

Bicameral legislature Lawmaking body made up of two chambers (houses). 274, 519

Bill A proposal presented to a legislative body for possible enactment as a law. 304, 530

Bill of Attainder Legislative act which inflicts punishment upon a particular person or group without a court trial. 138

Bill of Rights First 10 amendments to the Constitution, dealing mostly with civil rights. 59, 90

Block grants One type of federal grants-in-aid to the States and/or their local governments; block-grant monies are to be used in some particular but broadly defined area of public policy (*e.g.,* education or highways); see *categorical grants.* 76

Brief Document prepared by an attorney and submitted to a court, setting forth arguments and citing evidence in a client's behalf. 491

Budget Both a financial plan and a political document; a detailed statement of estimated receipts (revenue, income) and planned expenditures (spending, outgo) during a specified period (usually a fiscal year). 383, 609

Bureaucracy Any large, complex administrative structure; the hierarchical organization of positions and agencies in the executive branch of a government. 405

Cabinet Presidential advisory body, traditionally composed of the heads of the (now 13) executive departments and those other officers (*e.g.,* the Vice President) the President may choose to appoint to it. 384

Calendar Schedule of bills and other business in committees and on the floor of a legislative body. 306

Capitalism Economic system based on private (individual and corporate) ownership of the means of producing goods and services and upon private initiative, competition, and profit; often referred to as the free enterprise or private enterprise system; see *laissez-faire, mixed economy.*   15

Categorical grants   Type of federal grants-in-aid to the States and/or their local governments; categorical grant monies must be used for specific, narrowly defined areas (categories) of public policy (*e.g.,* adult literacy or post-natal health care); see *block grants.*   75

Caucus (legislative)   Meeting of all members of one party in a particular house of a legislature, to select floor leaders, fill committee posts, and plan strategy in the legislative session.   297

Caucus (nominating)   Meeting of party leaders (or of party members) to select candidates for office or to choose delegates to local, State, or national party conventions.   218, 361

Certiorari, writ of   Order issued by a higher court directing a lower court to send up the record of a case for its review.   491

Checks and balances   System of overlapping the powers of the separate legislative, executive, and judicial branches of a government, to permit each branch to check (restrain, balance) the actions of the others; see *separation of powers.*   52

Citizen   One who owes allegiance to a state and is entitled to its protection; American citizenship may be acquired by birth (1) in the United States or (2) to American citizen-parents abroad, and (3) by naturalization.   328

City charter   City's basic law, granted by the State, which defines its boundaries, sets out its powers, and outlines its form of government.   586

Civil law   That body of law relating to human conduct, including disputes between private persons and between private persons and government, not covered by criminal law.   566

Civil rights   Constitutionally guaranteed rights to freedom of expression, freedom and security of the person, fair trial, and fair and equal treatment by the law.   88, 122

Civil service   Collective term for most civilian employees of a government, especially those hired through a merit system, (elected officials, top-ranking policy-makers appointed by them, and judges are not considered part of the civil service).   432

Closed primary   Form of the direct primary in which only party members may vote; see *open primary, primary election.*   221

Cloture   Procedure that may be used to limit or end floor debate in a legislative body (especially to cut off a filibuster).   313

Coattail effect   Influence a popular candidate for a top office (*e.g.,* President or governor) can have on the voters' support of other candidates of his/her party on the same ballot.   227

Cold War   Period of political and ideological conflict, tensions between the United States and the Soviet Union since World War II.   463

Collective security   Basic purpose of the U.N. and a major goal of American foreign policy, to create a worldwide system in which all or most nations agree to take joint action to meet any threat to or breach of international peace.   462

Commerce power   Exclusive power of Congress to regulate interstate and foreign trade.   66, 324

Commission form   Form of city government in which elected commissioners serve collectively as the city council and separately as heads of the city's administrative department.   591

Common law   That body of law made up of generally accepted standards of rights and wrongs developed over centuries by judicial decisions rather than in written statutes; a major basis of the American legal system, often called "judge-made law"; see *equity.*   566

Communism   Economic and political system built on the theories of Karl Marx, based on the collective (centralized state) ownership and control of property and the means of production, with all individuals expected to contribute to society according to ability and receive from it according to need; an extreme form of socialism.   19

Concurrent powers   Powers held by both the National Government and the States in the federal system (*e.g.,* powers to tax and to define and punish crimes).   70

Concurrent resolution   Measure passed by both houses of a legislature that does not have the force of law nor require the chief executive's approval; often used to express the legislature's opinion on an issue or for internal rules or housekeeping purposes; see *joint resolutions.*   304

Concurring opinion   Written explanation of the views of one or more judges who support a decision reached by a majority of the court but disagree with the grounds for that decision.   492

Confederation   Form of government in which an alliance of independent states (regional governments) creates a degree of national unity through a central government of very limited power; the member states have supreme authority (sovereignty) over all matters except in those few areas in which they have expressly delegated power to the central government.   7

Conference committee   Temporary joint committee of both houses of a legislature, created to reconcile (compromise, iron out) any differences between the two houses' versions of a bill.   302, 314

Connecticut Compromise   Agreement reached at the Constitutional Convention in 1787, settling the conflict over the composition of Congress and providing for a House of Representatives with seats distributed among the States according to population and a Senate in which the States are equally represented.   42, 276

Constituency   Geographic area (usually, a district) and all of its residents (the constituents) represented by a legislator or other elected officeholder.   218, 286

Constituent power   Power of Congress and of State legislatures to propose constitutional amendments.   337, 528

Constitution   Body of fundamental (supreme) law, setting out the basic principles, structures, processes, and functions of a government and placing limits upon its actions; may be written (as in the United States) or unwritten (as in Great Britain). 50, 504

Constitutionalism Basic principle that government and those who govern are bound by (must obey) the fundamental law (the constitution); the rule of law; see *limited government*. 51

Containment Basic feature of American foreign policy since World War II, resistance to the expansion of Soviet power and influence in world politics. 464

Contempt Crime of obstructing the lawful processes of government, usually committed by violating a court order; see *subpoena*. 144

Cooperative federalism Process in which the National Government and the States share resources to meet public policy problems. 74

Council-manager form Form of city government with an elected council as the policy-making body and an appointed, professional administrator (city manager) responsible to the council for the running of the city's government. 592

Criminal law That body of law which defines crimes (public wrongs, offenses against public order) and provides for their punishment. 557, 566

De facto segregation Racial or other segregation (*e.g.*, in schools or housing) that exists "in fact," because of private rather than governmental actions; see *de jure segregation*. 152

Defendant In a civil suit, the person (party) against whom a court action is brought by the plaintiff; in a criminal case, the person charged with (accused of) the crime. 483, 557

De jure segregation Racial or other segregation that exists "by law," as a result of some governmental action (*e.g.*, a statute or an administrative decision); see *segregation*. 152

Delegated powers Those powers (expressed, implied, inherent) granted to the National Government by the Constitution. 66

Democracy System of government in which supreme authority rests with the people (popular sovereignty, the people rule); may be *direct*, where the people make public policies by their votes, or *representative*, where the people choose public officeholders to act in their behalf. 10

Detente Relaxation, lessening to tense relations between nations. 467

Deterrence Basic feature of American foreign policy, to maintain such massive military strength that that very fact will tend to prevent (deter) any attack upon this country or its allies. 463

Dictatorship Form of government in which the power to govern is held by one person or a small group; see *totalitarian*. 9

Direct primary See *primary election*. 221

Dissenting opinion Written explanation of the views of one or more judges who disagree with (dissent from) a decision reached by a majority of the court; see *majority opinion*. 492

Division of powers Basic principle of federalism; the constitutional provisions by which governmental powers are divided between units of government on a geographic basis (in the United States, between the National Government and the States); see *federalism*. 66

Double jeopardy Trial a second time for a crime of which the accused was acquitted in the first trial; prohibited by the 5th and 14th Amendments. 138

Due Process of Law Constitutional guarantee (in the 5th and 14th Amendments) that government will not deprive a person of life, liberty, or property unfairly, arbitrarily, unreasonably; see *procedural* and *substantive due process*. 122

Economic system Arrangements within a society that determine how goods and services will be/are produced and distributed. 15

Elections Procedures by which voters choose public officeholders. 216

Electoral college Group of persons (presidential electors) chosen in each state and the District of Columbia every four years who formally select the President and Vice President. 367

Electorate All of the persons entitled to vote in a given election. 191

Eminent domain Power of a government to take private property for a public use. 331

Equity That body of law developed to supplement the common law, to provide justice in cases where the common law falls short of that goal; see *injunction*. 567

Espionage Spying for a foreign power. 113

Excise tax Tax levied on the production, transportation, sale, or consumption of goods or services; see *sales tax*. 439

Exclusive powers Most of the delegated powers; those held by the National Government alone (exclusively) in the federal system. 70

Executive agreement Pact made by the President with the head of a foreign state; a binding international agreement with the force of law but which (unlike a treaty) does not require Senate approval. 396

Executive orders Rules, regulations issued by a chief executive (*e.g.*, the President or a governor) or his/her subordinates, based upon either constitutional or statutory authority and having the force of law. 391, 566

Expatriation Act by which one renounces (forfeits, gives up) his/her citizenship. 329

Ex post facto law Criminal law applied retroactively (before the fact) to the disadvantage of the accused; prohibited by the Constitution. 138

Expressed powers Those delegated powers of the National Government which are given to it in so many words (expressly, literally) by the Constitution. 66, 319

Extradition Legal process by which a fugitive from justice in one State is returned (extradited) to it from another State. 79

Federalism Form of government based on a constitutional division of powers on a geographic basis (*e.g.*, in the United States between the National Government and the States). 54, 65

The Federalist Papers   Collection of 85 essays written by James Madison, John Jay, and Alexander Hamilton in 1787-1788, in support of ratification of the Constitution.   46

Federalists   Those persons who supported the adoption of the Constitution in 1787-1788; most of them became members of the Federalist Party after the Constitution became effective in 1789.   45, 173

Felonies   Serious criminal offenses (*e.g.,* murder, robbery) punishable by correspondingly severe penalties; see *misdemeanors.*   577

Filibuster   Various tactics (usually prolonged floor debate) aimed at defeating a bill in a legislative body by preventing a final vote on it; this practice of "talking a bill to death" is most often associated with the U.S. Senate; see *cloture.*   312

Fiscal year   Twelve-month period used by a government for its record-keeping, budgeting, revenue-collecting, and other financial management purposes; the National Government's fiscal year now runs from October 1 through the following September 30.   383, 438

Franchise   Suffrage, the right to vote.   190

Full faith and credit   Constitution's requirement (Article IV, Section 1) that each State accept (honor the validity of, give full faith and credit to) the public acts, records, and judicial proceedings of every other State.   78

General election   Regularly scheduled election at which the voters choose (make the final selection of) public officeholders.   216, 226

Gerrymandering   Drawing the boundaries of election districts in a particular way in order to favor one party or some other group in the electorate.   199, 280

Government   That complex of offices, personnel, and processes by which a state is ruled, by which its public policies are made and enforced.   4, 6

Grand jury   Body of 12 to 23 persons convened by a court to decide whether or not there is enough evidence against a particular person to justify bringing that person to trial for a particular crime; see *indictment, petit jury.*   139, 564

Grants-in-aid   Financial aid given (granted) by one government to another (*e.g.,* by the National Government to the States and/or their local governments), with the funds available subject to certain conditions ("strings") and to be used for certain purposes; see *block grants, categorical grants.*   74, 607

Habeas corpus, writ of   Court order that a prisoner be brought before the court and that the detaining officer (*e.g.,* sheriff, warden) show cause (explain, with good reason) why the prisoner should not be released; designed to prevent illegal arrests and unlawful imprisonments.   137

Hearing   Session of a legislative committee at which witnesses give testimony on bills or other matters before the committee; also, a session of a court, *e.g.,* to determine if one accused of crime should be held for trial.   306, 558

Home rule   Powers of local self-government granted, in varying degree, by a State's constitution or statutes to cities and/or counties.   578, 588

Ideology   Set of political, economic, and social attitudes and beliefs, especially concerned with the form and proper role of government (*e.g.,* democracy, communism).   6, 170

Impeachment   Formal charge (accusation of misconduct) brought against a public official by the lower house in a legislative body; trial (and removal upon conviction occurs in the upper house.   337, 541

Implied powers   Those delegated powers of the National Government implied by (inferred from) the expressed powers; those "necessary and proper" to carry out the expressed powers; see *delegated powers, expressed powers.*   66, 334

Independent regulatory commission   Agency semi-independent of the executive branch, with administrative and also quasi-legislative and quasi-judicial functions, designed to regulate some important aspect of the economy (*e.g.,* the Federal Trade Commission, the National Labor Relations Board).   426

Independents   Voters who do not identify with or regularly support the candidates of any particular party.   212

Indictment   Accusation by a grand jury; a formal finding by that body that there is sufficient evidence against a named person to warrant his/her criminal trial.   140, 564

Information   Formal charge of crime brought against a named person by the prosecutor (directly, rather than by a grand jury); see *indictment.*   140, 565

Inherent powers   Those delegated powers of the National Government which, although not expressly granted by the Constitution, belong to it because it is the national government of a sovereign state.   67, 318

Initiative   Petition process by which a certain percentage of voters can put a proposed constitutional amendment or statute on the ballot for popular approval or rejection; available in nearly half of the States, in either the direct or indirect form.   511, 533

Injunction   Court order which requires or forbids some specific action; may be either temporary or permanent.   200, 568

Interest group   See *pressure group.*   257

Interstate compacts   Formal agreement between or among States, authorized by the Constitution (Article I, Section 10) subject to approval by Congress.   78

Isolationism   Basic part of American foreign policy until World War II; a policy of refusing to become generally involved in world affairs, of avoiding "entangling alliances."   445, 457

Item veto Power held by 43 State governors (but not the President) to eliminate (veto) one or more provisions (items) in a bill without rejecting the entire measure; see *veto*. 400, 546

Joint committee Legislative committee composed of members of both houses. 302, 529

Joint resolution Legislative measure which must be passed by both houses and approved by the chief executive to become effective; similar to a bill, with the force of law, and often used for unusual or temporary purposes. 304

Judicial review Power of the courts to determine the constitutionality of the actions of the legislative and executive branches of government; a basic feature of the American system of government. 53, 486

Judiciary Judicial branch of a government, its system of courts. 480, 556

Jurisdiction Power of a court to hear (to try and decide) a case; literally, its power "to say the law." 482, 557

Jury See *grand jury, petit jury*. 142, 564

Jus sanguinus Acquisition of American citizenship at birth, because of the citizenship of one or both parents; the "law of the blood," to whom born. 328

Jus soli Acquisition of American citizenship at birth, because of birth in the United States; the "law of the soil," where born. 328

Kitchen Cabinet Informal group of advisors, with sometimes greater influence on the President than that of members of the official Cabinet or the White House staff; the term dates from Andrew Jackson's administration (1829-1837). 387

Laissez-fiare Economic doctrine advocating little or no government intervention in the economy; based on Adam Smith's view that if everyone pursues his/her own self-interest all will benefit; literally (French) "to let alone"; see *capitalism*. 16

Libel Publication of statements that wrongfully damage another's reputation; see *slander*. 105

Limited government Basic principle of the American system of government; that government is not all-powerful, that it may do only those things the people have given it the power to do; see *constitutionalism, popular sovereignty*. 51

Literacy test Test of a potential voter's ability to read and write; once used in several States to prevent voting by blacks (and/or other minorities) but now outlawed. 196, 201

Lobbying Activities of an agent (lobbyist) for a pressure group, usually to influence the passage or defeat of legislation or the shape of administrative actions. 266

Major party One of the dominant parties in a governmental system (*e.g.*, the Republicans or Democrats in American politics); see minor party. 165

Majority At least one more than half (*e.g.*, over 50 percent of the votes in an election). 12, 169

Majority floor leader Leader of the majority party in a legislative body. 297

Majority opinion Written statement by a majority of the judges of a court in support of a decision made by that court. 492

Majority rule Basic tenet of democracy, that public policies must be made and public officials must act in accord with the popular will. 12

***Mandamus*, writ of** Court order commanding a public officer to do something required by law. 486

Mandate Support for and/or commands relating to policy stands that a constituency gives to its elected officials. 349

Mass media Those means of communication which reach (inform, influence the opinions of) large audiences, especially television, radio, and newspapers. 247, 250

Merit system Hiring and promotion of government employees on the basis of qualifications and performance (demonstrated merit) rather than political or other considerations; see *civil service*. 434

Minor party One of the less widely supported political parties in a governmental system (*e.g.*, the Libertarians and Socialists in American politics); see *major party*. 179

Minority Less than half of some total (*e.g.*, the number of votes received by a candidate who loses a popular election); see *plurality*. 169

Minority floor leader Leader of the minority party in a legislative body. 297

Minority group Segment of the population with some characteristic with distinguishes its members from the majority of people (*e.g.*, blacks or the handicapped). 122, 149

Minority opinion See *dissenting opinion*. 492

Misdemeanors Crimes less serious than felonies (*e.g.*, a traffic violation), punishable by a small fine and/or short jail term. 557

Mixed economy Economic system in which both private enterprise and government regulation play important roles. 17

Multi-party system Political system in which three or more major parties compete for public offices; see *one-party, two-party system*. 170

Naturalization Legal process by which a person born a citizen of one country becomes a citizen of another. 328

New Jersey Plan Proposed alternative to the Virginia Plan at the Constitutional Convention in 1787, reflecting the views of the smaller States and urging only some modifications in the Articles of Confederation (instead of a new constitution). 41

Nomination Process of selecting (naming) candidates for office. 182, 217

Nonpartisan election Election held to fill nonpartisan offices (most often, judicial, city, and school district offices), in which candidates do not represent or run as the nominees of political parties. 222

Obscenity   Written work or other expression that depicts sexual conduct in an offensive, unlawful way and lacks any serious literary, artistic, political, or scientific value. 105

Off-year elections   Congressional and other general elections held in the years between presidential elections; mid-term elections. 226, 287

One-party system   Political system in which only one party exists, or in which only one party has a reasonable chance of winning elections. 171

Open primary   Form of the direct primary in which any qualified voter may participate, without regard to his/her party allegiance; see *primary election.* 221

Ordinances   Laws made by local governing bodies (*e.g.*, a city council). 577, 586

Original jurisdiction   Power of a court to hear (to try and to decide) a case in the first instance, not on appeal from another court. 483

Pardon   Grant of a release from the punishment or legal consequences of a crime, by the President (in a federal case) or a governor (in a State case). 400, 547

Parliamentary government   Form of government in which the executive leadership (usually, a prime minister and cabinet) is chosen by and responsible to the legislature (Parliament), as in Great Britain. 8

Parole   Release of a prisoner short of the completion of the term of a sentence. 547

Party identification   Person's sense of attachment, loyalty to a political party. 212

Patronage   Use of government jobs, contracts, and other favors to reward political supporters; see *spoils system.* 433

Petit jury   Body of (usually) 12 persons who hear the evidence and decide questions of fact in a court case; the trial jury; see *grand jury.* 142, 565

Pigeonholing   Burying (killing) a bill in a legislative committee. 305

Plaintiff   In civil law, the party who brings a suit or some other legal action against another (the defendant) in court. 483, 557

Platform   Written declaration of the principles and policy positions of a political party (and its candidates for office), usually drafted at that party's convention. 364

Plurality   In an election, at least one more vote than that received by an other candidate; a plurality may or may not be a majority of the total vote; see *majority, minority.* 169

Pocket veto   Type of veto a chief executive may use after a legislature has adjourned; it is applied when the President (or the governor in 15 States) does not formally sign or reject a bill within the time period allowed to do so; see *veto.* 400, 546

Police power   Power of a State (and its local governments) to act to protect and promote the public health, safety, morals, and welfare. 125, 527

Political action committee (PAC)   Political arm of a pressure group, organized to raise and spend campaign funds and otherwise influence elections and public policy decisions. 235, 266

Political efficacy   Belief a person has that his/her participation in politics (*e.g.*, voting) can affect the workings of government. 205

Political party   Organized group that seeks to control government through the winning of elections and the holding of public office. 165

Political socialization   Complex process by which individuals acquire their political attitudes and opinions. 207, 245

Polling place   Particular location where those voters who live in a particular area vote in an election. 227

Poll tax   Tax (now unconstitutional) which had to be paid in some States before a person was allowed to vote. 59, 198

Popular sovereignty   Basic principle of the American system of government; that the people are the only source of any and all governmental power, that government must be conducted with the consent of the governed; see *constitutionalism, limited government.* 2, 50

Precedent   Previous court decisions which influence (usually are the basis for) the deciding of later and similar cases; see *stare decisis.* 492, 567

Presentment   Formal accusation of crime brought by a grand jury of its own motion (not, as in an indictment, on the motion of the prosecutor). 140, 546

Presidential government   Form of government characterized by a separation of powers between independent and coequal executive and legislative branches, as in the United States. 8

Presidential primary   Election at which a party's voters (1) choose some or all of a State party organization's delegates to that party's national convention, and/or (2) express a preference among various contenders for the party's presidential nomination. 225, 354

Pressure group   Private organization which tries to persuade government to respond to the shared attitudes (public policy positions) or its members. 256

Primary election   Election at which party members vote to select (nominate) the party's candidates to run for office in the next general election; often called the direct primary and/or the primaries; also used to select party officers and/or convention delegates; see *closed primary, open primary.* 221

Private bill   Legislative measure which applies only to certain persons or places, rather than to the country (or the State) as a whole; see *public bill.* 304

Procedural due process   Major aspect of the guarantee of due process of law; the constitutional requirement that government must act fairly, use fair procedures; see *substantive due process.* 123

Progressive tax Any tax in which the rate at which it is levied increases as the tax base (the amount subject to the tax) increases; a tax levied at varying (progressively higher) rates, with each step in the rate schedule geared to the taxpayer's ability (resources with which) to pay (*e.g.*, the federal income tax); see *regressive tax*. 438, 604

Propaganda Technique of persuasion, aimed at influencing individual or group views and actions. 264

Public bill Legislative measure which applies to the nation (or the State) as a whole; see *private bill*. 304

Public opinion Those attitudes held (shared) by a significant number of persons on matters of government and politics; expressed group attitudes. 244

Public policy Course(s) of action taken by government in response to the problem(s) it faces; the end product of governmental decision-making. 4, 404

Quasi-legislative, quasi-judicial agency Government body with certain executive (administrative) functions but which also exercises certain legislative-like (rule-making) and judicial-like (decision-making) powers (*e.g.*, the several federal independent regulatory commissions). 428

Quorum Least number of members who must be present for a legislative body to conduct business. 308

Quota sampling In scientific polling, drawing the sample to be interviewed so that the members of each of several groups (*e.g.*, blacks, women) are included in proportion to their percentage in the total population; see *sample*. 254

Random sampling In scientific polling, drawing the sample to be interviewed so that each member of the population has an equal chance to be included in it; see *sample*. 254

Ratification Formal approval, final consent to the effectiveness of a constitution, constitutional amendment, or treaty. 56, 395

Reapportionment New allocation (redistribution) of seats in a legislature; see *apportionment*. 278, 521

Recall Petition process by which voters can remove an elected State or local official from office in mid-term. 541

Referendum Process in which a measure passed by a legislature is submitted (referred) to the voters for final approval or rejection; may be mandatory, optional, or popular in form. 535

Registration Process by which voters establish their eligibility to vote in elections; also known as enrollment. 196

Regressive tax Any tax levied at a flat rate—*i.e.*, falls most heavily on those least able to pay it (*e.g.*, a sales tax); see *progressive tax*. 604

Representative government System of government in which public policies are made by officials who are selected by the voters and held accountable to them in periodic elections; see *democracy*. 10, 216

Republic See *representative government*. 10

Reserved powers Those powers held by the States in the American federal system. 68, 526

Resolution Measure relating to the internal business of one house in a legislature, or expressing that chamber's opinion on some matter, without the force of law; see *concurrent resolution*. 304

Revenue sharing Program in which one level of government gives a fixed portion of its income to another (usually with the funds to be spent as that other government chooses); see *grants-in-aid*. 76, 607

Reverse discrimination A description of affirmative action by critics of that policy, that giving preference to females and/or non-whites is unfair to (discriminates against) members of the majority group; see *affirmative action*. 157

Rider Provision, unlikely to pass on its own merit, added to an important bill certain to pass so that it will "ride" through the legislative process. 304

Rule of law See *constitutionalism*. 51

Sabotage Destructive act intended to hinder a nation's defense effort. 113

Sample In scientific polling, a small number of people chosen as a representative cross-section of the total population (universe) to be interviewed. 253

Scientific polling Measurement of public opinion by carefully selected and controlled sampling, interviewing, and reporting techniques. 253

Sedition Spoken, written, or other action promoting resistance to lawful authority; especially advocating the violent overthrow of a government. 113

Segregation Separation or isolation of a racial or other group from the rest of the population in education, housing, or other areas of public or private activity. 150

Select committee Legislative committee created for a limited time and for some specific purpose; also known as special committee; see *standing committee*. 300

Senatorial courtesy Unwritten rule that the Senate will not approve the appointment of an officer to serve within a State (*e.g.*, a federal district judge) if a Senator of the President's party from that State objects to the appointment. 392

Seniority rule Unwritten rule in both houses of Congress, that the top posts in the formal and the party organization in each chamber will (with rare exception) be held by "ranking members"—*i.e.*, those with the longest records of service; applied most strictly to committee chairmanships. 298

Separation of powers Basic principle of the American system of government, that the executive, legislative, and judicial powers are (must be) divided among three independent and coequal branches of government; see *checks and balances*. 52, 508

Shield law State law designed to protect reporters

against being forced to disclose confidential news sources. 109

Single-member-district Electoral district from which a single officeholder is chosen by the voters (rather than several, as in a multi-member district); see *at large selection.* 279

Slander Speech that wrongfully damages a person's reputation; see *libel.* 105

Socialism Economic and political system based on the public (collective, social) ownership of the means by which goods and services are produced, distributed, and exchanged. 17

Sovereignty Supreme, absolute power of a state within its own territory. 4

Special district Local unit of government, created to perform (usually) a single public function in a locale (*e.g.,* a school or library district). 582

Split-ticket voting Voting for candidates of more than one party in the same election; see *straight-ticket voting.* 212

Spoils system Practice of awarding government jobs, contracts, and other favors on the basis of party loyalty, political support, rather than merit; see *patronage.* 433

Standing committee Regular (permanent) committee in a legislative body to which bills in a specified subject-matter area are referred; see *select committee.* 299, 529

Stare decisis Rule of precedent; a policy generally followed by courts, that the precedents set by earlier decisions should be followed in deciding later and similar cases, literally (Latin) "let the decision stand"; see *precedent.* 567

State In international affairs, a sovereign member of the world community (often called a country or nation); in the United States, one of the 50 members (States) in the Union. 3

Statutory law Law (statutes) enacted by a legislative body; see *act.* 566

Straight-ticket voting Voting for the candidates of but one party in an election; see *split-ticket voting.* 212

Straw vote Unscientific measurement of public opinion; usually, asking the same question of a large number of people (who may, but probably do not, represent an accurate cross-section of the population). 251

Subpoena Order by a court or legislative body commanding one to appear and give testimony or provide evidence; literally (Latin) "under penalty"; see *contempt.* 306

Substantive due process Major aspect of the guarantee of due process of law; the constitutional guarantee that the law under which government acts is fair, reasonable; see *procedural due process.* 123

Suffrage Right to vote. 190

Survey research Method of obtaining information by polling (questioning, interviewing) a scientifically drawn sample of the population; see *scientific polling.* 207, 253

Symbolic speech Expression of beliefs, ideas by conduct rather than in speech or print (*e.g.,* by wearing an armband or flying a flag). 110

Tariff Tax (customs duty) levied on imports, to raise revenue and/or protect the domestic economy. 322, 441

Tax Charge (money demand) made by government on persons or property to raise funds for public purposes and/or to regulate conduct. 322, 601

Third party See *minor party.* 179

Totalitarian Form of government in which the power to rule embraces all (the totality of) matters of human concern; see *authoritarian, dictatorship.* 9

Trial jury See *petit jury.* 142, 565

Treason Crime of disloyalty which, says the Constitution (Article III, Section 3), "shall consist only in levying war against (the United States), or in adhering to their enemies, giving them aid and comfort"; can be committed only by a citizen and only in wartime. 113, 148

Treaty Formal agreement made between or among sovereign states. 71, 395

Two-party system Political system in which the candidates of only two (major) parties have a reasonable chance of winning elections; see *multi-party, one-party system.* 168

Unicameral legislature Lawmaking body with but one house; see *bicameral legislature.* 28, 519

Unitary government Form of government in which all of the powers of the government are held by (centralized in) a single agency, as in Great Britain; local governments are completely subordinate to and have only those powers given to them by the central government; see *federalism.* 6, 573

Veto Chief executive's power to reject a bill passed by a legislature; literally (Latin) "I forbid"; see *item veto, pocket veto.* 399, 546

Virginia Plan Series of proposals to the Constitutional Convention in 1787, favored by the larger States, calling for a stronger National government, and upon which much of the Constitution was then built; see *New Jersey Plan.* 40

Voter turnout Extent to which potential voters actually vote in an election, usually expressed in both absolute numbers and the percentage of eligible voters who cast ballots. 202

Ward Local unit of party organization; also, a district within a city for city council elections. 95, 590

Warrant Court order authorizing a public official to proceed in a manner specified by that order (*e.g.,* a search warrant); also, an order to pay out public funds (as in a check) issued by an officer with the legal authority to do so. 131, 550

Whip Assistant floor leader in a legislative body who serves as the link between the party leadership and the party's membership in the chamber.   297

Writ   Written court order directing the performance of or prohibiting some act.   137, 486

Zoning   Practice of dividing a city or other unit of government into districts (zones) and regulating by law (a zoning ordinance) the uses of land in each of them.   594.

APPENDIX

THE DECLARATION OF INDEPENDENCE

In Congress, July 4, 1776

THE UNANIMOUS DECLARATION OF THE THIRTEEN UNITED STATES OF AMERICA

When in the Course of human events, it becomes necessary for one people to dissolve the political bands which have connected them with another, and to assume among the powers of the earth, the separate and equal station to which the Laws of nature and of Nature's God entitle them, a decent respect to the opinions of mankind requires that they should declare the causes which impel them to the separation.

We hold these truths to be self-evident, that all men are created equal, that they are endowed by their Creator with certain unalienable Rights, that among these are Life, Liberty and the pursuit of Happiness. That to secure these rights, Governments are instituted among Men, deriving their just powers from the consent of the governed; That whenever any Form of Government becomes destructive of these ends it is the Right of the People to alter or to abolish it, and to institute new Government, laying its foundation on such principles and organizing its powers in such form, as to them shall seem most likely to effect their Safety and Happiness. Prudence, indeed, will dictate that Governments long established should not be changed for light and transient causes; and accordingly all experience hath shown, that mankind are more disposed to suffer, while evils are sufferable, than to right themselves by abolishing the forms to which they are accustomed. But when a long train of abuses and usurpations, pursuing invariably the same Objects evinces a design to reduce them under absolute Despotism, it is their right, it is their duty, to throw off such Government, and to provide new Guards for their future security.—Such has been the patient sufferance of these Colonies; and such is now the necessity which constrains them to alter their former Systems of Government. The history of the present King of Great Britain is a history of repeated injuries and usurpations, all having in direct object the establishment of an absolute Tyranny over these States. To prove this, let Facts be submitted to a candid world.

He has refused his Assent to Laws, the most wholesome and necessary for the public good.

He has forbidden his Governors to pass Laws of immediate and pressing importance, unless suspended in their operation till his Assent should be obtained; and when so suspended, he has utterly neglected to attend to them.

He has refused to pass other Laws for the accommodation of large districts of people, unless those people would relinquish the right of Representation in the Legislature, a right inestimable to them and formidable to tyrants only.

He has called together legislative bodies at places unusual, uncomfortable, and distant from the depository of their public records, for the sole purpose of fatiguing them into compliance with his measures.

He has dissolved Representative Houses repeatedly, for opposing with manly firmness his invasions on the rights of the people.

He has refused for a long time, after such dissolutions, to cause others to be elected; whereby the Legislative powers, incapable of Annihilation, have returned to the People at large for their exercise; the State remaining in the mean time exposed to all the dangers of invasions from without, and convulsions within.

He has endeavored to prevent the population of these States; for that purpose obstructing the Laws for Naturalization of Foreigners; refusing to pass others to encourage their migration hither, and raising the conditions of new Appropriations of Lands.

He has obstructed the Administration of Justice, by refusing his Assent to Laws for establishing Judiciary powers.

He has made Judges dependent on his Will alone for the tenure of their offices, and the amount and payment of their salaries.

He has erected a multitude of New Offices, and sent hither swarms of Officers to harass our people and eat out their substance.

He has kept among us in time of peace, Standing Armies, without the Consent of our legislatures.

He has affected to render the Military independent of, and superior to, the Civil power.

He has combined with others to subject us to a jurisdiction foreign to our constitutions, and unacknowledged by our laws; giving his Assent to their Acts of pretended Legislation:

For quartering large bodies of armed troops among us;

For protecting them, by a mock Trial, from punishment for any Murders which they should commit on the Inhabitants of these States;

For cutting off our Trade with all parts of the world;

For imposing Taxes on us without our Consent;

For depriving us, in many cases, of the benefits of Trial by Jury;

For transporting us beyond Seas, to be tried for pretended offenses;

For abolishing the free System of English Laws in a neighboring Province, establishing therein an Arbitrary government, and enlarging its Boundaries, so as to render it at once an example and fit instrument for introducing the same absolute rule into these Colonies;

For taking away our Charters, abolishing our most valuable Laws, and altering, fundamentally, the Forms of our Governments;

For suspending our own Legislatures, and declaring themselves invested with Power to legislate for us in all cases whatsoever.

He has abdicated Government here, by declaring us out of his Protection, and waging War against us.

He has plundered our seas, ravaged our Coasts, burned our towns, and destroyed the lives of our people.

He is at this time transporting large Armies of foreign Mercenaries to complete the works of death, desolation and tyranny, already begun with circumstances of Cruelty and perfidy scarely paralleled in the most barbarous ages, and totally unworthy the Head of a civilized nation.

He has constrained our fellow Citizens taken Captive on the high Seas to bear Arms against their Country, to become the executioners of their friends and Brethren, or to fall themselves by their Hands.

He has excited domestic insurrections amongst us, and has endeavored to bring on the inhabitants of our frontiers the merciless Indian Savages whose known rule of warfare is an undistinguished destruction of all ages, sexes, and conditions.

In every stage of these Oppressions We have Petitioned for Redress in the most humble terms. Our repeated Petitions have been answered only by repeated injury. A Prince whose character is thus marked by every act which may define a Tyrant, is unfit to be the ruler of a free people.

Nor have We been wanting in attentions to our British brethren. We have warned them from time to time of attempts by their legislature to extend an unwarrantable jurisdiction over us. We have reminded them of the circumstances of our emigration and settlement here. We have appealed to their native justice and magnanimity, and we have conjured them by the ties of our common kindred to disavow these usurpations, which, would inevitably interrupt our connections and correspondence. They too have been deaf to the voice of justice and of consanguinity. We must, therefore, acquiesce in the necessity, which denounces our Separation, and hold them, as we hold the rest of mankind, Enemies in War, in Peace Friends.—

We, therefore, the Representatives of the United States of America, in General Congress, Assembled, appealing to the Supreme Judge of the world for the rectitude of our intentions, do, in the Name, and by the Authority of the good People of these Colonies, solemnly publish and declare, That these United Colonies are, and of right ought to be Free and Independent States; that they are Absolved from all Allegiance to the British Crown, and that all political connection between them and the State of Great Britain, is and ought to be totally dissolved, and that as Free and Independent States, they have full Power to levy War, conclude Peace, contract Alliances, establish Commerce, and to do all other Acts and Things which Independent States may of right do. And for the support of this Declaration, with a firm reliance on the protection of Divine Providence, we mutually pledge to each other our Lives, our Fortunes and our sacred Honor.

JOHN HANCOCK

NEW HAMPSHIRE
Josiah Bartlett
William Whipple
Matthew Thornton

MASSACHUSETTS BAY
Samuel Adams
John Adams
Robert Treat Paine
Elbridge Gerry

RHODE ISLAND
Stephen Hopkins
William Ellery

CONNECTICUT
Roger Sherman
Samuel Huntington
William Williams
Oliver Wolcott

NEW YORK
William Floyd
Philip Livingston
Francis Lewis
Lewis Morris

NEW JERSEY
Richard Stockton
John Witherspoon
Francis Hopkinson
John Hart
Abraham Clark

PENNSYLVANIA
Robert Morris
Benjamin Rush
Benjamin Franklin
John Morton
George Clymer
James Smith

George Taylor
James Wilson
George Ross

DELAWARE
Caesar Rodney
George Read
Thomas M'Kean

MARYLAND
Samuel Chase
William Paca
Thomas Stone
Charles Carroll of Carrollton

VIRGINIA
George Wythe
Richard Henry Lee
Thomas Jefferson

Benjamin Harrison
Thomas Nelson, Jr.
Francis Lightfoot Lee
Carter Braxton

NORTH CAROLINA
William Hooper
Joseph Hewes
John Penn

SOUTH CAROLINA
Edward Rutledge
Thomas Heyward, Jr.
Thomas Lynch, Jr.
Arthur Middleton

GEORGIA
Button Gwinnett
Lyman Hall
George Walton

AN OUTLINE OF THE CONSTITUTION OF THE UNITED STATES

The American Constitution is the most wonderful work ever struck off at a given time by the brain and purpose of man.
William E. Gladstone

THE CONSTITUTION OF THE UNITED STATES OF AMERICA

PREAMBLE

We the People of the United States, in Order to form a more perfect Union, establish Justice, insure domestic Tranquility, provide for the common defence, promote the general Welfare, and secure the Blessings of Liberty to ourselves and our Posterity, do ordain and establish this Constitution for the United States of America.

Article I
LEGISLATIVE DEPARTMENT

SECTION 1. *Legislative Power; the Congress*

All legislative powers herein granted shall be vested in a Congress of the United States, which shall consist of a Senate and House of Representatives.

SECTION 2. *House of Representatives*

1. The House of Representatives shall be composed of members chosen every second year by the people of the several States, and the electors in each State shall have the qualifications requisite for electors of the most numerous branch of the State legislature.[1]

2. No person shall be a Representative who shall not have attained to the age of twenty-five years, and been seven years a citizen of the United States, and who shall not, when elected, be an inhabitant of that State in which he shall be chosen.[2]

3. Representatives and direct taxes[3] shall be apportioned among the several States which may be included within this Union, according to their respective numbers, [which shall be determined by adding to the whole number of free persons, including those bound to service for a term of years][4] and excluding Indians not taxed, [three-fifths of all other persons].[5] The actual enumeration shall be made within three years after the first meeting of the Congress of the United States, and within every subsequent term of ten years, in such manner as they shall by law direct. The number of Representatives shall not exceed one for every thirty thousand,[6] but each State shall have at least one Representative; [and, until such enumeration shall be made, the State of New Hampshire shall be entitled to choose three, Massachusetts eight, Rhode Island and Providence Plantations one, Connecticut five, New York six, New Jersey four, Pennsylvania eight, Delaware one, Maryland six, Virginia ten, North Carolina five, South Carolina five, and Georgia three].[7]

4. When vacancies happen in the representation from any State, the executive authority thereof shall issue writs of election to fill such vacancies.

5. The House of Representatives shall choose their Speaker[8] and other officers; and shall have the sole power of impeachment.[9]

SECTION 3. *Senate*

1. The Senate of the United States shall be composed of two Senators from each State [chosen by the legislature thereof][10] for six years; and each Senator shall have one vote.

2. Immediately after they shall be assembled in consequences of the first election, they shall be divided, as equally as may be, into three classes. The seats of the Senators of the first class shall be vacated at the expiration of the second year; of the second class, at the expiration of the fourth year; and of the third class, at the expiration of

---

[1]"Electors" means voters. Each State must permit the same persons to vote for United States Representatives as it permits to vote for the members of the larger house of its own legislature. The 17th Amendment (1913) extended this requirement to the qualification of voters for United States Senators.

[2]In addition, political custom requires that a Representative also reside in the district in which he or she is elected. The first woman to serve in the House, Jeannette Rankin (1881-1973), was elected from Montana in 1916; she did not seek re-election in 1918 but did run for and win a second term in 1940.

[3]Modified by the 16th Amendment (1913) which provides for an income tax as an express exception to this restriction.

[4]Altered by the 14th Amendment (1868).

[5]The phrase refers to slaves and was rescinded by the 13th Amendment (1865) and the 14th Amendment (1868).

[6]The Constitution does not set a specific size for the House; rather, Congress does so when it reapportions the seats among the States after each census. It fixed the "permanent" size at 435 members in the Reapportionment Act of 1929; see pages 278–279. Today (1984) there is one House seat for approximately every 540,000 persons in the population.

[7]Temporary provision.

[8]Although the Constitution does not require it, the House always chooses the Speaker from among its own members.

[9]Impeachment here means *accusation*. The House has the exclusive power to *impeach* (accuse) civil officers; the Senate (Article I, Section 3, Clause 6) has the exclusive power to *try* those impeached by the House.

[10]Modified by the 17th Amendment (1913), which provides for the popular election of Senators.

the sixth year; so that one-third may be chosen every second year; [and if vacancies happen by resignation, or otherwise, during the recess of the legislature of any State, the executive thereof may make temporary appointments until the next meeting of the legislature, which shall then fill such vacancies.][11]

3. No person shall be a Senator who shall not have attained to the age of thirty years, and been nine years a citizen of the United States, who shall not, when elected, be an inhabitant of that State for which he shall be chosen.

4. The Vice President of the United States shall be President of the Senate, but shall have no vote, unless they be equally divided.

5. The Senate shall choose their other officers, and also a President *pro tempore*, in the absence of the Vice President, or when he shall exercise the office of President of the United States.

6. The Senate shall have the sole power to try all impeachments. When sitting for that purpose, they shall be on oath or affirmation. When the President of the United States is tried, the Chief Justice shall preside; and no person shall be convicted without the concurrence of two-thirds of the members present.[12]

7. Judgment in cases of impeachment shall not extend further than to removal from office, and disqualification to hold and enjoy any office of honor, trust, or profit under the United States; but the party convicted shall, nevertheless, be liable and subject to indictment, trial, judgment, and punishment, according to law.

SECTION 4. *Elections and Meetings*

1. The times, places, and manner of holding elections for Senators and Representatives, shall be prescribed in each State by the legislature thereof: but the Congress may at any time, by law, make or alter such regulations, except as to the places of choosing Senators.[13]

2. The Congress shall assemble at least once in every year, [and such meeting shall be on the first Monday in December,][14] unless they shall by law appoint a different day.

SECTION 5. *Legislative Proceedings*

1. Each House shall be the judge of the elections, returns, and qualifications of its own members,[15] and a majority of each shall constitute a quorum to do business; but a smaller number may adjourn from day to day, and may be authorized to compel the attendance of absent members, in such manner, and under such penalties, as each House may provide.

2. Each House may determine the rules of its proceedings, punish its members for disorderly behavior, and, with the concurrence of two-thirds, expel a member.

3. Each House shall keep a journal of its proceedings, and, from time to time, publish the same, excepting such parts as may, in their judgment, require secrecy; and the yeas and nays of the members of either House, on any question, shall, at the desire of one-fifth of those present, be entered on the journal.

4. Neither House, during the session of Congress, shall, without the consent of the other, adjourn for more than three days, nor to any other place than that in which the two Houses shall be sitting.

SECTION 6. *Compensation, Immunities, and Disabilities of Members*

1. The Senators and Representatives shall receive a compensation for their services, to be ascertained by law, and paid out of the treasury of the United States. They shall, in all cases, except treason, felony, and breach of the peace,[16] be privileged from arrest during their attendance at the session of their respective Houses, and in going to, and returning from, the same; and for any speech or debate in either House, they shall not be questioned in any other place.[17]

2. No Senator or Representative shall, during the time for which he was elected, be appointed to any civil office under the authority of the United States, which shall have been created, or the emoluments whereof shall have been increased during such time;[18] and no person, holding any office under the United States, shall be a member of either House during his continuance in office.

SECTION 7. *Revenue Bills, President's Veto*

1. All bills for raising revenue shall originate in the House of Representatives; but the Senate may propose or concur with amendments as on other bills.

---

[11]Modified by the 17th Amendment (1913), which provides for the filling of vacancies by election and (if a State chooses) by a temporary gubernatorial appointment to fill the vacancy until the election.

[12]Those who object on religious grounds to the taking of an oath (for example, Quakers) are permitted to "affirm" rather than "swear."

The required "two-thirds of the members present" must be at least a quorum (Article I, Section 5, Clause 1). A quorum (the number of members who must be present in order to conduct business) is 51 in the Senate and 218 in the House.

[13]In 1842 Congress required that Representatives be elected from districts within each State with more than one seat in the House. The districts within each State must contain substantially equal numbers of persons—the "one-man, one-vote" rule; see page 281. The districts are drawn by the State legislators. Six States now (1984) have only one seat: Alaska, Delaware, North Dakota, South Dakota, Vermont, and Wyoming. In 1842, Congress directed that Representatives and, in 1914, that Senators be chosen on the Tuesday after the first Monday in November of every even-numbered year.

[14]Superseded by the 20th Amendment (1933), which fixes the date January 3rd.

[15]In 1969 the Supreme Court held that the House cannot exclude any member-elect who satisfies the qualifications set out in Article I, Section 2, Clause 2; see page 282.

[16]*Treason* is strictly defined in Article III, Section 3. A *felony* is any serious crime. A *breach of the peace* is any indictable offense less than treason or a felony; hence this exemption from arrest is of little real importance today.

[17]This "cloak of legislative immunity" extends to committee rooms and official publications of Congress, such as the *Congressional Record* and committee reports—but it does not extend to outside speech or publication.

[18]In 1909 President Taft appointed Philander C. Knox as Secretary of State. His eligibility for the post was challenged because Congress had raised Cabinet officers' salaries while Knox was in the Senate. Congress resolved the problem by reducing the pay of the Secretary of State to its former figure. This same procedure has been followed twice since: in 1973, when President Nixon appointed Senator William B. Saxbe Attorney General; and in 1980, when President Carter appointed Senator Edmund Muskie Secretary of State.

2. Every bill which shall have passed the House of Representatives and the Senate, shall, before it become a law, be presented to the President of the United States; if he approve, he shall sign it, but if not, he shall return it, with his objections, to that House in which it shall have originated, who shall enter the objections at large on their journal, and proceed to reconsider it.[19] If, after such reconsideration, two-thirds of the House shall agree to pass the bill, it shall be sent, together with the objections, to the other House, by which it shall likewise be reconsidered, and, if approved by two-thirds of that House, it shall become a law. But in all such cases the votes of both Houses shall be determined by yeas and nays, and the names of the persons voting for and against the bill shall be entered on the journal of each House respectively. If any bill shall not be returned by the President within ten days (Sunday excepted) after it shall have been presented to him, the same shall be a law, in like manner as if he had signed it, unless the Congress, by their adjournment, prevent its return, in which case it shall not be a law.

3. Every order, resolution,[20] or vote, to which the concurrence of the Senate and House of Representatives may be necessary (except on a question of adjournment), shall be presented to the President of the United States; and before the same shall take effect, shall be approved by him, or, being disapproved by him, shall be repassed by two-thirds of the Senate and House of Representatives, according to the rules and limitations prescribed in the case of a bill.

SECTION 8.   *Powers of Congress*

The Congress shall have power:

1. To lay and collect taxes, duties, imposts, and excises, to pay the debts, and provide for the common defence and general welfare of the United States; but all duties, imposts, and excises, shall be uniform throughout the United States;

2. To borrow money on the credit of the United States;

3. To regulate commerce with foreign nations, and among the several States, and with the Indian tribes;

4. To establish a uniform rule of naturalization, and uniform laws on the subject of bankruptcies, throughout the United States;

5. To coin money, regulate the value thereof, and of foreign coin, and fix the standard of weights and measures;

6. To provide for the punishment of counterfeiting the securities and current coin of the United States;

7. To establish post offices and post roads;[21]

8. To promote the progress of science and useful arts, by securing, for limited times, to authors and inventors, the exclusive right to their respective writings and discoveries;

9. To constitute tribunals inferior to the Supreme Court;

10. To define and punish piracies and felonies, committed on the high seas, and offences against the law of nations;

11. To declare war, grant letters of marque and reprisal,[22] and make rules concerning captures on land and water;

12. To raise and support armies; but no appropriation of money to that use shall be for a longer term than two years;

13. To provide and maintain a navy;

14. To make rules for the government and regulation of the land and naval forces;

15. To provide for calling forth the militia to execute the laws of the Union, suppress insurrections, and repel invasions;

16. To provide for organizing, arming, and disciplining the militia, and for governing such part of them as may be employed in the service of the United States, reserving to the States respectively the appointment of the officers, and the authority of training the militia, according to the discipline prescribed by Congress;

17. To exercise exclusive legislation in all cases whatsoever, over such district (not exceeding ten miles square) as may, by cession of particular States, and the acceptance of Congress, become the seat of the Government of the United States, and to exercise like authority over all places, purchased by the consent of the legislature of the State in which the same shall be, for the erection of forts, magazines, arsenals, dockyards, and other needful buildings;— And

18. To make all laws which shall be necessary and proper for carrying into execution the foregoing powers, and all other powers vested by this Constitution in the Government of the United States, or in any department or officer thereof.[23]

SECTION 9.   *Powers Denied to Congress*

[1. The migration or importation of such persons as any of the States now existing shall think proper to admit, shall not be prohibited by the Congress prior to the year one thousand eight hundred and eight; but a tax or duty may be

---

[19]The President must accept or reject a bill in its entirety; the President does not possess an *item veto*; see pages 399, 546.

[20]*Concurrent resolutions* (which usually relate to the internal management of Congress—for example, creating a joint committee) do not have the force of law and so are not submitted to the President; nor are joint resolutions which propose amendments to the Constitution.

[21]"Post" comes from the French *poste* meaning mail; "post roads" are those routes such as turnpikes, canals, rivers, streets, paths, and airways over which the mail is carried.

This power, "to establish post offices," which was granted to Congress, continued the precedent that had been established under the Articles of Confederation.

[22]*Marque* is the French for "boundary"; the word "reprisal" comes from the French *représaille*, meaning retaliation. Hence, originally "letters of marque and reprisal" were licenses to cross the boundary into an enemy country to capture or destroy. As used here it means a commission authorizing private citizens to fit out vessels (privateers) to capture or destroy in time of war. They are forbidden in international law by the Declaration of Paris, 1856, to the principles of which the United States subscribes.

[23]This is the Necessary and Proper Clause—or, as it is also known, the Elastic Clause. *Necessary* here does not mean absolutely or indispensably necessary, but rather *appropriate*. The Clause has made it possible for Congress and the courts to extend the meanings of other provisions in the Constition. The constitutional basis for the existence of the *implied powers*, those which are not specifically stated in the Constitution but which may be reasonably implied from the expressed powers, is found in this Clause.

imposed on such importation, not exceeding ten dollars for each person.][24]

2. The privilege of the writ of *habeas corpus*[25] shall not be suspended, unless when, in cases of rebellion or invasion, the public safety may require it.

3. No bill of attainder or *ex post facto* law shall be passed.[26]

4. No capitation, or other direct tax, shall be laid, unless in proportion to the census or enumeration hereinbefore directed to be taken.[27]

5. No tax or duty shall be laid on articles exported from any State.

6. No preference shall be given by any regulation of commerce or revenue to the ports of one State over those of another; nor shall vessels bound to, or from, one State, be obliged to enter, clear, or pay duties, in another.

7. No money shall be drawn from the treasury, but in consequence of appropriations made by law; and a regular statement and account of the receipts and expenditures of all public money shall be published from time to time.

8. No title of nobility shall be granted by the United States; and no person holding any office of profit or trust under them shall, without the consent of the Congress, accept of any present, emolument, office, or title, of any kind whatever, from any king, prince, or foreign state.

SECTION 10 *Powers Denied to the States*

1. No State shall enter into any treaty, alliance, or confederation; grant letters of marque and reprisal; coin money; emit bills of credit;[28] make anything but gold and silver coin a tender in payment of debts; pass any bill of attainder, *ex post facto* law, or law impairing the obligations of contracts, or grant any title of nobility.

2. No State shall, without the consent of the Congress, lay any imposts or duties on imports or exports, except what may be absolutely necessary for executing its inspection laws; and the net produce of all duties and imposts, laid by any State on imports or exports, shall be for the use of the treasury of the United States; and all such laws shall be subject to the revision and control of the Congress.

3. No State shall, without the consent of Congress, lay any duty of tonnage,[29] keep troops, or ships of war, in time of peace, enter into any agreement or compact with another State, or with a foreign power, or engage in war, unless actually invaded, or in such imminent danger as will not admit of delay.

Article II
EXECUTIVE DEPARTMENT

SECTION 1. *Term, Election, Qualifications, Salary, Oath of Office*

1. The executive power shall be vested in a President of the United States of America.[30] He shall hold his office during the term of four years, and together with the Vice President, chosen for the same term, be elected as follows:

2. Each State shall appoint, in such manner as the legislature thereof may direct, a number of Electors, equal to the whole number of Senators and Representatives, to which the State may be entitled in the Congress; but no Senator or Representative, or person holding an office of trust or profit, under the United States, shall be appointed an Elector.

[3. The Electors shall meet in their respective States, and vote by ballot for two persons, of whom one, at least, shall not be an inhabitant of the same State with themselves. And they shall make a list of all the persons voted for, and of the number of votes for each; which list they shall sign and certify, and transmit, sealed, to the seat of the Government of the United States, directed to the President of the Senate. The President of the Senate shall, in the presence of the Senate and House of Representatives, open all the certificates, and the votes shall then be counted. The person having the greatest number of votes shall be the President, if such number be a majority of the whole number of Electors appointed; and if there be more than one, who have such majority, and have an equal number of votes, then, the House of Representatives shall immediately choose, by ballot, one of them for President; and if no person have a majority, then, from the five highest on the list, the said House shall, in like manner, choose the President. But in choosing the President, the votes shall be taken by States, the representation from each State having one vote; a quorum for this purpose shall consist of a member or members from two-thirds of the States, and a majority of all the States shall be necessary to a choice. In every case, after the choice of the President, the person having the greatest number of votes of the Electors shall be the Vice President. But if there should remain two or more who have equal votes, the Senate shall choose from them, by ballot, the Vice President.][31]

4. The Congress may determine the time of choosing the Electors, and the day on which they shall give their votes; which day shall be the same throughout the United States.[32]

---

[24]Temporary provision; the phrase "such persons" was a euphemism (an agreeable substitute) for "slaves."

[25]A *writ of habeas corpus*, the "great writ of liberty," is a court order directing a sheriff, warden, or other public officer, or a private person, who is detaining another person to "produce the body" of the one being held in order that the legality of the detention may be determined by the court; see page 137.

[26]A *bill of attainder* is a legislative act which inflicts punishment without a judicial trial. See Article I, Section 10, and Article III, Section 3, Clause 2. An *ex post facto* law is any criminal law which operates retroactively to the disadvantage of the accused. See Article I, Section 10. See also page 138.

[27]See note 3, page 630, and the 16th Amendment (1913) which permits the levying of an income tax without regard to this prohibition.

[28]The phrase "bills of credit" means paper money; "tender" means *legal tender*—any kind of money that must by law be accepted in payment of a monetary debt.

[29]*Tonnage* is a vessel's internal cubical capacity in tons of one hundred cubic feet each. Tonnage duties are duties upon vessels in proportion to their capacity. These duties are paid as a ship enters a port.

---

[30]The Constitution did not originally set a limit to the number of times a person may be elected President. The 22nd Amendment (1951) now limits a President to two terms or not more than 10 years in office.

[31]Superseded by the 12th Amendment (1804).

[32]Congress has set the date for the choosing of electors as the Tuesday after the first Monday in November every fourth year and for the casting of electoral votes as the Monday after the second Wednesday in December of that year.

5. No person, except a natural-born citizen, or a citizen of the United States at the time of the adoption of this Constitution, shall be eligible to the office of President; neither shall any person be eligible to that office, who shall not have attained to the age of thirty-five years, and been fourteen years a resident within the United States.

6. In case of the removal of the President from office, or of his death, resignation, or inability to discharge the powers and duties of the said office, the same shall devolve on the Vice President, and the Congress may by law provide for the case of removal, death, resignation or inability, both of the President and Vice President, declaring what officer shall then act as President, and such officer shall act accordingly, until the disability be removed, or a President shall be elected.[33]

7. The President shall, at stated times, receive for his services a compensation, which shall neither be increased nor diminished during the period for which he shall have been elected, and he shall not receive, within that period, any other emolument from the United States, or any of them.

8. Before he enter on the execution of his office, he shall take the following oath or affirmation:

"I do solemnly swear (or affirm), that I will faithfully execute the office of President of the United States, and will, to the best of my ability, preserve, protect, and defend the Constitution of the United States."

SECTION 2. *President's Powers and Duties*

1. The President shall be Commander in Chief of the army and navy of the United States, and of the militia of the several States, when called into the actual service of the United States; he may require the opinion, in writing, of the principal officer in each of the executive departments upon any subject relating to the duties of their respective offices,[34] and he shall have power to grant reprieves and pardons[35] for offences against the United States, except in cases of impeachment.

2. He shall have power, by and with the advice and consent of the Senate, to make treaties, provided two-thirds of the Senators present concur; and he shall, nominate, and, by and with the advice and consent of the Senate, shall appoint ambassadors, other public ministers, and consuls, judges of the Supreme Court, and all other officers of the United States whose appointments are not herein otherwise provided for, and which shall be established by law; but the Congress may by law vest the appointment of such inferior officers, as they think proper, in the President alone, in the courts of law, or in the heads of departments.

3. The President shall have power to fill up all vacancies that may happen during the recess of the Senate, by granting commissions which shall expire at the end of their next session.

SECTION 3. *President's Powers and Duties*

He shall, from time to time, give to the Congress information of the state of the Union, and recommend to their consideration such measures as he shall judge necessary and expedient; he may, on extraordinary occasions, convene both Houses, or either of them, and in case of disagreement between them, with respect to the time of adjournment, he may adjourn them to such time as he shall think proper; he shall receive ambassadors and other public ministers; he shall take care that the laws be faithfully executed, and shall commission all the officers of the United States.

SECTION 4. *Impeachment*

The President, Vice President, and all civil officers[36] of the United States, shall be removed from office on impeachment for, and conviction of, treason, bribery, or other high crimes and misdemeanors.

Article III
JUDICIAL DEPARTMENT

SECTION 1. *Courts, Terms of Office*

The judicial power of the United States shall be vested in one Supreme Court, and in such inferior courts as the Congress may from time to time ordain and establish. The judges, both of the Supreme and inferior courts, shall hold their offices during good behavior, and shall, at stated time, receive for their services a compensation which shall not be diminished during their continuance in office.

SECTION 2. *Jurisdiction*

1. The judicial power shall extend to all cases, in law and equity, arising under this Constitution, the laws of the United States, and treaties made, or which shall be made, under their authority; to all cases affecting ambassadors, other public ministers, and consuls; to all cases of admiralty and maritime jurisdiction; to controversies to which the United States shall be a party; to controversies between two or more States, between a State and citizens of another State, between citizens of different States, between citizens of the same State claiming lands under grants of different States, and between a State, or the citizens thereof, and foreign states, citizens, or subjects.[37]

2. In all cases affecting ambassadors, other public ministers and consuls, and those in which a State shall be a party, the Supreme Court shall have original jurisdiction. In all the other cases before mentioned, the Supreme Court shall have appellate jurisdiction, both as to law and fact, with such exceptions and under such regulations as the Congress shall make.

---

[33]Modified by the 25th Amendment (1967), which provides expressly for the succession of the Vice President, for the filling of a vacancy in the Vice Presidency, and for the determination of presidential inability.

[34]The only authority in the Constitution for the President's Cabinet. There is no act of Congress which defines the membership of the Cabinet; rather, the matter is subject to the President's discretion.

[35]A *reprieve* is the postponing of the execution of a sentence; a *pardon* is legal (but not moral) forgiveness for an offense. The President may grant reprieves or pardons only in federal cases.

---

[36]*Civil officers* subject to impeachment include all officers of the United States who hold their appointments from the National Government, high or low, and whose duties are executive or judicial. Officers in the armed services are not civil officers; neither are Senators and Representatives so considered. Instead of the impeachment process, either house of Congress may expel one of its own members by a two-thirds vote (Article I, Section 5, Clause2).

[37]Restricted by the 11th Amendment (1795).

3. The trial of all crimes, except in cases of impeachment, shall be by jury; and such trial shall be held in the State where the said crimes shall have been committed; but when not committed within any State the trial shall be at such place or places as the Congress may by law have directed.[38]

SECTION 3. *Treason*

1. Treason against the United States shall consist only in levying war against them, or in adhering to their enemies, giving them aid and comfort. No person shall be convicted of treason unless on the testimony of two witnesses to the same overt act, or on confession in open court.

2. The Congress shall have power to declare the punishment of treason, but no attainder of treason shall work corruption of blood, or forfeiture except during the life of the person attained.[39]

Article IV
RELATIONS OF STATES

SECTION 1. *Full Faith and Credit*

Full faith and credit shall be given in each State to the public acts, records, and judicial proceedings of every other State. And the Congress may, by general laws, prescribe the manner in which such acts, records, and proceedings shall be proved, and the effect thereof.

SECTION 2. *Privileges and Immunities of Citizens*

1. The citizens of each State shall be entitled to all privileges and immunities of citizens in the several States.[40]

2. A person charged in any State with treason, felony, or other crime, who shall flee from justice, and be found in another State, shall, on demand of the executive authority of the State from which he fled, be delivered up, to be removed to the State having jurisdiction of the crime.[41]

3. No person held to service or labor in one State, under the laws thereof, escaping into another, shall, in consequence of any law or regulation therein, be discharged from

such service or labor, but shall be delivered up on claim of the party to whom such service or labor may be due.[42]

SECTION 3. *New States; Territories*

1. New States may be admitted by the Congress into this Union; but no new State shall be formed or erected within the jurisdiction of any other State, nor any State be formed by the junction of two or more States, or parts of States, without the consent of the legislatures of the States concerned as well as of the Congress.

2. The Congress shall have power to dispose of and make all needful rules and regulations respecting the territory or other property belonging to the United States; and nothing in this Constitution shall be so construed as to prejudice any claims of the United States, or of any particular State.

SECTION 4. *Protection Afforded to States by the Nation*

The United States shall guarantee to every State in this Union a republican form of government, and shall protect each of them against invasion; and on application of the legislature, or of the executive (when the legislature cannot be convened), against domestic violence.

Article V
PROVISIONS FOR AMENDMENT

The Congress, whenever two-thirds of both Houses shall deem it necessary, shall propose amendments to this Constitution, or, on the application of the legislatures of two-thirds of the several States, shall call a convention for proposing amendments, which, in either case, shall be valid, to all intents and purposes, as part of this Constitution, when ratified by the legislatures of three-fourths of the several States, or by conventions in three-fourths thereof, as the one or the other mode of ratification may be proposed by the Congress; provided [that no amendment which may be made prior to the year one thousand eight hundred and eight shall in any manner affect the first and fourth clauses in the ninth section of the first Article;][43] and that no State, without its consent, shall be deprived of its equal suffrage in the Senate.

Article VI
NATIONAL DEBTS, SUPREMACY OF NATIONAL LAW, OATH

SECTION 1. *Validity of Debts*

All debts contracted and engagements entered into, before the adoption of this Constitution, shall be as valid against the United States under this Constitution, as under the Confederation.

SECTION 2. *Supremacy of National Law*

This Constitution, and the laws of the United States which shall be made in pursuance thereof, and all treaties made, or which shall be made, under the authority of the United States, shall be the supreme law of the land; and the

---

[38]Trial by jury is here guaranteed in federal courts only. The right to trial by jury in *serious* criminal cases in the *State* courts is guaranteed by the 6th and 14th Amendments (see note 49, page 637). Crimes committed on the high seas or in the air are tried in the United States District Court for the judicial district in which the offender is landed or in which the offender is first apprehended.

[39]These very specific provisions are intended to prevent indiscriminate use of the charge of treason. The law of treason covers all American citizens, at home or abroad, and all permanent resident aliens. The maximum penalty is death, but no person convicted of the crime has ever been executed by the United States. Note that treason may be committed only in wartime; but Congress has also made it a crime for any person (in either peace or wartime) to commit espionage or sabotage, to attempt to overthrow the government by force, or to conspire to do any of these things.

[40]The meaning is made more explicit by the 14th Amendment (1868).

[41]This section provides for what is known as *interstate rendition* or *extradition*. Although the Constitution here says the fugitive "shall . . . be delivered up" custom and court decisions have changed it to read "*may* . . . be delivered up." Governors sometimes refuse to return a fugitive.

[42]The phrase "person held to service" referred to slaves. Since the ratification of the 13th Amendment in 1865, the Fugitive Slave Clause has been of historical interest only.

[43]Temporary provision, relating particularly to the slave trade.

judges in every State shall be bound thereby, anything in the constitution or laws of any State to the contrary notwithstanding.

SECTION 3.   *Oaths of Office*

The Senators and Representatives before mentioned, and the members of the several State legislatures, and all executive and judicial officers, both of the United States and of the several States, shall be bound, by oath or affirmation, to support this Constitution; but no religious test shall ever be required as a qualification to any office or public trust under the United States.

Article VII
RATIFICATION OF CONSTITUTION

The ratification of the conventions of nine States shall be sufficient for the establishment of this Constitution between the States so ratifying the same.[44]

Done in Convention, by the unanimous consent of the States present, the seventeenth day of September, in the year of our Lord one thousand seven hundred and eighty-seven, and of the Independence of the United States of America the twelfth. *In Witness* whereof, we have hereunto subscribed our names.

Attest: *William Jackson,* SECRETARY
    George Washington
    PRESIDENT AND DEPUTY FROM VIRGINIA

NEW HAMPSHIRE
John Langdon
Nicholas Gilman

MASSACHUSETTS
Nathaniel Gorham
Rufus King

CONNECTICUT
William Samuel Johnson
Roger Sherman

NEW YORK
Alexander Hamilton

NEW JERSEY
William Livingston
David Brearley
William Paterson
Jonathan Dayton

PENNSYLVANIA
Benjamin Franklin
Thomas Mifflin
Robert Morris
George Clymer
Thomas Fitzsimons
Jared Ingersoll
James Wilson
Gouverneur Morris

DELAWARE
George Read
Gunning Bedford, Jr.
John Dickinson
Richard Bassett
Jacob Broom

MARYLAND
James McHenry
Dan of St. Thomas Jennifer
Daniel Carroll

VIRGINIA
John Blair
James Madison, Jr.

NORTH CAROLINA
William Blount
Richard Dobbs Spaight
Hugh Williamson

SOUTH CAROLINA
John Rutledge
Charles Cotesworth Pinckney
Charles Pinckney
Pierce Butler

GEORGIA
William Few
Abraham Baldwin

AMENDMENTS

1ST AMENDMENT.   *Freedom of Religion, Speech, Press, Assembly, and Petition*[45]

Congress shall make no law respecting an establishment of religion, or prohibiting the free exercise thereof; or abridging the freedom of speech, or of the press; or the right of the people peaceably to assemble, and to petition the government for a redress of grievances.

2ND AMENDMENT.   *Bearing Arms*

A well-regulated militia being necessary to the security of a free state, the right of the people to keep and bear arms shall not be infringed.

3RD AMENDMENT.   *Quartering of Troops*

No soldier shall, in time of peace, be quartered in any house, without the consent of the owner; nor, in time of war, but in a manner to be prescribed by law.

4TH AMENDMENT.   *Searches and Seizures*

The right of the people to be secure in their persons, houses, papers, and effects, against unreasonable searches and seizures, shall not be violated; and no warrants shall issue, but upon probable cause, supported by oath or affirmation, and particularly describing the place to be searched and the persons or things to be seized.[46]

5TH AMENDMENT.   *Criminal Proceedings; Due Process; Eminent Domain*

No person shall be held to answer for a capital, or otherwise infamous, crime, unless on a presentment or indictment of a grand jury, except in cases arising in the land or naval forces, or in the militia, when in actual service, in time of war, or public danger; nor shall any person be subject, for the same offence, to be twice put in jeopardy of life or limb; nor shall be compelled, in any criminal case, to be a witness against himself;[47] nor be

---

[44]Ratified by the ninth State of June 21, 1788, but not immediately effective; see page 46.

[45]The first 10 amendments, the Bill of Rights, were each proposed by Congress on September 25, 1789 and ratified by the necessary three-fourths of the States on December 15, 1791. They restrict only the National Government—*not* the States. But beginning in 1925 the Supreme Court has held most of their provisions applicable to the States through the Due Process Clause of the 14th Amendment; see pages 92–94, 124–125.

[46]The guarantees of the 4th Amendment (including the Weeks Doctrine—the "exclusionary rule") apply against the States through the Due Process Clause of the 14th Amendment.

[47]The prohibition of double jeopardy and the guarantee against self-incrimination each apply against the States through the Due Process Clause of the 14th Amendment.

deprived of life, liberty, or property, without due process of law; nor shall private property be taken for public use, without just compensation.[48]

6TH AMENDMENT. *Criminal Proceedings*

In all criminal prosecutions, the accused shall enjoy the right to a speedy and public trial, by an impartial jury of the state and district wherein the crime shall have been committed, which district shall have been previously ascertained by law; and to be informed of the nature and cause of the accusation; to be confronted with the witnesses against him; to have compulsory process for obtaining witnesses in his favor; and to have the assistance of counsel for his defence.[49]

7TH AMENDMENT. *Civil Trials*

In suits at common law, where the value in controversy shall exceed twenty dollars, the right of trial by jury shall be preserved; and no fact, tried by a jury, shall be otherwise re-examined in any court of the United States than according to the rules of the common law.

8TH AMENDMENT. *Punishment for Crimes*

Excessive bail shall not be required, nor excessive fines imposed, nor cruel and unusual punishment inflicted.[50]

9TH AMENDMENT. *Unenumerated Rights*

The enumeration in the Constitution of certain rights shall not be construed to deny or disparage others retained by the people.

10TH AMENDMENT. *Powers Reserved to the States*

The powers not delegated to the United States by the Constitution, nor prohibited by it to the States, are reserved to the States respectively, or to the people.

11TH AMENDMENT. *Suits against States*[51]

The judicial power of the United States shall not be construed to extend to any suit in law or equity, commenced or prosecuted against one of the United States by citizens of another State or by citizens or subjects of any foreign state.

12TH AMENDMENT. *Election of President and Vice President*[52]

The Electors shall meet in their respective States,[53] and vote by ballot for President and Vice President, one of whom, at least, shall not be an inhabitant of the same State with themselves; they shall name in their ballots the person voted for as President, and in distinct ballots the person voted for as Vice President; and they shall make distinct lists of all persons voted for as President, and of all persons voted for as Vice President, and of the number of votes for each, which lists they shall sign, and certify, and transmit, sealed, to the seat of the Government of the United States, directed to the President of the Senate; the President of the Senate shall, in the presence of the Senate and the House of Representatives, open all the certificates, and the votes shall then be counted; the person having the greatest number of votes for President shall be the President, if such number be a majority of the whole number of Electors appointed; and if no person have such a majority, then, from the persons having the highest numbers, not exceeding three, on the list of those voted for as President, the House of Representatives shall choose immediately, by ballot, the President.[54] But in choosing the President, the votes shall be taken by States, the representation from each State having one vote; a quorum for this purpose shall consist of a member or members from two-thirds of the States, and a majority of all the States shall be necessary to a choice. And if the House of Representatives shall not choose a President, whenever the right of choice shall devolve upon them, [before the fourth day of March next following,][55] then the Vice President shall act as President, as in case of death, or other constitutional disability, of the President. The person having the greatest number of votes as Vice President, shall be the Vice President, if such number be a majority of the whole number of Electors appointed; and if no person have a majority, then, from the two highest numbers on the list, the Senate shall choose the Vice President; a quorum for the purpose shall consist of two-thirds of the whole number of Senators; a majority of the whole number shall be necessary to a choice. But no person constitutionally ineligible to the office of President shall be eligible to that of Vice-President of the United States.

13TH AMENDMENT. *Slavery and Involuntary Servitude*[56]

SECTION 1. Neither slavery nor involuntary servitude, except as a punishment for crime, whereof the party shall have been duly convicted, shall exist within the United States, or any place subject to their jurisdiction.

SECTION 2. Congress shall have power to enforce this article by appropriate legislation.

14TH AMENDMENT. *Rights of Citizens*[57]

SECTION 1. All persons born or naturalized in the United States, and subject to the jurisdiction thereof, are citizens of the United States and of the State wherein they reside.[58] No State shall make or enforce any law which shall abridge the privileges or immunities of citizens of the United States; nor shall any State deprive any person of life, liberty, or property, without due process of law, nor deny to

---

[48]Acting under its inherent power of *eminent domain*, the Government may take (condemn) private property for public use. This provision restricts the exercise of that power by requiring a fair payment to the owner of any property so taken.

[49]The rights to counsel, to speedy and public trial, to trial by jury (in *serious* criminal cases), of confrontation, and to compel witnesses apply against the States through the Due Process Clause of the 14th Amendment.

[50]The protection against cruel and unusual punishment applies against the States through the Due Process Clause of the 14th Amendment.

[51]Proposed by Congress March 4, 1794; ratified February 7, 1795 (but official announcement of the ratification was not made until January 8, 1798).

[52]Proposed by Congress December 9, 1803; ratified June 15, 1804.

[53]Modified by 23rd Amendment (1961), which provides presidential electors for the District of Columbia; see also the text of the proposed amendment relating to the representation of the District of Columbia, page 640.

[54]Only two Presidents, Thomas Jefferson in 1801 and John Quincy Adams in 1825, have been chosen by the House.

[55]Changed by the 20th Amendment (1933), which sets the presidential inauguration date as January 20th.

[56]Proposed by Congress January 31, 1865; ratified December 6, 1865.

[57]Proposed by Congress June 13, 1866; ratified July 9, 1868.

[58]This clause was primarily intended to make Negroes citizens, but it has much wider application. "And subject to the jurisdiction thereof" excludes children born to foreign diplomats in the United States or to alien enemies in hostile occupation.

any person within its jurisdiction the equal protection of the laws.

SECTION 2.   Representatives shall be apportioned among the several States according to their respective numbers, counting the whole number of persons in each State, excluding Indians not taxed. But when the right to vote at any election for the choice of electors for President and Vice President of the United States, Representatives in Congress, the executive and judicial officers of a State, or the members of the legislature thereof, is denied to any of the male inhabitants of such State, being twenty-one years of age, and citizens of the United States, or in any way abridged, except for participation in rebellion or other crime, the basis of representation therein shall be reduced in the proportion which the number of such male citizens shall bear to the whole number of male citizens twenty-one years of age in such State.[59]

SECTION 3.   No person shall be a Senator or Representative in Congress, or elector of President and Vice President, or hold any office, civil or military, under the United States, or under any State, who, having previously taken an oath, as a member of Congress, or as an officer of the United States, or as a member of any State legislature, or as an executive or judicial officer of any State, to support the Constitution of the United States, shall have engaged in insurrection or rebellion against the same, or given aid or comfort to the enemies thereof. But Congress may, by a vote of two-thirds of each House, remove such disability.

SECTION 4.   The validity of the public debt of the United States, authorized by law, including debts incurred for payment of pensions and bounties for services in suppressing insurrection or rebellion, shall not be questioned. But neither the United States nor any State shall assume or pay any debt or obligation incurred in aid of insurrection or rebellion against the United States, or any claim for the loss or emancipation of any slave; but all such debts, obligations, and claims shall be held illegal and void.

SECTION 5.   The Congress shall have power to enforce, by appropriate legislation, the provisions of this article.

15TH AMENDMENT.   *Right to Vote—Race, Color, Servitude*[60]

SECTION 1.   The right of citizens of the United States to vote shall not be denied or abridged by the United States or by any State on account of race, color, or previous condition of servitude.

SECTION 2.   The Congress shall have power to enforce this article by appropriate legislation.

16TH AMENDMENT.   *Income Tax*[61]

The Congress shall have power to lay and collect taxes on incomes, from whatever source derived, without appor-

tionment among the several States, and without regard to any census or enumeration.

17TH AMENDMENT.   *Popular Election of Senators*[62]

The Senate of the United States shall be composed of two Senators from each State, elected by the people thereof, for six years; and each Senator shall have one vote. The electors in each State shall have the qualifications requisite for electors of the most numerous branch of the State legislatures.

When vacancies happen in the representation of any State in the Senate, the executive authority of such State shall issue writs of election to fill such vacancies: Provided, That the legislature of any State may empower the executive thereof to make temporary appointment until the people fill the vacancies by election as the legislature may direct.

This amendment shall not be so construed as to affect the election or term of any Senator chosen before it becomes valid as part of the Constitution.

18TH AMENDMENT.   *Prohibition of Intoxicating Liquors*[63]

SECTION 1.   After one year from the ratification of this article the manufacture, sale or transportation of intoxicating liquors within, the importation thereof into, or the exportation thereof from the United States and all territory subject to the jurisdiction thereof for beverage purposes is hereby prohibited.

SECTION 2.   The Congress and the several States shall have concurrent power to enforce this article by appropriate legislation.

SECTION 3.   This article shall be inoperative unless it shall have been ratified as an amendment to the Constitution by the legislatures of the several States, as provided in the Constitution, within seven years of the date of the submission hereof to the States by Congress.[64]

19TH AMENDMENT.   *Equal Suffrage—Sex*[65]

The right of citizens of the United States to vote shall not be denied or abridged by the United States or by any State on account of sex.

Congress shall have power to enforce this article by appropriate legislation.

20TH AMENDMENT.   *Commencement of Terms; Sessions of Congress; Death or Disqualification of President-Elect*[66]

SECTION 1.   The terms of the President and Vice President shall end at noon on the 20th day of January, and the terms of Senators and Representatives at noon on the 3d day of January, of the years in which such terms would have ended if this article had not been ratified; and the terms of their successors shall then begin.

---

[59]The provisions of the second sentence here have never been enforced. Some authorities argue that they were nullified by the 15th Amendment (1870). The sentence is at least obsolete from disuse; also, it is not in accord with the 19th and 26th Amendments (1920, 1971).

[60]Proposed by Congress February 26, 1869; ratified February 3, 1870. The amendment was intended to guarantee suffrage to newly-freed Negro slaves but is of much broader application today.

[61]Proposed by Congress July 12, 1909; ratified February 3, 1913. The amendment modifies the restrictions on the power to levy direct taxes, set out in Article I. (Section 2, Clause 3 and Section 9, Clause 4).

[62]Proposed by Congress May 13, 1912; ratified April 8, 1913. The amendment repealed those portions of Article I, Section 3, Clauses 1 and 2 relating to the election of Senators by the respective State legislatures.

[63]Proposed by Congress December 18, 1917; ratified January 16, 1919.

[64]The 18th Amendment was repealed in its entirety by the 21st Amendment (1933).

[65]Proposed by Congress June 4, 1919; ratified August 18, 1920.

[66]Proposed by Congress March 2, 1932; ratified January 23, 1933. The provisions of Sections 1 and 2 relating to Congress modified Article I, Section 4, Clause 2, and those relating to the President, the 12th Amendment.

SECTION 2. The Congress shall assemble at least once in every year, and such meeting shall begin at noon on the 3d day of January, unless they shall be law appoint a different day.

SECTION 3. If, at the time fixed for the beginning of the term of the President, the President-elect shall have died, the Vice President-elect shall become President. If a President shall not have been chosen before the time fixed for the beginning of his term, or if the President-elect shall have failed to qualify, then the Vice President-elect shall act as President until a President shall have qualified; and the Congress may by law provide for the case wherein neither a President-elect nor a Vice President-elect shall have qualified, declaring who shall then act as President, or the manner in which one who is to act shall be selected, and such person shall act accordingly until a President or Vice President shall have qualified.

SECTION 4. The Congress may by law provide for the case of the death of any of the persons from whom the House of Representatives may choose a President whenever the right of choice shall have devolved upon them, and for the case of the death of any of the persons from whom the Senate may choose a Vice President whenever the right of choice shall have devolved upon them.

SECTION 5. Sections 1 and 2 shall take effect on the 15th day of October following the ratification of this article.

SECTION 6. This article shall be inoperative unless it shall have been ratified as an amendment to the Constitution by the legislatures of three-fourths of the several States within seven years from the date of its submission.

21ST AMENDMENT. *Repeal of 18th Amendment*[67]

SECTION 1. The eighteenth article of amendment to the Constitution of the United States is hereby repealed.

SECTION 2. The transportation or importation into any State, Territory, or possession of the United States for delivery or use therein of intoxicating liquors, in violation of the laws thereof, is hereby prohibited.

SECTION 3. This article shall be inoperative unless it shall have been ratified as an amendment to the Constitution by conventions in the several States, as provided in the Constitution, within seven years from the date of the submission hereof to the States by the Congress.

22ND AMENDMENT. *Presidential Tenure*[68]

SECTION 1. No person shall be elected to the office of the President more than twice, and no person who has held the office of President, or acted as President, for more than two years of a term to which some other person was elected President shall be elected to the office of the President more than once. But this Article shall not apply to any person holding the office of President when this Article was proposed by the Congress, and shall not prevent any person who may be holding the office of President, or

acting as President, during the term within which this Article becomes operative from holding the office of President or acting as President during the remainder of such term.

SECTION 2. This article shall be inoperative unless it shall have been ratified as an amendment to the Constitution by the legislatures of three-fourths of the several states within seven years from the date of its submission to the States by the Congress.

23RD AMENDMENT. *Presidential Electors for the District of Columbia*[69]

SECTION 1. The District constituting the seat of Government of the United States shall appoint in such manner as the Congress may direct:

A number of electors of President and Vice President equal to the whole number of Senators and Representatives in Congress to which the District would be entitled if it were a State, but in no event more than the least populous State; they shall be considered, for the purposes of the election of President and Vice President, to be electors appointed by a State; and they shall meet in the District and perform such duties as provided by the twelfth article of amendment.

SECTION 2. The Congress shall have power to enforce this article by appropriate legislation.

24TH AMENDMENT. *Right to Vote in Federal Elections—Tax Payment*[70]

SECTION 1. The right of citizens of the United States to vote in any primary or other election for President or Vice President, for electors for President or Vice President, or for Senator or Representative in Congress, shall not be denied or abridged by the United States or any State by reason of failure to pay any poll tax or other tax.

SECTION 2. The Congress shall have power to enforce this article by appropriate legislation.

25TH AMENDMENT. *Presidential Succession, Vice Presidential Vacancy, Presidential Inability*[71]

SECTION 1. In case of the removal of the President from office or of his death or resignation, the Vice President shall become President.

SECTION 2. Whenever there is a vacancy in the office of the Vice President, the President shall nominate a Vice President who shall take office upon confirmation by a majority vote of both Houses of Congress.

SECTION 3. Whenever the President transmits to the President *pro tempore* of the Senate and the Speaker of the House of Representatives his written declaration that he is unable to discharge the powers and duties of his office, and until he transmits to them a written declaration to the contrary, such powers and duties shall be discharged by the Vice President as Acting President.

SECTION 4. Whenever the Vice President and a majority of

---

[67]Proposed by Congress February 20, 1933; ratified December 5, 1933. This amendment is the only one which has thus far been submitted to the States for ratification by conventions rather than by the State legislatures. See article V. It is also the only amendment that specifically repealed a previous amendment. It also modified the scope of the commerce power, Article I, Section 8, Clause 3.

[68]Proposed by Congress March 24, 1947; ratified February 27, 1951. The amendment modified Article II, Section I, Clause 1.

[69]Proposed by Congress June 16, 1960; ratified March 29, 1961. The amendment modified Article II, Section I, Clause 2 and the 12th Amendment.

[70]Proposed by Congress September 14, 1962; ratified January 23, 1964.

[71]Proposed by Congress July 6, 1965; ratified February 10, 1967. This amendment contains the only typographical error in the Constitution. In the second paragraph of Section 4, the word "department" should properly read "departments."

either the principal officers of the executive departments or of such other body as Congress may by law provide, transmit to the President *pro tempore* of the Senate and the Speaker of the House of Representatives their written declaration that the President is unable to discharge the powers and duties of his office, the Vice President shall immediately assume the powers and duties of the office as Acting President.

Thereafter, when the President transmits to the President *pro tempore* of the Senate and the Speaker of the House of Representatives his written declaration that no inability exists, he shall resume the powers and duties of his office unless the Vice President and a majority of either the principal officers of the executive department or of such other body as Congress may by law provide, transmit within four days to the President *pro tempore* of the Senate and the Speaker of the House of Representatives their written declaration that the President is unable to discharge the powers and duties of his office. Thereupon Congress shall decide the issue, assembling within forty-eight hours for that purpose if not in session. If the Congress, within twenty-one days after receipt of the latter written declaration, or, if Congress is not in session, within twenty-one days after Congress is required to assemble, determines by two-thirds vote of both Houses that the President is unable to discharge the powers and duties of his office, the Vice President shall continue to discharge the same as Acting President; otherwise, the President shall resume the powers and duties of his office.

26TH AMENDMENT. *Right to Vote—Age*[72]
SECTION 1. The right of citizens of the United States, who are eighteen years of age or older, to vote shall not be denied or abridged by the United States or by any State on account of age.
SECTION 2. The Congress shall have the power to enforce this article by appropriate legislation.

---

[72]Proposed by Congress March 23, 1971; ratified July 1, 1971.

As of January, 1984, one proposed amendment was before the State legislatures. In 1978 Congress submitted an amendment to give the District of Columbia full voting representation in Congress:
SECTION 1. For purposes of representation in the Congress, election of the President and Vice President, and Article V of this Constitution, the District constituting the seat of government of the United States shall be treated as though it were a State.
SECTION 2. The exercise of the rights and powers conferred under this article shall be by the people of the District constituting the seat of government, and as shall be provided by the Congress.
SECTION 3. The twenty-third article of amendment to the Constitution of the United States is hereby repealed.
SECTION 4. This article shall be inoperative unless it shall have been ratified as an amendment to the Constitution by legislatures of three-fourths of the several States within seven years from the date of its submission.

The deadline for ratification of this proposed amendment is August 22, 1985. To 1984, it had been ratified by the legislatures of 10 States.

In 1972 Congress submitted the Equal Rights Amendment (ERA) to the States legislatures:
SECTION 1. Equality of rights under the law shall not be denied or abridged by the United States or by any State on account of sex.
SECTION 2. The Congress shall have the power to enforce, by appropriate legislation, the provisions of this article.
SECTION 3. This amendment shall take effect two years after the date of ratification.

In a separate resolution at the time, Congress placed a seven-year limit on the period for its ratification. That deadline (originally March 22, 1979) was later extended to June 30, 1982. Thirty-five of the State legislatures ratified ERA during that period—three short of the required 38. Congress is now considering the submission of this amendment a second time—and will likely do so some time in 1984.

INDEX

Note: Entries with a page number followed by an "n", as 365n, denote reference to a footnote on that page.

ACKNOWLEDGMENTS

Photo sources which have been abbreviated are as follows:

BA = Bettman Archive, Inc.
LC = Library of Congress
MA = MAGNUM
PR = Photo Researchers, Inc.
SB = Stock, Boston
SY = SYGMA
UPI = United Press International
WW = Wide World Photos

UNIT ONE: xvi–Shostal Associates. 2–National Park Service Photo. 3–SY/Diego Goldberg. 7–Liason/D. Halstead. 8–Woodfin Camp/Woolfit. 9–*Life Magazine*/Hugo Jaeger. 15–SB/Alper. 16–(left) SY/J.P. Laffont; (right) MA/Alex Webb. 18–MA/Leonard Freed. 24–LC. 25–BA. 27–BA. 31–LC. 33–LC. 35–After a painting by John Singleton Copley; from *Dictionary of American Portraits*, Dover Publications, Inc. 36–BA. 41–BA. 45–(all) LC. 47–Brown Brothers. 55–Woodfin Camp/J. Anderson. 55–Commonwealth of Massachusetts. 59–LC. 64–SB/Fred Bodin. 65–UPI. 71–LC. 73–Black Star/Ted Spiegel. 78–SB/James Holland. 83–Uniphoto/Jan Warbut.

UNIT TWO: 86–Shostal Associates. 88–SB/Stuart Cohen. 89–Black Star/Andy Levin. 93–National Archives. 96–(top left) SB/Owen Franken; (top right) Woodfin Camp/D. Budnik; (bottom) SB/Bohdan Hrynewych. 100–Paul Conklin. 103–Picture Cube/David Strickler. 106–(all) SY/Owen Franken. 109–Michael Sullivan; 110–SB/Michael Hayman. 113–UPI. 115–MA/Eve Arnold. 117–Click Chicago/Dale Bayles. 119–SB/ Jeff Albertson. 122–LC. 123–MA/Bruce Davidson. 126–Boston Globe. 127–Paul Conklin. 130–SB/Alan Mercer. 131–Paul Conklin. 133–Paul Conklin. 136–PR/Yvonne Freund; (insert) Michael Sullivan. 139–Paul Conklin. 143–Black Star/Michelle Bogre. 146–(both) Jeffrey Dunn. 150–LC. 152–(left) Black Star/Fred Ward; (right) Black Star/Flip Schulke. 158–Picture Group/Rick Browne.

UNIT THREE: 162–William McClenaghan Collection. 164–William McClenaghan Collection/Talbot Lovering. 165–Boatman's National Bank, St. Louis. 167–William McClenaghan Collection. 169–Michael Sullivan. 171.–(top) Click Chicago/Brian Seed; (bottom) McClenaghan Collection. 172–New York Historical Society. 174-175–(all) McClenaghan Collection. 176–McClenaghan Collection. 177–New York Historical Society. 179–UPI. 180–(both) McClenaghan Collection. 184–UPI; (insets) McClenaghan Collection/Frank Siteman. 186–(center) Michael Sullivan; (left and right) McClenaghan Collection and Jeanne Armin/Frank Siteman. 190–SB/Daniel Brody. 191–LC. 192–MA/Richard Kalver. 199–Tom Stack/J.C. Lejeune. 200–UPI. 213–(both) Liason. 216–BA. 217–Paul Conklin. 220–Sullivan Collection/Paul Conklin. 223–William J. Ranney. 226–Liason/Chris Harris. 227–McClenaghan Collection/Talbot Lovering. 229–(top) Indiana State Election Board; (bottom) Massachusetts Election Commission. 230–Liason/Penelope Breese. 231–Taurus/Frank Siteman. 233–Michael Sullivan. 237–Paul Conklin 239–(all) Sullivan Collection. 242–PR/Bettye Lane. 243–Paul Conklin. 249–(foreground) Picture Cube/Martha Stewart; (background) SB/Cary Wolinsky. 251–UPI. 254–Picture Cube/Richard Wood. 259–Paul Conklin. 263–(both) Paul Conklin.

UNIT FOUR: 272–Talbot Lovering. 274–LC. 275–Black Star/Fred Ward. 283–Paul Conklin. 285–(both) LC. 289–Paul Conklin. 291–Paul Conklin. 292–BA. 293–Black Star/Dennis Brack. 295–Paul Conklin. 297–Paul Conklin. 305–SY/Arthur Grace. 310–UPI. 313–WW. 314–Paul Conklin. 318–Paul Conklin. 319–BA. 321–(top) Culver Pictures; (bottom) Picture Cube/David Strickler. 330–SB/Chris Morrow. 331–U.S. Patent Office. 332–Jeffrey Dunn. 333–Paul Conklin. 337–SY/J.P. Laffont. 338–SY/J.P. Laffont. 339–SY/Arthur Grace. 340–Allyn and Bacon.

UNIT FIVE: 342–Paul Conklin. 344–Roloc Color Slides. 345–Bill Fitz-Patrick/The White House. 346–(left) Paul Conklin; (right) UPI. 347–McClenaghan Collection/Talbot Lovering. 351–SY/Randy Taylor. 352–Woodfin Camp. 355–Paul Conklin. 356–Sullivan Collection. 357–Liason/Michael Abramson. 361–Paul Conklin. 363–(left) SY/Arthur Grace; (all others) Paul Conklin. 364–Courtesy of Betty DeVito. 366–Liason/Leif Skoogfors. 367–Paul Conklin. 369–LC. 373–Picture Cube/Ed Hoff. 376–UPI. 377–WW. 380–UPI. 381–UPI. 383–(left) Michael Evans/The White House; (right) Paul Conklin. 385–Culver Pictures. 386–Paul Conklin. 389–Smithsonian Institution. 390–FPG/Jerry Hernani. 391–Paul Conklin. 393–SY/Rodney Mims. 395–Black Star/D.B. Owen. 397–Black Star/James Nachtwey. 399–SY. 401–UPI. 404–Paul Conklin. 405–Culver Pictures. 409–Paul Conklin. 411–Talbot Lovering. 412–(top) Paul Conklin; (bottom) SY/Tannea Baum. 413–Paul Conklin. 414–(both) Paul Conklin. 415–(both) Paul Conklin. 416–(both) Paul Conklin. 417–(top) Paul Conklin; (center) Picture Cube/Jonathon Goell. 418–Paul Conklin. 419–Paul Conklin. 420–Paul Conklin. 421–Paul Conklin. 422–Paul Conklin. 423–Paul Conklin. 429–Paul Conklin. 431–(left) Woodfin Camp/John Marmaras. 433–BA. 436–SB/Arthur Grace. 437–PR/Glynne Betts. 444–McClenaghan Collection/Frank Siteman. 445–Brown Brothers. 447–Paul Conklin. 449–Contact Press Images/Dilip Metha. 452–SY/J.P. Laffont. 455–UPI. 461–Culver Pictures. 465–WW. 467–MA/Phillip Griffths. 470–SY. 474–SY/Owen Franken.

UNIT SIX: 478–Paul Conklin. 480–UPI. 481–MA/Alex Webb. 487–UPI. 489–Liason/Penelope Breese. 493–Paul Conklin. 494–U.S. Customs Service. 497–Paul Conklin. 499–Paul Conklin.

UNIT SEVEN: 502–Marvin Rand. 504–Allyn and Bacon. 505–New York Historical Society. 511–Supervisor of Elections Office, Dade County, Florida. 518-Archive Pictures/Charles Harbutt. 519-State of Nebraska. 523–Paul Conklin. 528–Paul Conklin. 530–State of Georgia. 532–State of Wisconsin. 534–Jeffrey Dunn. 535–SB/Tyrne Hall. 538–UPI. 539–BA. 541–Michael Sullivan. 547–Peter Karas. 548–WW. 552–Paul Conklin. 555–Utah Tourist and Publicity Council. 556–Mary Lang. 557–U.S. Signal Corps. 559–SB/Bohdan Hrynewych. 562–(top) SB/Owen Franken; (center) Courtesy of Richard Riechard. 563–Indiana State Election Board. 564–Black Star/Michelle Bogre. 567–Woodfin Camp/Frostie. 572–Winston Pote from A. Devaney, Inc. 573–Black Star/Tom Ebenhoh. 577–Paul Conklin. 581–Michael Sullivan. 582–Michael Sullivan. 584–Black Star/Phil Huber. 587–SB/Peter Menzel; (inset) BA. 588–Liason/Frank Fisher. 591–Michael Sullivan/ Bob Daemmrich. 592–Paul Conklin. 594–SY/Alain Keler. 596–(top) PR/Michael Uffer; (bottom) PR/Jim Goodwin. 599–PR/Townsend Dickinson. 600–SB/Ellis Herwig. 601–Jeffrey Dunn. 607–PR/Will McIntyre. 608–(top) WW; (bottom) American Antiquarian Society, Worcester.